Inside the
Fashion
Business

SIXTH EDITION

Inside the Fashion Business

JEANNETTE JARNOW
Edwin Goodman Professor and Professor Emeritus
Fashion Merchandising
Fashion Institute of Technology

KITTY G. DICKERSON
Professor and Chairman
Department of Textile and Apparel Management
University of Missouri-Columbia

Merrill,
an imprint of Prentice Hall
Upper Saddle River, New Jersey   *Columbus, Ohio*

Library of Congress Cataloging-in-Publication Data

Jarnow, Jeannette A.
    Inside the fashion business / Jeannette A. Jarnow, Kitty G.
  Dickerson.—6th ed.
      p.   cm.
    Includes bibliographical references and index.
    ISBN 0-13-238148-6
      1. Fashion merchandising—United States.   2. Clothing trade–
  –United States.   I. Dickerson, Kitty G.   II. Title.
HD9940.U4J3   1997b
338.4'7687'0973—dc20   96-19717
                                                                           CIP

Cover art: Rita Chow/Irmeli Holmberg
Editor: Bradley J. Potthoff
Developmental Editor: Carol S. Sykes
Production Editor: Mary M. Irvin
Photo Researcher: Nancy Ritz
Design Coordinator: Julia Zonneveld Van Hook
Text Designer: Angela Foote/Julia Zonneveld Van Hook
Cover Designer: ORBIT Design
Production Manager: Patricia A. Tonneman
Director of Marketing: Kevin Flanagan
Advertising/Marketing Coordinator: Julie Shough

This book was set in Classical Garamond and was printed and bound by R. R. Donnelley & Sons Company/Willard. The cover was printed by Phoenix Color Corp.

 © 1997 by Prentice-Hall, Inc.
Simon & Schuster/A Viacom Company
Upper Saddle River, New Jersey 07458

Earlier editions © 1991, 1987 by Macmillan Publishing Company; © 1965, 1974, 1981 by John Wiley & Sons, Inc.

Chapter-opening photo credits: Courtesy of International Business Machines Corporation, 1; Anthony Magnacca/Merrill/Prentice Hall, 33, 69, 216, 233, 261, 305, 457; Courtesy of Burlington Industries, Inc., 106; Courtesy of Atlanta Apparel Mart, 153; Courtesy of Yves Saint Laurent, 346; Courtesy of Columbus City Center, 391.

Printed in the United States of America

10 9 8 7 6 5 4 3 2

ISBN: 0-13-238148-6

Prentice-Hall International (UK) Limited, *London*
Prentice-Hall of Australia Pty. Limited, *Sydney*
Prentice-Hall of Canada, Inc., *Toronto*
Prentice-Hall Hispanoamericana, S. A., *Mexico*
Prentice-Hall of India Private Limited, *New Delhi*
Prentice-Hall of Japan, Inc., *Tokyo*
Simon & Schuster Asia Pte. Ltd., *Singapore*
Editora Prentice-Hall do Brasil, Ltda., *Rio de Janeiro*

As I begin to assume authorship of the book with this edition, I would like to dedicate it to the original author, Jeannette Jarnow, and her coauthors. They have developed a book that has become known to virtually everyone who has studied the fashion industry. I am honored to have an opportunity to be a part of a book that has been so important to the field. Mrs. Jarnow has been an exemplary leader in the fashion field, as evidenced by her foresight in writing the first edition in 1965. Previous coauthors, Beatrice Judelle and Miriam Guerreiro, also made valuable contributions to this work.

Kitty G. Dickerson

We appreciate the readers of previous editions whose enthusiastic acceptance resulted in this new and revised edition.

Jeannette Jarnow
Kitty G. Dickerson

Preface

Inside the Fashion Business is a book for those who have a particular interest in what is called the *fashion industry*—that complex of enterprises concerned with the design, production, and marketing of men's, women's, and children's apparel and accessories.

As we approach the year 2000, we find a vastly different fashion industry from that which existed only 10 or 20 years ago. Although the fashion sector is known for its rapid change, we see an industry today that has been dramatically transformed by such things as new technology, globalization, and changing consumer values. Every segment of the industry has been required to change to meet new competitive challenges. As a result, we find a fashion industry that has restructured itself to respond to global competition. The industry is faster, is geographically more widespread, and can focus on understanding and serving the consumer more effectively than ever before. Through transportation and communications advances, the industry has become a worldwide production and distribution network. At the same time, new technologies permit close examination of consumer needs and have reduced the time it takes to respond to those needs.

New to This Edition

This sixth edition has been revised to incorporate the major changes taking place in the fashion industry in the 1990s. The book has been completely updated to prepare individuals for careers in this transformed industry. To that end, a new first chapter introduces the reader to the industry and covers a range of major trends that are transforming the industry and how it functions. The trends discussed in this chapter affect all segments of the industry, from the production of fibers through other stages of production and distribution, to the consumer purchase of finished merchandise from the retailer.

Because of increasing awareness that the consumer controls the success or failure of businesses in the fashion industry, this edition includes a new chapter on the consumer. This chapter covers changing population demographics and factors influencing consumer buying behavior. It includes information on new approaches being used to serve the consumer of the 1990s and beyond.

This edition, like previous ones, consists of the text plus industry readings. Our objectives are twofold: to develop an understanding of the workings of an industry that is a major segment of the national and global economies and to expose the reader to its inner workings as perceived through the eyes of recognized authorities and practitioners in the field.

By providing this knowledge, we also hope to help fashion business aspirants crystallize their career objectives and reach their own specific goals in the wonderful world of fashion.

Organization

The plan that we have followed is simple and consistent. An introductory overview of the fashion business is followed by chapters that each deal with one particular segment of the fashion industry. After the introductory chapter and another on principles of fashion, the book is organized to follow the stages through which a product goes. Because the consumer is the focal point around which the whole industry must be organized, we begin with a chapter on the consumer. Successive chapters go through the stages of production and distribution: the raw materials of fashion—the fibers, fabrics, and so on; apparel production, including global production; and finally distribution through various forms of retailing.

The chapters first include an organized fact-filled body of knowledge. Next comes a series of industry readings carefully selected to complement, supplement, and illustrate the subject matter of the chapter. The readings may describe the operations of leading companies or may reflect significant trends occurring in the industry. Then, to facilitate further research, each chapter has an updated bibliography, list of trade associations, and list of trade periodicals related to the subject. These have been expanded from the last edition to include some sources in other countries. In each case, the chapter concludes with suggested review activities. Following the final chapter are three appendixes and a fashion business glossary.

Content

Chapter 1, "The Business of Making and Selling Fashion," presents an overview of the fashion industry and its scope, economic importance, and major trends affecting the industry. The trends discussed are those of a broad nature that are reshaping the industry and that apply to virtually all segments of the fashion sector.

Chapter 2, "Principles of Fashion," discusses the generally accepted definitions of fashion and the principles governing its origin and dynamics, along with the implications for the marketers of fashion. It also discusses the role of designers today.

Chapter 3, "The Consumer," is designed to help the reader understand that the consumer is the reason the fashion industry exists. As consumers have changed their priorities and spending habits, fashion marketers must be increasingly sensitive to consumers' needs in order to succeed.

Chapter 4, "The Materials of Fashion," examines the industries that provide the raw materials from which apparel and accessories are made: fibers, fabrics, leathers, and furs. Each is discussed in terms of its economic importance, its method of operation, and its strategies for meeting present market conditions.

Chapter 5, "Women's and Children's Apparel," discusses the design, production, and marketing of women's and children's apparel. It includes the history, development, growth, and practices of this segment of the fashion business. This chapter has been revised significantly to incorporate new technological changes used in apparel manufacturing today.

Chapter 6, "The Menswear Industry," reviews the growth of this industry, the growing influence of fashion in menswear, changes affecting the industry, and its changing methods of operation.

Chapter 7, "Fashion Accessories and Intimate Apparel/Undergarments," deals with the economic importance and operations of these specialized industries that produce accessories and intimate apparel/undergarments.

Chapter 8, "Globalization of the Fashion Industry," considers why globalization has occurred for this sector, how it affects the industry, some of the issues involved including trade policies, and the importance of being prepared to function in a global economy.

Chapter 9, "Fashion Producers in Other Countries," discusses the fashion producers in other countries who supply fashion merchandise to the global market, with an emphasis on the U.S. market. These producers range from internationally famous designers to contractors in low-wage countries.

Chapter 10, "The Retailers of Fashion," explains the different types of retail operations, the circumstances and period of their origin, the part each plays in the business of fashion, and how retailing is changing. New forms of retailing are discussed.

Chapter 11, "Auxiliary Fashion Enterprises," covers the service enterprises that contribute to the effective functioning of the fashion business, such as news media, fashion advisory and information services, management consultants, advertising and publicity agencies, and buying/sourcing offices, among others.

Appendix A is an annotated list of influential designers. Appendix B, "Sources of Current Statistical Information," provides information for those who wish to keep current and update the figures presented in this edition. Appendix C, "Career Opportunities in Fashion," provides guidance for those seeking a niche in the fashion business. Entry-level opportunities are discussed in terms of personal qualities, skills, and preparation.

The authors feel strongly that readers need statistical yardsticks against which to measure the importance of the various industries, trends, and individual enterprises in the fashion business. We have sought to provide this in the text, within the limits of what was available up to the time of publication.

"Fashion Business Glossary" follows the appendixes. This provides help with the vocabulary fashion professionals need to master.

Acknowledgments

This book, like its predecessors, reflects the thoughts of many other people. We are grateful for the business leaders who shared their knowledge and insights with us and to the publications and organizations that granted reprint permissions for readings or other items. We appreciate the helpful comments provided by reviewers contracted by Prentice Hall to guide the revision for this edition: Jeannette J. Arbuthnot, Utah State University; Phyllis A. Eamons, Champlain College; Becky Greer, Steven F. Austin State University; Patricia A. Helms, University of Rhode Island; Nancy J. Miller, University of Nebraska-Lincoln; and Margaret Rucker, University of California.

Finally, we thank the many friends in the academic and fashion worlds who gave advice and counsel. These people helped us shape the previous editions and encouraged and guided us once again in this revision. A special thanks to Dr. Pamela Norum and Dr. Betty Dillard at the University of Missouri-Columbia for reviewing select chapters of the revision and providing helpful suggestions.

We appreciate the important role Editor Brad Potthoff played in launching this edition. Additionally, we are grateful to Production Editor Mary Irvin for her capable orchestration of the actual production of this edition.

Jeannette A. Jarnow
Kitty G. Dickerson

Brief Contents

Contents

CHAPTER 6
The Menswear Industry   216

CHAPTER 7
Fashion Accessories and Intimate Apparel/ Undergarments   261

CHAPTER 10
The Retailers of Fashion   *391*

CHAPTER 11
Auxiliary Fashion
Enterprises   *457*

The Business of Making and Selling Fashion

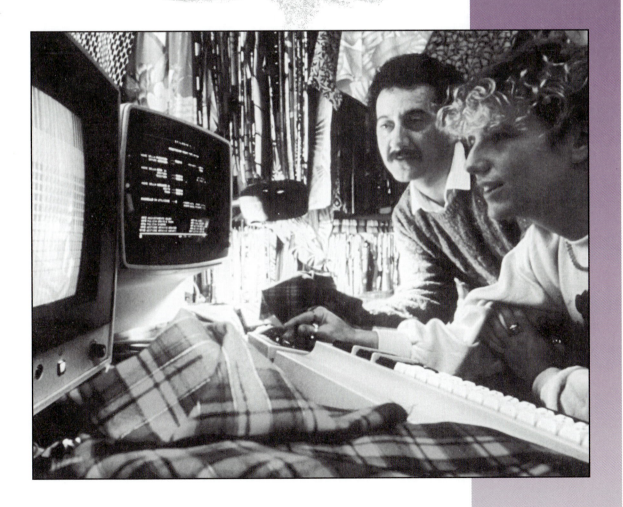

*F*ashion in the global market and the United States today is big business. Its component parts—the design, production, and distribution of fashion merchandise—form the basis of a highly complex, multibillion-dollar industry. It is a business that began with small entrepreneurs at the turn of the century and today is a huge, many-faceted business. It employs the greatly diversified skills and talents of millions of people, offers a multitudinous mix of products, absorbs a considerable portion of consumer spending, and plays a vital role in the country's economy. It is, moreover, a business of curious and exciting contrasts. On one hand, there is the rarefied air of Paris couture salons presenting collections of exorbitantly priced made-to-order designer originals; at the other extreme are giant factories that mass produce and distribute endless quantities of low-priced apparel to towns and cities across the country.

The fashion-related industries play a very important role globally. Almost every country in the world depends on the textile and apparel sectors as important contributors to the economy. Fashion products are made under an astonishing range of circumstances, from the high fashion houses of Europe to dreary, cramped sweatshops in the poorest developing countries.

This chapter presents an introduction to the fashion industry—its scope, economic importance, and trends that affect nearly all areas of the industry. The readings that follow address some of the changes taking place in the industry and encourage us to think about what the industry may be like in the future.

Subsequent chapters discuss in detail the various segments of the industry that are involved in the design, production, and distribution of fashion merchandise: fibers and fabrics, apparel and accessories production, foreign sources of supply, retailing, and related auxiliary services.

The Business of Fashion: An Overview

The impact of fashion is all-pervading, but when we speak of the *fashion business,* that term is generally understood to refer to all companies and individuals concerned with the design, production, and distribution of textile and apparel goods.[1] Unlike industries such as tobacco and automotive products manufacturing, the fashion industry is not a clearly defined entity. It is a complex of many different industries, not all of which appear at first glance to have anything of fashion among their products.

---

[1]Beauty and grooming products are sometimes included in the fashion industry. However, space does not permit including those in this book.

Scope of the Fashion Industry

Plainly recognizable as part of the fashion business are industries devoted to the making of inner- and outerwear articles of women's apparel; those involved in the production of menswear; those that make children's apparel; and those that make accessories such as scarfs, jewelry, handbags, shoes, gloves, wallets, and hosiery. Some of these industries serve one sex or the other; some serve both sexes.

When one moves back to an earlier stage of production—to the fibers, fabrics, leathers, furs, metals, and plastics from which the finished products are made—the line between what is and what is not the fashion business becomes harder to draw. Some textile mills that produce dress and coat fabrics also produce bedsheets, carpets, or industrial fabrics. Some chemical companies that produce fibers that are eventually spun and woven to make garments are also producers of explosives, fertilizers, and photographic film. Some producers and processors in fields normally remote from fashion find themselves temporarily with one foot in the fashion business when prevailing styles demand such items as industrial zippers, decorative chains, quilted fabrics, or padding materials, for example. A season or two later, these people may be as far removed from the fashion business as ever, but for the time being, they too are part of it.

The fashion business also includes different types of retailers, such as stores that sell apparel and accessories, and mail-order catalogs from which many consumer purchases are made. It includes businesses that neither produce nor sell merchandise but render advice, assistance, or information to those that do.

In this last category are consumer publications that disseminate news of fashion, ranging from the daily newspaper to magazines devoted primarily to fashion, such as *Glamour, Vogue, Harper's Bazaar,* and *Gentlemen's Quarterly.* Also included in this category are trade periodicals, such as *Women's Wear Daily, Stores,* and *Bobbin,* that carry news of fashion and information on production and distribution techniques to retailers, apparel manufacturers, and textile mills. It includes also publicists and advertising specialists, fashion consultants, and buying offices that represent retail stores in the vast wholesale centers.

All these and more are part of the business—farms and mills and factories, blue-collar and white-collar workers, tycoons, and creative artists. All play their parts in the business of fashion.

Economic Importance

Global Importance

Business sectors related to the fashion industry play important roles in the global economy. Since launching the Industrial Revolution in England centuries ago, the textile and apparel sectors have been, and continue to be, leaders in **industrialization** and trade in nearly all parts of the world. Beyond providing fashion products and textile home furnishings as basic human necessities, the manufacturing of these products provides the means of earning a living for an impressive portion of the world's population. *These industries are, by far, the world's leading manufacturing employer* (Dickerson, 1995).

The textile and apparel industries have been important engines of economic development worldwide. That is, the economies of many countries began to improve because they focused on these industries. In countries such as Pakistan and Bangladesh, for example, textile and apparel products count for nearly 70 percent of the country's total exports. In other words, those industries are the economic life blood for many individuals and families. Similar examples of the importance of the industry can be found around the world because *no other manufacturing sector today is even close to being as globalized as textiles/apparel.*

National Importance

The business of fashion contributes significantly to the economy of the United States both through the materials and services it purchases and through the wages and taxes it pays. In assessing the importance of this contribution, it helps to consider consumer expenditures, the number of people employed, and the amount of wages and salaries paid to them.

In 1995, U.S. consumers spent \$254.4 billion[2] for clothing, shoes, and accessories—an amount that constituted more than 5 percent of what they spent for all purposes from food to foreign travel. The outlay for fashion goods ran well above that for furniture, household equipment, or even personal savings for the year (U.S. Department of Commerce, 1996). Typically, the sales of men's, women's, and children's apparel and accessories account for well above half the total volume of general merchandise stores.

Still another indication of the industry's importance is the number of jobs it creates—and it creates them in every state of our country. Of the millions of people employed in manufacturing jobs in the United States, about one in nine is employed either in those industries that produce apparel for men, women, and children or in the textile plants that produce the materials from which the garments are made (U.S. Department of Commerce, 1994).

Apparel manufacturing alone employs more people than the entire printing and publishing field and more than the automobile manufacturing industry. Many additional workers are employed in producing such items as fur and leather garments, accessory items, shoes, and jewelry.

In addition to the industries that *make* fashion products, we find that the sectors that *sell* fashion products also add greatly to the economy and provide employment for large numbers of workers. More than 20 million Americans, 18 percent of the nation's workforce, are employed by retailers. Among these, more than 3.6 million are employed in general merchandising and apparel specialty stores (National Retail Institute, 1995).

To see the full picture of the fashion industry's contributions, we must add the employment in finance, transportation, advertising, utilities, and other essential services that devote part of their efforts to the fashion industry. It soon becomes obvious that the industry has an astounding impact on our economy.

The Democratization of Fashion: A Brief Historical Perspective

The textile and clothing industries have played an important role in the history of the United States. Besides contributing a great deal to the economy, the development of an industry that produced affordable clothing for the population added to the spirit of equality and democracy that were important principles of American life. Mass production of clothing has provided a majority of Americans with a more than adequate supply of good-quality garments. One should keep in mind, however, that the generous supply of ready-made apparel, as we know it today, was not available during a good portion of our country's early history.

---

[2]This figure is in current dollars.

In eighteenth-century America, two types of textile fabrics were available: the high-quality textiles for the rich and the low-quality textiles to clothe the poor. There was very little in between. Rich Americans took advantage of the products from the English textile industry, because the U.S. industry had only begun to develop by the latter part of the century. Not only was there virtually no U.S. textile industry at that time, but the apparel industry did not develop significantly for nearly a century. Therefore, early clothing for Americans varied both in the quality of the textiles and in the construction of the clothing. Wealthy Americans had their clothing custom produced from the fine fabrics. In contrast, those of less fortune wore clothing of fabrics characterized by a common quality of coarseness (Dickerson, 1991).

Kidwell and Christman (1974) noted that in colonial America, obtaining clothing was more difficult than securing food or shelter. A majority of families of ordinary means produced all their own clothing from raising flax and keeping sheep to provide fiber, which was transformed through time-consuming hand methods into fabrics and garments. Fabrics made from home-grown fibers were made into clothing for families by wives and mothers who had few tools and usually no training. Housewives made clothing to protect family members from the elements rather than to look fashionable. Consequently, in these early years, one's financial standing was readily apparent by one's clothing.

Kidwell and Christman's book, *Suiting Everyone: The Democratization of Clothing in America* (1974), focused on the development of the U.S. apparel industry and the role the industry has played in making "average Americans the best dressed average people in the world." The authors cited a quote by William C. Browning, a second-generation clothing manufacturer, as providing the essence of what they call the "democratization of clothing":

> And if it be true . . . that the condition of a people is indicated by its clothing, America's place in the scale of civilized lands is a high one. We have provided not alone abundant clothing at a moderate cost for all classes of citizens, but we have given them at the same time that style and character in dress that is essential to the self-respect of a free, democratic people. (p. 15)

In summary, the apparel industry that developed not only became a major U.S. industrial sector, providing employment and income for large numbers of workers through the years, but it also became an industry that manufactured products that enabled the population to have clothing that obliterated ethnic origins and blurred social distinctions. Although the apparel sector played a vital role in the economic development of the country, the industry contributed importantly beyond that to the spirit and climate of equality on which the new independent nation was founded (Dickerson, 1991).

The vast selection of fashion goods and the competitive prices found in the U.S. market are the envy of much of the world. Even today, individuals from almost any socioeconomic group can be well-dressed.

The Fashion Pipeline: Channel of Distribution

There are three main links in the production and distribution of fashion products. These are referred to as the **channel of distribution**—that is, the network of interrelated functions involved in moving products from where they begin to the consumer.

Other terms used to describe these linkages are the *production-distribution chain* or the *fashion pipeline*. The major segments are:

- **Component suppliers.** Companies in this group provide the raw materials of fashion, such as fibers, fabrics, leathers, and furs. They may also be the suppliers of buttons, zippers, threads, and other products required to produce finished items.
- **Finished product suppliers.** Firms in this group manufacture finished products of apparel and accessories.
- **Retail distributors.** This group includes all forms of retailing—stores, catalogs, television shopping, Internet shopping, and so on—that provide the link to get fashion products from the manufacturer to the consumer.

These three segments must work together closely to produce and deliver products quickly. The term **softgoods industry** often refers to the total network or chain of these interconnected segments. However, the softgoods industry label generally includes textile home furnishings and other textile products, as well as apparel and accessories.

All three segments of the industry are interdependent. The challenging business environment in recent years has forced all segments to work together more closely to respond to consumers' needs. The component suppliers depend on the finished product suppliers for the sale of their products; the finished product suppliers depend on the retailer, who is the final link between the consumer and the vast network of the fashion-producing industry. Within that network are enterprises of many different types. Figure 1–1 provides a flow chart to illustrate the main segments and the interrelationships of each. More competition and less **concentration** occur in the downward segments of the channel of distribution. That is, there are more companies to compete. Subsequent chapters discuss the activities of each in detail.

A detailed graphic inside the back cover of this book depicts the numerous segments of the industry involved in producing a garment. To obtain a four-color brochure featuring this graphic in greater detail, contact Textile/Clothing Technology Corporation, [TC]², at 211 Gregson Drive, Cary, NC 27511-7909 or FAX: 919-380-2181.

Figure 1–A Classification System for Various Segments of the Industry

Often it is important to be able to look at the overall business activities of specific segments of the fashion industry. The U.S. Office of Management and Budget has a classification system that lets us do that and also permits further designations for specific product categories. This scheme is called the **Standard Industrial Classification (SIC)** system, and it classifies industry groupings on the basis of their primary economic activity. The efforts of every establishment can be assigned to one of the SIC groups. The *major categories* in the fashion industry are:

- **Manufactured fibers** are in *SIC 28*, the *chemical and allied products grouping*, because of their chemical origin, rather than with other textile components.
- **Textile mill products** comprise *group 22 (SIC 22)*. These are the yarns, fabrics, and other textile components.
- **Apparel** constitutes *group 23 (SIC 23)*.
- **Retailing** of fashion products generally falls in *SIC 53, general merchandise stores*, or *SIC 56, apparel and accessory stores*.

Note that two digits represent each major industry segment. In later chapters, we shall see that two additional digits define the specific type of products within the major groups.

Figure 1-1 **The fashion pipeline**

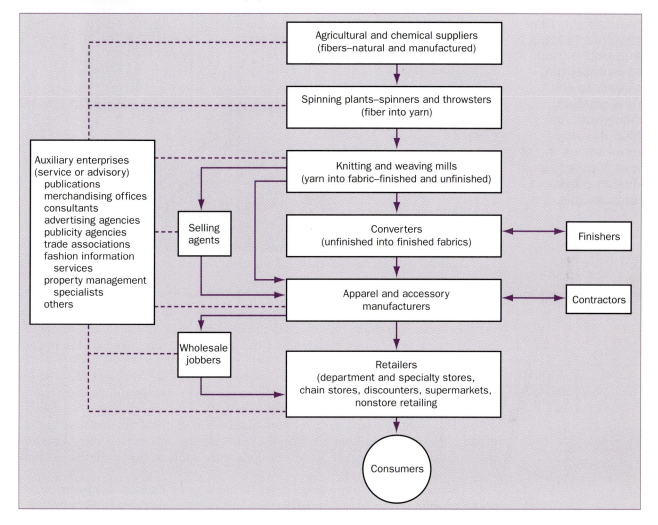

Timing of Product Development and Showings

Each link in the fashion industry chain periodically presents its new styles early to those in the next level of production, so that producers and sellers can in turn prepare their lines or collections in advance of the consumer buying periods. For example, the colors, weaves, and fabrics that are expected to receive consumer acceptance are researched and selected a year or more before the consumer will see them.

In the past, each branch of the industry announced its new lines according to a fairly traditional schedule based on several factors: the change of the season; the time required to produce goods after buyers placed their orders; and the time required by product developers (whose titles might have been fashion director, designer, stylist, or creative director) to assess the pulse of the market. Products often took a year or more to get from the design stage to the consumer.

Today, however, a changing market and new computer technologies have drastically changed traditional merchandising practices for apparel manufacturers and

Figure 1–2

Computers have reduced the time required to bring a garment from the conceptual stages to the final product. Designers can also develop more styles in less time using design programs such as this one.

Source: Courtesy of Gerber Garment Technology, Inc.

retailers. We have seen a dramatic compression of the time sequence required to develop new products and to get them to the customer. Many of the time-consuming activities now use computer techniques that reduce the time required for various stages. For example, using computer-aided design, the apparel manufacturer works with retailers to develop new lines that can be viewed on the computer and adapted on the screen, rather than going through time-consuming stages of making samples to see if designs give the desired effect (Figure 1–2).

Changes of this type have revolutionized the traditional timetable for getting products to market. Fashion merchandising has increasingly moved away from the traditional cycles and, instead, has evolved more and more toward a continuous flow of new products.

Using these newer approaches to producing fashion merchandise, many retailers and manufacturers have formed partnerships to make the flows work even faster. Both want to please the customer. As part of this, many companies use consumer style testing to determine through early, small orders if customers do actually like what is being produced. If they do, modern manufacturers can produce and ship quickly because they have new technologies that permit them to respond rapidly.

Fashion and the Profit Motive

Although the fashion industry is seen as a glamorous, dynamic field, companies are in the business for one reason only—to make a profit. If they do not succeed in being profitable, even the most dazzling fashion lines will not continue. Creativity and dedication mean nothing if an enterprise is not economically viable.

From Neiman Marcus in New York to Wal-Mart in Peoria, garments must appeal to customers willing to buy the merchandise. Customers who vote with their dollars are necessary so those who work in the production and retailing of fashion products find it financially worthwhile to be involved.

Although the fashion industry is among the most exciting fields in the world, it is also difficult, demanding, unpredictable, and exhausting. Despite the enchanting interplay of creativity, marketing wit, business acumen, and media hype, everything comes down to the bottom line. The accountant's financial statement must show a profit for an enterprise to continue. The fashion business is not a charitable business or a kind business. To be *in* business, a company—no matter how large or how small—must be a *profitable* business.

Companies must be profitable because those who own the firms are expecting profits. This applies to all segments of the fashion industry. Ownership may be considered in two major groupings:

- **Privately held companies** are owned by individuals, partners, or groups. Financial information about the company does not have to be made public, and profits go to the owners. In early days of the fashion industry, a majority of companies were started and owned by individuals; thus, they were of this type. Most small firms today still fall into this category. Two very large private U.S. companies are Levi Strauss & Co., one of the largest apparel firms in the world, and Milliken and Company, one of the largest textile firms worldwide.
- **Publicly held companies** are those owned by shareholders who have purchased stock in the company. Most of the largest textile, apparel, and retailing firms are of this type. Publicly held companies are required to report on their financial performance regularly to **shareholders** (or stockholders). Depending on how well the companies are performing, people may want to buy or sell stock in a company. If a company is doing well, potential buyers are attracted to buy that company's stock. If the company is doing poorly, shareholders may be inclined to sell their stock and invest in another firm earning higher profits. Therefore, large, publicly owned companies must strive to please their owners—the shareholders—who want a return on their investment in the form of **dividends.**

  Sometimes, publicly held companies in the fashion industry go through highs and lows of popularity with potential shareholders. For example, when Liz Claiborne products have been popular with consumers and selling well, investors are attracted to the company's stock. When the Liz Claiborne line loses some of its appeal and customers stop buying the company's fashions as they had before, the value of the company's stock declines. During the "low" time, potential shareholders may lose faith in the future of the company and are less inclined to buy the stock. Similarly, existing shareholders may sell.

  Publicly owned companies publish **annual reports,** which give a review of the firm's business activities for the year and a statement of the current financial position. These provide important profiles on companies. Annual reports also provide tangible evidence that the fashion business is also big business! Examples of annual reports from companies in the fashion industry are seen in Figure 1–3.

Anyone wishing to follow the stock of a company may do so through various ways. *The Wall Street Journal* is a primary source used to follow the performance of company stocks. A number of other services provide updates on companies' performance and even make recommendations on whether a company's stock is a good buy at the time. Examples of these are Value Line and Standard & Poor's. These services usually show a graph to illustrate the company's stock price over a period of time. An example is shown in Figure 1–4.

The Consumption of Fashion Goods

The fashion industries, like most other consumer goods industries in the United States today, have a productive capacity beyond what the public actually needs. At the same time, most consumers have incomes in excess of what their households require for such absolute necessities as food and shelter. This combination of ample productive capacity and ample discretionary spending power means that consumers have a wide choice as to how they will spend their money. A woman, for example, does not merely choose between one dress or another; she may also choose between a new dress and a new household appliance. Likewise, a man may choose between one jacket or another, or he may choose between a jacket and some new golf clubs.

The Role of the Consumer

The role of the ultimate consumer in the fashion business is an important one and, in the final analysis, controlling. This is a fact recognized by all successful fashion professionals. Ordinarily the part that consumers play is a passive one. People do not actually demand new products and designs of which they have little or no knowledge; neither do they demand change. Their individual and collective power is exercised in the selections they make, on the one hand, and in their refusals to buy, on the other. It is by their acceptance or rejection that they influence the goods that will be presented for their favor and even the methods of presentation. Consumers' collective acceptance or rejection results in annual figures on the industry, as shown in Table 1–1.

Figure 1–4

An example of Standard & Poor's *Stock Reports.* The report plots the trend in the stock performance and gives the Standard & Poor's analyst's views on whether the company appears to be a good investment prospect at the time.

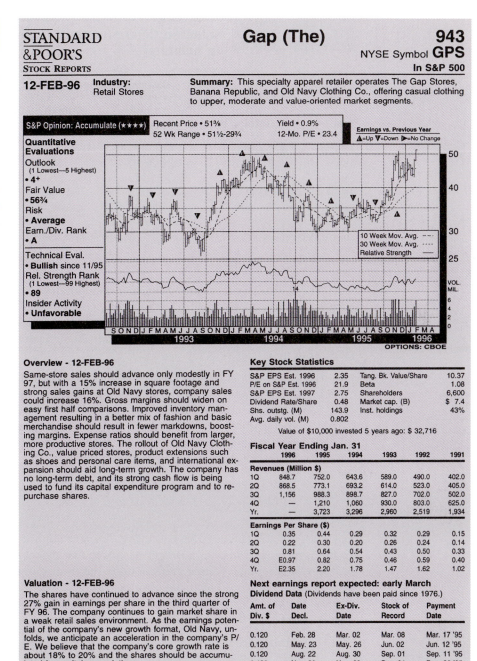

STANDARD & POOR'S
STOCK REPORTS

Gap (The)   **943**
NYSE Symbol **GPS**
In S&P 500

12-FEB-96   Industry: Retail Stores   **Summary:** This specialty apparel retailer operates The Gap Stores, Banana Republic, and Old Navy Clothing Co., offering casual clothing to upper, moderate and value-oriented market segments.

S&P Opinion: Accumulate (★★★★)   Recent Price • 51⅜   Yield • 0.9%
52 Wk Range • 51½-29¾   12-Mo. P/E • 23.4

Quantitative Evaluations

Outlook
(1 Lowest—5 Highest)
• **4+**

Fair Value
• **56¾**

Risk
• **Average**

Earn./Div. Rank
• **A**

Technical Eval.
• **Bullish** since 11/95

Rel. Strength Rank
(1 Lowest—99 Highest)
• **89**

Insider Activity
• **Unfavorable**

10 Week Mov. Avg. – –
30 Week Mov. Avg. ·····
Relative Strength —

S O N D J F M A M J J A S O N D J F M A M J J A S O N D J F M A M J J A S O N D J F M A
1993   1994   1995   1996
OPTIONS: CBOE

Overview - 12-FEB-96

Same-store sales should advance only modestly in FY 97, but with a 15% increase in square footage and strong sales gains at Old Navy stores, company sales could increase 16%. Gross margins should widen on easy first half comparisons. Improved inventory management resulting in a better mix of fashion and basic merchandise should result in fewer markdowns, boosting margins. Expense ratios should benefit from larger, more productive stores. The rollout of Old Navy Clothing Co., value priced stores, product extensions such as shoes and personal care items, and international expansion should aid long-term growth. The company has no long-term debt, and its strong cash flow is being used to fund its capital expenditure program and to repurchase shares.

Key Stock Statistics

S&P EPS Est. 1996	2.35	Tang. Bk. Value/Share	10.37
P/E on S&P Est. 1996	21.9	Beta	1.08
S&P EPS Est. 1997	2.75	Shareholders	6,600
Dividend Rate/Share	0.48	Market cap. (B)	$ 7.4
Shs. outstg. (M)	143.9	Inst. holdings	43%
Avg. daily vol. (M)	0.802		

Value of $10,000 invested 5 years ago: $ 32,716

Fiscal Year Ending Jan. 31

	1996	1995	1994	1993	1992	1991
Revenues (Million $)						
1Q	848.7	752.0	643.6	589.0	490.0	402.0
2Q	868.5	773.1	693.2	614.0	523.0	405.0
3Q	1,156	988.3	898.7	827.0	702.0	502.0
4Q	—	1,210	1,060	930.0	803.0	625.0
Yr.	—	3,723	3,296	2,960	2,519	1,934
Earnings Per Share ($)						
1Q	0.35	0.44	0.29	0.32	0.29	0.15
2Q	0.22	0.30	0.20	0.26	0.24	0.14
3Q	0.81	0.64	0.54	0.43	0.50	0.33
4Q	E0.97	0.82	0.75	0.46	0.59	0.40
Yr.	E2.35	2.20	1.78	1.47	1.62	1.02

Next earnings report expected: early March
Dividend Data (Dividends have been paid since 1976.)

Amt. of Div. $	Date Decl.	Ex-Div. Date	Stock of Record	Payment Date
0.120	Feb. 28	Mar. 02	Mar. 08	Mar. 17 '95
0.120	May. 23	May. 26	Jun. 02	Jun. 12 '95
0.120	Aug. 22	Aug. 30	Sep. 01	Sep. 11 '95
0.120	Nov. 20	Nov. 29	Dec. 01	Dec. 26 '95

Valuation - 12-FEB-96

The shares have continued to advance since the strong 27% gain in earnings per share in the third quarter of FY 96. The company continues to gain market share in a weak retail sales environment. As the earnings potential of the company's new growth format, Old Navy, unfolds, we anticipate an acceleration in the company's P/E. We believe that the company's core growth rate is about 18% to 20% and the shares should be accumulated for capital appreciation.

Source: Reprinted courtesy of Standard & Poor's, a division of McGraw-Hill Companies.

| Table 1-1 | Selected Components of Consumer Expenditures (in millions) | | | |

| Year | Total | Clothing and Accessories | | |
		Men's and Boys'	Women's and Children's	Shoes and Other Footwear
1970	$ 52,396	$15,539	$ 28,794	$ 8,063
1975	70,021	20,807	38,519	10,695
1980	102,831	30,142	56,909	15,780
1989	200,100	55,900	115,100	29,100
1995	254,400	77,900	140,300	36,200

Source: Department of Commerce, Bureau of Economic Analysis, *Survey of Current Business,* various years.

The controlling role of the consumer is not unique to the fashion industry. Every business that serves the public has to guide its operations in light of consumer demand. The fashion industry, however, moves at a fast tempo. The rewards of success are great and the cost of failure correspondingly high. As the late Dr. Paul H. Nystrom (1929) put it:

> Consumer demand is the guide to intelligent production and merchandising. . . . A knowledge of the fundamental facts of what consumers want and why, is clearly of the first importance . . . to those who plan the policies, design the product, determine the price lines, prepare the advertising and sales promotion, sell the goods and make the collections, in fact all who deal with the problems of the consumer.

The role of the consumer will be examined in greater detail in Chapter 3.

The Power of Fashion

Few words in any language have as many different implications as the word *fashion.* To the layperson, it implies a mysterious force that makes a particular style of dress or behavior acceptable in one year but quite the reverse in another. Economists view fashion as an element of artificial **obsolescence** that impels people to replace articles that still retain much of their original usefulness even though the new articles may not greatly differ from the old ones. As one writer noted:

> The economic, as distinct from social, *raison d'être* of fashion resides in the need to make people buy things they don't need. If the clothes can't be relied upon to wear out fast enough, something must be found that will wear out faster; that something is what we call fashion. But fashion is one form of the familiar capitalist technique of planned obsolescence which can be enjoyed with a clear conscience. Many of the world's people wear secondhand clothes, which are available in good condition at low prices because of the fickleness of their original buyers. (Gopnik, 1994, p. 16)

To sociologists, fashion represents an expression of social interaction and of status seeking (Barber & Lobel, 1952; Merton, 1949). Psychiatrists find indications of sex impulses in patterns of dress (Bergler, 1953). But whatever fashion may mean to others, it represents billions of dollars in sales to the group of enterprises concerned with the production and distribution of apparel and accessories. As one fashion scholar said, "Everything that matters, everything that gives their trade its nature and place in the world must be ascribed to fashion" (Robinson, 1962).

Fashion, in and of itself, does not create consumer purchasing power, but wherever there is such purchasing power, there is interest in fashion. In times past, when purchasing power was concentrated among the wealthy few, they alone pursued fashion. Today, with widespread ability to spend, the great masses of people follow fashion, and thus fashion determines both the character and the direction of consumption. Although such factors as price, durability, convenience of use, and quality of workmanship are also of concern to the consumer, they mean relatively little unless the purchased articles are also clearly identified with the prevailing fashions. Fashion is also an important factor in the replacement market for such utilitarian items as household goods; it is often more important than wear and tear in motivating discard and replacement of furniture, kitchen utensils, and automobiles, for example. Businesses that serve the consumer succeed when they go with the fashion, but are doomed to fail whenever they go against the tide.

Major Industry Trends

In recent years, the fashion production-distribution chain has undergone dramatic **restructuring**. The industry does not resemble the one that existed 25 years ago. Just as fashion products change, *the industry itself* keeps evolving. These changes reflect the dynamic nature of the industry as it responds to economic conditions, to business trends in general, and to consumers whose purchasing patterns vary from one time to another.

We shall discuss briefly some of the changes here to highlight trends that have affected the whole fashion industry. Many of these will be covered further in detail in later chapters.

Mergers and Acquisitions

Many companies, both manufacturers and retailers, have had **mergers** with others to form larger, stronger firms. Some companies have acquired others. The net result of these business moves has been the formation of many very large and very powerful firms. For example, Federated Stores purchased Macy's. Even before the **acquisition**, each was among the largest retailers in the industry. Together, these mega-merchants have enormous control over the marketing system and manufacturers' access to consumers. To illustrate this, Kurt Salmon Associates, a leading consulting firm for the industry, noted that in 1987, the five largest apparel retailers accounted for 35 percent of all retail sales; by 1991, the five took 45 percent of the market; and these experts estimated those five may now account for half of all apparel retail sales (Harris, 1994).

On the manufacturers' side, the large companies have also grown larger. For apparel firms, Kurt Salmon has noted that the top five apparel firms now account for about 75 percent of the total sales of all publicly held apparel firms (about half the total market). Similarly, the two top footwear firms account for 55 percent of the sales of publicly held footwear companies.

A leader in this movement toward becoming a mega-player in apparel, VF Corporation has continued to acquire apparel firms in many product categories in the United States and abroad. This strategy gives VF product lines that have been targeted at various channels of distribution. This means VF can sell its Girbaud jeans in up-scale stores, its Lee jeans to stores serving the middle-income consumer, and its Wrangler jeans to discount stores. In general, mergers and acquisitions lead to a concentration by a small number of firms, especially in some industry segments. In many areas, these industry giants have a major portion of the market. Although the move toward forming giants may lead to greater efficiency and productivity, there is also the risk that this strategy reduces the innovation and creativity needed in the industry. In other words, the growth of these giants has the potential of adding to the "sameness" which has characterized the industry in recent years. Consumers want fresh looks and grow tired of finding essentially the same thing everywhere they shop.

Although the high-fashion segments of the industry often receive a great deal of attention, those portions generally represent a relatively small portion of the total fashion industry business. On the other hand, the giants, often formed through mergers and acquisitions, dominate the industry. Most of these giants serve the mass market with mass-produced products and account for the major portion of the business in the industry. While the high-fashion part of the industry adds excitement and, often, the sense of fashion direction, the "big bucks" generally are connected to companies that serve the mass markets.

Vertical Operations

Companies in different segments of the industry have taken on activities that were previously handled by other players in the industry. For example, manufacturers have expanded into the retail business and retailers have entered the manufacturing area. Although these **vertical operations** are not new in the fashion industries, the dramatic increase in the number of firms using this strategy *is* a significant change. In the menswear industry, manufacturer-owned retail stores have existed for decades. More recently, however, these vertical ventures have proliferated in women's wear and accessories areas.

Examples exist at all levels in the industry, but it is most obvious and visible at the manufacturer-retailer interface. Some of the most successful companies on both sides of this divide are taking over functions that once were performed exclusively by their suppliers or customers. For example, a retailer such as The Limited is involved actively in designing and overseeing production of much of the merchandise it sells. Conversely, many manufacturers have opened their own retail stores. In a dramatic move, Levi Strauss & Co. opened retail stores in the mid-1990s. As evidence of this trend, outlet malls have sprung up around the country.

In the manufacturing sector, some apparel firms have become vertically integrated so they have control over the supply and quality of fabrics needed to produce their garments. Today, many yarn spinners, knitters, weavers, apparel producers, and retailers, who formerly were mutually exclusive and distinctive segments of the fashion industries, are losing their familiar identities and have taken over some of each other's roles.

Verticalization, like mergers and acquisitions, has led to a smaller number of companies—many of them giants. These vertical operations have added to the intensely competitive conditions of the fashion industry. Although verticalization may reduce the number of competing firms, those that remain are larger, more powerful industry players.

Globalization

Advances in communication and transportation systems have changed the world from a collection of fairly independent national economies to a global economy. In some respects, this is not new for the textile and apparel industries. The fashion industry has long functioned in response to international events such as the European couture showings, and for centuries, textile products played an important role in international trade.

Although textile and apparel products have been part of international commerce for decades, the earlier activities were hardly a warm-up for the rapid **globalization** of the industry today. Now, the fashion industry is very global in nature—requiring those of us who follow the industry to think globally. Today, the labels on our fashion products resemble a geography course. Consumers are wearing garments from countries they may be unable to find on a map. Apparel manufacturers frequently have their garments assembled in remote nations that were unlikely production sites a few years ago, such as the factory in India shown in Figure 1–5. Retailers travel worldwide to find products for their stores, often arranging for the production directly themselves, just as manufacturers do.

U.S. textile and apparel manufacturers are now setting their sights on the markets of other countries, after many years of focusing on just the domestic market. For many years, U.S. manufacturers spent a great deal of their time and resources fighting

Figure 1–5 | **Many garments sold in the market today are made by workers in other countries.**

Source: World Bank Photo.

imports rather than considering potential markets for their products in other parts of the world. Today, a number of U.S. textile and apparel firms sell their products in other parts of the world, including Levi, Russell, Lee, Sara Lee (for example, Playtex, Bali, Hanes), and many others. Designers, such as Donna Karan, Ralph Lauren, and Joseph Abboud, have opened their own stores in other countries.

Retailers are becoming increasingly global, too. U.S. retail chains such as Talbots, Kmart, J.C. Penney, and Wal-Mart are opening stores in many other countries as part of ambitious global expansion plans. A number of U.S. retailers have opened stores in Japan. L.L. Bean distributes its catalogs in more than 145 countries. Globalization of retailing is expected to continue.

Influence of the Electronic-Information Age

Communication technologies go hand in hand with the globalization of the industry. Through today's communication systems, a firm in New York can transfer via satellite its designs and markers (diagrams or layouts of pattern pieces to be cut from fabrics) to a firm in Hong Kong, where they are printed to be cut and produced. Or, a U.S. firm may communicate easily by telephone and fax with a company in Indonesia contracted to manufacture its line. Through video conferencing, retail buyers may view lines of fashions available to them from Asian producers without having to leave their offices. Retailers may conduct business with market showrooms via video conferencing (Figure 1–6). They may even do their buying through "on-line" services (Figure 1–7).

In the United States, some of the major apparel firms such as VF Corporation and Kellwood Company have computer systems that hook to those of retailers such as J.C. Penney and Wal-Mart. The reordering systems are so precise that when a pair of jeans is sold in a store, a replacement pair is back on the shelf in a matter of days.

Computer technologies have reshaped the fashion industry in nearly every aspect of the business. These advances have increased the variety and availability of products, shortened production time, improved design and manufacturing procedures, and in general eliminated many time-consuming manual operations in every facet of the industry. The Internet brings to both industry and consumers a plethora of new ways to find products and information (see Figure 1–8 on p.19).

The information age is even changing how consumers shop. The information super-highway has made possible electronic interactive retailing. The consumer can stay home and buy his or her new fashion products online via the Internet. If he or she is not connected to surf the Internet, a CD-ROM catalog or TV home shopping offers other choices (see Figure 1–9 on p. 20). These new options for shopping, along with a proliferation of printed catalogs, pose threats to traditional retailers who have built stores on the premise that consumers will come to them.

A Changing Consumer

The industry has found it difficult in the 1990s to cater to a consumer whose priorities seem to have changed. In the 1980s, consumers were eager fashion-spenders. Brand names were important, and consumers were willing to pay for status products. In the 1990s, however, consumers are value-driven, demanding more for less. As Mackey McDonald, President and CEO of VF Corporation, noted, "The consumer is now in control" (Maycumber, 1995, p. 9).

Consumers make apparel expenditures much more cautiously than in the past and are not easily manipulated by promotional efforts geared to encourage them to buy things they don't need or want. Caution is in part related to concerns over the

Figure 1–6

CaliforniaMart's video conferencing is an example of how the electronic age is transforming the way the fashion industry conducts business. Using video conferencing, retail buyers can view manufacturers' lines without the time and expense involved in travel to visit the Mart's showrooms.

INTRODUCING VIDEO CONFERENCING.
IT'S LIKE HAVING YOUR OWN RUNWAY ON
THE INFORMATION SUPER HIGHWAY.

The CaliforniaMart is coming to your neighborhood. Thanks to our new **VIDEO CONFERENCING CENTER**, a revolutionary communications technology, CaliforniaMart tenants can conduct business like never before. With over 3500 video conferencing centers nationwide, tenants can now meet face-to-face with buyers without having to meet in person, saving both time and money. Video conferencing is just part of the **$14 MILLION MODERNIZATION** plans for 1995. A **SATELLITE BROADCASTING STUDIO**, an **1,800 SEAT FASHION THEATRE**, and a new **BUYER'S LOUNGE** are in the works, not to mention a total renovation of the lobby. When completed, the CaliforniaMart will be transformed into the fashion center of the 21st century. Of course, some things won't change. We are still the only fashion center **OPEN 52 WEEKS A YEAR**, and we'll continue to be the world's destination for the latest in California fashion. Our **BUYERS' INCENTIVE PROGRAM** will continue to be the most generous in the industry. With all that's planned for 1995 and the future, the CaliforniaMart is the place to be — whether you're here in person or on video. Please call our new **AUTOMATED FAXBACK SYSTEM** for information at 1-800-404-0244. For **LEASING** information call: 1-800-CAL-MART, Ext 524.

CALIFORNIAMART *The World's Resource for Fashion*

Source: Figure courtesy of CaliforniaMart.

In this advertisement from a leading trade paper, we see another option provided by the electronic age. In this case, manufacturers may present their products on computers, permitting retail buyers to make their selections from their offices rather than having to travel to market.

Figure 1–7

 E.R.I.C.
Electronic Retail Image Catalog™

7th Avenue ON LINE and ON CD!

Vendor:
Adidas

Style Number:
027022

Phone Number:
507-797-4937

Price:
$10.00

The Newest Innovation Since E.D.I.!

RETAILERS Add Full Color Pictures To Your Existing Computer Systems!

- E.R.I.C.'s Technology has already made buying easier and cost effective! ADD COLOR IMAGES of current style assortments to all your existing computer systems: P.O.S., Inventory Control etc.

- AVOID COSTLY MARK DOWN MISTAKES! With pictures in your data base, store employees will always correctly identify styles to mark down - SAVE MONEY!

No Purchase or Lease of any Computer Equipment Required from E.R.I.C.!

For More Information and Member Application Write or Call:
E.R.I.C. • 1359 Broadway, Suite 1200, New York, NY 10018
212-244-0600 • 800-800-ERIC • FAX: 212-244-7600

See E.R.I.C. at MAGIC Booths #1122 & P-9727

Source: Figure courtesy of Electronic Retail Image Catalog.™

18

Figure 1–8

Check out these examples of Internet sites related to the fashion industry.

Consumer Shopping Venues

Fashion Magazine@Fashion:	http://www.delphi.com/news/fashion
Fashion Mall:	http://www.fashionmall.com/
Internet Mall:	http://www.mecklerweb.com
J.C.Penney:	http://www.jcpenney.com
MCI Marketplace:	http://www.internetmci.com
Shopping 2000:	http://www.shopping2000.com
Vintage Clothing:	http://www.cs.brown.edu/people/smh/vintage/vintage.html

Industry/Government Venues

The Apparel Exchange:	http://www.apparelex.com
Apparel.Net:	http://www.apparel.net/
Bobbin Magazine:	http://www.bobbin.com
Fabrics On-line:	http://www.fabrics.com
Technology Exchange:	http://www.webcom.com/tekguru/
Textile Information Management System:	http://www.unicate.com
U.S. Department of Commerce Office of Textiles and Apparel (OTEXA):	http://www.ita.doc.gov/industry/textiles/

Keep in mind that these are just a small sample of the resources available via the Internet. New ones are being created every day. You can find others in trade and consumer publications or in sources such as the *Internet Yellow Pages*.

economy. Priorities have changed; for many consumers, new clothing is no longer a high priority. Additionally, consumers are exerting a new independence. They are more likely to define their own styles and more likely to resist being dictated to by industry. Moreover, because they have so many choices, consumers have no reason to feel they have to buy a particular brand or shop at any special store.

Firms in all segments of the industry are scrambling to find ways to attract and satisfy an increasingly demanding consumer. Many are using new computer technologies to track the needs of more and more narrow segments of the consumer market in hopes of tailoring products more carefully to those individuals' needs.

Rapid Transfer of Fashion

Because of satellite communication systems, consumers see new trends and want them quickly. Before these communication advances, new trends from the European fashion shows might take two years to reach the mass markets. Now, consumers almost anywhere in the world can see the fashion shows in Paris and Milan as they occur. Rather than waiting for two years, the fashion-forward consumer wants the new fashions immediately. This rapid transfer of demand places pressure on the whole manufacturing-distribution chain to be able to respond more quickly than ever before.

Rapid worldwide communication of fashion trends also means that consumers in many parts of the world may also be wearing fairly similar new lines. For example, teenagers in Los Angeles, Jakarta, Mexico City, and Taipei may be listening to the same music and wearing clothes that look amazingly similar. In fact, they are likely to be wearing clothes more like their peers in other countries than like those of an older generation in their own countries.

(a) The electronic age is also changing how consumers shop. In the comfort of their homes, consumers may review merchandise via television and order directly. (b) Home shopping network QVC has been a leader in this field in creating electronic retailing "theater."

(a)

(b)

Source: Photos courtesy of QVC.

Reducing Response Time

All segments of the industry have had to rethink and reorganize the way products are made and distributed to reduce the time required to get merchandise produced and to the retail sales floor. These strategies go by names such as **Quick Response (QR)** and **rapid replenishment.** These quick turnaround schemes have become important because no company wants to have large investments tied up in inventories sitting in warehouses.

Retailers want to be able to get merchandise quickly from apparel manufacturers when needed rather than keeping large inventories themselves. Similarly, apparel firms do not want large inventories of fabrics sitting idle in warehouses; therefore, the garment manufacturers expect to obtain deliveries of fabrics and other components quickly, as needed. This pattern occurs throughout the industry, forcing each segment to respond quickly to its respective customers. Because of these schemes, the time required to get fashion items produced and to the customer is much shorter than was true only a few years ago. These strategies have also reduced consumers' out-of-stock shopping frustrations. Although these changes have required major adjustments from the companies involved at each stage, these new strategies are beneficial to an industry based on responding to consumers' never-ending desire for the latest trends.

Companies Have Redefined Their Businesses

In their quest for improved profits, a number of companies have taken on new identities. Some have expanded the types of products they produce or sell; others have narrowed their focus to serve a specific market more effectively; others have simply shifted in what they do.

DuPont, a major fiber producer, surprised the industry by announcing the company would become involved in some areas of apparel production (which the company later discontinued). Similarly, Guilford Mills launched an apparel firm in Mexico. Jockey, once a producer of only men's undergarments, now has a thriving business in women's lines. Sara Lee, once known for cakes and other baked goods, bought one apparel company after another, including names like Playtex and Hanes, making it one of the largest U.S. apparel firms. Hanes, once known for undergarments and hosiery, now has a very large knit activewear business. Nike, formerly known for athletic shoes, now produces a wide range of activewear and has also opened its own retail outlets. Similarly, Wilson, the maker of sports equipment, now has a line of activewear apparel.

Among retailers, J.C. Penney stores moved away from hard lines (appliances, furniture, automative areas, etc.) to emphasize primarily soft lines (apparel, textile home furnishings, and so on) and to serve a target market with somewhat higher incomes than had been true earlier. The chain has transformed itself from "a stodgy store for low-priced basics into America's favorite department store with a flair for fashion" (Haber, 1994, p. 8). Similarly, after many years of struggling to find a successful identity, in the early 1990s, Sears stopped selling through its "big book" catalog and also placed greater emphasis on fashion areas. In these new identities, both J.C. Penney and Sears have attempted to attract the traditional department store customer.

Improved Industry Relationships

In the past, manufacturers and retailers had many areas of disagreement and dissention. Prices, delivery dates, quality, terms of sale, advertising costs, and many other issues led to feelings of ill will toward one another. When business did not go well, it was easy to blame the other player.

More recently, however, many manufacturers and retailers have realized that both have a great deal to gain by working together. They now realize that both gain by cooperating in ways that permit them to serve the consumer more effectively. Today, we see many manufacturers and retailers connected via computers to share information on consumer purchases. When products are sold in the store, the manufacturer is able to replenish the store's stock. This way, the next consumers find what they want in the store rather than being disappointed. Today, we see a growing number of these industry partnerships that are built upon trust and a commitment to serve the consumer well.

Increasing Customization

As consumers have become less interested in shopping, they are expecting more from the softgoods industry. They have become more demanding of product value, quality, and service that meet their needs. Many consumers are tired of the "sameness" that is part of mass production and merchandising. They are tired of the "one-size-fits-all" approach. A number of companies are responding to consumer demands for more **customized** products.

Coca-Cola, for example, now offers a much more extensive array of products than in the past. Besides Classic Coke and regular Coke, each is available in choices that include with or without sugar and with or without caffeine. Similarly, the Lee Company offers women's jeans in an almost mind-boggling array of choices: denim, corduroy, or twills; denim in traditional, stonewashed, pepperwashed, or other spattered finishes; wrinkle-free or regular; short, regular, or long lengths; relaxed fit or close fit; narrow, medium, or full leg width; elastic waist or regular waistband; and jeans for women with full thighs or those with slim thighs.

The trend toward increased customization of products and service will continue, particularly as companies compete to win market share. Computer technology permits both retailers and manufacturers to track specific consumer groups and their needs. This increased customization will place added demands on firms, however, as they are required to produce and manage a wider array of products in smaller quantities.

Social Responsibility

As industries become increasingly global, and as segments of the industries become more powerful, a heightened need for social responsibility emerges. Moreover, consumers are becoming increasingly sensitive to the need for social responsibility among all segments of business. Many consumers are now beginning to demand ethical and socially conscious conduct from those enterprises that supply their goods and services. Among the issues of growing importance are sweatshops, child labor in some countries, prison labor, unsafe working conditions, harming the environment, and violation of trade policies.

Increasingly, industries, along with consumers, are faced with choices that have implications for the environment. These concerns include: manufacturing processes that pollute the air and streams, processes that use natural resources that are in short supply, and the proliferation of products and packaging that cannot be recycled.

Consumer and labor groups have begun to expose violations of environmental, labor, and human rights codes at both the national and international levels. Resulting negative publicity has focused on some of the United States' leading firms. In short, companies are expected increasingly to be responsible citizens, both globally and in their local communities.

This chapter has provided a brief overview of the fashion industry and has considered some of the major trends affecting most segments of the industry. We see that the industry itself is in transition. When we consider both the rapid turnover of fashion goods that propels the industry, along with the revolutionary transformation occurring in the way the industry goes about its business, the combination is indeed challenging. However, we must remember that most of the transformation of the industry continues to make it stronger and more efficient.

Individuals with careers in the various fashion fields must follow the major industry trends to be aware of how their own area of business is affected by the broader changes. We might say that the only thing constant about the industry *is the change*. The fashion industry provides many exciting careers for those who are informed, energetic, persistent, and resilient.

Readings

The fashion industry has been transformed greatly by new technology and competitive market forces. Changes to date are a preview of what lies ahead for the industry.

Technology Leads the Future

by H. Joseph Gerber

Changes are occurring in the textile and apparel industries at an ever-increasing rate in design software, production methods, networking, communications and the development of new materials.

Keeping pace with those innovations, we in the business are seeing dramatic changes in retailing and marketing as the industry changes in response to the demands of a global market. In the last decade we witnessed the beginning of the transition from mass production to short-run, quick-response production. In the decade ahead, we will continue to make that transition at an accelerated pace.

Expanding Business

In the expanding global market of the last decade, quick response manufacturing would have been impossible without CAD/CAM (computer-aided design/computer-aided manufacturing) technologies. Designers would still be locked into the laborious cycle of trial-and-error without computer-aided design systems. Manufacturers would still be faced with the compounded problems of labor, material waste and inventory control without technology such as CAD/CAM systems.

Problems will never be eliminated entirely, but often it is the speed with which manufacturers adopt and use the full range of automation options that is the key.

When and where the technologies have been fully implemented, manufacturers have seen dramatic improvements in quality, material savings, increased productivity, sewing room savings and faster turnaround times.

It is safe to say that technology has become an integral part of our industry. But where will technology lead us in the future? In my opinion, technology of the future will lead us to greater prosperity.

The Future of Technology

We have just begun to adopt the concepts of quick response in manufacturing, retailing, and marketing, and now we are being pressured to adopt concepts of even "quicker response" in the near future.

I foresee a time when the buyer for a fashion house, department store, or boutique will be able to have a private showing of new designs in virtual reality. This will reduce the costs of false starts, minimize the expense of bad guesses, and increase security against copying and knock-offs.

One day the consumer will walk into a boutique and view holographic, three-dimensional designs of apparel. An on-site designer will use projected images of three-dimensional parts to create personalized fashion on demand and choose colors, fabrics and detailing. The final design will be processed, digitized and sent to the manufacturer.

A major American retailer, L. L. Bean, already is working on a concept called the "virtual catalog" for its leisurewear fashions. It employs high-speed, digital communications to display fashions in broadcast-quality color, animation and stereo sound.

Several innovative American manufacturers, including VF Corp., have developed a computerized market response system that connects their own computers with thousands of retailers nationwide to track what shoppers buy. Each night the retailers send sales data collected on cash register scanners straight to the manufacturer, who then restocks their inventories automatically—usually in three days.

Design Horizons

But speed isn't the only advantage. By taking the guesswork out of reordering, this market response system ensures that retailers replenish only styles that sell. It takes a very small leap of imagination to conceive a data link between manufacturers, retailers, and consumers. Interactive television sets and home computers will make it possible.

One day the consumer will be able to view virtual catalogs at home. And the order for a made-to-measure garment can be sent directly to the manufacturer to be produced in a matter of hours.

In the last 30 years we created synthetics that look and feel like natural fibers. And recently we've created fibers from recycled materials. I can envision garments made of fibers with special materials embedded in the layers that respond to temperature, body perspiration and solar radiation.

In effect, our own bodies may power fashionable and functional environmental chambers made of composite materials.

Record Production Time

Designers will create the most imaginative designs, drape them in the material of choice, and display them in motion as three-dimensional images. Their creations will be compiled in digital form and sent over the information superhighway to fashion buyers, retailers, and consumers worldwide.

Physical dimensions of a buyer stored in a digital database will be used for made-to-measure orders. From a designer's database or a video catalog, the manufacturer will automatically generate markers. Automatically the fabric will be cut and the work pieces moved progressively through the sewing room and shipped to the customer in record time.

Spreading systems will not only match plaids and stripes, but will detect minute flaws in the roll and optimize the lay of plies with flaw management.

And speaking of waste: new fabrics are being produced from waste products that have enormous appeal to environmentally aware consumers and manufacturers. One day textile mills will supply manufacturers with cut parts from recycled materials to reduce their impact on the environment and to increase profitability.

Many Leaders

The advances I've commented on will come from a variety of sources. Some are here already.

Digital communication links are here thanks to the computer industry. Holographic, three-dimensional imaging, virtual reality motion and related techniques are a product of science and the entertainment industry.

To participate in this future, to fully realize the profit potential, manufacturers will not only have to be farsighted, but open-minded. To compete and prosper, manufacturers will have to integrate the various technologies as they evolve.

To benefit from the changes the manufacturers must demand open systems in order to link them with their mainframe computer. And they certainly must be flexible in terms of being able to meet the demands for quicker response in an ever-expanding global market.

Source: *From K/A, June 1995, pp 10–11. Reprinted by permission of America Textiles International.*

Catalogs Soar in Cyberspace

by Janie Brooks

In cyberspace apparel manufacturers now can offer retail clients or consumers what could never be experienced in a mall or a paper catalog: virtual "fashion shows on demand." And according to the early returns at New York-based ContentWare Inc., developer of Shopping 2000, an online mall, manufacturers who do not take advantage of this alternative distribution channel now will be left behind in the race for tomorrow's computer savvy consumers.

Whether a manufacturer needs to be on the Internet or a CD-ROM distribution service is a much harder question to answer. But it appears that venturing into cyberspace has a relatively low cost currently while the nascent industry is unsophisticated and major players have not staked out big turfs. For manufacturers with large retail outlet chains or others who simply want to explore alternative distribution channels, cyberspace offers some intriguing opportunities. For those that are already developing online catalogs for retail clients, it provides a way to increase the number of consumers with ready access to that catalog.

Since November, 1994, when Shopping 2000 was launched on the Internet, clothing has been an outstanding performer, says ContentWare President Ken Koppel. Among the companies in the virtual shopping mall are outdoor clothing and gear maker Recreational Equipment Inc. or REI, Sara Lee Intimates, including the hosiery brands L'Eggs and Hanes, as well as Spiegel's and J.C. Penney's catalogs, says Koppel. Total responses, or user accesses, to Shopping 2000's catalog service exceeded 100,000 log-ons its second full month.

Shopping 2000, which was also released on CD-ROM for personal computers a month after it joined the Internet, contains 51 advertisers, and is distributed by bundling and direct mail to users of multimedia personal computers. Ordering is done on 800 phone numbers or by faxing a computer-generated order form. Future Shopping 2000 editions—two more releases planned for 1995 will include on-line ordering—by modem, Koppel says.

Shopping 2000 software can feature music, voice-overs and product pictures. ContentWare already clearly sees that the more multimedia features and interactivity offered, the better a catalog will do.

"Imagine 100 or 1,000 SKUs on a disc sent to consumers. Browse them or search by categories, fabrics or similar parameters," Koppel describes. Consumers can view multiple images per item—front, back, lining, detailing, colors. They can select a video icon and put the garment in motion, or check prices, availability and promotions.

To participate in a shared CD program like Shopping 2000, "figure about $25,000 for a well produced catalog of 100 items, heavily illustrated and with some audio, going to about 20,000 consumers," Koppel says. The CD producer provides the distribution, and the advertiser (or its agency) provides text and graphics for conversion to multimedia.

Koppel advises his Shopping 2000 customers to give the software a test run, and have realistic expectations. "Electronic merchandising at the wholesale and retail levels is definitely coming," he says. "But don't look for instant payback," he warns, noting that proper combinations of merchandise, display, ordering mechanisms and distribution are still being developed. "On the other hand, not getting involved at this stage [will] guarantee falling behind more aggressive competitors—and the price now is right."

Source: From Apparel Industry Magazine, *May 1995, p. 8. Reprinted by permission.*

Teens Seen as the First Truly Global Consumers

by Cyndee Miller

Move over Generation X. Marketers have a new infatuation, the so-called global teens, a tribe of weened-on-MTV youngsters who show remarkably similar attitudes and shopping patterns.

From Rio to Rochester, today's teens can be found enmeshed in much the same regimen: watching "90210," drinking Coke, moshing to Green Day, dining on Big Macs, surfin' the 'Net on their Macintosh computers, and lining up to see *Ace Ventura: Pet Detective*. And then there's the international teen uniform: baggy Levi's or Diesel jeans, T-shirt, Nikes or Doc Martens, and leather jacket.

"Certainly from what I see in Europe, there's no doubt that there are much greater similarities among teens than there were 20 years ago," said Simon Fitall, president of Marketing Resources International in England. "There are huge similarities in the way in which teens look and in their consumption patterns."

The most common explanation for the phenomenon is that this is the first generation uniquely tied together by a worldwide media web that spreads trends faster than you can say, "I want my MTV."

"You see Beavis and Butt-head all over Europe," Fitall agreed, along with a slew of other teen-oriented TV shows such as "*Baywatch*."

Even with the rise of the global teen, marketing will "remain the same in some respects because you still have local differences that require subtle differentiations," Fitall said. "But I think you'll see more and more products taking a much more global approach."

To get the scoop on today's youth, DMB&B recently looked at the cultural attitudes and consumer behavior of more than 6,500 teenagers in 26 countries. The results revealed that "teens around the world are living very parallel lives," said Elissa Moses, the agency's senior vice president and director of strategic planning.

Anointing today's teens as the first truly global consumers, Moses declared their coming of age as "one of the greatest marketing opportunities of all time."

She agreed that media have been a powerful force in bringing them together and added that global events, including the Olympics, have been another influence. Yet another reason for the similarities is that they're all shopping at the same stores.

"From South Africa to Europe to the Far East, the malls all look alike," Moses said.

"From a targeting standpoint, this is wonderful news for marketers," she added. "There's much more common ground."

But, she warned, that "doesn't preclude the necessity to look at regional and country differences. I'm in no way advocating one-size-fits-all communications or advertising. That's just foolish. There will always be local forces that you can't ignore."

In the U.S., the teen population hit 25 million last year and over the next 15 years is expected to reach 30.8 million—about 900,000 more than during the baby boom's peak years. The market may be even more promising in Latin America and Asia, which have much younger populations.

Moses said she was interested in doing the study because she was convinced that teens weren't as "angst-filled and apathetic as they were being portrayed in ads." What Moses found was a "generation that's wise beyond its years. It's like these 35-year-old minds in 16-year-old bodies."

It's a generation best described as realistic, and Moses warned that marketers "better shoot straight with these kids." But that doesn't mean they don't want to yuk it up.

"They want to laugh," she said. "They like humor. They like fun. They want realism, but that doesn't mean to make it gritty. It means don't try to pull anything over on them. It means be candid."

The study also revealed a perceived "Americanization" of fashion and culture. When asked what countries had the most influence on fashion and culture, the U.S. was named by 54% of teens from the U.S., 87% of those from Latin America, 80% of the Europeans, and 80% of those from the Far East.

"It's not just Levi's and Nikes," Moses said. "Movies, TV, and music come from America. It's a cultural force as well as a consumer goods force."

She added that the "so-called American brands are made all over the world and customized so that despite the fact that these brands come from America, teens in [other] countries still feel like they're their brands."

International marketing researcher and consultant Gunilla Broadbent agreed that "this is the first generation where you can really talk about a global consumer." She doesn't think America dominates teen culture anymore, with the possible exception of Levi's, which is "*the* thing for teens to have, and that's true around the world."

Broadbent has held marketing positions in Indonesia, Japan, Tunisia, Switzerland, Sweden, and France. She is currently president of BAI International, Tarrytown, N.Y.

Broadbent sees an increasing influence coming from Europe, Asia, and Latin America. Even American kids are "much more keen on trying foreign brands and less prone to stick to American brands, but [foreign manufacturers] don't know that yet."

In addition, the emergence of the European Union (EU) has brought teens from those countries closer together. "Young generations of Spaniards, Italians, and French have much more in common. They feel European," she said, and use more European brands. Those teens aren't necessarily embracing American brands, "as opposed to 10 years ago, when everyone wanted to be just like an American kid," said Broadbent.

The increased nationalism "doesn't go against the global trend," but marketers have to "take great care with their advertising and how they position their products."

American ads, for example, typically use a lot of superlatives, and many Europeans and Asians prefer a more subtle tone. "Saying you're the best or you're number one doesn't go over very well," she said, and they don't care much for comparative ads, another staple in the U.S.

Not everyone, however, is buying into the global teen thing.

"Pay attention to who is promoting this idea and what they have to benefit from the prospect of the global teen," said Richard Leonard, vice president of The Zandl Group, a youth marketing consulting firm in New York.

"It's the ad agencies that are eager to improve their international business that are saying the youth market is global and that consequently they don't need to split their business among various local agencies," he said.

Leonard argues that there are "certain fundamental values that young people around the globe share, but the cultural differences are so prominent that it's extremely difficult to speak in one voice throughout the world."

"Look at the most popular recording artists, comedians, and movies in each country, and you'll find very different tastes," he said. Even MTV is moving in that direction with more localized broadcasts.

Teens also have different attitudes toward advertising, with those in the developed countries viewing it as entertainment, while those in Third World countries, "who don't have the experience as consumers that teens in the U.S., Western Europe, or Japan have, are much less cynical regarding advertising."

"Global marketing is a fallacy," he said. "It's a very popular idea because it appears to represent cost efficiencies." But few brands can attain that efficiency, he said, and they're usually prestige brands, such as Chanel, that are not primarily targeted to young people.

Source: From Marketing News, *March 27, 1995, p. 9. Reprinted by permission.*

Chapter Review

Key Words and Concepts

Define, identify, or briefly explain the following:

Acquisition
Annual reports
Apparel
Channel of distribution
Component suppliers
Concentration
Customization
Dividends
Finished product suppliers
Globalization
Industrialization
Manufactured fibers
Merger

Obsolescence
Privately held companies
Publicly held companies
Quick Response (QR)
Rapid replenishment
Restructuring
Retail distributors
Retailing
Shareholders
Standard Industrial Classification (SIC)
Softgoods industry
Textile mill products industry
Vertical operations

Review Questions on Chapter Highlights

1. Name the different types of industries involved in the business of fashion and explain the interrelationships.
2. How is the fashion industry important globally?
3. Explain the importance of the fashion business to the economy of the United States.
4. Name the three main links in the production and distribution of fashion merchandise and explain their interrelationships.
5. What is the likely fate of a company that has terrific fashion lines but is not profitable?
6. What is the difference between a publicly owned company and a privately held one?
7. How can one follow the success of a publicly held company that produces fashion-related products?
8. How have a growing number of industry mergers and acquisitions affected the fashion industry?

9. How have your fashion purchases been affected by globalization? By the electronic-information age?
10. How do today's consumers differ from those of a decade ago? What are the implications of these changes for the fashion industry?
11. What does Quick Response mean to a manufacturer? A retailer? A consumer?
12. What does it mean to say a company has "redefined its business"?
13. Are there reasons why fashion manufacturers and retailers should have positive working relationships? Explain your answer.
14. Do you purchase any "customized" products? What are they and why do you buy them?
15. Can you think of any social issue in the news in recent times that relates to the fashion industry? Identify the issue and how it relates to the industry.

References

Barber, B., & Lobel, L. (1952, December). Fashion in women's clothes and the American social system. *Social Forces.*

Bergler, E. (1953). *Fashion and the unconscious.* New York: R. Brunner.

Department of Commerce, Bureau of Economic Analysis. (Various years). *Survey of Current Business.*

Dickerson, K. (1991). *Textiles and apparel in the international economy.* Upper Saddle River, NJ: Merrill/Prentice Hall.

Dickerson, K. (1995). *Textiles and apparel in the global economy.* Upper Saddle River, NJ: Merrill/Prentice Hall.

Gopnik, A. (1994, November 7). What it all means. *The New Yorker, LXX* (36), pp. 15–16.

Haber, H. (1994, October). The best stores: The top ten. *Women's Wear Daily* Supplement, p. 8.

Harris, C. (1994, October). *Kellwood sourcing overview.* Paper presented at Kellwood Company Import-Export Conference, St. Louis, MO.

Kidwell, C., & Christman, M. (1974). *Suiting everyone: The democratization of clothing in America.* Washington, DC: Smithsonian Institution Press.

Maycumber, G. (1995, February 16). Add value or die, says VF president McDonald. *DNR*, p. 9.

Merton, R. (1949). *Social theory and social structure.* Glencoe, IL: Free Press.

National Retail Institute. (1995). *Retail industry indicators.* Washington, DC: Author.

Nystrom, P. (1929). *Economics of consumption.* New York: Ronald Press.

Robinson, D. E. (1962, August). The economics of fashion design. *Quarterly Journal of Economics*, p. 75.

United States Department of Commerce, Economic and Statistics Administration, Bureau of Economic Analysis. (1995, April). *Survey of current business*, Table 2.6, Personal consumer expenditures by type of product. Washington, DC: Author.

United States Department of Commerce. (1994). *U.S. Industrial Outlook.* Washington, DC: Author.

Selected Bibliography

Celente, G., & Milton, T. (1991). *Trend tracking.* New York: Warner Books.

Craik, J. (1994). *The face of fashion: Cultural studies in fashion.* New York: Routledge.

Davis, F. (1994). *Fashion, culture, and identity.* Chicago: University of Chicago Press.

Dickerson, K. (1995). *Textiles and apparel in the global economy.* Upper Saddle River, NJ: Merrill/Prentice Hall.

Feather, F. (1994). *The future consumer.* Buffalo, NY: Firefly Books.

Kotler, P., & Armstrong, G. (1994). *Principles of marketing* (6th ed). Upper Saddle River, NJ: Merrill/Prentice Hall.

Kurt Salmon Associates. (1995). *Vision for the new millennium . . . evolving to consumer response.* New York: Author.

Onkvisit, S., & Shaw, J. (1993). *International marketing: Analysis and strategy* (2nd ed.). Upper Saddle River, NJ: Merrill/Prentice Hall.

Peterson, R. (Ed.). (1992). *The future of U.S. retailing: An agenda for the 21st century.* New York: Quorum Books.

Standard & Poor's. (various years). *Industry survey: Textiles, apparel, and home furnishings* and *Industry survey: Retailing.* New York: Author.

The world of fashion. (1994, November 7). *The New Yorker, LXX,* (36).

Trade Associations

American Apparel Manufacturers Association, 2500 Wilson Blvd., Suite 301, Arlington, VA 22201.

American Textile Manufacturers Institute, 1801 K St., NW, Washington, DC 20006.

Canadian Apparel Federation, Suite 605, 130 Slater St., Ottawa, Ontario K1P 6E2, Canada.

Canadian Textiles Institute, 280 Albert St., Suite 502, Ottawa, Ontario K1P 5G8, Canada.

National Retail Federation, 325 Seventh St., NW, Suite 1000, Washington, DC 20004.

Retail Council of Canada, 210 Dundas St. W.#600, Toronto, Ontario M5G 2E8, Canada.

Trade Publications

Americas Textiles International, 2100 Powers Ferry Rd., Atlanta, GA 30339.

Apparel Industry Magazine, 6255 Barfield Rd., Suite 200, Atlanta, GA 30328-4300.

Bobbin, 1110 Shop Rd., Box 1986, Columbia, SC 29202.

Canadian Apparel Manufacturer, 1 Pacifique, Ste Anne de Bellevue, Quebec H9X 1CS, Canada.

DNR, 7 W. 34th St., New York, NY 10001-8191.

Stores, 325 Seventh St., NW, Suite 1000, Washington, DC 20004.

Textile World, 4170 Ashford-Dunwoody Rd., Suite 420, Atlanta, GA 30319.

Women's Wear Daily, 7 W. 34th St., New York, NY 10001-8191.

*P*rinciples of Fashion

F*ashion, which is as old as time* and as new as tomorrow, is one of the most powerful forces in our lives. It influences what we wear, the way we talk, the foods we eat, the way we live, how and where we travel, what we look at, and what we listen to. Fashion is what leads us to discard a product that is still useful but is no longer "in." It is also what makes us sometimes wear more clothes than we may actually need, and sometimes less than is needed to protect us from the cold or the sun.

The intensity with which changes in fashion are followed by people everywhere on all levels of society is evidence of its social significance and its impact on human behavior. To be "out of fashion" is indeed to be out of the world.

This chapter discusses the generally accepted definitions of fashion and the principles governing its origin and dynamics. It also suggests some of the many implications of the fashion process for the producers and sellers of fashion goods. The readings that follow the text cover changing trends in fashion and topics related to fashion design.

The Language of Fashion

Many definitions of fashion have been given by wise and witty or learned men and women. For example, to Oscar Wilde, "fashion is a form of ugliness so intolerable that we have to alter it every six months." And according to Ambrose Bierce, "fashion is a despot whom the wise ridicule . . . and obey." Thoreau philosophized that "every generation laughs at the old fashions but follows religiously the new." And Shakespeare wrote that "fashion wears out more apparel than the man."

Since an understanding of fashion is obviously of primary importance for fashion practitioners, let us begin by defining the terms that are used by everybody and confused by some. Although the definitions that follow are formulated largely with respect to textiles and apparel—the subject of this book—it must be emphasized that they also apply to music, painting, architecture, home furnishings, automobiles, telephones, and any other consumer goods or services that one can think of.

A Style: Distinctive Characteristics

The terms **fashion** and **style** are confused by many people who say, "That's the style," when they really mean "That's the fashion." There is a world of difference in the meanings of these two terms. *A style is a type of product that has one or more specific features or characteristics that distinguish it and make it different from other products of the same type.* For example, a crew neck is one style of neckline and a turtle neck is another. All blazer jackets have certain features in common—features that make them different from, say, safari jackets—just as bow ties differ from four-in-hands.

Baggy jeans have a common characteristic—fullness—that distinguishes them from other types of jeans. Shirtwaist dresses have a distinctive feature that makes them different from wrap, sheath, or other types of dresses.

Similarly, there are different styles of fabrics, each of which has its own distinctive features, such as denim, gabardine, chiffon, and seersucker, to name but a few. In automobiles, there are such styles as convertibles, station wagons, and vans. Art has such styles as pop art, art deco, and impressionism; houses may be colonial, ranch, Victorian, or other styles. There are styles in penmanship, interior decoration, advertisements. In any one category of product, there is usually an endless variety of styles.

A Design: Variations of a Style

Within a specific style, there can be many variations in trimmings, texture, decoration, or other details. A cardigan sweater, for example, is a distinctive style, but within that style, individual variations could include different types of knits, embroideries, pockets, and necklines, to name but a few. *These individual interpretations or versions of the same style are called **designs**.* Compared with the number of styles in any given product, the possible variety of designs is limitless. Each design is different from the others in detail; they are all individual interpretations of their respective style.

In the fashion industry, when a style becomes popular, many different designs or versions of that style may be produced. In the trade, each producer assigns a **style number** to each design in the firm's line, which is used to identify it in production, selling, and shipping.

Fashion Means Consumer Acceptance

Among the countless definitions of fashion, the one from Webster's latest unabridged dictionary comes very close to what professionals mean when they use the word: *the prevailing or accepted style in dress or personal decoration established or adopted during a particular time or season.* The most widely recognized fashion authority, the late Dr. Paul H. Nystrom (1928, p. 4), defined fashion in similar words as "nothing more or less than the prevailing style at any given time." Thus, a fashion is always based on a specific style. A style, however, does not become a fashion until it gains consumer acceptance, and it remains a fashion only as long as it is accepted.

For example, bow ties, tapered jeans, crinoline skirts, and chemise dresses are and will always be styles, but they can only be called fashions if and when they become prevailing styles. It is clearly possible, moreover, for a particular style to come in and go out of fashion repeatedly. Some examples of such "ins and outs" of fashion are peasant blouses, sheath dresses, padded shoulders, and circular skirts, to name but a few.

The element of social acceptance is the very essence of fashion. Acceptance, however, does not mean that a style is necessarily worn by everyone or even by a majority of the public. Acceptance can be and usually is limited to a particular group of people or to a particular location. For example, what New York men and women wear is often unacceptable in other parts of the United States that have markedly different climates or mores. Furthermore, what is popular among a particular age or occupational group may not be accepted by those of different ages or occupations.

Other Key Fashion Terms

There are, of course, many more key words commonly used in the fashion business, and it is necessary to understand their precise meanings to understand fashion itself and follow a discussion of fashion principles.

Classics and Fads

*A **classic** is a style that continues to be accepted, to a greater or lesser degree, over an extended period of time.* In the fashion world, this means that its acceptance endures for several seasons, or even longer. Typical of classics are blazer jackets, crewneck shetland sweaters, and men's oxford cloth button-down collared shirts. From time to time, some classics can achieve a peak in popularity and become a mass fashion. That happened to the examples just cited, which in 1983 constituted the "preppy look."

In contrast to classics, there are styles that sweep suddenly into popularity, are adopted with great fervor, and then just as quickly disappear. Their acceptance is generally for a brief period and among a limited following. *These short-lived fashions are called **fads***, and they seldom have any lasting impact on future fashions. An example is the Nehru collar, which was adopted by men almost overnight several years ago and died as abruptly as it was born. Often there is a capricious aspect in a fad, as in the case of "pet rocks" and "mood rings," which were briefly and suddenly seen everywhere, and then just as suddenly were gone. Fads go up like rockets and sink without a trace once their brief popularity is over.

Limited and Mass Fashions

The term **high fashion** is commonly used to describe a *very new style, whose acceptance is limited to those who want to be first to adopt the very newest fashions and can afford their often astronomical prices.* Some of these styles are limited in appeal primarily because of the high prices they command. Their intricate design and costly workmanship keep some of them out of reach of all but people in top income brackets.[1] Other styles may be limited because they are too sophisticated or extreme to be attuned to the needs of the average man or woman. In either event, high fashion styles are generally introduced, produced, and sold in relatively small quantities, until their newness wears off. If the style has the potential for appealing to a broader audience, it is generally copied and sold at lower prices. The originator and the early purchasers, meanwhile, have gone on to something new.

Karl Lagerfeld, head of three fashion houses—Chanel, Lagerfeld, and Chloé—and perhaps the most powerful designer in the world today, noted the role of high fashion houses. He reflected that the broader public would be unlikely to buy his clothes: "I don't buy. You don't buy. I propose" (Lane, 1994, p. 86). That is, the high fashion houses set the pace for trends through their creative offerings.

In contrast with high fashion, which accounts for a relatively small portion of the fashion industry's business, there are **mass fashions** or *volume fashions*. These are *styles that are accepted and worn by a large number of people.* Mass fashions are produced and sold in large quantities at moderate prices and constitute the bread and butter of the fashion industry.

Fashion Trend

Fashions are not static; there is always movement, and that movement has a direction, discernible to careful observers. *The directions in which fashions are moving are called **fashion trends**.* For example, skirt lengths have moved up from the calf to the knee

---

[1] Despite its glamour, high fashion is only a marginal money-maker. Design houses such as Dior, Yves St. Laurent, and Givenchy and many prestigious U.S. designers rely on fragrances and accessories bearing their names to provide their profits. More recently, many of these designers have created "secondary lines" within the reach of the upper middle class as a way to support their enterprises. Examples include Ungaro's Emanuel line, Anne Klein II, and Donna Karan's DKNY (Riemer, Zinn, & Dapner, 1991).

to well above the knee—perhaps almost imperceptibly from one season to the next, but generally in an upward direction. Short jackets, as another example, sometimes gain at the expense of hip-length styles. Men's lapels or ties may be getting wider or narrower; women's shoes may be getting clunkier or more elegantly slim; the athletic workout look may be getting more or less popular than other leisure-time clothes; fabrics may go from wrinkled to creaseless; and so on. The changes from season to season may be slight, but they generally have a direction. The ability to recognize that direction or trend is vital to fashion practitioners. Since these people must work far ahead of consumers' buying periods, much of their success depends on their ability to read the signs and recognize promptly the incoming and outgoing trends in fashion. The terms *prophetic,* **avant garde,** and *forward fashions* are often used to describe styles that are gaining in acceptance.

The Constant in Fashion Is Change

If there is one absolute constant pertaining to fashion, it is the fact that it is always changing—sometimes rapidly, sometimes slowly, but it is never static or dormant. This element of change is recognized in the definitions of fashion itself cited earlier, by the use of such words as *prevailing* or *a given period of time.* To ignore the element of change is like looking at a still photograph in place of a motion picture. The still tells you what is happening here and now; the motion picture shows you what came before and what may lie ahead.

Why Fashions Change

To understand the constant changes in fashion, it is imperative to understand that fashions are always in harmony with their era. As a famous designer expressed it, "Fashion is a social phenomenon which reflects the same continuing change that rides through any given age." Changes in fashion, he emphasized, "correspond with the subtle and often hidden network of forces that operate on society. . . . In this sense, fashion is a symbol" (Beaton, 1954, pp. 335, 379–381).

Differing views exist on how fashion changes are started. Sproles (1981; Sproles & Burns, 1994) categorized these views into two groups, as follows:

- *The industry as initiators of change.* Because the fashion industry thrives on change, this idea suggests that different segments of the industry "force" change on the consumer by dictating new trends. Traditionally, the European fashion houses exerted a powerful influence; the trade media such as *Women's Wear Daily* shaped the industry's choices and, therefore, consumers' choices; and retailers dictated what would be worn by what they carried. Although all these forces are important, Sproles noted, "changing fashion is a far more complex phenomenon than those with the industry-centered views might wish to believe" (1981, p. 118). In recent years, many consumers have become increasingly resistant to having new fashions forced on them. Often consumers now exert a spirit of independence in their dress by wearing what they feel is right for them, regardless of what the industry promotes.
- *Consumers as the initiators of change.* Others who study fashion change believe consumers are responsible for what becomes fashionable. Given an array of products from which to choose, certain trends develop because a group of consumers establish that these fashions are "right." Four major theories suggest how

consumers determine the course of new trends: (1) some trends may begin with the upper socioeconomic consumers; (2) others may occur simultaneously within all socioeconomic groups; (3) sometimes fashions rise from subculture groups such as urban African Americans, youth, blue-collar workers, and ethnic minorities such as Native American; and (4) nearly any creative or innovative individual can launch fashion trends if they are consistent with the social climate and life styles of the times (Sproles, 1981). Some of these theories are discussed further in this chapter.

Some of the factors that cause consumers to initiate change follow.

Psychological Reasons

Men and women are complex creatures whose actions are seldom governed by reason alone. Change comes about for psychological reasons. People grow bored with what they have; the eye wearies of the same colors, lines, and textures after a time; what is new and different appears refreshing; and what has been on the scene for a while appears dull and unattractive. Thorstein Veblen, writing at the beginning of the century, made this clear in his *Theory of the Leisure Class*. As he pointed out: "A fancy bonnet of this year's model unquestionably appeals to our sensibilities today more forcibly than an equally fancy bonnet of the model of last year; although when viewed in the perspective of a quarter of a century, it would, I apprehend, be a matter of the utmost difficulty to award the palm for intrinsic beauty to one rather than to the other" (Veblen, 1963, p. 97).

Changes for such psychological reasons occur also in the fashions for products other than clothing. Auto manufacturers introduce new colors because potential buyers tire of the same colors. Further, for example, nothing could be more utilitarian than a broom, a refrigerator, a telephone, a tea kettle, or a hand tool. Yet people about to buy such things will be attracted to, for instance, a broom with a coppertone handle to go with a similarly colored refrigerator that has recently been purchased to replace a quite adequate white model that they discarded. This element of change for the sake of change—artificial obsolescence, in fact—touches nearly all products today. Along with boredom, human curiosity or an innate desire for new sensations leads to change for its own sake.

Rational Reasons

Changes in fashion are also caused by rational reasons, such as environmental factors that create new needs. A classic example of a social change that brought about a drastic change in fashions occurred in the early decades of the twentieth century, when women sought, gained, and enjoyed new political and economic freedom. Their altered activities and concepts of themselves encouraged them to discard the constricting garments that had been in fashion for centuries and to adopt shorter skirts, relaxed waistlines, bobbed hair, and other fashions more appropriate to their more active lives. Generations later, as women moved into top executive positions in the business world, the tailored suit, femininely soft blouse, and attaché bags became the "dressing for success" fashion among career women.

Similarly, in the decade following World War II, when the great trek to the suburbs began, those who joined the exodus from the city found themselves needing cars and car coats, garden furniture, and casual clothes for backyard barbecues. The physical fitness movement in the 1970s and 1980s brought about a need for exercise clothing, and as the interest in jogging, hiking, tennis, and aerobic dancing mushroomed, so also did the need for new and different fashions appropriate to each of these active sports. "Casual Fridays" and a shift toward working at home have changed the way many people dress for work in the 1990s. Even environmental concerns influence fashion by avoiding the use of certain dyes and finishes harmful to nature.

Changes in Fashions Are Gradual

Although fashions change constantly and new ones appear almost every season, a full-scale changeover is never completed at any one time. In studying the pattern of change in fashions, scholars have observed that changes in fashion are **evolutionary** in nature, rather than revolutionary.

It is only in retrospect that fashion changes seem marked or sudden. Actually, they come about as a result of a series of gradual shifts from one season to the next. For example, when women's skirts began inching up from midcalf in the 1960s, this gradual shortening was not particularly noticeable at first. It was only when skirts moved thigh-high, in the form of minis and micro-minis, that people took notice of the approaching extreme. Similarly, when men begin to abandon ultranarrow ties and suit lapels in favor of more and more width, the changes are not noticed at first. Then, when wide ties and lapels begin to lose their appeal and progressively narrower styles make their appearance, people again mistake their belated recognition of these gradual shifts for a sudden change in fashion.

Even today, when the rate of fashion change has accelerated sharply, the pace of change is really slower than it appears to the unskilled observer who has failed to notice the early evolutionary movements in a new direction.

The evolutionary nature of fashion change is a fundamental principle that is recognized by fashion practitioners; it provides them with a solid, factual foundation for forecasting and identifying incoming fashions. When planning and developing new styling ideas, they always keep the current fashions and evolving directions in mind. Thus, the acceptance of a particular coat or dress fashion during a current season becomes a straw in the wind for experts in search of clues to next season's trends. The degree of its acceptance provides needed clues as to what will or will not be welcomed by the consumer in the next season. Knowing that people do not respond well to sudden changes, the fashion experts build gradually, not abruptly, toward new ideas.

An exception to this principle occurred just after World War II. During that cataclysm, fabrics were in decidedly short supply; fashion was at an enforced standstill; women's clothes were built along straight, skimpy lines. By 1947, however, fashion was on the move and making up for lost time. Dior introduced his famous "new look," with long, full skirts and pinched waists. The radical change was accepted overnight. This unique event in fashion history was possible because the years of wartime shortages had precluded the gradual changes that would otherwise have taken place.

Even the slowest, most gradual of evolutionary changes in fashion, however, do change direction eventually. Once an extreme has been reached, shifts begin to occur in a new and different direction—often a complete reversal, like the returning swing of a pendulum. "All fashions end in excess" is a saying attributed to Paul Poiret, an outstanding couturier of the 1920s, and his remark carries as much weight today as it did then.

Examples are readily found in both history and recent times. Eighteenth-century hoopskirts and the crinolines of the nineteenth century ballooned to diameters of eight feet. Later, both exploded into a fragmentation of trains, loops, and bustles that nevertheless provided a far slimmer silhouette. Similarly, when the miniskirts of the 1960s moved up to the micro-minis of the 1970s, hems began inching downward. Whether it be skirt lengths, silhouettes, suit lapels, or general fashion looks, all fashions tend to move steadily toward an extreme, at which point a new direction develops.

Fashion: A "Follow-the-Leader" Process

In the constant change and movement of fashion, there is a definite orderliness about the pattern of acceptance. Styles become fashions through a "follow-the-leader" process. Understanding the acceptance pattern is a key to understanding fashion movements; it explains how a look or idea begins with a few and spreads to many.

The Fashion Cycle

Every fashion has a life span, known as a **fashion cycle.** This consists of three major stages: a beginning, or rise; a peak or very popular stage; and a declining stage. The acceptance patterns of individual styles and of overall fashion looks both fall into this pattern.

Stages of the fashion cycle reflect the work of Everett Rogers, who focused on how innovations are diffused in a society (Rogers, 1962; Rogers & Shoemaker, 1971, 1983). Rogers developed a model in the form of a typical bell-shaped curve representing stages of adoption over time. Rogers proposed five typical categories: *the innovators,* who are the first to adopt a new idea (2.5 percent of the population), *the early adopters* (13.5 percent), *the early majority* (34 percent), *the late majority* (34 percent); and *the laggards* (16 percent). To simplify the curve for our purposes, these can be grouped into three stages (Figure 2–1).

In its first or beginning stage, the fashion is adopted by people who like or can afford to be first with what is new, or who are highly motivated by a desire to dress differently from others. These pacesetters are relatively limited in number. In this first stage, the new fashion is often called a "high fashion," as explained earlier in this chapter.

If and when the new fashion idea spreads and is widely imitated by the greater number of people who tend to follow rather than lead, we arrive at the second stage of peak or mass acceptance. The fashion is then in such demand that it can be mass produced and distributed at prices within reach of many consumers.

Figure 2–1

Fashion cycles differ. This figure depicts how the cycle may be different for Fashion X compared to Fashion Y.

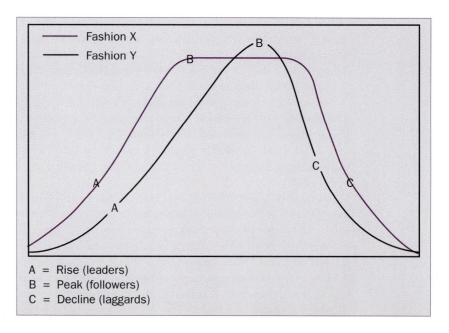

A = Rise (leaders)
B = Peak (followers)
C = Decline (laggards)

Ultimately, each fashion moves into its third or declining stage—usually the result of consumer boredom arising from seeing too much of the same thing. Some consumers will still be wearing it at this stage, but they are no longer willing to purchase it at regular prices. Meantime, other, newer fashions are going through the earlier stages of their cycles.

This pattern of acceptance and decline has been explained thus by sociology professor Neil J. Smelser:

> It is important to (style leaders) to be among the first in order to reap the psychological rewards of being in the forefront of fashion, and it is almost as important to flee from a new style when it is assumed by the masses. Further back in the procession, among the followers, the motivation is more purely sociable—persons adapt to styles to avoid being conspicuously traditional, rather than to be conspicuously original (as quoted in Ivins, 1976).

These stages of public acceptance tend to occur in all products that are subject to changes in fashion—not just in dress. Similar cycles can be traced in home furnishings, architecture, food, and even vacation spots, but the pattern shows up most obviously in what we wear.

Different fashions vary in their life spans, in the degree of acceptance they attain, and in the rate at which they move through their various stages. The length of time a particular fashion may remain in any of its three stages depends on the extent to which it is gaining or losing public acceptance. Some fashions may endure for a year or more; others for a season; and, indeed, some may never get beyond the first stage of acceptance by small groups of people. Therefore, if one were to draw a fashion cycle, it would include the three stages, but its shape would be different for different fashions. The rise and fall may be gradual or sharp; the peak may be narrow or wide. Although no one graph can depict the life story of all fashions accurately, all would have a wavelike appearance.

Scholars of fashion have sought to chart the ups and downs of fashions in an effort to determine the length of time a fashion movement takes to run its course. The time intervals, however, elude measurement. The spread of fashion, as of every new idea, is a complicated social phenomenon. The public's needs and interests do not change by clockwork.

The problem of applying the stopwatch technique to an analysis of fashion movements is also complicated by the fact that price differentials, which at one time tended to mark the different stages of style acceptance, have virtually disappeared. Moreover, while some cycles are in their peaks, their successors are already in the growing stage. Many new fashions often reach full growth without ever entirely displacing those that preceded them. A further complicating factor is that, owing to the evolutionary nature of changes, clearly definable shifts in fashion do not occur at a given time, and it is impossible to pinpoint the exact beginning or end of a specific fashion.

Application to Merchandising Fashions

An understanding of the fashion cycle is basic to successful merchandising of fashion goods, at wholesale or retail. Because very few concerns, if any, can successfully serve under one roof both the pacesetters and the followers, each firm must have a clear-cut policy on which fashion stages it wishes to deal in.

The main volume of business, in manufacturing and retailing alike, is done in fashions that are widely accepted or well on their way to the top or peak of the fashion cycle. A business that aims to attract a mass customers audience must concentrate on widely popular fashions, or on those that show promise of rising into the mass

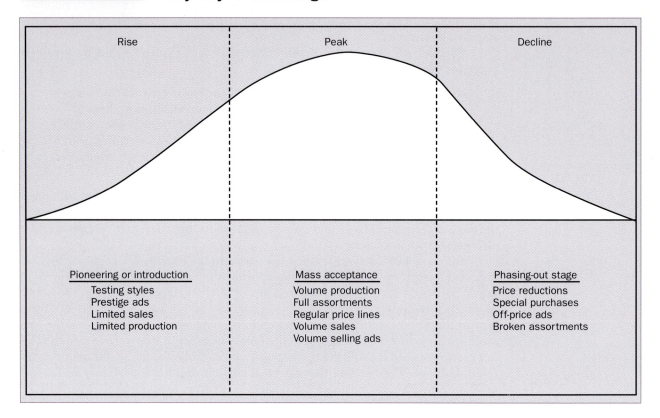

Figure 2–2 **Stages of the fashion cycle and how merchandising may vary for each stage.**

acceptance stage. These volume fashions constitute the major portion of the business done by the giant firms in the fashion industry. Conversely, those manufacturers and retailers that concentrate on being the first to carry the newest, the most individual, or the most extreme fashions cannot expect to do a large volume of business. Their appeal is to the limited group of customers who adopt such fashions. Their volume contributes only a small part of the total business done in the fashion industries, but a vital one indeed. Figure 2–2 depicts the relative importance of various stages of the fashion cycle and how merchandising varies for each stage.

Theories of Fashion Leadership

Social scientists explain the follow-the-leader element in fashion cycles in terms of an individual's desire to achieve status by choosing apparel similar to that chosen by an admired individual or group. This association through choice of fashion is a means of bridging the gap between social classes—that is, becoming in one's mind like "them" by wearing what "they" wear. Imitation and conformity in dress are also explained in terms of insecurity, since it takes more social courage than most of us possess to be conspicuously different from others in the appearance we present to the public. Thus, fashion gives expression to two basic human needs: the need for social status and the need to conform (Sapir, 1931; Tarde, 1903).

Three academically accepted theories categorize the admired groups or individuals from whom fashion leadership flows. These theories are "trickle down," "hor-

Figure 2–3

Theories of fashion leadership

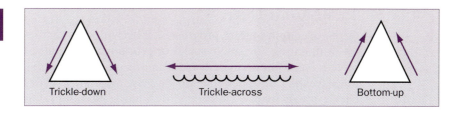

izontal, or trickle across," and "bottom up" (Figure 2–3). Each has its own claim to validity with respect to specific fashions and the fashion cycle.

Trickle-Down Theory

The **trickle-down theory** maintains that new styles make their first appearance among people at the top of a social pyramid and then gradually move down to progressively lower social levels.

Centuries ago, the persons at the top of the pyramid and therefore the setters of fashion were royalty. Fashions trickled down through the ranks of the nobility and those of the middle classes who had the means. The lower classes, of course, had neither the means nor the temerity to copy, or were even prohibited by law from doing so.

These days, royalty has practically disappeared, and the position at the top of the pyramid is held by individuals at the top of the economic, social, entertainment, and political ladders. Many such people make it their business to dress well, and their activities and appearance are highly publicized. To the large majority of the public, the fashions accepted by the glittering personalities at the top constitute a guide to what to wear, within the limits of their own more restricted budgets and social activities. For most consumers, innovation is risky but imitation is safe. Thus, fashions trickle down from higher to lower echelons, just as they did in the days of royalty.

Simultaneously, those at the top seek to dissociate themselves from those whom they consider socially inferior. They abandon a fashion once it has achieved popularity at less distinguished levels and introduce a new and different idea. This is perhaps why department store buyers will not carry a clothing brand that has become available in discount stores.

This type of social behavior was recognized and its implications for fashion were propounded by such early economists as Thorstein Veblen (1963), John Roe (1834), and Caroline Foley (1893), and by such sociologists as George Simmel, who spelled it out, step by step, in a paper published in 1904 (reprinted in 1957).

Behling (1992) reviewed fashion adoption research and constructed a profile of *early adopters* (also called *fashion leaders* or *fashion innovators*) based on the collective findings from the studies.[2] The profile that emerged suggests the early fashion adopter is relatively young, has a relatively high income and occupation, is not married or has no children (and, therefore, has funds available to purchase clothing and accessories), is likely to be female (although young males are also early adopters), is likely to read fashion magazines, and is mobile. Early adopters tend to be gregarious or social, conforming, and competitive; like or do not object to change; and tend to be exhibitionists or narcissistic.

[2]Behling's review provides a very useful overview of 20 studies based on Rogers' model conducted over three and one-half decades.

Trickle-Across Theory

As the twentieth century progressed, it became clear that fashion was no longer a matter of imitating any single social or economic class, but of choosing one's own role models—and not necessarily from among individuals with glittering genealogy or fabulous wealth. This phenomenon gave rise to another theory of fashion emulation: the **trickle-across theory,** enunciated by Charles W. King (1963). He observed that fashions spread horizontally within and across homogeneous groups, rather than merely vertically from one social level to another. He believes that each segment of our pluralistic society has its own leader or leaders whom it emulates. For example, a "Big Man" on campus may favor a certain type of jeans or baggy t-shirt and thus set a fashion for them among other students. In the business world, aspirants to the executive office tend to dress as the upper echelons do, be it the gray flannel suit of the 1950s or the colorful neckties of the 1990s. Even in so small a group as a suburban country golf club, the dominant members subtly influence the dress of the other members by the fashions they favor.

Bottom-Up Theory

The third and most recent theory espoused by many students of fashion and by fashion practitioners themselves is that the traditional trickle-down movement has reversed itself and many fashions now filter up. This **bottom-up theory,** as advanced by Greenberg and Glynn (1966), maintains that young people are quicker than any other social group to initiate new and different fashions and that fashions filter up, not merely from youth to older age groups, but also from lower to upper economic classes. Typical of fashions initiated by the young and less than affluent are jeans, sneakers, t-shirts, baggy shorts, military surplus and safari clothes, and black leather pants and jackets. Each of these started in the streets with young people of modest means and streamed upward to well-to-do middle-aged adults. The male espousal of flowing hair and beards similarly was initiated by the young in the 1960s, and that fashion spread to gray-haired, balding men as well. When younger men became reacquainted with razors, their elders soon followed suit.

Marketing Implications

These three different theories of how fashions spread have major significance for practitioners in the field, since they confirm that there is no single homogeneous fashion public in our pluralistic society. A number of distinctly different groups make up the fashion public, and each has its own leaders and its own perception of fashion. Although we continue to see many new styles introduced at high prices and eventually becoming fashions, this is less often the case than it once was. One successful new style may originate in the studio of a prestigious designer, but another may come into fashion from the stock of an Army-Navy store.

Leadership in fashion these days has less and less to do with price and high-priced merchandise. Therefore, producers and retailers can no longer look only to an elite group of traditional fashion leaders for incoming trends. They must also look at what people are wearing in the streets. They must be aware that some fashions flow upward and others flow across within special groups. Dominant individuals and dominant influences, wherever they reveal themselves within our society, are important influences on fashion. Success depends on identifying and watching these, not just the patrons of elite restaurants, resorts, and entertainments.

How Fashions Develop

There is no question that it is far easier to recognize what is fashionable at a given time and place than to say why or how it became a fashion. When we search for the influences that brought forth such fashions as the hobble skirts and crinolines of the past or some of the fashions of the present, we are confronted with a complex question indeed. Several things we do know, however. One is that esthetic appeal alone does not produce a fashion. Veblen (1963) made this point when he observed that there is no intrinsic difference between the gloss of a patent leather shoe and the shine of a threadbare garment. People, he observed, are ready to find beauty in what is in vogue; therefore the shine on the shoe is beautiful and the garment's shine is repulsive.

Another thing we know is that promotional efforts by designers, producers, or retailers cannot in themselves dictate what customers will accept. If there were such dictators in the past, there certainly are none today. And a third factor that we know is that a fashion does not just happen without a reason. It is a response to many things: attitudes, social changes and movements, major events on the world stage, and new technological developments, for example. Which of these is the most important, no one can say; their relative strengths vary with the times.

The Role of Designers

There are countless styles, each of which has its own distinctive characteristics and most of which have, at one time or another, or more than once, been a fashion. It is a common misconception, however, that all have been "created" by designers and only by them.

It is true, indeed, that many new fashions have been introduced by famous designers. Some examples include the boxy jackets of Chanel's 1920 suits; the bias cut dresses of Vionnet in the 1920s; and Dior's "new look" in the 1940s. More recently, at least two American designers have left a distinct mark on fashion: These include Ralph Lauren's look of casual elegance and Donna Karan's bodysuits.

Often, however, it is a functional garment rather than an individual designer that generates a new fashion. Some examples that have taken the fancy of the public and become fashions in their time are the bomber jackets of aviators, the pea coats of sailors and the trench coats of soldiers, the leg warmers of dancers, and the protective overalls of farmers. Similarly, denim pants. The ultrapractical style created by Levi Strauss in gold-rush days inspired the jeans that have enjoyed worldwide popularity in the second half of the twentieth century. And let us not forget that many examples of "street fashions" that started among young people and moved out to a wider following. A classic case is the miniskirt: the miniskirt and boots that London working girls adopted in the 1960s attained widespread popularity before being shown in Paris by Courreges.

Designers who acquire a reputation for "creating" fashion are simply those who have been consistently successful in giving tangible expression to the shapes, colors, fabrics, styles, and looks that are wanted and accepted by a substantial number of customers. The fact that a style may be widely heralded as a new fashion does not make it one. Even among the greatest of designers, it is recognized that it is only when customers accept a style, new or old, that the particular style becomes a fashion. Paul Poiret, one of the greatest Paris couturiers, once told an American audience the following:

> I know you think me a king of fashion. It is a reception which cannot but flatter me and of which I cannot complain. All the same, I must undeceive you with regard to the powers of a king of fashion. We are not capricious despots who wake up one fine day, decide on a change in habits, abolish a neckline or puff out a sleeve. We are neither arbiters or dictators. Rather we are to be thought of as the blindly obedient servants of woman, who for her part is always enamored of change and a thirst for novelty. It is our role and our duty to be on the watch for the moment at which she becomes bored with what she is wearing, that we may suggest at the right instant something else which will meet her taste and her needs. It is therefore with a pair of antennae and not a rod of iron that I come before you, and not so much as a master that I speak, but as a slave . . . who must divine your innermost thoughts (quoted in Bell, 1947).

Poiret was at his peak in the early decades of this century, but designers today still see things as he did—although they express themselves in less flowery language. Halston, an important designer for a part of this century, commented similarly: "I have always felt that all the designers can do is suggest; it is the consumer who accepts or rejects and is the ultimate maker of fashion" (*RAM Reports to Retailers,* 1977).

Fashions Reflect Their "Times"

Fashions in clothing have always been more than merely a manner of dressing. A study of the past and a careful observation of the present will make it apparent that fashions are social expressions; they document the taste and values of their era just as painting, sculpture, and other art forms do. Fashions are a fact of social psychology. They reflect the way people think and live, and are therefore influenced by the same environmental forces that act on any society (Table 2–1 pp. 48–49). Every fashion seems completely appropriate to its era and reflects the spirit of an age as no other symbol of the times does. This is true both for widely accepted fashions and for those that flourish only within small isolated or counterculture groups. To illustrate: Mennonite attire reflects Mennonite ideals; punk dress and hair styles reflect the attitudes of punk rockers.

Newsworthy Events and Personalities Make Fashions

Fashions are made by outstanding personalities and major happenings in the fields of entertainment, sports, art, and politics. Almost anything or anyone of newsworthy importance in the world of entertainment from prominent personalities to major television or motion picture productions has an effect on the fashions of the times. To cite but a few examples from the 1970s and 1980s: the Indian inspired fashions influenced by the widely watched television production of *Jewel in the Crown* and the Indian art exhibits in New York and Washington; the tremendous impact on hair and clothing styles of superstars whose personae are as closely identified with their clothes as with their music; the career fashions that received impetus from a new wave of television and movie productions that starred women in positions as business executives; the popularity of the black leather look, skull and crossbones imagery, and decorative metal studs resulting from the enthusiasm for "heavy metal" music. Youth of the 1990s, known as Generation X, were influenced by grunge dressing of bands like Nirvana, leading to popularity of flannel shirts, ripped jeans, Doc Marten boots, Teva sandals, reversed baseball caps, pierced noses, and tattoos.

Many new fashions have also emerged from the public's participation in sports and physical fitness activities. Each activity usually creates a need for different types of functional garments, many of which develop into everyday fashions. For example, sweatsuits and sweatshirts are an outgrowth of the functional running suits worn by joggers. A relatively short-lived fashion for dancers' leg warmers and cut-off t-shirts was generated by the active interest in aerobic dancing. Similar, also, are the fashions that developed for the brightly printed jams worn by surfers and skateboarders, and for the skin-tight bicycle pants of bicycle enthusiasts.

Emulation of personalities in the public eye, whose clothing and activities are featured in the media, also plays a part in the development of fashions. For instance, the pillbox hat and bouffant hair style of Jackie Kennedy, the young and much admired "first lady" in the 1960s, were widely imitated, as were the classic styles of dresses worn by Nancy Reagan in the 1980s, the faux pearls of Barbara Bush, and the classic suits of Hillary Clinton in the 1990s.

Social Movements Create Fashions

Fashions develop in response to social movements. For example, the focus on career fashions and specialized career shops for women in the 1980s was a direct response to the rise of women in the ranks of corporate executives. Similarly, the anti-establishment fashions of the 1960s—cut-off jeans, long hair, beards, the "hippie" look—were visible expressions of the anti-establishment attitude that developed as a reaction to the unpopular Vietnam War of the 1960s. The postindustrial thriftshop or grunge look of Generation X in the 1990s perhaps has reflected a spirit of pessimism about their prospects for jobs and the frequent burden of heavy college loans (Zinn, Power, Yand, Cuneo, & Ross, 1992).

In ways uniquely their own, hair styles have reflected social movements. In the Gay Nineties, women enhanced the luxurious look of their hair with pinned-on puffs, curls, rats, and other devices that have gone the way of tight corseting. In the 1960s, alongside the unkempt locks of the hippies, blacks let their hair grow long and full in the Afro styles that proclaimed that black was beautiful. In the 1970s many blacks, looking back to their roots, adopted corn-row hair styles and dreadlocks—two African hair styles almost impossible for Caucasians to copy. In the late 1970s, Mohawks and spiky pink and green hairdos were part of punk rock's way of thumbing its collective nose at the establishment.

Social Values and Attitudes Create Fashion

There is, of course, no one universal way of life in America today, even among those who constitute the mainstream. Except within fragmented groups, like those mentioned earlier, our values are varied. Some of us are hedonistic; others are antimaterialistic. Some are conservative; some are futurists. Whatever our values and life styles, our dress reflects that choice, consciously or otherwise. As one commentator points out, clothes nowadays are viewed "sometimes with almost mystical fervor, as the most basic expression of life style, indeed of identity itself" (Silberman, 1971 p. 95). Thus, fashions are a language that communicates self-identity and group identity with instant impact. When youth ideas are dominant, there is a tendency for people of all ages to dress, act, think like, and make believe they are young. The expanding use of hair dyes by both sexes and hair transplants by men reflect the desire to appear young, no matter what nature may say to the contrary.

The success of Victoria's Secret and other companies specializing in sensual attire perhaps reflects society's increasingly open attitude toward sexuality. The wearing

Table 2–1 Fashions Reflect the Times

Decade	Events	Entertainment	Looks
1920s	Prohibition The Charleston Art Deco Bootleg liquor "Showboat" on Broadway The Cotton Club in Harlem	"The Jazz Singer" "The Shiek" "City Lights" "Tea for Two" "Ol' Man River" "Swanee" "The Man I Love" "I'm Just Wild about Harry"	Short skirts Flapper chemises Bobbed hair Powdered knees
1930s	Hollywood glamour influences fashion Café society "Our Town" on Broadway Jazz	"Gone with the Wind" "The Wizard of Oz" "It Happened One Night" "42nd Street" "10¢ a Dance" "I Got Rhythm" "Night and Day" "Putting on the Ritz"	Streamlined silhouettes Body-conscious shape Bias cut Shirtwaists Draping and shirring Halters and hip wraps Hats and gloves Fox trimmed coats
1960s	Woodstock Pop art Psychedelics The Beatles Flower children "Hair" on Broadway	"2001: A Space Odyssey" "The Sound of Music" "Bonnie and Clyde" "The Graduate" "Z" "Let the Sun Shine In" "Strangers in the Night" "Moon River" "I Want to Hold Your Hand"	Ironed hair Nehru jackets Love beads Teased hair Go-Go boots Miniskirts Dark eyes, pale lips Pillbox hats Prints
1970s	Roller skating Disco "A Chorus Line" on Broadway	"The Godfather" "The Great Gatsby" "Annie Hall" "Rocky" "Butch Cassidy and the Sundance Kid" "Cabaret" "Send in the Clowns" "The Way We Were" "Losing My Mind" "Killing Me Softly"	Granny dresses Platform shoes Message t-shirts Midis "The Great Gatsby" "Annie Hall" Hot pants Designer jeans Punk

1940s

WW II ends	Short hemlines to long	"Casablanca"
Nylon stockings available	Dior's "New Look"	"Citizen Kane"
"Death of a Salesman" and "Street Car Named Desire" on Broadway	Hepburn pants	"Adam's Rib"
	Sarong drape	"Born Yesterday"
	Peplum jackets	"Notorious"
	Uniform style suits	"The Red Shoes"
	Hats with veils	"So In Love"
	Platform shoes	"If I Loved You"
		"Some Enchanted Evening"
		"Moonlight Serenade"

1950s

Television	The trapeze	"Rebel without a Cause"
The "Beat" generation	The chemise	"Some Like It Hot"
Abstract expressionism	The shirtdress	"Gigi"
Sock hops	Pennyloafers	"Singing in the Rain"
"My Fair Lady" on Broadway	Bobby sox	"Psycho"
	Capri pants	"High Society"
	Ponytails	"Hound Dog"
	The sheath	"Three Coins in a Fountain"
	Saddle shoes	"I Love Paris"
	Princess dresses	"Standing on the Corner"

1980s

MTV	"Rambo"	Menswear
New wave music	"Born in the U.S.A."	Sweaters
Michael Jackson	"Flashdance"	Preppy
Postmodern art and architecture	"We Are the World"	Leggings
"Cats" on Broadway	"Eraserhead"	Punk hairdo
Madonna	"Murphy Brown"	Torn jeans
Heavy Metal	"thirty-something"	Sweat clothes
"Phantom of the Opera"	"LA Law"	Athletic shoes
"Les Miserables"	"Cosby Show"	Earrings
	"Golden Girls"	Bodysuits
	"Wheel of Fortune"	
	"Batman"	

1990s

Globalization	Compact discs	Casual wear everywhere
Computerization	"Jurassic Park"	Grunge or post-industrial thrift shop look
Information age	"Forrest Gump"	Retro looks
AIDS/HIV grows	"Seinfeld"	Dress-down Fridays
Cautious consumer spending	"The Simpsons"	Baseball caps—men and women
The Internet and cyberspace	"Home Improvement"	'70s revival
NAFTA and GATT/WTO	O. J. Simpson trial	Doc Martens/Birkenstocks
Environmental concerns	"Lion King"	Tattoos and body-piercing
Gulf War	"Melrose Place"	Natural fibers
Health and fitness craze	"Schindler's List"	Healthy skin (no tan)
Political correctness	"NYPD Blue"	Wonderbra
Woodstock II	"Philadelphia"	Long, shapeless rayon dresses
	"Friends"	

of pants by women for many occasions is not merely a matter of dressing practically; it is also an expression of their freedom from the conventional restraints that they and their mothers had accepted in earlier years. When women, even those who wear trousers for most occasions, prefer to express their femininity, they move into fashions that are frillier, lacier, and sexier. When ostentation is seen as an expression of success, then rich clothes and elaborate home furnishings are "in." At other times, a revulsion against "conspicuous consumption" will express itself in understated clothes and home furnishings. And so it goes.

Technological Developments Create Fashion

New technological developments often spawn new fashions. So simple a thing as a digital clock, for instance, makes it possible to depart from the round-face design that prevailed for centuries. Some apparel fashions seem to have their origins in the development of new fibers and fabrics, new processes for utilizing familiar ones, and other fruits of the chemist's genius—plus a waiting need for the new or a weariness with the old. For example, the synthetic fibers that made wash-and-wear fabrics possible, and thus influenced fashion, might not have had such a rousing welcome if they had come on the scene early in the century, when domestic help was plentiful and when the stiffly starched, beautifully ironed garment was a symbol of a well-run household. More recently, the development of microfibers has led to a new luxury look in outerwear that resembles silk but has the easy-care features of manufactured fibers.

Other examples abound, such as the popularity of skintight bodysuits and activewear in the 1980s resulting from the rediscovery of stretch fabrics; and the proliferation of graphics on t-shirts, which were made possible by the advances in heat-setting technology. Plastics in their infinite variety influenced the development of such fashions as raincoats in bright colors, and the leather look of suede-like fabrics that offered the flexibility, easy care, and lightweight qualities of cloth.

The Prediction of Fashion

Analyzing and predicting which styles will become the fashions for coming seasons has been called an occupational guessing game for the fashion industry, with millions of dollars at stake. Fiber, textile, and leather producers must work from one to two years ahead of the consumers' buying seasons; apparel and accessory designer/manufacturers must prepare their lines from nine months to a year ahead in order to show them to retail buyers three to six months in advance of the consumers' wearing season. Without accurate forecasts and projections of what looks, colors, fabrics, silhouettes, and design details are likely to be acceptable to customers, they would not be able to produce and sell the massive quantities of textiles and apparel that they do.

Such forecasts and predictions of fashion, however, are neither guesswork nor a game, nor a matter of intuition. Rather, **fashion prediction** is one of the most vital activities in the industry. The successful forecaster recognizes that fashion is neither haphazard nor mysterious, but a tangible force whose progress can be charted, graphed, understood, explained, and projected. Basically, what fashion practitioners do is examine past experiences for clues as to what will happen today, and then analyze and evaluate today's activities for indications of what may happen tomorrow.

In Chapter 3, we shall focus further on how fashion firms determine their target customers and how they try to serve those target markets.

Recognizing and Evaluating Trends

The logistics of projecting current fashions are relatively simple. Whatever styles have been steadily rising in popularity during the last few months may be expected to continue to rise for a few months more—or at least, not to decline abruptly for some time. Figure 2–4 depicts "looks" that have lasted over several years to characterize a decade in each case. For instance, a rising trend for fur-trimmed coats at the end of a fall season is very likely to be followed by a high demand for fur-trimmed coats at the beginning of the next fall season. Likewise, whatever has been steadily declining in popularity up to the present offers little favorable prospects for the future. People in the fashion business seem to develop almost a sixth sense for weighing various factors and judging probable ups and downs of trends. Their apparently instinctive skill arises from years of experience in studying signs that may escape the untrained observer, just as a weather forecaster observes signs the rest of us may not have noticed and becomes adept in this work.

Sources of Information

Fashion practitioners base their predictions not only on their own selling records and preliminary sales tests, but also on facts and observations that are available from other segments within the fashion industry.

The fact-gathering procedure, to continue the analogy to weather forecasting, is similar to preparing a meteorological map, with its isobars, temperature readings, pressure systems, and other indicators of present and future conditions. On the fashion forecaster's mental map of present and future customer preferences are the factors below—in addition, of course, to a knowledge of the movement of fashions.

With respect to the firm's targeted customer group, the fashion forecaster calls on the following:

- Careful observation of current events that have captured or are likely to capture the imagination of customers and affect the styles they will prefer.
- Awareness of the current life styles and dress of those men and women most likely to influence what the firm's own customers will ultimately adopt.
- Study of sales trends in various sections of the country, not only for the forecaster's own company, but for competing companies to whatever extent is possible.
- An intimate knowledge of the fashion opinions of their sources of supply.
- Familiarity with professional sources of information, such as fashion reporting services, fashion periodicals, opinions of consultants, analyses offered by resident buying offices, and the like.
- Exchange of information with noncompeting concerns.
- Understanding of and constant awareness of the inevitable and evolutionary nature of changes in fashion.

Thus, a forecaster, whose official title may be designer, fashion director, product developer, magazine editor, or store buyer, may decide that brighter and livelier colors will be more acceptable than they were in the previous year, that oversized tops have run their course for the time being, or that sleek hairdos are coming in.

A fashion forecast, once made, whether in one's own mind or in print, is seldom final and immutable. The unexpected can often happen when some new factor enters the picture. In any forecasting, whether it be weather or fashion, all that can be hoped for is a high percentage of successful projections. Even the best informed and most successful designers, producers, buyers, and fashion reporting services make errors, resulting in merchandise that must be disposed of in some way—usually unprofitably.

Figure 2–4

The Looks from the 1920s to the 1990s

Consumers have given proof often enough that they have minds of their own and will reject a so-called fashion before it can even get going if it does not appeal to them. And if the industry had any doubts about this, it has only to look back a bit. Efforts to induce customers to wear hats when they preferred to go hatless achieved nothing. Similarly, an effort in 1970 to switch customers from miniskirts to the so-called midi, or midcalf length, met with disastrous results.

The importance of the customer in determining the course of fashion was stated effectively by Bill Blass, the American designer whose leadership has been legendary for decades. He said, after the midi fiasco:

I have never felt for one minute that the designers or the press or the industry could force or impose a new fashion on the customer, and that's never been more evident than now. The designer can only propose; the customer decides. This is a time of great individuality in customer buying, so the store merchant must pay more attention than ever to what his or her customers are looking for, and then find the designers who are making clothes that relate to their customers (*RAM, 1977*).

In summary, fashion is a dynamic phenomenon that drives the industry. Many factors influence fashion trends, but it is the customer who has the final word on whether a fashion lives or dies.

Readings

These readings consider the importance of design and having a good grasp of the business aspects of running a fashion firm. One article reports on the success of one designer who combined his fashion savvy with the business acumen of his staff to build a fashion empire. Other articles focus on U.S. consumers' growing emphasis on informality in dress.

Commentary: Design Matters

by Edward Newton

Fashion . . . design . . . styling. These are the essential dynamics of the clothing and textiles business. Design ensures that the aesthetic and functional factors are combined and organised with flair, style, timing and integrity using appropriate technology to produce successful clothing and textiles.

Design is the greatest asset that the clothing industry has and the major reason why consumers buy new clothing. The clothing industry needs to think more carefully about design and ensure that it is not treated in isolation but integrated with other management functions. Too many companies use design as an 'add-on' and lack a coherent policy for product development. It is important to use design as a full and integrated part of the business, equal to and as important as, sales and marketing, financial and production management. Fashion and design can assist a business to be profitable, successful and at the leading edge in its field.

Design is too important to be left as the sole responsibility of designers, it is an essential part of an organisation's strategy. There is no definitive formula or blueprint for managing design. Design, to be completely effective, should 'permeate' an organisation, but I think it is legitimate to suggest that there should be a top level commitment to design to be fully effective. Fashion and design are an integral part of the clothing and textile business, but often not fully understood or valued as highly as they should be. There are very few areas of business that can build into its production process an element that can make the commodity obsolete long before its time and the consumer buy a new product. This is the change and energy that 'fashion' contributes to the clothing and textile industry. Fashion is the essential element of design that is dependent on timing and acceptance and the only constant in reality is change.

It is important to understand fashion and how it is influenced and developed. A good parallel could be said to be the sensitivity and unpredictability of the stock market and, as in fashion, there is always a reason behind the change. To forecast and understand fashion change is both an art and a science and when defined there is always the possibility of a market change for some reason or other—the economy/the weather.

Therefore, it is very important for an organisation to develop an understanding of fashion awareness, fashion direction, fashion mainstream and fads in fashion. The appropriateness of the fashion direction is essential for the individual manufacturer or retailer in relation to their particular market section. The right or wrong direction can result in either success or failure. Fashion change moves at different speeds at the various market levels and it is important to forecast the rate of change and acceptance of new fashion. A sensitivity and awareness of fashion change has to be developed and nurtured to enable a company to be ready with replacement products before the life cycle of the current product reaches its end and thereby take full advantage of being in the clothing and textiles business.

The clothing and textile industry is a world business. Design and fashion are world commodities, passing freely without passport across frontiers and cultures. The pace of technological change and development, together with the communications revolution, will increase awareness and demand for design and fashion of the highest quality.

Source: From Textile Horizons, *1995, p. 5. Reprinted by permission of Benjamin Dent & Company Ltd.*

Advice to Aspiring Designers: Get Smart Before Getting Started

by Valerie Seckler

Talented designers too often underestimate the importance of business skills when seeking financing for their young businesses.

This was the consensus of factors, the most common source of funding for designers whose companies are in early growth stages. [See Glossary in back of book for a definition of the term **factor**]

These entrepreneurial ventures are often rich in design and sales talent, said factors interviewed by WWD, but sorely lacking in crucial back-room support like production proficiency, accounting expertise and sales organizations.

Such shortcomings typically undermine a designer's efforts to obtain financing and often explode the fledgling enterprise, factors noted.

Miles Stuchin, president of Access Capital, a factor that counts apparel designers among its clients, said, "We sometimes see design expertise but weak production skills. Often a company can produce, but is weak on bookkeeping. In smaller companies with limited funds, these can be big problems."

Observed Walter Kaye, president of Merchant Factors, "We don't see lots of designers going into business as we did in the past. Many who try don't know how to go beyond line development."

"They're not as able to market themselves and find funding as their predecessors," added Kaye, who founded Merchant 10 years ago at age 57.

In order to win the confidence and financing of factors, a young designer firm must build the proper business foundation and get at least one successful retail season under its belt.

After sinking $10,000 to $15,000 of their own money into their businesses, designers' next infusion of funds can come from a variety of sources, factors explained. They include family members, investors with roots in the apparel business, contract manufacturers seeking to boost production to cover overhead and joint ventures established with apparel companies that are looking to segment or trade up.

"All too often designers lose their initial investment because the new company doesn't have staying power," cautioned Kaye. "We've seen budding designers with lots of ideas but little capital, and we discourage them. They need adequate capital to develop their samples line, buy supplies and stay afloat until the money from their first season comes in."

A joint venture is one of the best ways for young designer firms with limited capital to get started, according to Kaye. The joint venture partner gets "very big leverage" in exchange for its business and financial support, resulting in "many deals that work out very well," he noted.

"Existing Seventh Avenue companies tend to be frequent and good sources of money," Stuchin agreed, assessing the joint venture route. "Complementary businesses and players tend to know and trust each other."

The good news for young designer firms is that their gross margins of 35 to 40 percent are far stronger than, say, the 15 to 20 percent achieved by mass market startups. So if they can survive the first season or two, designers' chances of finding funding from factors brighten considerably.

Factors lend money to young designer companies against their accounts receivable, typically offering financing for firms with sales ranging from $1.5 million to $5 million.

"Our average client has sales of about $2 million, but we've started funding $800,000 companies that are doing $15 million today," said Kaye.

Such firms can generally borrow 75 to 80 percent of the face value of their credit-approved receivables from factors. The fee is usually the prime rate plus a single-digit percentage. The percentage is determined by the principals' previous experience and the quality of the company's receivables and retail accounts, among other considerations.

Gary Wassner, president of Hilldun Corp., a niche factor for designer apparel resources, said his firm lends anywhere from $50,000 to $700,000. "The majority of our loans are about $150,000," he stated.

Assuming the business basics are in place, the criteria factors used to determine lending fees also help them to decide whether to lend money to a designer company in the first place. The most crucial: the ability to produce well-finished clothes that fit properly and deliver them on time to a range of quality retailers.

"We look for designers who are able to sell to a number of stores rather than to a guardian angel," said Stuchin.

For this reason, he noted, "We greatly prefer designers selling to department stores than to specialty boutiques. They take about the same amount of time to sell, and the department store has the much bigger pen. [having the finances to buy]"

When Hilldun's thinking about lending to a designer company selling $1,000 suits, for instance, "We have to be certain about the fit, finishing and timeliness of delivery," said Wassner. "The only way to know is if they've shipped for a season and the stores liked the merchandise."

As for on-time deliveries, the chief culprit creating slowdowns is the late arrival of supplies. "Designers have to be careful about their fabric suppliers," Wassner stressed. "This is where most of their delivery problems lie.

"Designers also have to know their factories will produce on time for them and not push them to the bottom of the heap," he added. "They need to use small shops where their orders carry more clout and to put an employee on site to monitor operations."

Another plus for designers seeking financing, said Stuchin, is the employment of an accountant specializing in the apparel business. "Credit suppliers look to see who's preparing a company's financials," he noted.

Most factors said it's usually harder for designer firms to secure funding than it is for other apparel businesses, because their higher cost results in a greater concentration of sales on fewer items.

"The odds of getting paid by a company making 10 dresses for $100 apiece are better than for a company making a single dress for $1,000," reasoned Stuchin. "If there's one rip in the $1,000 dress, that's it."

Moreover, even if factors are paid consistently, the size of the factoring volume generated by designers is far smaller than that of moderate or mass resources.

"Lots of factors avoid designer companies due to their lower overall sales volumes—factors won't do $50 million in volume with clients making $1,000 garments," said Wassner.

Nevertheless, Merchant's Kaye insisted, "It isn't necessarily harder for young designer companies to get financing, but they often lack the business acumen to secure the funds.

"Many times they get bad advice," he added. "They can only get started seeking loans from factors after their first season of orders are in from good retailers."

Source: From Women's Wear Daily, *March 27, 1995, pp. 30–31. Reprinted by permission.*

Ralph Lauren: From Ties to Riches

Ralph Lauren's fashion empire had humble beginnings, with a line of ties designed under the Polo label in 1967.

Today he designs men's and women's apparel, accessories and home furnishings that bear his signature, as well as a lucrative beauty business.

After founding his men's wear company in 1968, he went on to create Ralph Lauren Womenswear in 1971 and launched the Ralph Lauren Home Collection in 1983.

Lauren opened the first Polo/Ralph Lauren store in 1971. In April 1986 he opened his flagship store in the former Rhinelander Mansion on Madison Avenue and 72nd Street in New York. In the fall of 1993, Lauren opened the Polo Sport store directly across the street from his flagship to display his new activewear concept.

His international presence includes a shop on London's New Bond Street that opened in 1981 and a store in Paris that opened in 1986. There are currently 130 Polo/Ralph Lauren stores around the world.

In the fall of 1993, Lauren introduced Double RL, a new brand of men's jeans and apparel. The clothes are what he likes to call hard-to-find vintage pieces with character.

Polo/Ralph Lauren's men's apparel is distributed to over 32 countries.

Under the Chaps by Ralph Lauren label, introduced in 1974, Lauren designs a collection of men's clothing, shirts, sportswear and ties for young executives. Chaps by Ralph Lauren is distributed by licensees in Canada and Japan. In 1981, Lauren introduced Polo University Club, a line for the college student or aspiring businessman.

In women's Lauren presents his ready-to-wear in four lifestyle groups—Collection, Collection Classics, Ralph and Polo Sport.

Ralph Lauren's boys' wear was introduced in the fall of 1978. Polo girls' wear was introduced in the fall of 1981. Ralph Lauren footwear was launched in 1982. Lauren also makes women's and men's hats, scarves and hosiery in addition to swimwear, eyewear, sleepwear, underwear, jewelry, leathergoods, luggage and handbags.

The Ralph Lauren Home Collection includes bedding, blankets, fabrics, wall coverings, draperies, floor coverings, wood, wicker, rattan and upholstered furniture, bath and beach towels and giftware.

Lauren also licenses a sizable beauty business. Cosmair Inc., the U.S. licensee of the French beauty giant L'Oréal SA, owns the Ralph Lauren fragrance and cosmetics license and has built a business estimated by industry sources at nearly $400 million at retail worldwide.

The newest of Lauren's six fragrances, a men's scent called Polo Sport, was launched in the unlikely month of February. Despite the snowstorms, initial sales were so strong that Cosmair reportedly raised the full-year sales forecast from less than $35 million to $40 million wholesale.

Achieving that goal would give Polo Sport the Lauren sales record, edging out Safari for Men, which reportedly chalked up $38 million at wholesale in the 12 months following its September 1992 launch. That fragrance, in turn, had outperformed Safari for women, which did an estimated $25 million at wholesale in the year following its February 1990 introduction.

Source: From Women's Wear Daily, *August 24, 1995, p. 4. Reprinted by permission.*

Have We Become a Nation of Slobs?

by Jerry Adler

When Sam Albert went to work for IBM in 1959, he assumed he'd be wearing a suit for the rest of his life. In fact, the *same* suit (single-breasted dark blue or gray worsted), over dark socks suspended rigidly from garters and a white shirt with a detachable collar starched to the stiffness of an annual-report cover. Feet planted in black wingtips, heads encased in steel-gray fedoras, the men of IBM achieved an uncanny uniformity, signifying not just business, but business *machines*. When Albert retired in 1989 as a top marketing executive, he counted 35 dress shirts in his closet, all of them white. So when he returned as a consultant to IBM's Armonk, N.Y., headquarters last week, wearing a dress shirt, suit and tie, he was prepared for anything but the sight of employees lined up for lunch in sweaters and slacks. "They looked at me," he says, "like they were asking, 'Who is this guy with the suit on?' "

By rights, this age should mark the apotheosis of the suit. From Eastern Europe to Latin America, the broadcloth-backed armies of capitalism are on the march. Bustling Pacific Rim societies such as Singapore illustrate the perverse rule that the more inhospitable the climate of a given country, the more closely cinched the ties around the necks of the ruling class. America, for its part, has elected new leaders drawn from the ranks of the small-town Southern professionals and college teachers for whom drab gray suits are expressive of their very nature, like fatigues for Castro. The last election was a landslide for the values the suit stands for: tradition, hierarchy, conformity and, well, money.

Yet even as the idea of the suit has triumphed, the garment itself is losing ground. The most recent sign came on Friday, Feb. 3, when IBM chairman Louis V. Gerstner Jr. relaxed the inviolable, though unwritten, dress code for the 800 workers at the innermost sanctum of American capitalism. "Dress down" days, a phrase that first appeared in print barely five years ago, now affect, by some estimates, more than half of U.S. office workers. Major banks and law firms are among the companies that lift the burden of neckties and nylons on employees in honor of the impending weekend; so is the Central Intelligence Agency. At least one governor, Oregon's John Kitzhaber, has proclaimed casual Fridays for himself, keeping his normal schedule in crisply pressed Levi's button-fly jeans. American men bought only around 13 million suits last year, down by 1.6 million since 1989, according to NPD Research, Inc. This implies that every adult male in the country buys a suit every seven years. Since the average American doubles his weight in that time, he presumably has long since stopped buttoning the last one.

Hats and Gloves

Nor is this a phenomenon confined to office wear. You don't have to be very old to recall when middle-class men routinely wore a jacket and tie in public, even to a baseball game, or when women would put on a dress, hat, gloves, heels, nylons and jewelry to go to a department store. At a ball game today most people are grateful if the person in the next seat has on a *shirt*. Travel once called for dressing up—one is, after all, representing oneself to strangers—but now it seems to bring out people's worst fashion instincts. Bert Hand, chairman of the menswear company Hartmarx, identifies these as sweat pants and jogging suits. "Maybe," he says, "there should be a jogging-suit airline."

As tourists, Americans have given up pastel Bermuda shorts, only to replace them with Gap jeans, golf shirts, Nike jackets and $100 sneakers. These invite less ridicule but, if anything, even more contempt. Parisians assume not merely that Americans dress badly but that they don't even know the difference. The bright swirls and strips of American sports logos seem especially glaring in the gloom of an 800-year-old church. "People are pretending that dress has no symbolic significance," says Judith Martin, the "Miss Manners" columnist, "but it does."

As for worship, Americans who long ago gave up wearing ties to services are starting to treat socks as optional. "We have lost the ideal of adult self-respect, and we're dressing like rebellious children," remarks the fashion historian Anne Hollander ("Sex and Suits"). "When you go to church, or to the opera, you now have the idea that you do not need to express respect in your costume—that if you do, you somehow feel like one of the oppressed." Morticians are seeing more street clothes at funerals. That includes on corpses. Boston funeral director Arthur Hasiotis says families sometimes request casual burial wear for decedents who never put a tie around their necks while they were alive.

Shorts and Caps

Slovenliness jeopardizes our precious national iconography. Presidents used to dress like presidents, not like a guy from the block, lumbering by every morning in shorts and a baseball cap. Movie stars used to dress like stars; Brad Pitt, arriving for the première of "Legends of the Fall" last year in a baggy gray sweater, could have been mistaken for the projectionist. Many people's memories of Jackie Onassis will forever bear the nagging footnote that the day after her death, Daryl Hannah showed up at her apartment in jeans and a T shirt, looking like she was planning to clean out the closets. Hannah's controversial Rollerblading visit to Onassis just before she died was a watershed in casual history. Many people were offended, but Richard Martin, curator of the Costume Institute of the Metropolitan Museum of Art, came to her defense. "It seems to me that at the point of death one wants to affirm life," he says. "Rollerblading was an affirmation of life. Dressing mournfully is a pretty hollow ceremony."

Even gangsters don't dress up for work any longer. John Gotti showed that you can be an animal without dressing like one, but now mob power in New York has allegedly passed to Vincent (the Chin) Gigante, who wanders the streets of Little Italy in a bathrobe and bedroom slippers. Hollywood big shots used to dress like . . . well, never mind. But even on their worst days any three of them could have come up with more than the one necktie Jeffrey Katzenberg, Steven Spielberg and David Geffen

mustered last October to announce the formation of their colossal new studio.

The photograph of the moguls at their press conference is worth deconstructing, because it shows the many nuances of slovenliness. Katzenberg is relatively neat in a tie and a dress shirt with sleeves rolled up—a look that says, "OK, hey, I left my jacket in the office, you think starting a new studio is all I have to do today?" Geffen, known as "Mr. Gap," wears a shirt open at the collar and a casual vest, an outfit whose message is, "I can wear anything I want—you got a problem with that?" But Spielberg is dressed in rumpled pants and a plaid shirt that might have come from JCPenney, a white blotch of undershirt showing at the collar—a look that says only, "This was on the front hanger in my closet."

Of course, Spielberg, being Spielberg, can dress however he pleases. But that's the point: Americans used to *want* to dress up. Wearing a suit was a privilege of adulthood; Spielberg's outfit looks like something his mother might have dressed him in in fourth grade. One of the fastest-growing apparel categories is sweat suits, know in the trade as "fleece wear." Especially on airplanes, Americans love to curl up among their cuddly folds, like oversize babies, surrounded by the comforting sensations of infancy.

Collars and Garters

Comfort, of course, is the one unanswerable argument in favor of casual dressing. No one bothers putting on a suit or high heels to work at home, certainly. IBM's long-suffering employees of the 1950s didn't just sit at their desks in starched collars and garters; they rode to work in them on stifling buses or subways. You couldn't pay people enough to do that today—not, anyway, once they heard about how Lester Brown, president of WorldWatch Institute, works all summer in neat walking shorts. The other advantage of casual dress is that it is cheaper than suits—except, of course, for workers who may already have a closet full of suits, and find they now have to buy a bunch of sweaters as well. "Not having to wear nylons," an IBM worker in Atlanta told her boss, "is like getting a raise."

But comfort and economy are nothing new. What has changed is the maturing of the first generation that was allowed to wear blue jeans to high school. The formative moment for today's leaders, according to fashion editor Alan Millstein, was their first glimpse of a classmate's rear end in tight Levi's. "That was the ultimate sex symbol, the 501s," Millstein says, explaining that the experience permanently turned them away from baggy suits and dresses.

This is also a generation that defined itself by rebellion. Some of the earliest acts of student activism were directed at dress codes. For many people in their 30s and 40s, going without a suit is still a step on the road to self-actualization. Bart Kosko, a 34-year-old computer scientist, began his career in the aerospace industry, where a suit and tie was a badge of loyalty in the cold war. When he came to the University of Southern California in 1988 as an associate professor in "neural fuzzy logic," he began to question his old values, including what was in his closet. "I asked myself: 'Do you have the courage to dress as you please?' Was I afraid of what people think?" Over time Kosko pared his outfit to the irreducible minimum of tank top and shorts, something that would have been literally inconceivable a generation ago. In the 1950s a suit was not a lifestyle choice; it was just what men wore, unless they were manual laborers. "There was a much narrower view of the world," says Boston University sociologist Bernard Phillips. "You didn't step outside of your role. The role dominated you."

Unbuttoned Strap

It is also no coincidence that suits and ties became dispensable in the 1980s, just as people started seeing billionaires in khaki pants. High-tech start-up companies were notorious for being populated by overgrown college boys wandering the halls in socks, shorts and T shirts. "The first time I interviewed here there was a woman in bare feet and overalls with one strap unbuttoned," says Cindy Wilson of Velocity, a San Francisco multimedia company. The absence of ties is still linked in people's minds with creativity, imagination and $50 million Initial Public Offerings. "Your look is *entrepreneurial* when you dress down," says Timberland "wardrobe consultant" Barbara Seymour, using the hottest new catchphrase in fashion, "You can really *own your own look.*"

Of course, not everyone wants to look "entrepreneurial." In Dallas, where the chic thing is to look as if you already have all the money in the world, " 'casual' means you don't bring a gift," says Dallas Morning News columnist Maryln Schwartz. "A friend of mine called and said, 'I'm having people over for takeout,' and I'm thinking, you know, jeans. I go there and she was wearing pants, but they were Chanel pants."

But wearing a $1,200 outfit to eat chop suey at home is mere decadence. For sheer panache in dressing up, you can't beat a middle-class black church in the South. For generations church was the only institution where Southern blacks were allowed to dress up. On a recent Sunday the congregation arrived at Sardis Baptist in Birmingham, Ala., as if hoping to knock God's eyes out. The men wore immaculate black vested suits, French-cuffed shirts and top hats, the women . . . let's see: a formal black dress with matching blazer, saucer-shaped onyx earrings and a gold choker, a blue-black rhinestone-trimmed hat whose bobbing feathers stretched almost to the wearer's nose and, oh yes, a full-length black mink coat, on 53-year-old Laquita Bell, executive director of the Urban League of Birmingham. "You have to go to a little more trouble when you go to the house of the Lord," says Bell modestly. At around the same time, at First Baptist in a suburb north of Atlanta, a predominantly white congregation sauntered into the pews in jogging suits, jeans and sweaters. "It really doesn't matter what you wear," says Margaret Sulpy, strolling toward the "worship center" (a converted warehouse) in a pink and white warmup suit. "The Lord don't care, as long as you come."

There it is, in a nutshell, the philosophic question that everyone from the chairman of IBM to Daryl Hannah has to wrestle with: is "dressing down" a more democratic and authentic way of life, or a sign that we just can't get it together in the morning? Robert Goldberg, a senior research fellow at Brandeis University, has noticed the curious phenomenon that two people meeting for a business deal on a Friday will each put on a suit as a token of respect, even if it's dress-down day in their respective offices. To him, this signifies that the whole concept is flawed, because why should one's own co-workers be any less deserving of the minimal effort it takes to put on a necktie? More fundamentally, are clothes mere vanities, or do they express something essential about how we view ourselves and society? "In this country we say, 'To heck with facades, we have to have the truth'," Hollander says. "We have our Puritan Protestant ideals telling us that being vain is wicked. All this we have internalized hopelessly so that good people cannot wear earrings, they have to wear running shoes."

A lot is riding on the answers to these questions, because the fashion industry has ingeniously turned the "dress down" phenomenon into a way to sell people even more clothes—a new wardrobe *just for Fridays.* To the cotton industry, casual wear is the greatest boon since the Civil War. Eddie Bauer, the manufacturer of rugged out-doorsy sportswear, is starting two new lines to meet the demand for garments in such esoteric categories as "formal casual," "business alternative" and "dress sportswear." Hush Puppies, a company that has an obvious stake in casual wear, has produced a video guide to "the growing trend toward the unstructured." "The shift creates new challenges for human-resources professionals," the video notes cheerfully. "The human-resources department has got to do a better job of communicating what they mean by a Henley sweater or stretch leggings." Last year this kind of communication helped Hush Puppies sell the rest of the country 37 percent more shoes.

Frock Coats

And something else is at stake, the very face, if not the soul, of America. Fashion usually proceeds in cy-

cles, and so may the fashion for dressing down. But there is also a long-range trend toward informality that may prove unstoppable. What we know as the three-piece business suit was known at the turn of the century as the "lounge suit," a casual garment for wearing at home or in the country. A banker or senator would ordinarily wear a frock coat to his office. In "Sex and Suits," Hollander notes that in the middle of the last century, when formal dress consisted of white tie and tails, the bewigged footmen at a ball were dressed in the gentleman's costume of a century earlier. Today, the headwaiter in a fancy restaurant may wear a dinner jacket as he greets patrons dressed in business clothes. If the pattern continues, the ordinary suit may be fated to become a ceremonial garment, worn mostly by waiters in restaurants whose patrons wear . . . better not to think about it.

Source: From Newsweek, *February 20, 1995, pp. 56–62.* © *1995, Newsweek, Inc. All rights reserved. Reprinted by permission.*

Informal Immortals

Our sartorial slide didn't begin with leisure suits and gold chains. Some 20th-century low points:

1917: U.S. enters WWI and women donate their steel corsets to the effort; the 28,000 tons of steel they save are enough to build two battleships.

1920s: Bobbed hair waves across the nation, but snooty Chicago department-store Marshall Field refuses to employ women with hair cut above the shoulder.

1932: Paris police chief sees Marlene Dietrich walking by the Seine in man's jacket and pants; orders her to leave. Soon after, Katharine Hepburn popularizes trousers on screen.

1942: Baggy zoot suits, hip among teenage "hepcats," ignite parental protests, even race riots. Government bans zoots under wartime fabric-conservation standards.

1951: Marlon Brando bares chest in ripped T shirt; "Streetcar Named Desire" look later embraced by beer-swilling, belly-bulging football addicts. *Stella!*

1953: Witty Brothers, a men's clothier, turns out first polyester suit. To advertise it, model showers in it, wears it for 67 days. Granddaddy of '70s leisure suit.

1955: Disneyland opens. Look, Martha! Now we have somewhere to wear Aloha shirts and Bermuda shorts!

1961: JFK doffs inaugural top hat; men's hat sales plummet. (Jackie dons pillbox; hat sales skyrocket.)

1964: Shaggy-haired Beatles land in U.S.; barbers panic.

1966: Paper clothes add new wrinkle.

1967: Performance artist and cellist Charlotte Moormon arrested for indecent exposure while playing "Opera Sextronique" nude from the waist up.

1969: Woodstock I: long hair, bell-bottoms and love beads. Hippies in mud.

1970: Hot pants heat up; nowhere to hide.

1972: Rosemary Casals breaks the color barrier—appears at Wimbledon in dress trimmed in purple; loses to Billie Jean King, dressed in regulation whites.

1976–77: Punk look peaks. Spike haircuts, slam-dancing and safety pins. *Ouch!*

1978: Gloria Vanderbilt launches designer-jeans craze; a logo on every backside.

1980: NYC transit strike. Forced to walk, women pair sneakers with dress-for-success suits. Style takes a hike.

1982: Nancy Reagan sports flashy knickers at Big Seven confab in Versailles.

1984: Madonna wiggles into nation's psyche in bra tops, tight skirts and fingerless gloves. Material Girl wanna-bes stampede malls; Papa, don't preach.

1984: Don Johnson dudes up "Miami Vice" in pastel-tinted linen jackets, T shirts and sockless loafers. Hey, Sonny, real men don't wear pink.

1991: Nirvana's "Nevermind" album released; grunge band is way cool; grunge flannel shirts are not.

1992: Karl Kani designs first pair of baggy, hang-off-your-butt jeans, inspiring homeboys and homeboy wanna-bes (like Marky Mark) to bare their boxer tops.

1993: Bill Clinton jogs D.C. in too-short shorts. Um . . . Mr . President, some legs are better left under wraps.

1994: Woodstock II: Long hair and nose rings. Slackers, unite!

Source: From Newsweek, *February 20, 1995, pp. 58–61. © 1995, Newsweek, Inc. All rights reserved. Reprinted by permission.*

Global Grunge: It's Not Just Ugly Americans

Americans can get away with wearing jeans or warm-up suits in almost any setting—or at least *we* think we can. And our laissez-dress attitude seems to be spreading to other parts of the world. But some nations—poorer, perhaps, or less self-assured—don't want to dress down. Lucio Herredia always wears a dress shirt and slacks to drive his minibus in Mexico City. "Maybe in the United States people can afford to dress any way they like," he says, "but I can't." Below, a couple of countries that are going casual, then four more where folks wouldn't be caught dead in Ameri-wear.

France

Even the birthplace of haute couture is dressing down. Clothing is expensive, and it is hip to be "relax," as the French say. Blazers and slacks have become acceptable for executives in many offices. The most potent trend in *mode de la rue* (fashionable streetwear) is the puffy, insulated ski jacket, which can make even an elegant woman look like the Michelin man.

Britain

Though pockets of formality still hold out, Britain is embracing stylishly casual clothes. "Seven to 10 years ago, an unstructured Armani suit would have been inappropriate in the City," says Michael VerMeulen, editor of British GQ, referring to London's Wall Street. "Now it's a badge of status." For both men and women, there's less regimentation. Says a personal shopper for women at one of London's chicest department stores: "Even my mother wears leggings and a long sweater."

Israel

Most Israelis still dress down, to about the level of the Dead Sea; shorts, jeans and T shirts are even acceptable at funerals. But with kibbutzim going bankrupt and high-tech businessmen becoming cultural icons, some executives are actually beginning to wear suits.

Russia

In the Soviet era, the Russians were stuck with clothing that looked like potato sacks—a pan-slobbic nation. Now Yuppies and mobsters favor designers like Versace and Armani. Even the scrimping middle class dresses formally—and all too elaborately at times. When a group of Russians and Americans had a picnic last summer, the Americans showed up in jeans and sweat shirts. The Russians wore dresses and suit jackets with khaki trousers; one woman tottered across the grass in spike heels. Both sides were embarrassed.

Argentina

Looking one's best is still a rule of life in Argentina. "Vain and elegant—that's always been the Argentine," says Graciela Osorio, who owns a boutique in Buenos Aires. Pedestrians carry themselves like models. They keep their bodies trim and are extremely conscious of how they and others look. "I have always taken very good care of myself," says Osorio, who is 50 but could pass for 30. "And my daughter, who is 23, is the prototype of a generation even more hedonist than mine."

Japan

In a nation of conformists, fitting in matters. From CEO down to the most minor salaryman, the only acceptable look is "white shirt, bland necktie and dark suit, all worn so you don't stick out," says Tokyo management consultant Douglas Shinsato. Corporate Japan's biggest annual fashion decision is when to allow employees to switch to short-sleeved shirts for the sticky summer weather. Last summer

one foreign employee made the switch a day early and was asked to go home and change.

Chapter Review

Key Words and Concepts

Define, identify, or briefly explain the following:

Avant garde
Bottom-up theory
Classic
Design
Evolutionary
Fad
Fashion
Fashion cycle
Fashion prediction

Fashion trend
Forward fashion
High fashion
Mass fashion
Style
Style number
Trickle-across theory
Trickle-down theory

Review Questions on Chapter Highlights

1. Give examples of each of the following: a style, fad, classic, design, fashion, fashion trend. Explain the differences and relationships between these terms.
2. "The only thing constant about fashion is change." Explain why fashions change and cite examples.
3. Cite examples of products other than apparel and accessories that are currently being affected by fashion.
4. Do you agree or disagree that there are different fashions for different groups of people? Give examples to prove your answer.
5. Does your current wardrobe represent one or more stages of the fashion cycle? Which stage or stages and why?

6. Explain the following statement: "There are three accepted theories that categorize the admired groups from which fashion leadership flows." Give examples.
7. Do designers originate all fashions? Support your opinions.
8. Explain how fashions reflect their "times" and cite specific current examples.
9. Describe the factors that must be considered by fashion professionals in predicting coming fashions.

References

Beaton, C. (1954). *The glass of fashion*. Garden City, NY: Doubleday.

Behling, D. (1992). Three and a half decades of fashion adoption research: What have we learned? *Clothing and Textiles Research Journal, 10* (2), 34–41.

Bell, Q. (1947). *On human finery*. London: Hogarth Press.

Foley, C. (1893). *Economic journal,* Vol. 13. London: publisher unknown.

Greenberg, A., & Glynn, M. (1966). *A study of young people.* New York: Doyle, Dane, Bernbach, Inc.

Ivins, M. (1976, August 15). The constant in fashion is the constant change. *The New York Times.*

King, C. (1963). *Fashion adoption: A rebuttal to the "trickle down" theory.* Reprint Series 119. Reprinted from American Marketing Association Winter Conference, by Purdue University, Krannert School of Business Administration.

Lane, A. (1994, November 7). The last emperor .*The New Yorker,* 82–88.

Nystrom, P. (1928). *Economics of fashion.* New York: Ronald Press.

RAM reports to retailers (1977).

Riemer, B., Zinn, L., & Dapner, F. (1991, April 22). Haute couture that's not so haute. *Business Week,* 108.

Roe, J. (1834). *The sociological concept of capital.* London: Macmillan.

Rogers, E. (1962). *Diffusion of innovations.* New York: Free Press.

Rogers, E., & Shoemaker, F. (1971). *Diffusion of innovations* (2nd. ed.). New York: Free Press.

Rogers, E., & Shoemaker, F. (1983). *Diffusion of innovations* (3rd. ed.). New York: Free Press.

Sapir, E. (1931). Fashion. *Encyclopedia of Social Sciences, VI.* New York: Macmillan.

Silberman, C. E. (1971, March). Identity crisis in the consumer markets. *Fortune,* 95.

Simmel, G. (1957, May). Fashion. *American Journal of Sociology,* Vol. 62, pp. 541–558. Reprinted from the *International Quarterly,* Vol. 10, (October 1904), pp. 130–155.

Sproles, G., (1981, Fall). Analyzing fashion life cycles—principles and perspectives. *Journal of Marketing,* 45, pp. 116–124.

Sproles, G. & Burns, L. (1994). *Changing appearances: Understanding dress in contemporary society.* New York: Fairchild Publications.

Tarde, G. (1903). *The laws of imitation.* New York: Henry Holt & Co.

Veblen, T. (1963). *The theory of the leisure class* (mentor edition). New York: New American Library of World Literature.

Wool Bureau. (1989) *Wool Bureau special report.* New York: Author.

Zinn, L., Power, C., Yand, D., Cuneo, A., & Ross, D. (1992, December 14). Move over Boomers: The Busters are here—And they're angry. *Business Week,* 74–82.

Selected Bibliography

Adburgham, A. (1966). *View of fashion.* London: Allen & Unwin.

Anspach, K. *The why of fashion.* (1967). Ames: Iowa State University Press.

Batterberry, M., & Batterberry, A. (1977). *Mirror mirror: A social history of fashion.* New York: Holt, Rinehart & Winston.

Beaton, C. W. H. (1954) *The glass of fashion.* Garden City, NY: Doubleday.

Behling, D. (1992). Three and a half decades of fashion adoption research: What have we learned?" *Clothing and Textiles Research Journal,* 10(2), 34–41.

Bell, Q. (1976). *On human finery,* 2nd ed. London: Hogarth Press.

Bergler, E. (1953). *Fashion and the unconscious.* New York: R. Brunner.

Boehn, M. von. (1932). *Modes and manners.* Philadelphia: J. B. Lippincott.

Boucher, F. (1967). *2,000 years of fashion.* New York: Harry Abrams.

Broby-Johansen, R. (1968). *Body and clothes: An illustrated history of costume.* New York: Reinhold.

Carter, E. (1980). *Magic names of fashion.* London: Weidenfeld & Nicolson.

Celente, G., & Milton, T. (1991). *Trend tracking.* New York: Warner Books.

Coleridge, N. (1988). *The fashion conspiracy.* New York: Harper & Row.

Contini, M. (1965). Fashion: *From ancient Egypt to the present day.* New York: Odyssey.

Craik, J. (1994). *The face of fashion: Cultural studies in fashion.* New York: Routledge.

Cunningham, C. W. (1979). *Why women wear clothes.* New York: Gordon Press.

D'Assailly, G. (1968). *Ages of elegance: Five thousand years of fashion and frivolity.* London: MacDonald.

Davis, F. (1994). *Fashion, culture, and identity.* Chicago: University of Chicago Press.

Diamond, J., & Diamond, E. (1990). *The world of fashion.* Niles, IL: Dryden Press.

Everyday Fashions of the Twenties as Pictured in Sears and Other Catalogs. (1981). New York: Dover.

Fairchild, J. (1989). *Chic savages.* New York: Simon & Schuster.

Flugel, J. C. (1966). *The psychology of clothes.* New York: International Universities Press.

Harris, C., and Johnston, M. (1971). *Figleafing through history: The dynamics of dress.* New York: Atheneum.

Hollander, A. (1994). *Sex and suits.* New York: Knopf.

Kaiser, S. (1990). *The social psychology of clothing* (2nd ed.). Upper Saddle River, NJ: Merrill/ Prentice Hall.

Kaiser, S., Nagasawa, R., & Hutton, S. (1995). Construction of an SI [symbolic interactionist] theory of fashion: Part 1: ambivalence and change. *Clothing and Textiles Research Journal, 13* (3), 172–183.

Khornak, L. (1982). *Fashion, 2001.* New York: Viking Press, 1982.

Klensch, E. (1995). *Style.* New York: Berkley.

Kohler, C. (1963). *A history of costume.* New York: Dover.

Lagner, L. (1959). *The importance of wearing clothes.* New York: Hastings House.

Laver, J. (1938). *Taste and fashion.* New York: Dodd, Mead.

Laver, J. (1950). *Dress.* London: J. Murray.

Laver, J. (1964). *Women's dress in the jazz age.* London: H. Hamilton.

Laver, J. (1969). *Modesty in dress.* Boston: Houghton Mifflin.

Laver, J. (1983). *The concise history of costume and fashion,* rev. ed. New York: Oxford University Press.

Laver, J., & Provert, C. (1983). *Costume and fashion,* rev. ed. New York: Oxford University Press.

Lurie, A. (1981). *The language of clothes.* New York: Random House.

McDowell, C. (1985). *McDowell's directory of twentieth century fashion.* Englewood Cliffs, NJ: Prentice Hall.

Milbank, C. R. (1990). *The evolution of American style.* New York: Harry Abrams.

Moore, J. (1988). *Perry Ellis: A biography.* New York: St. Martin's Press.

Murray, M. P. (1990). *Changing styles in fashion: Who, what, why.* New York: Fairchild.

Nystrom, P. F. (1928). *Economics of fashion.* New York: Ronald Press.

Roach, M. E., & Eicher, J. B. (1965). *Dress, adornment and the social order.* New York: John Wiley & Sons.

Roach-Higgins, M., Eicher, J., & Johnson, K. (1995). *Dress and identity.* New York: Fairchild.

Rubinstein, R. (1994). *Dress codes: Meanings and messages in American culture.* Boulder, CO: Westview Press.

Rudofsky, B. (1971). *The unfashionable human body.* New York: Doubleday.

Schnurnberger, L. (1991). *Let there be clothes: 40,000 years of fashion.* New York: Workman.

Solomon, M. R. (1985). *The psychology of fashion.* Boston: D. C. Heath.

Sproles, G. (1981, Fall). Analyzing fashion life cycles—Principles and perspectives. *Journal of Marketing, 45,* 116–124.

Sproles, G., & Burns, L. (1994). *Changing appearances: Understanding dress in contemporary society.* New York: Fairchild.

Tortora, P., & Eubank, K. (1994). *A Survey of historic costume.* 2nd Ed. New York: Fairchild.

Tozer, J. (1985). *Fabric of society: A century of people and their clothes, 1770–1870.* New Jersey: Laura Ashley.

Trachtenberg, J. A. (1988). *Ralph Lauren: The Man behind the mystique.* New York: Little, Brown.

Trade Associations

Council of Fashion Designers of America (CFDA), 1412 Broadway, New York, NY 10018.

The Fashion Group, 597 Fifth Ave., New York, NY 10017.

International Association of Clothing Designers, 7 E. Lancaster Ave., Ardmore, PA 19003.

Trade Publications

DNR, Fairchild Publications, 7 W. 34 St., New York, NY 10001-8191.

Women's Wear Daily, Fairchild Publications, 7 W. 34 St., New York, NY 10001-8191.

The Consumer

T*he fashion business exists for* one reason only—the CONSUMER. Although the industry makes important contributions to the economy and provides a host of fascinating jobs, these reasons alone do not justify the existence of this large, diverse sector. Jobs and profits occur only because they are part of the process through which the industry produces and sells products and provides services *for people—the customers.*

Textile producers are in business because the consumer buys the end products. Apparel manufacturers would not survive without the consumer to buy their products. Retailers would have no need to carry merchandise, or for that matter even open their doors each day, were it not for the consumer. The whole industry must keep its eye on the consumer and have a strong service commitment to that consumer to survive and to thrive.

Business conditions of the 1990s have made it more important than ever for companies to have a strong emphasis on the consumer and on service. If one company doesn't serve customers well, another will. Similarly, some segments of the industry itself have customers *within* the softgoods industry (before products reach the end consumer) whom they must serve well. For example, the textile company that makes fabric for apparel must think of the apparel firm as its customer, as well as the person who later purchases the finished garment.

In contrast to the free-spending 1980s, the lackluster economy of the 1990s has created cautious consumers who have changed their buying habits. Another factor that may have influenced consumer spending is that the bulk of the population is older. Whatever the reasons, consumers have changed and their expectations have changed. Companies are learning they gain in the end by satisfying customers first.

In short, the 1990s has been dubbed as the "Decade of the Consumer." Some sources refer to the consumer as "King Customer" (Phillips, Dunkin, Treece, & Hammonds, 1990).

Articles at the end of this chapter focus on various ways in which the industry is attempting to understand the needs of consumers and respond effectively to those needs. Forward-thinking companies know this is an important ingredient in being successful.

Background: Never Take the Consumer for Granted

Through the 1960s and into the 1970s, U.S. manufacturers in all industries experienced the luxury of a booming economy. This strong economy, plus a growing population and only limited competition from imports, meant that manufacturers could sell just about anything they could produce. Consequently, many began to focus their attention on the *production* part of the business—how to make products faster and most cost-effectively. Many began to emphasize winning a greater share of the market. Manufacturers who had this approach thought of the "market" as a collection of competitors, not customers. Many companies forgot about the customer after the sale (Phillips et al., 1990).

The fashion industry has always been very competitive because of the large number of companies competing for business. However, like industry in general, the 1960s and early 1970s were a prosperous time for segments of the softgoods industry. Compared to most of the rest of the world, the U.S. market is a very large and affluent collection of consumers who spend a great deal of their incomes and save very little. A combination of the large market and the thriving economy caused many companies in this industry to begin to take the consumer for granted. They even took their intermediate customers in the industry for granted. For example, the textile industry often provided apparel firms with the fabric selections the *textile mills wanted to produce* rather than what the *garment companies wanted*. The textile firms had, after all, invested heavily in high technology production equipment so they could efficiently produce thousands of yards of the same fabric.

By the mid-1970s, market conditions began to change for U.S. textile and apparel firms. Imports provided the first stimulus for the softgoods industry to begin to think more seriously about its customers' needs. Although imported products had been entering the U.S. earlier, these garments filled a small part of the market. By the 1970s, products from other countries began to be seen as a serious threat by domestic producers. Parts of the U.S. industry actually fostered growth of imports. Apparel firms, tired of the take-it-or-leave-it attitude of many textile mills, often found that companies in other countries were willing to provide what they wanted and worked hard to please. Retailers, too, began to turn increasingly to imports for part of their fashion merchandise.

By the mid-1980s, various segments of the industry began to realize that all could benefit by working together to serve the customer. New partnerships developed between textile and apparel manufacturers, and between apparel firms and retailers. A new **customer orientation** began to emerge in the industry. Apparel manufacturers began to work more closely with retailers to develop and make products based on customer preferences. This information was in turn fed back to textile producers who tailored production around what the customer wanted. The consumer began to have more influence in determining what would be available. **Style testing, focus groups,** and various other strategies became increasingly important in gauging consumer likes and dislikes.

The sluggish economy of the 1990s added to the need to be more sensitive to the customer. A new emphasis on value and service emerged. Consumer confidence plummeted, and many people no longer felt optimistic about the future. Higher taxes, medical costs, housing, and other costs of living left consumers with less to spend on apparel (Figure 3–1). Sobered by recession-like conditions and widespread job layoffs related to "downsizing" of companies, consumer spending changed dramatically. Shopping at prestigious stores and wearing designer-label clothes became less important. Priorities changed. Consumers began to place greater emphasis on personal fulfillment than on material status. As a result, consumers became more value-oriented and price conscious. All segments of the fashion industry felt the impact of the slowdown in spending, the shift in the types of products bought, and where they were being bought. Another new phenomenon has been the emergence of a new breed of consumer called the **cross-shopper.** These are the consumers who may want prestigious items in some product areas but look for bargains when buying other items. This customer may go to prestigious stores for suits and to discount stores for hosiery.

Figure 3–1

U.S. household expenditures. This figure illustrates the decline in clothing expenditures as a percentage of household income, while other areas such as medical costs increase.

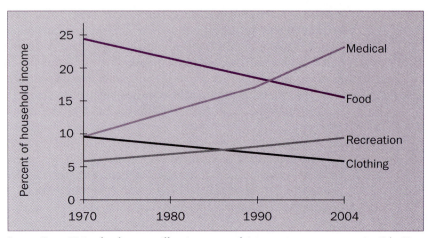

Source: From *Vision for the new millennium . . . evolving to consumer response* (p. 2) by Kurt Salmon Associates, Inc., 1995, New York: Author. Reprinted courtesy of Kurt Salmon Associates, Inc.

Figure 3–2

Consumers' attitudes have changed toward fashion. Consumers' values have shifted from outward expressions of success to longer lasting and deeper concerns.

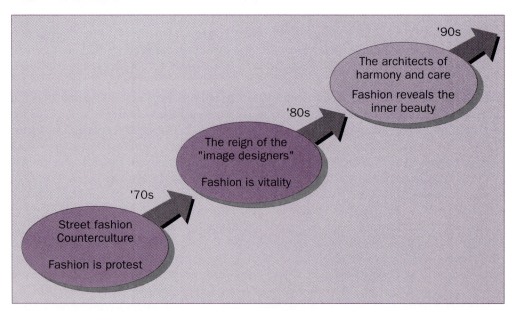

Source: From "Who Are Tomorrow's Consumers?" 1992, *Textile Horizons, 12*(10), p. 3. Reprinted courtesy of Benjamin Dent & Company Ltd.

The Research Institute of Social Change (RISC) identifies sociocultural trends in 17 of the world's most-developed countries and interprets these in terms of implications for society. RISC has charted the changes in attitudes toward clothing and fashion as shown in Figure 3–2. A reading at the end of the chapter, "Who Are Tomorrow's Consumers?," is related to this model.

Fashions of the 1970s (particularly street fashion of the counterculture) represented the protest mood of that decade. In the 1980s, when Wall Street and Main

Street were bustling, consumers used certain looks to project images of success—the "dress for success" approach. Fashion manufacturers experienced healthy demand for their products, and retailers opened stores at a very rapid pace (Esquivel, 1995). According to the RISC conclusions, the 1990s is a time for greater introspection and emphasis on authenticity as people conclude that "a good design in the 90s is one that cares for people, for their body, their soul, their health, and their comfort" ("Who Are Tomorrow's Consumers?," 1992, p. 3).

The Power of the Consumer

The success or failure of the fashion industry depends on consumers' purchase of its products. To illustrate the power of the consumer, we might think of the whole fashion pipeline as a train (Figure 3–3). Different cars in the train represent various segments of the fashion industry: the fiber producers, fabric manufacturers, apparel makers, and apparel retailers. The train goes nowhere without an engine, however, and the consumer represents that engine.

The consumer provides the momentum to make things happen for the rest of the train. Consumer demand for products creates sales for the retailer, who then needs to buy more garments from the apparel manufacturer. As the garment firm produces more merchandise to send to the retailer, more fabric is needed from the fabric producer. As the fabric mill fills orders, it requires more fiber from the fiber producer. When consumer spending occurs at a healthy pace, the whole fashion pipeline experiences prosperous times. When business conditions are favorable, the segments of the chain usually respond and work together with remarkable speed. It is, after all, an industry that must move its products quickly because of the importance of fashion timing.

A few decades ago, various segments of the industry kept large inventories on hand so they could respond readily at each stage to fluctuations in consumer demand. Changes in the economy and the costs of doing business have changed that greatly, however. Retailers, apparel firms, and textile companies have experienced having large inventories on hand when spending dropped sharply, leaving companies at all these levels stuck with inventories that could not be sold in the next fashion season.

Figure 3–3 **When the consumer spends, all segments of the fashion industry move with healthy momentum.**

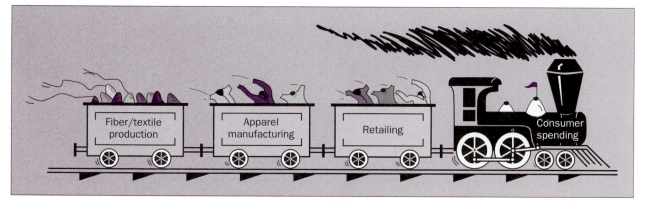

Companies took great losses as they disposed of these inventories by selling them very cheaply just to clear them out. Secondly, companies have become sensitive to the high costs involved in having huge investments tied up in inventories that sit in a warehouse. Because of these changes in the economy and in ways of doing business, retailers, apparel producers, and textile firms all work with much smaller inventories than in the past. Fewer keep large inventories in warehouses awaiting orders. Instead, firms are now more inclined to match their orders to consumer demand. Because the large inventories may not be on hand to accommodate demand, this means that the segments of the industry (the cars of the train) must work together closely to keep the train moving (to respond to the consumer).

Sometimes, however, conditions change. The train may not move along smoothly. Changes in the economy or in consumers' needs may influence consumer spending patterns and create conditions that cause the industry to lose its momentum. Just as consumer demand keeps the train moving, a slowdown in consumer spending reduces activity throughout the fashion pipeline. An abrupt slowdown in spending results in the braking effect we see in Figure 3–4.

A number of factors may cause this abrupt stoppage or slowdown in fashion business activity. Sometimes these are widespread occurrences that affect the entire industry. For example, a downturn in the economy may dampen consumers' spending patterns. This type of change tends to affect the industry broadly, as witnessed in much of the early 1990s. Nearly everyone involved in the industry is affected by this kind of slowdown—all the way back to the fiber suppliers, fabric producers, and, of course, the apparel firms and retailers. Other suppliers to the industry are affected—those who provide zippers, buttons, threads, hangers for new garments, or transportation services for merchandise. Workers may experience layoffs or reduced work weeks.

Sometimes a slowdown in fashion spending occurs when the population reaches a stage when consumers begin to emphasize spending for areas other than apparel. For example, a widespread interest in building or refurnishing homes often results in reduced apparel spending in many households.

Momentum in certain segments of the industry (that is, our "train") is affected when the industry miscues seriously in having products that consumers want in a season. These changes can affect specific segments of the industry or companies, with a ripple effect back through the pipeline. For example, manufacturers may introduce

Figure 3–4

When consumer spending slows, this causes a slowdown in the whole fashion industry.

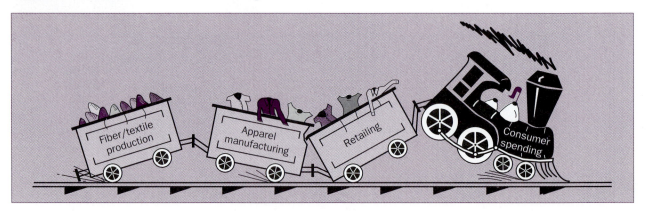

their lines with only very short skirts, and many women avoid purchases altogether because they find nothing they feel is suitable for them. Firms that offer a variety of skirt lengths may have more customers than those offering only very short skirts. In other cases, fashion trends may shift business from one group of producers to another. Firms that produced only traditional tailored menswear felt this slowdown in spending when men began to wear more casual office wear.

Sometimes the industry is not prepared to move as quickly as the consumer expects. We might think of this as a train with an engine that is moving so fast that the rest of the train has difficulty keeping up. Sara Lee's Wonderbra of the early 1990s created this kind of consumer demand when it was first introduced. Customers actually waited in long lines to buy the bras. Although the company had expected healthy sales, they simply had not anticipated the incredible consumer demand that followed. Sara Lee scrambled to manufacture bras quickly enough to keep them in stock in stores, and, as might be expected, other bra companies quickly developed their own versions.

Organizing the Industry Around the Consumer

Old industry strategies that focused just on improving manufacturing processes or gaining an increasing share of the market may have been fine in their time. However, in the 1990s, companies have been forced to think about how their business structures and strategies are organized to serve the new independent, sophisticated consumer.

Mackey McDonald, president of VF Corporation, the world's largest publicly held apparel firm,[1] spoke on the role of the consumer in the 1990s:

> "Business as usual is not an option, because the consumer is now in control.
> For some years now, the retailers have been calling the shots. That has ended
> now. The consumer is really the center of the decision-making process for
> the textile, apparel, and retail industries. Consumers have changed. They are
> time-poor, aging, have less money, are very, very value- and quality-driven,
> seek personalized products and, what is very important, are faced with a lot
> of shopping alternatives" (Maycumber, 1995, p. 9).

As these 1990s consumers asserted themselves in the marketplace, forward-thinking companies in the fashion industry began to grapple with how to serve this new independent customer. For many firms, old strategies did not work anymore. Many began to realize that they needed to be more customer-focused. For some, it was much harder to understand that the organization itself generally needed to change. Management consultants and authors of a plethora of new books have made a specialty of helping companies learn to serve the customer more effectively.

Like companies in all industries, many firms in the fashion industry have, in fact, become more sensitive to satisfying customers. Leading companies gave customer *service* a top priority in their business strategies—with the ultimate commitment for this coming *from the top*. Some companies restructured their entire firms around giving customers what they want. Some tried creative ideas to learn more about service. For example, a few executives tried a stint answering complaint calls to learn more about

---

[1]Sara Lee is also a very large publicly held apparel firm, but because the company produces many other products, it frequently is not listed among the apparel firms *per se*.

what customers are saying. A mail-order firm learned a great deal from analyzing the customer returns. More importantly, customer returns became seen as a source of information rather than just a bother.

One of the authors recalls an experience with a leading apparel firm that functioned under the old mentality when customer returns were a nuisance. The shoulder pads in her name-brand jacket failed miserably after the first drycleaning. The dry cleaner felt responsible and made an honorable attempt to try to substitute new shoulder pads. However, because of a particular shoulder design, it was deemed that only the manufacturer could remedy the problem. Together, the dry cleaner and the author determined the original shoulder pads were faulty anyway. Believing the manufacturer would welcome feedback to prevent further use of this type of shoulder pads, the author went to great effort to find the New York address of the apparel firm, drive across town to the UPS shipping point, and pay the costs of returning the jacket to the company. The package included a letter indicating that the primary purpose of the return was to let the company know of its problem. Replacing the shoulder pads was secondary. A few days later, the company returned the jacket—same shipping box and all—with a terse letter that the garment should be returned to the retailer where it was purchased. Such a return was no easy feat—the jacket was purchased in another state while on a business trip. Today's consumers will no longer tolerate this sort of callous response; they will take their business elsewhere. Manufacturers, retailers, or any other components of the fashion industry who are indifferent to consumer feedback will lose in the end.

For companies seriously committed to service, such strategies have meant training and rewarding employees who fulfill their roles well. It often involves giving employees the power to handle customer problems on the spot. For example, Montgomery Ward customers were frustrated in the past by having to wait for store managers to approve checks and merchandise-return problems. To solve this, the company's chairman authorized all sales clerks to handle these transactions. To reward good service, companies like Montgomery Ward are linking performance reviews and bonuses to customer-satisfaction ratings (Phillips, et al., 1990). Many of Wal-Mart's earliest sales associates became millionaires through the company's profit sharing plan, which gave employees a stake in doing a good job of creating and keeping faithful shoppers.

If we think of the fashion industry as one that is becoming increasingly consumer-centered, we might envision the entire pipeline as revolving around those consumers (Figure 3–5). As this illustration depicts, all segments of the industry must try to remain close to the consumer. This means that although the fiber producer does not sell directly to the end-use consumer, it is important to know what the consumer wants in terms of aesthetics, comfort, and performance of garments made of that company's fiber. Fabric producers also must be sensitive to what the consumer likes and dislikes in fabrics for different purposes. If consumers are frustrated by pilling (formation of small "balls" on the surface of a fabric after repeated wear and laundering), textile firms must resolve this problem if they want repeated business. Every player in the industry has a stake in creating products that satisfy the consumer.

A survey of U.S. textile CEOs indicated that textile firms are placing high priority on serving the end-use customer. CEOs ranked the consumer *first* among the groups with whom they wished to improve business relationships (Figure 3-6, p. 78). This is particularly significant because in most cases the end-use customer is relatively far-removed from the textile firm. One might expect textile executives to place greater emphasis on an industry segment with which their companies work more directly. This emphasis on the end-use customer, however, likely reflects the industry's growing marketing orientation in recent years (Dickerson, Hooper, & Boyle, 1995).

Figure 3–5

The entire fashion industry must be consumer-centered. All segments of the industry must revolve around consumers' needs and wants.

Source: Illustration by Dennis Murphy.

Figure 3–6

Textile CEO priorities for improving working relationships. In a survey of textile CEOs, researchers found that these executives indicated the group with whom they felt they most needed to improve working relationships was end-use consumers.

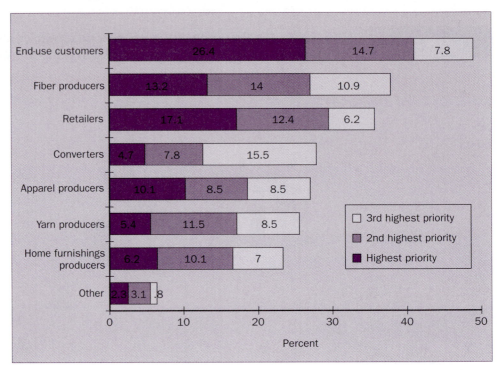

Source: "A New Approach for Manufacturers" by K. Dickerson, C. Hooper, and R. Boyle, April 1995, *America's Textiles International (ATI)* p. 29. Reprinted by permission of *ATI.*

When a company has a true service orientation, this is evident to all who do business with that firm. This commitment will be evident in the way the textile mill works with the apparel firm or how the apparel firm works with the retailer on matters of what will be produced, quality, prompt deliveries, and handling of problems that arise. Producers of intermediate components have another important reason to treat their business customers well. For many parts of the industry, the only way a company gets its products to market is through companies in another stage of the industry. Many segments are far removed from actual sales to the consumer. For a fabric producer to get its fabric to the consumer, an apparel firm must make it into garments. Consequently, treating the business customer well is as important as how the end-use consumer is served.

The Marketing of Fashion

Most of our discussion so far in this chapter actually deals with the shift toward a **marketing orientation** for the fashion industry. This is a change from the earlier **production orientation** when apparel firms and others in the industry "thought of their business and markets in terms of *what their plants could produce*" (American Apparel Manufacturers Association, 1982, p. 55).

Import competition caused U.S. firms to develop more thoughtful marketing plans. Increasingly competitive conditions no longer permitted the losses that accompanied a less-focused, hit-or-miss approach used by some. The fashion industries were slow to awaken to the marketing approaches that sparked growth in many other sectors. In recent years, however, there has been a major change in fashion marketing philosophy. Sophisticated marketing research techniques have been applied to the study of consumer wants.

These marketing activities take place at all levels of the fashion industry—from the producers of fibers, fabrics, and apparel to the retailers of fashion merchandise. A basic difference is that producers are concerned with what to manufacture, whereas retailers are concerned with what to select and purchase for resale. (However, in recent years, as a number of retailers develop and contract production for many of their own lines, they are also concerned with what to *manufacture*).

The Marketing Approach

When companies have had a production orientation, they relied on "persuasive salesmanship" to move as much of the company's goods as possible. Such production and selling focused on the needs of the seller to produce goods and make profits. The distinction of a few terms may be useful here:

- **Marketing** identifies the customer and determines what products to offer that customer and how to do so while meeting the financial return objectives of the company.
- **Merchandising** is the process through which products are designed, developed, and promoted to the points of sale.
- **Sales** operations implement marketing and merchandising activities by physically selling the line to retail customers according to marketing plans (AAMA, 1982).

Marketing focuses on the needs and wants of the consumer, and the customer-centered approach is known as the **marketing concept.** This concept is based on the philosophy that achieving the company's goals depends on determining the needs and wants of customers and delivering the desired satisfactions more effectively and efficiently than competitors do. A firm's **marketing strategy** will look at customer needs and that company's ability to satisfy them. This approach means that all parts of a company function with the customer at the *center* of its activities (Kotler & Armstrong, 1994).

The model shown in Figure 3–7 shows marketing's role and activities in a company. This model summarizes the whole **marketing process** and the forces influencing company marketing strategy. Components of this marketing process will be discussed in sections that follow.

Target Customers

Given what we have said so far, it is logical that the **target market** (this could also be customers that are companies at various stages in the fashion pipeline) is at the center of the model in Figure 3–7. Whether one is designing, producing, or selling, the first step is to have a clear picture of the customer market segment that constitutes the firm's targeted customers. Since no business can be all things to all people, it must identify a group of customers as its target. For a high fashion business, this group may be very small and homogeneous. For a mass marketing company, this targeted group of consumers will be large and quite diverse. Everything that follows in the marketing process is then geared to the target group or market segment. In general terms, a **market** means a meeting of people for the purpose of buying and selling. Such a meeting is not necessarily physical or personal. Specifically, a market for fashion merchandise refers to people with money (some more, some less) and with an inclination to buy fashion-related goods. Fortunately, the potential fashion market in the United States is so large that there is enough business for a company to operate successfully by satisfying even a small percentage of that market.

Figure 3–7

Factors influencing a company's marketing strategy. In this model, we see that the company's target consumers are the center of all the firm's activities.

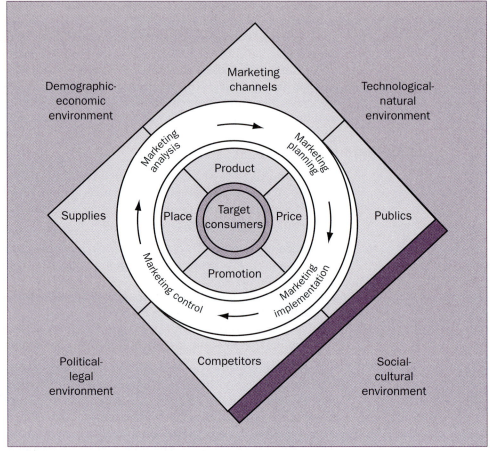

Source: From *Principles of Marketing,* 6th ed. (p. 43) by D. Kotler and G. Armstrong, 1994, Englewood Cliffs, NJ: Prentice Hall. Reprinted courtesy of Prentice Hall.

Just as there can be no universal weather forecast, but only one that is specific as to time and area, the fashion firm must identify its market segment—that is, its part of the whole market. **Market segmentation** means dividing the heterogeneous market into smaller customer divisions that have relatively homogeneous characteristics the firm can satisfy. The segment will consist of a group of customers (not necessarily physically in one community) who react in a similar way to a given set of market stimuli. The segment may be based on such characteristics in common as income level (high, middle, upper middle, etc.), life style (suburban, city), fashion preferences (*avant garde* or classic), special interests (jogging, aerobic dancing, disco), sizes (extra large, petite, junior, misses), occupation (career executive, homemaker), and so on. The potential categories are many more than can be illustrated here, and the kinds and types within each category are also more numerous than our necessarily limited examples.

Usually, a market segment includes a combination of two or more of such characteristics as were mentioned here. The individuals who constitute a segment may differ in other respects, but they have a commonality of interests and wants that makes each one a potential customer for the business concern that is courting that particular market. A market segment can even be large and powerful enough that producers and retailers prepare whole new categories of clothing for it. For example, in the 1980s as the baby boomers born in the 1950s and early 1960s entered the workforce, they created a market segment for executive career apparel.

If a business, either manufacturing or retailing, is large enough, it may cater to several different market segments at once, creating separate divisions or departments for each. An obvious example is the special shops, both freestanding and within department stores, for "big is beautiful" women and for extra-tall, extra-large men.

It must be realized that segments do not always remain static. One of the costliest errors a business can make is to take its market for granted. Economic and social conditions change; competitors develop new market strategies; new products arise and affect consumer purchasing patterns. The only way for a business to expand or even maintain its market position is to keep up with, and even ahead of, such changes. Products, services, and pricing policies must continuously be reevaluated in terms of changing market influences.

The need to target consumer groups is threefold: (1) to identify consumer characteristics most suited to the goals and capabilities of the firm; (2) to provide a basis for formulating and, if necessary, adjusting the firm's policies and products to satisfy these characteristics; and (3) to pinpoint consumer characteristics that affect patterns of buying behavior.

Market segmentation in itself will not ensure success in the fashion business, since it is only one of a combination of many factors in the equation. Not to segment, however, is to choose a sure way to failure. The principle of segmentation is based on the fact that people are different and that, to make the point again, no one company can be all things to all people. A choice must be made as to which segment of the market a particular business or division or department can most effectively serve.

With a specific targeted customer group in mind, the next step is to collect all the facts one can get. What are they buying this season? What are the activities and occasions for which they need clothes? What are their priorities? Are they innovators or imitators? What people, periodicals, or environmental influences will affect their choice? And so on. The more answers one has to such questions, the clearer the picture becomes, and the easier it is to forecast.

Marketing Mix

After the company identifies its target market, then it designs a **marketing mix** made up of factors under its control—product, price, place, and promotion—shown in the middle ring in Figure 3–7. The company finds its own combination of these factors that will do the job it wants to do in serving the market identified. The marketing mix is determined by management as they go through marketing analysis, planning, implementation (putting the marketing plan into action), and control (evaluating strategies and making adjustments to be sure marketing efforts are doing what they intended). These management functions are shown in the outer ring of the model (Kotler & Armstrong, 1994). Elements of the marketing mix are:

- *Product* refers to the fashion items and services that a company will offer its target market. Company history may play a major role here; many firms have a long-standing record in producing specific lines. For example, jeans makers may venture into related sportswear lines but will not usually decide also to make and sell bras or evening gowns.
- *Price* refers to what customers who buy the product will be charged. Firms in the fashion industry have had to think carefully about prices of their products aimed toward the 1990s consumer. Consumers have resisted paying inflated prices for so-called prestige label merchandise. Instead, they expect good value for their money

and even like to boast about their ability to get quality they like for cut-rate prices. Many manufacturers have felt squeezed on prices in the 1990s. As the prices of cotton and other fibers increased, the apparel firm's cost of materials have risen dramatically, but apparel firms found it difficult to pass these higher costs on to consumers, who balked at paying higher prices for garments.

- *Place* indicates where the product will be sold. Companies may produce products to be sold only in department stores or only in discount stores. Large apparel firms may make various lines geared at specific channels of distribution, with the intent of covering all major retail channels. For example, Sara Lee sells its L'eggs hosiery in supermarkets and discount stores, its Hanes Silk Reflections in department stores, its Donna Karan line in upscale specialty stores, and several acquired international brands in other countries (e.g., Dim in Europe). For a retailer, *place* may mean that certain products may be sold in some of its branch stores and not in others. For example, a Dillard's store may not offer its Ellen Tracy collections in stores located in predominantly blue-collar sections of a city.
- *Promotion* includes all the efforts of a company to establish the identity and enhance the demand for specific brands and designer name products or to encourage buying from certain retailers. The fashion industry has spent vast amounts to achieve these goals.

The Marketing Environment

The **marketing environment** includes all the factors that affect how a company is able to meet its goals in developing and maintaining successful business relationships with its target customers. As Kotler and Armstrong (1994) note, these can be either opportunities or threats. A company must monitor these environmental factors at all times to be able to respond by changing its marketing strategies. If we refer back to the marketing model in Figure 3–7, we see that these environmental factors are of two types.

1. The **microenvironment**, which consists of the forces *close to the company* that influence its ability to serve its target market—suppliers, marketing channel firms, customer markets, competitors, publics, and even other parts of the company. We might consider each of these briefly. *Suppliers* affect the availability of certain fabrics and trims, thus, influencing what a company can produce. *Marketing channel firms* might include ways to ship and store merchandise. *Customer markets* refers to determining the type of customers the firm will serve and studying the characteristics of those customers; the customers may be end-use consumers, businesses, government sources, those who may resell the product, or buyers in other countries. For *competitors,* a firm must position itself to have certain advantages over others to win the customer's business; for example, Levi Strauss & Co. must be able to persuade consumers their jeans have superior points to Lee jeans (and vice versa). Examples of *publics* are the financial community, the media, and the general public. *Other parts of the company* refers to all the other divisions that must cooperate and be supportive in order to implement the marketing plan (Kotler & Armstrong, 1994).

2. The **macroenvironment**, which consists of factors in the larger societal setting in which the company functions—**demographic**-economic influences, technological-natural factors, political-legal environments, and social-cultural forces (Kotler & Armstrong, 1994). In the next section, we shall consider some of these influences.

Macroeconomic Factors that Affect Consumption of Fashion

Let us consider some of the macroeconomic forces that affect the fashion business. Although we might easily have a chapter on just this topic, space permits us to consider just a few of these important factors.

The growth of the fashion business in the United States directly reflects the vast social and economic changes that have taken place in this country's lifetime. As one noted social commentator expressed it, "Few societies in history have been as fashion conscious as the American, and there have been few in which styles and clothes changed so often. Students of human society know that changing fashions are an index of social change within a society" (Lerner, 1957).

Keeping up with the changing social and economic trends is not a one-time or a once-in-a-while research project for fashion professionals. Instead it is necessarily as much a part of their day-to-day activity as keeping sales and inventory records. The fashion industry must be aware of the various macroeconomic factors that influence the needs and wants of consumers; it must also be aware that, as consumers react to these influences, their fashion needs and wants change. The industry must constantly finetune its awareness of these changes and its responses to them.

The consumer market is the source of all ultimate demand. Significant changes that take place in the consumer market have had and will continue to have significant impact on the fashion industries. For example, the age mix of the population, both present and projected into the future, has a definite bearing on the current fashions and those to come. The baby boom that followed World War II gave us the rise of the "Yuppies"—or young, upwardly mobile urban professionals—who became a major economic and fashion force in the 1980s. Marketers in all areas of business have followed population demographics, watching the baby boomers go through changing stages of their lives, with attempts to respond to this group at various stages because it represents a very large potential market for all kinds of goods and services.

Baby boomers began the strong thrust of women in the workforce, and especially into executive positions. This trend not only changed the status of women but also affected the way they dress. By the same token, the younger men of this age group increasingly participated in home and leisure activities, and accordingly adopted more varied styles in dress. Early generations, it is true, had working wives and husbands who participated in home activities, but not in the numbers or with the impact of this group. The rise in the number of dual-income households was accompanied by a decrease in time available to shop, as shown in Figure 3–8.

Now the baby boomers are aging. Many are growing wealthier— not only from their own earnings, but also from substantial inherited wealth. Many have become what some writers are calling a new development in American sociology—the "overclass." Although the United States has always had a wealthy segment of the population, the new elite in the "overclass" are different. Members of this group share a common culture and interests, and are different from the "underclass" with the obvious difference that no one is trying to get out of the "overclass." This group places great value on competitive achievement, and has a tendency to judge people on "merit," as defined by a continual and strenuous accumulation of academic and professional credentials. For many in this group, success began by graduating from Ivy League schools and then scrambling up the merit ladder through intense work. They lead a life style that might be called "Yuppie taste updated" to take into account their increased affluence and sophistication. The "overclass" are prominent in the upper 5 percent group of U.S. incomes, which in 1995 started at $113,182. Members of this group want prestigious private schools even for their preschoolers; they often want housing that separates them from the middle-class and below; they eat gourmet food and drink gourmet coffee (Adler, 1995). Members of this group are obvious prospects for the upscale end of the fashion business, both for themselves and their children. As an example, Bloomingdale's, Neiman Marcus, Nordstrom, and Saks Fifth Avenue tap their vast customer databases to identify their most profitable customers. Some of these retailers extend special perks and shopping services to this group (Bird, 1995).

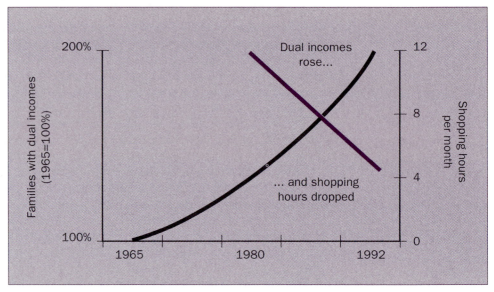

Source: From *Vision for the new millenium . . . evolving to consumer response* (p. 3) by Kurt Salmon Associates, Inc., 1995, New York: Author. Reprinted courtesy of Kurt Salmon Associates, Inc.

Figure 3–8

The rise of dual incomes and the decline in shopping time. As this graph indicates, dual incomes increase spending potential but greatly reduce the amount of time available for shopping.

Another related significant socioeconomic trend is that there is a growing gap between the incomes of the richest and the poorest Americans. Middle-class income is growing slowly, incomes of "the poor are stagnating, and the rich are getting richer, very rapidly" (Adler, 1995, p. 43). This pattern, too, has important implications for the fashion industry. We must keep in mind, however, that the upper income group represents a relatively small percentage (5 percent) of the population. Despite high spending potential of the affluent, the majority of the fashion market is not in this group.

A generation that followed the baby boomers—given labels such as the twentysomethings, Generation X, slackers, and baby busters— have moved into the mainstream of American life. This group represents the second-largest group of young adults in the country's history, some 46 million of them. Zinn, Power, Yang, Cuneo, and Ross (1992) describe this group as follows:

> Busters are the first generation of latchkey children, products of dual-career households, or, in some 50% of cases, of divorced or separated parents. They have been entering the work force at a time of prolonged downsizing and downturn, so they're likelier than the previous generation to be unemployed, underemployed, and living at home with Mom and Dad. They're alienated by a culture that has been dominated by boomers for as long as they can remember. They're angry as they look down a career path that's crowded with thirty- and fortysomethings who are in no hurry to clear the way. And if they're angry and alienated, they dress the part, with aggressively unpretty fashions, pierced noses, and tattoos (pp. 74–75).

Generation X launched the "grunge" look consisting of "slovenly, asexual, antifashion fashion" (Zinn et al., 1992, pp. 75, 77). Variations of the look include items suggesting a "postindustrial thrift-shop look": baggy clothes, faded flannel shirts, clunky work boots, ripped sweaters, old jeans and corduroys, long flowing skirts, body piercing, and tattoos.

Although those who follow population patterns have been fixated on the baby boomers for many years, another youthful group—teenagers—has begun to grow

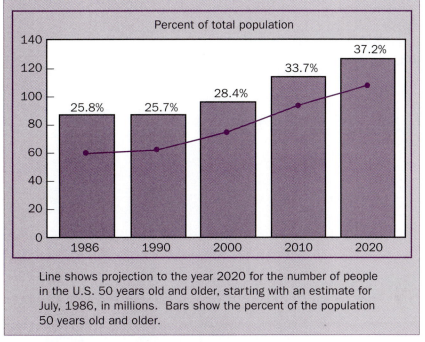

Figure 3–9

50 and over, a growing force

Line shows projection to the year 2020 for the number of people in the U.S. 50 years old and older, starting with an estimate for July, 1986, in millions. Bars show the percent of the population 50 years old and older.

Source: U.S. Department of Commerce; U.S. Census Bureau.

again. Children of boomers entered their teen years in the early 1990s, ending a 15-year decline among the teen population. When the bulge of teenagers reaches its peak of 30.8 million teens in 2010, this group will exceed the baby boom teen explosion of the 1960s and 1970s both in size and duration. Teens in this group will be a powerful force in fashion markets and have already made their preferences known for Doc Martens, Reebok Air Pumps, Big Smith overalls, concert t-shirts, thermal underwear, flannel shirts, and bead necklaces. As a cover of *Business Week* proclaimed, "Get ready: Once again, they will shake our culture—and our economy" (Zinn et al., 1994).

At the same time, an increasing portion of the U.S. consuming population is growing older. First, there is the "middle age" group, with a larger percentage in the 50-plus group than ever before (Figure 3–9). The baby boomers are entering their fifties, and many are attempting to defy the aging process through "exercise, diet and dye." Efforts seem to be paying off because this "middle age" group looks, feels, and acts younger than previous generations did. Most Americans will have more years of adult life *after* their children leave home than they spent parenting (Anderson, 1992). For many, the fifties is the most productive and rewarding decade of their lives (Beck, 1992). At this age, consumers generally have their highest spending potential, and their continued interest in remaining active and youthful bodes well for the fashion industry.

The so-called "senior citizen" group accounts for a growing proportion of the population, as Figure 3–10 indicates. Today, about one in eight Americans is 65 years or older, compared to one in 25 at the turn of the century. The 85-and-over group is growing especially fast. By 2030, *one in five* Americans will be elderly, and senior citizens will live longer. People who used to be considered old at 65 are usually still in their prime at that age today. Healthier life styles mean that older consumers are leading active, vital lives and retain their interest in being well-dressed. The senior citizen market is viewed by many as an economic bonanza (Bureau of Census, 1995; Farrell, Palmer, Atchison, & Andelman, 1994).

Figure 3–10

Coming soon: Age of the aged.

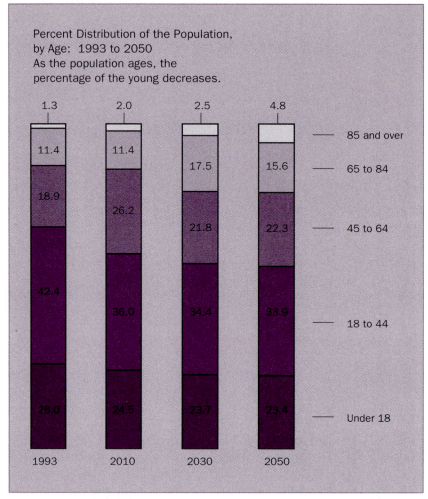

Percent Distribution of the Population, by Age: 1993 to 2050
As the population ages, the percentage of the young decreases.

Source: From *How We're Changing—Demographic State of the Nation: 1995* (Current Population Reports, Special Studies, Series P-23, No. 188) (p. 1) by Bureau of Census, December 1994, Washington, DC: U.S. Dept. of Commerce.

Life styles are another important macroeconomic factor affecting purchase of fashion goods. Family life has been turned inside out by the rush of married women, many of them mothers, into the workforce. Households made up of single individuals, once a rarity, are commonplace today; so are single-parent households, in which the unmarried or divorced parent drops the child off at a daycare center and spends the major part of the day in the business world rather than in the nursery and the kitchen. Customers have changed from the conventional mother-at-home shopping during the week in downtown or suburban stores to the working woman, the senior citizen, and the single adult, each with his or her preferences in clothing, food, and life styles in general.

Changing life styles affect fashion purchases in other ways. The health and fitness craze in recent decades provides terrific boosts to sweatsuit and other activewear manufacturing and sales. As baby boomers began to age and have demanding careers, many adopted a life style known as *cocooning.* This means they are spending more time at home, often taking advantage of food delivery and other services that permit them to spend time at home. This trend affects demand for comfortable clothes, shoes, and home products that create a comfortable environment. Moreover, it means that catalogs and on-line shopping services appeal to this group. When these consumers do shop in stores, they want quick, convenient, affordable shopping. According to a MasterCard study, consumers are frustrated by the dizzying array of indistinguishable products, and many women are moving toward a "male" pattern of shopping. Men tend to avoid haphazard or confusing shopping environments. Consequently, retail stores, mall developers, and others must attempt to respond to these concerns (Vandeventer, 1994).

Fashion marketers must also take into account that the U.S. population is becoming more ethnically diverse, with new target markets that are growing in explosive numbers demographically and socially. The 1990s census provided data that sparked all consumer product marketers to think of the growing importance of minorities. In 1990, 24.4 percent of the U.S. population were members of minority groups, compared to 20.4 percent in 1980 (Dunn, 1992). The U.S. Census Bureau forecasts that by the year 2050, Asians, Hispanics, African Americans, and other nonwhite groups could represent 47 percent of the total population. The Asian/Pacific Islander group is the fastest growing segment of the population, whose numbers are expected to increase fivefold to roughly 12 percent of the population by 2050. Moreover, a surge of the Hispanic and Asian groups are expected to affect total population projections because those families tend to have larger families (Bremner & Weber, 1992). African-American consumers represent a growing percentage of the U.S. population and have increasing collective economic clout. Up to now, companies have only made modest efforts to develop and market products specifically for various ethnic groups. As these groups' spending power increases, companies will find it is increasingly important to stop regarding them as "dark-skinned white people" (Mallory & Forest, 1992, p. 70). Many members of these ethnic groups do not want to assimilate with the rest of the population. They are proud of their ethnic heritage, want products of their own, and are willing to spend to get them (Gordon, 1993).

Analysis of Customers' Fashion Preferences and Trends

An important part of the fashion marketer's job is the analysis of what customers are actually buying. In the fashion industry there is a constant flow, back and forth, of information about these purchases. The systems that producers and retailers have today for this purpose are extremely rapid and accurate, thanks to the development of the computer. In most retail stores, a record is kept as to the styles, colors, fabrics, and so on that have been purchased for resale. On this record are also entered the day-to-day sales. Every garment bought by a consumer thus becomes a ballot cast by the customer for the desired size, color, fabric, silhouette, and style. Computerized registers provide this important **point-of-sale (POS) data** from every purchase made. Bar coding provides this data (Figure 3–11).

From the point-of-sale records, retailers can discern sudden or gradual changes in the preferences of their own customers. These changes become apparent whether the same customers are turning to different fashions, or whether there is a change in the kind of people who make up the store's clientele. In either case, the proprietor or buyer sees that there is less demand for Item A and more for Item B.

These variations in what consumers are buying at that store are reflected in what the store buys from the manufacturers of fashion merchandise. Multiply that store's ex-

Analyzing fashion purchases at point of sale (POS). Retail sales ticket showing manufacturer, style number, classification, season, size, and price. This information is fed into a POS register and the data appear on sales and inventory reports. POS data are also being used to enable replacement of merchandise as it is sold.

Figure 3–11

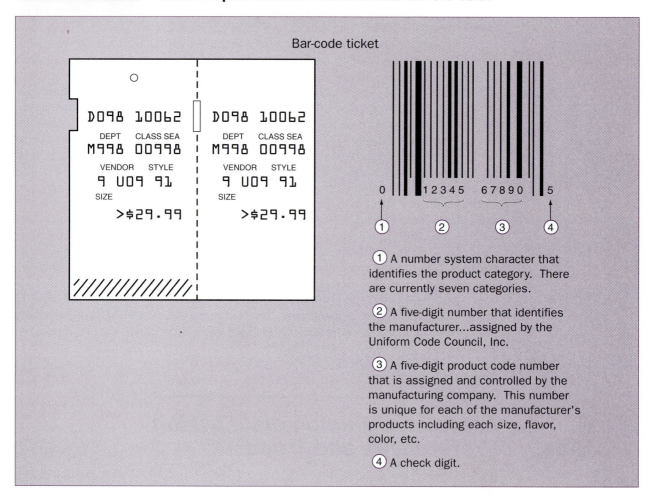

Bar-code ticket

① A number system character that identifies the product category. There are currently seven categories.

② A five-digit number that identifies the manufacturer...assigned by the Uniform Code Council, Inc.

③ A five-digit product code number that is assigned and controlled by the manufacturing company. This number is unique for each of the manufacturer's products including each size, flavor, color, etc.

④ A check digit.

perience by the hundreds or even thousands of stores that buy from one manufacturer, and you see that producers have a relatively broad spectrum of consumer response as represented in the rate at which their various styles are sold. If they have countrywide distribution, they may see that certain areas are buying certain colors, styles, or fabrics faster or more slowly than others. If they have no reason to believe that this is due to special effort (or lack of effort) on the part of their retail outlets in those areas, they can assume that a regional difference is influencing sales. Typical of such differences are the West Coast's quickness to accept what is new, and especially what is casual and relaxed, or the Middle West's fondness for shades of blue to go with the blue eyes that predominate among the German and Scandinavian groups who have settled there.

From the manufacturer of the finished garment, information about customer preferences, as expressed in customer purchases, flows in several directions. One flow is back to the retail stores, by means of the manufacturer's salespersons, to alert them to trends they may not have noticed for themselves. Another flow is to the fabric producers, in the form of the garment maker's reorders for the most accepted fabrics and colors.

The POS data provide the basic information needed for Quick Response (QR) systems to operate. As these electronic linkages among producers and retailers have become more prevalent, a number of large apparel manufacturing firms are actually connected to retailers' computer systems. When certain products are sold by the retailer, this information informs the apparel firm that it should replace those items in the retailer's supply of that apparel firm's lines. For some mail-order firms, orders for certain products will be sent *directly* to the manufacturer, who ships the product to the customer. In those cases, the mail-order retailer may hold none of the apparel firm's product in the retail inventory.

Information about the customer and the balloting that he or she does from day to day at the retail cash register is also collected by other people in the fashion field. Editors of consumer magazines, for instance, check regularly on trends with manufacturers of raw materials and finished products. They do this to see whether their own previous editorial judgments of fashion trends have been right, and to establish a basis on which to select styles to be featured in future issues. What the customer does or does not buy is watched as closely in the fashion industry as Wall Street transactions are watched by stockbrokers.

Often the customer is a guinea pig on whom the experts test their judgment. Sometimes he or she is a member of a committee formed by retailers or editors to represent a particular section of the public and to be available for consultation or reaction to new ideas, or just to sound off on any subject. Consumer surveys are also conducted by stores, producers, and publications. More often, the customer serves unknowingly as a test subject. When a new style, color, fabric, or silhouette is introduced, makers and retailers usually proceed on a "sample, test, reorder" system. This means that only small quantities are made up and placed for sale in retail stores. At the first inkling of customer reaction, the retailer reorders the acceptable styles and discontinues whatever other styles may have evoked little customer enthusiasm. The manufacturers, meanwhile, are watching the retail reorders to see which styles they should cut in quantity and which ones should be discontinued.

No one, least of all the customers, may fully understand why one style is chosen in preference to another, but everyone in the fashion industry is observing their selections and thus determining what the current fashions are and evaluating their degree of popularity and their directions.

Quick Response as a Marketing Strategy

Although the industry's Quick Response program encompasses production operations and employs new computer technologies in a range of activities to fulfill its promises, the *objectives of the QR effort rely on a marketing concept: getting the right merchandise to market at the right time.* Even more fundamental, QR is based on the marketing principle of *serving the customer more effectively by focusing on the customer's needs.* The apparel industry is concerned with serving more effectively both the retail customer and the end-use customer, and QR provides an important strategy for doing that (Dickerson, 1991).

Push System

Quick Response represents a dramatically different marketing strategy from that employed by most apparel manufacturers in the past. Traditionally the apparel industry expected merchandisers to be able to predict a year in advance what the consumer would want in the next year's selling season. Given the transient nature of fashion and the fickle tastes of the apparel consumer, choosing styles, colors, and other aspects of a line that far in advance was risky. Despite the risks and inconveniences, the softgoods chain was structured to support the **push system.** The push system depended on force feeding a product line through the multistage production and marketing process in hopes that the consumer would like the end product. If the consumer did not like it, markdowns resulted (Figure 3–12). Whether planned or forced, markdowns are said to approach 25 to 30 percent of total U.S. apparel sales (Dickerson, 1991).

Pull System

In contrast, the **pull system** is based on observing the consumer and translating the consumer's wishes back through the pipeline to determine what will be produced. The pull system relies on using retailers' point-of-sale data to record consumer reactions and

Figure 3–12   **The push system is based on force feeding a product line through the manufacturing and marketing process in hopes the consumer will like it.**

preferences. Consumer preferences, as indicated through purchases of introductory lines, are transmitted quickly back through the information pipeline so that merchandise is produced promptly to respond to what the consumer wants (Figure 3–13).

The entire QR system is based on tracking, analyzing, understanding, predicting, and responding to consumer demand. The system depends on electronic communication systems for transmitting data through the softgoods chain, a willingness of retailers and suppliers to share information, and a cooperative spirit among members of the production and marketing chain (Dickerson, 1991).

Another reference to the earlier train analogy may be useful in considering the push/pull systems. Under the *push system,* the engine (consumer) ran the train, but the train (fashion pipeline) was not geared to respond quickly and effectively to the engine's activity. The cars had tried to second guess the path of the engine, and, on occasion, the back cars tried to divert the engine to where the cars wanted to go. Under the *pull system,* the train recognizes that the engine is in control. Rather than try to second guess the engine or divert it, the train responds to the path being charted by the engine (Dickerson, 1991).

Figure 3–13　**The pull system is based on determining the consumer's needs and wants and basing production on that information.**

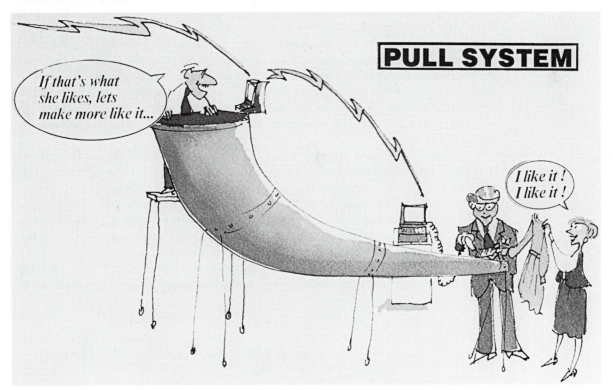

Source: Reprinted with permission from *Bobbin.* Copyright © Bobbin Blenheim media. All rights reserved.

The Marketing Concept and Manufacturing/Distribution

When an apparel company adopts the marketing concept as a vital part of company philosophy, this provides a focus for the firm and serves as a guide for the company's production and distribution of its lines—both domestically and globally. The manufacturer must understand the markets and the firm's role in those markets. Furthermore, as the company develops a marketing strategy, this targets the firm's customers, providing focus so the company can concentrate on serving that customer or group of customers. Obviously, a company must take the firm's capabilities into account in making these plans. The marketing strategy may also provide guidance on markets to avoid because of oversaturation, excessive import competition, or other reasons (Dickerson, 1991).

The marketing strategy determines the manufacturing strategy—including sources of production—rather than the reverse. The marketing strategy will take into account a full range of production alternatives including manufacturing in the firm's own plants, contracting, or perhaps **offshore production.** Or, a company may use a combination of production alternatives suitable to serving its customers well. For example, it may produce more fashion-oriented merchandise in its domestic plants so that it can get time-sensitive lines to the retailer and consumer quickly. When timing is not as critical, the company's lines of a more "staple" nature might be made in another country to take advantage of lower production costs.

A number of U.S. apparel firms have placed added emphasis on marketing and service while de-emphasizing manufacturing. This means that some apparel firms have little or no manufacturing base; instead, products are manufactured to a company's specifications by independent contractors both in the United States and other countries. In these firms, a product development team generally develops the lines, selects fabrics, and makes other specifications on how garments should be made. All of this occurs with the target market in mind. Then, the production occurs elsewhere. Finished garments are sent to the firm's distribution center and from there are shipped to the apparel firm's retail customers. Nearly all Liz Claiborne garments are made in this manner.[2]

Distribution operations play a very important role in customer-centered firms. The company's distribution area is responsible for getting the right merchandise to the retail customer in a timely fashion so that it is available for quick-turn fashion trends, promotional sales, to replenish the retailer's inventory, or other needs. Distribution operations monitor the company's available inventories to be sure a supply is available to respond quickly to the customer. Distribution areas of a firm often handle returns and other service matters related to the retail customer.

In short, the marketing strategy helps the firm identify who it is and what it does, and then it keeps the company on target as it proceeds with production and distribution.

---

[2]Today many retail firms are engaged in contracting the production of their lines, just as apparel firms are. This means that the retail firm's marketing strategy will determine how and where garments will be produced, just as it does for apparel firms.

Serving Consumers in the Next Millennium

Kurt Salmon Associates (KSA), a leading consulting firm for the fashion industries, has identified a number of anticipated visionary changes in how these sectors will serve their customers in the year 2000 and beyond. These experts predict that the production-distribution chain with its distinct segments, as we know it today, will give way to a more integrated, interlocking complex with the consumer as the focal point. Companies will develop differentiated competitive business expertise, focus on their core businesses, and link with other companies without regard to ownership. Products will be more customized rather than mass produced where one or a few sizes are expected to fit all.

Today, many retailers expect manufacturers to send merchandise to them **floor-ready,** with packaging and ticketing ready to move directly to the sales floor. The KSA team predicts that links directly between the producer and the consumer will grow, with a shift to **consumer-ready** manufacturing. According to KSA predictions, retail stores will become the shopping "theater" in which the consumer makes buying decisions, and customized products will be sent directly from the manufacturer to the consumer.

KSA experts have coined a term to describe a new replenishment model based on the consumer: Automatic Consumer Replenishment^{SM}. KSA calls this the "next generation of relationship marketing" (Kurt Salmon Associates, 1995, p. 10.) This takes the customer-centered company a step closer to the consumer compared to today's automatic replenishment schemes that replace garments in the retail store as soon as they are sold. In KSA's visionary model, new relationships between producers and consumers will permit automatic replenishment of a variety of items on a regular periodic basis: toiletries, food, underwear, hosiery, dress shirts, and activewear. The producer might approach the customer in the following manner: "Mrs. Johnson, you normally order 10 pair of Hanes panty hose, style 485, size B, color black, from us about every 3 months. Would you like us to send those to you, automatically, on a regularly scheduled basis?" (KSA, 1995, p. 7). For consumers who are increasingly pressed for time to shop, this convenient, time-saving approach is likely to be very well-received, particularly in certain product areas.

Federal Legislation Affecting the Fashion Business

Under the American systems of government and economy, businesses enjoy certain rights and freedoms. Although business in America originally operated in a *laissez-faire* economy (i.e., noninterference by government), the emergence and abuses of trusts and monopolies in the late nineteenth century, which minimized competition and made it difficult for small business to survive, created the need for regulation. Two basic categories of federal legislation affect the fashion industry: (1) laws that regulate competition and (2) labeling laws designed to protect consumers. In essence, those laws that regulate competition help consumers also by assuring market conditions that provide competitive prices and other conditions to serve them fairly.

Federal Laws Regulating Competition

Sherman Anti-Trust Act—1890: This was our first law enacted to restrain unfair competition. It outlawed monopolies and practices that restrained competition.

Clayton Act—1914: This law reinforced the Sherman Act by spelling out some specific restraints pertaining to price fixing, price discrimination, and interlocking directorates.

Federal Trade Commission (FTC) Act—1914: This law created the **FTC** to serve as a "policing" agency to enforce the Sherman and Clayton acts, to investigate alleged unfair methods of competition, to conduct hearings, and to issue cease-and-desist orders. This law was amended by the Wheeler-Lea Act of 1938 and gave the FTC authority to prohibit fake advertising and made it an additional offense to injure the general public.

Robinson-Patman Act—1936: According to this law, which was aimed primarily at giant retailers, large purchasers of goods may not be given so large a discount as to give them monopolistic advantage. This act makes price discrimination between purchasers of like grade or quantity illegal (e.g., it outlawed "phony" advertising allowances).

Celler-Kefauver Act (or Antimerger Act)—1950: This law made it illegal to eliminate competition by creating a monopoly through the merger of two or more companies.

Product Labeling Laws to Protect Consumers

In addition to regulating business to promote competition, the federal government has enacted various product labeling laws intended to protect consumers by requiring that the materials used be listed, that they be safe and accurately identified, that the percentage of natural and synthetic fibers be shown, and that clear instructions to consumers about the care and maintenance of articles be provided. Examples of these labeling laws are as follows:

Wool Products Labeling Act—1939; amended in 1984
Fur Products Labeling Act—1951
Flammable Fabrics Act—1953
Textile Fiber Products Identification Act—1966; amended in 1984
Fair Packaging and Labeling Act—1966
Care Labeling of Textile Wearing Apparel Act—1972; amended in 1984

Readings

Competitive conditions in the fashion industry in the 1990s have made companies increasingly interested in understanding consumers, learning their needs, and focusing on how to best serve those consumers' needs.

Who Are Tomorrow's Consumers?   96

The fashion industry can best serve consumers by understanding their changing attitudes toward fashion. The consumer market can be viewed as going through stages of attitude changes toward fashion in the 1970s, 1980s, and 1990s.

Database Marketing   97

Through database marketing, fashion retailers can learn more about their consumers to better serve their target markets. By profiling existing customers, retailers can identify target markets for promotions.

Jeans Firms Target Baby Boomers with Special Labels, Styles, Fits   99

As the baby boomers move through various stages of their lives, marketers have followed their needs carefully. As the boomers have matured, the fashion industry has responded with specific product lines geared toward this market.

Cotton Inc. Lifestyle Monitor, To Survey Consumer Attitude   101

Cotton Incorporated has an ongoing effort to monitor consumer attitudes on fashion and shopping. Information from these surveys can be helpful to all segments of the fashion industry.

Who Are Tomorrow's Consumers?

As part of its ongoing programme, RISC identifies socio-cultural trends in 17 of the world's developed markets and maps how they develop, spread and change during their progression through the fabric of society. It also projects the profile of those who are likely to compose tomorrow's mainstream consumers. Among the thirty trends currently under observation, the Institute has pinpointed an interlocking cluster of five that illustrate the attitudes towards clothing and fashion of the new, post-materialistic consumer. What are these consumers' values identified by RISC, and what are their significance to the clothing industry?

Personal Growth Looks Deeper

The '80s were individualistic in a 'look-at-me-I-made-it' sense. The accomplished individual wanted to excel in several domains at once. In this highly demanding world there was a 'look' for each situation and life-style group to which the individual belonged. In the '90s, while eclecticism and sensuality are expected to remain strong, people are attaching greater importance to longer lasting and deeper concerns [refer to Figure 3-2]. Self-development is becoming less frantic. Time, intimacy and responsibility are growing values. There is a search for meaning and spiritual content. As a result, the addiction to fashion change is likely to give way to a more thoughtful use of clothing, concludes RISC.

From 'Look' to Authenticity

As already suggested, in the narcissistic and eclectic '80s, assertiveness and development of all the facets of one's individuality were key. People wanted to be perceived as 'more' than they might actually be, so appearance was of primary importance.

Since the early '90s, however, preferences have shifted away from being up-to-date towards a more classic style. 'Being' is becoming the cultural focus in Europe rather than 'representation'. Personal appearance is less a matter of look than a balancing of the inner and outer self, comfort and stylishness, transparency and protection. A good design in the '90s is one that cares for people, for their body, their soul, their health and their comfort.

From the Addicted to the Mature Consumer

The long-announced end of the consumer society is upon us and will obviously have an impact on purchase behavior.

Nonetheless, this reluctant new consumer may well buy as much as before, although his/her choices and expectations are likely to move towards greater selectivity and quality, more meaningful instead of fun products, connoisseur products instead of ostentatious luxury. The research indicates that to make their informed choices, consumers in the '90s will look for orientation, information and benchmarks.

Co-existence of Hard and Soft Hedonism

While the above trends apply equally to women and men, this one affects the sexes differently despite common roots in the hedonism of the '80s. This was the decade when contact with oneself and the outside world was triggered by the body and all its senses, it was the time of the 'total look' for a fit, mobile body. In the '90s this hard hedonistic line is still likely to be pursued by a young male population seeking instant gratification through numerous interests and activities and bodes well for hi-tech performance fabrics in active sportswear.

On the other hand, a softer variety of hedonism is taking shape and is linked to a new sense of holistic well-being and ethical values, says RISC. Here we see well-educated women up to the age of forty in search of environments where they can interact on many levels, savour time and communicate through their feelings. In clothing terms, their preference should go to high quality products which are meaningful to them: 'real clothes' through which to express their own authenticity.

From 'Convenience' to 'Creative' Shopping

The '70s saw the birth of consumerism and a growing focus on efficiency and convenience—supermarkets, frozen food, easy care textiles, etc. As consumers began asserting more individuality in the '80s, flexibility became the marketing response. Shoppers also became more actively opportunistic, seeking premium brands at a discount.

In the '90s, hyper-choice has bred a degree of saturation. Rather than search through the offering for the item best suited to their needs, the new consumers will be drawn to products they can adapt creatively to their unique lifestyles and habits. This expectation of product adaptability is also related to the physical and psychological well-being described in the second trend.

Consumer Attitudes to Clothing*

In a recent survey, consumers representing the better educated, more affluent and travelled, more sophisticated portions of the female population throughout Europe, were questioned about their attitudes to clothing. Out of several statements submitted to them for evaluation, the highest level of agreement went to the seven listed [here], confirming that attitudes identified by RISC for future development are already present today among the more progressive consumers[:]

% AGREE	STATEMENT
95%	The trend is towards comfortable clothing
92%	I look for fashion and comfort combined
90%	Comfortable clothing moves with me
79%	I will pay for higher quality
77%	I read hang-tags
74%	I like to have information on fabrics
74%	I won't pay more than I have to

In conclusion, RISC reported to Du Pont and its audience that today's progressive and tomorrow's mainstream consumers are, and will continue to be, in tune with the comfort and the 'look better, feel better' qualities which they believe Lycra* brings to clothes. These consumers tend to go beyond the superficial appearance of things and seek out hidden values—which means that the more they comprehend the benefits of Lycra** and how it fits their lifestyle expectations, the more likely they will be to look for, and be willing to pay for, this invisible ingredient in the clothes they buy.

* Du Pont European Survey, July 1991
** Du Pont's registered trademark
Source: From Textile Horizons, October 1992, pp. 93–94. Reprinted by permission of Benjamin Dent & Company Ltd.

Database Marketing

by Gary Robins

Most retailers today who are planning to be around tomorrow have started to address database marketing. There are not going to be increasing numbers of customers coming into your store, so you better make sure those who are coming into the store are happy. And you better learn as much as you can about them so you can get others who look like them into the store."

That quote, from Dana Katz, owner of Miltons, a six-store off-price apparel chain based in Braintree, Mass., illustrates an important characteristic about database marketing in the '90s: Small retailers are just as passionate about database marketing as their larger competitors.

A number of factors have led retailers to the use of database marketing, which takes large files of names, addresses and attributes and picks out those people who are more likely to respond to direct mail or telemarketing efforts.

For the most part, retailers are not selling to the general public, but to databases of customers. Therefore, their databases are of purchase histories, and the trick for those without in-house credit has been to link historic sales transactions to identifiable customers.

As Katz points out, one of the primary movers is the realization that as a result of too many stores and increased competition, growth is not necessarily going to come from new customers, but from leveraging relationships with old customers.

Katz, who has been actively using database marketing for about a year and a half, has used database marketing to promote to his best customers. One example was a mailing that thanked the group for being good customers and notified them that, because they were good customers, a clearance sale would be available to them several days before it was advertised to the general public.

Hard benefits amounted to a $100,000 increase in sales. Another benefit to the database marketing approach is that after the promotion is over, there is the ability to track its effect on sales so that a return on investment can be evaluated. Results also can be tracked at the customer level, so that marketers can learn which types of customers responded to this particular promotion and use that to improve response rates in the future.

To find his best customers and for all other database marketing activities, Katz uses a company specializing in database marketing, Retail Resources Database Marketing, Carlstadt, N.J.

Although Miltons is not unsophisticated when it comes to merchandise information systems—the chain is running Island Pacific software on an AS/400 and Fujitsu Atrium registers on the front end—the small chain turned to a service bureau because of the resource and expertise requirements needed to successfully run database marketing.

To build a database from scratch, Retail Resources accessed Miltons' historical sales transaction records. The credit card numbers were then used to acquire names and addresses. Miltons currently is not tracking all customers, just those using third-party credit cards.

The sales transaction information is sent monthly to Retail Resources to update the database. Retail Resources maintains the database and executes all database analyses and segmentation.

According to Claude Johnson, president of Retail Resources, the next step for many of his clients is to track customers on an ongoing basis by telephone number, since telephone number can also be used to acquire name and address.

Johnson indicates that for small retailers without computerized systems, there are a number of options. A database can be built from paper copies of bankcard receipts. Customers can be tracked by telephone number on an ongoing basis, and in some cases his clients are capturing this information on a dedicated credit-card authorization terminal that is set up to transmit the telephone number and transaction information to Retail Resources.

Lists can also be obtained from special order documents, rain checks, and contest entries. To build on a list, one option is to purchase demographic information about the names on the list.

You would first do this, explains Jim Peyton, account manager with DynaMark (St. Paul, Minn.), a service bureau with both catalog and store-front retail clients, in order to learn as much as you can about the people on the list so that you could then go out and purchase additional names that fit a similar profile.

In most cases, the best data will come from internal sales records. Whether internal or external, the problem the retailer then faces is finding the programming resources to deal with manipulating, sorting and preparing the database for marketing purposes.

The preparation before a mailing goes out, says Peyton, is a multi-step process that involves cleaning the lists to remove incomplete and duplicate records and passing it against postal information in order to correct and confirm addresses and append postal codes.

DynaMark has been recently acquired by San Raphael, Calif.-based Fair, Isaac that has a long history of developing scorecards in the credit area. It is expected that both companies will be working together on response scorecards to be used in database marketing, and that Fair, Isaac will build on its experience with response models in the credit solicitation area.

Source: Reprinted from Stores Magazine, May 1994, pp. 32, 34, NRF Enterprises, Inc., 1994.

Jeans Firms Target Baby Boomers With Special Labels, Styles, Fits

by Rachel Spevack

Jeans companies are increasingly targeting products to maturing baby boomers—men born between 1946 and 1964—on the grounds that these men grew up wearing denim and are not about to stop just because they're now in their forties and fifties.

Manufacturers are taking different approaches to this customer, however.

Some companies have introduced sub-brands targeted to this market, such as Levi Strauss Signature. Others introduce styles within their core jeans lines for this customer, such as Lee and Big Smith Brands, parent company of the Big Smith, Caterpillar and Wolverine jeans lines.

One controversy concerns whether boomer men will wear stretch jeans. Williamson-Dickie thinks they will—its Dickies Comfort Classics Stretch Jeans line, for example, is entirely stretch. Others use special fits to target this customer, but no stretch fabrics. Lee, for example, came out with an Easy Fit targeted to 25-to-45-year-old men. It's a little looser in the seat and thighs and fits a little lower on the hips.

Manufacturers also disagree about where boomer men shop for denim. Some contend they still shop in the young men's area; others see them buying their jeans in mainfloor men's departments.

The Levi Strauss Signature sub-brand is about two years old. Steve Goldstein, vice-president, research and development, Levi's brand, described it as "a line of jeans that are designed to fit a man comfortably." It includes wrinkle-resistant jeans that retain their center crease after washing. Fabrics include 100 percent cotton denim and denim blended with polyester.

The Signature line is in "all of our major department store accounts and Penney's as well," Goldstein said. "It's a service to our older jeans loyalists who prefer shopping in the men's department. It's a nice little business."

The "primary effort" has been at point-of-sale, he continued. Levi's has worked with its accounts to establish Signature in-store shops, "which are typically in mainfloor men's departments as opposed to young men's denim areas. We also have worked with retailers on a direct mail campaign so that we're reaching this target audience in their mailboxes with catalogs and information." The direct mail campaign is not a "broad blanket mailing." Rather, it goes out to "people who are in the Levi Strauss Signature target who also happen to live near retailers who carry the line."

Levi's uses the same techniques to determine the preferences of these customers as it uses for its other products: focus groups, observations in the field, and panel data, Goldstein said. "Even though we see it as a smaller business for us, we still put a lot of research into establishing what it is he likes."

The "vast majority" of these customers are former heavy Levi's jeans loyalists, he explained. "We want to keep them happy with the Levi's product. They're probably buying Dockers. We've seen a lot of interest in the explosion of casual businesswear in the U.S. Guys are seeing that they can wear jeans to work as they've never been able to do before. We're seeing an upsurge in men in this target age group wearing jeans not only for casual occasions, but also for work occasions."

VF Corp.'s Lee division's Easy Fit is targeted to 25-to-45-year-old men, "which would include boomers and younger brothers of boomers," said Gary Dawson, vice-president and general manager of the Lee brand. "Baby boomers are pretty much reacting to jeans the way that younger men are. They like bleached finishes. They like lower rise jeans just like younger guys do. They like looser fits, not baggy fits but relaxed fits. As far as finishes go, we don't see any differences. We believe baby boomers and young men like the same finishes. We think both of them want to wear progressive finishes—worn washes, blasted finishes."

Dawson said that baby boomers have slightly thicker waists than younger men. "In most men that's usually compensated for by buying a bigger size."

Lee doesn't offer much in the way of stretch jeans because it doesn't think that there's a consumer demand or need for it, he said. "Basically the looser fits have really allowed more mature men to still wear rigid fabrics without needing stretch." Dawson said that he himself is a baby boomer, as are all of his friends. "I don't know a single person including myself who would ever contemplate wearing a stretch jean. I just don't see frankly a consumer desire out there for stretch jeans. We sell a lot of jeans to baby boomers. That really is one of our core franchises. We don't feel the need to address the consumer with stretch."

The company does merchandise a little bit of stretch in its men's line, but it's for a much older, more traditional consumer.

Fort Worth-based Williamson-Dickie Manufacturing Co. launched a mass market denim line called Dickies Comfort Classics Stretch Jeans about six months ago. Through market research studies, the company determined that about a third of all stretch jeans purchases are made by men in the 35-to-45 age group, said Jim McLaughlin, senior vice-president of sales and marketing. "We're doing it specifically to capture this fast-growing population segment of aging baby boomers. This is our attempt, our product strategy for that market. We're shipping now for back-to-school. We've got pretty strong placement already."

The Comfort Classics Stretch Jeans line is made entirely from Burlington denim fabrics, including 50/50 cotton/E.S.P. (Extra Stretch Performance polyester yarn) and 80/20 cotton/E.S.P. McLaughlin said the blends have the appearance of being 100 percent cotton. "To the layman's hand it has the same feel as cotton." Approximate retail price points for the jeans are $21.99 and $22.99.

Dickies is definitely competing with other stretch jeans in the mass market, McLaughlin conceded. Its major selling point is that it's a branded product supported by national advertising. The company contends that Dickies is one of the 10 most recognized brands in the mass merchant channel.

Big Smith Brands of Carthage, Mo., is introducing three new fits (loose, easy and baggy) targeted to baby boomers for holiday selling. Ray Patterson, senior vice-president of sales, said that the company will be running the new fits in its Big Smith, Caterpillar and Wolverine jeans lines.

The company does make stretch jeans, but Patterson said they're not aimed at boomers. "That guy's older than baby boomers. That guy would be in the 55-to-70-year-old crowd."

Patterson said the new fits are part of a major effort to attract those customers who are accustomed to wearing brands like Guess and Girbaud.

Source: From DNR, May 2, 1995, pp. 2, 5. Reprinted by permission.

Cotton Inc. Lifestyle Monitor, To Survey Consumer Attitude

by Michael McNamara

Cotton Incorporated has launched a major ongoing effort to measure consumer attitudes on fashion and shopping, and in its first installment has found:

- Most people want to dress casually, even at the office.
- Denim apparel is the favored casual type of dressing.
- There's more concern about function and comfort, as opposed to fashion.
- Shopping balances out as a neutral experience for consumers generally. The highest percentage of respondents, 36 percent, said they shop when they need something, while 33 percent said they enjoy it.

The study is called Cotton Inc.'s Lifestyle Monitor and will track behavioral attitudes behind purchasing patterns in both apparel and home furnishings.

While the information will be used to help the organization formulate future advertising and promotion plans, the findings can also be accessed for use by retailers, apparel manufacturers and mills, said J. Nicholas Hahn, president and chief executive officer. Cotton Inc. is the research and promotional organization supported by the 30,000 U.S. cotton growers.

The research, conducted by Bellomy Research, Raleigh, N.C., is based on telephone interviews with a national sampling of 3,600 consumers, ages 16 to 55. The interviews last from 20 to 25 minutes, and from 120 specific questions, barometer indices are formulated that can be tracked to detect shifts in behavior. Barrye Worsham, Cotton Inc.'s director of market research and business information, said Cotton Inc. had been working with Bellomy for a year on developing this research.

The initial benchmark findings were based on 3,600 interviews conducted from last October through December. For each subsequent report, Bellomy will conduct 300 per month for a total of 3,600 per year. The next findings, based on 900 interviews conducted in the January–March quarter, should be released in mid-to-late April, Worsham said.

Of the 3,600 initial interviews, 2,000 were done with women. Worsham said since women do more apparel and home furnishings purchasing, more women than men were interviewed.

The monitor, using a scale of zero to 100, tracks eight consumer attitude barometers—shopping, casual dressing, fashion versus function, denim dressing, appearance effort, fiber awareness, natural fiber preference and influences on fashion decisions.

For example, the benchmark casual dressing barometer has an index of 58, revealing consumers have a decided preference for dressing casual versus dressing up. If the barometer had been 50 or below, it would have indicated that people prefer to dress more formally.

In response to specific questions regarding casual dressing, 79 percent of consumers said that casual days are appropriate for the office, while 43 percent who work in offices said they currently do not have the opportunity for even one casual day per week at work. Fifty-two percent of consumers surveyed said they would rather be underdressed for an occasion than overdressed.

The denim index reached even higher, hitting 65, showing consumers are extremely positive towards the fabric. When consumers were asked whether they agreed that denim was their first choice for casualwear, 67 percent concurred.

While the numbers indicate general consumer preferences, the same findings can be broken out into specific groups, such as age, sex, income, education level and race, said Hahn.

Among other topics, the index for fashion versus function was put at 38, showing Americans are more concerned about function. However, researchers pointed out the finding is not definitive, since many of the respondents equated function with fashion.

The influence of fashion trends carries an index of 39, suggesting that consumers are only moderately influenced by external factors, including fashion magazines, television shows and what their friends wear.

Source: From Women's Wear Daily, February 9, 1995, p. 11. Reprinted by permission.

Chapter Review

Key Words and Concepts

Define, identify, or briefly explain the following:

Consumer orientation	Marketing orientation
Consumer-ready	Marketing process
Cross-shopper	Marketing segmentation
Demographic	Marketing strategy
Focus groups	Merchandising
FTC	Offshore production
Floor-ready	Point-of-sale (POS) data
Market	Production orientation
Market segmentation	Pull system
Marketing	Push system
Marketing concept	Robinson-Patman Act
Marketing environment	Sales
Marketing macroenvironment	Style testing
Marketing microenvironment	Sherman Anti-Trust Act
Marketing mix	Target market

Review Questions on Chapter Highlights

1. Why is it important for a company to place serious emphasis on serving the consumer well?
2. What role have textile and apparel imports played in causing the U.S. fashion industry to think more about satisfying the customer?
3. How is the consumer of the 1990s different from the 1980s consumer? What implications does this difference have for the fashion industry?
4. How does the consumer play a powerful role in affecting the whole fashion pipeline? Give an example of how this can affect a textile firm, an apparel manufacturer, and a retailer.
5. What does it mean to "organize the industry around the consumer"?
6. What does it mean to say that a company's whole organizational structure could be restructured around giving customers what they want?
7. Contrast what is meant by a "marketing orientation" and a "production orientation."

8. Distinguish between marketing, merchandising, and sales.

9. What is the marketing concept? Why is it important for the fashion industry?

10. Give examples of consumers who might be identified by a fashion firm's market segmentation efforts.

11. What are the elements of the marketing mix? Think of a fictitious product and define how you would identify elements of the marketing mix for your product.

12. Contrast the marketing microenvironment with the macroenvironment. Give examples of each.

13. Give examples of current social and economic factors that are affecting the consumption of fashion.

14. What are some of the demographic factors that affect the business of fashion? Why?

15. Why have marketers in all industries followed the baby boom generation?

16. How is the growing teen population or the increased number of senior citizens likely to affect the fashion industry?

17. Give an example of marketing fashion products to minority markets.

18. How do marketers follow consumer preferences and buying trends?

19. Contrast the push system with the pull system used in the industry.

20. How is the fashion industry likely to be serving its customers in the year 2000 and beyond?

21. Why does federal legislation exist that may affect the fashion industry?

References

Adler, J. (1995, July 31). The rise of the overclass. *Newsweek*, 32–45.

American Apparel Manufacturers Association. (1982). *Fashion apparel manufacturing: Coping with style variation*. Arlington, VA: Author.

Anderson, W. (1992). Retailing in the year 2000: Quixotic consumers? Exotic markets? Neurotic retailers? In R. A. Peterson (Ed.), *The future of U.S. retailing: An agenda for the 21st century* (pp. 27–84). New York: Quorum Books.

Beck, M. (1992, December 7). The new middle age. *Business Week*, 50–56.

Bird, L. (1995, March 8). Department stores target top customers. *The Wall Street Journal*, B1, B4.

Bremner, B., & Weber, J. (1992, December 21). A spicier stew in the melting pot. *Business Week*, 29–30.

Bureau of Census. (1995, December). *How we're changing—Demographic state of the nation: 1995* (Current Population Reports, Special Studies, Series P-23, No. 188). Washington, DC: U.S. Department of Commerce.

Dickerson, K. (1991). *Textiles and apparel in the international economy*. Upper Saddle River, NJ: Merrill/Prentice Hall.

Dickerson, K., Hooper, C., & Boyle, R. (1995, April). A new approach for manufacturers. *America's Textiles International (ATI)*, 28–32.

Dunn, W. (1992, July). The move toward ethnic marketing. *Nation's Business, 80*(7), 39–41.

Esquivel, J. (1995, January). Theme for 1990s: Dress for survival. *America's Textiles International*, K/A 2–K/A 10.

Farrell, C., Palmer, A., Atchison, S., & Andelman, B. (1994, September 12). The economics of aging. *Business Week*, 60–68.

Gordon, M. (1993, May 21). Ethnic mags: A tough sell. *Women's Wear Daily*, 4.

Kotler, P., & Armstrong, G. (1994). *Principles of marketing* (6th ed). Upper Saddle River, NJ: Merrill/Prentice Hall.

Kurt Salmon Associates. (1995). *Vision for the new millennium . . . evolving to consumer response*. New York: Author.

Lerner, M. (1957). *America as a civilization*. New York: Simon & Schuster.

Mallory, M., & Forest, S. (1992, March 23). Waking up to a major market. *Business Week*, 70–71.

Phillips, S., Dunkin, A., Treece, J., & Hammonds, K. (1990, March 12). King customer. *Business Week*, 88–94.

Vandeventer, E. (1994, February 3). Textiles, apparel, & home furnishings. *Standard & Poor's Industry Surveys, 162*(5), Sec. 1, 75–125.

Who are tomorrow's consumers? (1992). *Textile Horizons, 12* (10), 3.

Zinn, L, Berry, J., Murphy, K., Jones, J., Benedetti, M., & Cuneo, A. (1994, April 11). Teens: Here comes the biggest wave yet. *Business Week*, 76–86.

Zinn, L., Power, C., Yang, D., Cuneo, A., & Ross, D. (1992, December 14). Move over boomers. *Business Week*, 74–82.

Suggested Bibliography

Anderson, W. (1992). Retailing in the year 2000: Quixotic consumers? Exotic markets? Neurotic retailers? In R. A. Peterson (Ed.), *The future of U.S. retailing: An agenda for the 21st century* (pp. 27–84). New York: Quorum Books.

Baker, S., & Baker, K. (1995). *Desktop direct marketing.* Hightstown, NJ: McGraw-Hill.

Boutilier, R. (1993). *Targeting families: Marketing to and through the new family.* Ithaca, NY: American Demographics.

Bureau of Census. (annual). *How we're changing—Demographic state of the Nation: (annual)* (Current Population Reports). Washington, DC: U.S. Department of Commerce.

Celente, G., & Milton, T. (1991). *Trend tracking.* New York: Warner Books.

Dunn, W. (1993). *The baby bust: A generation comes of age.* Ithaca, NY: American Demographics.

Dychtwald, K., & Gable, G. (1990). *The shifting American marketplace.* Emeryville, CA: Age Wave.

Esquivel, J. (1995, January). Theme for 1990s: Dress for survival. *America's Textiles International*, K/A 2–K/A 10.

Evans, C. (1993). *Marketing channels: Infomercials and the future of televised marketing.* Upper Saddle River, NJ: Prentice Hall.

Feather, F. (1994). *The future consumer.* Buffalo, NY: Warwick.

Gale, B. (1994). *Managing customer value.* New York: Free Press.

Guber, S., & Berry, J. (1993). *Marketing to and through kids.* New York: McGraw-Hill.

Hines, J., & O'Neal, G. (1995). Underlying determinants of clothing quality: The consumers' perspective. *Clothing and Textiles Research Journal, 13* (4), 227–233.

Hughes, A. (1991). *The complete database marketer.* Chicago: Probus.

Hughes, A. (1994). *Strategic database marketing.* Chicago: Probus.

Kincaid, D. (1995). Quick Response management system for the apparel industry: Definition through technologies. *Clothing and Textiles Research Journal, 13* (4), 245–251.

Kotler, P., & Armstrong, G. (1994). *Principles of marketing* (6th ed). Upper Saddle River, NJ: Merrill/Prentice Hall.

Kurt Salmon Associates. (1995). *Vision for the new millennium . . . evolving to consumer response.* New York: Author.

Leeming, E., & Trip, C. (1994). *Segmenting the women's market: Using niche marketing to understand and meet the diverse needs.* Chicago: Probus.

Longino, C. (1995). *Retirement migration in America.* Houston, TX: Vacation Publications.

Mallory, C. (1991). *Direct mail magic.* Menlo Park, CA: Crisp Publications.

Mergenhagen, P. (1994). *Targeting transitions: Marketing to consumers during life changes.* Ithaca, NY: American Demographic.

Meyers, G. (1993). *Targeting the new professional woman: How to market and sell to today's 57 million working women.* Chicago: Probus.

Mowen, J. (1992). *Consumer behavior* (4th ed). Upper Saddle River, NJ: Merrill/Prentice Hall.

Morgan, C., & Levy, D. (1993). *Segmenting the mature market.* Chicago: Probus.

Nystrom, P. (1929). *Economics of consumption.* New York: Ronald Press.

Ostrow, R., & Smith, S. (1987). *The dictionary of marketing.* New York: Fairchild.

Perna, R. (1987). *Fashion forecasting*. New York: Fairchild.

Peterson, R. (1992). A context for retailing predictions. In R. A. Peterson (Ed.), *The future of U.S. retailing: An agenda for the 21st century* (pp. 1–25). New York: Quorum Books.

Popcorn, F. (1991). *The Popcorn report*. New York: Bantam Doubleday Dell.

Popcorn, F. (1995). *Clicking*. New York: Harper Business.

Ritchie, K. (1995). *Marketing to Generation X*. Greenwich, CT: Lexington Books.

Rossman, M. (1994). *Multicultural marketing: Selling to a diverse America*. Saranac Lake, NY: AMACOM Books (American Management Association).

Smith, D. (1992, Spring). Changing U.S. demographics: Implications for professional preparation. *Journal of Home Economics*, 19–23.

Smith, T. (1995, January). Marketing in 2004. *Textile Asia*, 107–110.

Stanley, T. (1993). *Networking with the affluent and their advisors*. Burr Ridge, IL: Irwin Professional Publishing.

Templeton, J. (1994). *The focus group*. Chicago: Probus.

Vavra, T. (1992). *After-marketing: How to keep customers for life through relationship marketing*. Burr Ridge, IL: Irwin Professional Publishing.

Weinstein, A. (1994). *Market segmentation*. Chicago: Probus.

Trade and Consumer Associations

American Council on Consumer Interests, 240 Stanley Hall, University of Missouri-Columbia, Columbia, MO 65211.

American Marketing Association, Suite 200, 250 S. Wacker Dr., Chicago, IL 60606–5819.

Direct Marketing Association, 1120 Ave. of the Americas, New York, NY 10036–6700.

Direct Selling Association, 1776 K St., NW, Suite 600, Washington, DC 20006.

Consumer Federation of America, 1424 16th St., N.W., Suite 604, Washington, DC 20036.

Consumers Union of the U.S., Inc., 101 Truman Ave., Yonkers, NY, 10703–1057.

International Organization of Consumers Unions, Emmastraat 9, 2595 EG The Hague, The Netherlands.

Trade and Consumer Publications

American Demographics, P. O Box 2888, Boulder, CO 80322–2606.

Consumer Reports, Consumers Union of the U.S., Inc. 101 Truman Ave., Yonkers, NY, 10703–1057.

Marketing Communications Magazine, 475 Park Ave. S., New York, NY 10016.

Marketing News, Suite 200, 250 S. Wacker Dr., Chicago, IL 60606–5819.

Journal of International Consumer Marketing, Haworth Press, Inc., 10 Alice St., Binghamton, NY 13904–1580.

Sales and Marketing Management, Bill Communications, Inc., 355 Park Ave. S., New York, NY 10010–1789

*T*he Materials of Fashion

*T*he expression of every fashion in the form of a garment or accessory owes as much to the fabrics, furs, or leathers that are available as it does to the idea that inspires its birth. As Christian Dior once said, "Many a dress of mine is born of the fabric alone" (Dior, 1953, p. 35).

To grasp the importance of the producers of the raw materials in the business of fashion, one must recognize that many of the changes are primarily variations in colors, textures, or fabrics rather than changes in style.

This chapter is concerned with the components industry that provides the fibers, fabrics, leathers, and furs that enable designers to give substance to their ideas. The text discusses the most important segments of the components industries and indicates how each of these influences fashion and is influenced by it. The readings that follow illustrate the operations of leading companies and developments in the field.

From Fiber to Fabric

The making of fabrics involves a great many processes, uses machines of many different types, and employs the skills and knowledge of a variety of producers and processors.

No matter what the end result, every textile product originates as fiber. Fibers fall into two main categories: (1) **natural fibers,** such as cotton, wool, ramie, silk, and flax, which come from plant and animal sources and have been used for thousands of years, and (2) **manufactured fibers,** previously known as "man-made" fibers, which are basically chemical products and whose development and utilization are twentieth-century phenomena. Whether fibers are natural or manufactured, however, they undergo the same basic fabrication processes in the course of their transformation into textile products: the spinning of fibers into yarns, the weaving or knitting of yarns into fabric, and the finishing of fabric to impart color, texture, pattern, or other characteristics. *Weaving* is the interlacing of two sets of yarns, vertical and horizontal. *Knitting* involves machines that make fabric by interlooping of either vertical or horizontal sets of yarns.

Before being made into a fabric, fibers must first be spun into yarns. **Yarn** is produced by twisting together strands of fiber into a continuous thread or filament. This may be as coarse as rug backing or finer than sewing thread. To manufacture cloth, the yarns are knitted or woven together. Figure 4–1 shows a modern weaving facility.

Some natural fiber yarns are dyed before being made into fabric. This is particularly true of wool, but sometimes manufactured fibers receive similar treatment. In the latter case, the fibers are **solution-dyed,** which means that dye is introduced into the chemical "dope" from which the fiber is made. In **yarn dying** the yarn is first spun,

Figure 4–1

In today's modern weaving plants, computers are used extensively to maintain quality and efficiency.

Source: Photo courtesy of Burlington Industries, Inc.

then put on cones, then dyed on the cone prior to the fabric production process. More commonly, however, yarns are employed in their undyed state to produce **greige goods,** which is undyed, unfinished fabric that is later dyed in the piece and subjected to a variety of finishing processes. At every step of the way, from fiber production to finished product, fashion is the primary influence in determining what materials will be used, how they will be treated, and what the end product will be.

Fiber Producers

Much of the fashion industry's ability to respond promptly and accurately to changes in consumer preferences for apparel and accessories is due to the immense variety of textile products available for use. In turn, the textile industry can more readily present its impressive range of textures, colors, weights, lusters, and other characteristics because the fiber producers are also aware of and responsive to fashion's requirements. That responsiveness, this far back in the production process, was slight in the days when only natural fibers were available, but it has reached enormous proportions now that manufactured fibers have opened new doors in the industry.

Suppliers of Natural Fibers

The natural fibers are cotton, wool, silk, ramie, and flax. The amounts and qualities available at any given time and place are influenced by environmental conditions, such as climate and terrain suited to the animals and plants that are their source. Suppliers of natural fibers are many, are located all over the world, and tend to be relatively small in size. They generally sell their products in local markets to wholesalers who, in turn, may sell them to other wholesalers in regional markets. In the case of cotton and wool, commodities dealers may buy these fibers from central wholesalers throughout the world and sell them to mills. Thus, it is possible for an American

Figure 4–2

Examples of natural fiber logos: (a)Woolmark pure wool logo and (b)Mohair Council logo.

WOOLMARK

PURE NEW WOOL

(a)

(b)

Source: Woolmark logo courtesy of Wool Bureau, Inc., and mohair logo courtesy of Mohair Council of America.

textile producer to create a shirting fabric from Egyptian cotton, or a Japanese knitter to offer a sweater of Australian lambswool.

Before the entrance of manufactured fibers, the suppliers of natural fibers were scarcely a part of the fashion industry. Their traditional role was only to produce and sell their raw materials. They were not concerned with the making of these raw materials into yarns for weaving or knitting fabrics, and they had no relationship with the garment makers or ultimate consumers. They certainly were not attuned to fashion. All of this changed with the entrance of manufactured fibers into the business of fashion.

The need to compete with manufactured fibers forced the cotton and wool growers into reevaluating their marketing procedures. They were impelled to take a more aggressive role and become proactive in reaching the textile producers, the garment makers, and the ultimate consumers. In addition to improving the desirable properties of their fibers, the suppliers of wool, cotton, and other natural fibers each began efforts to compete more favorably with the manufactured fibers. Today natural fiber producers, through their trade associations, act as a source of information about the fabrics processed from their respective fibers and about fashion in general. They also promote their fibers to the trade and to the general public by directing attention to the virtues of their product. Figure 4–2 shows examples of natural fiber logos.

For example, there is an International Wool Secretariat supported by wool growers from all over the world. Their headquarters, which are located in London, are staffed with fashion specialists who advise fabric manufacturers of new developments in weaves, patterns, and colors. This association also publicizes wool in all media and by all means—films, fashion presentations to the trade and to the press, and cooperative advertising programs with makers and sellers of wool garments. Cotton Incorporated, which is headquartered in New York City, acts as an information and promotional center for cotton. They prepare and distribute advance information about fashions in cotton and cotton-blended fabrics to designers, manufacturers, the fashion press, and retail stores. They also advertise cotton fashions in consumer and trade publications. In addition, both associations encourage producers and retailers to use their distinctive logos (a ball of yarn in the one case, a cotton boll in the other) in the advertising of fashion garments made of their particular fibers. The promotional activities of their trade associations have drastically changed the part played by natural fiber producers in the world of fashion.

Manufactured Fiber Producers (SIC 28)

As defined by the Textile Fiber Products Identification Act, manufactured fiber is "any fiber derived by a process of manufacture from any substance which, at any point in the manufacturing process, is not a fiber." This is in contrast to the term *natural fiber,* meaning a fiber that exists as such in the natural state.

As we noted in the Chapter 1, all U.S. industries are classified by a number system, the Standard Industrial Classification (SIC), that designates what each does. Manufactured fiber companies tend to be part of large chemical complexes that in some cases produce chemical components for everything from fertilizers to aspirin. Because of the nature of manufactured fiber production, this industry is part of the *chemical and allied products grouping (SIC 28)* rather than with other textile or apparel production.

For hundreds of years, humans have toyed with the possibility of duplicating the work of the silkworm by mechanical or chemical means. These small creatures feed on mulberry leaves and are able to produce a thick liquid, which they force out through tiny openings in their heads in the form of silk fiber. Thus, in 1855, a Swiss chemist named Audemars attempted to produce synthetic silk by using the fibrous inner bark of the mulberry tree.

It was not until 1891, however, that the French Count Hilaire de Chardonnet built the first "artificial silk" plant in France. He eventually earned the title of "father of the rayon industry" when, in 1924, artificial silk was renamed *rayon:* "ray" to suggest sheen and "on" to suggest cotton. Rayon was followed by a deluge of manufactured fiber experiments and developments in the 1920s and 1930s. The giant breakthrough came with the first public showing of nylon hosiery, introduced by DuPont, at the 1939 Golden Gate Exposition in San Francisco. Not only did nylon hosiery immediately become one of the most wanted articles of feminine apparel, but nylon itself played a significant role in World War II for such uses as parachutes and uniforms.

With the development of manufactured fibers, the importance of natural fibers declined dramatically, whereas the growth of the manufactured fiber industry was phenomenal. These figures illustrate the point: At the end of World War II, manufactured fibers accounted for only 15 percent of all fibers used in the textile mills of the United States. By 1965, the manufactured fiber industry was providing 42 percent of the nation's fiber needs and by 1980, manufactured fibers accounted for 63.7 percent of total fiber consumption. Since that time, however, a shift in consumer preferences toward natural fibers, plus aggressive promotion by the cotton industry, had reduced manufactured fiber consumption to 57 percent (includes interior and industrial uses for manufactured fibers). Figure 4–3 gives a graphic comparison of these trends (Fiber Economics Bureau, 1990; U.S. Department of Commerce, ITA, 1990).

Impact of Chemical Fiber Producers

The continuing development of an unending procession of new manufactured fibers took place and continues to do so in the laboratories of giant chemical companies such as DuPont, Hoechst-Celanese, Monsanto, BASF, and Eastman Chemical, for example. The entrance of these chemical producers into the fashion industry brought about many changes in the fashion business, along with a whole new world of textiles. Since few in

Figure 4–3

U.S. total fiber consumption in 1950, 1980, and 1994 (percentages based on weight)

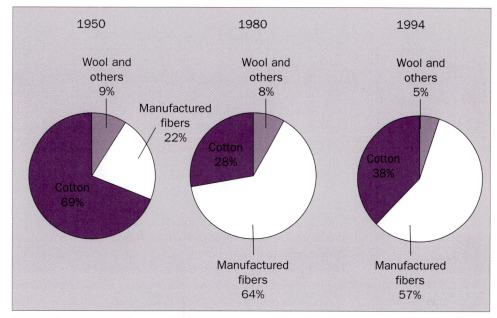

Source: Fiber Economics Bureau, *Textile Organon* (various years, including April 1995 issue for 1980 and 1994 data, p. 81).

the textile industry knew how to handle new synthetic fibers, the manufactured fiber producers had to teach and guide spinners, weavers, and knitters in the processing and fabrication of new fibers. They also have to create a demand among garment producers for the fabrics made with their fibers and provide them with guidance and encouragement. Finally, they have to educate and create a demand among consumers as well. In short, they not only supply their fibers to yarn makers, but with their enormous facilities for financing and research, they assume a dominant role in how these fibers are used in yarns, fabrics, and fashion apparel. Unlike the suppliers of natural fibers, the manufactured fiber producers made fashion their business from the start.

The entrance of giant chemical companies into the business of fashion has added new dimensions to the fashion industry. The concept of creating whatever kind of fiber is needed or wanted to develop new and different fabrications opened up a whole new world of textiles such as "stretchable," "wash and wear," "durable press," "heat-set pleats," and "wrinkle-resistant," with more to come. The promotional funds provided by manufactured fiber producers to help finance the advertising of fabrics and/or garments that feature their fabrics generate more fashion advertising than would otherwise be possible. The financial resources of giant chemical companies are such that they can support continuing research and development of new concepts in technology, merchandising, and fashion, the results of which are made available to fabric and apparel producers.

Flexibility of Manufactured Fibers

Two basic types of manufactured fibers are used for apparel: cellulosic and noncellulosic. Cellulosics are produced from cellulose, the fibrous substance found in plants such as softwood trees, and are made with a minimum of chemical steps. They include rayon, triacetate, and acetate. Noncellulosic fibers are made from chemical derivatives of petroleum, coal, natural gas, air, and water. Fiber chemists link the molecules from these sources into long chains called polymers. In this category are nylon, acrylic, and polyester fabrics.

Manufactured fibers have been improving the quality of fashion goods by offering a variety of characteristics unavailable in natural fibers. Their production, moreover, is not affected by the vagaries of weather or other natural conditions. They can be manufactured in quantities as large or as small as anticipated demand requires, and they can be endowed with desirable characteristics not necessarily found in natural fibers. For example, triacetate can be used to produce fabrics that are washable and wrinkle-resistant, or with pleats that are heat-set for permanency; it can also be used in fabrics with brushed or napped surfaces and textured effects. Acrylic fibers can be employed in pile fabrics that are used in fleecewear and that simulate furs. Modacrylics, inherently flame-resistant, are excellent for use in children's sleepwear, upholstery, blankets, and draperies.

An example of how a fiber can constantly be improved to meet changes in consumer demand is offered by nylon and polyester. Today, high-filament nylon is blended with stretch fibers such as spandex to create new swimwear, exercise wear, and dance clothing. The qualities of these fibers have fostered a whole new look in sleek activewear. Nylon reflective yarn is used in clothes that reflect the headlights of oncoming cars when worn by nighttime joggers and bicycle riders. In the home, nylon has become the leading fiber for carpets; 99 percent of all domestic carpets are made of it.

In the early 1990s, new **microfibers,** filaments of less than one denier—two or three times thinner than a human hair—were introduced, leading to the creation of yarns and fabrics with greater softness and silk-like characteristics than previous fiber filaments provided. Although DuPont developed the technology to produce microfibers in the 1960s, the Japanese first introduced these to the markets. By the early 1990s, DuPont first introduced microdenier polyester, with a number of other companies not far behind, some of which applied microdenier technology to other types of fibers besides polyester. Development of microfibers opened the door to a range of new "looks" for manufactured fibers. Because the filaments are so fine, many more are combined to form the yarns used in weaving and knitting fabrics; this gives fabrics a much more natural look than the shiny, "plastic"effect sometimes associated with manufactured fibers. Not only do the fabrics look more elegant, they also feel better. They have more breathability and better performance characteristics than previous products from manufactured fibers (Brunnschweiler & Hearle, 1993; Maycumber 1991).

Emphasis on Brand Names

Under the Textile Fiber Products Identification Act, the Federal Trade Commission establishes generic names for synthetic fibers. A **generic name** is one that designates a general group of fibers with similar chemical composition and properties. Of the more than 20 generic names established, however, relatively few are used for apparel fabrics. Polyester, nylon, and rayon, in that order, are the most widely used for clothing; other fibers used include acrylic, acetate, modacrylic, and triacetate. Within any of the basic broad categories, fiber producers can modify the basic chemical and physical composition to produce a new fiber. Although the same generic names may apply to the newer creations, these *variants,* as they are called, are usually identified by a **brand name** given them by the manufacturer (Table 4–1).

From the first, the producers of manufactured fibers have been very aggressive in promoting their brand names. A *brand* is a device, sign, trademark, or name that is used to identify and distinguish products as a means of building a market for them. Each company uses its brands to build recognition and acceptance of its product, to differentiate it from other similar products in the customer's mind, and to lessen price competition. To accomplish these ends, producers of manufactured fibers advertise

Table 4–1	Manufactured Fibers and Examples of Trade Names

Acetate	Nylon	Olefin	Strialine
Ariloft	Anso-Tex	Herculon	Trevira
Avron	Antron	Marvess	Ultra Glow
Celafil	Blue "C"	Patlon	Ultra Touch
Celaperm	Cadon	Tyrex	**Rayon**
Chromspun	Cantrece	**Polyester**	Absorbit
Estron	Caprolan		Avril
Loftura	Captiva	Avlin	Absorb
Acrylic	Celanese	Caprolan	Beau-Grip
	Cordura	Ceylon	Coloray
Acrilan	Cumuloft	Crepesoft	Courcel
Bi-Loft	Eloquent Luster	Dacron	Courtaulds HT
Creslan	Eloquent Touch	Encron	Durvil
Fi-Lana	Enkacrepe	Fortrel	Enkaire
Mann-Aeryl	Enkalon	Golden Glow	Enkrome
Orlon	Enkalure	Golden Touch	Fibro
Pa-Qel	Enkasheer	Hollofil	Narco
So-Lara	Hydrofil	Kodaire	Viloft
Zefkrome	Lurelon	Kodel	Vincel
Zefran	Multisheer	KodOfill	Zantrel
Aramid	Natural Luster	KodOlite	**Spandex**
	Natural Touch	KodOsoff	
Kevlar	Shareen	Lethasuede	Lycra
Nomex	Shimmereen	Matte Touch	**Triacetate**
Modacrylic	Softalon	Micromattique	
	StayGard	(microfiber)	Arnel
SEF	Ultron	Natural Touch	**Vinyon**
	Zefran	Plyloc	
	Zefsport	Polyextra	Teviron
	Zeftron	Shanton	
		Silky Touch	

Source: Updated from *Man-Made Fibers—A New Guide,* Man-Made Fiber Producers Association, Inc.

their brands in trade and consumer magazines and other public media in their own names, or in conjunction with fabric firms or makers of finished products. Anything from a multipage advertisement in a trade paper to an elaborate fashion presentation on TV may be used. In addition, their cooperative advertising money pays for much of the trade and consumer advertising of textiles and apparel in which their branded fibers are employed and identified. They also arrange or participate in fashion presentations staged by textile firms that identify their fibers, and they distribute free educational booklets to both retail employees and the consumer to acquaint people with the properties and names of their fibers. Some branded fibers are sold under a licensing arrangement that restricts the use of the brand name to products that comply with standards set by the fiber producer. An example of such a brand is Fortrel. At the other extreme are fibers that are sold as unbranded products, with no specified or implied performance standards or restrictions on their end use.

Textile Mill Products Producers (SIC 22)

Textile mill products is a broad term that describes fabrics and yarns made from fiber by any of a number of different methods. First, fibers are made into yarns. Then, thousands of yards and millions of pounds are produced annually in the United States, in infinite variety: fabrics include wovens and knits, polka dots and stripes, reds and blues, chiffons and seersuckers, and on and on, in every kind and color and texture fashion can demand. In providing the materials with which to express the designers' ideas, textiles are the very essence of fashion. Without denim, for instance, the fashion for jeans could not have come into being. Nor could there be sweatsuits and jogging outfits if the appropriate sweatshirt materials were not available.

All textile mill products fall into the SIC 22 grouping. For the SIC system, the additional digits after the first two for the group designate the specific segments of the industry. For example, Category 2281 represents all yarn spinning mills; 2253 includes all knit outerwear mills; and 2251 represents all producers of women's hosiery, except socks. These SIC categories are very useful in studying the performance of any segment of the textile mill products industry. For example, we might look at government data and determine the sales, number of employees, and so on for any specific part of the industry, using these numbers. If we were employed in a specific segment of the industry, we could see what portion of the total our company represents.

Economic Importance

The basic function of the textile mill products segment of the fashion industry is the transformation of fibers—natural or manufactured—into yarns and then into finished fabrics. At one end of the industry spectrum are thousands of manufacturing plants that perform one or more of the three major processes involved in the production of fabrics: spinning fibers into yarns, weaving or knitting yarn into fabric, and finishing fabric to provide color, pattern, and other desirable attributes. At the other end of the spectrum are the sales offices that market the finished cloth to apparel and accessories producers, fabric retailers, and the home furnishings industry.

The textile industry plays a vital role in the economy of the United States. It encompasses companies operating approximately 5,000 plants and gives employment to more than 660,000 people. Its output was valued at the manufacturing level at almost $75 billion in 1995 (U.S. Department of Commerce, Bureau of Census, 1996).

Although the bulk of the manufacturing facilities are on the East Coast, some phase of textile activity is carried on in nearly every state of the union, with the largest concentration in the Southeast. Marketing, styling, and design activities are centered in New York City as the number one location, with Los Angeles second, but selling activities reach into many other major cities.

The textile industry consumes fibers and dyes, machinery and power, services and labor to produce cloth that finds its way into a myriad of end uses—fashion apparel and accessories, to be sure, but also such diverse products as inflatable buildings, tire cord, space suits, sheets, carpets, heart valves, and diapers. Clothing and accessories take up more than one-third of the industry's output, with products for the home ranking second and increasing rapidly. Some textile companies are well known for producing specific fabrics, such as Guilford Mills' Lycra fabrics used in swimwear and activewear (Figure 4–4).

History and Growth

Although the U.S. textile industry today is one of the largest in the world, textile production by factory methods had its beginnings in England. During the eighteenth century, while the United States was establishing its own identity and struggling for its independence, a series of inventions, each a closely guarded trade secret, had mechanized the spinning of yarn and the weaving of cloth in England and had moved production from the home to the factory in that country. The American colonies were, as England intended, a dependent market for one of the mother country's major products.

Figure 4–4

Many textile companies specialize in specific types of products. In this case, Guilford Mills, Inc. is well known for its quality Lycra fabrics.

Source: Photo courtesy of Guilford Mills, Inc.

Colonial America imported most of its fashion materials: silks from Italy, China, and France; woolens, calico, and cashmere from England; feathers and artificial flowers from France. Prosperous settlers took full advantage of such imports; those who were less prosperous produced their own crude materials with which to clothe themselves. The men raised and sheared sheep, grew flax, tanned leathers, made shoes, and cured furs. Women did the spinning, weaving, dyeing, cutting, and sewing of the family garments.

Eighteenth Century: From Hand to Machines

The transition from handcraft to factory production of textiles had its start in the United States when the first cotton **spinning mill** was built in 1790 at Pawtucket, Rhode Island, by **Samuel Slater** (Lewton, 1926). Slater was a young Englishman who had worked in one of England's leading mills and memorized the machinery his country refused to export. Declaring himself a farmer rather than a mechanic, he was allowed to emigrate to the United States, carrying his knowledge in his head to build the spinning equipment and a mill. In 1793, Slater expanded his plant to house all the processes of yarn manufacture under one roof. That same year Eli Whitney introduced his cotton gin, a machine that pulled fibers free of seeds and helped to make a bountiful supply of cotton available to Slater and other early American textile producers.

Slater's spinning mill, now a textile museum, not only was the first successful spinning or yarn-making plant in this country but was also considered to have started the **Industrial Revolution** in America. His contribution to the industrialization of this country was recognized by President Andrew Jackson, who called him the "Father of American Manufacture" (American Textile Manufacturers Institute, T*extiles—An industry, a science, an art*. date unknown.)

Rapid Growth in the Nineteenth Century

The nineteenth century saw a period of great development in textile manufacturing activity. The country was growing rapidly and the continuing improvement of textile machinery and factory methods made it increasingly economical to produce textiles outside the home. Fundamental to this development was the introduction and perfection in 1814 of the power loom by **Francis Cabot Lowell,** a Boston merchant, importer, and amateur scientist, who visited England and memorized the system in factories there (American Textile Manufacturers Institute, *Mankind's,* no date). Lowell's factory in Massachusetts was the first in America to handle all operations from raw cotton to finished cloth under one roof. Before Lowell, spinning mills contracted out the weaving of yarn into cloth to individuals or small groups of workers. Spinning was thus a factory industry, and weaving a cottage industry before Lowell. The nineteenth century also saw the rise of a domestic wool industry as a result of the introduction of Merino sheep into America early in that century. By 1847, more Americans worked in textiles than in any other industry (American Textile Manufacturers Institute, *All about textiles,* 1996). Textiles was clearly the leading industry prior to the Civil War, with nearly all the industry centered on cotton (Poulson, 1981).

Additional impetus was given to the industry by the Civil War, which made great demands on American mills for fabrics for soldiers' uniforms, over and above the country's normal requirements. By the end of the war, the textile industry was firmly established and mass production of fabrics, although not yet of top-quality goods, was well on its way. As late as 1858, England and France were still our sources for better grade textiles, notably fine broadcloth, and the New York Chamber of Commerce reported "that American wool, when used alone, cannot produce cloth of equal quality and finish as that made of foreign wools" (Heaton, 1929; p. 147).

By the end of the nineteenth century, however, woolens became available in a great variety of patterns and in great quantities, and cotton fabrics were even more abundant and variegated. In the relatively small silk industry, in which imports dominated the market as late as the 1860s, domestic production provided the overwhelming share by the turn of the century (Alderfer & Michl, 1957).

The Evolution of an Industry

Spurred on by the booming postwar economy in the late 1940s and an increasingly affluent consumer market, leading firms in the industry began to expand by means of mergers and acquisitions and to "go public" by offering shares in their companies on the stock exchanges. For some companies, the objective was diversification, such as by acquiring carpet and hosiery mills in addition to those that produced garment fabrics. Burlington Industries, for example, originally specialized in weaving rayon fabrics. In 1939, it moved into hosiery production. During World War II it made nylon parachute cloth. After the war it continued to expand, acquire new plants, buy up other companies, and diversify. Later, another company tried to take over Burlington, which had become the world's largest textile firm. To fend off the hostile offer, the company resorted to a leveraged buyout to go private. The company had to sell off major divisions to pay for these moves. For several years, Burlington's future was shaky and uncertain. In recent years, however, the company has recovered greatly and has once again become a publicly held firm. At present, as one of the largest textile producers, it produces many different types of fabric and is a vertically integrated operation.

The drive toward integration and diversification that began in the 1940s continued in the 1950s and 1960s. Between 1955 and 1966, when acquisitions were perhaps at their height, the Federal Trade Commission reported that about 365 textile companies were acquired by other companies (U.S. Department of Labor, no date). In the 1970s, the Federal Trade Commission moved against excessive mergers and acquisitions, in this and many other industries, to avoid the lessening of competition that could result.

From the mid-1980s on, one saw a total restructuring of the American textile industry. Many public companies went private either through leveraged buy-outs, or as a result of acquisitions by other textile companies or major investment companies. Of the top 15 U.S. textile companies that were publicly held in 1981, only a handful among them (Springs Industries, Guilford Mills, Burlington Industries, Westpoint Pepperell, and Fieldcrest Cannon) remain.

Acquisitions, Mergers, and Consolidation

Merger mania in the textile industry has been encouraged in part by the flood of imports of fabrics and also by a desire on the part of many giant companies to increase market share and thus their ability to compete against other giants by combining similar products.

Some of the acquisitions and mergers include Springs Mills, which bought converter M. Lowenstein and also consolidated their Springmaid with Wamsutta Brands. Dominion textiles bought Swift Textiles; Fieldcrest bought Cannon; Collins and Aikman was purchased by Wickes Co.; Cone Mills, together with Odessey Partners, purchased J. P. Stevens and Forstman and Co.; and the list goes on.

Sara Lee, one of the largest firms in the industry today, was never thought of as a player in the textile industry little more than a decade ago. Through acquisitions of the Hanes Group, Pannill Knitting, Champion, and a number of other companies, Sara Lee—through its Knit Products Division—is a major force in the industry.

Consolidations have changed the nature of the textile industry from a manufacturing-driven industry into a more marketing-driven sector, with huge market shares now in the hands of fewer and stronger players. For example, five firms dominate the denim market (Cone Mills, Swift Textiles, Burlington, Graniteville, and Thomaston). Only two independent texturizers (providing texturized yarns to weaving and knitting operations), Unifi and Madison, dominate this segment of the industry compared to 200–250 independent texturizers in the early 1980s. Although concentration and specialization have helped many firms stay competitive, this strategy is no guarantee for success, however, as shown by the bankruptcy of Crompton and Co., the largest corduroy and velvet/velveteen fabric producer in the United States (Finnie, 1992).

Most textile companies have seen the marketing advantages of specializing in either home furnishings and domestics or apparel textiles and of becoming a more important presence in one or the other. Milliken and Dan River remain the major holdouts that continue to market in both areas.

The 1970s and 1980s were difficult indeed for the textile industry. Some companies went out of business; some drastically restructured; and some new ones even emerged. As a result of these changes, the textile industry remains an important manufacturing sector whose productivity or other measures of performance often surpass those of manufacturing in general. Most companies have been transformed to meet changing markets and those efforts have paid off. The largest U.S.-based textile firms are identified in Table 4–2.

Table 4-2	Major U.S.-based Textile Firms[a] (by sales)
Company	**1995 Sales[b] ($ in millions)**
Milliken & Company	2,706[c]
Shaw Industries	2,630[d]
Springs Industries	2,233
Burlington Industries	2,207
Westpoint Stevens	1,650
Unifi	1,597
Wellman	1,109
Cone Mills	910
Guilford Mills	774
Dixie Yarns	671
Delta Woodside	614[d]
Galey & Lord	460
Dan River	385
Johnston Industries	296
Thomaston Mills	205
Texfi	263
Forstman	237[d]

[a]Some of the textile components produced by these firms also go into home furnishings products. For example, Springs Industries focuses primarily on the home textile market.
[b]Except as noted below.
[c]Milliken & Co. is privately held; however, this estimate for 1993 came from: "Private Lives" by S. Kichen and T. McCarthy, December 5, 1996, *Forbes,* pp. 184–220.
[d]From "Textiles, Others Outperform Retailers in 1994," July, 1995, *Textile World,* pp. 11–12. Original source of data, Kurt Salmon Associates, Inc.
Source: From "Textile Mills' Results for the Fourth Quarter and Full Year," March 19, 1996, *DNR,* p. 12. Reprinted courtesy of Fairchild Publications.

Geographic Location

Throughout the nineteenth century, the industry was located principally in New England, where it began. Cotton, however, was grown in the warm southern states, and the transportation northward to the mills was slow, inconvenient, and costly. Industry leaders began to turn their eyes southward but, although there were small textile mills in virtually every southern state in the early nineteenth century, they were not especially welcome. Plantation owners found industrialization repugnant, perhaps seeing it as a threat to their way of life and as competition for slave labor.

After the Civil War, however, southern leaders recognized the need for industrialization and offered textile companies special inducements, such as low taxes and utility rates, if they would build plants in the South. The movement of cotton manufacturing plants gained momentum after World War I, and by 1920 more than half the spinning and weaving capacity of cotton textile manufacturing was found in the South (Adams, 1957). Woolen and worsted plants, attracted by an improved spinning system developed in the South for woolen manufacture, followed suit shortly after World War II. Today, the three southern states of North and South Carolina and Georgia are the largest employers of the textile industry's labor force.

Along with the growth of the industry came changes in the selling and distribution of its output. Merchants who had originally started as importers of European fabrics gradually became selling agents for the domestic mills or bought their goods outright for resale. The expansion of domestic output after the Civil War stimulated the establishment of a textile center in downtown Manhattan, on and near Worth Street, that became the heart of the textile trade. The name *Worth Street* became synonymous with the body of textile merchants on whom American mills depended for their orders and often for the financing. After World War II, however, when fashion's impact hit the industry, the textile showrooms began moving uptown, where they are still located, right on the doorstep of the women's apparel industry.

Today, the textile mills are largely situated along a broad arc reaching from New England through the Southeast, but their designing, styling, and sales activities are heavily concentrated in New York City.

Different Types of Textile Producers

In its early history, the U.S. textile industry was highly fragmented. Different companies specialized in different stages of production, each of which required different machines, processes, and skills. Spinning mills bought fibers, which they spun into yarn. Fabric mills purchased such yarns and performed the weaving or knitting into cloth. Much of what the fabric mills produced was greige goods, or unfinished cloth. At this point, finishing plants took over, doing the dyeing, printing, or whatever other treatments were required. In the case of yarn-dyed fabrics, commonly woolen cloth, the fabric usually required less finishing than piece-dyed fabrics.

Today more and more fabric producers seem to be utilizing a wider range of fibers or combinations of fibers, and more companies are producing more diversified product lines.

Vertically Integrated Firms

During and immediately after World War II, problems of scarcity and price made the prewar production and marketing procedures of fragmented operations infeasible. The industry began to become more integrated. In some cases, fabric mills ceased to rely on spinning mills, selling agents, and finishing plants, and acquired or set up their own operations. Burlington Industries was one such company. In other cases, independent selling agents such as J. P. Stevens acquired textile mills and finishing plants.

In still others, converting firms such as Cohn Hall Marx bought mills to be sure of having fabrics to sell.

Today the textile industry includes companies that engage in all processes of production and distribution—spinning, weaving, knitting, finishing, and selling. This all-encompassing operation is called **vertical integration** and it enables a company to control its goods through as many processes as are potentially profitable. Russell Corporation and Fruit of the Loom are two well-known firms that have high levels of vertical integration. Even in these integrated firms, however, operations are specialized in their different plants, each of which performs a single function in the production of fabric, and different products are distributed by their different specialized marketing divisions.

Specialized Firms

There are still, however, many more companies that specialize in a single phase of production. Some are large firms that employ hundreds of workers, such as spinners like Dixie Yarns and Wintuk Yarns; weavers such as Dan River; giant converting companies such as Concord Fabrics; and printers such as Cranston. There are also many small firms, some of which limit themselves to narrow product lines, such as velvets and velveteens, or to such dressy fabrics as chiffons, taffetas, and silk failles. Other firms deal only in knits, brocades, metallics, or novelty fabrics. Their limited specialization seems to make some of the firms less attractive acquisition targets for very large firms.

Converters

Converting is a specialized textile operation whose function it is to style greige goods and arrange to have it finished. The unfinished goods are contracted out to finishing plants for processing as ordered by the **converter** (i.e., dyeing, printing, waterproofing, etc.). The finished goods are then sold by the converter to apparel and home furnishings manufacturers or to fabric retailers. The converter may be either a division of a vertically integrated textile company or an independent company that owns neither fabric mills nor finishing plants but serves as a middleman between these two stages of production. In that capacity, the converter specifies all aspects of the finished fabric, such as design, color, and other treatments considered necessary to make the goods salable to apparel producers or fabric retailers. Independent converters are usually relatively small operators, but there are big names among them, such as Concord, Loomskill, Erlanger Blumgart, and Pressman-Gutman.

There are three basic types of converting organizations, each of which performs essentially the same functions. One is the *independently owned converting company,* which has contractual relationships with the mills from which it purchases greige goods, or the finishing plants it uses, or both. A second is the *converter-jobber,* also independently owned, who does not have any contractual arrangements. The third is the *integrated converter,* which is a division of a vertical textile firm. Such a converter works primarily with greige goods from mills of the parent organization and, as a general rule, has the finishing done in its own plants. It may also use outside sources, however, for greige goods or finishing.

Converters fulfill an important function in the textile industry. Since they enter the fabric production process in its end stages, they can work quite close to the time of need and adjust quickly to changes in fashion. Converters (company or independent) keep in contact with clothing producers, seeking indications of colors, patterns, and finishes that are likely to be wanted. For this reason, most of them are located in major apparel markets, with more than 90 percent represented in New York City. The successful converter is a keen student of fashion, observes trends, anticipates demand, and is one who senses and responds to fashion directions.

Fashion Research and Development

Apparel designers say that fabric is the designer's creative medium, just as pigment is the painter's. A good designer responds to new fabric and searches for the quality that will make it—and his or her designs—come alive. To make possible fabrics that will evoke such response and that will ultimately be acceptable to the consuming public, fiber and textile producers must keep many fashion steps and several years ahead of the design and production of apparel. By the time fashions are featured in stores and magazines, they are old hat to textile designers and stylists, because these are the people who created these patterns and colors at least a year earlier. And probably two years before the public sees the fashions, the fiber companies and their associations were working with fabric mills on the kinds of cloth to be presented. At that time or even earlier, fiber companies were working on color projections and fiber variants for seasons still further ahead.

Specialized Fashion Staffs

Fiber and textile producers invest a great deal of time and money in fashion research to guide the development of salable fabrics, blends, textures, colors, finishes, and whatever other properties are expected to be wanted. All of the large producers, textile as well as fiber, maintain specialized fashion staffs in menswear and women's wear to research and report on trends in fashion.

Although their individual responsibilities and titles—fashion merchandisers, creative directors, fashion coordinators, stylists, and others—vary from one company to another, the recommendations of these fashion experts guide their company's design and production activities. These fashion specialists tour the world fashion centers looking for fashion inspiration and direction, observe what fashion leaders are wearing, exchange ideas with apparel designers and manufacturers and fashion editors, and generally use every resource available to anticipate what will be wanted by their customers and eventually by the public. At the same time, many large producers conduct market research in order to analyze consumer attitudes and their ever-changing tastes and preferences as to performance characteristics. Thus armed with their research findings about the performance and fashion features that are likely to be wanted, producers design, develop, and produce fibers and fabrics long before they become available to ultimate consumers.

Early Color Decisions

Fashion decisions in the primary markets begin with color. Color is a sensation—a mood—and one of its attributes is that it helps sell clothing. Fairly typical of the procedures followed in determining the colors to be used are those described by Ed Newman, then vice president and creative director of Dan River, Inc., in the comment:

> When putting together a color line we review the best and worst sellers of the last season, check computer readouts, have informal discussions with manufacturers and check the racks of department and specialty stores. We think of what colors have been missing from the palette for a while and which shades seem "new again." Many colors make the natural progres-

sion through the seasons; a wine becomes purple, the purple moves to magenta and the magenta to a pink. No mystery—just logic. The final choice of a color line is logic, research and "gut feeling." With it lies the success or failure of your next season (Newman, 1981, p. 92).

The Color Association of the United States (CAUS), a major force in guiding industry color decisions, has been issuing color projections for textiles and apparel for more than 80 years and has been forecasting home furnishings and appliance colors for nearly 35 years. It is a nonprofit service organization whose board of directors consists of top industry executives, each from a different industry, and all of whom donate their time. Seasonal forecasts for women's wear, menswear, children's wear, and the interior design industries are developed by committees of experts from each industry segment from fiber producers to retail. These forecasts are arrived at by committees of volunteers who evaluate what they call the "color climate." To arrive at their decisions, they consider everything from politics to the economy to cultural events and movements. Among the members of their committees are such distinguished persons as Mary McFadden, the well-known fashion designer, and Jack Lenor Larsen, a famous textile designer.

CAUS makes its predictions at least two years in advance and sends them to 1,500 subscribers, including design companies, textile mills, and paint manufacturers. The choice of colors will rule everything from women's fashions to desktop accessories.

Intercolor, an association of representatives from the worldwide fashion industry, arranges meetings in Paris twice each year. There, these experts analyze color cycles and the natural evolution of color preferences to determine specific color palettes for their target season two years in the future. Another color prediction service offered to textile and apparel producers is the **International Colour Authority** (ICA). They, too, meet twice a year to establish their color predictions for fiber, yarn, and fabric producers. Six months later, they send a modified version of their selected colors to member apparel producers.

Textile Design

In addition to the color story, fabric stylists must also be aware of the silhouettes coming into fashion, so that the fabrications they recommend will be appropriate. For example, if the trend is toward a tailored or structured look, firm fabrications are necessary, whereas soft, light fabrics are needed for a layered look.

Once the stylists have their color story set and the fabrications determined, the next step is designing the fabric. Textile designers, unlike apparel designers, are primarily concerned with two-dimensional surfaces, rather than with the three-dimensional human form. A further consideration is the capabilities of the knitting machines or weaving looms to be used. If a printed design is to be applied to the fabric, the designer must also consider any problem the pattern may present to the garment cutter. The pattern, usually a continuous repetition of a motif, is planned so that it does not entail unnecessary waste or difficulties in the cutting of garments.

Textile designers tend to specialize in print, woven, or knitted design. Some are full-time employees of fabric mills, converters, or textile design studios. Others work free-lance and sell their sketches to textile companies.

Fashion Presentations

Fiber and fabric producers have developed considerable skill in utilizing their fashion expertise to sell their products. And through the fabrics they make available and the fashions they promote, they exert an important and continuing influence on the fashion industry's chain of production and distribution.

Large producers (both fiber and fabric) are very active in disseminating the fashion information they have collected to all segments of the industry. Most maintain fabric libraries in their showrooms that contain swatches of fabrics currently available or scheduled for production for an upcoming season. In addition, producers and retailers are invited to visit, inspect, and consult special displays of new yarns and fabrics that are set up periodically. These libraries and exhibits are used by apparel makers and their designers, retailers, and fashion reporters as sources of information about future fabric and color trends.

Some conduct seasonal clinics and workshops at which they visually present their fashion projections and illustrate them with garments they have had made up for this purpose and in which their fibers or fabrics are featured. These clinics are open to all segments of the industry: producers, retailers, and fashion reporters.

Seasonal Lines and Sales Presentations

Once a fabric line is set and sample yardage is in process, the work of the sales and merchandising staff is put into motion. In the fabric and other component suppliers' markets, two new seasonal lines a year are customary. Fabrics for seasonal apparel lines are shown from six to nine months in advance.

The actual selling of piece goods is broken down into two phases. The first of these, called *preselling*, is a presentation by the textile company's merchandising staff to its key accounts—the decision makers. Presentations take the form of color swatches (small fabric samples made on sample machines), croquis (painted samples on paper), color puffs, and sketches set up on story boards for approval. Presentations are made either in the fabric mill's own showroom or in the showrooms of their customers. At this point, all samples shown are **open-line** goods, available for selection. If a customer chooses to have a particular sample "confined" and not available to others, and agrees to purchase an amount of yardage considered adequate by the mill, then no other customers may purchase it. Exceptions are sometimes made, however—for example, for a very prestigious designer label.

The second phase of fabric selling is the sales presentation to all other customers, regardless of size. Appointments are made six to eight weeks in advance of these customers' market weeks (selling periods), and presentations are made to apparel designers, stylists, and even the apparel companies' marketing staffs. Sample yardage is then ordered by the apparel producers for use in making up sample garments. After such garments have been shown to retail store buyers, apparel producers decide how much goods to buy and place their fabric orders. By the time this takes place, the textile creators are well into work on the next season's goods.

Textile Trade Shows

American producers participate in trade shows both in the United States and abroad. Held semiannually, these shows are attended by designers, manufacturers, and retailers who come to look at and perhaps buy the new fabrics (Figure 4–5). At this writing, the most comprehensive such shows are the **Interstoff** Textile Fair held in Frankfurt, Germany; the **PremièreVision** in Paris, France; the **Ideacomo** in Como, Italy; **Texitalia** in Milan, Italy; the **New York Fabric Show;** and the **Canton Trade Fair** in Canton, China. Each host country presents the latest lines of textiles developed within its own borders, along with whatever else producers from other countries choose to exhibit. Other, smaller shows include the Knitting Yarn Fair in New York City, which features new yarns, dyeing, and knitting techniques; and Cotons de France in New York City.

Source: Reprinted courtesy of The Larkin Group.

Figure 4–5

The International Fashion Fabric Exhibition—a textile trade show featuring both U.S. fabrics and those from other countries. Apparel manufacturers might visit this trade show to shop for components and services needed for their garment production.

In addition to stimulating sales of fabrics, these shows result in further benefits. First, they make all related industry branches aware of changing fashions. At the same time, they unify and coordinate the thinking of related areas within the industry, so that they change in phase with one another and thereby facilitate the mass production that mass demand requires.

Electronics: The Technologies Required to Compete

Although we still have a long way to go before we can produce a million yards of fabric by a simple verbal command, the fashion industry has been in the process of modernizing itself with new electronic capabilities that are reshaping its present and its future.

Because the textile industry requires modern technology to stay competitive, the U.S. industry has invested a great deal in state-of-the-art production facilities and equipment. Figure 4–6 shows the extent to which the industry continues to invest in modernization efforts. These investments have paid off. Textile mill **productivity**—which is measured by total fiber processed per employee—has more than *doubled* since 1978 (Standard & Poor's, 1994). These continued investments have made the U.S. textile industry among the most modern and efficient in the world.

Quick Response (QR): Computerized Partnerships

The late 1980s witnessed the introduction of a new industry-wide strategy called Quick Response. No recent industry development has created as much interest, publicity, and reams of printed materials as QR.

QR is a strategy whose aim is to achieve quick and precise replenishment of fast-selling merchandise by means of computerized partnerships between fabric suppliers, apparel producers, and retailers. Companies that participate in this strategy are linked electronically to each other so that each can speedily exchange, in computer language, information about the merchandise that is currently being purchased by the ultimate consumers. Its purpose is to considerably shorten the time it takes for currently desired merchandise to arrive in retail stores and to keep inventories at each level in balance with consumers' current needs and wants. Its development was spearheaded by the textile industry in order to meet the competition from apparel imports that involved the use of foreign-made fabrics.

A QR program begins with an agreement among a textile company, an apparel producer, and a retailer to participate in a computerized partnership after the fabric producer has shown its line to an apparel producer who then prepares and shows his or her line to a retailer. The preparation and presentation of these lines are done many

Figure 4–6

Textile industry capital spending

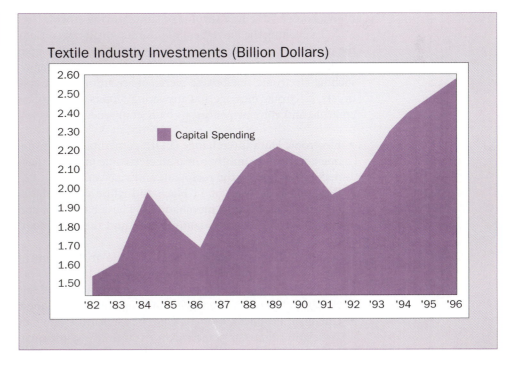

Textile Industry Investments (Billion Dollars)

Source: From "Good Year Ahead for Textiles" by C. Soras, January, 1996, *America's Textiles International.* Based on U.S. Department of Commerce data, with 1995 estimated. Reprinted by permission of *ATI.*

months in advance of a retail selling season. At this point, the retailer decides only on the styles and fabrications to be produced and establishes the quantities that will be needed for specific time periods, subject to timely revision. Colors and sizes, however, are not yet specified.

After the apparel manufacturer knows the styles, fabrics, and quantities, he or she works with the fabric supplier and establishes the types of fabrics to be used and the estimated quantities of as yet unfinished fabrics to be held in reserve and finished as needed for future use. Before the garments are put into production, the retailer establishes model stocks by style, fabric, size, color, and quantities for specified time periods, all of which are subject to needed revisions. The apparel producer now details the ordered fabrics by the colors and quantities wanted by the retailer for his or her opening inventories and goes into production.

When the merchandise is received by the retailer, it is ticketed with an identification code. When a sale is made, a scanner at the cash register decodes the ticket and records the key elements of the sale such as the price, the vendor number, and the size, color, and classification. This information is relayed to the store's central computer, where a running inventory of goods on hand is maintained. It is also transmitted through **electronic data interchange (EDI)** to the apparel manufacturer's computer, which enables the producer to replenish the styles, colors, and sizes that are needed, based on planned stock levels. Now that the producer knows which fabrics and colors need replenishing, this information is then quickly transmitted to the textile company's computer; the company will finish and quickly deliver the unfinished goods that have been reserved for the apparel producer.

This preplanning at all market levels makes it possible to stock smaller lots of goods close to the time of consumer purchases, thereby eliminating heavy inventories of untested goods at all market levels. The advantages to all participants are increased sales as a result of being able to respond quickly and accurately to consumer wants, reduced investments in raw materials and finished goods inventories, and a reduction of markdowns due to a surplus of slow-moving stock.

Expediting the movement of information about consumer purchases back through the production system involves a great deal of computer input and cooperation at each level. Although the concept of Quick Response involves many companion developments such as electronic mailboxes, merchandise information systems (MIS), automatic reorders, electronic message and answering centers, automatic warehousing and inventory controls, and voice activators, its basic components are as follows:

- **Electronic Data Interchange (EDI):** A method of transmitting computer data from one company to another into an electronic mailbox that unscrambles the data and makes it usable by the recipient, and vice versa.
- **Bar coding:** A series of 11 black-and-white vertical bars printed on a ticket or label that is attached to merchandise. These bars are a code that identifies the merchandise category, the manufacturer, and the individual item down to the details of size and color.
- **Scanners:** Devices that read the bar code at the point of sale (POS), transform it into numbers, and transmit the product code into a computer. By means of EDI, retailers and producers can instantly keep track of all sales data on individual purchases and thus monitor styles and current or emerging trends.
- **Universal Product Code (UPC):** The Uniform Code Council is a nonprofit trade association that sets standards for transmitting information by computer and administers a Universal Product Code. See Figure 3–11. The UPC is a 12-digit numeric code that identifies the product. The first digit in the UPC code is a number

system that serves to key the other numbers as to meaning and merchandise category. The next five digits are the manufacturer's identification number, which is assigned by the Uniform Code Council. The item or product code is the next-to-the-last five digits which are assigned and controlled by the supplier and are unique to his or her item. The last bar is a checking digit.

This QR strategy, using high technology data exchange and inventory controls, and based on industry-to-industry cooperation, and coordination has proven to be successful. The formation of two industry groups has contributed to its success, and both groups contributed to the development of the third.

TALC/SAFLINC

TALC/SAFLINC is a network of U.S. apparel, sundries, and textile industries that work together to establish and maintain bar coding uniformity, EDI standards, ticket design, and other standards necessary to transmit uniform and accurate information from computer to computer. The group emphasizes Quick Response strategies and partnerships as overall critical business issues. This group resulted from a merger of the Textile and Apparel Linkage Council (TALC) and the Sundries and Apparel Findings Linkage Council (SAFLINC). Many major companies such as Oxford Industries, Milliken & Company, Levi Strauss & Co., Burlington Industries, and Haggar Apparel are members.

VICS

Voluntary Interindustry Communications Standards is an outgrowth of the Crafted with Pride organization. This committee includes representatives from Kmart, Sears, Bullocks, Dayton-Hudson, Blue-Bell, VF Corporation, Levi Strauss, Milliken, and Wal-Mart. Their efforts are directed toward improving customer service through voluntary standards for identifying and marking products and for communicating across all industry segments involved in bringing goods to consumers in a more timely manner.

ANSI X 12: American National Standards Institute

ANSI X 12 is the result of a committee, cutting across many major industries, that was formed to apply a set of conventions that establish the format of an electronic document. For electronic data interchange to take place, a format or set of conventions must be uniformly established and accepted by all. This enables all companies, regardless of size, computer type, or computer language used, to accept and understand each other's data. Using a specific set of data keys with its accompanying dictionary, all businesses (both big and small) can receive and interpret the numbers transmitted. For example, the first three-digit number describes the type of document being transmitted (purchase orders, invoice, etc.); the next 10 digits give the sender's identifying code for its own name; and so on through the document. This system has already been accepted by the automotive, electronics, textile, apparel, retailing, and footwear industries, for a total of 44 industries.

Thus ANSI X 12 is the backbone of QR since it makes the industry capable of both receiving and sending immediate electronic information to its customers, be they General Motors, Levi Strauss, or Wal-Mart.

Computer Aided Design (CAD)

The introduction of computer aided design (**CAD**) systems in textile designers' studios provides the capability to experiment with weave, color, and yarns directly on a computer monitor. High definition printers can print on paper full-color fabric designs that are so realistic that they are sometimes mistaken for an actual swatch of fabric. Once a fabric printout is accepted, the computer can prepare and deliver exact instructions for replication in the sample weaving department.

This provides a textile company with the ability to offer an endless supply of new and innovative designs tailor-made to each customer's particular wants and needs.

Computer Aided Manufacturing (CAM)

The computer aided manufacturing **(CAM)** system is used to guarantee that the colors on the CAD printout of the design are identical to those used in the weaving of an actual sample fabric, or blanket. A textile industry blanket is a series of preselected color combinations all in the same pattern. Data from dyeing used to calibrate color matching programs can be fed into color simulation computers. (Calibration data defines the dye's coloristic attributes. This, along with the colorant's performance specifications, produces an "electronic shade card.")

Shuttleless Weaving

The high-speed shuttleless loom has increased productivity dramatically, with each new shuttleless loom capable of weaving more than twice as many yards per hour as the old shuttle loom.

There are different types of these looms, and each offers different benefits.

- *Projectible looms.* These looms weave a broad assortment of fabrics from basic poplins and twills to a variety of fibers and blend levels.
- *Rapier shuttleless looms.* More versatile and less productive than the others, they can take all types of colored yarn for many end market uses.
- *Air jet shuttleless looms.* The workhorses of all of these types of looms, these are the most productive and widely used shuttless looms. They cannot weave multicolor or decorative fabrics.
- *Water jet looms.* These looms produce synthetic silk-like fabrics for blouses. They are characterized by good productivity and fine quality, but they lack flexibility.

The next generation of shuttleless looms are likely to be fully robotic, with the ability to insert several different colored yarns into the weave. When combined with CAD-CAM, the future holds superior fashion styling with shorter required minimum yardage, and shorter production times at competitive prices (Figure 4–7).

ISO 9000

ISO 9000 refers to a set of international standards that companies must meet to be "ISO certified." Under the International Organization for Standardization (ISO), this certification program does not focus on product standards; rather, companies must have *systems in place to scrutinize quality.* Standards are generic and may apply to any industry. Although ISO 9000 is generally not a requirement to do business in the United States, many European companies will not buy products from firms that are not ISO 9000 certified. Although this is a relatively new concern for most U.S. textile firms, as more companies increase **export** efforts, they will find it necessary to be certified, especially if they wish to sell in Europe.

Figure 4–7	**Modern textile mills are highly automated and can produce large amounts of fabric with few workers.**

Source: Photo courtesy of Guilford Mills, Inc.

Environmental Issues

Historically, as the textile industry used various chemicals in the production of fibers, dyeing, finishing, and so on, many pollutants were released in the environment. In fact, the largest U.S. rayon producer, Avtex, was forced to close down because of chemical runoffs in streams.

Today's textile industry is both sensitive and committed to preserving the environment, as illustrated by the large expenditures on environmental controls to reduce or eliminate contamination of the air, water, or land. New methods of applying dyes and finishing treatments reduce water usage and chemical discharge. Additionally, an industry-wide program called Encouraging Environmental Excellence (or "E-3") encourages companies to promote environmental awareness and responsibility. To qualify for E-3 recognition, companies must meet 10 requirements, from having a corporate policy in support of the environment and detailed environmental audits of their facilities to the development of employee education and community outreach programs. Participation also entitles companies to use the distinctive Encouraging

Source: American Textile Manufacturers Institute (ATMI). Reprinted courtesy of ATMI.

Environmental Excellence logo (Figure 4–8) in their communications and marketing efforts. This distinction may be a plus for companies awarded it because of rising consumer interest in environmental responsibility.

Additionally, many companies have been required to rethink their product packaging so they are using materials that are environment friendly. Consumers' concern for the environment now influences what many individuals buy. The previous distinctive plastic egg-shaped package for L'eggs hosiery is one example of product packaging that had to change. Landfills can no long accommodate millions of non-degradable packages like plastic L'eggs "eggs"; therefore, packaging was changed to recycled paper (Ramirez, 1991).

Textile firms have responded to environmental concerns in another creative way. A few firms have developed processes to recycle plastic soda bottles to make fiber to be used in textile products. Early efforts produced fibers used in carpets.

In 1993, the Fibers Division of Wellman, Inc., a leader in the recycling movement, introduced Fortrel® EcoSpun™, polyester fiber manufactured from recycled PET (polyethylene terephthalate), including two-liter plastic soda bottles. Fibers are being used in a variety of consumer products: home furnishings, sleeping bags, and apparel. Patagonia, well-known maker of outdoor clothing, was one of the first apparel firms to develop a line using the new recycled fiber. Wellman recycles approximately 2.4 billion PET bottles annually, going through the stages shown in Figure 4–9

Figure 4–9	**Lifecycle of EcoSpun, the polyester fiber manufactured from recycled plastic soda bottles.**

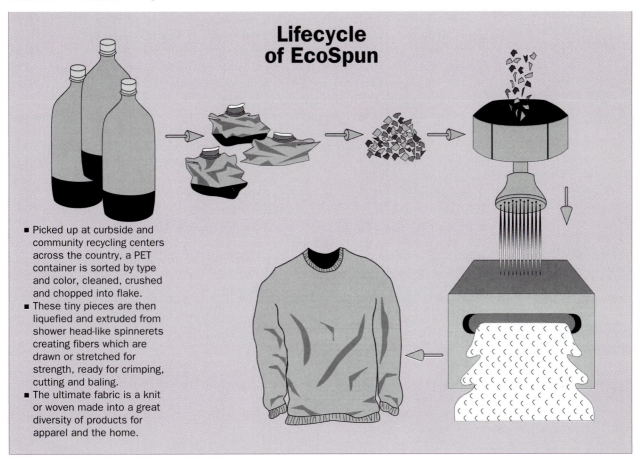

Lifecycle of EcoSpun

- Picked up at curbside and community recycling centers across the country, a PET container is sorted by type and color, cleaned, crushed and chopped into flake.
- These tiny pieces are then liquefied and extruded from shower head-like spinnerets creating fibers which are drawn or stretched for strength, ready for crimping, cutting and baling.
- The ultimate fabric is a knit or woven made into a great diversity of products for apparel and the home.

Source: Wellman, Inc. Reprinted courtesy of Wellman, Inc.

to produce EcoSpun. The oil saved yearly by using these bottles instead of virgin raw materials (petroleum is used in production of polyester fiber) is enough to power a city the size of Atlanta for one year (Wellman, 1995).

In 1995, Swift Textiles introduced Soda Pop Denim™, promoted as the "denim with a conscience"; "pop" also stands for Protect Our Planet. Swift's new denim combines 80 percent cotton and 20 percent PET from recycled plastic soda pop bottles. The company reports that a pair of jeans keeps a pair of two-liter bottles out of the landfill (Dominion Textiles, 1994).

Imports and Exports

Global competition has been a difficult matter for many U.S. textile firms. For decades, the industry had a nearly captive market—the large, relatively affluent U.S. market. Compared to most of the rest of the world, U.S. citizens have a fairly high standard of living, with incomes that permit them to buy many things beyond the most basic items for survival. For a long time, the domestic textile industry was in an enviable position of having customers willing to buy almost anything they produced. The only competition was from other U.S. producers.

By the late 1950s and 1960s, the textile industry's captive market began to erode. Textile and apparel items appeared in the U.S. markets from Japan, Hong Kong, Taiwan, South Korea, and a number of other countries where wages were low. Because of the low production costs, merchandise from these other countries was being sold at prices below those the U.S. industry could offer for similar products. Consumers bought the imported goods because of the affordable prices.

Over the years, **imports** continued to grow. Many more *types* of textile and apparel products were being imported, compared to just a few in the earlier years. Merchandise came from a *growing number* of low-wage countries. Many retailers soon came to see other countries as good places from which to secure merchandise for their stores. Additionally, some apparel manufacturers began to have their own production occur in low-wage countries as a way to reduce manufacturing costs. And, for all these reasons, the percentage of the U.S. textile and apparel market being filled by imports continued to increase, as shown in Figure 4–10.

U.S. textile leaders have been very successful over the years in securing government support for trade policies to restrict imported textile products from the domestic market. Despite these restrictive measures, imports have continued at very significant rates. In 1995, $47.3 billion in textile and apparel products were imported into the U.S. market, while $13.1 billion was exported. This means the textile/apparel

Figure 4–10   ## U.S. Textile and apparel trade

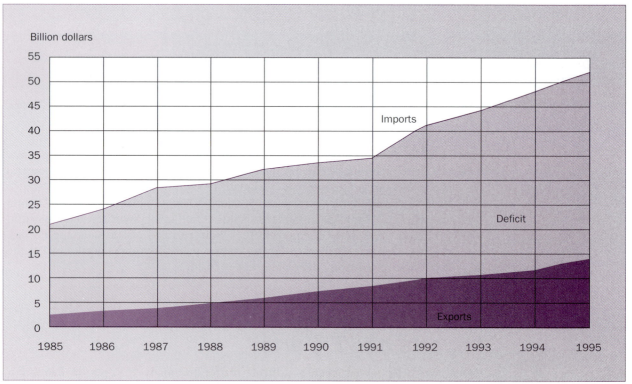

Source: From *Textile HiLights* (p. 24) by American Textile Manufacturers Institute, March 1996, Washington, DC: Author. Reprinted with permission.

trade balance, or in this case trade deficit (imports minus exports), was $34.2 billion for the year (U.S. Department of Commerce, OTEXA online trade balance report[1]).

Textile producers have felt they are losing their markets in many ways. First, they have seen many of their industry customers buying imported textile components. For example, weavers and knitters may buy imported yarns. Second, when garments are imported, textile manufacturers feel they lose the market for their fabrics—compared to the past when domestically made garments were made from U.S. fabrics.

In the mid-1990s, the U.S. textile industry embarked on a very different plan to counter the growing loss of its domestic markets. For many years, industry leaders had been preoccupied with fighting imports and most had given little attention to the prospects of selling *their products* in other countries. The change was that many companies adopted an export orientation for the first time. This means many of the companies began to think about products that would sell in other markets, started opening offices to represent their firms in other regions of the world, and began to think of their global neighbors as their potential *customers* instead of competitors.

Furs and Leathers

Furs and leathers were used for garments long before textiles were developed, and they are still major raw materials in the fashion industry. Both materials share certain basic qualities: they utilize the skins of animals; the natural habitat of the individual animal determines the part of the world in which the material originates; high degrees of skill are required in selecting, treating, and making garments and accessories of the material; there can be great variations over the years in the availability of a particular animal skin; there has not yet been a way to produce truly equivalent materials in laboratory or mill.

The qualities with which nature has endowed both furs and leathers make them uniquely desirable in today's sophisticated, mechanized age, just as they were in the dawn of history. In the fashion field, dominated by textiles and other machine-made products, each of these two materials occupies a small but important place. Although both materials require skilled handling and slow processing, the fashion industry curbs its appetite for speed when dealing with fur and leather. It has no real choice.

The Fur Industry

The wearing of fur as a status symbol goes back to the ancient Egyptian priests, if not further. Present-day use of fur for prestige and fashion is evidenced most clearly in the parade of sable, chinchilla, mink, and other expensive furs on such occasions as inaugural balls, opera openings, and other gatherings of the socially and financially elite.

Nature of the Industry

Sales of fur garments within the United States reached a historic high of $1.8 billion in 1986–1987 (Fur Information Council of America [FICA], 1995). In the years that followed, sales declined as low as $1 billion in 1991 but have risen again in recent years. Sales for 1993 were $1.2 billion but dropped again to $1.1 billion in 1994. More than 60,000 jobs are provided by the fur industry. This includes retailers, manufacturers, buyers, brokers, dealers, fur farmers, skin buyers, and trappers. Slightly under 300 U.S. firms produce fur garments today (FICA, 1995; "Fur Sales," 1994).

[1]For annual updates, check this Internet site: http://www.ita.doc.gov/industry/textiles/

In recent years, animal rights groups have sought media attention and have attempted to defame the fur industry. Two groups, the Friends of Animals and the People for the Ethical Treatment of Animals (PETA), have staged demonstrations at fur showings in the United States and other countries. For example, activists from the United States and Britain staged protests outside the Hong Kong International Fur & Fashion Fair, one of the largest for fur sales. Activists, half stripped and wearing a banner which read, "We'd rather go naked than wear fur," were arrested (Sung, 1994).

The fur industry responded to activists by establishing various trade associations to promote fur apparel: the Fur Retailers Information Council, the American Fur Industry, and the Fur Information Council of America. These associations have set about to educate consumers about the industry's philosophy, which encourages the use of fur as long as animal species are not endangered (Vryza & Hines, 1994).

Fur industry leaders believe the impact of antifur activists has been vastly overblown. Furriers insist that their lean years had little to do with the antifur campaign. One industry group says its research shows that fur sales reflect the state of the economy rather than the impact of the animal activists. Warm winters are also detrimental to sales. Industry leaders believe the drop in sales in 1994 was related to 60-degree weather in December, when cloth and leather coat sales were also sluggish (FICA, 1995; Reilly, 1993).

Manufacturing of Fur Garments

At every step of the way, from the living animal to the finished fur garment, the industry requires specialized knowledge, plus skills that are acquired through a long learning process (Figure 4–11). In many phases of the work, hand operations prevail. Mass production methods have little application.

Figure 4–11

Fur industry flowchart

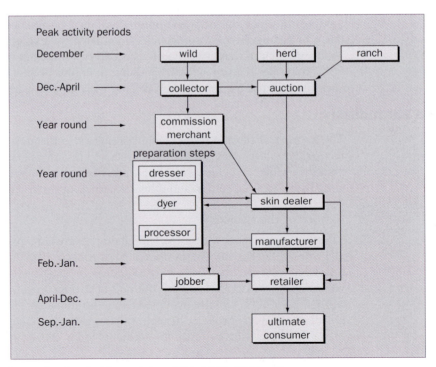

Source: Reprinted with permission of Fairchild Publishing Company.

The process begins with a trapper who obtains animals in the wild by methods that do not damage the **pelts,** or with a breeder who raises certain species under controlled conditions on a fur ranch. According to the Fur Information and Fashion Council, about 80 percent of the furs used in the United States are from ranch-bred animals, notably mink and fox. The fur business is necessarily worldwide in scope, with each country offering pelts of animals indigenous to its area. To secure desirable pelts, fur traders attend auctions all over the world: in Russia and Finland; Oslo, Sweden; Montreal, Canada; and Frankfurt, Germany.

Once purchased, the raw skins are prepared for use by *dressers*—firms that prepare skins for use by the garment producer. These companies first immerse skins in a salt-water solution, then scrape off excess fat and flesh from the hide. Next, the pelts go into revolving, sawdust-filled drums that remove grease and dirt. Oils are then added to keep the skins soft and pliable. Finally, the fur itself is combed and blown to raise its pile. Only after the furs become part of a finished garment is the last step taken—glazing, to add to the natural luster by drawing the oils to the surface.

To enhance their natural beauty, some furs are subjected to other steps. Beaver or nutria, for instance, may be plucked, to remove the guard hairs and enhance the underfur. On furs like beaver or nutria, shearing may also be used to clip the fur into an even pile.

Colors, too, may be subjected to change. White furs may be bleached to remove stains or discolorations, at least until a few years of exposure to air causes them to yellow. Other furs may be given a dye bath, to change the color entirely. In such cases, a federal law, the Fur Products Labeling Act, requires appropriate labeling. Other beauty treatments are tip dyeing or blended color. The latter is a matter of brushing dye over the fur to even out the color or give additional color depth. All this before the making of a garment begins!

Production of the actual garments involves a number of skills. First comes the selection and matching of bundles of pelts for each individual garment. Then the skins are cut individually by hand, sewn together in garment sections, and wetted, stretched, and nailed by hand, fur side down, to a board and allowed to dry in the desired shape. Only then are the sections sewn together to complete the garment.

For some expensive furs, like sable and mink, the expensive **letting-out** process precedes the garment construction. Again, this is a hand operation that requires great skill. Each skin is cut in half through the dark center stripe. Diagonal cuts are then made down the length of the skin at intervals of 1/8 to 3/16 of an inch apart. When the resulting strips are sewn together at a different angle, a longer, narrower skin is formed, presenting the striped effect that is wanted, for example, in mink garments.

Marketing Fur Garments

There is one major market period when fur garment producers present their wares to retailers—the period from May 15 to June 15—in New York City. Showings are usually held in the manufacturers' showrooms, generally on live models in the larger companies. The majority of fur wholesalers are located on or near Seventh Avenue, between 27th and 30th streets. In that area, messengers carrying thousands of dollars worth of furs and fur garments stroll through the streets as casually as if they were bringing a bag lunch to the office.

There are approximately 1,500 fur retailers in the United States (FICA, 1995). Because of the huge investment in merchandise required to present an adequate assortment to the consumer, the practice of consignment selling is common in the fur trade. This means that the manufacturer ships a supply of garments to the retailer and is paid for them only when they are sold; unsold garments are returnable at a specified date.

Department stores and large specialty shops almost universally lease out their fur departments, thus calling upon the capital and the expertise of the lessee. Under such an arrangement, the lessee supplies stock, hires and trains salespeople, and pays for the advertising. All activities are subject to store policy and approval. The lessee benefits by the drawing power of the store's name and location, and pays a percentage of sales plus rent.

In addition to the advertising done by retailers, the industry launches advertising and publicity through its trade associations, many of which concentrate on a single type of fur—for example, EMBA (the Eastern Mink Breeding Association), GLAMA (Great Lakes Mink Association), SAGA (Scandinavian mink and fox breeders), the Canadian Majestic Mink Association, and the British-Irish-Dutch conglomerate.

The Impact of Fashion

Many factors influence the fashion for furs. When there is a fashion for opulence, furs are "in." When there is a revulsion against ostentation or against wanton killing of animals for their skins, people swing away from furs. When the fashion world, as it has done in the past, goes overboard for an exotic fur to the point that the animal involved is threatened with extinction, the conservationists and sometimes the government itself will bring pressure to bear against the use or importation of such furs. This happened with leopard, which zoomed into prominence in the 1960s, causing such indiscriminate slaughter that by 1969 the animal was an endangered species. Similarly, revulsion against the use of certain types of seal fur, for which trappers kill very young pups, curtails the market to some extent—but not enough to stop the annual slaughter. These days, a retailer may add a footnote to the store's advertising, stating that no endangered species are among its offerings.

A fashion development since the late 1970s has been the introduction of major American apparel designers into the fur business. Through licensing arrangements with major fur producers, Valentino, Oscar de la Renta, and Adolfo, among others, now have their names on a variety of high priced fur garments. Where formerly terms such as *quality* and *luxury* got major emphasis in the industry, today a new fashion dimension has been added—designer names.

The fur industry realizes it needs to be more innovative and not rely on the basic, classic designs year after year. They believe there is a need now to respond more to fashion trends and new life styles. Now that people are dressing down, they need coats they can wear with jeans and sneakers. Furriers have learned to offer lower price ranges in the last decade to market to young working women (Feitelberg, 1995).

Imports and Exports

United States fur sales account for one third of the world market. In the world fur market, the United States ranks behind Italy (FICA, 1995).

Once a fur garment gets into the channels of trade in the United States, it is not easy to identify its source. The Federal Fur Products Act requires that a garment be tagged with the following information: the name of the fur in plain English, the country of origin of the pelts, any processing such as dyeing or shearing, and whether full, partial, or pieced pelts were used. In addition, secondhand furs must be marked as such. However, it does not require information about where the garment was made. It could be presented or even labeled "U.S.A." yet have been made elsewhere.

The Leather Industry

Leather is one of humankind's oldest clothing materials. Long before people learned to plant cotton and make fabrics, they were skilled in the tanning and use of leather for sandals and crude garments. Leather apparel in this country goes back to the Native Americans, who made moccasins and cloaks out of deerskin. Renowned frontiersmen like Daniel Boone and Davy Crockett and other early settlers wore deerskin and buckskin pants, shirts, shoes, and jackets.

Nature of the Industry

The leather tanning and finishing industry is made up of establishments primarily engaged in tanning, curing, and finishing animal hides and skins to produce leather. Also included are leather converters and dealers who buy hides and skins and have them processed under contract by tanners or finishers. Figure 4–12 shows stages of leather production and distribution.

The supply of cattle hides used in the leather industry depends solely on the demand for meat because the hides are only a by-product of the meat-packing industry. The meat packinghouses derive their primary revenue from the carcas; the hides and skins, which have no food value, are sold to the leather trades. A long-term decline in U.S. consumption of red meat has reduced the hides available to the industry and, furthermore, has discouraged growers from rebuilding cattle herds. Also part of this industry, but of far less importance, are the hides from goats, sheep, lambs, horses, fish, birds, and reptiles (U.S. Department of Commerce, ITA, 1994).

Industry shipments of leather and leather products were about $9 billion in 1994. Between 1982 and 1987, the U.S. tanning industry decreased and consolidated, going from 342 companies to 308, and the number of plants dropped from 384 to 338. Production declined about 25 percent during this period. About 12,000 people worked in the tanning and finishing segment of the industry in 1994, and the output from this segment was valued at more than $2.7 billion. Only slightly more than 100 establishments of any size are involved in the wet-processing part of the industry that turns hides and skins into leather (U.S. Department of Commerce, 1994).

Processing of the hides and skins is done largely in small plants located mostly in the north central and northeastern states. Three major types of companies are involved: (1) converters, who buy the hides and skins from meat packers and contract

Figure 4–12

Leather industry flowchart

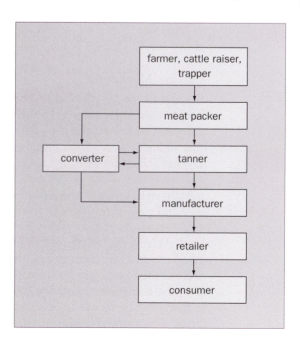

them out to tanneries for finishing, (2) contract tanners, who finish skins but do not market them directly, and (3) regular or complete tanneries, which purchase and process skins and hides and sell finished leathers.

Like the fiber and fabric producers, the leather industry promotes and sells its products to manufacturers of apparel and accessories. Yet, unlike fiber and fabric companies, the tanning companies do not make their names known to the consuming public. Advertising for leather garments and accessories may include the name of the fashion designer, the manufacturer, and the type of leather, but never the name of the producer of the leather.

Hides and Skins

These terms, used interchangeably by the layperson, have very specific meanings within the leather industry. **Hides** come from animals whose skins weigh more than 20 pounds, such as cattle, horses, and buffalo. These hides are so thick they are frequently split into two or more layers, called **splits.** Under Federal Trade Commission regulations, the under pieces must be identified as splits and cannot be called genuine leather or genuine cowhide. **Kips** is a term applied to skins weighing between 15 and 25 pounds. The term **skins** designates still smaller skins, from such animals as calves, pigs, sheep, and goats (Tanners' Council of America, date unknown).

Processing of Leathers

There are three basic steps in processing leather: pretanning, tanning, and finishing. **Pretanning** is basically a cleansing process in which the leathers are soaked and rid of all flesh, hair, and dirt. Next is **tanning,** which both preserves the skin and improves its natural physical properties. The varied tanning methods employ such substances as oil, vegetable substances, alum, formaldehyde, zirconium, and, most commonly used in the United States, chrome. The technical term "in the blue" refers to hides, skins, or kips that have been chrome-tanned but not yet finished. Final steps after tanning include dyeing and a variety of finishes. Among these is aniline, the most expensive, used only on the finest, smoothest skins to impart a highly polished surface. Other finishes include embossing, which presses a pattern onto the leather, often to simulate expensive alligator or snakeskin; also sueding and napping to raise the surface; or pressing, to give a shiny glazed finish. That last, called glacé leather, is often used for accessories.

Leather Marketing

Because of the length of time required to purchase and process its raw material, the leather industry is among the earliest to research and anticipate fashion trends. Its decisions as to colors, weights, and textures are reached early and are presented early. The industry as a whole participates in this process through its strong association, Leather Industries of America (LIA). The LIA offers color seminars semiannually and sells swatches of its colors to industry members at nominal cost, some 18 to 24 months in advance of the season concerned. As experienced observers of fashion signals and early forecasters of trends, the leather industry is looked to for guidance by other segments of the fashion industry.

At least one to one and a half years before the ultimate consumer sees the finished products in retail stores, there are leather trade shows at which tanners show and sell their latest products to professional buyers. For example, the *Semaine du Cuir* is a long-established major annual show in which tanners from around the world participate and to which buyers come from all over the world, along with the fashion press. This show is held in Paris, usually in September.

The Hong Kong International Leather Fair is a more recently established trade show. It is held in June in Hong Kong and attracts buyers and sellers from many countries, including the United States.

The Tanners' Apparel and Garment (TAG) Show is held in New York City in October of each year and attracts garment manufacturers, suppliers, and retailers, among others.

Imports and Exports

U.S. imports of leather products increased about 6 percent in 1993, to about $13.9 billion (this figure includes shoes, luggage, gloves, etc., as well as apparel). Most of the imports come from developing countries, accounting for 71 percent of the total—of which 41 percent came from China. Lower wages in those countries mean that it is less costly to make products there.

U.S. import levels have been especially high for leather wearing apparel—imports accounted for 83 percent of the leather apparel sold in the U.S. market. Although the U.S. leather industry exports some of its products, imports are much greater. In 1992, leather imports exceeded exports (a trade deficit) by about $12.5 billion. The United States is the world's largest *hide* exporter, but many of these are shipped back in the form of finished products (U.S. Department of Commerce, 1994).

Environmental Concerns

Many of the chemicals that have been used to process leathers are very damaging to the environment. In recent years, however, the industry has developed new ways of processing that do not produce toxic pollutants and has learned how to pretreat liquid wastes from the tanning process before releasing them into publicly owned waste treatment facilities.

Readings

The textile industry is taking a variety of approaches to be competitive in the future. The following articles reveal some of the strategies being used by major companies or segments of the industry.

Textiles, Fibers Are in a Global War: Woolard Tells ATMI   141

Globalization of the textile industry is a fact of life, and global competition in this sector continues to intensify. This article features some of the strategies DuPont is using to compete.

New CEO Puts Burlington on Fast Track   143

Burlington Industries, Inc. has been through a dramatic transformation in recent years. In this article, the CEO discusses his plans to keep Burlington as a major successful supplier of fabrics for the apparel industry.

ITC: Asian Power   145

Although the United States is still the world's largest manufactured fiber producer, a number of Asian countries are making rapid gains as major producers for the global market.

Regal Comeback: King Cotton Reigns Once Again in South As Production Surges   146

As demand for cotton around the world continues to grow, many U.S. farmers are switching from other crops to cotton. Cotton production for domestic consumption and for exporting has grown significantly in the 1990s.

Textiles, Fibers Are in a Global War: Woolard Tells ATMI

by S. Gray Maycumber

As far as international trade is concerned, and textiles and apparel trade in particular, Edgar Woolard, chairman and CEO of DuPont, believes, "we are in a global war— if you're not positive you'll win in this global war, there is a good chance you're losing it."

Woolard did an excellent job with the unenviable position of being the final speaker at the closing business session of the American Textile Manufacturers Institute's annual meeting, last weekend. Woolard kept his audience with a discussion of the steps and, in some cases, missteps in DuPont's recent three-year reorganization, and related it to what is needed for most companies in the fabric/fiber industries to survive in a global economy.

"I believe, without a doubt, that the stiffest competition in the next decade will come from parts of the world that are just developing, using technology that hasn't been invented yet. Companies from these areas don't have to adapt to a changing environment, they don't have to unlearn anything. All of their energies are going into winning the contest. Winning the contest for them is knocking you out of your business and us out of ours."

He warned, "Globalization of the textile industry is a fact of life. Global sourcing is a reality."

Major factors in this contest, he feels, are the increase in the sophistication of information technology and the decrease of trade barriers.

But Woolard believes that "this is a great opportunity to use the technology to repatriate more and more apparel sourcing back to the U.S. We must be competitive and creative."

He added, "we must try to shape markets the way we want them to be, instead of reacting to what they are going to be."

As an example, he cited the Swatch Watch company of Switzerland. That country had lost a great deal of its watch business to Asia, but won a chunk back with the Swatch watch. Woolard said, according to the Swatch people, "our cost is 1 percent of our selling price, so if the Chinese and Japanese work for free, we can still beat them."

Woolard feels that the watch is a universal symbol, because, "it's the only thing we wear when we make love."

He described the recent reshaping of DuPont, particularly its fiber operations, as how his company is preparing for the global challenge. But he noted, "restructuring and reshaping will not be sufficient alone to succeed long-term. We must also revitalize our companies."

Calling the restructuring, "one of the most dramatic changes in DuPont's 150 years," Woolard noted that it included a reduction in fixed costs by $3 billion, to $10 billion last year. "We had the most successful year in DuPont's history, with record earnings, on sales that were up by 6 percent."

This included a reduction in the fixed cost of Dacron polyester "by $100 million."

"What have we done with that $100 million? We have taken this and put it back into the business—modernizing our Dacron facilities. All together, we have put $400–$500 million back into the polyester business to make it world competitive," Woolard said.

He noted the work by Rich Angiullo, vice-president and general manager of the world wide Dacron business, in reducing costs, but said, "now we are fighting escalation in costs of ingredients."

Noting past speculation that the major fiber businesses, particularly polyester, were considered mature businesses that companies such as DuPont might move away from, Woolard said, "It continues to be an excellent business for us and it strongly reflects our goals of continuing technology improvement, world class competition, and global growth. We remain highly committed to our fiber business in our continuing efforts to be world class competitors."

He added, "I don't believe that there are mature businesses, only mature people that don't have the creativity to make businesses grow."

For DuPont, Woolard said, "The last few years have been a big learning experience.

"One of the first lessons was that it was an absolute necessity to face reality. When we did, we saw a company with too much cost and some unfocused businesses. We were losing our ability to compete. We were fat, lazy and blind.

"In the summer of '91, we faced the reality and announced that we were going to reduce fixed cost by $1 billion. This sent shock waves through Wilmington [the Delaware headquarters of DuPont], where we had 25,000 employees at that time—very few of whom made anything or sold anything."

"In 1991," Woolard said, "We realized that we had to compete globally with all of our businesses, or get out of them. Four years ago, typically, DuPont did 40 percent of our business in the U.S., 15 to 20 percent in Europe, and less than 5 percent in Asia. We knew that was unacceptable. We knew that quality and customer service had to be improved."

"We also had to reduce the complexity of our business. A lean company is meaningless unless it is determined to simplify everything it does—lean is meaningless unless it is focused.

"We reduced the number of our employees by about 30,000," Woolard said. "We never told any business unit how many people to reduce. We told them 'anything that doesn't add value to customers has got to go.' An awful lot of the things we did were for our own satisfaction and the customers didn't want to pay for them."

An example, he noted was the Seaford, Del., nylon plant, where nylon was first produced about 55 years ago. "Before reorganization, it did pretty much what it had always done. One employee proudly said, 'I have the same job my father had and I am doing the same thing.' This is a great tribute to loyalty, but proved to be a prime reason for the reorganization."

Woolard added, "In the last two years, we reduced Seaford's fixed costs by $50 million, a 30 percent reduction. At the same time production was up and quality was up. This amounted to a 15 percent reduction in the cost of nylon per pound."

There were also mistakes in the reorganization. "Speed was one," Woolard said. "It took us three years

to go through it. Looking back I would have liked to have done it in half the time. In reorganization, speed is very important. Slow change is detrimental. Change doesn't take time, it takes commitment."

Woolard also addressed a problem that was the focus of an old adage around the industry for some time, that "DuPont created and made wonderful products, and marketed them badly."

"Another problem we had to correct was focus. There was a strong internal focus in the company. This was bad. We worked very hard to shift to an external focus—particularly to a customer focus. Our aim was to get everybody as close to the customer as possible.

"We had a lot of people at DuPont that felt DuPont would be successful, regardless of what the customers thought and did. So we made dramatic changes."

One of the early casualties was the famed DuPont Executive Committee, "which was held in high esteem by the business schools. We found that nobody would move without the approval of the Executive Committee, so we eliminated the damn thing.

"A second major thing we did was to blow up our big departments into smaller separate business units. The old fiber organization is now three separate but closely connected business units—Dacron [polyester], Nylon and Lycra. This improved accountability. If you screw up now, there is no place to hide. In the old organization, there was a lot of places to hide skeletons."

Another change resulting from the reorganization, Woolard noted, was that, "we now send production associates out to see the customers. Now if there is a problem in a customer's plant, he calls our production associates, not his own engineers, and this is working.

"If there is one point I want to make about this, it is that much of this transformation is aimed at making us an outstanding supplier to the textile industry. From New York and around the world, customers say they see a dramatic shift in DuPont."

Woolard also noted that in addition to greatly improved communications with their customers, DuPont has also worked to improve communication within the company. "When Jerry Blumberg [head of the fibers operations] wanted to revitalize the nylon business, he got together the best people in all parts of our company, Agricultural Chemicals, Lycra, etc., and asked how can we grow nylon, which has only grown at 2 to 3 percent a year. How can we get it to 6 to 7 percent? The input helped him a great deal."

Source: From DNR, March 30, 1995, p. 8. Reprinted by permission.

New CEO Puts Burlington on Fast Track

by S. Gray Maycumber

Fashion alone is not enough to stimulate retail apparel sales, said a major textile leader. "You need fashion plus speed," according to George W. Henderson 3d, president and CEO of the world's largest apparel fabrics company, Burlington Industries.

"We must do a better job as an industry in providing newness and fashion to the consumer," he said.

Henderson, in an interview last week at Burlington's New York office, discussed the challenge confronting the textile-apparel-retail pipeline in improving apparel sales in the U.S.

"Burlington is heavily committed to apparel fabrics, and to the U.S. market," he told DNR, but "there is just not enough newness, and not enough fashion, at apparel retail now."

That, he indicated, is why prices of apparel are so low and sales flat. "This is the first time that apparel prices have gone down since the Eisenhower administration. They have actually dropped from last year.

"I don't think this is a consumer problem. I think it is a result of extreme competition at retail. There is over 19 square feet per capita of retail space in the U.S., it has tripled over the past 20 years. Competition tends to focus on price. We must find a better way to merchandise apparel. It doesn't compute that the customer is driven only by prices when he buys apparel.

"People go into stores not just for bargains but for entertainment. They must feel good doing it. We must make it more exciting to shop. If we don't, the customer will not go into stores, and just sit home and buy by computer."

He feels the reason there is not enough fashion at retail is that "fashion requires risk. When you get your fashion from overseas, you have to do it eight to nine months in advance. That's a lot of risk." To minimize this long-distance risk, he feels, retailers are too careful, and fashion suffers, or it ends up as markdowns.

Henderson's and Burlington's answer to this problem is to produce fashion apparel fabrics, and deliver fast.

"Fashion plus speed is our plan," he said.

"The largest market for apparel fabrics is in the U.S. We think there is a tremendous opportunity for growth here. Burlington has a major commitment to it. We are growing the business and increasing our capacity. We see it as a good opportunity for us.

"The type of fabrics we are offering the market are fashion fabrics, offering performance and value-added factors. There is no way we are going to be the cheapest. We have been working on this for many years."

He feels that "you need more than just creativity to market fashion fabrics on a major scale. You need the infrastructure to produce the fashion fabric and to deliver it. We build on strength of value. Fashion alone is not enough. It must also be very quick. Why there is no fashion at retail now is that garments have to come from halfway around the world. Fashion can be sourced closer to the market.

"We are trying to take a lot of the risk out of the business with speed," he emphasized.

How is Burlington actually getting real fashion with speed? "We have been working on Quick Response for many years. We've been setting goals, eliminating unnecessary steps, concentrating on everything we can do to bring fashion fabrics to the marketplace faster. With GATT, we have a very realistic timetable—10 years [phaseout]. Then it will be a completely open market."

Is Burlington getting enough information from its customers to really add the speed to its fashion fabrics? DNR asked.

"We are getting sales information from some customers, where we have close linkages. Others are not so good. We are working on it."

He stressed, "As a company, we are very customer-focused. We are also realistic. We want to know, from our people, what is going on out there, including unfavorable things. We want to know what is not selling. We don't shoot the messenger."

Those who knew Burlington several years ago will note a change here.

"A big part of the speed factor," Henderson said, "is the foundation on how we are organized—to be fast and functional. We are a very flat organization. Decisions must be made as close to the market as possible. We've looked into why things take so long and found that often it is communication—too long to make decisions. We are taking decision-making down to those in the market." Backing his claim that Burlington is growing its apparel fabric businesses, Henderson detailed growth in the fabric divisions.

"We have grown the denim business every year since 1983. And we will continue investing heavily in it. We think the denim market will continue to grow. The casual look will help, as will the opening of the Mexican market.

"The Klopman division is much bigger today than four or five years ago. It is continuing to diversify. We are expanding dyeing and finishing operations and quality."

Burlington Menswear (the worsted and woolen operation) is also growing, he said, citing the *esenzia* collection, a new fabric for casual fashion apparel and specialty suitings for both men's and women's wear. "It is a U.S. fabric with a European look," Henderson said. "Finishing is an important key to this fabric."

The *esenzia* collection is offered in a wide range of fibers and blends, including all-cotton, all-silk, all-linen and blends for spring '96, and wool, rayon and nylon blends for fall '96. It has found its way into designers' lines, including Joseph Abboud's. It is a major departure from the division's usual wool and worsted lines.

The Knitted Fabrics division has been a problem, he admitted. "It was a large production operation the way we had been running it. It is rapidly changing. There is a new management team in there now and they are focusing on several things, including taking cost out of the operation; concentration on the day-to-day operations (there was too much off-quality fabric); creating products with a differ-ence that will give people a reason to buy from Burlington Knits. And finally, and very important, improvements in service, delivery and quality have come about in only four months."

Henderson feels there are plenty of opportunities for all four divisions to grow. Mexico also figures big in Henderson's plans. Burlington has had plants there for more than 40 years and now operates three plants there that produce apparel and home fashion fabrics and floor coverings. "These plants won't be technologically competitive with our U.S. plants until later," he said. "Now we are using them to support our U.S. plants." He doesn't feel that the peso devaluation will have a long-term effect on Burlington's Mexican business.

"We know the market and the cost structure there, and we see it as a long-term market," Henderson said. He feels that NAFTA has paved the way for import growth in his company's sale to Mexico.

"Since the passage of NAFTA, Burlington's fabric exports to Mexico are up by 150 percent, and the volume of imported apparel assembled in Mexico using U.S. fabric has grown 38 percent." He also sees the Caribbean Basin countries, and Central and South America, as important fabric markets for Burlington.

In 1994, Burlington's export business was $131 million, about a 32 percent increase over '93, and about 6 percent of the company's overall sales.

A major challenge not only to Burlington but the entire textile industry has been raising raw material costs. In fact, Henderson said it was the first subject brought up by anyone who discusses Burlington with him, including customers and analysts.

Cotton has been running over $1 a pound, the highest since the Civil War, and polyester staple has had several hikes, three in the last few months.

To illustrate how prices have affected Burlington, Henderson said, "Our sales for first quarter are up by 13 percent, but our earnings are down. Rising raw material costs are the reason for this. We haven't been able to pass them along fast enough and there is a squeeze. We are getting prices up, but there is a lag.

"Raw materials are about 30 percent of the cost of a fabric. There is an awareness of this problem at retail, and we are getting prices up.

"The cotton problem will be with us until October. Maybe it will go back down to 75 cents in the fall. They [the USDA] expect a record crop this year. We hope the worst is behind us in cotton, but there is a lot of uncertainty.

"The polyester problem should also improve. There is more capacity coming onstream. Also there is new capacity in fiber raw materials coming along, which should help. Right now the polyester producers are making very nice money. We would hope this would moderate.

"In wool, in some grades, the price is up by 70 or 80 percent. There is trading-down [by cutters] in wool grades, and blends are becoming more acceptable. They went out of favor when wool prices went down. Now this is changing. But the workhorse grades of wool continue to go up."

Burlington is somewhat of a family business to Henderson. His father, George Henderson 2d, also became a Burlington executive when the company acquired Galey & Lord and made it a division several years ago.

But, while steeped in the U.S. textile industry, and Burlington in particular, Henderson 3d has had an international outlook from the very beginning.

He joined Burlington in 1974, and in 1978 was named head of the company's sportswear operations in Europe, a post he held until 1982, thus spending about half of his first eight years with the company overseas. In '82 he became head of Burlington Denim and later added responsibility for the floor coverings operations. He was named a corporate group vice-president in 1986 and was elected to the board in 1990.

Henderson, 46, served as president and chief operating officer from April 1993 until Jan. 1 of this year, when he became CEO, succeeding Frank Greenberg.

With annual sales of over $2 billion, Burlington is one of the largest and most diversified textile companies in the world, and the largest producer of apparel textiles.

Source: From DNR, *March 7, 1995, pp. 1, 8. Reprinted by permission.*

ITC: Asian Power

by Joanna Ramey

While the U.S. remains the world's largest producer of man-made fibers, accounting for 18 percent of the world's output in 1993, Asian producers continue making inroads in the market.

In fact, the Asian producers as a group are expected to provide most of the expected 14 percent increase in world capacity from 1993–1995, according to a recent International Trade Commission report on the world man-made fiber industry.

Asian producers—principally China, Korea, Taiwan, India, Indonesia and Thailand—in 1993 alone saw their share of world man-made fiber production increase to 42 percent from 31 percent in 1989, the study said.

By comparison, in 1980 these countries comprised 15 percent of world man-made fiber output.

The ITC report, focusing on the world man-made fiber market from 1989–1993, recounts how the U.S. fiber industry evolved into a sector dominated by nine large producers accounting for 70 percent of the nation's total capacity, with 85 firms manufacturing the balance.

As part of its restructuring, the industry increased its capital expenditures on new equipment and plants to $915 million annually in 1992 from $796 million in 1989. In turn, the industry increased productivity to an average of 167,200 pounds a year from 136,400 pounds.

Greater efficiencies also figured in the reduction of workers in the U.S. by 22 percent to 42,600 employees from 54,300.

Although the industry from 1989–1993 supplied more than 90 percent of U.S. consumption, the nation's huge trade surplus in man-made fibers has deteriorated sharply, declining from a peak of $870 million in 1990 to $267 million in 1993.

The ITC contended the surge in imports is largely due to increased economic activity in the U.S., increasing demand for foreign-made materials and a weakness in major foreign markets.

Source: From Women's Wear Daily, *May 23, 1995, p. 11. Reprinted by permission.*

Regal Comeback: King Cotton Reigns Once Again in South As Production Surges

by Andrea Gerlin and Scott McCartney

The last cotton gin shut down in this corner of Arkansas in 1975. Plagued by low prices and boll weevils, cotton-farming families such as the Haigwoods abandoned a way of life that stretched back to the 1800s. "I thought it was gone" for good, says Dennis Haigwood, at 40 years old the first of many generations of Haigwood farmers never to have planted cotton.

On a recent day, though, Mr. Haigwood and two brothers were busily jury-rigging a corn planter to dispense cottonseeds. "The market is just screaming at us to plant cotton," Mr. Haigwood says.

Once the king of the South's crops but later a symbol of its rural decline, cotton is making a big comeback. Contract prices paid to farmers are up 40% since 1992, as China, the world's biggest cotton grower, and other major producers have been devastated by insect-related crop failures. In February, the cash price topped $1 a pound for the first time since the Civil War. Yesterday, it closed at $1.0783 on the Memphis Cotton Exchange.

Fields of Dreams

Little wonder many farmers can think of little else. "They're going to have new trucks, and their wives will have new diamond rings," says J. W. Kellar, manager of Farmers Gin Cooperative in Cotton Plant, Ark.

As planting now begins in earnest, some farmers from California to the Carolinas are giving up soybeans, sweet potatoes, rice, peanuts, corn and even tobacco in favor of cotton. Cotton acreage here in Newport is expected to rise tenfold from last year to 2,500 acres. Alabama's farmers probably will increase their cotton plantings 28% and Georgia's 58%, according to the U.S. Department of Agriculture.

"It's just cotton-crazy," says Richard Petcher, an agricultural extension agent in New Brockton, Ala., an area where 60 farmers are planting cotton this year, up from eight in 1990.

Last year, U.S. production jumped 22% from 1993 to 19.7 million bales, and exports surged 46%

to 10 million bales. This year, production could well jump as much as 15%. In Georgia, the value of the 1994 cotton crop exceeded that of peanuts.

The failure of foreign crops is coinciding with record usage in the U.S., driven by fashion trends toward loose-fitting, casual cotton clothing. And the high cotton prices are driving up clothing prices. Fruit of the Loom Inc. says the cost of its cotton has risen 10% this year, bumping up retail prices 6.5% on all its clothing. Other big textile companies, including Fieldcrest Cannon Inc., WestPoint Stevens Inc. and Russell Corp., are charging 5% to 8% more.

The boom is also raising prices that farmers must pay. Seed and fertilizer dealers report sales up as much as 30%, and there is some talk of shortages. Ed Mason, DuPont Co.'s northeast Arkansas herbicide salesman, says his computer screen flashes "revise your forecast" almost weekly. Prices of cotton fertilizer are up 50% since last year.

Equipment Scarce

Cotton-picking machines and cotton gins, which remove the seeds from the fibers, are sold out for the rest of this year. Deere & Co. and Case Corp. say factories turning out pickers, which cost $150,000 to $200,000, can't keep up with demand. And gins are sprouting up in new cotton-growing areas—15 of them are being built in Georgia alone—even though the giant machines cost $3 million to $4 million and typically are purchased by co-ops of farmers who borrow against their land and homes.

Economists are beginning to fear another classic boom-to-bust cycle, with farmers taking on heavy debt during good times, then defaulting on 15-year and 20-year loans when prices fall and ending up losing their farms. Several marketwatchers expect prices to crash as early as 1997, when other cotton-producing nations return to full production. And feeding fears of an even earlier glut are county agricultural agents' reports of more and more U.S. farmers jumping on the cotton bandwagon.

"If we have a good crop year, we will flood the market," says Carl Anderson, an economist and marketing specialist with the Texas Agricultural Extension Service. "High prices usually cure high prices."

Industry experts expect the USDA to raise its 1995 cotton-crop estimate next week to more than 22 million bales from the current February forecast of 19.5 million to 21 million bales. Even though world stocks are low and China, India and Pakistan aren't ex-

pected to overcome all their insect problems this year, Mr. Anderson believes that such a harvest could depress prices. "If the weather's good, we could see 24 million, and that would be the place where we see an overflow of cotton," he says. By 1997, "prices may not cover the cost of production," he adds.

Watching farmers in Darlington County, S.C., make huge investments to convert to cotton worries Dave Gunter, an agricultural extension agent. Farmers typically invest $250,000 or more in new equipment to switch to cotton, which requires so much fertilizer, herbicide, pesticide and care that it is among the most expensive crops to grow. "If something turns around here with all this expense and prices drop heavily, you're going to have a lot of people hurt," Mr. Gunter says.

Another worry: a drop in demand. If cotton stays around $1 a pound, textile mills are likely to shift some production to other fibers. "I always tell farmers: 'Gentlemen, enjoy this but don't say your prayers at night for dollar cotton because dollar cotton is going to screw up your dreams,' " says Murray Robinson, president of Delta & Pine Land Co., a seed supplier.

In what many consider a danger sign, cotton-seed prices are already falling, pushed down by excess 1994 production. Even William B. Dunavant Jr., a closely watched cotton merchant in Memphis who two months ago predicted a U.S. cotton shortage by mid-August, forecasts an eventual softening. "It always works that way," he says.

Try telling that to farmers, bankers and merchants scrambling to cash in. To them, the future looks like the distant past, when all over the South gins emitted pungent odors and cotton created fortunes.

In recent years, Bill Veazey picked up where his ancestors left off. Planting cotton in Cotton Plant, 45 miles south of Newport, he says he "hit the jackpot" last year; his income jumped 25%, and he bought a new Chevrolet pickup. In addition, Mr. Veazey's brother paid off $30,000 of debt and purchased new cotton-harvesting equipment. But this year's profits are going to better use, John Veazey jokes: "Clothes, cars, trucks. . . ."

For most farmers, the break-even point for cotton is 50 cents to 60 cents a pound. While prices were stuck in the low end of that range until recently, government subsidies kept many cotton farmers afloat.

Today's prices, however, exceed the government's 72-cent-a-pound target price; so, the government is saving money. And the economics of cotton farming are changing dramatically. Record numbers of farmers are locking in contracts at nearly 80 cents a pound for December, a level at which each acre harvested can produce a 25% to 50% return on their investment. Based on last year's average yield, just 1,000 acres could make a profit of $100,000 to $200,000 this year, after all expenses (including interest and depreciation), farm economists say.

Cotton is also easier and cheaper to grow now that the dreaded boll weevil has been largely eradicated. The bug was so devastating for so many decades that the town of Enterprise, Ala., in grudging admiration, has a monument to it. But improved pesticides and full-scale eradication programs have gained the upper hand. Now, instead of twice-a-week sprayings, each costing $7 to $8 an acre, most farmers spray only twice a year.

Small wonder, then, that Arkansas farmers are switching over from soybeans and rice. Here in Newport, Mr. Haigwood decided to act while visiting a trade show last winter; there, he heard Mr. Dunavant's prediction of a cotton shortage this summer and watched brokers pick up cellular phones and place orders from the audience. "I said to myself, 'Cotton,'" he recalls. "The numbers just jump off the page at you."

But there's a problem. Few Arkansas farmers retained any cotton-growing equipment from the old days, and new equipment is hard to come by. The Haigwood brothers drove as far as Louisiana and Tennessee to hunt for machinery and came up empty-handed. None available, dealers said over and over. So, the brothers set about modifying their corn planter.

Outside his machinery-strewn equipment shop, a metal-sided shed off Highway 367, Mr. Haigwood struggled one recent day to widen the space between the chutes that will feed nearly five tons of cottonseed to 750 acres on which he used to grow soybeans. Then, aided by his brothers and farmhands, he strapped aboard huge yellow barrels that will deliver chemicals.

"Everything we have to farm is wrong for cotton," Mr. Haigwood says. Come harvest time in September, the Haigwoods will plunk down about $35,000 at the local supply store to rent a cotton picker. "If you want a new picker, you order it for next year," he says.

Another problem: Not many here remember how to grow cotton. "There are very few folks here with any experience in cotton; there might be some who saw it on the farm as kids," says Bob Pleasants, an agricultural extension director in Wayne County, N.C., another new cotton hotbed.

Cotton isn't an amateur-friendly crop. The first mistake is to neglect to prepare the soil, which must be far looser for cotton than for rice or soybeans. The second mistake is to fail to nurture the fiber, which requires intensive fertilizing and spraying. "Cotton takes a lot more management, more business acumen" than rice or soybeans, Mr. Pleasants says.

Like others, Mr. Haigwood vaguely recalls 25 to 30 gins in Jackson County; all are shuttered. He recalls cotton moving up and down the White River and his father and uncle tending fields. He recalls the worry about the autumn temperatures vital to a good crop.

But he never actually learned how to grow cotton. "We'll be short on know-how," he says. "We're going to make mistakes. I think Tagamet is going to help," he adds, referring to the ulcer medicine.

To bone up, Mr. Haigwood and his brothers visited veteran cotton farmers and attended cotton trade shows last winter. They studied cotton-growing techniques and found they had to learn a whole new vocabulary. At the Memphis show, Mr. Haigwood was laughed at for talking about "bedding up cotton." Now, still befuddled, he chuckles, "It's not 'bedded up'; they told me it's 'rowed up.'"

Already, Mr. Haigwood, who with his brothers farms 5,500 acres, is proselytizing about cotton's wonders. Like a politician, he has been handing out bumper stickers around Newport, urging people to advertise that "This is Cotton Country." If enough farmers switch, Newport will have enough acreage in cotton to support a new gin. Although five new gins have been built in the state since 1990, the closest to Newport are in Cotton Plant and Bay, Ark., both about an hour's drive away.

In this gently sloping slice of Arkansas between the Ozarks and the Mississippi River, cotton has already reclaimed its old status. Banks are making larger-than-usual production loans because cotton requires more capital. And retailers and auto dealers can't wait until harvest. "It is unusual for an industry that's left an area to come back," marvels Bill Elliott Jr., senior vice president at Union Planters Bank in Newport.

Some can't help fantasizing. If 2,500 acres are planted this year, next year it could be 10,000—enough to justify building a gin. The year after that, locals are predicting 20,000 acres—an amount that could add $8 million to the local economy at the present price of cotton. To support their dreams, they look no farther than nearby Mississippi County, which three years ago built a $14 million "super gin" that is said to be the world's largest.

"I'll show you what cotton can do," says Shirley Haigwood, Dennis's 61-year-old father. Driving deep into Mississippi County, he points out gleaming new sheds, large new homes and fancy new equipment on farms that converted to cotton a few years ago. Along the way, he also notes some dilapidated rice farms. "I can see a great big turnaround coming," he says.

Source: From The Wall Street Journal, *May 2, 1995, pp. A1, A8. Reprinted by permission.*

Chapter Review

Key Words and Concepts

Define, identify, or briefly explain the following:

Bar coding	Microfibers
Brand name	Natural fibers
CAD	New York Fabric Show
CAM	Open-line
Canton Trade Fair	Pelt
Converter	Première Vision
Converting	Pretanning
Electronic data interchange (EDI)	Productivity
Export(s)	QR
Export orientation	Scanners
Generic name	Skins
Greige goods	Samuel Slater
Hide	Solution-dyed
Ideacomo	Spinning mill
Imports	Splits
Industrial Revolution	Tanning
Intercolor	Textalia
International Colour Authority	Textile mill products
Interstoff	Trade balance
ISO 9000	Trade deficit
Kips	Universal Product Code (UPC)
Letting-out	Vertical integration
Francis Cabot Lowell	Yarn
Manufactured fibers	Yarn-dyed

Review Questions on Chapter Highlights

1. Give examples of current and past fashions that prove the following statement: "Many of the changes in fashion are primarily variations in colors, textures, or fabrics rather than changes in styles."

2. In their correct sequence, name the steps in the production of fabrics.
3. Explain the statement that "unlike the suppliers of natural fibers, the manufactured fiber producers made fashion their business from the start."
4. What was Samuel Slater's role in the Industrial Revolution in the United States?
5. How is the textile industry involved in environmental concerns?
6. How has the domestic industry met the competition of imports?
7. What are the competitive advantages and disadvantages of a vertical operation?
8. Describe the function of a converter and explain the various ways in which different types of converters perform the same function.
9. Discuss the various fashion activities of the textile industry.
10. What are new technological developments in the textile industry, and what are their advantages?
11. Discuss the controversy associated with fur fashions. Take a position on this and defend your position.
12. What is there about the processing of leather that causes the leather industry to be among the earliest to research and anticipate fashion trends?
13. Select one or more of the readings in this chapter and explain their relationship to the content of this chapter.
14. Discuss and explain the relationships between apparel producers and the textile producers.

References

Adams, W. (1957). *Structure of American industry.* New York: Macmillan.

Alderfer, E., & Michl, H. (1957). *Economics of American industry* (3rd ed.). New York: McGraw-Hill.

American Textile Manufacturers Institute. (1995). *Textile HiLights.* Washington, DC: Author.

American Textiles Manufacturers Institute. (1996). *All about textiles.* Charlotte, NC: Author.

American Textiles Manufacturers Institute. (date unknown). *Textiles—An industry, a science, an art.* Charlotte, NC: Author.

Brunnschweiler, D., & Hearle, J. (1993). *Tomorrow's ideas and profits: Polyester 50 years of achievement.* Manchester, UK: The Textile Institute.

Dior, C. (1953). *Talking about fashion.* New York: G. P. Putnam's Sons.

Dominion Textiles, Inc. (1994). *Dominion Textiles, Inc. annual report.* Montreal: Author.

Feitelberg, R. (1995, May 23). Fur week sets stage for rebound. *Women's Wear Daily,* p.7.

Fiber Economics Bureau. (various years). *Textile Organon.*

Finnie, T. (1992). *Textiles and apparel in the U.S.A.: Restructuring for the 1990s.* London: The Economist Intelligence Unit.

Fur Information Council of America (FICA). (1995). Unpublished information packet.

Fur sales rise for second year in a row. (1994, March 7), *Women's Wear Daily,* p. 3.

Heaton, H. (1929, November). Benjamin Gott and the Anglo-American cloth trade. *Journal of Economics and Business History,* 2, 147.

Kichen, S., & McCarthy, T. (1994, December 5). Private lives. *Forbes,* pp. 184–220.

Lewton, F. (1926). Samuel Slater and the oldest cotton machinery in America. *The Smithsonian Magazine.*

Maycumber, G. (1991). Microfibers—what they are and what they are not. *Daily News Record.*

Newman, E. (1981). Development of a fabric line, *Inside the fashion business* (3rd ed.). New York: John Wiley & Sons.

Poulson, B. (1981). *Economic history of the United States.* New York: Macmillan.

Ramirez, A. (1991, July). L'eggs makes a big switch: From plastic to cardboard. *The New York Times*, pp. 1, 7.

Reilly, P. (1993, September 21). Furriers hustle to keep sales warm. *The Wall Street Journal*.

Soras, C. (1995, January). Good year ahead for textiles. *America's Textiles International*.

Standard & Poor's. (1994). *Industry surveys: Textiles, apparel and home furnishings*. New York: Standard & Poor's.

Sung, V. (1994, April). Rather nude than furred. *Textile Asia*, p. 128.

Tanners' Council of America. (date unknown). *Dictionary of leather terminology* (4th ed.). Publication location unknown.

Textile and apparel financial directory. (published periodically). New York: Fairchild.

Textile mills' results for the fourth quarter and full year. (1996, March 19). *DNR*, p. 12.

Textiles, others outperform retailers in 1994. (1995, July). *Textile World*, pp. 11–12.

United States Department of Commerce, Bureau of the Census. (1994). *M-3*. Washington, DC: Author.

United States Department of Commerce, Bureau of the Census. (1996). *M-3*. Washington, DC: Author.

United States Department of Commerce, International Trade Administration (ITA). (1990). *U.S. industrial outlook*. Washington, DC: Author.

United States Department of Commerce, International Trade Administration (ITA). (1994). *U.S. industrial outlook*. Washington, DC: Author.

United States Department of Labor. (date unknown). *Technology and manpower in the textile industry of the 1970s*, Bulletin No. 1578. Washington, DC: Author.

Vryza, M., & Hines, J. (1994). The use of fur for apparel: An attitudinal study. *Journal of Family and Consumer Sciences, 86* (3), 45–50.

Wellman, Inc. (1995). *Wellman, Inc. profile*. Unpublished material.

Selected Bibliography

Berkstresser, G., Buchanan, D., & Grady, P. (Eds.). (1995). *Automation in the textile industry: From fibers to apparel*. Manchester, UK: The Textile Institute.

Bona, M. (1995). *Textile quality*. Manchester, UK: The Textile Institute.

Brackenbury, T. (1992). *Knitted clothing technology*. London: Blackwell Science.

Ewing, E. (1981). *Fur in dress*. England: Batford.

Feitelberg, R. (1995, May 23). Fur week sets stage for rebound. *Women's Wear Daily*, p. 7.

Harris, J. (Ed). (1993). *Five thousand years of textiles*. London: British Museum.

Higginson, S. (Ed.). (1993). *World review of textile design*. London: I.T.D.B./Textile Institute.

Hudson, P., Clapp, A., & Kness, D. (1993). *Joseph's introductory textile science* (6th ed.). Niles, IL: Harcourt Brace.

International leather guide (1993). Kent, UK: Benn Publications.

Jerde, J. (1992). *Encyclopedia of textiles*. New York: Facts on File.

Kadolph, S. (1993). *Textiles* (7th ed.). Upper Saddle River, NJ: Merrill/Prentice Hall.

Montgomery, F. (1984). *Textiles in America 1650–1870*. New York: Norton.

Powers, S., & Mitorja, R. (1988). *The designer's fabric and trim resource guide*. New York: Trends in Progress.

Textile Institute. (1992). *Tomorrow's fabric, tomorrow's people*. Manchester, UK: Author.

Textile HiLights. (quarterly). Washington, DC: American Textile Manufacturers Institute.

The textile industry: An information sourcebook. (1989). Phoenix, AZ: Oryx Press.

Thornton, A. (1994). *Index to textile auxiliaries*.

Tortora, P. (1992). *Understanding textiles* (4th ed.). Upper Saddle River, NJ: Merrill/Prentice Hall.

Tortora, P., & Merkel, R. (1995). *Fairchild's dictionary of textiles* (7th ed.). New York: Fairchild.

Walton, F. (1953). *Tomahawks to textiles: The fabulous story of Worth Street*. New York: Appleton-Century-Crofts.

Trade Associations and Other Groups

American Association of Textile Chemists & Colorists, P.O. Box 12215, Research Triangle Park, NC 27709.

American Association for Textile Technology, Inc., P.O. Box 99, Gastonia, NC 28053.

American Fiber Manufacturers Association, 1150 17th St., NW, Washington, DC 20036.

American Printed Fabrics Council, 45 W. 36 St., New York, NY 10018.

American Textile Manufacturers Institute, Inc., 1801 K St., NW, Suite 900, Washington, DC 20006.

American Wool Council, 6911 S. Yosemite St., Englewood, CO 80112.

American Yarn Spinners Association, Inc., P.O. Box 99, Gastonia, NC 28053.

Canadian Textile Institute, 280 Albert St., Suite 502, Ottawa, Ontario K1P 5G8, Canada.

The Color Association of the United States, 409 W. 44 St., New York, NY 10036.

Cotton Incorporated, 1370 Ave. of the Americas, New York, NY 10019.

Fiber Economics Bureau, Inc., 1150 17th St., NW, Washington, DC 20036.

Fur Information Council of America (FICA), 655 15th St., NW #320, Washington, DC 20005.

International Silk Association, U.S.A., 200 Madison Ave., New York, NY 10017.

Knitted Textile Association, 386 Park Ave. S., Suite 901, New York, NY 10016.

Leather Industries of America, 1000 Thomas Jefferson St., NW, Suite 515, Washington, DC 20007.

Mohair Council of America, 499 Seventh Ave., 1200 N. Tower, New York, NY 10018.

National Association of Hosiery Manufacturers, 200 N. Sharon Amity Rd., Charlotte, NC 28211.

National Cotton Council of America, P.O. Box 12285, Memphis, TN 38182.

Northern Textile Association, 230 Congress St., Boston, MA 02110.

Textile/Clothing Technology Corporation [TC]^2, 211 Gregson Dr., Cary, NC 27511.

The Textile Institute, 10 Blackfriars St., Manchester, M3 5DR, U.K.

Textile Distributers Association, 45 W. 36 St., New York, NY 10018.

Textile Fabric Association, Inc., 36 E. 31 St., New York, NY 10013.

Wool Bureau, Inc., 330 Madison Ave., New York, NY 10017-5001.

Trade Publications

America's Textiles International (ATI), 2100 Powers Ferry Rd., Atlanta, GA 30339.

Canadian Textile Journal, 1 Pacifique, Ste. Anne de Bellevue, Quebec H9X 1C5, Canada.

DNR (Daily News Record), 7 W. 34 St., New York, NY 10001-8191.

Journal of the American Leather Chemists Association, Leather Industries of America Research Laboratory, Campus Station, Cincinnati, OH 45221.

Journal of the Textile Institute, 10 Blackfriars St., Manchester, M3 5DR, U.K.

International Textiles, 23 Bloomsbury Sq., London WC1A 2PJ, U.K.

Knitting International, 23 Bloomsbury Sq., London WC1A 2PJ, U.K.

Knitting Times, 386 Park Ave. S., New York, NY 10016.

Leather Industry Statistics, Membership Bulletin, 1000 Thomas Jefferson St., NW, Suite 515, Washington, DC 20007.

Leather, International Journal of the Industry, Sovereign Way, Tonbridge, Kent TN9 1RW, U.K.

New York Connection, 1 Times Square, New York, NY 10018.

Textiles, 10 Blackfriars St., Manchester, M3 5DR, U.K.

Textile Horizons, 23 Bloomsbury Sq., London WC1A 2PJ, U.K.

Textile News, 9629 Old Nations Ford Rd., Charlotte, NC 28273.

Textile World, 4170 Ashford-Dunwoody Rd., Suite 420, Atlanta, GA 30319.

*T*he Women's and Children's Apparel Industry

*A*lthough the apparel industry works closely with the textile industry, the two are really quite different in nature. The apparel manufacturing sector consists of far more firms, many of which are very small, and employs far more people than the textile industry. Also known by terms such as the garment trade, the needle trades, and the "rag trades," the clothing-producing industry is a sizable force in our nation's economy. The apparel industry is also a major employer worldwide—almost no country in the world is without a garment industry that contributes significantly to the local economy through the jobs it provides. Although we shall focus on primarily the U.S. industry, the apparel sectors in many other countries would have similarities.

As we noted in Chapter 1, the development of the U.S. **ready-to-wear** industry meant that fashionable clothes were mass produced and affordable to a large portion of the population. As Kidwell and Christman (1974) noted in quoting William C. Browning, a clothing manufacturer near the end of the 1800s, "abundant clothing at a moderate cost for all classes of citizens . . . [is] essential to the self-respect of a free, democratic people" (p. 15).

This chapter deals with the development, location, operations, and economics of the women's branch of the apparel industry, including the subdivision concerned with children's wear. Much information in the early sections of the chapter applies also to the men's and boys' industry covered in Chapter 6. The readings following the text discuss topics related to significant new developments in the apparel industry.

Economic Importance

By any of a number of yardsticks, the importance of the women's fashion business is clear. In terms of how consumers spend their money, it is estimated that in 1995, the outlay for women's and children's clothing and accessories, exclusive of shoes, was $174 billion (American Apparel Manufacturers Association, 1996). In terms of the value of its production, the women's fashion industry also ranks high. In 1994, the value of factory shipments of apparel, accessories, and fabricated textiles for women and children was over $45 billion. Another yardstick—employment in the apparel industry as a whole (men's, women's, and children's wear combined)—is just under 900,000. The women's and girls' segment of the apparel industry account for well over half the total figures for clothing expenditures, employment, and value of factory shipments.

Numbers alone, however, do not tell the full story of the importance of the fashion industry as an employer. Historically, the industry has been a haven for women, the foreign-born, and minorities in search of work; it is a vast source of jobs in all parts of the country for semiskilled labor; and it is notable for hiring and training unskilled workers.

Not only is the women's apparel industry, with which we are primarily concerned here, of considerable size itself, but its activities have great influence on many other business areas. Its productive facilities, as is discussed later in this section, are distributed throughout the United States. It provides an outlet for the talent of gifted, creative individuals and employment for workers who are happiest at routine jobs. In addition, it is an industry that has changed fashion from what was once for the privileged few to something within reach of all but the most deprived women in this country. It was in the United States that the development of mass markets, mass production methods, and mass distribution of fashion merchandise was most rapid. It is to this country that manufacturers and retailers from many other countries turn for the know-how of making and selling fashionable ready-to-wear merchandise.

Women's and Children's SIC Groupings

The Standard Industrial Classification system for all manufacturing activities designates certain categories for apparel; these are shown in Table 5–1. The first two digits define the major SIC classification (i.e., "major group"). Nearly all apparel is in SIC 23, except for a few items knitted in textile mills (SIC 22). As we can see in the table, the third digit defines a grouping (i.e., a "group") of products. For example, the SIC 233 group consists of women's, misses, and juniors' outerwear, and the 234 group consists of women's, misses, and juniors' undergarments. Men's and boys' apparel and furnishings are in the SIC 232 group. The SIC category concept is important to understand because all industry production, employment, and trade are tracked by these codes.

Table 5–1	Select Branches of the Apparel Industry by Standard Industrial Classification Code Number

SIC Code	Branch of Industry
23	Apparel
231	Men's and boys' suits and coats
232	Men's and boys' apparel and furnishings
2321	Shirts and nightwear
2322	Underwear and nightwear
2323	Neckwear
2325	Trousers and slacks
2326	Work clothing
2329	Other clothing, nec[a]
233	Women's, misses' and juniors' outerwear
2331	Blouses and shirts
2335	Dresses
2337	Suits and coats
2339	Outerwear, nec[a]
234	Women's and children's undergarments
2341	Underwear
2342	Bras, girdles, and allied garments
236	Girls' and children's outerwear
2361	Dresses, blouses, and shirts
2369	Outerwear, nec[a]

[a]Not elsewhere classified.
Source: From *Standard Industrial Classification Manual* by United States Executive Office of the President, Office of Management and Budget, 1987, Washington, DC: Author.

History and Growth of the Women's Industry

Until the mid-nineteenth century, ready-made clothing was virtually nonexistent, and fashionable clothing was something that relatively few people in the United States wore or could afford. The wants of these few were supplied by custom-made imports, usually from England or France, or by the hand labor of a small number of custom tailors and dressmakers in this country. The dressmakers worked at home, in the homes of their customers, or in small craft shops. The fabrics they used for their wealthy clients were generally imported from Europe.

Ready-to-Wear in the Nineteenth Century

From colonial times to the end of the 1800s, the majority of American women wore clothes made at home by the women of the house; every home in modest circumstances was its own clothing factory. Aiding these home sewing operations were the instructions for constructing garments printed in such early American women's magazines as *Godey's Lady's Book* and *Graham's Magazine.* And in 1860, Ebenezer Butterick developed paper patterns that provided the home sewer with help with styles and sizes. Home dressmaking continued to prevail.

Early Ready-to-Wear

In contrast to custom-made apparel, which is constructed to the exact measurements of the garment's wearer, the term **ready-to-wear** applies to apparel made in standardized sizes and usually produced in factories. An advertisement for early ready-to-wear is shown in Figure 5–1.

As we shall note in the chapter on menswear, the first ready-to-wear clothing in the United States was produced for men. Not until the U.S. Census of 1860 was the commercial manufacture of women's ready-to-wear deemed worthy of enumeration. In that year, mention was made of 96 manufacturers producing such articles as hoopskirts, cloaks, and mantillas. What was available was of poor quality and completely lacking in good design. Although once started, the industry grew rapidly, home dressmaking continued until into the early twentieth century, and it was not until well into the 1900s that the term *store clothes,* applied to early ready-to-wear, was used in other than a derogatory manner.

The women's ready-to-wear business in the United States is indeed young, and its early beginnings were anything but fashion inspired. In not much more than a century, the industry that once served only the lowest income levels of society has worked its way up to acceptance by the very richest of women.

From Hand to Machine Production

The major event that opened the way to ready-to-wear production was the development of the sewing machine by **Elias Howe** in 1845. Howe's machine was further perfected by **Isaac Singer,** whose improvements made it suitable for use in factories. Singer also promoted it aggressively, thus bringing it to public attention. These machines, first operated by footpower with a treadle and later by electricity, revolutionized production by making volume output possible in machine-equipped factories.

Figure 5–1

An early advertisement for women's ready-to-wear.

Source: From a city directory, circa 1855. Courtesy of the Bettmann Archive.

Immigrants: A Source of Manpower

A plentiful supply of labor is essential to growth of any industry. This is especially true of an industry like apparel production, which was, and still is, heavily dependent on hand-guided operations such as machine sewing. Workers to perform those tasks became available in vast numbers, beginning in the 1880s, in the person of immigrants from Central and Eastern Europe. Many of the newcomers were Jews, fleeing Czarist persecutions and bringing tailoring skills with them; others, without a trade and with no knowledge of the language, were ready and willing to master the sewing machine and work at it to survive in their new country. Hundreds of thousands of immigrants came each year, and the stream never slackened until restrictions were placed on immigration in 1920. This influx of immigrant labor, both skilled and unskilled, made possible an accelerated pace of industry growth.

Developments in the Twentieth Century

During the first two decades of the twentieth century, a number of developments combined to give additional impetus to the industry. In the 1920s, the industry came of age and the output of apparel passed the billion-dollar mark, representing one-twelfth of the country's total output of manufactured goods (U.S. Department of Commerce, 1966).

Improvements in Technology and Retail Distribution

Continuing improvements in textile technology in both Europe and America made available a wide variety of fabrics. Improvements in machines for sewing, cutting, and pressing made garment production faster, easier, and cheaper.

Along with the improvements in textile and apparel production technology, there were advances in mass distribution. Retailers began to learn the ready-to-wear business. Dry goods merchants learned to sell apparel; department and specialty stores that prided themselves on their custom-made operations began to establish ready-to-wear departments. Continuing innovation in retail salesmanship and advertising stimulated the demand for the industry's products and contributed to the further expansion of women's apparel manufacturing.

Increasing Need for Ready-to-Wear

As manufacturing improved, ready-made clothing overcame the stigma of inferiority and cheapness that had originally been attached to it. It became an acceptable answer to a growing need for reasonably priced and respectably made apparel.

An important reason for this need was the changing role of women. Prior to 1900, there were relatively few women who looked beyond the confines of home and family. Many of those who did work held miserably paying domestic or farm jobs. To be well dressed was the privilege primarily of the wives and daughters of well-to-do men.

At the turn of the century, a whole new breed of busier and more affluent women began to emerge: women in colleges, women in sports, women in politics, and women in factories, offices, and retail stores. World War I further gave many women their first view of an occupation outside the confines of their homes, and stimulated the need for ready-made clothing. Their expanding interests and activities made ready-to-wear for themselves and their families a great convenience, and thus accelerated its acceptance among nearly all classes and incomes.

Recognition of American Designers in the 1940s

In the early years of the twentieth century, the American apparel industry had demonstrated an awareness of fashion but had not yet reached the point of sponsoring or participating in its development. Instead, producers and retailers looked to Parisian couture designers for inspiration. Twice a year, heads of apparel-producing firms went to view the Paris collections and bought samples for copying or adapting into mass-produced garments. At the same time, buyers from leading retail stores also bought lavishly from the Paris collections and arranged for manufacturers to copy or adapt the garments chosen. American fashion publications also concentrated their publicity almost solely on what was being shown. The phrase *Paris inspired* was the key to fashions and their promotion.

Inevitably, however, American design talent had been attracted to the industry. By the 1930s, many capable and creative designers were at work in the trade, but so great was the enthusiasm for Paris that their names were rarely mentioned in the press or by the stores. In the war-ridden years of the 1940s, with Paris blacked out by the German occupation, Dorothy Shaver, then president of Lord & Taylor and an outstanding fashion merchant, smashed the tradition of idolizing Paris designers. Her store, for the first time in retail history, advertised clothes designed by Americans and featured their names: Elizabeth Hawes, Clare Potter, Vera Maxwell, Tom Brigance, and Claire McCardell, considered by many to have been the first true sportswear designer. The rule that only French-inspired clothes could be smart had been broken.

Publicly Owned vs. Privately Owned Apparel Firms

Development of publicly owned giants in the 1960s.   Until the 1950s, the women's apparel industry consisted almost entirely of relatively small, privately owned, single-product businesses, each concentrating its efforts on its own specialized product. Large or publicly owned firms were virtually nonexistent. In the late 1950s and throughout the 1960s, however, the situation changed and huge, publicly owned, multiproduct corporations made their appearance in the apparel field, usually by means of mergers with and acquisitions of existing companies (Table 5–2). Many influences contributed to this phenomenon. Among them was the increase in consumer apparel spending resulting from an expanding economy. Another factor was the need to become large enough to be able to deal successfully with ever-larger textile suppliers, on the one hand, and enormously large retail distributors, on the other.

The rise of publicly owned giants in the apparel field during the 1960s is reflected in the fact that, in 1959, only 22 such publicly owned firms existed in the women's apparel field but, by the close of the 1960s, some 100 multiproduct apparel companies were listed on the stock exchanges and inviting public investment as a source of capital for further expansion.

Going private in the 1980s: Leveraged buyouts.   In the mid-1980s, the trend toward going public began to reverse itself, and some large manufacturing firms began to "go private" again through **leveraged buyouts.** In a typical leveraged buyout, a group of investors, aided by an investment firm specializing in the field, buys out a company's public shareholders by leveraging or borrowing against the company's own assets. The investors put up between 1 and 10 percent of the total price in the usual case. The rest of the purchase price, up to 99 percent in some cases, is financed

Table 5–2	Women's Apparel[a] Producers: Selected Examples
Company	**1995 Sales (in $ millions)**
Sara Lee Corporation	7,259[b]
Liz Claiborne, Inc.	2,081
Kellwood Company	1,451
The Warnaco Group	916
Jones Apparel Group	776
Leslie Fay	700[c]
Cygne Designs, Inc.	516[c]
Carole Little	368[c]
Esprit Holdings, Inc.	303[c,d]
Norton McNaughton	228
Donnkenny	210
Bernard Chaus	168
Jessica McClintock	151[c]
JH Collectibles, Inc.	131[c]
St. John Knits	128[c]
Fritzi of California	125[c]

[a]Some produce other products, but are for the most part women's apparel firms.
[b]Figures are from Sara Lee Personal Products Division; data are not available on women's apparel alone.
[c]From "Top 100 Sewn Products Companies '95," June 1995, *Apparel Industry Magazine,* pp. 17–40. Figures from this source are for 1994.
[d]1993 estimate.
Source of information not noted elsewhere: "Apparel Manufacturers' Results for the Fourth Quarter and Year," March 4, 1996, *Women's Wear Daily,* p. 22.

by layers of long-term loans from banks and insurance companies. The company's assets and cash flow are then used to pay back the loans, with or without the sale of bonds. The company's management has reclaimed their autonomy, albeit with a load of debt and interest payments, but without the need to submit their operating decisions to the review of outside stockholders. Some examples of leveraged buyouts were those of Levi Strauss, Leslie Fay, and Puritan, among others.

New companies go public.   In the early 1990s, a number of privately held companies decided to go public. Companies generally decide to do this so they can sell shares in the company, and through those sales generate capital for the company's growth. When stock is sold for the first time this is called an **initial public offering (IPO).** Examples of well-known companies that issued stock in recent years were Tommy Hilfiger, Danskin, St. John Knits, and Haggar Corporation.

Industry Restructuring

The apparel industry has faced many challenges that have forced changes—changes that cause today's industry to be very different from that of 20 years ago. Competition from imports has created difficulties for many companies. However, the business climate is tough for firms, even if imports were not considered because of the large number of U.S. companies competing in the market. Additionally, sluggish consumer spending has hurt companies.

Because of the challenges, the apparel industry has restructured in many ways in recent years. Many small companies were trying to survive without adequate capital to keep them afloat. As a result, a number of companies and apparel plants have gone out of business. Others have merged, and some have acquired smaller companies. Some have sold off unprofitable parts of their businesses. In general, these changes have resulted in larger and stronger firms with funds to hire professionals to manage the businesses.

Development of the Unions

In the early days of the women's apparel industry, working conditions, as in many other industries of the period, were generally extremely bad. Men and women worked 12 hours and more a day, seven days a week, in damp, disease-breeding places, referred to in disgust as **sweatshops,** such as the one shown in Figure 5–2. The hourly wage was five cents. Some provided their own machines and paid for thread and needles, for the water they drank, and sometimes even for the "privilege" of working in the factories. Work was also taken home to dark, unsanitary tenements that often doubled as sweatshops, and in which children worked long hours side by side with their parents. It was in this environment in the early 1900s that the International Ladies' Garment Workers' Union (**ILGWU**) developed. At that time the union represented fewer than 2,000 workers and was founded after two decades of desperate struggle.

But the union did not achieve strength until after several major strikes and the monumental disaster of the **Triangle Shirtwaist Fire** of 1911. This tragic event took place in a factory where 146 persons lost their lives because of locked exit doors, inadequate fire escapes, and one fire escape that actually ended in midair. The shock of this holocaust was the turning point in the sweatshop era, because it awoke the public conscience to labor conditions in the garment industry.

Since the 1920s, industry-wide strikes and lockouts have been all but non-existent. Reports vary as to the proportion of apparel industry workers in unions, with the range generally between 20 and 60 percent (anonymous union source). Unionized workers are more likely to be in the Northeast, in major metropolitan areas, and on the West Coast—but are not commonly found in the South. After all, many firms lo-

Courtesy of the Bettmann Archive

cated in the South to take advantage of less costly labor. Wages of unionized workers are generally somewhat higher than those of nonunionized workers.

In 1995, the ILGWU merged with the Amalgamated Clothing and Textile Workers Union (ACTWU)[1] to form one union with 355,000 members. The merger gave birth to the **Union of Needletrades, Industrial & Textile Employees (UNITE),** which became one of the largest unions in the United States. The unions combined their strengths to have more power to fight imports and the rash of sweatshops that have developed in recent years in several major U.S. cities. UNITE also represents its members on wage and other labor issues of concern (Friedman, 1995a).

From Design Concept to Consumer

As garments go through the process of being designed and produced, many of the processes are similar from one company to another. A great deal of difference exists,

---

[1]The ACTWU included apparel workers who produced men's and boys' wear. Also included were employees in men's tailored wear firms that later produced women's tailored garments. The small portion of textile industry workers who were unionized were in this union.

however, in *how* the processes are organized and *how* they occur within the industry. For example, the way a company is organized affects how designs are developed and sewn.

How an Apparel Firm Is Organized

Apparel manufacturing firms must perform a certain number of basic functions regardless of the size of the firm or the product being made. Kunz (1995) has developed the following model to depict the functional areas within a modern apparel firm: executive management, merchandising, marketing, operations, and finance. Figure 5–3 illustrates the necessary interaction of these main areas and that activities of a company must be built around the needs and demands of the target market. All this must occur in a way that produces a profit.

Kunz (1995) provides the useful summary of each area's responsibility below. Following this summary, each area will be covered somewhat more in detail.

executive	establishes the firm's goals and administers activities to achieve them
merchandising	plans, develops, and presents product lines
marketing	defines target customer(s) and develops positioning and promotion strategies
operations	manages people and physical property
finance	manages financial resources (p. 257)

Figure 5–3

Functional areas and interactions within a modern apparel firm

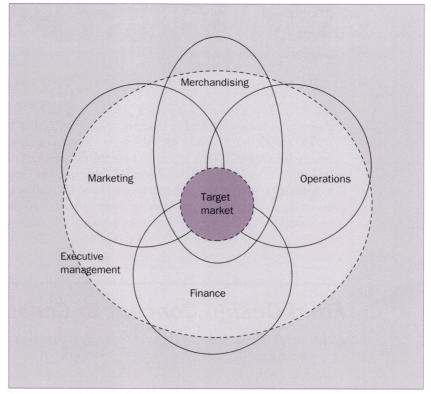

Source: From "Behavioral Theory of the Apparel Firm: A Beginning" by G. Kunz, 1995, *Clothing and Textiles Research Journal, 13*(4), p. 255. Reprinted courtesy of *Clothing and Textiles Research Journal.*

- *Executive management* sets the direction for a company and oversees the running of the company. This group makes decisions on such basics as the target markets to serve and product lines to produce. Position titles include chairman, president, chief executive officer (**CEO**), chief operating officer (**COO**), vice presidents of the major areas, director, and manager (Kunz, 1995).
- *Merchandising* in a manufacturing firm is more specific than marketing, concerning itself with the development, execution, and delivery of the product **line.** With its close ties to the market segment it serves, the merchandising function is not only able to adjust to market variations rapidly, but is capable of anticipating and helping to create market changes (Frank, 1985, p. 10). In short, merchandising includes directing and overseeing the development of product lines from start to finish. Position titles in this area may include designer, product development manager, merchandiser, product manager, and merchandise manager (Kunz, 1995, p. 256).
- *Marketing and sales.* Marketing focuses on (1) defining a company's market and identifying new opportunities for growth, (2) establishing the position of a company's products in relation to its competitors, and (3) determining advertising and promotional plans to reach sales goals. The sales division provides the link to get products to the retail customer and to give feedback on merchandise to appropriate personnel in the company. Position titles in this grouping may include market researcher, advertising manager, manufacturer's representative, sales manager, and sales representative (Frank, 1985; Glock & Kunz, 1995; Kunz, 1995).
- *Operations* manages people and physical property. These include human resources, physical facilities and equipment, inventories, and quality control. In many companies, operations is responsible for all activities associated with getting garments made and ready for the customer. Among the range of position titles are personnel manager, inventory controller, receiving manager, plant manager, apparel engineer, line manager, and sewing machine operator (Kunz, 1995). Sewing operators are the backbone of the company—the people who transform everyone else's plans into products to be sold (Figure 5–4).
- *Finance* personnel manage the financial aspects of the apparel firm to be sure enough profit is earned and to assure the company's financial future. This includes setting financial goals, monitoring financial performance, borrowing and spending money, managing **accounts receivable** and **accounts payable,** and keeping others in the company informed on financial matters. Among position titles often found in this area are controller, treasurer, accountant, and financial auditor.

In a very large apparel firm, experienced and more specialized staffs (usually teams) carry out these functions. In a smaller company, one individual may be responsible for a whole area or even multiple areas.

How Lines Are Developed

In the women's apparel industry, producers have traditionally prepared and presented (or "opened") new **seasonal lines** to be shown to retail store buyers. A line is a collection or group of styles designed for a specific season. In the women's apparel industry, four to six new lines or collections have been customary in the past: Spring, Summer or Transition, Fall I, Fall II, and Resort or Holiday. The opening dates and number of new lines have varied from one segment of the industry to another, but, as a general rule, higher priced lines have been presented before lower priced lines.

However, computer technology has revolutionized the whole idea of developing new lines. Now, because of computers, apparel firms can learn quickly from retailers what is selling. This permits the apparel firm to continually update its lines.

Sewing operators perform tasks that yield finished garments.

Source: Photo courtesy of Kellwood Company.

This strategy means that companies are thinking less and less in terms of discrete seasons and are moving toward a seasonless continuum of introducing new lines closer to the selling season.

Product Development and Design

In today's apparel industry, many variations exist regarding who does the designing and other aspects of developing a line. The size of the firm, the nature of the apparel produced, and the fashion orientation of the company influence how lines are developed.

In large apparel firms, **merchandisers** are responsible for developing new lines. Merchandisers plan the overall fashion direction for the coming season and give directions to the design staff about seasonal themes, types of items to be designed, and colors. A **product development** team is responsible for the planning and development of a particular product, product line, or brand. In the product development team, **designers** are primarily responsible for the creative aspect of product development. In a smaller company, the owner or sole designer may perform these tasks.

Designers: Owners or Employees

The authority, position, and name recognition of the designer vary greatly from one firm in the industry to another. In the majority of apparel firms, the designer is simply a hired talent, perhaps only one of several responsible for developing lines that will be presented under the manufacturer's firm name or brand name. Manufacturers generally hesitate to build up the name of a designer who could be working elsewhere next season. Therefore, the vast majority of the industry's designers are nameless as far as the public is concerned. Also in the industry are many small firms that do not even employ designers but rely on free-lance design services or on a patternmaker with a good sense of fashion.

Today the number of American designers whose names are well known to the public has increased. This is because they have become owners, partly or completely, of their own producing companies, operating in their own names, and featuring their names on labels, in national advertising, and in the fashion press. Among the best known and most successful are the companies of Calvin Klein, Ralph Lauren, Bill Blass, Oscar de la Renta, James Galanos, Nicole Miller, Adrienne Vittadini, Arnold Scaasi, Donna Karan, and Liz Claiborne.

Typical of the way a designer wins recognition by operating his or her own company is the story of Liz Claiborne. During the many years she worked for Jonathan Logan, she was unknown to the consuming public. In 1976, in conjunction with several partners, she formed her own company under her own name, and since then has become well known among manufacturers, retailers, the apparel-buying public—and even among investment strategists who take a lively interest in trading shares in her company which has a sales volume of more than $2 billion a year.

Designer-name firms generate relatively small sales volume, because their products are aimed and priced for a limited, affluent group of customers. Their importance, however, goes far beyond the dollars in their respective tills, because of the impact of their ideas on the fashion business and the fashion consumer. They are like the icing on the cake—a small but important part of the whole, and a part without which the cake would have little appeal.

Responsibilities of Designers

The designer, whoever he, she, or they may be, is expected to develop a group of new designs in advance of a marketing period—which, in turn, is in advance of the consumer buying period. In many instances, because fashion is basically an evolutionary process, each seasonal collection may include "new" designs that are simply updated versions of the current or past season's best sellers. Also included may be copied or revised versions of some other company's best sellers.

The designer's responsibilities go beyond ideas alone, and there are many practical obstacles to overcome. In addition to creating styles that will fit into the firm's price range and type of merchandise, the designer is responsible for the selection of fabrics and must give consideration also to the availability and cost of materials, the availability of production techniques, costs of labor, and the particular image that the company wishes to present. Great designers are those who can apply their creative talents and skills to overcome business limitations and produce salable merchandise.

Developing and Making a Garment: Major Stages

Product Development.

Design.   In high fashion apparel firms, designs may originate on the drawing board of its designers, who create new ideas and execute new lines four to six times per year. In these companies, the designer's ideas are made into sample garments by expert seamstresses known as sample makers. Revisions are made during these stages to give the effect the designer wants.

In a very large company a merchandiser plans the overall fashion direction for the coming season and gives directions to the design staff about seasonal themes, types of items to be designed, and colors and fabrics to be used. In a smaller company the owner or the designer will fulfill this function. Among less original manufacturers, designs often start life in the form of someone else's merchandise that has been sketched or purchased for copying.

For most other firms these days, designing takes place on computers that store many basic styles, including designs from previous lines (Figure 5–5). **Computer-aided design (CAD)** systems have led to many changes in the development of a design

Figure 5–5

(a) Pattern making with computer speed and accuracy are provided by pattern design systems, such as Gerber Garment Technology's AccuMark™ shown here. Patterns are easily drafted from scratch or modified from existing styles. (b) Computer systems such as Gerber Garment Technology's Product Data Management (PDM) system automate the entire product development cycle. PDM organizes fabric, sketches, patterns, sizing data, and labor and costing information. The information is available on a central database and can be accessed from any geographical location.

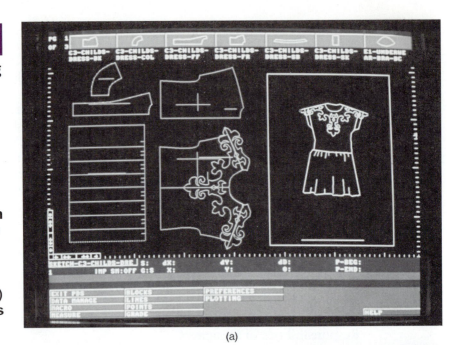

(a)

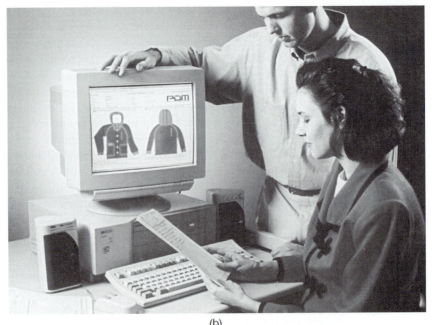

(b)

Source: Photos courtesy of Gerber Garment Technology, Inc.

up to the stage when production occurs. When creating new ideas for a line, the designer can sketch new garments on the screen and manipulate lines, silhouette, fabric patterns, color, and other design features. Although new designs will be made into samples and perfected through that process, the computer permits shortcuts for a significant portion of many companies' lines. Designs stored in the computer can be modified without having to go through the time-consuming process of making sample garments. By not having to go through the sample-making stage, a great deal of time is trimmed from the schedule for developing a line. Additionally, the computer sketches can be printed for use in meetings with company executives and retail buyers or for use in printed materials showing the line.

After tentative designs are developed, whether by computer or by the more traditional way, key teams in the company review garments for cost, production feasibility, **sourcing** for production, fabric requirements and availability, and profit potential. The decision is made at this point whether the garment will be accepted as part of the new line. Again, in small companies, one or two individuals may make these decisions.

Preproduction Operations. **Preproduction operations** are those between the stage when a style is accepted in the line and when the cut garment pieces are sent to the sewing floor (Glock & Kunz, 1995).

Making the pattern. If a design is to be produced, it moves to the next stage of having a pattern made for the garment. Traditionally, a highly skilled pattern maker made the master production pattern for the garment—in one size only (whatever size the firm used for its samples). Some high style design houses may still use this traditional way extensively. Other firms may use this only in the very early stages of developing patterns for designs for which no similar pattern exists in the computer's memory.

Again, computers have revolutionized this stage for much of the industry. Many companies today store a large portion of their basic patterns in the computer's memory. In the product development stage, a company can modify an existing pattern for many new styles without having to start from the beginning. Additionally, patterns made by more traditional ways can be entered into the computer by digitizing or scanning them into the computer. Then, the designer can manipulate and modify those patterns on the computer.

Making samples for sales representatives. After designs are selected for the line, duplicate samples (in the sample size) are produced for sales representatives. Samples are shown to buyers in showrooms in New York and/or some of the regional marts, or sales representatives may take samples with them on the road as they call on retailers. Orders placed with sales representatives determine the quantity of various styles to be produced.

Pattern grading. After a basic pattern is perfected, **grading** occurs to produce a pattern for that garment in all the sizes in which it will be offered. Traditionally, pattern graders were highly skilled individuals whose tedious work made a great deal of difference in how wearers felt about the fit of garments. Grading is equally important now, but computers expedite this task greatly in most firms.

Body scanning technology, already in use to a limited extent, will permit manufacturers to scan the customer's body and generate a pattern uniquely sized for that person's body. When this process is more commonly available, pattern grading may seem old fashioned.

Marker making. The next step after grading is **marker** making. The marker is made according to the ratio of orders. The marker is a long paper diagram that shows placement of all of the various pattern pieces for all the sizes produced as they should be laid out in order to cut the cloth economically and with bias and straight **grainlines** where each is needed. Computers generate most of today's markers because of the great savings in fabric achieved through more efficient markers (Figure 5–6a).

Spreading. In preparation for cutting, layers of fabric are rolled out on long tables, often as many as 100 or more plies high. In the past, spreading occurred manually as workers moved fabric rolls from one end of the cutting table to the other. Now, automatic spreading machines are available to perform this step.

Figure 5–6

(a) Computer technologies permit efficient marker making. The placement shown on the screen is transmitted to a printer that prints the marker in full scale for manual cutting or transfers it to a computerized cutter with this layout stored in its memory. (b) Automated cutters, such as this GERBERcutter®, cut garments with precision and speed.

(a)

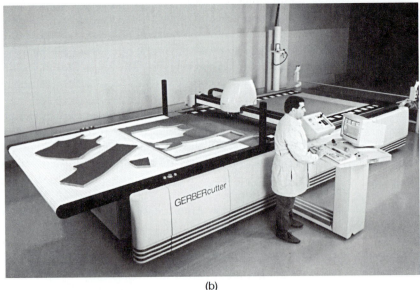

(b)

Source: Photos courtesy of Gerber Garments Technology, Inc.

Cutting.   Cutting occurs next, with the marker providing the cutting plan. The number of orders received or realistically anticipated determines the number of garments to be cut at this stage. The decision on the number of units to be produced must fit the company's broad business plan—that is, the number of units that must be produced to meet the company's financial goals. Risk is a concern. Companies do not want excessive inventory left over if they produce too many units in the line. In recent years, firms tend to be conservative on the number to cut at this stage. Instead, they test the market with a limited number of units. Unless items are basic, the company is more likely to make garments according to orders received rather than making them to have in stock.

Firms vary on the minimum number of garments they will cut. For example, producers whose dresses retail at medium to higher prices say that they require orders of 100 to 500 units of a number before cutting. On the other hand, one producer whose coats employ carefully hand-cut leather in their designs and whose retail prices are very high stated that he will start production with orders for as few as 10 units. For manufacturers that are producing for mass distribution, the number of units considered a minimum for a production order may be counted in the thousands. Each producer has to work out its own minimum, in terms of how many units can be expected to be sold to customers and how much must be realized in profit on the sales of a given number to offset the costs of putting it into production, in addition to other costs.

For actual cutting, layers of fabric are rolled out on long tables. The way in which cutting occurs depends on the size of the company and the extent to which it spends money to buy modern time-saving equipment. In traditional methods, the marker is placed on top of the layered fabric. In these cutting methods, a person called a cutter uses electrically powered portable knives and follows lines on the marker to cut through fabric layered several inches deep, sometimes as many as 150 plies.

Newer cutting technology automates and expedites the cutting step. Among these, the most common is the computerized cutter, which has the marker stored in its memory; therefore, the paper marker is not required (Figure 5–6b). An automated cutting head quickly moves about, cutting multiple layers of fabric and stopping from time to time to resharpen the cutting blades. Laser cutters are also available, and although these do excellent precision cutting, most types cannot cut through thick layers of fabrics. High-tech cutting equipment is very costly, frequently placing it out of reach of smaller companies.

Production: Garment Assembly.

The cut parts of the garments are then collected, identified, and passed along for the sewing operation. This is done in the firm's own plant if it is an **inside shop** or to a contractor—either in the United States or another country—for the sewing. If it is an **outside shop,** in some instances, contractors do the cutting, working from the marker and continuing on from that point.

Firms vary in the type of production systems used to sew the garments. The basic types follow.

Single operator. In this system, sometimes known as the tailor system, a single operator does all the machine sewing on a garment. This system is used for expensive or customized garments that require highly skilled workers.

Progressive bundle system. In this system, workers generally sew one part of the garment in an assembly line manner. The name for this system comes from the cut bundles of garment pieces that are distributed to operators who sew their part and then pass the item on to the next operator. In this system, workers are usually paid by the number of items they produce (also known as the *piece rate* system).

Modular production system. In this system, small teams of operators work in a group to produce garments from start to finish. Workers in the module generally are able to perform more than one task. They often have autonomy to set their own production goals. Many companies have shifted from the bundle system to the modular approach. Pay systems vary, but often bonuses are given to the team based on quality, productivity, and meeting deadlines.

Final Stages.

Inspection. Garments are inspected after final assembly. This occurs either in the module or in a separate inspection department for the progressive bundle system. This stage is a final check to be sure garments meet the quality standards expected.

Finishing. After inspection, workers trim loose threads and prepare the garment for pressing.

Pressing.   Garments are pressed to give a pleasing appearance to shoppers who will view finished items. Many retailers now want garments ready to put on the floor without additional pressing in the store.

Ticketing.   As more and more retail stores are demanding that garments be preticketed by the manufacturer, the price tag and other hang tags may be attached at this stage.

Shipping.   Garments are prepared for shipping to retail customers. Sometimes items are shipped in boxes, but for some kinds of garments, retailers now demand they be shipped in hanging cartons so they are ready for the sales floor.

As our discussion has indicated, a great many decisions and activities are part of the apparel development and production process. Each step is important in producing merchandise customers will find in their favorite stores. The women's apparel industry is distinguished by the rapidity with which it produces and distributes its goods. In a business that must keep up with changing fashion, it is vital to surmount time and distance factors by speed and flexibility in production. The industry maintains an impressive record in doing so.

Although consumers usually do not understand all the steps involved in getting a garment to the sales floor, many people have contributed in important ways to produce and deliver that garment. Figure 5–7 provides an estimate of the cost of each of these aspects that go into making and selling a garment.

The Role of Computers in Revolutionizing the Industry

Computers are dramatically transforming the apparel industry in ways not seen since the invention of the sewing machine. Nearly every aspect of the industry now incorporates some form of computerization. New technology enables the industry to speed up the product development process, preassembly operations, manufacturing processes, and finishing operations while reducing labor time per garment. Computers also contribute in these other areas: production planning, marketing, sales, financial management, inspection of fabrics, costing, programmable sewing machines, unit production systems that move garments in a conveyor manner from one operation to another during the sewing process, and state-of-the-art automated warehouse facilities. For many companies, the computer makes possible easy communication and transfer of information from one company location to another—even when some facilities are located halfway around the world.

Early computer applications for the industry focused mostly on a single aspect of the product development or production process. Computerization in one activity was not linked to that in others. Data had to be reentered at each stage. Today the goal is to integrate multiple computerized activities, a concept known as **computer integrated manufacturing (CIM).**

Large apparel firms have an advantage over smaller ones in being able to buy and use the range of new technologies. A company must have adequate capital to be able to buy costly equipment and to employ specialists who can operate it.

Quick Response

As described in a previous chapter, **Quick Response (QR)** is an industry-wide strategy for quick and precise replenishment of fast-selling merchandise. Today, many apparel companies are participating in computerized partnerships with retail customers and fabric suppliers, which is enabling them to accelerate their manufacturing process and provide customers with more timely delivery of currently wanted merchandise. By

| Figure 5–7 | **Behind the price tag of a $73.00 skirt** |

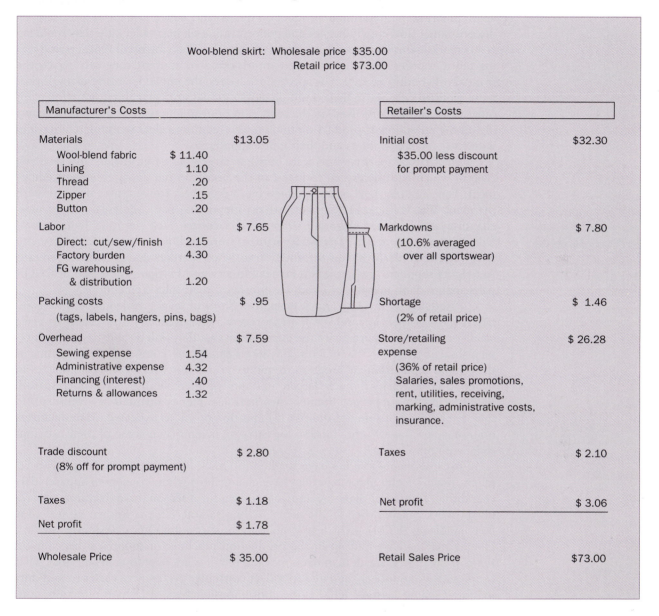

Wool-blend skirt: Wholesale price $35.00
Retail price $73.00

Manufacturer's Costs		
Materials		$13.05
Wool-blend fabric	$ 11.40	
Lining	1.10	
Thread	.20	
Zipper	.15	
Button	.20	
Labor		$ 7.65
Direct: cut/sew/finish	2.15	
Factory burden	4.30	
FG warehousing, & distribution	1.20	
Packing costs		$ .95
(tags, labels, hangers, pins, bags)		
Overhead		$ 7.59
Sewing expense	1.54	
Administrative expense	4.32	
Financing (interest)	.40	
Returns & allowances	1.32	
Trade discount		$ 2.80
(8% off for prompt payment)		
Taxes		$ 1.18
Net profit		$ 1.78
Wholesale Price		**$ 35.00**

Retailer's Costs	
Initial cost	$32.30
$35.00 less discount for prompt payment	
Markdowns	$ 7.80
(10.6% averaged over all sportswear)	
Shortage	$ 1.46
(2% of retail price)	
Store/retailing expense	$ 26.28
(36% of retail price) Salaries, sales promotions, rent, utilities, receiving, marking, administrative costs, insurance.	
Taxes	$ 2.10
Net profit	$ 3.06
Retail Sales Price	**$73.00**

Note: These calculations vary from firm to firm. Assumptions for the **manufacturing** portion of this example: returns and allowances=3.8% of wholesale price, total costs of goods sold (materials, labor, factory burden, FG warehousing and distribution)=70.1% of wholesale price, and net profit=5.8% of wholesale price. Assumptions for the **retailing** portion of this example are: markdowns=10.6% of retail price, shortages=2% of retail price, store expenses=36% of retail price, taxes=40% of gross income, and net profit=4.1% of retail price.

Source: The authors wish to express appreciation to the following executives at Kellwood Company who provided updated calculations for this figure: John Turnage, Deane Thompson, Roseanne Grady, and John Henderson (formerly with May Department Stores). These figures reflect business conditions for both industry sectors in the 1990s.

means of electronic data interchange, participating apparel producers receive an instant and continuing flow of information about what their "retail partners" are selling by style, sizes, and colors, and what needs to be replenished. This information enables them to predetermine production plans and schedules more precisely by discontinuing slow-moving styles and concentrating on best sellers, thereby reducing costly markdowns and increasing turnover. Also, by receiving retail reorders and giving fabric reorders directly into their interlocking computers, they can bypass the manual order entry process. For apparel producers, the implementation of a QR program requires a change in their traditional operational strategies and production planning which formerly focused on the reduction of production costs and is now focusing on the reduction of production time. It also requires a clear working relationship with their retail customers and their fabric suppliers.

The first QR partnerships were between large-volume producers and retailers, each of which had the capital to invest in the necessary but costly electronic equipment. For example, Levi Strauss, which has a computer-to-computer network with the giant Wal-Mart retail company, affixes identifying bar code labels on its merchandise and provides elaborate software services to track the sales in its stores. Dillard's, one of America's largest department stores, is linked to major suppliers with which it electronically shares information to place reorders and to pinpoint trends. Among its suppliers are Sara Lee's Hanes Hosiery and Haggar. These and other QR participants claim that the program has increased their sales tremendously.

Fast delivery (through Quick Response) is one of several added expectations retailers have of their apparel suppliers in recent years. Retailers now prefer to place smaller orders for apparel, with the expectation that they will be able to get quick replenishment from the manufacturer as items sell. Some companies refer to this as their **rapid replenishment** program. Retailers prefer this over previous strategies in which they purchased much larger amounts of merchandise early in a season. Retailers like this approach because they have less money invested in inventory and they are relieved of some of the risk if items do not sell as expected. Manufacturers often have to assume more burden for carrying inventory in some of their relationships with retailers.

Because manufacturers have worked in Quick Response partnerships with retailers, much shorter planning cycles have changed the whole concept of apparel merchandising. Instead of planning and committing for a season, manufacturers and retailers work much closer to the actual selling season. This is known as **real time merchandising (RTM)**—which is at the core of successful Quick Response systems. Having merchandise tied up in the production pipeline for months is becoming a thing of the past. Instead, manufacturers and retailers are operating in *real time*. That is, lines are continuously updated to reflect consumer preferences closer to and during retail selling seasons. RTM is the continuous analysis of fashion direction, consumer style testing results, and current retail sales. Under real time merchandising, the line planning calendar becomes a flexible and more responsive tool for merchandisers, not a strait jacket (Brown, 1989). Figure 5–8 depicts the basic steps in real time merchandising.

Industry consultants Kurt Salmon Associates (KSA) predict that Quick Response, as the industry knows it today, someday will not exist as a chain with its distinct functions (i.e., different segments in the softgoods chain). Instead, we will have an interlocking complex that revolves around the consumer. Speed, electronic linkages, and strategic alliances among companies will be "givens" in the future. KSA concludes that companies *will have to be quick to survive* (Kurt Salmon Associates, 1995).

Figure 5–8 ### Quick response real time merchandising

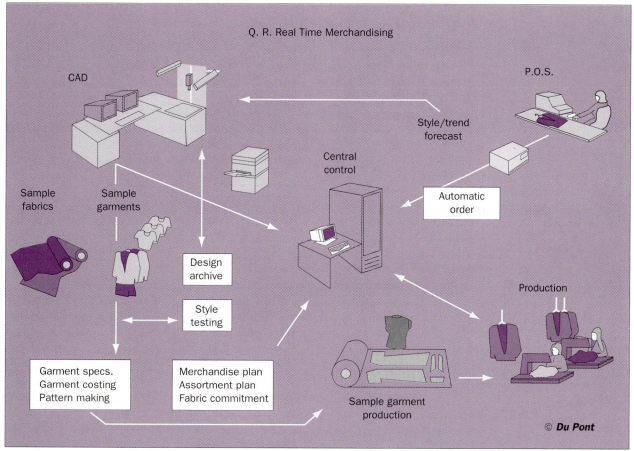

Q. R. Real Time Merchandising

CAD

P.O.S.

Style/trend
forecast

Central
control

Automatic
order

Sample
fabrics

Sample
garments

Design
archive

Style
testing

Production

Garment specs.
Garment costing
Pattern making

Merchandise plan
Assortment plan
Fabric commitment

Sample garment
production

© *Du Pont*

"Real time merchandising" starts with analysis of what is selling, proceeds to consumer style testing of sample designs, and follows with short-lot production of styles that proved most popular in consumer tests. Initial sales, monitored by size and color, guide production for fill-in stock and provide styling guidance for following seasons.

Source: Reprinted by permission of DuPont.

Another strategy called **agile manufacturing** was introduced to the industry by the Textile/Clothing Technology Corporation, [TC]^2, in late 1993. [TC]^2 is an industry/government-funded program that develops leading-edge competitive strategies for the apparel industry. The agile manufacturing concept might be considered Quick Response with a higher rate of flexibility, or QR made-to-order. It is considered a strategy for twenty-first-century manufacturing, which may go from the cash register to design, to cut fabric, to screen printing, to assembly, and to shipping in a matter of hours. As [TC]^2 managing director Joe Off noted:

> "In an agile . . . world, we need to be able to design and deliver new products very quickly. Products are designed to evolve. Patterns on shorts today, for example, are not selling well tomorrow. We can immediately redesign that pattern and start shipping a new product in a day's time. It's designed to evolve so it's produced to order" (Clune, 1993, p. 8).

Marketing Procedures

Over the years, the women's apparel industry has established a pattern of selling directly to retailers, supplementing the efforts of producers' salespeople with advertising and publicity. This practice of direct selling, from producer to retailer, is related to the need for speed in the marketing time for ever-changing fashions. Since timing in fashion is of utmost importance, there is no real place for wholesale middlemen in the marketing of fashion goods. Such middlemen would have to buy, warehouse, and sell—distribution procedures too time-consuming to be practical except for staple items such as basic hosiery and undergarments, and any other articles in which fashion change is fairly slow.

Presentation of Lines

The methods of introducing new lines to buyers vary. Some firms show their new collections accessorized, dramatized, and professionally modeled in elaborate fashion shows. These shows may be staged in ballrooms, chic restaurants, discos, and other "in" locations. Other companies simply have their lines ready in their showrooms, where the garments are on racks, to be taken down and shown to individual retail buyers for inspection and possible purchase. Some firms stage press previews of their new collections, to which they invite fashion editors in order to get publicity to the consuming public. Others show their lines only to publications in which they are eager to have a "credit"— an editorial mention of one of their numbers. The method and timing of presenting new lines varies from firm to firm, and from one branch of the industry to another.

The initial presentation of a line, however, is only the beginning of a manufacturer's selling effort, since relatively few retail store buyers will be present at the opening. For the benefit of late-comers, the line will continue to be shown at the company's headquarters or showrooms, although without the initial fanfare and probably without live models. For the benefit of retail store buyers who may not have seen the line while in the market, or who may not have come at all, the firm may send it out with traveling sales representatives, or exhibit it at regional showrooms and trade shows, or it may do all of these.

Beginning in 1992, nearly all major U.S. designers banded together to centralize and unify their fall and spring fashion showings. Today, most leading U.S. designers are collaborating and staging their opening seasonal runway shows under large tents in Bryant Park, which is next door to New York's Public Library. The Bryant Park showings are under the auspices of "Seventh on Sixth," a non-profit organization put together for the seasonal shows by the Council of Fashion Designers of America. Important cogs in this event are corporate sponsors that underwrite costs in addition to rental fees from the participating designer companies, which range from $13,000 to $25,000, depending on showing time and seating capacity of the tents.

Reliance on a Sales Force

By and large, women's apparel producers rely on their own salespeople to bring the products to the attention of retail store buyers. Most firms maintain selling staffs in their showrooms to wait on visiting retail store buyers and to build a following among retailers who are potential customers. Some firms also employ road salespeople who travel with sample lines to show their merchandise to retailers within their assigned territories. These men and women may also set up temporary displays in any regional trade shows that take place in their territories. In addition, many of the larger firms supplement their headquarters showrooms with regional showrooms.

For those manufacturers who do not have their own sales staffs or regional sales offices, there are independent selling representatives that maintain permanent show-rooms and represent several noncompeting lines in given areas.

The industry usually pays its salespeople on a commission basis, except for those who staff the showroom in the headquarters office.

Advertising and Publicity: National and Trade

Before the 1960s, the names of American designers and garment manufacturers were not generally well known to customers; apparel was purchased by a combination of approval of a garment's appearance and confidence in the retail seller. The source of a garment or accessory was considered the retailer's trade secret; the store's label was of paramount importance.

The rise of giant apparel firms in the 1960s gave impetus to the development of brand names and their promotion by national advertising campaigns. This advertising was aided by the **cooperative advertising** funds made available by the giant producers of manufactured fibers such as Dacron (by DuPont) and Kodel (by Eastman). These were (and still are) arrangements under which the manufacturer and fiber company share the cost of advertising, which is run in the manufacturer's name and features the fiber brand in order to promote it to the consumer. The national advertising of "names" became increasingly important when designers of higher priced merchandise went into business for themselves, either alone or with partners, and established the manufacturing companies that today bear their names. The amount of brand- and designer-name national advertising done by the apparel industry today is very impressive in comparison with this almost nonexistent type of industry advertising prior to the 1960s, but it is still small alongside what is spent by such other major industries as food, drugs, autos, and electronics. In addition to the national advertising done by large brand- or designer-name companies, all fashion manufacturers make widespread use of trade publications as advertising media to bring their names and products to the attention of retailers. The small and specialized circulation of these publications brings their advertising rates far below those of consumer publications, and thus an apparel producer does not have to be large to make good use of them. Among those widely used are *Women's Wear Daily, California Apparel News,* and *Body Fashions/Intimate Apparel.* All of these are supported by the advertising of small and large producers.

Also common in the apparel business are cooperative advertising arrangements between retailers and apparel manufacturers. In these arrangements the advertising appears under the store's name and features the manufacturer's name or brand. In such an arrangement, the retailer enjoys more advertising space than is paid for out of pocket; the manufacturer enjoys advertising that is run in conjunction with the name of a locally known and respected retail store and that is usually backed up by the store with a substantial stock of that maker's goods. The retailer, moreover, as a large and consistent purchaser of space in the local papers, pays a much lower rate for this space than the manufacturer could obtain for its occasional insertions. "Co-op" money buys the producer more space for less cost.

Other promotional techniques include providing retailers with selling aids: customer mailing pieces and newspaper advertising mats and photographs for use in store advertisements, for example.

Many of the larger firms also employ publicity agents. It is through their efforts that many of the fashion articles that appear on the life-style pages of newspapers have their origin. Press releases, often accompanied by fashion photographs of high quality, are sent directly to newspaper editors or, in some cases, to local stores for forwarding to the editors.

Designer Trunk Shows

Another marketing technique used by many well-known designers is the **trunk show.** A trunk show is a showing by a manufacturing company of its complete line to consumers assembled in a major retail store. A key company salesperson is in attendance, and often the designer makes a personal appearance. There are also live models to exhibit the garments. Such shows are backed by heavy local advertising and publicity. The consumer has the opportunity not only to see the manufacturer's complete line, but also to order through the store any styles, sizes, and colors not available in the store's stocks, since it is usually impossible for any store to stock an entire line. Designers get a firsthand view of consumer reaction; retailers observe consumer response to style numbers they did not select as well as to those already chosen for resale; producers and retailers gain sales from the impact of the promotion. Many designers say there is nothing like a trunk show for stimulating interest in and sales of their merchandise.

New Technology

New computer and communication technologies provide many new ways to view a line. These might include fashion shows via communication satellite, viewing a line on the Internet, or a compact disk.

Manufacturers into Retailing

Today, many apparel-producing companies, dissatisfied with the capabilities of their retail customers to efficiently market their products, are taking an increasingly active role in retailing their own merchandise. Instead of depending exclusively upon retail accounts to buy and sell their products, more and more apparel manufacturers are also selling directly to the consumer through company-owned retail shops, factory outlets, and their own separately run shops within the retail stores that buy their merchandise. Some reach the consumer directly through catalogs, the Internet, or television home shopping. Usually these retail activities represent a small portion of the company's total sales, and there appears to be no intention on the part of these producers to abandon manufacturing in favor of retailing. Their aims are to seek a larger share of the consumer market, to "showcase" their entire line, and to be less dependent upon retailers to buy and distribute their merchandise.

Manufacturer-Owned Retail Stores

The manufacturer-owned retail stores have long been an established channel of distribution in the menswear industry, as is discussed in Chapter 6. In the women's apparel field, however, the trend toward company-owned retail stores accelerated in the 1980s as more and more women's apparel manufacturers moved into their own retail operations in ever-increasing numbers. These company stores are located in prime shopping areas, carry a large and complete stock of the firm's products at regular prices, have an attractive environment, and offer many customer services.

Some industry observers believe that these company-owned stores essentially bring them into direct competition with their retail accounts. For many retailers, this trend is very distressing. Table 5–3 reflects the significant growth of this trend, with data for selected firms.

The relatively new company stores that have been discussed above should be distinguished from the manufacturers' underselling factory outlets that have been around for decades. These older factory outlets were usually sparsely located, in out-of-the-way factory town locations, and were stocked with an incomplete assortment of irregulars, seconds, and excess out-of-season merchandise—an inevitable by-product of mass-produced ready-to-wear that was unsalable at regular prices. Today's newer factory outlet developments, however, generally carry a good deal of new, first-quality merchandise. The current proliferation of factory outlets is discussed in the retailing chapter.

Manufacturers' Shops within Stores

Producers with strong images are further playing an increasingly active role in the presentation and sale of their own merchandise by means of their own separate "named" (i.e., brand or designer) shops within the large retail stores to which they sell. In co-operative operations such as these, the retailer provides the "real estate" (the space within the store) and is credited with the sales volume of the department. Although financial arrangements vary, the vendors participate in the design and fixturing of their department and pay all or part of the cost for setting them up as well as the costs of advertising. The department's selling personnel either are employed and paid by the manufacturer directly or are the retailer's employees whom the manufacturer has specially trained. The quantity and quality of the merchandise assortment, as well as its presentation, are determined by the manufacturer.

In order for manufacturers to be given their own department within a store, their merchandise must appeal to the store's targeted customers, and the vendor must guarantee the retail company that it can provide continuity as well as a minimum

Table 5–3	Selected Apparel Manufacturers That Operate Retail Stores	
Company	**Full-Price Stores**	**Factory Outlets**
Calvin Klein	4	15
Elisabeth	21	0
Liz Claiborne	28	56
Nike	4	33
Original Levi Store	11	0
Osh Kosh B'Gosh	1	65
Ralph Lauren	130*	—
Reebok	3	55
Speedo	58	0

*Includes international stores and factory outlets.
Source: From "When Vendors Become Retailers" by S. Reda, June, 1995, Stores, p. 21.
Reprinted from Stores magazine, NRF Enterprises, Inc., 1995.

amount of sales on which the retailer will achieve a required gross profit. The ability to provide enough merchandise to keep the shop filled and to keep that merchandise moving is also a vital consideration for the retailer.

The companies of Liz Claiborne and Ralph Lauren have been leaders in this "shop-within-a-shop" concept with their creation of "Liz Shops" and "Polo" shops. Their success encouraged other manufacturers to follow suit.

Nature of the Industry

Apparel producers vary widely as to size, product, and type of operation. Small companies coexist with giant firms. Specialists rub shoulders with firms that, through their various divisions, can dress a person from the skin out and for every conceivable occasion. Self-contained operations and plants that perform no more than a single step of the production process, publicly owned giant companies and small privately owned firms, fashion creators and flagrant copiers—all are found in the industry.

Different Types of Producers

Apparel manufacturers do not always handle the entire production of a garment in their own factories; they may contract out some of the work. The U.S. Census of Manufacturers, therefore, divides the industry's firms into three classifications according to the comprehensiveness of their production activities: manufacturers, apparel jobbers, and contractors. Common usage, however, employs different criteria and terminology.

Manufacturers

Classified as **manufacturers** by the census are those firms that buy fabric and do the designing, patternmaking, grading, cutting, sewing, and assembling of garments in factories that they own. In the industry, factories that are wholly owned by a manufacturing company are known as **inside shops,** whether or not all steps in production are performed on the same premises. A major advantage of such integrated operation is that there is complete control over the production quality of the product. A disadvantage is that the necessary factory facilities and machinery require large capital investments.

In reality today, however, few large firms commonly considered "apparel manufacturers" would qualify under the census terminology as *manufacturers*. In common usage, firms considered apparel *manufacturers* in the 1990s by industry executives, trade associations, industry publications, Wall Street analysts, and others who follow the industry may actually perform a very limited number of the tasks in the census definition. For example, in a summary of the top U.S. apparel firms' sales for 1995 in *Women's Wear Daily* ("Apparel Manufacturers'," 1996), a leading trade publication for the industry, perhaps only one of the top 10 companies is not actively involved in contracting production outside the respective firms' own facilities. Some use domestic contractors, and nearly all of them use extensive overseas contracting. For example, the Liz Claiborne company invariably appears on the list of apparel manufacturers in industry sources; however, all production is contracted outside the firm's facilities—and a very large portion of that production is performed by overseas contractors.

Therefore, the term *manufacturer,* as it is generally used within the industry today, has a much broader interpretation than the census definition. Industry use of the term refers to any firm that develops garments, controls production, sells to retailers (and, in some cases, directly to end-use customers), and ships and bills merchandise. Firms may or may not buy the fabrics to be used. Today, mostly only smaller apparel companies conform to the limited census definition for apparel manufacturers.

Apparel Jobbers

What the census defines as an **apparel jobber** is a firm that generally handles all processes but the sewing, and sometimes the cutting, and that contracts out these production processes to independently owned outside contracting facilities. The majority of women's apparel firms, both small and large, high priced and low priced, contract out their sewing and often their cutting, as well as any other highly specialized production processes such as embroidery, quilting, and pleating, which require special machinery. One advantage of using outside facilities in this way is that minimal capital investment is required. A disadvantage is that there is less quality control.

The Contracting System: Outside Shops

There are independently owned factories that own their machinery and employ operators to sew and often cut goods from the designs, materials, and specifications of the apparel jobbers that hire them. Both the census and the industry refer to such factories as **contractors.**

The contracting system evolved early in the history of the industry. Prior to 1880, the manufacture of women's apparel was generally accomplished, in all its steps, under one roof. However, as ready-made clothing began to be produced in volume, it became common practice to perform in one place only such key operations as designing, patternmaking, grading, cutting, inspection, selling, and shipping. Most of the sewing tasks were contracted out to individual women who worked in their homes. This was a "cottage industry" procedure in which women added to the family income by doing piece work sewing at home. Eventually, this production shifted to privately owned factories that were devoted entirely to such work. This system of employing outside production facilities—the contracting process—continues to play an important role. The burden of seasonal idleness and production peaks can be shifted to entrepreneur contractors, along with the investment in sewing machines and the dealings with labor.

Contractors are used by both small and large firms, and a large individual company may use hundreds of different sewing shops at the height of the producing season (Figure 5–9). Even firms with their own "inside" production facilities hire independent contractors for extra capacity in busy periods; still others subsidize contracting shops. This system of using outside production facilities also enables manufacturers to diversify their product mix to meet changing consumer demands. For example, sportswear producers may one season need jackets in their lines and the following season need sweaters. The contracting system makes it possible for them to adjust and change their lines without making large dollar investments in new equipment. Most contractors specialize in a particular category of merchandise. Some of them work only for one company; others do contract work for several different firms.

Today the women's clothing industry is a maze of inside and outside shops, of contracting and subcontracting and contracting beyond that. This system makes it possible for newcomers with salable ideas but limited capital to swing into large-scale production almost overnight, through the simple device of hiring the contractor's plant, labor, and production know-how. Contractors need not be located in the major market centers. Nowadays, they are located not only in every section of this country, but almost everywhere in the world where labor is abundant, facilities are available, and wages are reasonable.

Figure 5–9

Examples of the contracting system

Contract Work Wanted

ATTN: MFRS
Long est. contractor in NYC doing business w/K-Mart, Limited, Express, etc. Exp in all phases of sewing & finishing. Production capacity 2000 dozen/week. Quick turn. Specialize in knits.   608-555-1240

America's most advanced contract service for all apparel
Contract Apparel Network
555-488-9122
FAX 319-555-9141

CUT & SEW FACTORY
In Dominican Republic is looking for long term 807 relationship. We can handle small or large programs.
515-555-8070

CUT & SEW
Small orders. Will pick up & deliver. Or you cut, I sew. Call (608)555-3266

Immediate Production - Private Label Program. Sportswear - Outerwear.
Ph: (312) 555-1834   Fax (608) 5554910

L. I. Cutting Service. Large & small lots, markers & copies. Good prices.
319-555-1795.

Contractors Wanted

Children's Activewear
Mfr seeks contractors in NY/NJ, Carolinas area. Please contact Russell
515-555-4551

Not all contractors abide by accepted labor standards of how workers are treated and paid. Unfortunately this means no one is looking after the welfare of the workers employed in these shops.

Size of Apparel Companies

In matters of size, as in almost every other characteristic, the apparel industry presents enormous variety. There are huge companies that devote themselves entirely to the women's wear business; there are other enormous companies that have one or more divisions in this field; and there are the small fry. Despite the emergence of giant firms, the trend toward consolidation, the presence of conglomerates, and all the other indications of bigness, the women's apparel industry remains a stronghold of small business—more so perhaps than any other major industry.

Dominance of Small Specialized Firms

The U.S. apparel industry consists of nearly 25,000 establishments, more than half of which employ fewer than 20 workers (American Apparel Manufacturers Association, 1995).

Many of these firms are contractors whose very existence makes it possible for an enterprising and creative person with a flair for fashion and selling ability to set up an apparel company and hope to prosper. Except for the purchase of fabric, little else is needed in the way of capital outlay, since the cutting and sewing can thus be farmed out. The key to success is in producing styles that will find acceptance. In that respect, the small firm is viable and has an equal chance with a large one. The small entrepreneur has the further advantage of being able to move quickly to exploit sudden fashion shifts. On the other hand, a single poor season can wipe out a small, undercapitalized firm—and often does.

Today, small reputable specialized producers continue to set the fashion pace for the industry as some of the country's leading designers give splendid proof of how a small firm can flourish. The companies such as those of Bill Blass, Anne Klein, Geoffrey Beene, and Oscar de la Renta, for example, are relatively small; their individual sales volume figures exclusive of licensing royalties are in most cases less than $100 million. Although their target customers are women who spend a great deal on a single garment, their combined spending for fashion is a drop in the bucket compared with the volume done by moderate-priced apparel companies that cater to the great mass of American consumers. Dollar volume alone, however, does not measure the importance of the designers and their firms. The publicity they generate in the news media, plus the impact of the fashion news embodied in their garments and their licensed names, constitutes a major element in keeping the general public aware of fashion and the American fashion industry.

No matter how much the future holds for further merging and giantism in the apparel industry, one can be sure that there will always be a pool of small manufacturers that are innovative and flexible and have a clear view of what their small, special target customer group wants. As an element in the apparel industry, the small producer will survive. Those who fall by the wayside are sure to be replaced by newcomers.

Multiproduct Giant Companies

Although the greatest majority of apparel companies have an annual sales volume of less than $100 million, today there are some multiproduct giant companies involved in the production of apparel whose sales volume is far in excess of that figure. All have expanded either by diversification or by acquiring other companies. Three outstanding examples of giant companies that have diversified their product mix are Liz Claiborne, with sales in excess of $2 billion; Kellwood Company, with sales of $1.5 billion; and Levi Strauss, whose 1995 sales were $6.7 billion ("Apparel Manufacturers," 1996). Liz Claiborne, who began her business in 1976 as a sportswear producer, expanded into dresses, menswear, and accessories. Kellwood went from a producer of moderate-priced apparel primarily for Sears, Roebuck, and Co. to one that now sells merchandise to all retail levels from upscale to discount stores. Levi Strauss added women's wear to their menswear.

A second type of diversified giant company, exemplified by Warnaco and Vanity Fair, each of which started as undergarment producers, moved into new fields by acquiring other companies already active in the area in which they wished to function. For instance, under the $5 billion corporate umbrella of VF Corporation (which evolved from Vanity Fair) one will find the following separate divisions: Lee Jeans, Wrangler Jeans, Girbaud, Jantzen, and Bassett Walker, among others (Table 5–4). VF's companies are positioned to serve different types of retailers. For example Girbaud sells jeans in up-market stores, and Rustler is sold by discounters. In the table, we see how both VF's jeans brands and its lingerie brands are targeted to span the distribution spectrum. VF Corporation owns additional companies besides those shown in the table.

A third type of giant company is composed of conglomerates whose business activities involve companies operating in widely diversified fields. For example, Sara Lee, originally a food company, owns Hanes, Playtex, L'eggs, Bali, Coach Leathergoods, Mark Cross, and Isotoner.

Giant apparel companies, however, are actually multiproduct aggregates of small and medium-sized business divisions, each of which concentrates on a range of products targeted to a specific consumer market segment and operates quite autonomously. Conglomerates such as VF Corporation, Sara Lee, and Kellwood are each a "family" of companies held under a corporate umbrella. In such setups, each specialized product division draws on the parent firm for financing and for policy decisions, but each

Table 5–4	**VF Corporation: Multiple Brands and Distribution**				
	Department Stores	Mass Merchandiser	Discount	Specialty	International
Jeans Brands					
Girbaud	☐				
Lee	☐	☐			☐
Riders			☐		
Wrangler-Hero			☐		
Wrangler-Western				☐	☐
Wrangler-Rugged Wear				☐	
Timber Creek			☐		
Rustler			☐		
Maverick					☐
Lingerie Brands					
Vanity Fair	☐	☐			☐
Eileen West	☐				
Vassarette			☐		
Barbizon				☐	
Lou					☐
Bolero					☐
Variance					☐
Carina					☐
Siltex					☐
Silhouette					☐
Belcor					☐
Intima Cherry					☐
Gemma					☐
Private Label	☐	☐	☐	☐	

Source: From *VF annual report 1994* by VF Corporation, 1995, Wyomissing, PA: Author.

one has its own name, its own clearly defined product area, its own design staff, its own contractors, its own selling force, and even its own advertising.

Specialization by Products and Prices

Traditionally there has been a high degree of product and price line specialization among industry firms. Small companies generally limit themselves to a particular category of garments such as sportswear, evening wear, bridal dresses, coats, or suits within a narrow range of prices, and also in particular size ranges, such as juniors, children's, misses, women's, and the like. Even multiproduct giant producers and retailers tend to follow this pattern by maintaining separate divisions or departments for different categories of merchandise. Although specialization still continues, over the years producers have tended to broaden their assortments as a result of changes in fashion. Many of the giants mentioned above have a broad range of products, but their member companies or divisions may be quite specialized.

Product Specialization

The following are typical products in the women's apparel industry in which companies or divisions of multiproduct companies specialize:

- Outerwear—coats, suits, rainwear
- Dresses
- Sportswear and separates—active wear, pants, tops, sweaters, jackets, blouses
- After-five and evening clothes
- Bridal and bridesmaid attire
- Uniforms and aprons—career (other than office) apparel, daytime dresses
- Maternity
- Swimwear and beachwear
- Intimate apparel—foundations, lingerie, robes
- Blouses
- Sweaters and knitwear

Wholesale Price Specialization

Within the wide spectrum of wholesale prices for garments, there are *price ranges* in which individual manufacturers specialize. Elements in the wholesale price of a garment are (1) the quality of workmanship, (2) the cost of labor, and (3) the quality and amount of fabric and trimmings. The women's apparel industry generally divides itself into the following five price ranges (or groups of individual prices per garment):

1. *Designer* (highest priced merchandise). This includes the lines of American name designers such as Calvin Klein, Bill Blass, Oscar de la Renta, Donna Karan, Ralph Lauren, and Geoffrey Beene.
2. *Bridge* (high prices but lower than designer). This includes the lower priced or secondary lines of designers such as Anne Klein II and Donna Karan's DKNY. It also includes such lines as Ellen Tracy, Adrienne Vittadini, Dana Buchman, and David Dart.
3. *Better* (medium to bridge prices). The lines of Evan Picone, Liz Claiborne, Jones New York, JH Collectibles, and Ciao would fall into this price range.
4. *Moderate* (or lower than better but higher than budget). This includes such lines as White Stag, Russ Togs, Jantzen, Levi Strauss, Gitano, Norton McNaughton, Chaus, and Sag Harbor.
5. *Budget* (the lowest prices in which one would find advertised brand names). This includes firms such as Rustler jeans, Cape Cod women's wear, and the Kathie Lee line.

Prevalence of Style Piracy

Apparel designs cannot be copyrighted; therefore, copying the work of creative designers is standard operating procedure for many firms, both large and small. Design and styling are such important competitive weapons in the fashion industry that **style piracy,** against which U.S. laws provide no protection, is considered a way of life in the garment business. In the language of the industry, however, a design is never "stolen"; it is "knocked off." It is copied, adapted, translated, or even pirated, but the **knock-off** is never considered as having been "stolen." This is not hypocrisy but simply the garment trade's way of acknowledging that copying dominates the industry; it is done openly and without apology. The late Norman Norell, who produced garments in very high price lines, indeed, and who was considered in his day the dean of

American designers, expressed his philosophy about style piracy: "I don't mind if the knock-off houses give me a season with my dress. What I mind is if they bring out their copies faster than I can get my own dresses to the stores" ("He's a," 1964).

Aside from the absence of copyright protection for apparel designs, there are several reasons for this copying practice. Plunging into a fast-selling style, regardless of whose design it was originally, is one way to make a modest investment work to the limit. Another reason style piracy is rife is the highly specialized nature of the firms themselves. If, for example, a dress intended to retail at $200 has features that would make it a fast seller at a lower price, the originator of the style is in no position to produce or market inexpensive versions. The originator's entire purchasing, production, and distribution are geared to customers who are willing to pay for the particular grade of fabric, workmanship, and details in which he or she has specialized. In addition, apparel firms' labor costs may be established by the union, based on the companies' normal wholesale price lines, and they cannot be reduced. On the other hand, a maker specializing in garments to retail at $75 has much lower labor costs, enjoys access to sources for much less expensive fabrics, knows how to cut corners in production, and has established distribution among retailers catering to the price-conscious consumer. And if a style can be copied down to a still lower level, or can be marketed at some intermediate levels, makers specializing in those levels are likely to step in.

Occasionally, the copying process is reversed, and a style that originates in the lower priced lines will have features that make it desirable for higher priced manufacturers to adapt. Normally, however, the procedure is for a style that originally retailed for hundreds of dollars to be "knocked off" at successively lower prices, if it shows signs of popular acceptance by customers.

Proliferation of Industry Licensing Agreements

The 1970s witnessed the burgeoning of the "name game"—the licensing by prominent American apparel designers of their names for use by manufacturers of accessories and of lower priced clothing. **Licensing** is a legal arrangement covering a specific period of time, during which a manufacturer of goods in a particular generic category is given exclusive rights to produce and market a line of merchandise bearing the name of a licensor. For this privilege, the **licensee** pays a **royalty fee**—that is, a percentage of the wholesale sales of the goods concerned. According to *The Licensing Letter* (1995) royalty fees for apparel average 7.3 percent, ranging from 4 to 12 percent. In addition, a guaranteed minimum payment is usually specified.

The **licensor,** however, is not required to confine his or her name to only one product category. For instance, a licensing arrangement with a jewelry manufacturer does not preclude similar arrangements with producers of jeans, sunglasses, shoes, bed linens, scarfs, hosiery, fur coats, perfume, swimwear, or any other product that can profitably become part of the name game (Figure 5–10). Apparel and accessories, nevertheless, are a major field for such arrangements. It is estimated that in 1994 licensed apparel and accessories represented 29 percent of all licensed name products sold at retail, out of a total of $70.01 billion a year, an amount still on the rise (*The Licensing Letter,* 1995).

Licensing arrangements are not new to the European couture; some of the most famous among them have long had income of this sort from American manufacturers and stores. For American designers, however, this is a relatively new development and one that has grown enormously. Today, some designers are receiving royalty fees that equal and in some cases even exceed the total sales volume of their own apparel enterprises.

Figure 5–10

Licensing: Sales of licensed products by category

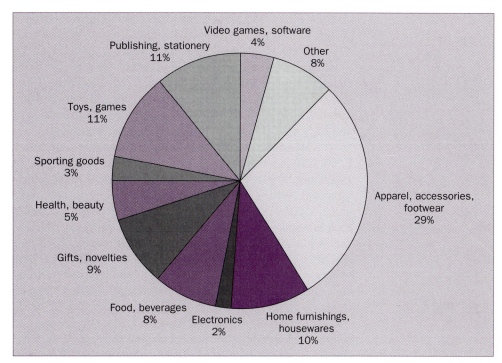

Source: From *The Licensing Letter* (p. 6), 1995, New York: EPM Communications, Inc. © Copyright 1995 EPM Communications, Inc.

The proliferation of licensing by both American and European designers has arrived at the point that their names now appear on apparel priced well below the high prices level of the merchandise for which they became famous. Past examples included the Calvin Klein jeans line manufactured by Puritan Inc.[2] and the Halston name marketed by J.C. Penney, to name but two. In 1995, the top licensed names in fashion were: Guess, Calvin Klein, Donna Karan,[3] Tommy Hilfiger, Liz Claiborne,[3] Ralph Lauren, and B.U.M. (*The Licensing Letter,* 1995).

Apparel producers do not necessarily limit themselves to licensing one designer's name alone. They may have several arrangements during the same period. For example, Fairbrook Enterprises, a prominent coat producer, makes coat lines under licenses with Perry Ellis, Anne Klein II, and Calvin Klein while at the same time manufacturing other branded lines of their own.

The practice of licensing in the apparel industry is not limited to designer names. There are firms whose company names are so well known that they are able to license them to makers of other products. As but one example, Jordache produces and promotes its own line of jeans but licenses its name for some 46 other products to U.S. manufacturers and 55 to foreign producers. These range from women's undergarments produced by a lingerie company to sunglasses made and marketed by an optical company.

Also into the licensing act today are legions of widely recognizable names such as cartoon characters, sports figures, movie and television idols, and corporate names and logos. For example, Halmode of Kellwood Company and Wal-Mart signed entertainer Kathie Lee Gifford for a line of clothing to bear her name. Among the foremost is the licensing of the different characters of Disney Enterprises and those of

---

[2]Calvin Klein now owns Puritan, Inc.
[3]A very small percentage of sales based on these designers is licensed.

Looney Tunes. Although cartoon and story characters are the most popular licensing group, a *Stores* magazine survey found that Michael Jordan had replaced Mickey Mouse as the single most popular licensed name ("From Michael," 1995).

The major value of a licensing arrangement to the licensees is that the merchandise carries a highly recognizable, presold name. To consumers, the name often symbolizes status, achievement, and quality. To the licensors, of course, it means additional income from royalty fees and extended name exposure without the hassles and high cost of having to produce and market the goods themselves.

Among the most active American designer-name licensors are Bill Blass, Anne Klein, Calvin Klein, Ralph Lauren, and Oscar de la Renta. The designer's input varies. For example, the Anne Klein company supplies its 28 licensees with color, fabric, design, and display ideas, and it retains final approval on all merchandise bearing its name. Others merely "edit" their licensed collections, reserving the right to approve such factors as color, quality, and design approach. With a few exceptions, very few actually design every item sold under their name. These items are more often than not designed by the unknown designer of the licensed company. What they all have in common is a very profitable royalty fee income amounting to many millions of dollars. Today Bill Blass licenses generate more than $750 million at retail, Oscar de la Renta more than $500 million (*Women's Wear Daily*, 1995).

It must be remembered, however, that the licensing value of a designer's name is directly dependent on the success and prestige of the licensor. Almost any designer entrepreneur can have an unsuccessful collection. A series of unsuccessful collections can put any such firm out of business and also put an end to licensing, since licensees have no reason to renew an arrangement with a designer whose name has lost its glamour or status. No licensing agreement is forever.

Today, with the thousands of licensed names and licensed products plus the licensing brokers who serve as the liaisons between licensors and licensees, licensing has almost become an industry unto itself.

Financing by Factoring

Many garment manufacturers rely heavily on outside sources for operating capital. This is necessary for many companies because products must be made and delivered before the apparel firm collects for the merchandise. These sources are called **factors.** The manufacturer engages a factor to become its credit and collection department. Orders are submitted to the **factoring** company for approval and are shipped as designated. The invoices are assigned to the factor, who supplies immediate cash, usually equal to 90 percent of receivables' net value. (The 10 percent reserve of outstanding receivables is usually held to cover returns, allowances, etc.) The factor then proceeds to collect payment from the manufacturer's customers and takes the credit risk. For their services as a credit and collection department and guarantor of credit risks, factors receive a fee known as a factoring commission, as well as interest on money loaned out before collecting on the receivables.

A highly publicized example illustrates the role factors play in the industry. When Sarah Phillips designed the Presidential Inaugural Ball gown for Hillary Clinton in 1992, she was a 37-year-old designer who had opened her own shop just three years earlier. Although she had worked for Yves St. Laurent, Ralph Lauren, and Christian Dior, she was a relative unknown at the time. Although the inaugural gown brought Sarah Phillips into the limelight, like most starting designers who wanted to develop her business, she was operating on a shoestring. Becoming the first lady's couturiere didn't attract the seed

"The last thing a small company wants to be treated like is a small company."

Bruce Gifford
Leslie Gifford

Bruce and Leslie Gifford,
Molto Fino, Inc.

At CIT Commercial Services, we measure companies by the size of their dreams, not the size of their revenues.

That's important to Bruce and Leslie Gifford, owners of Molto Fino, Inc. Their small, quality company needs a factor that's responsive, flexible, and able to provide the quick turnarounds their business demands.

Since 1928, we've made it our business to serve small business. So while you may have thought that our impressive growth has been fueled only by our relationships with large corporations, the fact remains that nearly 75% of our clients have less than $10 million in factored volume with us.

With CIT, people like Bruce and Leslie can be confident that they'll get the financial clout and the services that help them stay competitive. And just as importantly, they'll never feel like their small business is of little concern to us.

To find out how we can serve your company, call us at (213) 613-2420.

THE CIT GROUP

AMERICA'S
MOST EXPERIENCED
ASSET-BASED
LENDER

ATLANTA • CHARLOTTE • DALLAS • DANVILLE • LOS ANGELES • LOUISVILLE • NEW YORK • HONG KONG

© 1994 The CIT Group, Inc.

Source: Reprinted courtesy of The CIT Group, Inc.

money Phillips needed to grow her business. She needed equity capital of several million dollars to go forward. Phillips was able to expand her business through the assistance of a factor. The factor (in this case a pre-factor because Phillips's business was still in early stages) supported her on a purchase order basis to help in the initial financing. This provided the funding to buy the fabrics and other components as well as to support production facilities. That is, the factor approves the credit and loans money to the client before collecting on receivables (i.e., collecting from retailers for the products they buy from the client). Although factors generally work with more established companies than Sarah Phillips, this example helps to illustrate the role of factors (Abend, 1993).

Factoring is a very large business in itself. For example, the factoring industry reported its 1993 volume of business just under $57 billion. The largest factoring firm is The CIT Group, which acquired Barclays Commercial, with more than $12 billion in business (Figure 5–11). The top five factors now account for about 70 percent of the business, down from some 38 major players in the early 1980s (Thorton, 1993).

Location of Fashion Market Centers

Although some phase of apparel production (i.e., contracting and subcontracting) can be found in many states of the Union, the design and marketing activities of domestic apparel companies are concentrated in relatively few major cities throughout the United States. It is in these cities that one finds an enclave of apparel companies, also known as **vendors,** that produce and sell merchandise at the wholesale level to retail buyers. Known as **market centers** in the trade, these centers are the very heartbeat of the industry since they are the marketing link between apparel manufacturers and retail distributors.

New York, the Leading Market Center

The oldest, largest, and best-known wholesale fashion center in the country is located in the heart of New York City. Whereas other sections of the country have been whittling away at its base, insofar as women's and children's ready-to-wear is concerned, it is still the U.S. fashion capital.

It is not entirely an accident that New York occupies this dominant position. When Elias Howe first perfected his sewing machine, factory production of garments was not limited to any one city or area. But then came the great wave of immigration, as mentioned earlier in this chapter. New York was a major port of entry for newcomers, eager to find work in the city where they landed. Their assimilation into the garment industry there was often immediate, with some manufacturers and contractors actually meeting incoming vessels to recruit whole families for work in their factories. This pool of labor, growing out of the steady stream of immigrants, was the circumstance that enabled New York to leave its rivals behind in the production of apparel.

New York had the further advantage of being close to both the cotton mills of the South and the woolen mills of New England. It was also the nation's largest city and the center of fashionable society. Once New York had gained dominance, it became a magnet, attracting such auxiliary businesses as embroidery, pleating, and trimmings, as well as textile showrooms, consumer and fashion periodicals, trade associations, and the like. With these advantages, the city became the hub of the women's garment industry.

Today, New York still remains and will probably continue to remain the dominant center of the U.S. fashion industry. It is only in that city that one can find the showrooms of an estimated more than 5,000 apparel firms, the showrooms of all major fiber and fabric producers, the headquarters of consumer and fashion magazines, and the offices of many major trade associations. Add to that the countless opportunities for fashion practitioners to engage in New York's other important activity—"shop talk" with suppliers, friends, competitors, editors, and other sources of fashion information—and it becomes clear why the city retains its position as the hub of the fashion industry. Most of the leading American fashion designers work in New York-based firms because, as Donna Karan explained it: "Everything is here. . . you have to commute to see what kinds of clothes are needed for commuting and working. You have to live through the seasons to design clothes for the seasons. New York is just like fashion: dirty and clean, casual and uptight, alive and changing" ("The City," 1976).

Seventh Avenue

So much of New York City's garment and accessories business is concentrated within a distance of one block east or west of **Seventh Avenue (SA),** from West 41 Street south into the low West 30s, that the term *Seventh Avenue* has become synonymous with the women's fashion industry. The street itself was renamed Fashion Avenue in 1972. Within this area, there are literally thousands of showrooms presenting every known type and price line of women's ready-to-wear and accessories. These showrooms include not only those of New York firms, but also those of many producers whose headquarters are in other parts of the country and even in other parts of the world. There are other apparel centers elsewhere in the country where women's garments are produced and sold, but to those in the fashion business, no other center has the color, tension, activity, or merchandise variety of Seventh Avenue.

Individual buildings within the garment center tend to be specialized, each housing producers of more or less the same categories of merchandise and wholesale price ranges (Figure 5–12). For example, 1410 Broadway (the next street east of Seventh Avenue) is the market for moderate-priced sportswear, sweaters, and budget apparel; 1407 and 1411 Broadway house the showrooms of more than 2,000 sportswear companies; 1400 Broadway is the main building for medium-priced misses and junior dress firms; 1375 houses many bridal and evening dress firms; and 1350 contains many producers of lower priced apparel, of the type sold by the dozens, sometimes called "daytime" dresses.

The upper end of Seventh Avenue has a range of coat and suit firms and higher priced designer-name companies, with the overflow spilling into West 39 Street. Coat

Figure 5–12

New York's Garment District

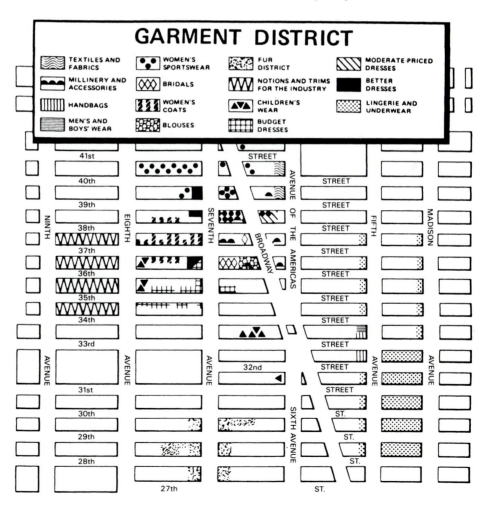

and suit firms are in 500 and 512 Seventh Avenue. Designer-name companies like Bill Blass, Trigère, Ralph Lauren, Geoffrey Beene, and their peers are in 530 and 550 Seventh Avenue. At the lower end of Seventh Avenue are makers of lower priced apparel whose names are generally unknown to the public. Children's wear showrooms are mostly on the south and west fringes of the area, with many of them concentrated in a specialized children's wear building at 112 West 34 Street.

The garment center's tenants, however, have been pushing out its boundaries. For example, two buildings on West 35 Street have attracted many young designer firms, and 1441 Broadway now houses three floors of the Liz Claiborne company and other better-sportswear producers.

Decentralization of Production

At one time, practically every New York-based firm had its design, showroom, production, and shipping facilities in the garment district, and even all in the same building. Increasingly in recent years, apparel firms locate their cutting and, to a larger extent, their sewing operations in areas outside the city, and even outside the country, whether these production facilities are owned by the companies or simply contracted for. This trend is noticeable not only in New York, but in other large cities as well. The high cost of rent, the unavailability of space that can be adapted to newer methods and equipment, the rising cost of taxes and labor, the almost unbelievable traffic congestion on city streets—all these have encouraged the establishment of factories in small towns in New York State and the surrounding states, in the Southeast, and in other countries—Mexico, the Caribbean, or Asia, for instance. No matter where the goods are produced, however, the finished garments are sent back to the parent firm for selling and distribution. Seventh Avenue remains the nerve center of the design, marketing, and management operations, regardless of how far afield the production facilities may be.

Secondary Fashion Centers

There are other regional market centers outside New York City. Although some of these are very important, no one of them can compare with New York in terms of the number of companies based there or the variety, quantity, and dollar sales. Each of these other centers tends to be fairly specialized as to the types and price ranges it produces. Many of the manufacturers in these **secondary fashion centers** have sales representation in New York City.

Los Angeles

Los Angeles, following close on the heels of New York City, has emerged as the second most important design and manufacturing center, known for its "California look." Once limited mostly to swimsuits and active sportswear, it now turns out a wide range of garments, including blue jeans, "trendy" junior-sized garments, and boutique items.

California has greatly surpassed New York in the number of persons employed in the industry. California's industry had 142,000 employees in 1994, compared to 94,000 in New York (AAMA, 1995). Los Angeles manufacturers have some advantages over New York: less expensive and abundant space and a large pool of Mexican workers. Unfavorable factors include a shortage of the small specialized fabric and findings firms that are plentiful in New York. California manufacturers, however, have developed their own "look" and are noted for their creative innovations in sportswear styling and colorations. Particularly in the casual wear areas, California designs have influenced the entire country.

Miami

Miami's major role in the apparel industry today is that of being the "gateway to the Caribbean." Under U.S. **tariff** rules (formerly 807 of the tariff regulations, now 9802), apparel manufacturers send cut garments to other countries to have them sewn and pay tariffs on only the value added during those operations. To use this strategy, still commonly called **807 production,** much of the garment cutting occurs in Miami and the sewing takes place in various low-wage Caribbean countries. Then finished garments are sent back to the U.S. markets through Miami, completing the cycle that has made Miami a major hub of industry activity in recent years.

Miami has a relatively important children's wear industry, resulting from early relocation there in the 1940s. In the 1960s, some 30 children's wear firms founded the Florida Children's Wear Manufacturers Guild, which sponsors a successful trade show each year for retail buyers. Additionally, a number of leisure and active wear firms are located in Miami.

Like New York, Miami became an important apparel center because of immigrants. Whereas European immigrants were instrumental in founding New York's industry, Cuban immigrants contributed similarly in Miami. In the 1960s, many Cuban immigrants fled from the Castro regime and needed jobs when they arrived in Miami. As one children's wear manufacturer put it, "The Cuban immigration of the Sixties was the catalyst that allowed us to grow. Once we got the Cuban labor working for us, we could take orders from major stores and know that we could deliver the merchandise" ("More than," 1985). Today, many Cubans have moved from positions as machine operators to become principals in their own companies—a modern parallel to the European immigrant saga in New York.

Dallas

Once a design and production center primarily for lower priced polyester knit garments distributed through large-volume apparel chains, Dallas has changed. Most of the manufacturers headquartered in Dallas have made a shift to a mix of moderate-priced dresses and sportswear in a greater variety of fabrications to meet the changing demands of a large segment of mainstream customers. As one of Dallas's leading manufacturers explained it: "Dallas is a market that caters to middle America, only middle America has changed, and we've noticed. None of the merchandise we produce is faddish, because the middle American customer we're trying to reach isn't faddish" ("Dallas," 1985). In recent years, however, a cadre of young designers who live and work in Dallas are breathing new life into their local industry and are becoming known for their creative and innovative designs. To date, the best-known Dallas-based designer is Victor Costa.

Chicago

Chicago has changed. At one time it had a reputation for conservatively styled and well-made dresses for misses and women, at higher than moderate prices. But here is how an article describes the Chicago market:

> Gone are the days when traditional and polyester were the fashion watchwords here. Gone are the days when moderate-priced volume manufacturers and their multi-million dollar business along the crowded banks of the Chicago River were the ONLY game in town. Today Chicago is fashion. From the fresh young talent not long out of design school, like Richard Dayhoff, Kate Jones, and Peggy Martin, to the long established designers rapidly gaining a national reputation, like Maria Rodriguez, Mark Hester, and Gina Rossi, Chicago is making a new fashion statement.

Other Fashion Design Centers

Some other secondary design centers, even more distant from New York in terms of both the value of output and the variety of merchandise, are Boston, whose local manufacturers have developed a reputation primarily for well-made, moderate-priced classic sportswear and rainwear; and Philadelphia, for moderately priced sportswear and children's wear.

Apparel Marts: Regional Selling Centers

An industry development that began in the late 1960s is the marketing importance of **apparel marts,** or large regional selling centers. Located in major cities throughout the United States, their purpose is twofold: (1) to reach out for and sell to small fashion retailers in the surrounding areas and (2) to serve as a wholesale selling facility for apparel producers, wherever the headquarters of the companies may be.

In addition to the lines of local producers, these marts house **regional showrooms** of hundreds of apparel firms from other parts of the country and even those of some foreign fashion producers. The showrooms bring the current and incoming seasons' lines of these companies within easy reach of the area's small retailers, most of whom do not have the time or money to go to New York more than once or twice a year, if that often. Buyers for nearby large retail organizations also find the marts a convenience, as it is often more practical to fill some of the special or urgent needs from a nearby source of supply.

Showrooms are leased both on a year-round basis and for temporary use during major seasonal buying periods. The temporary showrooms are particularly convenient during regional **market weeks** (Figure 5–13). Such weeks are scheduled periodically as a means of introducing the new lines of hundreds of out-of-town producers to the retailers of the area at the start of a buying season. Separate market weeks are usually held for different categories of merchandise and range in number from two to five a year. Merchandise categories include accessories, sportswear, intimate apparel, infants' and children's wear, and dresses, among others. A typical calendar of market weeks in major marts is shown in Figure 5–13. These schedules appear in trade periodicals such as *Women's Wear Daily.*

The past two decades have seen Los Angeles, Dallas, Atlanta, and Chicago emerge as important regional selling marts, challenging what was once New York's exclusive domain. To attract buyers to market weeks, these marts stage many special events, such as fashion shows, merchandising seminars, and entertainment galas. In the sluggish economy of the early 1990s, most of the marts have struggled to keep tenants.

The Dallas International Apparel Mart

The Dallas International Apparel Mart[4] is part of the Dallas Market Center. The total 125-acre complex ranks as the world's largest wholesale apparel and merchandising complex with approximately 7 million square feet of space in six buildings. In addition to the Apparel Mart, the complex boasts the International Menswear Mart, a separate facility for the menswear industry (Vargo, 1994).

The Dallas International Apparel Mart has 1,200 showrooms and is home to more than 10,000 apparel and accessories lines. In a year, about 27,000 stores will have shopped in the Apparel Mart, writing orders for more than $2.5 billion in business from

---

[4]The Dallas Apparel Mart added "International" to its name in 1992 to reflect increasing efforts to draw international buyers, particularly those from Mexico and other Latin American countries.

Figure 5–13

Market Week Schedule for 1996

Location	Summer	Fall I	Fall II	Resort	Spring
Atlanta (Atlanta Apparel Mart)	Jan. 25-29	April 11-15	June 13-15	Aug. 22-26	Oct. 24-28
Birmingham (Birmingham Jefferson Civic Center)	Jan. 21-22	March 24-25	June 9-10	Aug. 18-19	Oct. 13-14
Boston (Bayside Expo Center)	Jan. 14-17	April 14-17	June 16-19	Aug. 18-21	Oct. 13-16
Charlotte (Charlotte Merchandise Mart) (children's market)	Jan. 19-23 Jan. 19-22	March 22-26 March 22-25	June 7-11 June 7-10	Aug. 16-20 Aug. 16-19	Oct. 11-14
Chicago (Chicago Apparel Center)	Jan. 26-30	March 29-April 2	May 31-June 4	Aug. 16-20	Oct. 25-29
Dallas (International Apparel Mart)	Jan. 18-22	March 21-25	June 6-10	Aug. 15-19	Oct. 17-21
Kansas City (Kansas City Market Center)	Jan. 13-15	April 13-16	June 22-24	Aug. 24-27	Oct. 26-29
Los Angeles (California Apparel Mart)	Jan. 12-16	April 19-23	June 21-25	Aug. 9-13	Nov. 1-5
Miami (Miami Merchandise Mart)	Jan. 14-17	March 16-19	May 31-June 3	Aug. 9-12	Oct. 12-15
Minneapolis (Hyatt Merchandise Mart)	Jan. 21-24	March 10-12	April 14-17	June 9-11 Aug. 11-14	Oct. 20-23
New York (For New York updates, contact Fashion Calendar, 212-289-0420)	Jan. 8-19	Feb. 19-March 1	March 25-April 12	July 29-Aug. 9	Oct. 28-Nov. 15
Pittsburgh (Monroeville Expo Mart)	Jan. 21-23	April 14-16	June 9-11	Sept. 8-10	Nov. 3-5
San Francisco (The Fashion Center)	Jan. 6-9	April 13-16	June 15-18	Aug. 17-20	Oct. 19-22
Seattle (Seattle International Trade Center)	Jan. 20-23	March 30-April 2	June 8-11	Aug. 3-6	Oct. 26-29

The 1996 general women's and children's apparel market weeks at the various regional marts and in New York are listed above. In addition to these general markets, various specialized events are held throughout the year at some of these venues. Dates are subject to revision, and individual marts should be contacted for confirmation and more information.

Source: From *Women's Wear Daily,* January 18, 1996, p. 15. Reprinted by permission.

the mart tenants. To maintain a flow of customers for the exhibitors, the mart spends millions on promotion. The Dallas Mart was one of the first to open a site on the Internet to disseminate information about the complex to retailers and to permit retailers to place orders with the mart tenants via computer. The Dallas Mart has encouraged major chain retailers to shop there by offering them free offices in the building; retailers must pay taxes and utility bills (Haber, 1995; Williamson, 1994).

Although large Texas retailers such as Neiman Marcus may shop this mart, the typical and best customers of any mart are not the buyers from the major stores, but a host of small independently owned specialty store retailers from the surrounding areas. Dallas draws these customers primarily from Arkansas, Louisiana, Oklahoma, and Texas, with these states accounting for 78 percent of the mart's traffic. Another 17 percent comes from other states, 4 percent from Mexico and other Latin American countries, and about 1 percent from the rest of the world (Williamson, 1994).

The CaliforniaMart

Located in downtown Los Angeles' garment district, the California apparel center, known as the CaliforniaMart, contains some 1,200 permanent showrooms, plus 300 or so that are available for temporary rentals. This mart is not only a regional selling facility for New York manufacturers but also the showcase for West Coast producers whose merchandise is not exhibited in other marts or even shown in New York. Retail buyers are drawn from the Southwest, the whole of California, Washington, Oregon, and New York.

Various incentives are offered to retail buyers to attract them to the mart: rebates on airfare or gasoline, free meals, and other inducements. Attendance is also promoted by means of a newsletter, a calendar of special events, and market directories. As a service to exhibitors, the mart also publishes a buyer registration list, which manufacturers can use as a mailing list.

By the early 1990s, managers of a number of showrooms became disenchanted with CaliforniaMart for what they considered poor service, high rents, and facilities that lacked contemporary appeal. Under new management since late 1994, these concerns have been addressed.

The Atlanta Apparel Mart

The newest of these apparel selling centers is the Atlanta Apparel Mart, which opened in 1979 with seven floors of showrooms. The Apparel Mart is part of a larger complex, the Atlanta Market Center, which draws heavily from southeastern states. In 1987, the Center announced a major $43 million expansion of the Apparel Mart. This expansion, completed in 1989, consisted of adding seven additional floors on top of the original seven (Lloyd, 1994b).

Apparel Mart managers planned the expansion during the boom years of the 1980s. However, by the time it was finished, the economy took a nose-dive. Many specialty stores in the Southeast went out of business, and retailing was restructuring in other ways. As the Apparel Mart was in the process of expanding, retailing was changing in ways that meant fewer users for the Mart. Department stores throughout the United States were consolidating, many of these in the Southeast. Long-time names disappeared when companies merged, including Loveman's, Cain Sloan, and Ivey's. Macy's closed its buying offices in the South. All these changes resulted in reduced traffic from retailers who had been customers for the Mart's tenants. Consequently, by late 1994, the Apparel Mart was only 53 percent leased (Lloyd, 1994b).

The Atlanta Mart developed a number of strategies to fill the expanded building. Showrooms were consolidated on upper floors, and the first four floors became the International Sports Plaza, creating a trade center for the sporting goods industry. Timing coincided with the 1996 Olympic Games, and the Atlanta Committee for the Olympic Games designated the Sports Plaza as the Main Press Center for the games. Other strategies to improve business included hosting mini-trade shows for major stores, the first being for Mercantile. Additionally, the Mart leased a permanent showroom to Fashion Consul, Inc., a Miami-based international buying service with 100 retail accounts in South America and the Caribbean (Lloyd, 1994a; 1994b).

The Chicago Apparel Center

The Chicago Center is a 25-story building, opened in 1977. It has 11 floors of showrooms, plus a hotel and a 140,000-square-foot exhibition hall. There is also a 3,000-square-foot exhibit, set up as a modern retail store, to offer ideas for store plans, fixturing, color effects, and the like.

At its peak, some 4,000 resources were represented on a year-round basis. These spanned all price levels and covered a wide spectrum of manufacturing firms from all over the world. Well-known tenants have been Oscar de la Renta, Geoffrey Beene, Yves St. Laurent, and others of similar stature. As in other marts, there are several hundred showrooms available for temporary rentals.

Industry changes have affected the Chicago mart, just as it has its counterparts. The decline of small retail stores and the mergers of large retailers has resulted in much less traffic for market weeks and for year-round showroom business. Consequently, future demand for showroom space is uncertain (Sharoff, 1994).

Other Merchandise Marts

In addition to the four major apparel marts described above, there is a smaller specialized apparel mart in Boston and a new Fashion Center in San Francisco. There are also general merchandise marts in other cities that have several floors devoted to apparel showrooms. Like the specialized marts, these more general ones aim to promote their local industries and house both permanent and temporary showrooms for local, national, and international producers. And like the apparel centers, the general merchandise marts hold regularly scheduled market weeks that are attended mostly by smaller retailers from the surrounding regions. Some examples are the Miami Merchandise Mart, the Carolina Trade Center in Charlotte, North Carolina, the Kansas City Trade Center, and the Radisson Center in Minneapolis.

Future of New York as a Fashion Center

Although a good deal of the buying and selling action has moved to regional apparel marts, New York is still firmly entrenched as the key marketplace of the United States because it offers buyers their choice of more than 175,000 lines of goods, an amount that no other area can ever begin to match. It still remains to be seen whether the proliferation of regional marts will affect the frequency with which buyers for major stores throughout the country shop the New York market. Some New York-based manufacturers feel that market weeks at the regional marts detract from the business that could be done in New York. They feel there is an "overkill" of market weeks (Feitelberg, 1994).

The manufacturing segment of the New York apparel industry has declined over the years because of the high costs of doing business there—real estate, labor, utilities, and so on. However, a core group of manufacturers, particularly makers in the higher-end market, are committed to keeping their production in the city. For many, having production there is an integral strategy enabling them to respond quickly to hot trends and to meet the demands of retailers who want to buy close to the season.

Realizing the economic importance of its apparel industry, the City of New York has funded special projects in recent years to boost the long-term health of the industry. The mayor of New York has been involved in various efforts to promote the city's industry. Civic and industry leaders have launched a "Made in New York" campaign to promote New York–made fashions (Friedman, 1995b). Efforts are also being made to entice buyers from other countries, particularly those whose customers are attracted to upscale merchandise.

Children's Wear

In the not-too-distant past, when children were expected to be seen but not heard, they were dressed in miniature versions of adult apparel. Parents chose their clothes. Today, largely as a result of their exposure to television, children have become customers in their own right and have definite opinions about the toys they want, the foods they eat, and the clothes they wear. This "liberation" of children has had a direct effect on the styling of children's wear.

Nature of the Industry

The development of the children's wear segment of the industry and its methods of operation, as far as the presentation of seasonal lines and the production methods

Figure 5-14

The children's wear market represents a significant component of the apparel industry. Today this market gives children an opportunity for creative choices and self-expression in their clothing.

Source: Courtesy of Kellwood Company.

Table 5–5	Top Five Children's Apparel[a] Producers
Company	**1994/95 Sales (in $ millions)**
Oshkosh B'Gosh	432[b]
Bugle Boy Industries, Inc.	414[c]
William Carter Co.	271[c]
Gerber Childrenswear, Inc.	185 (estimate)[c]
Garan, Inc.	173[c]

[a]Some produce other products, but are for the most part children's apparel firms.
[b]1995 sales From "Apparel Manufacturers' Results for the Fourth Quarter and Year," March 4, 1996, *Women's Wear Daily,* p. 22.
[c]1994 sales from company annual reports and "Top 100 Sewn Products Companies '95," June 1995, *Apparel Industry Magazine,* pp. 17–40.

used, follow much the same pattern as the women's sector. However, the children's industry has a relatively small volume of output and many fewer companies, is less competitive and less aggressive in its marketing practices, and puts emphasis on the ages of the ultimate consumers.

There are close to 1,000 companies that produce children's wear. The total value of output is more than $4 billion (AAMA, 1995).[5] With the notable exception of a few giant firms such as Oshkosh, Carter, and Healthtex, the majority of companies are small (Table 5–5). Most manufacturers produce three seasonal collections per year—Spring/Summer, Fall, and Holiday. Many children's wear firms are located in New York City, but there is a substantial contingent in the Miami fashion industry, many of which maintain sales representatives in New York.

Some large-scale multiproduct producers of adult apparel have entered into some phase of children's wear. Among them are such companies as Levi Strauss, Lee, Russ Togs, Guess, and Esprit. As explained previously, these large producers set up separate divisions for each of their product categories, and their children's wear is no exception. The design, production, and marketing of children's products has its own division in these firms.

Industry Specializations

As in the women's wear industry, manufacturers tend to specialize by price range, sizes, and types of merchandise. In terms of price levels, most companies fall into low, moderate, or higher priced categories. In regard to type, the most common specializations are by age or size groups rather than by merchandise categories. Children, it should be understood, have different body proportions at different stages of growth, and their garments must be designed accordingly. For example, two girls of the same height and weight may require garments from different ranges, because one still has toddler proportions and the other has small-girl proportions.

---

[5]The exact output is difficult to determine because some SIC categories (e.g., undergarments) have women's and children's apparel in the same grouping.

Thus, the size ranges are related to the age or stage of growth. The following sizes are the same for girls and boys:

Infants: 3 to 24 months
Toddlers: T2 to T4

From children's size 4, the sizes for the two sexes diverge. Children's sizes for girls go from 4 to 6x, then go on to girls' 7 to 14, and preteen 6 to 14. Boys' wear is sized 4 to 7 and 8 to 12, and their garments are made in the children's wear industry. When they pass this age and size, however, the boys move into the menswear industry, wearing boys' sizes 14 to 20, and going on to young men's and students' wear.

In a large retail store, each age or size grouping is often in a section of its own, usually within the infants' and children's department, and usually under one buyer unless the store is quite large. Clothes for boys who have outgrown the children's size ranges are generally bought, displayed, and sold with or near menswear.

Marketing Activities

Marketing practices are similar in many respects to those of the women's wear industry. For example, seasonal lines are presented in showrooms, at company headquarters, and sometimes also at regional marts. The merchandise, however, is not usually dramatized and accessorized as is done in the women's industry. Advertising and sales promotion are relatively minor, with the exception of the few very large firms, which have made their names well known through national advertising. Most producers in this industry leave consumer advertising to the retail stores.

The industry has its own specialized publications: *Earnshaw's Infants-Girls-Boys Wear Review* plus a periodic section in *Women's Wear Daily*. These focus on trade and product news and carry advertising to the retail trade.

There are three trade shows a year, held in New York; more than 300 lines are usually exhibited at each. These are the International Kids Fashion Shows, which are in addition to the Florida Children's Wear Manufacturers' Guild Show, an annual trade show held in Miami.

As in the women's industry, the licensing "name" game is very prevalent. Character licensing is a practice so rampant in the industry that very few t-shirts, sweatshirts, sleepwear, and similar items are without the licensed names of a Mickey Mouse, Star Wars, Lion King, Looney Tunes, Snoopy, Pocahontas, and *ad infinitum*. Also important is the licensing of sports figures and designer names. Today, many children's wear manufacturers have licensing agreements with both European and American designers. European luminaries such as Christian Dior, Pierre Cardin, Yves St. Laurent, and Givenchy have licensed their names to producers of higher priced children's wear, as have some well-known American designers.

It is interesting to note that in recent years many large retailers of adult apparel have gone into the children's wear business such as The Limited, Gap Kids, Benetton's 012, and Laura Ashley's Mother and Kids.

Both manufacturers and retailers of children's wear (including teens) have room for improvement in serving this market, according to a Kurt Salmon Associates study. In this study on the purchasing power of 8- to 17-year-olds, researchers found that this group controls about $120 billion in disposable income annually. This group of young consumers reported, however, that their special needs are often ignored by retailers. The age group represents 36.6 million young consumers and will grow another 15 percent by 2005. Each spends 32 percent of his or her income on apparel, about $1,031 annually or about $25 each shopping trip. The group reported that it chooses stores in the following order of importance: price, quality, styles, and variety ("Kids Feel," 1995).

An advertisement for the International Kids Fashion Show, a trade event that shows products for retailers who cater to young customers.

Source: Reprinted courtesy of The Larkin Group.

Readings

Not only has the apparel industry experienced radical changes in the ways it goes about its business, but many changes are also taking place in the manner in which the industry interacts with its business partners. The following articles address examples of both types of these changes.

CAD Comes of Age

by Laurel Gilbert

Throw away that pencil and paper. Forget messy charcoal and watercolor. You need a computer aided design (CAD) system to get up to speed in today's competitive marketplace.

This is the collective opinion of 15 CAD users recently surveyed on the numerous benefits they have achieved through automating the design process. The participants—who represent a wide variety of manufacturers from apparel to shoes to furniture—were asked questions regarding CAD's benefits and were queried for recommendations on successful implementation of this technology.

Among CAD's benefits, as reported by these companies, are a savings in time and money (at the top of the list), along with more creative freedom. In fact, many companies begin to explore new areas with CAD once they become acquainted with the technology. The ability to improve and embellish merchandising and design presentations to vendors and customers also was noted, as well as enhanced precision and better quality output.

Save Time

A CAD system allows you to illustrate a concept or line without ever making a sample. Let's face it, the name of the game in today's marketplace is Quick Response. By eliminating the sample making process, you can get early numbers from key accounts for use in forecasts, which will greatly reduce lead times and overruns.

One large jeans manufacturer, for example, who used to spend months on its conceptual development phase, now is able to complete the entire process in three weeks with a CAD system. This includes everything from conceptual design to graphic presentations for merchandising and sales with fabrics, styling and colorways. The company now is producing all artwork in-house without having to make sacrifices as a result of time constraints. If designers want to change the colors of a line from red to blue, it can be done in a matter of minutes. If that's not quite right, other colors can be tried at no extra charge.

Another company, Spiegel, a catalog house, also has been able to reduce its lead time tremendously with CAD. According to Bill Scully, "We can now design a fabric or a print and drape it over a figure. Our buyers do not have to wait through mill, print house or sample making lead times to see their concept visualized into a communicable format.

"Sending computer renditions of our prints and garments greatly reduces the amount of interpretation that we expect of our vendors," Scully continues. "This is a win/win situation from both perspectives, which shortens lead times and reduces development costs."

Enhance Creativity

There is no limit to your imagination with a design system. The user has the same capabilities as if drawing by hand, but with many more options. It is simple to create textures that would be difficult to do manually. And existing textures can be scanned and used in new ways. When designing fabrics and prints by hand, a repeat must be kept in mind the entire time; this is not the case when using a CAD system.

Irene Iglesias from Sigallo, a manufacturer of men's and boys' sportswear and swimwear, says, "Using a CAD system, we can better accomplish tasks that we have done [manually] in the past. We also seem to be coming up with new uses for many of its functions. . . . Without this technology, people will have a hard time catching up."

Even people without artistic inclinations find CAD systems very easy to use. Dave Herr of Kinney Shoe says, "Our design system brought a new creative side to my job. I am not an artsy person; I am more of an engineer than a designer. The system and its tools have enhanced what little natural ability I have and made me creative."

Cut Costs

Once CAD is implemented, artwork costs drop dramatically. The jean manufacturer mentioned herein says that it used to pay up to $500 per image for hand paintings by an outside source. Additionally, it would take nearly two weeks for the results. Now, the designers can create their own images in-house in less than a day, and then come up with 10 different colorway variations of that image in minutes. With four seasons in the company's selling year, the savings add up very quickly.

Perfect Presentation

People often express reservations about the ability for CAD systems to create images that look like real garments and generate believable presentations. However, CAD technology now has reached a level of sophistication that allows buyers to accurately see a complete design in the correct fabric or texture. As a result, buyers don't have to guess how a swatch will look on the finished product.

One uniform manufacturer uses its CAD system to create presentations for buyers that visualize what the uniforms actually will look like in a particular environment. If the presentation is for a hotel, for example, the company would show a model wearing a selected uniform standing behind a desk in that hotel's lobby. This is accomplished by scanning a photograph of the property and calling up an image from the company's catalog. It is then possible to change colors or drape an entirely new fabric onto the garment.

According to a company representative, "It makes a big impression on our customers to be able to show them the garments in their environment. It also helps a great deal with presentations to large groups or committees if you come prepared with a demonstration like this.

"We can show the full concept without ever having to make an investment, and ultimately, we can get back to the customer faster with the finished product."

Improve Quality

CAD systems provide more precision and more control over designs than manual methods. This level of

accuracy is vital in the creation of prints and yarn dyes. CAD also allows communication with vendors using detailed sketches and artwork, instead of words, to get a quality product the first time.

Julie LaRoche of Patagonia Inc., a performance sportswear manufacturer, points out that CAD has allowed her company to improve the design quality of both fabrics and prints. As a standard, LaRoche and other Patagonia designers always try to design two-directional fabrics so that they can increase cutting efficiency and reduce fabric waste. Designing the repeats in-house ensures that there are no surprises, such as a motif that creates an unwanted diagonal or pattern when the fabric is finally printed. They also can meet the specific repeat standards from a vendor by creating precise screening modules, whether for a rotary process or flat screening.

"CAD increases the quality of designs by allowing greater control during development, therefore improving the quality of the end product," says LaRoche, who also notes that CAD has helped the company in its well-noted environmental improvement efforts in recycling and minimizing waste. "CAD allows us to cut down on as much waste as possible," adds LaRoche. "We can filter through a lot of designs, but only print out what we think are working ideas."

Any type of artwork can be created with the right CAD system, including rough sketches, dramatic fashion illustrations, colorways and textiles, as well as sales and marketing materials. With CAD, rough sketches are created quickly to record ideas and concepts, while simple line drawings typically are used to accurately communicate ideas between the designer and pattern maker. With a CAD system, a designer can sketch new flats and bodies, modify existing drawings and build libraries of commonly used art. These drawings can be used to show details of the style. Color or fabric drape also can be added to these flat sketches.

In the creation of fabrics, companies use CAD systems to develop everything from textile concepts to specific textile measurements for mills. For the uniform company mentioned earlier, the addition of textile design capabilities has opened new possibilities. A representative explains that before implementing CAD, "We used to just utilize what was available out in the market or take the time and expense to pay a service to do the paintings. Now we are able to create our own conversational prints and colorways and have the fabric mill produce them for us."

The creation of technical illustrations, a key part of quality assurance during the actual construction of the product, is another area where CAD has achieved widespread use. These illustrations can be used for many purposes, including the training of internal staff and customers. Kinney Shoe, for example, uses technical illustrations to help educate salespeople by documenting key points about the product with technical drawings such as cutaway and exploded views.

CAD systems also feature a wide array of tools designed to create fashion illustrations: pastels, colored markers, paints, inks, watercolors, etc. Images and photographs can be scanned and manipulated to give a very realistic effect, while screen prints and graphics can be created and original embroideries designed to scale.

Once the artwork is designed, it is possible to create complete storyboards and catalog sheets for selling products. For instance, Triboro Quilt Manufacturing Inc., a producer of infant bedding products, develops presentation boards to "tell a story." This helps the customer visualize the entire group of bedding items together.

In another case, Sigallo is producing artwork for marketing materials using its CAD system. Instead of simply having one large piece of expensive artwork to display only in the showroom, the company now features mini illustrations, colorways and images on small-scale catalog sheets. These can be duplicated for the sales force to carry or mail to customers.

Patagonia uses its CAD system to create sales books for early-buy projections in its adult and children's lines. These books are distributed to the sales force and include printouts of color palettes for the season, yarn dyes, printed fabrics, garment sketches and basic style descriptions. To emphasize how successful these books are, consider that Patagonia sells solely from these sales books for its children's line.

Says LaRoche: "Our sales books provide a visual aid for our accounts when sales samples are not yet available. The sales reps and customers rely on these visual aids. Without them, it would be much harder to sell."

Retail designing, including logos, hangtags and packaging, is another hotbed of CAD activity. County Seat, for example, uses its CAD system to design buttons, rivets and woven and paper labels for its men's and women's lines. The company also de-

velops point-of-purchase items such as hangtags, sticky size-strips, pocket flashers and matchbooks for jeans and other garments.

A CAD system also can be used to create store plans and layouts. Triboro Quilt Manufacturing Inc., for example, designs "Plan-O-Grams" to help mass merchants visualize groupings together in the retail environment. Since bedding items are so space intensive, it is important to determine how a group of items can work together in a small amount of space.

Making It Work

Combine creative energy with CAD's efficiency, speed, ease of use and quality—and you have the designer's dream. So, what is the best way to go about implementing all of this?

When asked for their recommendations on how to implement a CAD system, the manufacturers interviewed herein stressed that one should put a lot of thought and research into selecting the right CAD system. Not every company has the same needs. They also suggested installing the system to the vendor's specifications, as much research is conducted by vendors to determine the best hardware and operating systems.

Next, it is important to select the best operator for the CAD system. Do this by selecting the person that is the most interested, not necessarily the one that is the least busy or has been there the longest. Also, take the time to train that person properly. Most companies interviewed agreed it is a waste of time to train someone, and then not allow for sufficient time to get him or her up to speed on the system. Be willing to commit the time for the user to work on the system in addition to normal duties.

Whether tangible or intangible, the benefits received from automating the design process are tremendous. In his 25th year at Kinney Shoe, Dave Herr sums it up saying, "This is a technology that is vibrant and alive. It has brought excitement back into an industry that I would have otherwise thought was dying, by giving it a whole new creative dimension. Being a part of it gives me a real sense of personal growth."

L.S.&Co. Tries On Custom-Fit Jeans

by Mark Henricks and Susan Hasty

Levi surprised the apparel industry with the announcement this past November that it was testing a custom-fit capability for women's jeans in its Levi's Only Stores. A consumer comes into the store, tries on jeans, has some measurements taken, and within three weeks, she receives the custom-fitted jeans.

In between, the customer's data is electronically sent to CAD Cut, a Montpelier, Vt., cutting plant, where the parts are cut on Cutting Edge single-ply cutters. The cut parts are sent to L.S.&Co.'s Mountain City, Tenn., sewing plant.

Is this the future of apparel? "I don't know and nobody else knows," says Thomas Fanoe, vice president of customer relations for Levi Strauss U.S.A. "If anyone says they know how big it's going to be, they're guessing."

L.S.&Co. reports that customers have responded well to the idea. There are two obvious disadvantages: the $10 premium L.S.&Co. charges and the three-week wait. Levi promises the jeans within three weeks but is turning the orders in about 10 to 12 days.

In the scheme of things, $10 isn't much to pay for custom-fitting. But does it pay Levi's costs? Fanoe won't say, but it appears not. "We're satisfied with it, but it's an investment at this point," he says.

The three-week wait period is not likely to get much shorter, Fanoe says. And there are other hindrances to an explosion of custom-fit apparel. Retailers have to maintain large, costly inventories of sample jeans to provide customers with a good fit. Salespeople have to be extensively trained.

While Levi officials are cautious with prognostications for their made-to-order business, Sung Park is not. Park is the 35-year-old entrepreneur who designed the turnkey system that Levi has licensed to do its custom-fit jeans. Park heads up 3-year-old Custom Clothing Technology Corp., Newton, Mass., a seven-employee software company with one customer—L.S.&Co.

Park is a Tufts University graduate who has spent most of his working life in what he describes as "geek software companies. . . . I usually leave when they bring in the personnel manuals and start wearing ties. That's when it stops being fun," he says.

Three years ago, he was vacationing in Hong Kong, where he had a suit made in a day, and he came home with the germ of an idea. He spent the next months researching the apparel business and designing a system that would allow an apparel company to take point-of-sale measurements, design a customized garment, generate markers and cut files, track the garment through sewing and then ship.

Park will not divulge how his CAD system tailors the jeans, but Levi North America President Robert Rockey told an audience at the November Apparel Research Conference that the system has 4,200 size variations, which implies that templates are used in some fashion. Park says the system may be expanded to include several thousand more variations, but beyond that he is silent. He has applied for patents.

Park believes there is a huge untapped market for custom-fit apparel, and he is aggressively pursuing new licensees for his system in such areas as bridal gowns, men's shirts and swim suits. "This is an approach that will work for anything that the customer needs to have made-to-fit," Park says. "And the cost of the technology is such that even small companies can do this."

Brian Tyrol, general manager at CAD Cut, the cutting contractor for L.S.&Co.'s program, agrees. He says Park is a "very bright guy" who brought together all the parts necessary in one package. "I have to applaud Levi for having the courage and conviction to do it."

Mass customization will "completely flip the economic equation normally involved in apparel," Tyrol says. Instead of having money tied up in product development and design, manufacturers can have "a lot less money hanging out in the breeze and more in their pockets up front to play with."

Ironically, Tyrol is slated to lose his Levi business as the jeans giant plans to install its own Cutting Edge cutters in the Mountain City plant this month, as well as an additional site in Stoney Creek, Canada. "I guess I'll get left out in the cold," Tyrol chuckles.

But he adds, "The world is full of opportunities. Levi is not the only customer."

For more information, contact Custom Clothing Technology Corp., (617) 630-8109; CAD Cut, (802) 223-4055; Cutting Edge, (617) 631-1390.

Source: From Apparel Industry Magazine, *January 1995, pp. 32–34.*

Brand Names

by Susan Reda

In a volatile business environment where nobody wants to close the door on a potential customer—regardless of what tier of retail they operate in or what their shoppers expect to pay—corporate executives overseeing brands are in the throes of some hard and fast decisions.

The opportunity to do more business is tempting, but most executives are vigilant about brand image and equity. They don't want to tarnish what has taken years to build. Stories of what has happened to brands such as Izod and Gitano—labels once coveted by retailers and consumers—weigh heavy in their decision-making process.

"In the '60s and '70s we were manufacturing-driven. The goal was to sell what you made to whatever takers were out there," recalls Tim Lambeth, president of the Lee Corp. "Now the consumer has so many choices that it's imperative for a manufacturer to hit a responsive chord, to talk to specific consumers with specialized products and marketing."

In short, it has become essential for megabrands such as Lee, Levi, and Vanity Fair to develop multiple brands for myriad consumers.

Needless to say, vendors approach segmentation from different angles.

At Vanity Fair Mills, executives have worked to keep the Vanity Fair brand firmly positioned in the department store sector. But understanding shifts in the retail marketplace, and changing consumer shopping patterns, they sought out a well-known label that would provide them with entree into the discount market. Vassarette fit the bill.

The combination of VF's marketing and manufacturing prowess combined with consumer recognition of the Vassarette brand, has resulted in a winner. Today Vassarette is among the top three brands sold at discount stores.

Executives at Liz Claiborne, long-time champions of department store retailing, have similar aspirations for the Villager and Crazy Horse labels recently acquired from Russ Togs. With a mature department store business, executives suggest that the prudent marketing of these brands toward shoppers with a somewhat tighter budget, may hold the key to the corporation's future success.

At Lee, where overexposure of the Lee brand had become a problem, executives recently decided to develop a new brand for discounters and to keep the Lee brand exclusive to the upstairs market. Playing off the Lee Riders name, a segment already established within the product line, the decision was made to launch a new brand, Riders, at discount stores in spring '93.

"The Riders brand is working extremely well, and I think part of the reason for that is that Riders was already a recognized brand, associated with Lee. It gave us a tremendous leg up at the outset," says Lambeth.

He admits that retailers on both sides of the fence were skeptical at first, but the success of this strategy has mellowed them.

"Discounters were not happy when we told them that we were taking the Lee brand out of their stores, but they were professional enough to give the new brand a shot," explains Lambeth. "Today the Riders brand has replaced about 75 percent of the volume previously done with Lee and that's still growing."

Apparently all their strategizing has paid off. Jeans volume at the Lee Corp. grew by more than 10 percent by the close of 1993.

The strategy at Sara Lee Corp., front runners in market segmentation and the development of highly successful brands, seems to be a combination of acquiring meaningful brand names and building them, and spinning off new brands that the consumer has some predetermined inclination toward.

Brands such as Champion, Jogbra and Henson Kickernick have benefited from Sara Lee executive marketing prowess. While Hanes Her Way and Just My Size, new brands which were developed as a result of the success of other Sara Lee products, are perfect examples of the corporation's ability to build from within.

Other companies have adopted still different strategies in an effort to segment their goods at retail.

Silver tab Levi's for instance, are offered to better department stores and some specialty store retailers. Red tab jeans, the company's premium, authentic five-pocket styles, are sold to most department and specialty store merchants. Orange tab denims are just a notch below red tabs in terms of styling, and retail for a few dollars less at discount stores.

Though San Francisco-based Levi's executives have been known to tweak the positioning in certain circumstances, most retailers have been pleased with their method of differentiation. It also proved sufficient for Macy's. The New York-based retailer, which refused to sell Levi's for many years because of gripes about their distribution, recently reopened its selling floor to Levi's.

With the retail landscape in a constant state of flux, new channels emerging, and hybrid retailers playing an increasingly important role, determining where a brand should be distributed can be a sticky issue.

Sears, Kohl's and Mervyn's are among the chains that manufacturers describe as falling into a sort of gray area. Does Mervyn's get Levi's red tab or the orange tab? Does Sears get Vanity Fair or Vassarette?

The question of branded distribution at Sears is one which vendors are grappling with today and will continue to try to sort out over the next few years. The 360-degree turnaround which the national retailer has made in apparel has raised some eyebrows to say the least, but at what point will they be on a par with JCPenney? With other department store competitors?

Manufacturers also have to guard their current business. Many question how their accounts would feel if they began selling their brand at Sears.

One manufacturer that came to grips with this issue is Healthtex. The brand, which is in the throes of a comeback, recently opted to sell Healthtex playwear at Sears.

"We took a look at what they've done and where they're going. We feel that it fits with our mission to be responsive to meeting the needs of consumers and retailers in middle market retail chains," explains Gary Simmons, Healthtex president.

"The relationships we've built with our customers are of utmost importance, so we told them one by one of our decision to sell Sears. No one said, 'Hey, that's great,' but they didn't threaten to pull our brand from their shelves either," says Simmons. "GMROI [Gross Margin Return on Inventory] is driving the product mix at retail and Healthtex is producing excellent turn and strong margins. I think that retailers in today's economic environment would rather compete than give that up."

John Freudenthal at Carson Pirie Scott doesn't buy into his thinking. "We really look for brands that keep their distribution clean. Obviously, a department store has a different expense structure from other types of operations and that's critical when you assess the steps we have to take to be competitive."

Another challenge which manufacturers face as they develop new brands for other retail tiers is to be certain that the product offering is noticeably different from goods they are producing for other types of retailers. Several merchants charge that in the rush to cash in on the fast growing discount tier many manufacturers have done little more than slap a different hangtag on a garment.

"I would be willing to bet that if you were shopping for a bra and you went to a discounter, Sears, and a department store you could buy the exact same bra for $8.99, $15.99 and $22," claims one

Midwest-based intimate apparel dmm [divisional merchandise manager]. "Even those manufacturers who do differentiate their products don't provide enough distinction."

Needless to say, vendors who fall into this trap will soon learn the shortsightedness of selling the customer short. Today, customers are cross shoppers and they are increasingly savvy about the products they're purchasing and the price value equation. Manufacturers who do not develop different products for different retail tiers risk the erosion of brand equity and the crumbling of customer loyalty.

Obviously, a brand's reputation can be a tough thing to rebuild, but one lesson that both manufacturers and retailers have learned is that it is not impossible.

The re-emergence of the Healthtex brand is testimony to that. When the Healthtex brand came up as a possible acquisition by VF Corp. back in 1990, executives were reticent. Quality had slipped, deliveries were unpredictable, and marketing was questionable. VF executives weren't sure there was life left in this brand. Ellen Rohde, then a corporate director of operations and later president of Healthtex, convinced VF to purchase the brand and over the last three years she has managed to turn the tide significantly.

Sales are up by 80 percent since the acquisition and Healthtex is expected to emerge profitable by the close of the 1993 fiscal year. In addition, the company's work force has grown by 69 percent.

Source: From Stores, *January 1994, pp. 35–38. Reprinted from* Stores *magazine, NRF Enterprises, Inc., 1994.*

When Vendors Become Retailers

by Susan Reda

When Robert Rockey, president of Levi Strauss North America, announced earlier this year that his giant manufacturing company would open a total of 240 stores over the next five years, he was following in the footsteps of Speedo, Liz Claiborne, Sony and a host of branded makers who are launching major moves into retailing.

At about the same time, Terry Lundgren, chief executive officer of Federated Merchandising, was unveiling plans for the $14 billion Federated Department Stores to raise its private label sales to 15 percent companywide—a steep rise from the 4 percent to 5 percent PL contributed to Federated's sales prior to its merger with Macy's.

As these prominent developments illustrate, manufacturers and retailers are engaged in a high-stakes game of trading places. In an effort to control their own destinies, diversify risk and build consumer awareness, both are moving at an accelerated pace toward vertical marketing.

The integration of manufacturing and retailing is hardly new. Factory outlets selling off-price goods, seconds and closeouts have been around for a long time. And speciality stores like The Gap and The Limited and department stores such as JCPenney and Macy's have emphasized private brands for years.

But what does seem different is the intensity of the effort and marketing skill going into these latest moves. For a manufacturer to have a factory outlet up in the mountains is a far cry from opening a glitzy new store with state-of-the-art merchandising across the street from a department store with which it has done business for years.

So far, the strains produced by these changes are most evident on the part of retailers, who complain that their long-time business partners are turning into competitors and cutting into their market share. But there are potential costs for manufacturers as well, and for both sides the results of these campaigns may be crucial in positioning them for control of the interactive retail market of the future.

"Good or bad, as resources open more stores they take away from what we're supposed to do and blur the lines between our job and theirs," says Michael Gould, chairman of New York-based Bloomingdale's. "Why should I spend money to build a shop for a brand that is out there opening its own stores? I think the time is fast approaching when we're all going to say, 'Time Out.'"

Manufacturers say they have no intention of eroding their brands' sales at department stores or of establishing a major new profit center through their retail ventures. Their goal, they maintain, is to boost their brands' identity at a time when retailers are consolidating and competition from private label goods is getting stronger.

"Philosophically and ethically, we've handled our stores at arm's length," says Jerome Chazen, chairman of Liz Claiborne, which currently operates 28 Liz Claiborne stores and will add five by the end of the year. "We do less for our own stores than we do for department stores.

"Since we began opening Liz Claiborne stores," he adds, "we've done everything we can to try to make sure that the main thrust of our business doesn't suffer."

But even if that is true in the short run, it seems clear that both sides are positioning themselves for a game with much higher stakes over the long term.

"The issue boils down to control," says Kate Murphy, vice president at Fitch, a Columbus, Ohio-based international consulting firm. "Manufacturers and retailers are utilizing vertical integration to control their brand, their image and their conversation with the consumer. The successful ones have the strongest prospects for survival."

Some analysts suggest that manufacturers that are now taking the vertical marketing track will have an edge in the future as selling direct to the consumer via interactive retailing gains a foothold.

"Clearly, manufacturers that are successfully operating retail stores are learning how to interact with shoppers and gaining valuable merchandising and marketing experience," points out Steve Johnson, a managing partner in Andersen Consulting's consumer

industry practice in Chicago. "When all the kinks have been worked out on the information superhighway, these suppliers will be right there saying, 'Give me a shot, I know what to do,' and they will because of the knowledge they've gained by going direct to the consumer with their stores."

But Ira Kalish, senior economist at Management Horizons, a division of Price Waterhouse, gives traditional department store retailers the upper hand in the battle for vertical marketing supremacy.

"Consolidation in the department store realm has resulted in a handful of very large retail companies with an enormous amount of power," says Kalish. "They can say we want this and that and manufacturers don't have much choice but to listen."

Moreover, department store merchants could turn the tables once again and open free-standing private brand shops in an attempt to bump up awareness of their own labels. JCPenney, for example, could develop stores focused on its popular Arizona line of jeans, going head to head with The Gap, or take a step further and set up an Arizona channel to reach consumers through interactive retailing.

Executives at companies such as Liz Claiborne and Nike say they are using stores as laboratories to test merchandising techniques and new products. Then they share information with national department store accounts.

"At the core of each Nike Town store is a very simple and specific objective: Enhance the Nike brand image," says Kevin Kutcher, retail spokesman for Nike, which operates four stores now and has four more on the drawing board.

Chazen says Liz Claiborne is applying the same approach to Elisabeth, its chain of large-size women's apparel stores. "We're opening Elisabeth stores for two reasons. First, we want to reap the benefits of the merchandising-laboratory concept for this collection. Second, we're concerned about the presentation of large-size sportswear in department stores.

"We've always believed that this customer would respond to a little TLC and some real service," Chazen adds. "And, guess what? We were right."

As the company prepares to add 25 to 30 Elisabeth stores this year, Chazen stresses that programs are being set up and special attention is being paid to working with the department stores in the malls where these stores will be located.

Beth Ravit, president of the Speedo retail division of Authentic Fitness, says the company opened stores in part out of frustration over its difficulty in getting retailers to view Speedo as a total fitness collection. "Our channels of distribution were driven by our image as a racing swimwear resource, and we couldn't seem to convince merchants that we were more than that," she says.

Speedo has opened 54 units over the past three years, and Ravit expects that number to climb to 100 by the end of the year. The success of the stores, she argues, has created a win-win situation for both the brand and the retailers that stock it.

"The immediate feedback we get from customers is shared with our accounts and as a result we've had some real product success stories," says Ravit.

Some retailers say this sharing of information has been beneficial.

Jack Guze, group vice president-men's apparel, children's wear and footwear at Sears, says he is not sure how many is too many when it comes to branded suppliers opening their own stores. Right now, though, he views this trend as part of an evolutionary process.

"Manufacturer stores are raising brand awareness and showcasing some creative ideas in store design and merchandise presentation—neither of which hurts our business," Guze observes.

Shortly after joining Sears, Guze spent some time in the Original Levi's store on Lexington Avenue in Manhattan. The store sparked some ideas, he recalls, and served as a springboard for talks with executives at Levi's about plans for Sears' Ultimate Jeans shops.

"We were able to incorporate a merchandising technique in our shops that we learned from their stores. By making our jeans bins deeper, we doubled the inventory capacity on the selling floor," Guze says. "We also borrowed some ideas that enable us to effectively merchandise tops with jeans."

Despite the perceptions of many retailers, there isn't currently any hard evidence that the new competition is actually stealing sales. In fact, Claiborne, Nike and Levi Strauss cite research showing the opposite.

"In many cases that I'm aware of, manufacturers that have opened stores in malls have not only been successful, but sales have increased in department stores in the same mall," says Bill Ress, a consultant for Levi Strauss. "I'm not sure I can explain it, except to say that the more strongly a brand is positioned, the louder the message is to the consumer that this is an important label."

The great equalizer is that operating retail stores and developing, manufacturing and marketing products are both so difficult.

"Manufacturers are learning that retailing is a very different business from manufacturing and vice versa. There will be failures and rethinkings on both sides," says Irwin Cohen, chairman of the Deloitte & Touche TRADE Retail Group.

"There's no wrong or right here. It's just a time in life when everyone is searching for answers," Cohen continues. "Manufacturers are concerned about the future of the distribution channels they sell through, and retailers are fixed on developing a competitive advantage at a time when brand and product parity is running rampant."

Source: From Stores, *June 1995, pp 18–21. Reprinted from* Stores *magazine, NRF Enterprises, Inc., 1995.*

More Stores to Shift Marking Costs to Vendors

by Jeff Black

If you're interested in a partnership with Federated Department Stores, you'd better get acquainted with the Universal Product Code (UPC).

That's the word from Allen Questrom, chairman and chief executive officer of the retail giant, who made clear the growing importance of vendor-marked merchandise at the recent National Retail Federation Convention.

Small manufacturers, he stressed, "may handicap themselves if they aren't into UPC. Smaller companies are where the jobs are being produced. We need to make sure they're educated about UPC."

In a nutshell, the UPC is the code most retailers and/or vendors use to create bar codes for merchandise. UCC bar codes are used for cartons. That's not new.

What's new is the pressure retailers generally—not just Federated—are putting on vendors to assume the cost of marking merchandise and cartons.

Questrom said it's critical for vendors to use the UPC if they want to participate in programs with Federated. According to marking machine makers, other stores are insisting as much.

"Retailers have identified marking as a costly enterprise," said Jacqueline Simmonds, a market manager for the Soabar Systems division of Avery Dennison, Philadelphia, Pa., "so a lot of apparel people are now being asked to do marking."

Fact is, as accuracy, cost cutting and efficiency continue to dominate retail boardroom discussions, more stores are making marking a condition of doing business, she said.

Consequently, "we've identified vendor marking as a growth area for us this year," said Simmonds.

According to one study, vendor marking is already catching hold.

Deloitte & Touche, in its fifth annual Bar Code/EDI/Quick Response survey, found that the number of companies scanning vendor-marked goods more than doubled in 1992, from 20 percent to 52 percent among retailers who scan.

Mass merchants and department stores are leaders in implementing the scanning of vendor-marked UPC bar codes, according to the study.

It's broad in scope, but the survey, coupled with comments by apparel retailers and marking machine suppliers, indicates that vendor scanning is on the rise.

Marking systems aren't cheap. At the very least, they require a printer and usually software, which together can run anywhere from $4,000 to $15,000.

Little wonder, then, that small vendors—especially those not already on EDI—get nervous when faced with the decision to mark or be dropped from the matrix.

Marker machine executives say there is little cause for worry. By working closely with retailers, many packages have been put together that make the transition easier.

Avery Dennison is one company offering packages to vendors. It sells marking machines, printers and the labels, tags, and softwear packages necessary to work with J.C. Penney, for instance. Packages for other retailers are also available.

Monarch Marking Systems has just introduced Vendor Connect, a windows-based PC product that allows a vendor to code a package or container, send it, and download the purchase order receipts, which are recorded on EDI and transferred into the Vendor Connect system, which can then be recorded and analyzed for vendor use.

All of this isn't just for the benefit of the retailer. By bar coding merchandise, the vendor stands to gain a lot. Accuracy, chargebacks, tracking merchandise—all can be helped by bar coding goods.

"We want to convince apparel makers that it's a good idea for them for their internal businesses as well," said Richard Rosen, director of business development at Monarch.

"With these systems, you get instant verification your goods arrived, what arrived, and eventually, what was sold. This cuts down dramatically on returns, and it serves as a verification system."

But the question whether to buy a marking system or not may be moot.

According to some, the smaller players should resign themselves to the change, even though, for many, it's fundamental. "The vendors that hop onto this and move forward are the ones that'll be around for the long haul," said Simmonds.

Source: From DNR *special issue, "Shifting the Costs," 1993, pp 6–7. Reprinted by permission.*

Chapter Review

Key Words and Concepts

Define, identify, or briefly explain the following:

Accounts payable	Manufacturer
Accounts receivable	Marker
Agile manufacturing	Market center
Apparel jobber	Market weeks
Apparel marts	Merchandisers
Body scanning	Modular production system
CEO	Outside shop
Contractor	Preassembly operations
COO	Preproduction operations
Cooperative advertising	Product development
Computer-aided design (CAD)	Progressive bundle system
Computer integrated manufacturing (CIM)	Quick Response (QR)
Designers	Rapid replenishment
Elias Howe	Ready-to-wear
807 production	Real time merchandising (RTM)
Factoring	Regional showroom
Factors	Royalty fee
Grainline	Seasonal line
Grading	Secondary fashion centers
ILGWU	Seventh Avenue (SA)
Initial public offering (IPO)	Sourcing
Inside shop	Style piracy
Isaac Singer	Sweatshop
Knock-off	Tariff
Leveraged buyout	Triangle Shirtwaist Fire
Licensee	Trunk show
Licensing	UNITE
Licensor	Vendor
Line	

Review Questions

1. Explain the economic importance of the women's and children's apparel industry to the United States.
2. Why is the SIC system useful to one who is studying the apparel industry?
3. In chronological order, give the major developments that contributed to the growth of the women's ready-to-wear industry and explain the importance of each.
4. What forms of industry restructuring have we seen in recent years?
5. What changes have occurred in the 1990s for the industry's union?
6. Describe the five major functional areas of an apparel firm as covered in this chapter.
7. Give the major steps involved in the development and production of apparel.
8. Identify as many ways as you can that computers have drastically changed the apparel industry.
9. Contrast the progressive bundle system of production with modular production. If you were a sewing operator, which would you prefer? Why?
10. Describe the role Quick Response has in today's apparel industry.
11. What is real time merchandising?
12. Discuss the strategies that may be used by an apparel producer to market a line to retailers.
13. Discuss the methods by which manufacturers are selling directly to consumers and give an example of each.
14. Explain the difference between a manufacturer, an apparel jobber, and a contractor. What are the advantages of each?
15. Is the practice of style piracy good or bad for the fashion industry? Why?
16. Why is licensing so prevalent in the fashion industry?
17. Explain why New York developed into the fashion capital of the United States. Do you think it will retain its present status?
18. What is the role of regional marts in the marketing of apparel?
19. Find an article in a current trade publication that relates to the information in this chapter. Explain how your article relates to the new information you learned.

References

Abend, J. (1993, June). Factors report vigorous business. *Bobbin*, pp. 70–73.

American Apparel Manufacturers Association. (1995). *Focus: Economic profile of the apparel industry*. Arlington, VA: Author.

American Apparel Manufacturers Association. (1996). *Focus: Economic profile of the apparel industry*. Arlington, VA: Author.

Apparel manufacturers' results for the fourth quarter and year. (1996, March 4). *Women's Wear Daily*, p. 22.

Brown, P. (1989, February/March). Quick Response: Fashion's quickening pulse. *Fairchild supplement: Retailing technology & operations*. New York: Fairchild.

The city that dresses a nation. (1976, February 15). *New York Sunday News*.

Clune, R. (1993, October 5). [TC]^2's agile manufacturing to give preview of 21st century production. *Daily News Record*, p. 8.

Dallas, the business of fashion. (1985, October 15). *Women's Wear Daily*.

Feitelberg, R. (1994, December 13). NY gripe: Regional schedules. *Women's Wear Daily*, pp. 21, 22.

Frank, B. (1985). *Profitable merchandising of apparel* (2nd ed.). New York: National Knitwear and Sportswear Association.

Friedman, A. (1995a, February 21). Apparel unions "UNITE." *Women's Wear Daily*, pp. 10–11.

Friedman, A. (1995b, May 25). New York gives push to private label plan, cuts funding to GIDC. *Women's Wear Daily*, pp. 1, 10.

From Michael to Mickey, licensed products show broad appeal. (1995, June). *Stores*, pp. 34–37.

Glock, R., & Kunz, G. (1995). *Apparel manufacturing: Sewn product analysis* (2nd ed.). Upper Saddle River, NJ: Prentice Hall.

Haber, H. (1995, May 25). Dallas Market Center getting @ address. *Women's Wear Daily*, pp. 2, 14.

He's a fashion purist with the golden touch. (1964, September 12). *Business Week*.

Kids feel ignored by retailers. (1995, April). *Apparel Industry Magazine*, p. 16.

Kidwell, C., & Christman, M. (1974). *Suiting everyone: The democratization of clothing in America*. Washington, DC: Smithsonian Institution Press.

Kunz, G. (1995). Behavioral theory of the apparel firm: A beginning. *Clothing and Textiles Research Journal, 13* (4), 252–261.

Kurt Salmon Associates. (1995). *Vision for the new millennium. . . evolving to consumer response*. Atlanta: Author.

Levi Strauss & Co. (1995, February). *NewsWatch*. San Francisco: Author.

The Licensing Letter. (1995). New York: EPM Communications, Inc.

Lloyd, B. (1994a, August 3). Atlanta Market Center positioning itself for future growth. *DNR*, p. 5.

Lloyd, B. (1994b, November 8). Marts face uphill battle in muddled market: Atlanta Apparel Mart. *DNR*, pp. 8, 10.

More than just kid stuff. (1985, May 26). *Women's Wear Daily*.

Reda, S. (1995, June). When vendors become retailers. *Stores*, pp. 18–21.

Sharoff, R. (1994, November 8). Marts face uphill battle in muddled market: Chicago Apparel Center. *DNR*, pp. 8, 10.

Thornton, M. (1993, January). Factoring: Which service is best for you? *Apparel Industry Magazine*, pp. 71–76.

Top 100 sewn products companies '95. (1995, June). *Apparel Industry Magazine*, 17–40.

U.S. Department of Commerce. (October 1966). *Long term economic growth 1860–1965*. Washington, DC: Author.

Vargo, J. (1994, November 8). Marts face uphill battle in muddled market: Dallas Market Center. *Women's Wear Daily*, pp. 8, 11.

Williamson, R. (1994, September 26). Mart's keys for growth. *Women's Wear Daily*, pp. 22–23.

Select Bibliography

American Apparel Manufacturers Association. (annual). *Focus: Economic profile of the apparel industry*. Arlington, VA: Author.

Brown, P. (1991). *Ready-to-wear apparel analysis*. Upper Saddle River, NJ: Merrill/Prentice Hall.

Carr, H., & Latham, B. (1994). *The technology of clothing manufacture*. Oxford, UK: Blackwell Science.

Carr, H., & Pomeroy, J. (1992). *Fashion design and product development*. Oxford, UK: Blackwell Science.

Chuter, A. (1995). *Introduction to clothing production management*. Oxford, UK: Blackwell Science.

Chuter, A. (1995). *Quality management in clothing and textiles*. Oxford, UK: Blackwell Science.

Cooklin, G. (1991). *Introduction to clothing manufacture*. Oxford, UK: Blackwell Science.

Dickerson, K. (1995). *Textiles and apparel in the global economy* (2nd ed.). Upper Saddle River, NJ: Merrill/Prentice Hall.

Dubinsky, D. (1977). *David Dubinsky: A life with labor*. New York: Simon & Schuster.

Fairchild Publications. (annual). *Fairchild's textile & apparel financial directory*. New York: Author.

Fairchild Publications. (annual). *WWD buyer's guide: Women's apparel and accessories manufacturers*. New York: Author.

Fairchild Publications. (annual). *WWD supplier's guide: Women's apparel and accessories manufacturers*. New York: Author.

Finnie, T. (1992). *Textiles and apparel in the USA: Restructuring for the 1990s*. London: The Economist Intelligence Unit.

Gaines, S. (1991). *Simply Halston—the untold story*. New York: G.P. Putnam's Sons.

Geoello, D., & Berke, B. (1979). *Fashion production terms*. New York: Fairchild.

Glock, R., & Kunz, G. (1995). *Apparel manufacturing: Sewn product analysis* (2nd ed.). Upper Saddle River, NJ: Prentice Hall.

Guber, S., & Berry, J. (1993). *Marketing to and through kids*. New York: McGraw-Hill.

Hunter, N. (1990). *Quick Response in apparel manufacturing*. Manchester, UK: Textile Institute.

Mass, M. (1991). *Fashion designers*.

Morgenson, G. (1992, May 11). The feminization of Seventh Avenue. *Forbes*, pp. 116–120.

Solinger, J. (1988). *Apparel manufacturing handbook* (2nd ed.). New York: Van Nostrand Reinhold.

Stegemeyer, A. (1995). *Who's who in fashion* (3rd ed). New York: Fairchild.

Stein, L. (1962). *The Triangle fire*. Philadelphia: Lippincott.

Tate, S., & Edwards, M. (1990). *Inside fashion design*. New York: Harper Collins College.

Ulrich, P. (1995). "Look for the label"—The International Ladies' Garment Workers' Union label campaign. *Clothing and Textiles Research Journal, 13* (1), 49–56.

ZuHone, L., & Morganosky, M. (1995). Exchange relationships between apparel retailers and manufacturers. *Clothing and Textiles Research Journal, 13* (1), 57–64.

Trade Associations

American Apparel Manufacturers Association, 2500 Wilson Blvd., Suite 301, Arlington, VA 22201.

American Coat and Suit Manufacturers Association, 450 Seventh Ave., New York, NY 10123.

Bureau of Wholesale Sales Representatives, 1801 Peachtree Rd., NE, Suite 200, Atlanta, GA 30309.

California Fashion Creators, 110 E. 9th St., Los Angeles, CA 90015.

Canadian Apparel Federation, 130 Slater St., Suite 605, Ottawa, Ontario K1P 6E2, Canada.

Canadian Association of Wholesale Sales Representatives, 1712 Avenue Rd., Box 54546, Toronto, Ontario M5M 4NS, Canada.

Children's Apparel Manufacturers Association, 8270 Mountain Sights, Room 101, Montreal, Quebec H4P 2B7, Canada.

Color Association of the United States, 409 W. 44 St., New York, NY 10036.

Council of Fashion Designers of America, 1633 Broadway, New York, NY 10019.

Ladies Apparel Contractors Association, 450 Seventh Ave., New York, NY 10001.

National Association of Blouse Manufacturers, 450 Seventh Ave., New York, NY 10001.

National Association of Uniform Manufacturers and Distributors, 1156 Ave. of the Americas, New York, NY 10036.

National Dress Manufacturers Association, 570 Seventh Ave., New York, NY 10018.

National Knitwear and Sportswear Association, 386 Park Ave. S., New York, NY 10016.

The Fashion Association, 475 Park Ave. S., 17th Floor, New York, NY 10016.

United Infant's and Children's Wear Association, 520 Eighth Ave., New York, NY 10018.

Trade Publications

Apparel Industry Magazine, 6255 Barfield Rd., Suite 200, Atlanta, GA 30328-4300.

Apparel International, The White House, 60 High St., Potters Bar, Herts EN6 5AB, U.K.

The Apparel Strategist, Apparel Information Resources, 101 E. Locust St., Fleetwood, PA 19522.

Bobbin, 1110 Old Shop Rd., Columbia, SC 29202

California Apparel News, 110 E. 9th St., Suite A-777, Los Angeles, CA 90079.

Canadian Apparel Manufacturer, 1 Pacifique, Ste. Anne de Bellevue, Quebec H9X 1C5, Canada.

CAMA Review (Children's Apparel Manufacturers Association), 3110, 6900 boul. Decarie, Montreal, Quebec H3X 2T8, Canada.

Chicago Apparel News, Ste. 1045, 350 N. Orleans St., Chicago, IL 60654.

The Discount Merchandiser, 233 Park Ave. S., New York, NY 10003.

Earnshaw's Infants-Girls-Boys Wear Review, 475 Fire Island Ave., Babylon, NY 11702.

Fur Age Weekly, P.O. Box 868, Glenwood Landing, NY 11547.

International Colour Authority, 23 Bloomsbury Square, London WCIA 2PJ, U.K.

Kid's Fashions, Larkin Group, 100 Wells Ave., Newton, MA 02159.

The Licensing Letter, 160 Mercer St., 3rd Floor, New York, NY 10012-3212.

Outerwear, 19 W. 21 St., #403, New York, NY 10010.

Private Level Development, 19 W. 21 St., #403, New York, NY 10010.

Sourcing News, 110 W. 40 St., New York, NY 10018.

Women's Wear Daily, 7 W. 34 St., New York, NY 10001-8191.

World Clothing Manufacturer, 23 Bloomsbury Square, London WC1A 2PJ, U.K.

*T*he Menswear Industry

*U**ntil the 1950s, the average* man's wardrobe consisted of one or more dark suits with vests, white shirts, subdued colored ties, highly polished shoes, an overcoat, and a hat. Whatever changes in fashion did take place usually expressed themselves in little more than variations in the width of lapels, the number of buttons, the style and flap of a jacket pocket, and the location of a vent in the suit jacket. The industry that produced men's garments did not consider itself to be in the fast-changing business of fashion.

Change came dramatically after World War II. Surfeited with khaki drabness, many of the younger men yearned for color, even in undershirts. Suburban living, the shorter work week, and the trend toward family-oriented leisure activities set up a demand for sports and leisure wear and resulted in a much freer style of dress even during business hours. By the 1960s, the presence of a large and highly visible generation of young adults sparked a demand for greater variety, faster change, and new opportunities for expression of individuality. Through the 1970s and on into the 1980s, the winds of fashion change continued to blow up a storm in the men's field. From the late 1980s and into the 1990s, active sportswear has created a casual dress code that has revolutionized and revitalized the menswear industry. Special-purpose wardrobes abound in the closets of fashion-conscious males who want to make a "statement" about themselves, with different wardrobes for work, sports, evenings out, shopping, and just hanging out. (The same is true for females, but this is relatively new for males.)

Today men's interest in fashion has become increasingly pronounced and the industry that serves them has responded accordingly. Obviously then, no book about the fashion business would be complete without a discussion of the menswear industry—the subject of this chapter and the readings that follow it.

Economic Importance

The menswear industry's importance as a segment of the U.S. fashion business is demonstrated by such figures as these: More than 2,500 separate companies are engaged in the production of men's and boys' clothing and furnishings. They employ nearly 300,000 people, the majority of whom are engaged directly in production activities. Factory output is estimated at about $21 billion (wholesale value) for 1994 (American Apparel Manufacturers Association, 1995).

Another measure of the importance of the industry is that there is scarcely an area of the United States in which it does not have production facilities. Some segments of the industry, such as tailored clothing, require highly skilled workers. Others, such as shirts and work clothing (including the ever-present jeans), can provide employment even for people with minimal skills, as long as they can guide a seam through a sewing machine.

Still another indication of the industry's importance: Consumer expenditures in 1994 for men's and boys' clothing and accessories were more than $50 billion, exclusive of shoes. Not all of this was domestic production, of course, nor did all of the domestic industry's output necessarily go to consumers in this country (U.S. Dept. of Commerce).

Men's and boys' clothing has been the bright spot in the apparel industry in the 1990s, outperforming the apparel industry in general. Although the women's and children's wear industry sales have generally been sluggish, sales in the men's and boys' segments have been strong. Many in the apparel industry have taken special note of this and made special efforts to capitalize on this strong business and to serve those related to that business. Figure 6–1, for example, shows an example of a leading trade publication's efforts to provide consumer information useful to firms in the industry.

A number of factors are credited for the strong menswear market. An important one has been men's and boys' increasing interest in clothing—a trend to be discussed further in this chapter. Other explanations include the trends toward casual "office wear," the appeal of wrinkle-resistant apparel, and a move toward European styling in the suit and coat areas.

History and Development

The U.S. ready-to-wear apparel industry started with clothing for men; it was born in the early 1800s, almost half a century before women's ready-to-wear had its beginnings. Until that time, all men's apparel in this country either was custom tailored, for those who could afford this service (Figure 6-2), or was made at home for those less affluent.

Early Beginnings in the Nineteenth Century

Like so many other segments of the fashion industry, menswear manufacturing began with the efforts of some enterprising individuals who saw a need and proceeded to fill it. In this case, the need was to supply clothes for men who either had no access to the then-customary source of supply—the housewife's nimble fingers—or could not afford custom-made clothing.

Development of Men's Ready-to-Wear

In such port cities as New Bedford, New York, Boston, Philadelphia, and Baltimore, a few venturesome tailoring shops conceived the idea of producing and selling cheap ready-to-wear trousers, jackets, and shirts for sailors who needed to replenish their wardrobes inexpensively and immediately during their brief stops in port. These clothes were poorly made in low-quality fabrics. The cutting was done in the dealers' shops and the garments were then sent out to local women for hand sewing.

This early ready-made clothing was referred to as "**slops**," a term from which the word *sloppy* developed, with the same connotation then as now. It was remarked that these garments "could be readily recognized about as far as the wearer could be seen. Hence, there was a sort of shame in the purchase and wear of such clothing, and it was considered almost disreputable to wear it; it was at once a reflection upon a man's taste and a supposed indication of his poverty" (Kidwell & Christman, 1974). Nevertheless, the market for ready-made clothing soon expanded to serve bachelors

Figure 6–1

An advertisement in DNR depicts the growing attention paid to the menswear industry.

SPECIAL ISSUE AUGUST 2, 1995

Why Men Buy

DNR'S NATIONAL SURVEY OF CONSUMER ATTITUDES TOWARDS BUYING MEN'S WEAR

The DNR national survey of consumer attitudes towards men's wear and men's wear retailers will consist of 1000 telephone interviews in the nations 20 top metropolitan areas.

THE SURVEY:

- Attitudes towards purchasing, including sales and mark downs.
- Attributes consumers consider important in purchasing men's wear.
- Frequency of shopping/purchasing.
- Factors influencing men's wear purchases like advertising, significant others.
- Favorite store for shopping for men's apparel and reasons for this selection.
- Attitudes towards brands and private label.
- Attitudes towards new products like WR slacks, shirts.
- Favorite apparel items.
- Attitudes toward changes in dress codes, if appropriate.
- Concepts of "Fridaywear". What is "casual" for office?

The exclusive presentation of the survey findings will be presented at the **Chicago Men's Wear Collective**
Monday, August 7
Continental Breakfast 8:00 AM
Presentation 8:30 AM
RSVP: Sonja Nelson (312) 527-7759

The survey will be conducted by America's Research Group and the results will be presented by its Chairman, C Britt Beemer.

For advertising information please contact: Susan Stolar at (212) 630-4824 or your DNR sales representative

- NEW YORK (212) 630-4700 • DALLAS (214) 227-1344
- LOS ANGELES (310) 442-6735 • ATLANTA (404) 633-8461
- CHICAGO (212) 630-4824 • MILAN (39) (2) 760-05-078
- PARIS (33) (1) 44.51.13.00

DNR

THE DNR NATIONAL MEN'S WEAR SURVEY REPORT
ISSUE DATE: AUGUST 2
Ad Close: July 17

Bonus Distribution at the Chicago Men's Wear Collective, August 6-8

Source: From *DNR* (1995, July), p. 8. Reprinted courtesy of Fairchild Publications.

The Cut of The Coat

Tells the taste of the tailor. The garment that strikes your fancy may not be the one that you should wear. In the mirror of the retail clothier you cannot see yourself as others see you. Is it safe to trust your appearance to the judgment of the ready-made salesman; biased by the necessity of fitting you to the clothing rather than the clothing to you? Individuality and character are subtly expressed in every garment I make. Years of experience in serving the best dressers guarantee that clothing made by me is perfect in style and finish, and is of the color and cut best suited to the wearer's complexion and figure.

BLENHEIM

Tailor of Taste

Source: Courtesy of the Bettmann Archive

who had no one at home to sew for them and plantation owners who needed cheap clothing for their slaves.

From Tailors to Manufacturers

Since no firms then existed that produced clothing for others to sell, these early shops functioned as both retailers and manufacturers. Some of the proprietors were custom tailors who produced ready-made garments from cheaper grades of cloth in addition to carrying on their primary business of made-to-measure clothing. Others cut the cloth on store premises and contracted to have the sewing done outside by people who worked at home.

As industrialization developed in the early nineteenth century, cities grew and a new mass market began to emerge among middle-class or white-collar city dwellers. To attract these customers, some of the more resourceful shop owners offered higher priced and better made garments. The quality of "store clothes" improved and their acceptance increased. By 1830, the market for "store bought" apparel had expanded so greatly that there were firms specializing in the manufacture of garments for others to sell at retail. The first steps in the establishment of the men's clothing industry as we know it today had been taken. By 1835, some manufacturers in New York City, then the nation's leading center for ready-made men's clothing, reportedly employed from 300 to 500 workers (Cobrin, 1971). Boston, Philadelphia, Newark, and Baltimore also progressed rapidly as manufacturing centers, as did Rochester and Cincinnati, toward the middle of the century. Impetus was gained when the sewing machine was developed in the middle of the 1800s.

Among the early producers of men's ready-mades was one of today's most famous and prestigious retailers of men's apparel—Brooks Brothers. Founded in 1818 as a custom-tailoring shop, the company got its start in ready-to-wear during the early period of industrialization. By 1857, it employed 78 tailors who worked on the premises and more than 1,500 outside workers (Kidwell & Christman, 1974).

Work Clothes for Laborers

A development that contributed in a special way to the growth of the menswear industry was the Gold Rush of 1848, which drew thousands of men to the West to pan or dig for gold. Anticipating that these prospectors would need tents to shelter them, a man named Levi Strauss went to California with a supply of heavy fabrics from which to make tents. Among these fabrics was one from France, then called *de Nime,* later Americanized to *denim.* Seeing a need for workclothes, he used his fabrics not for tents but to make workpants that featured large back pockets to hold mining tools. When he added metal rivets to the pockets to hold them securely, the success of his pants was ensured. The menswear industry grew in a way typical of American frontier life—with workclothes for laborers. Aside from Levi Strauss' contribution, the industry grew generally as a result of the westward migration. The men who pushed the frontier westward, not just in California but in the prairies and the mountain states, became a promising market for ready-made clothing. Plants to produce such clothing developed in Chicago and St. Louis to meet the demand.

Standardization of Sizes

The manufacture of ready-to-wear is based on **standardized sizes** in sufficient variety so that almost any figure can be accommodated by one of them. In the early years of the industry, each manufacturer worked out its own set of sizes and made garments to its own specifications, hoping to fit as many people as possible. The fit of these early garments was far from perfect.

One of the biggest boosts to the men's ready-to-wear clothing industry came from the government orders for soldiers' uniforms during the Civil War. Because hand sewing could not keep pace with the Army's needs, factories had to be built and equipped with the then-new sewing machines. Also, in order to facilitate the production of its uniforms, the Army surveyed the height and chest measurements of more than a million recruits, and thus provided the first mass of statistical data on the form and build of American men. After the war, the results of the Army study were made available to producers of men's civilian clothing. This put the sizing of men's ready-to-wear on a scientific basis and, by making improved fit possible, hastened the change from homemade and custom-made to factory-made garments.

Twentieth-Century Developments

By the time the menswear business entered the twentieth century, it was no longer an industry of small entrepreneurs; it had its share of large enterprises. As the present century progressed, there came such developments as unionization, public ownership, and, in time, a return to private ownership on the part of some of those who had earlier gone public.

"The Amalgamated" (ACTWU)—Now UNITE

Like the women's garment industry, the men's clothing industry presented a dismal labor picture at the beginning of this century, with sweatshops prevalent. Producers contracted to have the sewing of garments done outside their plants, either by individuals who did the work in their tenement homes or by contractors who gathered sewing hands together in equally uncomfortable and unsanitary lofts.

In 1910, a strike that started at the Hart, Schaffner & Marx plant in Chicago spread and eventually drew 35,000 workers from their jobs. Settlement of the dispute brought improved working conditions, reduced working hours to 54 hours a week, and set up machinery for adjusting grievances. A few years later, in 1914, the craft union that formerly represented the men's clothing workers yielded its place to the Amalgamated Clothing Workers of America, an industry union, and one that has established a record of labor peace and pioneering effort.

"The Amalgamated" worked for arbitration and industry-wide bargaining; it sought stable labor relations with management as a means of keeping its people employed. It has encouraged scientific techniques in industry management, and it has provided extensive and innovative social welfare services to its members. The union points with pride to its relationship with that same Hart, Schaffner & Marx, at whose Chicago factory a strike triggered the events that led to the Amalgamated's birth. For more than 50 years, that plant, now the world's largest in the men's clothing field, did not have a strike.

In the 1970s, the Amalgamated merged with the Textile Workers of America and the United Shoe Workers of America to form the Amalgamated Clothing and Textile Workers Union (ACTWU). In 1995, this union merged with the International Ladies Garment Workers Union to form the Union of Needletrades, Industrial, & Textile Employees (UNITE). Virtually all factories in the United States that produce men's tailored clothing (suits, tailored sports coats, formal wear, top coats, etc.) are unionized today. This is not true, however, of other segments of the men's apparel industry, such as sportswear. In that respect, the union does not have control over its industry. In part, this situation arises because production of men's apparel is widespread throughout the United States; and in part, it is due to the varying patterns of production in the different segments of the industry.

Public Ownership in the 1960s

Until the 1960s, publicly owned firms were the exception rather than the rule in menswear. Just as was the case in women's apparel at that time, most concerns were individually owned enterprises, partnerships, or closely held corporations. During the 1960s, many firms in the men's field went public, for much the same reasons as prevailed in the women's field. In some instances, it was a way for a proprietor with no family successor to ease his way into retirement; in others, it was a need for expansion capital. The lure of expansion capital is a strong one. Without it, firms can expand only to the extent that they plow back the profits of their operations year after year. Drawing on the public's invested capital is a faster way.

Private Ownership in the 1980s

Like the women's industry, in the ultracompetitive atmosphere of the 1980s, some major men's apparel producers began to see public ownership as more of a liability than an asset. Publicly owned companies have a responsibility to shareholders, and this includes public disclosure of new marketing plans and strategies to the extent that swift, silent changes of course are difficult to execute. Some firms, therefore, decided to go private—that is, to buy back their corporation's stock. **Levi Strauss & Co.** took this step. By returning a company to private ownership, a firm is freer in decision making; it is no longer in the spotlight turned on public companies by investment experts; it is protected from the possibility of hostile takeovers.

Nature of the Industry

The menswear industry, which also includes garments for boys and youths, resembles the women's wear industry in some ways and differs from it in others. Their points of resemblance include the following: (1) manufacturers usually specialize in clearly definable categories of garments, (2) producers in the various industry branches present seasonal lines, and (3) designer names are featured. Still another point of resemblance is the importance of collections that feature complete, coordinated groups of merchandise, all of which are produced, sold, and ultimately displayed in retail stores under a single brand or designer name. A still later development is the growing importance of classification (pants, t-shirts) merchandising to avoid excessive markdowns sometimes caused by buying complete collections. This development mirrors a prior development from decades ago in women's sportswear as the sportswear market was growing and expanding.

Points of difference from the women's field are numerous: (1) the larger firms account for a larger share of the men's industry's total output; (2) manufacturers' brand names have been long established, may be better known, often are more important to the consumer, and frequently are more influential in marketing than they are in the women's field; and (3) the contracting system, so much a part of the women's field is somewhat less common. On the last point, however, the growing importance of sportswear is increasing the use of the contracting system.

Like other parts of the apparel industry, the men's and boys' segment has become increasingly global. Various lines, even for some of the leading firms, may be produced by overseas contractors. Similarly, a number of retailers may develop their own men's and boys' lines and contract production just as U.S. manufacturers do.

Men's and Boys' SIC Groupings

Just as the women's and children's apparel industry has Standard Industrial Classification (SIC) categories for firms by garment type, so does the men's and boys' wear industry. The menswear industry differs from women's wear because the types of firms are not as clearly defined. That is, women's wear has more distinct categories that clearly identify product groupings included. Categories for firms in the men's and boys' wear industry are shown in Table 6–1.

In the lexicon of the men's apparel industry, the term **tailored clothing** refers to structured or semistructured suits, overcoats, sports jackets, and separate slacks, the production of which may involve some hand-tailoring operations. This division at one time so dominated the industry that, to the consumer, the term *men's clothing* was synonymous with tailored clothing. Not so today, as we shall discuss later in this chapter.

Types of Firms

Many of the largest menswear firms began as just that. They produced garments for men, and sometimes boys. In recent years, however, many firms have expanded into women's wear, either by creating or acquiring women's divisions. Some of these major firms are shown in Table 6–2.

Table 6–1	Men's and Boys' Apparel Industry by Standard Industrial Classification (SIC) Codes

SIC Code	Branch of Industry
23	Apparel
231	Men's and boys' suits and coats
232	Men's and boys' apparel and furnishings
2321	Shirts and nightwear
2322	Underwear and nightwear
2323	Neckwear
2324	Trousers and slacks (jeans included)
2325	Work clothing
2326	Other clothing, nec[a]

[a]Not elsewhere classified.
Source: From *Standard Industrial Classification Manual* by United States Executive Office of the President, Office of Management and Budget, 1987, Washington, DC: Author.

Table 6–2	Major Menswear Producers[a]: Selected Examples

Company	1994/1995 Sales (in $ millions)	Principal Menswear Products
Levi Strauss & Co.	6,708	Jeans, sportswear (all products in total)
Phillips-Van Heusen	1,256[b]	Shirts, sportswear (includes retail stores)
Hartmarx	595	Tailored clothing (and office casual wear)
Oxford Industries	676	Shirts, sportswear
Williamson-Dickie Mfg. Co.	500[b] (est.)	Sportswear, industrial wear
Tommy Hilfiger Corp.	441	Casual wear, relaxed dress clothing
Haggar Corp.	426	Slacks, casual wear
Farah, Inc.	242	Slacks, casual wear
Hugo Boss, U.S.A.	112[b]	Suits, casual wear

[a]Although menswear is a major focus of these firms, in nearly all cases, they also have women's wear divisions that account for a significant portion of annual sales.
[b]From "Top 100 Sewn Products Companies '95," June 1995, *Apparel Industry Magazine,* pp. 18–40. These figures are for 1994 sales.
Source of data, except as noted: "Apparel Manufacturers' Results for the Fourth Quarter and Year," March 4, 1996, *Women's Wear Daily,* p. 22.

Levi Strauss & Co. expanded from a men's jeans firm to one that later produced jeans for women and children, and later still other apparel for both men and women. Today few people would think of this company as a "men's" company because of the large volume of sales to women and children. Ralph Lauren also started in menswear, expanded into women's wear and boys' clothing, and then expanded further into retailing by opening his own stores and franchising stores to sell Ralph Lauren, Polo, and Chaps products.

Geographic Locations: Decentralized

Menswear firms are not heavily concentrated but rather are widely distributed throughout the United States. The industry's largest, Levi Strauss, is headquartered in San Francisco. **Hartmarx,** a major producer of tailored clothing, is headquartered in Chicago. Philadelphia is headquarters for Greif & Company, After Six, and Pincus Bros. Maxwell. In the Pacific Northwest are White Stag and Pendleton. Haggar and Farah are in Texas. Oxford Industries is one of the many companies in the South. Production facilities, as well as headquarters offices, are so widely scattered that the industry is truly national and there is scarcely a state that is not involved in menswear. All the firms mentioned, however, have showrooms in New York City, as do many, many others.

Importance of New York

New York City is the hub of the industry's marketing efforts and houses the sales office of virtually every important producer in the United States. In just a single building, 1290 Avenue of the Americas, several hundred menswear firms have their offices. As the industry has grown, its showrooms have spilled over into surrounding office buildings on 51st, 52nd, and 53rd streets, from Fifth Avenue to Seventh Avenue. Farther downtown, in the Empire State Building at 34th Street and Fifth Avenue, there are sales offices for a major share of the men's furnishings companies. Meantime, the area around 23rd Street and Fifth Avenue, which was once the heart of the industry, has been abandoned to retail and housing uses.

What draws merchants to New York City is the presence of showrooms, showrooms, and more showrooms. The typical retailer has little need or desire to visit production facilities. A few, however, such as L.L. Bean and Lands' End make frequent visits to work out details of production of products specifically for their respective companies and to monitor quality.

Centers of Production

The production of menswear, as has been mentioned, takes place all over the United States. Certain areas, however, are more important than others for specific types of apparel. Tailored clothing is produced primarily in the Northeast, with New York, Pennsylvania, and Massachusetts being the major areas. Together with Georgia, these states produce more than 50 percent of all domestically-made tailored clothing (U.S. Census of Manufacturers, 1989).

As to other categories: A large percentage of men's and boys' shirts and nightwear are produced in North Carolina, Alabama, Georgia, and Tennessee; almost three-fourths of separate trousers are produced in Georgia, Texas, Tennessee, and Mississippi; and the main U.S. production of all men's and boys' neckwear takes place in New York, North Carolina, California, and Louisiana (U.S. Census of Manufacturers, 1989).

Design and Production Procedures

The procedures in the design and production of men's tailored clothing and in the design and production of men's sportswear differ greatly. In tailored clothing, changes are simple and subtle; in sportswear, changes tend to be more rapid, more drastic, and more trendy. Throughout the entire menswear field, however, men remain slower and less willing than women to accept radical fashion changes in their wardrobes. What has been changing, however, is men's attitudes toward their bodies, with emphasis on health. Exercise became a fact of life in the 1980s. Fitness, says designer Bill Blass, "is a major preoccupation of people in our time" ("The Impact," 1985).

This new body awareness manifests itself in menswear in a number of ways. There is, of course, the demand for jogging suits, tennis and running shorts, and workout outfits. So strong is the interest in athletics and athletic clothes that the warmup suit became known as the leisure outfit of the 1980s. At the same time, men's tailored clothing has changed to reflect the interest in fit bodies. Shoulders are wider, waists are narrower, and the drop has increased. The **drop** is the difference between the chest measurement and the waist measurement. Traditionally, this was six inches, but nowadays manufacturers are changing their specifications to seven or eight inches.

Tailored Clothing

The tailored clothing segment of the menswear industry presents a completely different picture from what prevails in other branches, and certainly a picture utterly unlike that which prevails in the women's fashion industry. Production is slow and painstaking; highly skilled operators are required; handwork is still a factor; sizing is complex; emphasis is on selection of fabrics rather than styles alone; and styles change slowly and gradually. With all these elements to consider, it is not surprising that this segment of the industry operates on the basis of only two seasons a year.

Seasonal Lines

The tailored clothing industry, with its long and complex production methods, traditionally presents its lines to retailers only twice a year. Fall/Winter lines are shown to the trade in December and January; Spring/Summer lines are shown in July and August. This long-established calendar prevails today and continues to do so because the apparel concerned remains largely classic in style. If fashion changes were swifter and more marked in this field, necessitating more frequent introduction of new styles, the calendar might change—and the industry's methods of operation would undoubtedly have to change along with it.

Development of a Line

The development of a tailored clothing line starts with a decision as to the bodies, or basic styles, that will be featured for the coming season. Each major suit and coat manufacturer employs at least one master tailor/designer whose job is to make the subtle changes in last year's bodies that may be needed to produce this year's new shape. Changes may include adding or subtracting length in the jacket and lapels; bringing the garment closer to or farther from the body; making the shoulders fuller or less so; choosing between flap and patch pockets; deciding on whether there will be side vents, back vent, or no vent; and so on.

Once the newly modified bodies are ready, the designer, the piece goods buyer, and the principals of the company set to work to choose the fabric assortment. These assortments are quite extensive, as retailers expect to see a broad range when they come in to make their selections for a major season. Finally, sample garments may be made up in a few of the fabrics, so that the bodies can be shown in plaids, stripes, and solids. However, with today's computer technologies, not all variations may need to be made into sample garments. This is the line that is shown to the retailer, along with a swatch book of additional fabrics that are available.

Production of Tailored Clothing

The process of producing men's tailored clothing is long, complex, and quite different from the procedures followed in women's apparel or in other divisions of menswear. Many hand operations are involved in the construction of structured garments, the sizing system is more complicated, and it is fabric rather than shape or silhouette that differentiates one tailored style from another (Figure 6–3). The manufacturer commits itself in advance to 100 fabrics or more. These are presented to the retail customers, and the retail buyers select those they want and the basic bodies in which they want them made up. To that extent, the retailer designs its own exclusive line. The producer, moreover, may offer PGR (Piece Goods Reservation), a system whereby the manufacturer sets aside fabric for a specific retailer during or immediately after showing the line. The manufacturer does not begin production until sufficient orders have been accumulated for a fabric to justify a cutting ticket. A quality maker will put a fabric into production, if it has been ordered in one or several different models and runs of sizes, as long as there are at least a minimum number of garments to cut. Each producer sets its own figure, of course.

Even after the cutting has been done, production goes slowly. The hand operations involved in tailored clothing are time consuming; as much as an hour or more may be needed for the pressing operation alone. Quality control is maintained throughout the construction of tailored clothing—a factor that explains why many producers in this division of the industry are inside shops, using their own production facilities rather than those of outside contractors. This is in sharp contrast with the men's sportswear field, where style and design features are emphasized rather than exact fit and meticulous workmanship.

Figure 6–3

Tailored menswear

Source: Courtesy of Andrew Gordon/The Diamond Company

Complex Sizing

The dual sizing system that prevails in tailored clothing is a further factor in making production procedures slow and cumbersome. Men's suits are cut in different chest measurements, each one of which is combined with different figure types. This is in sharp contrast with the situation that prevails in the women's apparel industry, in which each producer tends to concentrate on a single figure type, such as misses, junior, or half-size, and cuts possibly five or six sizes for that figure type. A tailored suit producer, however, has to cope with all these sizes for any one number in the line:

- *Short.* 36, 37, 38, up to 42 chest measurement.
- *Regular.* 36, 38, 39, 40, up to 46 chest measurement.
- *Long.* 38, 39, 40, 41, up to 48 chest measurement.
- *Extra Long.* 40, 42, 44, up to 48 chest measurement.
- *Portly.* 39, 40, 41, up to 50 chest measurement.

Even in the case of separate slacks, the sizing is not simple. Many in the tailored category are sized by waist alone, it is true, depending on the retailer or the customer to measure off the inseam length and hem the garment. But there are also many men's pants that are sold finished at the hem, and these are sized in waists from 26 to 42 for the most part, and in inseam lengths of 29 to 36 inches.

This enormous variety of sizes is important to the retailer seller, since many menswear stores continue to alter men's suits to fit individual customers and to absorb the cost of such alterations. This, too, is changing, as the mix of stores selling men's tailored clothing changes to include discounters and others who charge for alterations. Also, stores that have traditionally provided free alterations now charge for some types of alteration in order to keep expenses down. Even Brooks Brothers now charges for some alterations.

The enormous variety of sizes stocked by retailers that desire to have a presence in the tailored clothing marketplace has necessitated huge investments of capital in slow-turning stock. Consequently, the broad range of sizing in men's tailored wear makes this a complex and expensive segment of the industry for both manufacturers and retailers.

The custom of doing free alterations goes back to the made-to-order beginnings of menswear, when accurate fit was expected by the consumer. (In contrast, women, who are supposed by tradition to be competent seamstresses, have nearly always had to pay for any needed alterations.) To minimize alterations, menswear retailers have sought to carry stocks that permit almost any size or figure type to be fitted with a minimum of adjustments. Although it is unlikely that any one style will be carried in all sizes, the average number of sizes bought in one garment ranges from 15 to 25, depending on the type and size of the store and the importance placed on the model and fabric in relation to the total inventory.

Simplifying Sizes

The growing importance of young men as suit buyers is slowly leading the way into S/M/L/XL sizing, introduced at the MAGIC show in 1986 to poor results, to replace the myriad of sizes carried in traditional tailored clothing departments today. This trend to date is confined to makers that market to the customers who desire a more formal version of the contemporary soft suit, but do not want fully constructed clothing. However, traditional manufacturers such as Southwick, Lanvin Studio by Greif, Joseph Abboud, and Bill Robinson among others are producing soft-construction tailored clothing.

At the base of this S/M/L/XL sizing, which can be done in regulars and longs, is "Small," which has a 40 shoulder and a 38 body; "Medium," which has a 43 shoulder and a 41 body; and "Large," which has a 49 (or equivalent) shoulder and a 44 body. In a way, this is another way of responding to the desire for increased "drop" in tailored clothing. It may also be the retailer's way to respond to the desire to keep inventories as lean as possible without giving up the tailored clothing business.

Hand Tailoring

The production of men's tailored clothing traditionally has involved many hours of hand tailoring. In the past, tailored clothing was given *grades* from 1 to 6+, based on the number of hand operations that went into the production. In recent years, the practice of identifying suits by grades has disappeared, due to technological developments. Today, many hand-tailoring processes have been eliminated because there is machinery that simulates hand stitching of lapels, turning of pockets, or finishing of buttonholes. Such procedures speed up production and reduce costs. However, top-quality men's suits still involve a great deal of hand tailoring.

Custom Tailors and Tailors-to-the-Trade

Because men's apparel required a more precise fit than women's clothes, custom tailoring remained important in the men's field longer than custom dressmaking did in women's wear. Most of the men's tailors who did custom work in this country in the early years of this century had been trained in Europe under the apprentice system; they could design a suit, sponge the fabric to preshrink it, cut the garment, run up the seams, sew on buttons, make buttonholes by hand, and supply the fine stitching on lapels. Until the 1920s, a man could enjoy the excellent fit of a made-to-order suit at prices and in qualities that compared very favorably with ready-made clothing.

The supply of custom tailors, however, began to dwindle in the 1920s and 1930s. Immigration had been restricted and, as the older European-trained tailors died or retired, very few new ones crossed the Atlantic to take their places. Work in the factories of this country did not produce craftsmen capable of making complete garments. Efficient methods of operation required some men to specialize in cutting, others in sewing, and still others in the hand finishing.

Today, a growing number of **custom tailor** (made-to-order) shops still exist in the United States, principally in large cities and at the upper end of the price scale. An example is Barneys New York (Figure 6–4). Another outstanding example is Dunhill Tailors of New York City featuring suits that sell for $2,000 or more each. To quote Leon Block, one of Dunhill's principals: "Custom is bigger than ever; eight years ago, we planned to phase it out but we couldn't because so many clients wanted it" ("At $1,500," 1982). The store's customer list has included such names as Cary Grant, Paul Newman, Walter Hoving, and some of New York's leading politicians.

Sulka, a venerable haberdashery shop that made only custom-made shirts in the past, opened a custom-made suit department selling suits from $1,250 to $3,000. This store is owned by Sy Syms of Syms discount retailing. In Washington, D.C., the traditional men's clothier of Lewis and Thos. Saltz Co. opened a prototype store that offers 500 swatches from which a customer may choose a custom-made suit costing from $500 to more than $1,000, and this company expects to open 100 more such stores in major cities nationwide over the next 10 years. This company, as does Sulka, also offers custom-made shirts. The trend for custom-made clothing is indeed expanding.

In addition to the retail custom tailors who produce a complete garment on their own premises, there are also **tailors-to-the-trade** or *made-to-measure firms*.

Figure 6–4

Many men enjoy the merits of made-to-measure clothing.

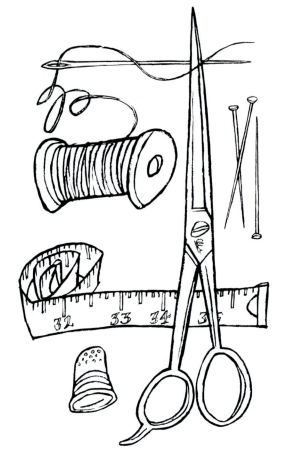

Made-to-Measure
at no extra charge

BARNEYS
NEWYORK

Source: Courtesy of Barneys New York Advertising. Art by Robert Clyde Anderson, permission granted.

These are factories that specialize in cutting individual garments according to the exact measurements of customers who place their orders through retail stores serviced by these firms. The customer selects style and fabric from fashion books and swatches that he consults in the retail store; the retailer relays his selection and his measurements to the factory; and in due course the garment is made up. Although there are still some tailors-to-the-trade, their output is only a small portion of the industry's total and is no longer reported separately in census figures. Much of the made-to-order business nowadays is handled by large producers of ready-made apparel that have set up separate divisions for this special made-to-measure business.

Casual Office Wear

A major new trend in men's dressing has resulted from what started as a perk in computer companies—casual dress on Fridays. As the idea spread, a new term in the fashion industry vocabulary developed: **FridayWear.** Men discovered what women had known for some time—one can be properly dressed but still comfortable. Large numbers of Fortune 500 and smaller companies developed some form of alternative dress code for at least part of the work week. In 1995, even IBM, known for its formal dress codes, relaxed its expectations for employees' clothing, resulting in marketing efforts directed specifically to men at that long held bastion of proper attire (Figure 6–5).

As men in many U.S. companies enjoyed the freedom and comfort of FridayWear, many decided to extend the trend to other days of the week, leading to what some have called **Everyday Wear.** By whatever name or when it is worn, this trend has had a major impact on the menswear industry. Tailored menswear firms have felt the change in business. Many have introduced new lines of softly tailored, relaxed apparel, such as that shown in Figure 6–6, to fill this need. Retailers, too, felt the effect of shifts toward more casual wear in the workplace (Courter, 1995; Gellers, 1994).

Confusion surrounded the definition of casual wear for the workplace. A number of menswear manufacturers helped customers by introducing coordinated lines with flexibility in mixing and matching jackets, slacks, shirts, and accessories. To help the befuddled shopper, some apparel makers provide guidance on labels to tell when and how to wear the garment. For example, a Pepe Jeans sleeveless lumber jacket label reads, "This shirt must be worn as an overshirt." A "relaxed dress shirt" by Joseph Abboud comes with a booklet that states the shirt "can be worn with jeans or without a tie, perfect for a relaxed day at the office" (Brown, 1994, p. 158).

Sometimes companies have been embarrassed by their employees' over-interpretation of casual wear. Although jeans, t-shirts, and running shoes may fit the California life style or in the development laboratories at computer firms, most companies had something less casual in mind for employees.

At any rate, this fast-growing category of menswear, somewhere between formal business attire and leisurewear, has represented new opportunities for apparel firms. For example, Phillips–Van Heusen created a "Corporate Casual" program that has proven very successful. Hartmarx, Grief, Haggar, and Farah have responded with new lines. Arrow makes "Friday shirts," and Brooks Brothers has a whole line called "Soft Classics" (Brown, 1994). Textile firms benefit from the trend, too, because many of the casual work wear lines incorporate fabrics with increased texture and other design interest.

Sportswear Design and Production

It was only a few decades ago when men's sportswear emerged from the dark ages. The mod explosion of the 1960s transformed the business. The old-furnishings-oriented (ties and shirts) business-clothing-only look gave way to the jeans generation of baby boomers.

The designer revolution of the 1960s, which brought names like Oleg Cassini, John Weitz, Pierre Cardin, and Yves St. Laurent to the forefront, later swept in Ralph Lauren and Calvin Klein in the 1970s, and Perry Ellis, Alexander Julian, and Georgio Armani in the 1980s. Joseph Abboud, Donna Karan, and Jhane Barnes are important names in the 1990s.

**An advertisement
that followed
IBM's relaxed
dress codes.**

An
open letter to
the men
of I.B.M.

It's welcome news that I.B.M. will relax its dress code.
The menswear industry thrives on creating clothing
that allows men self-expression, personal style and comfort.
Since casual style is far from sloppy, the men
of I.B.M. and every company with relaxed dress codes will
want to build new wardrobes. They'll find the 'Easy Friday' Collection
by Bagir, dedicated to the art of dressing down,
exactly what they need in stylish, easy clothing that's perfect
when the business dress isn't suits. Have 'Easy Friday' ready and
waiting for them at your store. Call 212-307-1900.
Outside New York 1-800-828-2244.

BAGIR
for men.

Source: Reprinted courtesy of Bagir.

From California came the young men's revolution and Brittania (later to become Generra) and Union Bay. The active boom brought in names such as Nike, Wilson, and Adidas to the apparel industry. Names once important, such as Merona, Bruce, and McGregor, lost their luster and gave way to names such as Nautica, Guess, Tommy Hilfiger, and Levi's/Dockers.

The demand of male customers for a more fashionable look—for clothes suited to the multifaceted multidimensional lives they lead—has made the sportswear segment of the men's clothing industry increasingly important. Clothes for activity, the outdoors, casual evening dressing, biking, hiking, running, and working out all require appropriate clothing. Even "hanging out" needs the right clothes depending on where you do your hanging out. These clothes do not require careful shaping and

Figure 6–6

With its roots in tailored clothing, this example illustrates the dressed-down, relaxed look many men began to wear to the office in the mid 1990s.

hand operations; the shape is supplied by the wearer. What is required is more fashion awareness and producers that can quickly respond to changing customer demands.

Seasonal Lines

In men's sportswear, the quickening desire of consumers for fashion newness has resulted in a quickening pace of style change. Because of its ability to respond to changes in silhouette, pattern, color, and trend, sportswear provides faster inventory turnover.

In the quickening fashion pace of the men's sportswear market, the need has developed for more newness more often. Instead of the three seasons that were prevalent just six short years ago, sportswear now has four seasons. Fall (shown in March) is delivered in August; Holiday (shown in June) is delivered in November; Spring (shown in October) is delivered in February; and Summer (shown in January) is shipped in April or May. Claiborne, the menswear division of Liz Claiborne, offers five men's lines a year: Fall I is shown in March for June delivery; Fall II is shown in June for September delivery; Holiday/Pre-Spring is shown in August for November delivery; Spring I is shown in October for January delivery; and Spring II is shown in January for March delivery. The menswear industry is gradually becoming "seasonless" in much the same way as women's apparel, with a constant stream of new products offered.

Figure 6–7   An example of a men's sportswear line, illustrating potential for mixing and matching various pieces in the line.

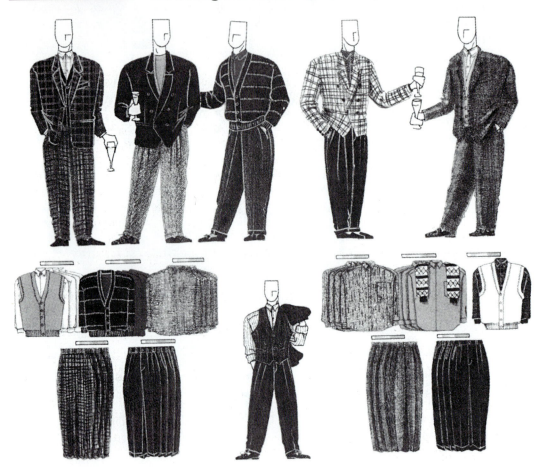

Development of a Line

The preparation of a sportswear line differs a great deal from the development of a tailored clothing line. In sportswear, as in women's wear, the producer has already preselected the fabrics for the various numbers in the line, and the emphasis is on offering a selection of styles rather than a choice of fabric (Figure 6–7).

In preparing a line of coordinated sportswear, or of men's separates (such as trousers, shirts, or sweaters), there are both similarities and differences between one company and another. Where a designer's name is involved, the designer usually oversees the sketching, selection of fabrics, making of samples, and selection of colors. A company that specializes in separates, such as Haggar, uses house designers who prepare a line of pants by adding or removing front pleats, narrowing or widening pants legs, or making whatever other modifications are needed to achieve the new season's look. Fabric selection is usually handled by the designer, working with the company's principals and the sales manager, each of whom contributes his or her special expertise to the final selection. Pricing is usually done by the same group, but with the production manager replacing the designer on the team for this task.

Production

Since no hand tailoring is involved in the production of sportswear, the sewing (and often also the cutting) is likely to be farmed out to independent contractors (domestic and overseas), much as is done in the women's apparel industry. However, in addition to using outside shops, many large producers such as Haggar, Oxford Industries, and Levi Strauss also handle some of the production in their own plants.

With fashion changes, the scope of a line expands or contracts. There may be more or fewer sweaters, fewer t-shirts, more or less activewear, and so on. In such cases, it is necessary merely to find new contractors for the expanded categories and to drop those no longer needed for fading areas of demand. And, as in the women's industry, both international and domestic contractors are used.

Simplified Sizing

The sizing in some sportswear categories is fairly simple; in others, it is becoming so. Men's sweaters are usually sized Small, Medium, Large, and Extra Large. Sports pants are sold by waist measurement in inches. Some trousers carry both waist and length sizes, in inches, such as 29/30, 29/31, and so on. In these designations, the first figure is the waist measurement and the second is the inseam, or length from trouser rise to hem. More expensive trousers often come without hems, so that the leg length can be adjusted for the individual customer.

Sports shirts are produced in only four sizes: Small, Medium, Large, and Extra Large. Sleeve lengths are standard for each size. Makers of men's dress shirts have been following the lead of the sports shirt makers in simplifying their sizes, but with limited success. Dress shirt manufacturers had been accustomed to making their entire lines with neck sizes ranging from 14 (inches) to 17 1/2 or even larger. For each neck size, they produced sleeve lengths ranging from 31 to 37 inches, at one-inch intervals. Such a wide range of sizes represented a slow production process for the manufacturer and a formidable inventory problem for both retailer and manufacturer.

To permit quicker response to fashion change and to permit lower inventories, shirt producers have sought to pay less attention to fit and increased attention to fashion. They simply produce a very large percentage of their styles with average rather than exact sleeve lengths. This system of producing only average sleeve lengths (ASL) has not been too well received by some customers. Today, major men's shirt retailers carry both types—fashion shirts in average sleeve lengths only and classic dress shirts in the customary collar and sleeve length sizing.

Importance of the Collection Concept

In the past, male shoppers in professional careers tended to build their wardrobes around tailored clothing and regarded such items as sweaters or sports trousers as merely extra purchases. Today, they may very well make all their purchases in sportswear departments, where they can achieve a look that is properly put together, even if the fabrics in the various garments are different. This has become possible because of the **collection concept.**

Originally in the realm of licensing designers such as John Weitz, Giorgio Armani, and Allan Flusser, the collection concept has grown to the point that it encompasses almost all menswear, whether designer sponsored or manufacturers' brands, and at all price levels. A menswear retailer nowadays buys and presents a collection from a company that produces jackets, trousers, shirts, sweaters, and even ties and belts, thus ensuring that the customer will be offered varied items, all of which can be worn together and are color coordinated.[1]

For example, Henry Grethel, a New York designer licensed by Hartmarx, designs a complete clothing collection including trousers, jackets, shirts, sweaters, and t-shirts, all geared for weekend wear. Perry Ellis America produced by Manhattan Shirt Co., a division of Salant Corp., creates complete coordinated collections, as does Andrew Fezza for GFT America. Other designer collections include those by Barry Bricken, Jhane Barnes, Jeffrey Banks, and Claiborne. Giorgio Armani does three collections, each geared to a separate target market by price and life style: Armani Couture, the highest priced and most elegant; Armani Boutique, moderate to high priced, geared to the man on his way up the corporate and fiscal ladder; and Mani, the most fashion-forward line in department store price ranges. Similarly, Hugo Boss has three distinct groupings targeted toward different consumers: the classic consumer, the "fashion aware," and the *avant garde* (Silverman, 1995).

Increase of Classification Merchandising

Because of the growth of the menswear customer today who has confidence in his own fashion expertise and taste, and because retailers want the freedom to pick and choose from a line to satisfy their target market, we see a return to classification buying and merchandising. This approach lowers potential markdown, lowers stock investments in slower selling classifications, and speeds inventory turns.

Marketing of Menswear

The way to achieve growth is to find new markets or to win business away from competing companies. Thus there is greater emphasis on marketing, instead of on production alone, and this in turn has speeded up the industry's use of contractors to facilitate quick response to the changes in demand. As the apparel industry develops and emphasizes marketing strategies rather than production capabilities alone, the field of menswear becomes an ever more important area of potential growth. Today's menswear customer, at every age and economic level, is more interested and involved than ever before in the building of a wardrobe and in the process of selection. Fashion shopping is no longer for women only; it has truly become an activity for both sexes.

Manufacturers' Brands

Brand names in the men's field are older and better established, and have been longer promoted, than those in the women's field. Men have been conditioned for generations to purchase apparel in terms of grade, quality, fit, and durability rather than style alone. Thus, until a dozen or more years ago, consumers gravitated to brand names that were associated in their minds with quality: Arrow and Manhattan shirts, Hickey-Freeman and Society brand suits, for example, and such stores labels (private brands) as those of retailers such as Brooks Brothers, major department stores, outstanding menswear shops, chains, and mail-order companies.

---

[1]Similarly, a number of retailers may produce their own coordinated collections by contracting directly with domestic or overseas producers.

Some of the brand names still prominent in menswear date back to the beginning of this century or earlier. Hart, Schaffner & Marx, now known as Hartmarx, began promoting its name through national advertising in 1890. In 1901, Joseph & Feiss (now owned by Phillips–Van Heusen) embarked on a national campaign to sell its "Clothescraft Clothes," retailing $10 and upward, by telling their retail customers that "the wearer will be brought to you by judicious advertising. We pay for it" (Cobrin, 1971). This, of course, was an early and simple form of cooperative advertising.

Responding to a vastly different department and specialty store climate created by mergers and acquisitions on the part of retailers, manufacturers are developing new marketing strategies to maintain the consumer awareness of their brand names. Greif companies, which include licensed labels such as Chaps by Ralph Lauren and Colours by Alexander Julian among others, has added a new layer of service people who will act as liaison between the retailers and the company to provide marketing intelligence for themselves and their customers, thus keeping their brand names highly visible. For example, Levi Strauss spends millions of dollars a year to advertise just one style jean, and Guess spends millions each year to promote what it describes as "image advertising."

Targeted Customer Approach

As menswear purchases in apparel changed from replacement purchases to impulse fashion purchases, manufacturers had to develop much more knowledge about their customer. A very focused and targeted approach is developing and is replacing the commodity thinking that was prevalent in the menswear industry. Major producers such as Hartmarx have developed customer profiles for different divisions of their company, as shown in Table 6–3. Similarly, Generra, has separated its business into a young men's market (the 15-to-24 age range) and a men's market (geared to men in the 25-to-45 age range). As noted earlier, Hugo Boss has developed lines for three distinct market segments.

Designer Labels and Designer Licensing

Fashion in menswear took on new importance in the mid-1960s. For the first time, designers gave serious attention to menswear—and consumers noticed. Up to then, men tended to look for favorite brands, placing their confidence in stalwarts like Arrow, Van Heusen, and Palm Beach. These national brands contributed to market growth for many apparel companies but did not provide the market excitement that designer lines added. Important early designers whose work influenced the menswear industry included John Weitz, Pierre Cardin, Hardy Aimes, Oleg Cassini, and Bill Blass. Menswear companies worked with many of these designers under various arrangements, often licensing the designers' names (Gellers, 1995). Bearing a designer's name, sometimes ordinary garments took on a special aura and customer appeal. The designer influence launched an excitement in the menswear industry that continues today. Celebrating its 30th birthday, *DNR*, the leading daily trade publication serving the menswear industry, conveyed on its special anniversary issue cover the importance of this designer influence (Figure 6–8).

Some designers whose names were well established in the women's wear industry took the logical step of moving over into the menswear area. The first steps were made by designers such as Calvin Klein, Pierre Cardin, and Yves St. Laurent, soon followed by Perry Ellis, Christian Dior, and others who signed licensing agreements with various menswear tailored clothing and sportswear producers for the use of their

Table 6–3	**Hartmarx Brand and Product Segmentation**		
Upper*	**Upper Moderate***	**Moderate***	**Popular***
Suits $675+	Suits $450-$675	Suits $325-$450	Suits Under $325
Sportcoats $450+	Sportcoats $300-$450	Sportcoats $200-$300	Sportcoats Under $200
Dress Slacks $125+	Dress Slacks $75-$125	Dress Slacks $50-$75	Dress Slacks Under $50
Casual Slacks $90+	Casual Slacks $60-$90	Casual Slacks $40-$60	Casual Slacks Under $40
Classic			
Hickey-Freeman	*Hart Schaffner & Marx*	*Sansabelt*	*Suburbans*
Tailored Clothing	Tailored Clothing	Slacks	Women's Separates
Bobby Jones	Slacks	Tailored Clothing	*John Alexander*
Blazers and Slacks	Dress Furnishings	*Barrie Pace*	*Tailored Clothing*
	Jack Nicklaus	Women's Career Apparel	*Slacks*
	Blazers and Slacks	*Allyn Saint George*	Kuppenheimer
		Tailored Clothing	Tailored Clothing
Traditional			
Gieves & Hawkes	*Tommy Hilfiger*	*Racquet Club/Wimbledon*	*J.G. Hook*
Tailored Clothing	Tailored Clothing	Tailored Clothing	Tailored Clothing
	Slacks		
	Austin Reed		
	Tailored Clothing		
	Rovers		
	Women's Separates		
	Graham & Gunn		
	Tailored Clothing		
	Society Brand, Ltd.		
	Tailored Clothing		
Fashion			
Karl Lagerfeld	*KM by Krizia*	*Perry Ellis*	*Daniel Hechter*
Tailored Clothing	Tailored Clothing	Tailored Clothing	Tailored Clothing
	Slacks	*Nino Cerruti*	*Henry Grethel*
		Tailored Clothing	Tailored Clothing
		Pierre Cardin	Dress Furnishings
		Tailored Clothing	*Fumagalli's*
		Slacks	Tailored Clothing
			Confezióni Risèrva
			by Luciano Franzoni
			Tailored Clothing
Sportswear			
Bobby Jones	*Nicklaus*	*Jack Nicklaus Signature*	*Henry Grethel*
Sportswear	Men's Golfwear	Sportswear	Sportswear
Men's Golfwear	Women's Golfwear		
Women's Golfwear	*KM by Krizia*		
	Sportswear		

*Men's apparel retail prices only.
Source: From *Hartmarx Annual Report 1994* (p. 15) by Hartmarx, 1994, Chicago: Author: Reprinted by permission.

Figure 6–8

DNR's 30-year anniversary supplement to celebrate the impact of key designers on menswear.

Source: Reprinted courtesy of Fairchild Publications.

names. Only occasionally did the name designer have much input into the actual designing of the line. Soon celebrity sports and entertainment names such as Johnny Carson and Bobby Jones, both licensed by Hartmarx, entered the menswear arena. In addition, names such as Indiana Jones and Batman come and go as the movie industry grinds out new licensable heroes. These licensing agreements, of course, have added a great deal of additional income for the designers and, hopefully, luster to the apparel producers' products.

Liz Claiborne and Donna Karan are among the more recent entries into the menswear area with the introduction of the Claiborne division in late 1985, Donna Karan Menswear in 1991, and DKNY Men (her sportswear line) in 1992. Using designing talent and marketing know-how learned in the women's wear area, these businesses have emerged as very successful menswear enterprises.

Although designer names continue to be important, the consumer's response is only as strong as the continued importance of the designer's name. The designer business has become "more *business* than designer" (DiPaolo, 1988).

Retail Channels of Distribution

In the past, the largest percentage of the retail menswear business was done in the strictly masculine confines of the men's specialty stores. As men became more interested in presenting an appearance that reflected both the current fashions and their own personalities, and as they sought alternatives to the conventional business suit, they began to shop in other types of stores. And to enjoy shopping! At the same time, that bastion of men's privacy, the menswear store, began to solicit female customers. Examples include Brooks Brothers, Hastings, Paul Stuart, and Barneys.

A parallel development has occurred in the traditionally feminine environs of the department store and women's specialty shops. Department stores have become more aggressive in menswear. For a time, they were losing ground to mass merchants. Retail analyst Steidtmann noted, "Bill Clinton is the comeback kid of politics and the department stores are the comeback kids of [menswear] retailing" (Palmieri, 1994, p. 30). Most major department stores have responded to men's growing fashion awareness and have arranged their stores to be more appealing and convenient to male shoppers. Many have devoted prime floor space to men's areas, whereas in the past, menswear was less likely to occupy key spots. Neiman Marcus now devotes a large part of the main floor of its flagship Dallas store to menswear. At Bloomingdale's in New York, menswear gets nearly half the main floor, plus another area that was once a low-priced basement sales area. Department stores are devoting more space and more attention to menswear because these have become some of the most profitable areas. Because of competition from off-price menswear retailers such as Men's Warehouse and Today's Man, department stores are offering suits at prices that compare favorably with some of the off-pricers. This, in turn, is bringing back customers in some cases at the expense of off-price retailers (Palmieri, 1994).

At the same time, those specialty chains whose units are primarily located in malls are appealing to young men who shop with young women for the fun of it. Both sexes watch MTV and both react to the same fashion images. Nevertheless, there are still many small men's specialty shops that are an important outlet for men's clothing.

Men's specialty shops, large or small, remain important for several reasons. For one, many men still hesitate to enter the predominantly feminine confines of the department store, or feel so uncomfortable there that even special entrances and special elevators do not entirely break down their reluctance. Another reason is that men's specialty shops are usually arranged in such a way that furnishings and clothing are

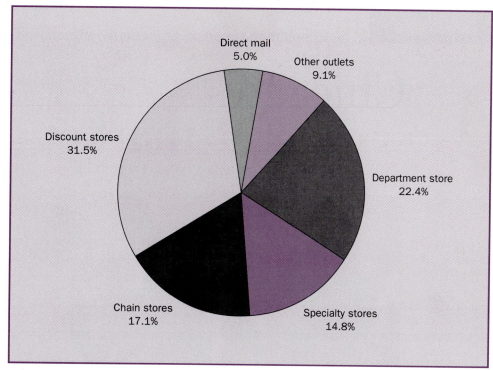

Figure 6–9

Menswear sales by type of retail channel

Source: Based on data from *Apparel Marketing Monitor,* (pp. 7–8) by American Apparel Manufacturing Association, 1996, Arlington, VA: Author. Adapted by permission.

placed near one another, and a single salesperson can escort the customer throughout the entire store and assist him in all his purchases. Such procedures save time for the customer and make suggestion selling of second, third, fourth, or add-on items infinitely easier. Still another reason is the convenience of location; men's shops can be found everywhere and anywhere—in business districts, residential areas, and shopping centers.

The menswear business pie, once heavily weighted toward men's specialty stores, is now giving a slightly larger slice to the discounters, with department stores, specialty stores, and chains each holding its own shares, as illustrated in Figure 6–9.

Menswear Marketing at Apparel Marts

As the menswear market has grown, the regional apparel marts have given increasing emphasis to this segment of the business. In some marts, specific floors are designated for men's apparel and accessories. **Menswear weeks** are scheduled at select times of the year; Figure 6–10 offers an example of the Chicago Apparel Center's promotion for menswear shows. These shows are held when menswear retailers know they can find manufacturers' new lines and can place orders for the coming season.

Manufacturer-Owned Retail Stores: Dual Distribution

Firmly entrenched in the menswear field is the **dual-distribution** system, whereby some large menswear manufacturers own and operate retail stores through which they sell their products—the same products that they also sell to other independent retailers for resale. Manufacturer-owned stores include in their assortments merchandise produced by other apparel makers—men's furnishings, for example, and

Figure 6–10 An example of a promotion for menswear market weeks.

Chicago's the market
for all your men's wear needs

Photography: Andrew Martin

February 5-7

Chicago Men's Wear Collective,™ Fall Market

Experience the nation's premier fall specialty store show.

April 7-11

Ultra Show of America™
April 9-11
Men's Show

Find everything for fall at this ultimate, all-inclusive men's, women's & children's market.

August 6-8

Chicago Men's Wear Collective,™ Holiday/Spring Market

Return to the national specialty store market for an impressive showing of first-rate resources.

November 3-7

Men's, Women's & Children's Spring Market
November 5-7
Men's Show

Shop the season's most comprehensive selection of resources at one incredible show.

CHICAGO APPAREL CENTER

Call 800/677-6278 for Market details and registration or 800/528-8700 for travel discounts.

Source: Reprinted courtesy of Chicago Apparel Center.

women's wear. A prominent example is Phillips-Van Heusen, the giant shirt company that owns many stores. Hartmarx previously owned nearly 500 stores but has sold those to concentrate on its manufacturing business. Many manufacturer-owned stores are given names that do not identify them to the public as belonging to the producer concerned.

Marketing Activities by Trade Associations

An important point of difference between the menswear and women's apparel fields lies in the role of trade associations. In menswear, several trade associations are actively concerned with the marketing of the merchandise, acting more or less as go-betweens for producers and retailers. In the women's field, trade associations generally work only at single levels of distribution—that is, retail organizations work only with their retail members, and industry associations only with producers, as far as marketing is concerned.

Clothing Manufacturers' Association

The oldest trade association in the menswear field is the **CMA**. This was formed originally in 1933 by producers of tailored clothing to represent manufacturers in negotiations with the union—"the Amalgamated." Although it still performs this function with UNITE, the CMA's activities have been greatly expanded. CMA is the tailored clothing industry liaison with the federal government on labeling and other matters. The association coordinates and publicizes the two New York market weeks each year: the January/February showings for Fall/Winter and the August/September showings for Spring/Summer. Twice a year, in January and July, the association publishes, in cooperation with *Newsweek* magazine, a trade periodical for international distribution. Appearing in three languages—English, French, and German—it undertakes to inform retailers about major fashion trends in tailored clothing. Another association function is to compile and distribute periodically to its members statistical and technical reports on developments in tailored clothing. And, of course, like most major trade associations, it is the lobbying voice of its industry.

NAMSB

A second trade association that is very active in marketing menswear is the National Association of Men's Sportswear Buyers (**NAMSB**). This organization was founded and is financially supported by store buyers of menswear as well as owners of men's stores. It was founded in 1953 to give status and identity to a then-new category of menswear—sportswear. In its early years, it helped give direction to the styling of men's and boy's sportswear by recommending themes and colors the retailers considered most likely to succeed.

The NAMSB stages four show weeks a year: in January at the Sheraton Center and New York Hilton hotels, and in March, June, and October at the New York Javits Center. At each of these **trade shows**, exhibit booths are set up on several floors for the use of manufacturers in showing their lines. Although the association was founded by sportswear buyers and originally concentrated on that single category, its function has expanded to include all types of men's and boys' apparel and furnishings, including accessories and shoes. At each show week, more than 1,200 exhibitors buy space. The opportunity to view so many lines draws more than 25,000 countrywide retailers from establishments of every size and type. NAMSB estimates that more than half of these are store owners and reports that all who come to the shows come to buy. Since show weeks attract more menswear buying power than any menswear trade event, they have become a key marketing tool not only for domestic producers and retailers, but also for importers, producers from other countries, and groups of overseas suppliers exhibiting under sponsorship of their governments.

The Fashion Association (TFA)

Until the early 1990s, **TFA** was known as the Men's Fashion Association of America (MFA). In many ways, this association's development paralleled that of the menswear industry. A few promotional activities for the menswear industry began in the 1950s, but it was the expanding interest in men's apparel in the 1960s that launched the MFA. The group served as the public relations arm of the menswear industry, organizing press shows, providing press kits, sponsoring design awards, and coordinating a range of activities to promote men's apparel and accessories (Parola, 1991).

The Fashion Association is no longer limited to menswear. Rather, it continues the same activities as in earlier years but promotes the whole apparel industry. It is funded by members drawn from fiber, mill, apparel manufacturing, and retail organizations, and its purpose is to make fashions newsworthy and to provide information on the subject to the press. Press previews are held twice a year—in an area near New York City in June and on the West Coast in January or February. Each preview entails three-day seminars, supplemented by elaborate press kits, to acquaint the media with upcoming trends in fashions. In addition, material is supplied to the press from time to time as the seasons progress. Activity is not limited to the print media; scripts and slides are also provided to television programs. Further encouragement to the media is the award each year of an "Aldo" for outstanding fashion journalism in various newspaper, television, and radio categories.

The "MAGIC" Trade Show

Another important menswear enterprise has moved into women's apparel also. The Men's Apparel Guild of California, once an association and trade show for West Coast producers, began in 1979 as a national men's apparel show with emphasis on sportswear. Its "**MAGIC**" designation is, of course, an acronym for the name of this increasingly important industry show held in Las Vegas (Figure 6–11). Factors in its development were the energetic promotion of the "California look" by producers and the growing appeal of sportswear. The MAGIC show has expanded into all men's product lines since those early days. Already the world's largest menswear show, MAGIC fills nearly two million square feet of show space. Attendance has reached more than 75,000 people per show. In 1995, the first MAGIC show for women's apparel took place. MAGIC management's ultimate goal is to position this show as the most important apparel trade show in the world so that a buyer anywhere in the world will want to attend the show ("Great," 1995).

California International Menswear Market (CIMM)

The latest menswear trade show to make an appearance is **CIMM**, which started in 1988. This show hopes to give major competition to the MAGIC shows. CIMM meets in Los Angeles.

Menswear Trade Showings

In addition to the menswear group trade shows described above, menswear manufacturers also have the opportunity to show their wares at fashion trade shows held in various fashion centers around the world. In the United States, the **Designers' Collective**, a trade association, presents seasonal shows in New York City, with

Figure 6–11   For many years, the MAGIC Show was a market for menswear only.

Source: Reprinted by permission of MAGIC.

emphasis on fashion newness and innovation. Participants are a constantly growing group of menswear designers, both established and newcomers.

Other trade shows are staged by European menswear trade associations. Among them are the European Menswear Show (SEHM) in Paris, Pitti Como in Florence, the English Menswear Designers' Collection in London, the Scandinavian Menswear Fair in Copenhagen, and the International Men's Fashion Week in Cologne. These are seasonal showings that are presented twice a year for the major seasons—Fall/Winter and Spring/Summer.

Fashion Explosion in Men's Accessories

Great as the impact of fashion has been on men's clothing, the American male still wears essentially the same articles of dress that his father and grandfather did before him: coat, pants, shirts, ties. Color, pattern, line, and other elements may have changed, but not the basic costume. Where men have really broken loose from regimentation, however, is in accessories. Not only do they have their hair styled instead of simply cut, and not only do they use perfumes (whose very presence in the home would have scandalized the earlier generations), but they also have let themselves go in wearing medallions, gold chains, and decorative bracelets, in carrying shoulder and tote bags if they choose to, or in wearing western-look hats and boots if they like the idea. Fashion in neckties has exploded, with designs that include everything from colorful abstract art to cartoon characters, Harley-Davidson motorcycles, and hot chili sauce. Not since the days of Beau Brummel have men so much indulged in creative things to wear and in uninhibited colors.

Perhaps the most important development in the total men's market is that fashion has become more important in men's lives than it ever has been before.

Readings

The menswear industry experienced a revolution in the last 30 years, resulting to a great extent from the design pioneers. Moreover, men's attitudes about clothing have changed, with many much more interested in fashion than in the past. These articles focus on menswear design pioneers, their efforts in bringing their designs to the masses, and new trends in the menswear industry.

Men's Wear's Designer Pioneers   248

Contemporary menswear designers in the 1960s were the first to attach their names to men's clothing. This group of designers also changed the rules regarding silhouette, color, pattern, and cloth in menswear.

The Big Brand Era   251

Menswear firms learned how to capitalize on the popularity of designer names to enhance their business. For many companies, the menswear market has become tremendously successful.

Clothing Men Use Soft Suit to Play Hardball   254

The shift toward casual office wear has been detrimental to many firms that make men's tailored suits. However, many of these firms are now producing clothing for the dress-down era.

34 Joseph Abboud In-Store Shops Open in Japan   256

Well-known U.S. menswear designer Joseph Abboud has joined the globalization trend by opening in-store shops in Japan. Other menswear designers have also joined this global movement.

Men's Wear's Designer Pioneers

by Barry Van Lenthen, with contributions from Sophie D'Aulnay and James Fallon

They used to be known as tailors and seamstresses.

But 30 years ago, in a similar codification that transformed mailmen and stewardesses into postal workers and flight attendants, they became fashion designers, moving out of the gritty backrooms and into the limelight.

The women's field had been comfortable with the role of couturiers dating back to the European monarchs, but in 1965 the concept of one person's actually taking credit for designing a man's suit—a two- or three-piece labeled business uniform—was rather odd. A suit is tailored, for God's sake: That took a tailor, not a designer.

Which was exactly the point made over and over by the man generally acknowledged as the first contemporary American men's wear designer, John Weitz.

John Weitz

In 1970, brandishing a gigantic pair of pinking shears at this reporter, John Weitz boomed, "Are these the tools of an artist? No, they belong to a craftsman; a tailor."

So be it. Weitz considers himself the longest-existing licensed designer, incorporated in 1952 with children's and women's wear, with sporadic forays into the men's area. In 1965 Weitz contracted his own merchandise for pilot men's shops in Lord & Taylor, John Weitz *Clubs,* the term *boutique* being considered and discarded as too slight.

Shortly thereafter, Weitz incepted a manufacturing/licensing venture, LWL Corp., to stretch the categories. At the time, Weitz had distinguished himself and his business by stratifying licenses by price point within a category, like tailored clothing or dress shirts, through one or more producers. He saw no confusion in this arrangement: "GM has five price levels, and both Chevrolet and Cadillac have bodies by Fisher," he said. "I'm not confused."

Pioneering an international reputation, a few missteps naturally occurred. A string of European boutiques opened within the aegis of Austin Reed between 1967–1976 that Weitz calls "more effort than fact." But Weitz made those steps in going forward.

Today Weitz manages an East-West network involving 24 domestic licenses for men's, boys, women's and home fashions, plus The Daimaru in Osaka for Weitz's extensive Japanese business. Estimated at some $250 million at retail, the great Weitz way with clothes, bedsheets, cutlery, aircraft interiors and more examples of design—"We are a design firm and always have been," he reminds—continues as inexhaustedly as does the man.

"There are interesting new winds of change blowing in America," Weitz says. "It's comforting to have the dependability of a name."

On the good and bad of design sensibility today, Weitz says, "That one can make a living on it is, of course, good; what is bad is that some, particularly the young, are unsure of what the function is. To be creative with a capital 'K' and playing to the press is not making money. They should have their heads stuck under the shower head to remind them—pay attention to the consumer."

Weitz has always known his audience. Early on, promulgating a no-nonsense one-button silhouette, Weitz's scrunch-it-up-in-a-gym-bag traveler's "unconstructed" jacket at the onset was as much of function as form. His all-American concept of a man with broad shoulders and narrow hips was directly antithetical to the nipped-waist models issuing from England and France. "American men are not nymphs," he had declared back then.

Since Weitz worked within the system, the branded U.S. clothing establishment accepted him as one of their own. So what if he grandstanded one individual's talent over that of generations of family-firm craftsmanship. It was business, so they neither damned nor deified this "designer/tailor" idea.

Their crucifixion awaited Cardin.

Pierre Cardin

At tailored clothing firms from Chicago to Rochester, the backrooms emptied as the master tailors convened in Philadelphia in 1967 at the annual meeting of the International Association of Clothing Designers. Frank Toscani, vice-president, Design & Quality Control, at H. Daroff & Sons, then-maker of the Botany 500 label, took a large easel board and with two curvy lines drew a voluptuous silhouette. "This is not what a man is built like," he said, ripping it off the easel. The audience cheered. Then, drawing an upside-down triangle on a fresh sheet, he growled, "That is a man." They cheered louder.

This is what Pierre Cardin was up against with his International Line, licensed to Intercontinental Men's Apparel, then housed on Astor Place in Manhattan's Greenwich Village.

Essentially a slim French cut with narrow shoulders, suppressed waist and tapered pants, it was clearly a look for city sophisticates and, though cut for a fuller frame than the French originals sold in the trendsetting men's shop at Manhattan's Bonwit Teller, it developed a following. American men won't wear it, said the establishment, but boy did they hear about it as the press began to trumpet the news: International style had arrived on these shores.

"What was important was to bring the French approach [to fashion] because at that time it was all about the English and the Italians," Pierre Cardin says today about the launch of his men's ready-to-wear collection in the U.S. "I was doing ready-to-wear, which was an event in itself. There were no real collections then—it was only tailors doing made-to-measure," he adds.

Cardin's open-minded vision remains his driving force. From haute couture he went into ready-to-wear and then spread his scope via multiple licenses. "What I'm interested in is mass distribution," he states, something others look down upon, especially in the fashion world. "It's thanks to my creativity that I became a businessman," he says. "I'm entirely free from A to Z. I have complete freedom as a designer as well as a businessman. It's an enormous advantage."

Today the Cardin empire represents 904 licenses, a global number that, despite contractual realignments, has remained stable over the past five years. The house employs 190,000 people worldwide and Cardin products are present in 171 countries. In France, the Cardin label can be found in some 2,500 doors [stores] and the shirt brand alone represents 32 licensed contracts throughout the world.

Cardin entered Japan in 1957, the U.S. in 1960, China in 1978, Russia in 1983 and more recently India where he now has 40 shops. He also exports men's wear to Estonia, Lithuania, Ukraine and Latvia and has Cardin shops in Croatia, Romania, Vietnam and Kazakhstan. The country that generates the largest turnover [annual sales] is Japan.

In the U.S., Cardin operates 32 licenses, of which the suit license with the IBA division of Hartmarx is the most profitable. "It's working well in the U.S.—we're up 4 percent this year," enthuses Cardin, adding that the only turnover decrease was due to low currencies. For 1994, U.S. sales will hit $200 million.

Estimates for Cardin's total turnover run around $2 billion at retail and from $800 million to $1 billion gross, from which royalties are calculated between 5 and 12 percent. Monsieur Cardin also owns several prize pieces of real estate around the world, including buildings in Paris's Golden Triangle and his cosmic Palais Bulle hosting the Cardin Foundation on the French Riviera.

His latest licenses include car-seat covers in France, mineral water from Himalayan rain water and Cuban cigars signed Maxim's. Next to launch is a license contract for fine jewelry in France.

Cardin products run the range from cigarettes to haute couture, and vehicles from airplanes to cars. "My latest prospect is Cuba, which has great potential for North and South America. After that there's nothing left except maybe Albania and Burma," says Cardin, always on the lookout for virgin territories to civilize.

Hardy Amies

In London, at No. 14 Savile Row, Sir Hardy Amies, Dressmaker to the Queen, has been also tailoring outfits for British gents for almost 40 years.

Color coordination became the benchmark of the U.S. line the dapper Amies had licensed to the Phoenix Clothes division of Genesco in 1966, which was then showcased in Genesco's Roger Kent and

Whitehouse & Hardy men's shops. The statement therein, steeped in solid-toned dress shirts of larkspur, claret and avocado, threaded those revolutionary shades from hatbands to hosiery.

"I've noticed a distinct change takes place on the fashion scene every 20 years," says the grand couturier, who this year celebrates the 50th anniversary of the opening of his Savile Row house.

"The last was the double-breasted suit, but that is now distinctly passe. The single-breasted coat reigns supreme and it keeps going higher. We now are selling five-button coats very successfully." Aimes predicts the dominance of the single-breasted look will last until the year 2000. "After that I can't predict."

Prediction is what has made him a standout in the men's wear field, ever since he signed on with the English suit retailer Hepworth in the late '50s to design a Hardy Amies line.

That caught the attention of the world and Amies became one of the forerunners of licensing in men's wear, signing deals from New York to New South Wales. He now has 50 licenses worldwide for everything from men's suits to bridalwear. And the main change since he started in men's wear has been in attitude more than fashion, Amies says.

"It is overwhelmingly clear that street fashion has made its mark; whether it's pretty or not is another question," he says. "The difference now is more a question of manners than of clothing. It has become acceptable that casual gear can be worn on many more occasions than when I started.

"On the other hand, because I have gone up in the world since I began, I frequent grander circles than I did 50 years ago. And there the tie rule reigns supreme. There still is a firm clinging to the old rules in those circles."

In suits, Amies believes there is a harking back to the custom-made look that was prevalent 40 years ago. Hence the demand for five-button styles, which has a custom-made appearance even if it is ready-to-wear. "Men want that look again, which the English provide," Amies says. "An Italian suit still has a ready-to-wear appearance, even Armani. That is why no Italian gentleman wears Armani; he comes to London to get his suits made."

Amies last year signed a new master licensing deal in America with Philadelphia's Pincus Bros.-Maxwell, which shows that even at 85 years young the world still beats a path to his door seeking stylistic wisdom. Amies says his staff recently has been wading through a raft of licensing requests from Thailand. "We're very much alive, old boy," Sir Hardy says, chortling.

Bill Blass

Pattern play became the business of Bill Blass, a successful American couturier and savvy promoter of the total look for men. One of the longest continuing licensed men's wear lines, Bill Blass of PBM began with the Philadelphia-based clothier in 1965. Toothy checks, mammoth windowpanes and woodsy country suits never seemed like overkill when handled by the Blass staff, who organized trunk shows tied to charity events at the best stores around the country. Basking in the glow of his female customers, Blass would wax on about Indiana, meatloaf and clothes for real guys, and sold a fortune coast to coast.

Ralph Lauren

Change the patterns, colors and even the silhouette of the businessman's bib and you have the beginning of Ralph Lauren's amazing transformation of the culture of men's clothes.

"I could have called it Schwartz," Lauren said in 1969 when asked if the tony name Polo had anything to do with his neckwear line's popular acceptance. "The line was good; I could have called it anything and it would have sold," he had said modestly. It was certainly different; made from fabrics the former Brooks Bros. salesman had culled from the home dec market, Lauren's big beefy ties so overwhelmed most customers' typical dumb-dumb suits that a new set of wardrobe components was required and shortly began to appear under that Polo label, and later under nearly every other decent label in the business.

Oleg Cassini

To break the men's wear color code—specifically dress shirts and specifically white—took the amazing acceptance in 1968 of the dark-toned dress shirt labeled Oleg Cassini, though designed and sold by Barry Boonshaft, Inc.

The name of Cassini, as a favorite designer of Jacqueline Kennedy, not only splashed through the headlines as the couturier of the Camelot wedding gown, the man's dark sets of highly photographed furnishings got plenty of exposure.

His deep-blue dress shirt therefore became a favorite of any American man who, if leery about springing for a total look outfit (then costing about $225), could go for the shirt at $17.50. And go they did.

Source: From DNR, January 18, 1995, pp. 16–20. Reprinted by permission.

The Big Brand Era

by Stan Gellers

The 1960s sizzled for the men's wear business.

Right after the Mod explosion, in the middle of this decade, the designer was suddenly discovered—not only as a talent, but as a cash cow that later gave many anonymous men's wear manufacturers celebrity status.

The timing couldn't have been better for an industry mired in ultra-conservative Ivy League fashions.

Americans' first taste of British Mod style might have been the Beatles in their knockoffs of the now-famous Pierre Cardin cardigan suit on the *Ed Sullivan Show* in 1964. The Beatles made the American clothing community take a hard look at Europe, where fashion was happening.

At first, U.S. suit manufacturers begrudgingly acknowledged the new fashion trend—the Continental—that changed the shape of American tailored clothing. And sportswear and jeans makers took quick note of the low-slung bell-bottom jeans and skinny rib-knit T-shirts.

The excitement was there, but for no-nonsense American retailers and manufacturers, something was missing—a merchandising handle. For the most part, fashion in the early '60s was faceless and nameless.

After all, American consumers at every level were weaned on brands and they looked for their favorite names as a sign of trust, quality and dependability.

Brands also meant money in the bank for stores and manufacturers, and America had a well-stocked storehouse of famous men's names: Arrow, Van Heusen, Palm Beach, Wembley and Stetson, to name just a few.

Still, with all their stability, respect and recognition, they couldn't match the pizazz and excitement of America's next wave of brands that were actually the names of the living designers who created the fashions. Three designer greats—Pierre Cardin in Paris, Hardy Amies in London and John Weitz in New York—had a lot in common. First was the talent to translate their country's mood and lifestyles to men's clothes.

Second, and perhaps equally important as the years have proven, an innate commercial sense to bring their fashions to the masses.

Third, the knack to team up with savvy manufacturers via licensing arrangements that turned designers into international celebrities—and not long after, celebrities into designers (or so many thought).

More important, the famous brands of the past had to move over and make room for the designer labels, which often offered snappier fashions and fat margins for both the licensed manufacturer and the retailer.

Consider Oleg Cassini, who became an overnight celebrity after his stint designing Jacqueline Kennedy's first White House wardrobe. He signed a long-term licensing deal with Burma Bibas, the neckwear company.

Then there was Bill Blass and his long association with Pincus Bros.-Maxwell, the Philadelphia tailored clothing company that became the master licensor for the designer's label, which has become a perennial performer in men's wear.

These designers, and others, got the licensing balloon off the ground by the end of the 1960s and, at the same time, their names fueled the new Big Brand Era.

The race to cash in on the designer boom heated to the boiling point in the mid-'70s and names suddenly surfaced all over the map.

Certainly, many designers had the valid credentials and a list of credits alongside their names in men's as well as women's wear. But as eager and talented as many designers were, surprisingly few were able to link up with licensees and build a lasting home in the market.

This included some of the best names here and in Europe that never progressed beyond getting their labels on suits or ties. Of those that did, most designers had a fairly short run. Included here are such former European luminaries as Caraceni, Litrico and Vitucci from Rome, or Franceso Smalto, Philippe Venet, Ted Lapidus, Jeff Sayre and Marcel Lassance, from France.

Across the channel in England, some of the entries were Tommy Nutter, Walter Holmes, John Stephen of Carnaby Street and Michael Fish of Mr. Fish fame.

Somehow, they all managed to elude the web of licensing that brought many designers into the big time of the U.S. They weren't alone either, because the same was true for many American women's wear designers who never shared in the fat payoff that men's wear licensing and branded status produced.

Adrian, Don Loper, Luis Estevez, John Fredericks of Hollywood, Donald Brooks and Giorgio Sant' Angelo are some of the old-timers. More recently, other women's wear hopefuls who never made it in men's wear: Isaac Mizrahi, who had a season or two in the sun; the late Carmelo Pomodoro; and Ronaldus Shamask, now mostly involved at Revlon, and with his own men's exclusive label for Barneys.

On the flip side of the coin are the elite American and European women's designers whose names became a hot brand for men's stores. Their names continue to be very marketable because they have the visibility and reputation that preceded them into stores.

Among these perennials are such designer-turned-celebrities as Yves Saint Laurent, Calvin Klein, Perry Ellis, Gianfranco Ferre, Valentino,

Gianni Versace and Emanuel Ungaro. Or taking the reverse route, Ralph Lauren, Alexander Julian, Sal Cesarani and Stanley Blacker, among others, who began in men's wear and later became hits in women's wear.

Yet, as effective as licensing became in the '70s and '80s in bringing designer labels to the general marketplace, some designers did it on their own.

Taking the solo route were some of the biggest names in the business who decided to take their sub-licensing in-house, such as Perry Ellis, or to manufacture and market their collections on their own. Both Ralph Lauren and Calvin Klein led the corps to designers who also happened to have some sharp business brains in their ranks.

The Adolfo-to-Zegna roster of designer brands has changed a lot over the years.

In the '70s and '80s, the labels included Don Robbie, Calvin Klein, Ralph Lauren, Ron Chereskin, Jeffrey Banks, Christian Dior, Nino Cerruti, Geoffrey Beene, Cacharel, Sal Cesarani, Dimitri, Jean-Paul Germain, Givenchy, Henry Grethel, Halston, Nick Hilton, Daniel Hechter, Alexander Julian, Lanvin, Valentino, Egon von Furstenberg and Allyn Saint George, among many.

Most have survived the years, others are in a holding pattern, and several have even turned into comeback kids, such as Hechter signing on with Hartmarx and von Furstenberg cutting a licensing deal with Lubiam, the Italian clothing maker.

But some designers became casualties in the war to win brand supremacy for a number of reasons.

Even in the years when the men's wear market was desperate for new design talent, some designers never could connect with men's wear companies. The litany of excuses offered by the designers as well as the would-be licensees all had the same ring.

Hard-nosed manufacturers complained the designers were "too far out" to become a commercial reality in men's wear. That's still the case with such talents as Jean Paul Gaultier and the late Franco Moschino, whose labels are still apparently underutilized.

Most designers, meanwhile, fell into the ranks of the unknown, except for their own markets, and consequently won only moderate success in men's wear. Then there were even names that some considered box-office poison for one reason or another.

But the bottom line for many designers—one that stopped many in their tracks—was the funding needed to promote as a men's wear brand. Designers with solid reputations were everybody's goal and there simply weren't enough Calvins and Ralphs to license.

Also, the added cost of designer royalty payments became part of inflated wholesale prices. Marketing people felt that if American consumers wanted to enjoy the snobby appeal and mystique of a designer name, they should pay for it.

By the mid '80s, designer licensing abuses caught up with the industry. The many questionable "homemade" labels, inflated prices and an overload of names-for-names'-sakes derailed the gravy train that carried many in the market for years.

As a result, many hard-pressed manufacturers were forced to let down the bars and sell their stable of labels to the growing number of discounters and off-pricers, which continue to have a huge appetite. And they pay their bills fast.

Some designer brands made no bones about going mass with class and the late designers Halston and Lee Wright both broke the mold by penning fat contracts with J.C. Penney in 1982. Other designers tried to walk both sides of the street with two-tier pricing and licensing deals: marketing their labels both upstairs at department and specialty stores and also at the chains and in the mass market.

Other designers whose labels made the brand stand at the chains were Alan Flusser at Penney's in the early '80s; Gil Truedsson's Boston Athletic Club at Sears, Roebuck; and Jean-Paul Germain at Montgomery Ward.

The rule had always been that once the designer brand became "tainted" by chain or off-price distribution, it could never climb back into the pricier specialty and department store world.

Wrong! Flusser, for one, is happily ensconced in Saks Fifth Avenue and Robert Stock is another name that has successfully rounded this turn. And other designers rattling comparable skeletons in their closets have moved upstairs again.

Then there were the people, like Ralph Lauren, Perry Ellis and Alexander Julian, who skirted the price issue in the '80s by coming up with sub-labels for different retail distribution. Lauren invented "Chaps," Perry Ellis simply added "America" and Julian, "Portfolio" to their names.

After designer licensing almost slammed to a halt in the late '80s, Giorgio Armani came on the scene from Italy and revitalized the entire label concept on the strength of his visionary silhouettes and fabrics.

American manufacturers again looked to the Continent for designer names and they were there for the picking, such as the Missonis, Mariuccia Mandelli at Krizia, Karl Lagerfeld, Marco Wachter at Mondo, and more.

At the same time, new designer brands emerged that are as American as apple pie. For example, Tommy Hilfiger, Liz Claiborne, Nautica's David Chu, Liz Claiborne and Peerless's Kasper are just a few of the U.S. talents spreading their wings via licensing into many other categories.

What hasn't changed over the decades is the major role that neckwear and tailored clothing continue to play in turning licensed designer names into brands.

Both industries built large stables of designer brands that opened many retail doors for them and also enabled many manufacturers to lift the lid on their price points.

Most designers earned their stripes in neckwear and many have endured. But today, there's a split between the designers who market their own ties and the many others who license their labels.

The major neckwear companies monopolizing the licensing end of the designer business are Salant (Perry Ellis, John Henry); Superba (Tommy Hilfiger, Claude Montana); Wemco (Evan-Picone, Oscar de la Renta, as well as nine other labels); Randa (Bill Robinson, Geoffrey Beene, Oleg Cassini); Fashion Point Neckwear (Anne Klein, Enrico Coveri); Mallory & Church (Bill Blass, Karl Lagerfeld, and Colours/Sporting Colours by Alexander Julian); Park Lane (Nigel's by Nathan David, Christian Dior); and Zanzara (Jhane Barnes).

In the same way, the tailored clothing market has been infatuated with labels for years. And whether it's a relative newcomer like Peerless International licensing Kasper, Chaps by Ralph Lauren and Ralph; or Hartmarx with almost a dozen licensees, designer labels are thriving.

Back in the '80s, when Bidermann Industries was at its peak, the French-owned clothing company led the market with a star-studded list including Yves Saint Laurent, Calvin Klein, Daniel Hechter and Jean-Paul Germain.

Today Hartmarx holds on to first place in the designer league. The Chicago company, which recently signed on Perry Ellis and Hechter for its new Novapparel division, also markets Karl Lagerfeld, KM by Krizia, Nino Cerruti, Tommy Hilfiger, Pierre Cardin, Henry Grethel, Confezioni Riserva/Luciano Franzoni and Allyn Saint George.

Not to be outdone, Plaid Clothing Group now has Christian Dior, Evan-Picone, Nautica by David

Chu, Hanae Mori, John Weitz, Nicole Miller and Liz Claiborne [Plaid had since lost some of these as a result of filing for bankruptcy in June of 1996].

And the embattled GFT Corp. continues with some of the best names in the clothing business: Giorgio Armani, Calvin Klein, Valentino, Joseph Abboud, Ungaro, Louis Feraud and Andrew Fezza.

What's next? More niches to be filled by the seemingly endless tunes designers are ready to play in the Big Brand Era.

Source: From DNR, October 18, 1995, pp. 30–32, 62–63. Reprinted by permission.

Clothing Men Use Soft Suit to Play Hardball

by Stan Gellers

Casual has become a curse word among tailored clothing manufacturers.

They blame casualwear as the chief cause for clobbering the suit business and they're pointing fingers at the many Fortune 500 companies giving their employees the green light to dress down on Fridays.

They admit this isn't something that's going to go away, either. And because of this, they agree their big challenge for '95 is to get the suit business back on track.

But everybody feels they can't do it with "last year's suits." They claim their biggest challenge is to come up with soft suits to keep the consumer in *clothing* and not sportswear.

And at every level, the feeling is that *soft* is about the best way to reflect the growing relaxed, easy attitude in today's business scene.

How is the market meeting the casual invasion?

James Stankovic, president, Schoeneman/Palm Beach Cos., reports, "Frankly, I feel Friday dressing as almost passe. I think it's only a blip on the screen and our challenge is much greater than just Friday Wear.

"There's no question that the clothing business we once knew has changed dramatically. And there's no question that today's casual attitude is reflected in poor suit sales.

"The suit as we knew it—the typical boardroom-type suit—is being challenged the most."

Stankovic points out, "We have got to give the retailer clothing that reflects the sportswear mentality. What do I mean? If you watch any hip person on TV today, you'll see them still wearing a suit for the most part.

"But they're wearing them in ways we've never seen before—with T-shirts, banded collars, no ties or even no shirts. As an industry, we certainly should be able to play in that market."

The executive reports that "virtually every one of the collections will reflect some of that thinking—and some, all of it.

"The clothing attitude today requires fabrics with surface interest, crepes and the kind of things you've seen for years in women's wear. And these fabrications, married to a now silhouette either in two, three- or four-buttons with softness and drape that will make the consumer feel he's wearing sportswear."

From Homi Patel, president and chief operating officer, Hartmarx Corp. "First and foremost, there's the issue of casual dressing facing us in terms of what it will do to the components that we produce.

"We already see some shift from suits to softer sport coats and odd slacks. In our particular case, being that we are big in the tailored clothing business and also the largest dress slacks manufacturer, this trend doesn't concern us other than as to how we capitalize on it and move the various product categories."

From Steve Kurtzman, president and CEO, American Fashion, which markets Jhane Barnes and Nick Hilton Standards clothing, "I think the slowdown in suits is a change in lifestyle. As a Californian, this is something I've been subjected to all my life.

"That's why our fancy sport coat business has always been so strong."

But he adds, "Today, there's another element. It's not just the design of the model or the construction. Now it's the fabrication that says casual. You just don't take a navy-blue pinstripe fabric and sell it as a soft model.

"As far as we're concerned, what casual has done for us is to develop a whole new classification of clothing. And to me, it's the leisurewear of the '90s. We're doing it with really soft jackets without chest pieces. And it's probably taking away from clothing."

Kurtzman notes that the company's real thrust is with regular clothing with "a much softer construction that we began doing five years ago when we reengineered our factory.

"Soft now represents 20 percent of our fashion business and it's stronger in sport coats."

Soft will also be an issue for next year at Cliftex Corp., explains Joshua Weiss, executive vice-president. "I think the industry hasn't responded to the move to casual lifestyle and comfort. Look at how many four-wheel-drive sport vehicles are being sold in the suburbs and not for practical use in the mountains. It's a lifestyle.

"The challenge is how to make men enjoy wearing clothing and not look at it as a chore. And the way to do it is with soft, comfortable garments. And soft can relate to suits as well as it relates to sport coats."

Weiss continues, "Ultimately, soft really relates to something that may not be evaluated by the consumer as to how many years he will get out of the garment. But soft is part of his thinking right now and his desire for comfort.

"For our part, we're launching a collection of softwear-related separates . . . sport coats and slacks that are both soft that don't match. We'll also have match-ups. And they'll be designed to sell in the clothing classification."

At The Greif Cos., Henry Siegal, president and CEO, confesses, "Our biggest worry is the continu-

ing trend towards casualwear in the workplace, which is still where the majority of suits and tailored sport coats are worn.

"Our challenge is to offer the consumer exciting, fashionable clothing that satisfies his new workwear requirements.

"It's not necessarily the price or where he buys his clothing but the look and feel and expression of his wardrobe. That's why we are aggressively updating our line with soft make, luxury fibers and new models."

Siegal notes, "We don't see the average male consumer going back to a store and buying basic suits like he used to. He'll buy new fashion-driven clothing that is soft, relaxed, exciting, yet still presentable for the workplace. This translates to both suits for the beginning of the week and fun sport coats for Friday—or any day he wants to wear them.

"To say the rules have changed is an understatement."

As Peter Marziano, president, Individualized Apparel Group, puts it, "It's going to be a tough next three years for everybody. Not only are piece goods prices and labor costs going up, we're also facing some big changes in distribution.

"But maybe the biggest one of all is the workplace. Sure, soft clothing is happening. But I think we're going to see a new kind of business sport coat happening once again. I don't mean dumb airport coats, but neat checks and similar fabrics in flatweaves and subtle textures with a casual feeling.

"And these new sport coats will fit in to the business scene and feel as casual and comfortable as sportswear."

Echoing this thinking, Carl Freedberg, one of the principals at Freedberg of Boston, feels that "FridayWear was born out of the fact that the consumer was completely bored with what was available for Monday through Friday.

"If stores had evolved into fresher silhouettes and fabrics, there would have been no need for FridayWear. It would have been an evolution into another kind of clothing.

"What we're really talking about is a new kind of soft clothing that's right for any day of the week and not just Friday."

Noting that the company launched its lightly constructed Caravan sport coat line four years ago, he reports, "We did it when we began to see the erosion of the classic clothing that we used to produce over the past 60 years. The response has been huge and today it's 60 percent of our business.

"We just call it today's clothing."

The firm's Caravan model is softly constructed with or without a lining. Adds Freedberg, "The important things in clothing today are the silhouette and the fabric and the make, just so long as it's clean. That's sufficient for today's consumer.

"They don't need to spend a lot of money on extra hand tailoring. They don't need it or want to spend on it. There are too many other things to spend on."

Summing up the situation is Bill D'Arienzo, vice-president of marketing and strategic planning: "Quite simply, soft is modern clothing. We're not giving it any handle that implies sportswear or even Friday dressing because our Lineage Collection of soft clothing is for every day of the week."

Source: From DNR, October 31, 1994, pp. 10–11. Reprinted by permission.

34 Joseph Abboud In-Store Shops Open in Japan

by Don Kaplan

Joseph Abboud has launched the first 34 of 35 in-store boutiques in Japan, with one more slated to open on Oct. 1.

The venture, orchestrated through a licensing agreement with Onward Kashiyama Co. Lt., a Japanese manufacturing company, allows for the manufacturing and marketing of J.O.E. by Joseph Abboud in Japan. The new boutiques will feature the company's new line of J.O.E. sportswear, the designer's men's tailored clothing collection and furnishings made for the Japanese market.

Sources at Abboud say the company is eyeing an unspecified number of stores throughout Korea for a similar expansion in fall '96. No details were available.

Last March, the company presented the fall '95 collections to Japanese retailers and secured commitments to open some 35 in-store boutiques throughout Japan. At the time, the company estimated approximately $7 million in volume for fall '95 and based its projection on only 15 units. More current figures are not available, company sources said.

Some department stores in the country that have participated in the launch include Seibu, Isetan, Tobu and Takashimaya.

"This is our most significant license to date," the designer told DNR last spring. He added that eventually Onward Kashiyama might handle Abboud's other categories in Japan, such as its women's line and its fragrance.

"The Japanese are terrific at interpreting," Abboud said. "They built the line from the fall '95 collection in the same fabrics. It's the authentic product."

The Joseph Abboud Co., a joint venture between the designer and GFT USA Corp., already has distribution agreements for all of its men's wear collections in Australia, Great Britain and Canada, and for its women's collection in Canada.

The company also has a licensing agreement for the Joseph Abboud Fragrance for Men with international distribution throughout Europe, the Middle East, Australia, Canada and the U.S., and licensing agreements for belts, socks, braces, coats, eyewear, women's footwear and, most recently, a bed and bath collection called Joseph Abboud Environments.

Robert Wichser, president and chief operating officer of Abboud, said the agreement with Onward Kashiyama, which has been in the works for more than a year, is part of the firm's "process of development. We looked at a number of different options," said Wichser. "It's more than a licensing agreement; it's a partnership. It's more about developing a product than licensing a name."

The Abboud lines will be sold in shop environments only in Japan and be coupled with an aggressive marketing campaign, Wichser said.

Onward Kashiyama is the third-largest apparel manufacturer in the world. It is involved in the manufacturing or distribution of several designer names in Japan, including Jean Paul Gaultier, Calvin Klein, Nino Cerruti, Yves Saint Laurent and Polo by Ralph Lauren, among others.

_____

Source: From DNR, September 28, 1995, p. 5. Reprinted by permission.

Chapter Review

Key Words and Concepts

Define, identify, or briefly explain the following:

CIMM	Everyday Wear	Standardized sizes
CMA	FridayWear	Tailored clothing
Collection concept	Hartmarx	Tailors to the trade
Custom tailors	Levi Strauss & Co.	TFA
Designers' Collective	Menswear weeks	The "MAGIC" show
Drop	NAMSB	Trade show
Dual distribution	"Slops"	

Review Questions on Chapter Highlights

1. Why were the shops that produced men's ready-to-wear in the early nineteenth century known as "slop shops"?
2. Name two developments of the nineteenth century that contributed to the growth of the menswear industry and explain their effect.
3. How does the menswear industry differ from the women's apparel industry? In what ways are they similar?
4. How do the procedures of the men's tailored clothing segment of the industry differ from those of the other segments of the menswear industry?
5. If you were the CEO of a major company today, how would you define casual office wear for your employees? How would you handle it if their definition differs from yours?
6. How do the sizes of men's tailored clothing differ from those of men's sportswear? Why?
7. What is the meaning of the "collection concept" in men's clothing? Why has it developed?
8. What important changes began to occur in the menswear industry in the 1960s? How has this affected the menswear industry today?

9. What trade associations play an important role in the marketing of menswear? What is their importance?
10. Name and compare two of the major menswear companies discussed in the readings.
11. Why is fashion today more important to men than it was formerly? Is it as important to men as it is to women? Why or why not?
12. Who attends the MAGIC show and why?

References

American Apparel Manufacturers Association. (yearly). *Apparel Marketing Monitor.* Arlington, VA: Author.

American Apparel Manufacturers Association. (1995). *Focus: Economic profile of the apparel industry.* Arlington, VA: Author.

At $1,500, his clothes make the man. (1982, July 9). *The New York Times.*

Brown, C. (1994, December 5). Dressing down. *Forbes,* pp. 155–160.

Cobrin, H. (1971). *The men's clothing industry: Colonial through modern times.* New York: Fairchild.

Courter, E. (1995, March 1). Dressing down drives some stores out of biz. *DNR,* p. 4.

DiPaolo, N. (1988, September 1). Quotation in *Daily News Record,* citation information unknown.

Gellers, S. (1994, October 31). Clothing men use soft suit to play hardball. *DNR,* pp. 10–11.

Gellers, S. (1995, January 18). The big brand era. [Special issue: 1965–1995: The Designer Decades], *DNR,* pp. 30, 62, 63.

Great business . . . great selection . . . great MAGIC! (1995, June). *MAGIC News, 10* (18), 1.

The impact of fitness on the cut of clothes. (1985, September 5). *The New York Times, Men's Fashions of the Times.*

Kidwell, C., & Christman, M. (1974). *Suiting everyone: The democratization of clothing in America.* Washington, DC: Smithsonian Institution Press.

Levi Strauss & Co. (1995). *NewsWatch.* San Francisco: Author.

Palmieri, J. (1994, September 5). Financial analysts give high marks to dep't stores' new emphasis on men's. *DNR,* p. 30.

Parola, R. (1991, April 30). MFA at 35. *DNR,* pp. 3, 11.

Silverman, E. (1995, June 13). *Production, sales, and marketing strategies of Hugo Boss.* Unpublished paper presented at the 11th annual International Apparel Federation meeting, Washington, DC.

Top 100 sewn products companies '95. (1995, June). *Apparel Industry Magazine,* pp. 18–40.

U.S. Census of Manufacturers, 1989. Washington, DC: Author.

U.S. Department of Commerce, Bureau of Economic Analysis. Washington, DC: Author.

United States Executive Office of the President, Office of Management and Budget. (1987). *Standard Industrial Classification Manual.* Washington, DC: Author.

Selected Bibliography

Aldrich, W. (1990). *Metric pattern cutting for menswear: Including computer aided design.* London: Blackwell Science.

Bennett-England, R. (1968). *Dress optional: The revolution in menswear.* Chester Springs, PA: Dufour.

Brown, C. (1994, December 5). Dressing down. *Forbes,* pp. 155–160.

Boyer, B. (1984). *Elegance: A guide to quality in menswear.* New York: Norton.

Carlson, P., & Wilson, W. (1977). *Manstyle: The GQ guide to fashion, fitness, and grooming.* New York: Clarkson.

Chenoune, F. (1993). *A history of men's fashion.* London: Flammarion.

Cobrin, H. (1971). *The men's clothing industry: Colonial through modern times.* New York: Fairchild.

Cooklin, G. (1992). *Pattern grading for men's clothes: The technology of sizing.* London: Blackwell Science.

Cray, E. (1979). *Levis.* New York: Houghton Mifflin.

Dolce, D. (1983). *The consumer's guide to menswear.* New York: Dodd.

Dyer, R., & Dyer, S. (1987). *Fit to be tied: Vintage neckwear of the forties and early fifties.* New York: Ron Abbeville Press.

Edelman, A. (1990). *The fashion resource directory* (2nd ed.). New York: Fairchild.

Feldman, E. (1960). *Fit for men.* Washington, DC: Public Affairs Press.

Flusser, A. (1985). *Clothes and the man.* New York: Villard.

Hollander, A. (1994). *Sex and suits.* New York: Knopf.

Hyde, J. (1990). *Esquire's encyclopedia of 20th century men's fashions* (2nd ed.). New York: Abrams.

Jackson, C., & Luow, K. (1984). *Color for men.* New York: Ballantine.

Laver, J. (1968). *Dandies.* London: Weidenfeld & Nicholson.

Martin, R., & Koda, H. (1989). *Men's styles in the twentieth century.* New York: Rizzoli International.

McGrath, C. (1994, November 7). The suit doctor. *The New Yorker,* pp. 91–96.

Molloy, J. (1975). *Dress for success.* New York: P.H. Wyden.

1965–1995: The designer decades. (1995, January 18). *DNR* [Special issue].

Pope, J. (1970). *The clothing industry in New York.* New York: Burt Franklin. (Original work published in 1905.)

Shapiro, H. (1956). *Man, culture and society.* London: Oxford University Press.

75 years of men's wear fashion 1890–1965. (1965). *Menswear Magazine.* New York: Fairchild.

Stegemeyer, A. (1995). *Who's who in fashion* (3rd ed.). New York: Fairchild.

Tolman, R. (1982). *Selling men's fashion.* New York: Fairchild.

Updike, J. (1994, November 7). The seriousness gap (a review of *Sex and Suits*). *The New Yorker,* pp. 243–246.

Wagenvoord, J. (1978). *The man's book: A complete manual of style.* New York: Avon.

Wilson, W., & Editors of *Esquire Magazine.* (1985). *Man at his best.* Reading, MA: Addison-Wesley.

Winnick, C. (1968). *The new people: Desexualization in American life.* New York: Pegasus.

Trade Associations

American Apparel Manufacturers Association, 2500 Wilson Blvd., Suite 301, Arlington, VA 22201.

Clothing Manufacturers Association of the U.S.A., 1290 Ave. of the Americas, New York, NY 10104.

MAGIC International (has moved beyond its origins as the trade association, Men's Apparel Guild in California), 100 Wilshire Blvd., Suite 1850, Santa Monica, CA 90401.

Men's Clothing Manufacturers Association, 555 Chabanel W. #801, Montreal, Quebec H2N 2H8, Canada.

National Association of Men's Sportswear Buyers, Inc., 500 Fifth Ave., Suite 1425, New York, NY 10110.

The Fashion Association (formerly the Men's Fashion Association), 475 Park Ave. S., 17th Floor, New York, NY 10016.

Trade Publications

Apparel Industry Magazine, 6255 Barfield Rd., Suite 200, Atlanta, GA 30328-4300.

Apparel International, The White House, 60 High St., Potters Bar, Herts EN6 5AB, England.

The Apparel Strategist, Apparel Information Resources, 101 E. Locust St., Fleetwood, PA 19522.

Bobbin, 1110 Shop Rd., Columbia, SC 29202.

DNR, 7 W. 34 St., New York, NY 10001-8191.

For Him, Tayvale Ltd., 9-11 Curtain Rd., London EC2A 3LT, England.

Men's and Boys' Wear Buyers, Box 31, New Providence, NJ 07974.

Men's Clothing Retailer, Key Note Publications, Ltd.; Field House, Old Field Rd., Hampton TW12 2HQ, England.

Men's Guide to Fashion (MGF), 805 Third Ave., 28th Floor, New York, NY 10022-7513.

Men's Wear of Canada, Laurentian Media, Inc., 501 Oakdale Rd., Downsview, Ontario M39 IW7, Canada.

Menswear Retailing (MR), Business Journals; 50 Day St., Box 5550, Norwalk, CT 06856.

*F*ashion Accessories and Intimate Apparel/Undergarments

*L*ike a pebble dropped in a lake, every fashion change in apparel creates a ripple of change in the industries that produce fashion accessories and intimate apparel. The total look that the wearer seeks to achieve demands such change. For example, a blazer jacket may invite the use of a tucked-in scarf; a long skirt may require a long slip; short skirts may focus enough attention on the leg to suggest eye-catching patterns in hosiery; shoes may change shape and heel height to become good companions to current clothes; belts may be wide and colorful when waistlines are important, and vanish when dresses hang straight. Jewelry, too, must conform, playing to the high or low neckline, the short or long sleeve, or whatever are the important features of the garment. Even precious heirlooms may be consigned to the vault for a time if the prevailing "look" is wrong for the treasured pieces. Accessories conform to and accentuate apparel fashions to be viable; they cannot afford to lag or clash with the dress or coat or other garment that is the star of the show.

Although changes in men's fashions also require modifications in accessories, the less dramatic changes in menswear generally mean that accessories vary less from season to season than in women's wear. Ties vary in patterns and width; sometimes suspenders are "in" and other times not; and jewelry—from gold chains to cuff links—vary from one time to another. So, although the men's accessory area has become an important one in the fashion industry, changes are much less noticeable than in women's areas.

Accessories, intimate apparel, and the industries that produce them are an integral part of the fashion business. This chapter discusses the economic importance and methods of operation of each of these industries. The readings that follow are concerned with different aspects of this segment of the fashion business.

The Accessories Industries

When designers show their collections on models, and when retail stores put important fashion garments on display, they "accessorize" each dress, suit, or other featured garment to emphasize the total look that is being presented. Consumers also use **accessories** both to accentuate the important fashion points of their appearance and to give individuality to mass-produced clothes. Jewelry in the newest trend, a color-coordinated scarf, a very special handbag, newly textured hosiery—these and similar touches help each woman feel that the outfit she wears is uniquely her own.

Every fashion in the accessory category changes its look as clothing fashions change. Shoes may go from unadorned flats to elegantly pointed highheeled styles; scarfs and jewelry may vary in size, color, and materials; hosiery may go from neutral to colorful or from plain to textured—all in terms of what best suits the current apparel fashions. Success in accessories production and sales is a matter of moving quickly and surely in step with apparel fashions. Conversely, no amount of promotion and invention can create acceptance for a particular accessory when it simply does not fit into the current fashion picture.

Many accessories have experienced dramatic ups and downs as fashions changed. Belts, for example, went into eclipse for many years when chemise dresses hung from the shoulder, ignoring the natural curves of the body. Millinery, too, has had its problems, reaping only a thin harvest from its industry promotional efforts at times when women preferred to go hatless. Accessories as a whole have had lean years at times when there was little room for them in the fashion picture.

In recent years the accessories business is being perceived as an ever more vital and important part of the fashion industry. Accessories are considered by some to be the most necessary part of dressing because they define the style and character of the wearer. Another indication of accessories' growing importance is that the licensing concept has flourished as designers want to increase their share of this rich pie. Examples include Echo Design, which has licensed Ralph Lauren for scarfs, Alpert Nipon for belts and small leather goods, and Sarah Coventry for neckwear; Vera produces Perry Ellis and Anne Klein neckwear; and Victoria Creations holds licenses for Diane von Furstenberg, Givenchy, and Karl Lagerfeld in jewelry. The list grows monthly.

The Business of Accessories

The design, production, and marketing of fashion accessories are not a single business, but several. Each category of accessories is produced in its own industry, and these individual industries are as diverse as the merchandise itself. Some, like shoes and hosiery, are large and dominated by big producers. Others, like gloves, handbags, jewelry, scarfs, and millinery, are the domain of small firms. Some of the industries are highly mechanized; others still use hand operations not much changed from those used 50 or even 100 years ago. Some have plants in or near New York City; others are hundreds of miles from that center or even in other countries and merely have showrooms there. This industry has its own trade shows (Figure 7–1). This segment of the fashion industry has its own site on the Internet (http://www.nfaa-fasa.org). The web page called "Accessory Web" is an online source sponsored by the National Fashion Accessories Association, Inc. and the Fashion Accessories Shippers Association, Inc. for retailers, wholesalers, and consumers.

The accessories industries as a whole, however, do have several elements in common:

1. All are extremely responsive to fashion and very quick to interpret incoming trends. Their success depends on how well they reflect the look of the apparel with which they will be worn.
2. All present a minimum of two new seasonal lines a year.
3. All domestic accessory manufacturers, as is the case with other segments of the fashion industry, are confronted with increasing competition from imports.
4. Almost all major accessory producers have entered into licensing agreements with leading apparel designers to produce and market styles bearing the designer's name.

Economic Importance

According to the *Accessories Market Guide* (1995), published by *Accessories* magazine, this segment of the fashion industry represented a $21.2 billion retail business in 1994.

Figure 7–1

Trade show for the accessories industry

C ome feel the creative pulse that fuels today's hottest fashions at America's most comprehensive women's fashion trade event ... including the most up-to-date collections of jewelry, accessories and apparel.

INTERNATIONAL
FASHION
BOUTIQUE SHOW
Javits Convention Center
NEW YORK CITY

January 6-7-8-9, 1996
Immediate
Spring
Summer

March 16-17-18-19, 1996
Immediate
Early Fall

June 1-2-3-4, 1996
Immediate
Fall

August 22-23-24-25, 1996
Immediate
Holiday
Resort

October 19-20-21-22, 1996
Immediate Holiday
Early Spring

Photography: Ronen Ackerman

To attend any of the above shows, call 617-964-5101.

Call 1-800-4NY-SHOW to exhibit!

THE LARKIN GROUP

Corporate Headquarters, 100 Wells Avenue, Newton, MA 02159, 617-964-5101, FAX: 617-964-5295, E-mail: larkind@wtm.com
New York Office, 485 7th Avenue, Suite 1400, New York, NY 10018, 212-594-0880, FAX: 212-594-8556
California Office, 112 West 9th Street, Suite 418, Los Angeles, CA 90015, 213-623-SHOW (in CA, 800-262-SHOW), FAX: 213-623-9468

Trade only. No one under 14 admitted, including infants. Two forms of business ID required, plus personal ID.

Source: Reprinted courtesy of the Larkin Group.

An additional $4 billion in sales came from the men's accessories segments ("Accessories Report," 1995). For women, the total sales figure included handbags, small leather goods, scarfs, hosiery, hats, gloves, and jewelry, but does not include shoes and fine jewelry. For men, the categories included were similar where appropriate.

In the last decade, the accessories industry has grown a great deal. For example, in 1978, the women's accessories industry accounted for $7.2 billion in retail sales (inflation accounts for part of what appears to be growth). During the 1980s, retail space devoted to accessories expanded, and a number of apparel firms added accessory lines. Examples have been Liz Claiborne, DKNY, Ralph Lauren, and J.G. Hook.

By the mid-1990s, however, most segments of the accessories industry felt the same consumer reluctance to spend that plagued the apparel industry. Despite improvements in disposable income, slow economic recovery hindered consumer spending. Many department stores tried to improve business in the accessories areas by continuing to lower prices. Mass merchants moved into the territories once held mostly by department stores, with about one-third of the sales now coming from mass retailers (*Accessories Market Guide '95*, 1994).

Marketing

Accessories firms have used a number of approaches to attract consumers. Some companies have made a concerted effort to build brand recognition of their products. This approach has been successful in many cases, to name a few: Arias gloves, Monet jewelry, Ray Ban sunglasses, Dooney & Bourke leather goods, and L'eggs hosiery. Another approach has been for an apparel firm to build an accessories line around its established name, such as J.G. Hook, Liz Claiborne, and DKNY. Or, in some cases, an accessories line may be developed around a well-established name in another sector. An example of this is the men's personal leather goods line made by Samsonite. In other cases, a firm may have a licensing agreement with a well-known designer to make the products and sell them under the designer's name. Examples here are Givenchy jewelry, Pierre Cardin sunglasses, or Dior scarfs.

When *Accessories* magazine ("1995 National Consumer," 1995) conducted its first-ever survey on consumer accessories purchases, some results were surprising. In the survey of female consumers between the ages 26 and 44,[1] respondents were asked to identify their favorite accessories brands, designers, or labels (Table 7–1). Most consumers, regardless of age, *had trouble naming more than one or two categories.* Consumers were most likely to be able to identify brands for pantyhose. Aside from this category, almost all other brands for products were department store-oriented. Many consumers named Liz Claiborne as one of the leading brands. Coach was a very popular handbag brand ("1995 National," 1995). "Favorite brands," as identified in the survey, included those respondents *aspired* to buy; they may not have actually bought them.

Shoes

If we had no other indication of the importance of the shoe industry, consider the leather industry's estimate that each of us walks the equivalent of twice around the world in the course of a lifetime. No wonder foot protection has always been of prime

[1]Consumers were a random sample of subscribers to *Working Woman* magazine, a consumer publication that targets women in middle and upper management with a median age of 38.

Table 7–1	Favorite Accessories Brands by Household Income			
	$15,000–$30,999	**$31,000–45,999**	**$46,000–$64,000**	**$65,000+**
Handbags	Coach, Dooney & Bourke, Gucci, Rolfs	Coach, Liz Claiborne, Contessa, Craft	Coach, Liz Claiborne, Stone Mountain	Coach, Dooney & Bourke, Stone Mountain, Perlina, Perry Ellis, Louis Vuitton, Capezio, Aigner
Costume Jewelry	Monet	Trifari, Monet, Anne Klein, Liz Claiborne, Express, Limited, 1928	Monet, Anne Klein, Christian Dior	Anne Klein, Monet, Trifari, Liz Claiborne Contempo label, Ralph Lauren, Napier
Pantyhose	L'eggs, Hanes, No Nonsense	L'eggs, Hanes, Hanes Alive, Hanes Ultra Sheer, Liz Claiborne, Donna Karan, Gloria Vanderbilt, Evan Picone	L'eggs, Hanes, Givenchy, No Nonsense, DKNY	L'eggs, Hanes, Hanes Alive, Hanes Silk Reflections, Calvin Klein
Scarfs	none identified	none identified	Hermes	Liz Claiborne, Vera, Hermes
Belts	none identified	Coach, Marshall's	Ann Taylor, Ellen Tracy, DKNY	Liz Claiborne, Dunn Dee, DKNY, Nordstrom
Sunglasses	none identified	Ray Ban, Gucci, Vuarnet	Liz Caliborne, Ray Ban, Foster Grant	Ray Ban, Serengeti, Anne Klein, Vuarnet, Liz Claiborne
Wallets	Coach, Liz Claiborne, Dooney & Bourke, Lady Buxton	Coach, Liz Claiborne, Princess Gardner	Princess Gardner, Coach, Dooney & Bourke	Coach, Louis Vuitton, Esprit

Source: From 1995 National Consumer Accessories Survey, July, 1995, *Accessories,* p. 37. Reprinted by permission.

importance to mankind and shoes take a prominent place in our legends, proverbs, and fairy tales! We are cautioned not to criticize a man until we have walked a mile in his shoes; we grow up on tales of seven-league boots, glass slippers, and red dancing shoes; we tie shoes to the cars of newly married couples as symbols of good luck. Aching feet remind us of the importance of being comfortably shod; a glance into a full-length mirror highlights the importance of shoes appropriate to one's outfit.

The first American shoemaker was Thomas Beard, who landed in the Massachusetts colony on the second voyage of the *Mayflower* and opened his shop to produce made-to-order shoes. Others followed, some of whom became "visiting shoemakers." These men lived with a household until all members had been shod. Leather for the purpose was usually supplied by the farmer or householder and was obtained from the cured skins of animals killed for meat. During the eighteenth century, shoemakers began producing "sale shoes," made without waiting for specific orders and brought to market to be offered for

Table 7–2	The Shoe Industry Is Dominated by Large Firms
Company	**Annual Sales (1994)**
Nike	$3,789,668
Reebok International Ltd.	3,280,418
Nine West Group	652,028
Timberland Company	637,545
Stride Rite Corporation	523,877
Justin Industries	483,009
Converse	437,307
L.A. Gear	415,966
Woolverine World Wide	378,473
Phillips Van Heusen	371,517

Source: Kurt Salmon Associates (1995, May), *Profile Highlights,* Atlanta: Author, p. 9.
Reprinted courtesy of Kurt Salmon Associates.

sale. Thus, ready-made shoes were introduced. These, however, were made only in three widths and five lengths. The well-to-do, therefore, almost universally had their shoes custom-made as late as 1880 (Quimby, 1936).

The oldest and still active retail shoe organization in the United States is Thomas F. Pierce & Son of Providence, Rhode Island, established in 1767.

Nature of the Industry

The largest dollar volume of business in the accessories group occurs in the shoe industry. This is an industry dominated by large firms (Table 7–2). It is not unusual to find among them companies with many divisions, each of which produces and distributes footwear under its own brand name. For example, Joyce is a division of the U.S. Shoe Company, which also produces Pappagallo and Red Cross Shoes. Thom McCann is a division of Melville Shoe Corp., which also produces footwear under several other labels. The Brown Group manufactures Buster Brown shoes for children, Naturalizer and Airstep for women, and Roblee and Regal shoes for men.

Production facilities are located primarily in Missouri, Maine, Tennessee, Texas, Pennsylvania, New York, New Hampshire, and Massachusetts, with total payroll dollars of $1.2 billion in direct manufacturing alone (Footwear Industries of America, 1995). As with most segments of the fashion industry, the major marketing center for shoes is New York City, and most producers maintain permanent showrooms there. For decades, the 34th Street area was the center of activity for American footwear manufacturers. Headquarters were in the Marbridge Building, at 34th Street and Sixth Avenue, and in the Empire State Building, on the corner of Fifth Avenue. Since the mid-1970s, however, many companies have moved uptown to the 50s, close to the hotels where out-of-town retail buyers stay when they come to attend the industry's semiannual trade showings. Most of those who have remained in the 34th Street area are producers of children's and men's shoes. Companies such as Ferragamo, Golo, and Joan and David prefer the more fashionable 50s.

Development of Athletic Shoes

Not too many years ago, athletically inclined people bought a single pair of sneakers in which to run, jump, bike, or scramble up the side of a hill. Today, all are specialized.

There are biking shoes that are stiff enough to direct all the rider's energy into the pedal, cross-country running shoes with spiked soles for traction, high-laced shoes for skateboards, and on and on to a variety of special-purpose sports shoes. Some athletic shoes, such as the models with air pockets, are highly engineered, often incorporating a curious blend of high and low technology.

The phenomenal interest of the American consumer in physical fitness has created an entirely new segment within the formerly traditional shoe industry. This segment has its share of giants, such as Reebok International Ltd., whose subsidiaries include Rockport and Avia, and Nike. Also important, but to a much lesser degree are Converse, L.A. Gear, Adidas, and Keds.

Economic Importance

The **nonrubber footwear** industry includes production of all footwear that is deemed to contain more than 50 percent nonrubber in the upper part of the shoe. Thus, athletic shoes with more than 50 percent of the shoe itself made of suede, leather, vinyl, or any other fabric are considered part of the nonrubber footwear industry. On the other hand, shoes such as "jellies" or those that are produced by a vulcanizing process, or those that have more than 50 percent rubber in the uppers are classified as part of the rubber shoe industry. With the enormous growth of athletic shoes, these distinctions are increasingly difficult to perceive. However, a tariff advantage is currently granted to imported rubber footwear, and many canvas-topped athletic shoes contain just enough rubber to qualify for this category (Treber, 1990).

In 1995, the domestic shoe industry produced 159.1 million pairs of nonrubber footwear that included shoes for men, women, and children. This production resulted in $7.8 billion in retail shoe sales. The industry employed about 53,800 people compared to employment of 158,400 in 1978. Currently the industry consists of nearly 200 manufacturers operating 341 plants in 31 states (Footwear Industries of America, 1996).

Shoe Construction

Shoes consist of a number of different parts, all of which must be joined together with precision to make for a comfortable fit. These parts include the shoe **uppers** (the visible outside material) and linings cut to fit inside the uppers. These two elements are joined and draped over a **last**—the form that gives the finished shoe its size and shape. Also included are the toe box, which protects both the wearer's toes and the shape and contour of the shoe, and the **vamp,** which is the front of the shoe from toe to instep.

The lasting of a shoe is one of the most important processes in making shoes, since it gives the finished shoe proper fit, removes wrinkles, and ensures comfort and good appearance. Each size is made on a different last, and it is not unusual for a shoe manufacturer to have thousands of pairs of lasts in a factory. Originally, lasts were constructed of wood, but today newer lasts are made of lightweight plastic or aluminum.

At the bottom of the shoe is the outsole, the surface that hits the ground with each step. Above this is the insole, the lining on which the foot rests. Between these two layers is sandwiched a shank—a metal, leather, or plastic strip that protects and forms the arch of the foot within the shoe itself. Some shoes also contain additional padding within the two sole layers for further cushioning and comfort.

The method by which the sole of a shoe is attached to the upper varies within the industry. Each method is referred to as a "construction," to identify the process used: stitching, cementing, vulcanizing, injection molding, nailing, or stapling. About 60 percent of shoes made today use the cement process, applying adhesives to attach the sole to the upper with a permanent bond. This construction is found primarily in men's and women's casual and lighter-weight dress shoes. The most expensive shoes are usually of hand-sewn construction and are referred to as "bench made."

Heel heights of shoes vary, of course; the industry builds them and refers to them in terms of eighths of an inch. Flats measure up to 7/8 inch, low heels are 8/8 to 14/8 inch. Medium heels are 15/8 to 19/8 inch; high heels are 20/8 inch and up. Heels are made of many materials, including leather, wood, plastic, and rubber.

A most important distinction in shoe construction is whether the various parts are made of leather or synthetic material. Leather is highly valued, because it molds to the wearer's foot, is supple and resilient, and breathes to allow moisture to evaporate. Thus, leather is generally used in footwear of the finest quality. Shoes are generally labeled to identify the areas in which natural and synthetic materials are incorporated.

Marketing

The shoe industry is extremely fashion and marketing oriented and each season presents a wide variety of new colors, shapes, and designs, geared to apparel trends. Perhaps this is why many women seem to be intensely susceptible to the lure of new shoes and to buy them as often as or even more often than they buy the other major components of their wardrobes. The industry does not rely on fashion alone to sell its products, however. Major emphasis is also placed on manufacturers' brand names in selling and in trade and consumer advertising.

Seasonal Showings

New lines are brought out twice a year. Because shoe production is a slow process, manufacturers develop and show their seasonal lines in advance of ready-to-wear. Fall/Winter lines are shown in January/February and Spring/Summer lines in August. In addition to presenting their lines in their own showrooms, manufacturers participate in semiannual cooperative trade shows, such as the National Shoe Fairs held in New York. These shows attract thousands of shoe store owners and buyers from all over the country, not only to see the new merchandise but also to attend merchandising clinics and discuss new fashion trends with the fashion directors of the participating manufacturers. A regular feature of the New York shows is fashion presentations, at which retailers see how the new shoes coordinate with apparel fashions. All this is done six months before so much as a pair of the new shoes is likely to turn up in a retail store. In addition, there are other, less elaborate regional showings and clinics throughout the country.

Leased Shoe Departments

Because of the expertise needed to fit and sell shoes, and also because of the tremendous inventory needed to stock a shoe department, department and specialty stores have traditionally leased out some or all their selling space to experts in the field. Many of these are manufacturers of well-known national brands, such as the U.S. Shoe Company, which uses leased departments to stock and sell its Cobbie, Red Cross, and Pappagallo lines, and the Brown Shoe Company, whose leased departments feature its Buster Brown, Regal, and Naturalizer shoes. Other leaseholders are simply shoe merchants, who operate their departments as they would operate freestanding stores, with as many or as few brands as they deem appropriate.

Many of the leased shoe departments, manufacturer-owned or otherwise, also stock related accessories, such as handbags, hosiery, and small leather goods, which they purchase for resale from producers in these various industries.

Figure 7–2

U.S. Consumption of nonrubber footwear: imports vs. domestic production

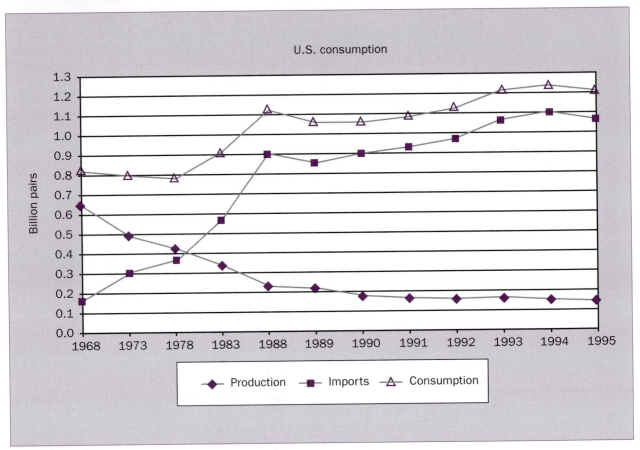

Source: From *Current Highlights of the Nonrubber Footwear Industry* (p. 1) by Footwear Industries of America, 1996. Washington, DC: Author. Reprinted by permission.

Manufacturer-Owned Retail Chains

As has happened in the apparel industry, the growth of manufacturer-owned stores has been a fast-developing trend in the accessories area. The shoe classification, as the largest segment of the accessories industry, was the first to get into this business and remains in the forefront.

The advantages shoe companies see in this type of operation include creating a stronger brand franchise for their stores, protecting their share of the market in the wake of a diminishing number of mom-and-pop specialty shoe stores, and providing target consumers with a tightly focused assortment to fit their needs.

As a result, many of the leading names in footwear including U.S. Shoe, Stride Rite, Jumping-Jack Shoes, and Nike either are operating their own stores or are aggressively pursuing franchisees to operate stores for them. U.S. Shoe operates about 600 stores nationwide, 80 percent of which are franchised. Brands include Joyce/Shelby, Pappagallo, Red Cross, and Cobbie. Stride Rite itself operates 270 stores and additionally has about 400 individual dealers across the country that are licensed to operate a Stride Rite store ("Footwear," 1988).

Figure 7–3

Shoe making requires a great deal of labor, therefore many shoes are produced in low-wage countries. This photograph shows shoe production in Indonesia.

Source: Photo by Kitty Dickerson.

An even newer development is the trend to outfit the targeted consumer from head to toe as shoe manufacturers expand into apparel and activewear. Nike has opened stores where "we're trying to merchandise appropriate footwear and apparel together as a collection, so consumers can see how it coordinates" (McGuire, date unknown). Others such as Reebok, which in 1987 purchased Ellesse and L.A. Gear, are opening stores to do the same thing.

Extensive Competition from Imports

In 1995, shoe producers in other countries shipped more than 1.2 billion pairs of shoes into the United States. Imports now account for 89 percent of U.S. shoe consumption, compared to only 22 percent in 1968 (Footwear Industries of America, 1995, 1996). Increased imports have led to an all-time low in domestic production. Thus, the footwear industries have felt the effects of import competition just as the fashion industries in general do. (Further discussion on trade for the industry is found in a later chapter.) Figure 7–2 illustrates that as U.S. consumption has increased, a growing percentage of the market has been taken by imports.

The fashion appeal of Italian and other European styling is important; so is their expertise. Important competition is also a result of the price appeal of low-wage-labor countries (Figure 7–3). A further complication faced by shoe producers is that other countries are often quick to buy up hides and leather in the United States, where our meat-eating habits make us an important provider of these commodities. Then those producers manufacture shoes and other leather goods in their own countries, at a lower price than is possible here, and compete on a favorable price basis with domestic producers.

Figure 7–4 shows where shoes purchased in the U.S. market originated. China now produces more than five times as many shoes for the U.S. market as domestic producers. These figures include shoes imported and resold by domestic manufacturers who find they are unable to compete with high cost labor in this very labor-intensive industry. A large portion of the imports is contracted or purchased directly by

Figure 7–4

Percent share of U.S. footwear market by country of origin, 1995

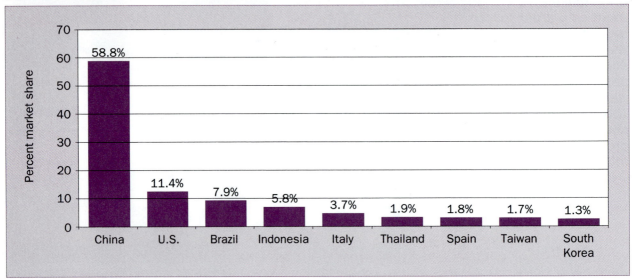

Source: From *Current Highlights of the Nonrubber Footwear Industry* (p. 5) by Footwear Industries of America, 1996. Washington, DC: Author. Reprinted by permission.

retailers. For example, the May Company's Payless Shoe division buys a large volume of shoes from China. The low cost production in China and other low-wage countries enables Payless to sell shoes to consumers at very competitive prices.

Some U.S. manufacturers contract their production with offshore producers. There are those who own their own facilities in Italy, Spain, or South America. An example of the first type is the fashion-oriented firm of Joan and David, whose shoes are produced by the Martini factories, among the oldest and finest in Italy.

Although the footwear industry's competition from imports parallel those of the textile and apparel industries, the footwear sector has had far less protection from imports. That is, there are no import quotas.

Although the outlook appears grim for the domestic footwear industry, an occasional manufacturer in this country is able, by ingenuity and enterprise, not only to meet foreign competition, but also to sell domestic shoes abroad. More than 22 million pairs of U.S. shoes were exported in 1994. Major countries buying U.S. shoes were Canada, Japan, Mexico, the United Kingdom, and Germany (Footwear Industries of America, 1995). Timberland is an example of a company that has exported successfully.

Hosiery

The introduction of nylon stockings in 1938 set the stage for vast changes in hosiery, in the industry that produces it, and in its importance as a fashion accessory. Before nylon, stockings were made primarily of silk and also of wool, rayon, and cotton. Yarns were knitted into pieces of flat fabric, each shaped so that when it was folded in half and seamed down the back, a stocking in the form of a leg resulted. Colors were limited and fabric surfaces were plain.

Early nylon stockings for women were made much as silks and rayons had been. Except during the World War II years, when civilian use of nylon was ruled out to make way for military needs, nylon has made steady progress in hosiery, to the point that it has virtually crowded out other fibers for dress wear. With continuing technological progress, women's nylon stockings became sheerer, took on more colors, were produced in sandal-foot and other styles, and developed patterns and textures undreamed of in earlier years. In the 1960s, the development and popularity of pantyhose substantially added to the growth and fashion importance of hosiery. Again the development of panty-hose resulted from a change in fashion—women's skirt lengths. When skirts were very short in the 1960s, nylon hosiery that stopped at mid-thigh was no longer suitable.

Nature of the Industry

The business of hosiery is one of chemistry, filaments, yarns, knitting machines, technology, big production, big promotion, and big competition. It is also the second largest industry in the accessories field, after footwear. And like the shoe industry, it is dominated by large firms. Among the largest are Sara Lee (notably L'eggs, Just My Size, and Hanes), Round-the-Clock, Bonnie Doon, Hot Sox, and Kayser-Roth (No Nonsense). Perhaps it is significant that in a national survey asking consumers to identify the most recognizeable brands in all women's apparel, two *hosiery* brands topped the list: L'eggs and Hanes ("Fairchild 50," 1993).

Most manufacturing plants are in the Southeast—notably North Carolina, a state that accounts for more than half the industry's output (National Association of Hosiery Manufacturers, 1995). Nevertheless, the marketing center for the industry is New York City. There the larger firms have their showrooms and smaller companies also have sales representation. It is there that retail buyers go during market weeks, not only to select merchandise, but also to learn about national advertising programs that producers plan to run and to assess the opportunities for tying in at the local level.

Economic Importance

The hosiery industry produced and shipped more than $4.4 billion (wholesale value) in 1994 (American Apparel Manufacturers Association, 1995). The National Association of Hosiery Manufacturers (NAHM) noted that its member companies contributed $7 billion (retail value) to the retail environment in 1994. Of the NAHM retail figure, socks represented the largest category with $3.7 billion, followed by women's sheer hosiery sales at $2.8 billion. This volume represents the output of 341 companies, operating 455 plants. Of these, 19 percent or 94 plants are in the women's sheer hosiery business, and the other 81 percent or 392 plants produce socks. The industry employs 65,000 people in 28 states (NAHM, 1995). Hosiery consumption was estimated at 17.9 pairs per person in 1994 compared to 15.7 pairs in 1979 (NAHM, 1988, 1995).

Hosiery Construction

Hosiery is knitted, either full-fashioned or seamless, in the greige state. Full-fashioned stockings are knitted flat to the desired shape, length, and size; sewn into the shape of the leg; next heat-set or boarded; and then packaged. Seamless hosiery is knitted on a circular machine, at high speed, and then dyed. The same procedure is used for pantyhose, some of which are knitted as stockings and then attached to separate panties. Full-fashioned hosiery had the advantage of a better fit than seamless until the introduction of stretch yarns in the 1960s. With them, the fit of seamless hosiery and pantyhose was greatly improved. Stretch yarns also made possible stretch hosiery, support hose, control tops, and comfortably fitted knee-high stockings.

Automation in hosiery production is constantly increasing, to the point that computerized machines can turn out hosiery that features graphics, patterns, and textures and employs many novelty yarns.

Marketing of Hosiery

As hosiery moved from almost entirely functional purposes toward becoming an important fashion accessory, the marketing strategies of the industry changed along with its product. Manufacturers' brands acquired new influence; producers' advertising took on greater importance to the retailer; fashion became the watchword of the industry.

Nationally Advertised Brands

Manufacturers' brand names in the hosiery field are older and better established and have been longer promoted than those in other accessories areas. But whereas women had been conditioned to purchase a brand for its fit and durability, they are now bombarded with advertising that stresses the fashion points of the brands. Major producers advertise consistently in national magazines, on television, and, through cooperative advertising with retail stores, in newspapers.

One of the most phenomenal success stories of the entire apparel industry has been Sara Lee's quiet movement into the hosiery and intimate apparel business by acquiring well-known brands and building them into commercial successes through high profile marketing efforts. Through these efforts, nearly all women in the United States would recognize names like L'eggs, Just My Size, and Hanes. More than that, a very large number *buy* those brands. Marketing strategies turned relatively mundane products and brands into megabrands—a strategy that has paid off handsomely for the company. Through wise acquisitions and well-planned marketing, Sara Lee has become one of the largest (or possibly *the* largest) U.S. apparel firms—with women's hosiery as a major component of its business. Additionally, Sara Lee has acquired well-established hosiery and foundations firms in Europe and Latin America—providing access for its U.S. brands in those markets and bringing some of those brands to the United States.

Retailers have capitalized on women's devotion to brand names by not only featuring national brands but also creating their own. These are known as **private labels.** This approach gives them greater price flexibility, removes them from direct competition with other stores in the national brand arena, and creates a certain exclusivity for their stores. Usually, the same manufacturer will produce both the store's private brand and its own national brand that is also carried in the same department. For example, Macy's has its Clubhouse but it carries an impressive array of nationally advertised brands side by side with its own. And in that array, the maker of the house brand is sure to be represented. Its source of supply, however, remains the store's secret. The same situation prevails in discount houses, chain drug stores, supermarkets, and others, except that these latter outlets seldom carry as many brands as department stores and major women's specialty shops.

Impact of Fashion and Designer Names

As hosiery has moved into the fashion spotlight, both retailers and manufacturers have been treating legwear much as ready-to-wear is treated. For example, the industry has changed from two to three market weeks a year: March for the presentation of Fall lines; August for the opening of Holiday and Early Spring lines; and November for Spring lines. This change in the marketing calendar is a natural outgrowth of the increased number of fashion items attuned to the seasonal apparel fashions. More and more emphasis is put on decorative legwear in a wide variety of textures, colors, and patterns. To coordinate with active sportswear, the industry offers leg warmers in colors coordinated with the clothes themselves. And in response to women's body-building and other exercise activities, the industry produces bodywear in attractive colors, to be sold in hosiery departments.

Inevitably, as the total look became important in fashion, leading apparel designers, both European and American, moved into designer-name hosiery—for the most part under licensing arrangements with producers of national brands. For example, Donna Karan hosiery is licensed by Hanes, which is owned by Sara Lee; Round-the-Clock has legwear bearing the name of Givenchy; Bonnie Doon has Geoffrey Beene socks; Kayser-Roth produces the Calvin Klein line; and Hot Sox has a Ralph Lauren collection.

Package Marketing

Hosiery, like so many other products, has been affected by packaging and self-service techniques. For decades, it was sold over department and specialty store counters by saleswomen who slipped their beautifully kept hands into the stockings to show how they would look on the leg. Then came packaging, notably L'eggs by Sara Lee. These were pantyhose, folded into egg-shaped containers, for sale from self-service fixtures conspicuously placed near checkout counters in supermarkets and drugstores. With the marketing success of L'eggs, other producers soon followed. Kayser-Roth developed the No Nonsense brand for similar distribution. Presently, the consumer can find a packaged hosiery rack in almost any self-selection store.

The success of these nontraditional channels of distribution has led hosiery producers to seek out more innovative packaging and marketing techniques. Another factor is that consumers have changed in general in terms of *where* they are buying apparel. Together these trends have affected the retail distribution of hosiery. Discount stores have gained at the expense of department stores and national chains (the latter consists of Penney, Sears, and Montgomery Ward). Distribution for all hosiery is shown in Figure 7–5. To compete with the price appeal of discounters, supermarkets, and others, department stores and national chains are using a two-pronged attack. One effort is to push their own brands to meet price competition; the other is to emphasize designer or decorative legwear as a major accessory of fashion.

Global Activities

Pantyhose, hosiery, and basic socks constitute one area of domestic production that has resisted the inroads of import competition. This is true because the industries involved are capital intensive. Less costly labor, the competitive edge that many producers in other countries enjoy, has less impact in this segment of the industry compared to most others. However, imports grow each year. Competition also comes from industrialized countries such as Japan, England, and France. These produce goods of high quality, have great technical expertise, and use sophisticated dyeing techniques. Despite attempts by the domestic industry to keep imports to a minimum, some manufacturers say they will bring goods in from offshore because of the quality of yarns from some countries, the quality of finishing, and the greater sophistication of dyeing techniques.

In 1994, hosiery imports totaled 26 million dozens of pairs, up 22 percent from the 21 million imported in 1993. Imported hosiery represented 7 percent of the domestic hosiery market in 1994. Of the total hosiery imported, 33 percent were **9802 (formerly 807) transactions,** hosiery partly made in the United States, shipped elsewhere for completion, then brought back to this country to be sold. Sock imports represented 47 percent of the total hosiery imported, pantyhose 44 percent, and tights 6 percent (NAHM, 1995).

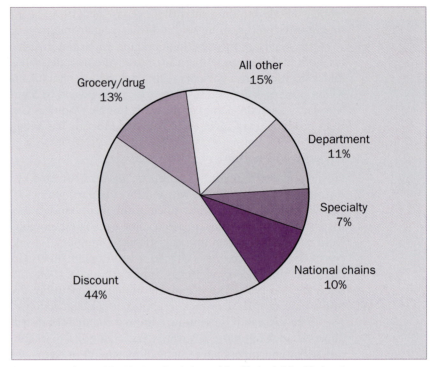

Figure 7–5

Retail distribution channels for all hosiery

Source: Data from *1994 Hosiery Statistics and Profile* (p. 31) by National Association of Hosiery Manufacturers, 1995, Charlotte, NC: Author.

Handbags and Small Leather Goods

From earliest history, people have needed receptacles of some kind in which to carry with them various personal possessions and necessities. Quite possibly, a pouch made of skin or leather and suspended from a belt or girdle was used by primitive peoples who had not yet ventured into clothes, much less clothing with pockets. Handbags as we know them are a creation of the twentieth century; before that, women had only a belt from which to suspend housekeeping keys and slit pockets in their voluminous skirts to accommodate whatever a lady wanted to carry with her. As women's activities grew more varied in the twentieth century, and as their garments became slimmer and sleeker, handbags became necessary and developed into accessories that would complement and coordinate with the apparel. Today, most women have a wardrobe of handbags in a variety of materials (leather, fabric, and plastic, for example), and in a diversity of sizes and shapes, such as clutch, envelope, satchel, box, duffle, tote, pouch—and the woman executive's briefcase-like carryall.

Although men do not generally have as many items, they do have wallets, key holders, agenda organizers, toiletry cases, and other pieces. Therefore, this segment is also an important part of the industry.

Nature of the Handbag Industry

For the most part, the handbag industry consists of relatively small specialists, the majority of whom are headquartered in New York—primarily in the 30s, between

Broadway and Fifth Avenue. They present their lines in two major showings a year: in May for Fall and in November for Spring and Summer. Supplementary collections, smaller than the main seasonal ones, are shown for Holiday/Transitional in August, for Early Fall in March, and for Summer in January.

The majority of buyers for retail handbag departments also buy other accessory items, such as gloves, belts, or small leather goods. Such buyers demand and usually get coordination in both color and silhouette among the various markets they shop, and they also seek to purchase accessories that will relate well to the upcoming season's ready-to-wear. The handbag industry establishes market dates that dovetail with apparel openings. It also uses its openings as an opportunity to disseminate both industry and fashion information to the retail store buyers.

Economic Importance

In 1994, U.S. manufacturers produced handbags valued at an estimated $441 million at wholesale. In 1995, $949 million in handbags were imported, accounting for about three-fourths of U.S. consumption. Retail sales of handbags was $4.2 billion in 1994. National chains and alternative retailers (off-pricers, mail order, etc.) continue to slowly increase their share of the handbag market at the expense of department stores (*Accessories Market Guide,* 1994, 1995).

Handbag Construction

Years ago, leather was the principal material from which bags were made. This meant a large amount of hand-guided work and demanded considerable resourcefulness in cutting, since the operator had to work with a natural product, irregular in shape and sometimes with scars to be worked around. Today, vinyl is the leading material used. Vinyl and fabric offer advantages of uniformity in width and quality that vastly simplifies the cutter's task. Cost is, of course, the main reason for using vinyl and fabric over leather.

Today's handbags range from classic, constructed types to unconstructed, unframed bags of leather, canvas, or other materials. The number and difficulty of the operations required varies with the styling. All, however, begin with a design from which a muslin sample is made. From the muslin, a paper or metal pattern is made, and this is used to cut the handbag materials. The actual cutting is done either by hand or with metal dies, depending on the complexity of the design and the quantities to be produced. Each handbag shape, such as the clutch, envelope, tote, and satchel, for example, requires different types of construction and parts. If the design requires a frame, then all of the inside and outside parts must be fitted into the frame; after that, closures and straps are added.

Global Activities

Imported handbags now account for 76 percent of all those sold in the U.S. market. China supplies about 80 percent of those imports; South Korea, 6 percent; and India, 4 percent (U.S. Department of Commerce, 1994). Many handbags require a good deal of labor in sewing and other aspects of assembly; therefore, many high-wage countries such as the United States have difficulty competing in this segment of the industry. Most large accessory firms and retailers buy directly from the factories abroad, primarily in the Far East, or, increasingly, contract with Asian firms to have lines produced.

Exports increased in recent years, particularly to Mexico. However, these are generally believed to be largely cut parts for handbags, which are being shipped to Mexico to be assembled and then returned to the U.S. market. Other exporting does occur.

Coach bags, a division of Sara Lee, has developed recognition of its quality products in upscale markets in other countries. Coach sells in department stores and operates its own shops in locations frequented by upscale consumers in numerous countries.

Small Leather Goods

Fashion and changing activities of both men and women have had strong impacts on the industry that produces **small leather goods** (sometimes called personal leather goods), such as wallets, credit card cases, billfolds, key cases, jewelry and eyeglass cases, cigarette cases, and similar items for both sexes. Although historically the largest producers of these types of products were Prince Gardner, Buxton, and Swank, the recent addition of Liz Claiborne Accessories, Bosea, and Bond Street has added to the fashion look of these items. Upscale lines such as Coach and Bally are also available.

In today's world of fashion, many women choose to match such items with the handbags they carry. This is especially true of designer-licensed lines, which coordinate the various items by fabric and color. And among women climbing the success ladder in the business world, special needs are developing for which the small leather goods industry is providing some answers: calculator wallets, credit card cases, pocket appointment calendars, work-and-date organizers, notebooks, and all sorts of handbag and briefcase accessories that project both fashion and businesslike efficiency. Professional men are also buying many of these items.

This industry's domestic production for 1994 was $301 million (wholesale), a decline from $365 million in 1990. Imports of personal leather goods was estimated at $301 million, an increase from $255 million in 1990. Leading suppliers of these leather products are China, representing 52 percent of the imports; and South Korea, Italy, and India, each about 7 percent. Most of the $21 million in 1993 exports went to Canada and Japan (*Accessories Market Guide,* 1994, 1995). Men's personal leather goods accounted for $420 million in retail sales. Women buy 84 percent of ladies' units and 50 percent of men's ("Accessories Report," 1995).

Gloves

One can trace the wearing of gloves before and through recorded history. In ancient times, they were worn as protection and adornment—as they are today. Objects in pyramids dating back to Egypt's twenty-first dynasty include gloves. In ancient Rome, ladies protected their hands with gloves. In medieval times, kings and church dignitaries wore richly ornamented gloves, symbolic of their status. A knight wore gloves, or gauntlets, reinforced with armor. When he threw one down before another knight, that constituted a challenge to battle.

Gloves today have many purposes, many of them functional. Foundry workers use insulated gloves to protect their hands from heat; Eskimos need mittens to keep out the cold; racing drivers wear gloves that give them better wheel grip; skiers use waterproof kinds to protect them from frostbite. In fashion, gloves play a role that changes in importance, taking a share of the spotlight when dress becomes elegant and fading out when the look is at a casual extreme.

Nature of the Industry

The glove industry suffered a severe blow during the 1960s and 1970s, when fashion took on an ultracasual look and gloves became almost obsolete as fashion accessories.

The hard times this situation imposed on the glove industry dealt it a blow from which it has not recovered.

Many of today's gloves, especially those made of fabric, are produced by divisions of multiproduct companies that also manufacture small leather goods and handbags, such as Etienne Aigner, or by firms such as Kayser-Roth that produce intimate apparel and hosiery. There are still, however, some specialists that are glovers exclusively. Among these are Aris Glove, producers of a line of fine leather gloves and also the Isotoner glove. Hansen Gloves is another well-known specialist. Other important names here are Fownes and Grandoe, both important producers of fashion gloves, as is LaCrasia, producer of a line of trendy gloves that are unquestionably more fashionable than functional. Companies such as these, which are glovers first and foremost, flourish or suffer according to whether fashion smiles on or ignores the glove as an accessory to the total look.

The plants that produce leather gloves are located principally in the Northeast. Gloversville, New York, was the site of the first glove production facility in the United States, as far back as 1760, and it is where, by 1900, some 80 percent of American gloves originated (Pelz, 1980). Production of fabric gloves, on the other hand, is more widely distributed throughout the country, with 65 percent of the factories being located in North Carolina, Mississippi, Alabama, and Tennessee.

Economic Importance

The glove and mitten industry is largely a business of warm hands and work gloves. That is, the fashion motivation for buying gloves is virtually a thing of the past. The market may vary from year to year—an unusually cold winter can boost sales significantly.

The U.S. *leather* glove and mitten industry is composed of two product segments: work gloves and mittens, which account for approximately 85 percent of domestic production, and dress gloves, which account for the remaining 15 percent. Some 2,300 employees produced $143 million worth of gloves and mittens at factory value in 1992. Imports accounted for about 62 percent of the glove/mitten market. Major supplier countries are China, the Philippines, Mexico, and South Korea (*Accessories Market Guide,* 1994; U.S. Department of Commerce, 1994). The U.S. *fabric* dress and work glove industry produced $279 million at factory value in 1992, employing another 3,552 workers (AAMA, 1995).

Men's gloves accounted for $270 million in retail sales in 1994. Oddly, men's glove sales by type of retail outlet shifted more toward department stores at the expense of the discounters and off-price outlets. The *MR* "Accessories Report" (1995) speculated that department store promotions and markdowns have permitted consumers to buy gifts for friends and relatives at reasonable prices and to do so with the status of a top department store box and wrapping.

Glove Construction

Of all accessories, gloves are among the most labor intensive to manufacture. Although made on an assembly line, they require great skill on the part of production workers and involve many steps, since a glove must fit when the hand is closed in a fist and yet not be baggy when the hand is open.

Gloves are made up of numerous small pieces, such as the trank, or hand and finger piece, both front and back; the thumb part, which may be made in any of several ways; the fourchettes, or pieces that shape the fingers between front and back; and quirks, tiny triangular pieces sewn at the back of the fingers to provide flexibility and give additional fit. Only the very inexpensive gloves use few pieces; they consist merely of a front and back sewn together—a procedure that earns them the name of "sandwich gloves" in the trade.

Because there are so many pieces in the usual glove and because they are so small, a great deal of handwork is involved in cutting. This may be done on a table, using a ruler to measure each part, or with the use of a die. The former method is known as table cutting, the latter as clicker cutting. Actual sewing is done on several types of machines and uses lock stitch, chain stitch, and overstitching, depending on quality and style. Since gloves are curved, high-speed production equipment cannot be used.

Because gloves require a great deal of labor to produce, especially high quality ones, U.S. manufacturers have found it difficult to compete with imports. The lower wages in other countries make production more affordable in those nations.

Glove Marketing

The major marketing center for gloves is New York City, where most glove producers maintain permanent showrooms of their own or use the facilities of sales representatives. These showrooms are usually located in the East 30s, where many of the other accessories industries are also located. Seasonal lines are shown at the same time as the handbag showings. Compared with the promotional outlays and activities of other fashion accessories manufacturers and retailers, the money devoted to promoting gloves is relatively insignificant.

Some of the more aggressive producers, however, have followed the example of the hosiery industry and are packaging "one size fits all" stretch gloves that can be displayed and sold in self-service fixtures. Others are increasing their volume by packaging their gloves with matching hats or scarfs, or both—a combination with strong consumer appeal during cold winter months.

Millinery/Hats

Until the middle of the present century, it was unthinkable for a well-dressed woman to be seen on the streets or to enter a store or office without a hat. Every department or women's specialty store devoted a great deal of prime space to millinery[2] departments, which featured both ready-made and custom-made hats and were usually located adjacent to apparel departments. In the 1950s, there was an enormous exodus from the city to the suburbs and, with it, an emerging fashion for casual living and casual clothes. The outdoor barbecues of the 1950s called for a very different style of dress from the garden tea party of an earlier suburban generation. Country casual dress spread to the city, and the habit of wearing hats declined. The millinery industry, after many years of prosperity when women had whole wardrobes of hats, declined too—from which it has just recently begun to recover somewhat.

Men's hats are also considerably less popular than in earlier decades. Some men are inclined to wear them in colder seasons and cooler climates for functional purposes. However, this industry segment is also very small compared to what it once was.

Nature of the Industry

The millinery industry today is small because of the diminished demand for its wares. It is made up, as it always has been, of small firms, numbering fewer than 100, all of which

---

[2]The term *millinery* generally refers to women's hats.

are specialists in this one field. The industry has been untouched by the drive to bigness and diversification that has affected other areas of the fashion business. Smallness is no handicap in this industry, however, as there is little opportunity to mechanize, automate, or develop huge runs of individual styles. The ability to move quickly on a new idea—the strong point of small operations—is an important asset in the millinery field.

Periodically, the importance of the total look in fashion sparks renewed interest in millinery. Designers dutifully put appropriate headwear on their models as they parade the runways; retailers show millinery with other outer apparel; some customers even buy hats. But one still sees few, indeed, on the streets and in other public places. That tide may turn, as tides often do in fashion. Meanwhile, even the most prestigious of fashion retailers gives only minimal space to millinery departments. The day of the huge millinery department—in which expert salespeople helped women choose the right hats for their outfits, or the right hat to enhance their morale for an important occasion—has not yet returned. Until it does, the millinery industry will remain small.

The men's headwear industry generally responds to more functional needs. The industry has some fluctuations as fashions change—but in general the industry is more stable than women's millinery.

Economic Importance

Retail sales of millinery for 1994 were estimated at $700 million, which represents a healthy increase over the $58 million production in the late 1970s (Millinery Information Bureau, 1995). The production of millinery domestically takes place primarily in New York City, although a small number of companies are located in St. Louis, Dallas, and Los Angeles. The fewer than 80 companies operating today represent a continued decline from the more than 400 companies operating in the 1960s when hats were always worn by a majority of the women (Millinery Institute of America, 1989).

Men's hat sales for 1994 were $227 million. This figure included baseball caps, which enjoyed remarkable popularity among young people, both men and women, in recent years. Worn both forward and backward, these caps—like t-shirts—have become a place to express one's support for a favorite team or cause.

Construction of Millinery

Basically, the millinery industry's output falls into two categories: hats and caps, and millinery. The former category can be made by machine or by hand. Millinery-type hats are made by sewing velvet, satin, or other fabric and trimmings over buckram frames, or by shaping and trimming felt or straw bodies. Millinery made by the latter methods involves a great deal of handwork, and the processes lend themselves readily to custom work for consumers or for sale through retail shops. The industry is headquartered mostly on a single street in New York City: West 37th Street, between Fifth and Sixth avenues.

At one time, the industry had its share of well-known designers. Adolfo and Halston, for example, began their fashion careers as milliners. These days, however, the glamorous names bypass the millinery industry and concentrate in the apparel field, where opportunities and rewards are much greater.

Marketing of Millinery/Hats

An unusual factor in the millinery industry is the millinery syndicate of Consolidated Millinery, which operates 250 leased departments. Such a firm leases space for millinery departments in retail stores across the country and provides these stores with a continuing supply of new styles. In order to obtain such styles, the buyers for these firms are constantly in the wholesale markets, not only to seek out actual merchandise but also to find and develop talented new producers and stylists. Help, advice, and sometimes even operating capital will be made available by the syndicate to potentially creative resources.

Unlike other fashion accessories, millinery does not function on two lines a year. Seasonality has its influence, of course, but the life of a hat as an accessory is usually short and, as a rule, the faster a firm gets into and out of a good selling style number, the better the operation is. In millinery, the important element is an unending procession of new styles or new versions of currently accepted styles. At one time, when millinery was in its heyday, retailers sought to have completely new assortments every three or four weeks, and the term *millinery turnover* was used in retail circles to describe extremely fast-moving merchandise.

Today the millinery market has four specific seasons, currently labeled Fall I, Fall II, Spring I, and Spring II, which roughly correspond to the traditional seasons in ready-to-wear. However, since millinery is such an impulse purchase on the part of most consumers, constant new additions serve to increase the turnover.

The great unknown for millinery today is the customer. It still remains to be seen whether promotion, publicity, and fashion creativity can reverse the trend toward hatlessness and convince women that smart millinery is essential to the total fashion look.

Men's headwear is sold through all major retail channels, including sporting goods stores for caps and casual hats. Mail-order merchants have also increased sales. Industry leaders hope that the baseball cap craze reacquainted a previously hatless American male with the joys of wearing a hat and that this market might continue to grow ("Accessories Report," 1995).

Jewelry

The wearing of jewelry is believed to antedate the wearing of clothes; in fact, among primitive peoples today, even if one sees little that could be called clothing, there is usually a ring or two or ten on the body, the neck, the ears, or the nose. In modern times, jewelry has become a sign of worth and status—and a very important fashion accessory. No fashion costume is complete without it, whether it be the understated string of cultured pearls worn with a woman executive's office clothing, or the exaggerated four-inch earrings hanging from the earlobes of the latest MTV star. More men wear jewelry today, ranging from gold chains to earrings.

The jewelry industry divides itself into two distinct parts: fine jewelry, made of precious metals and gemstones, and costume jewelry. In recent years, a third category has entered the picture: bridge jewelry, which spans the gap between the other two.

This segment of the fashion industry has its own trade shows, as noted in Figure 7–6. In addition jewelry firms have showrooms in New York and regional marts.

Precious or Fine Jewelry

The metals used in **fine jewelry** are gold, silver, and platinum, worked alone or in combination with gemstones. The approximately 2,300 firms operating in this field in the United States produced more than $4.0 billion of merchandise at factory value and employed more than 33,000 people in 1993 (U.S. Department of Commerce, 1994). More than 60 percent of the factories are located in New York, Rhode Island, California, and Massachusetts.

Figure 7–6 A trade show for the jewelry segment of the industry.

UNITED JEWELRY SHOW

Where Fashion Jewelry Begins

Prime Source

The Fashion Jewelry Mart is located in Providence, RI, the fashion jewelry and jewelry accessories capital of the United States.

Style

The Mart features over 300 fashion jewelry and jewelry accessory manufacturers and importers.

Value

Buy direct from the prime sources. ❖ **FOR VOLUME BUYERS ONLY.**

UNITED JEWELRY SHOW, INC.

FASHION JEWELRY MART
DAVOL SQUARE

1996 MARKETS ❖ JANUARY 12-14 ❖ MARCH 9-16

3 DAVOL SQUARE • Unit 177 • PROVIDENCE, RI 02903 • 401-331-7630 • Fax 401-521-7488

Source: United Jewelry Show, Inc. Reprinted by permission.

Gold, the metal of first choice for fine jewelry, is too soft to be used by itself and is therefore usually combined with base metals. The gold content is expressed in terms of carats, or **karats.** Solid gold is 24 karats, or **24K.** The most commonly used alloys are rated 18K, 14K, or 12K, and are arrived at by mixing gold with copper (to produce reddish yellow metal), silver (to produce greenish yellow), or palladium or nickel (to produce white gold). Any alloy of less than 10K may not be called karat gold. In the United States, 14K is favored; in European jewelry, 18K is customary.

Platinum, a silvery metal, is rarer, heavier, and more expensive than gold and is a favorite for diamond settings. It, too, is generally alloyed, primarily to reduce its price, with palladium, iridium, rhodium, or ruthenium—all white and hard metals.

Silver, the least expensive of the precious metals, is usually combined with copper. The term **sterling** may be used where there are at least 925 parts of silver per thousand.

Gemstones

Precious stones include diamonds, emeralds, sapphires, rubies, and real pearls. With the exception of pearls, stones are measured in carats, one carat being the equivalent of 100 points. Pearls are measured in millimeters and length.

Semiprecious stones include amethysts, garnets, opals, lapis, jades, topaz, and aquamarines, among others. Today, fine jewelry uses more of these than ever, because of the high prices of precious stones.

In addition to natural gemstones, wide use is now made of synthetic gemstones. Laboratories can produce synthetic corundum to look like garnets and amethysts, and synthetic spinel to look like emeralds, diamonds, and aquamarines, among others.

An important element in the value of a piece of fine jewelry is the workmanship that goes into it. It is a hand-made product, with a jeweler creating each setting for each stone at the workbench, one piece at a time. The creativity and skill of the workman are major factors in the cost of the finished piece.

Marketing of Fine and Precious Jewelry

In recent years the fine jewelry industry has seen a major consolidation at the retail level through the steady growth of jewelry store chains. These chains are growing both through internal growth and through acquisitions. Examples here are Kay Jewelers; Peoples Jewelers, a Canadian owned company; Ratner's Group, a British owned company; Reeds Jewelers; and Barry's Jewelers, among others.

Bridge Jewelry

With the price of fine jewelry climbing and the demand for jewelry increasing, a new area of jewelry has developed to fill the need. This is **bridge jewelry,** which involves silver, gold-plated metals, or 14K gold, and which uses less expensive stones, such as onyx, ivory, coral, or freshwater pearls. Much of the fashion leadership comes from designers such as Celia or Karen Sibiri, Elsa Perretti, and M. J. Savitt, who, among others, create hand-made and signed pieces. Also important here are items such as gold chains; gold combined with the less expensive semiprecious stones; and jewelry that sets many small diamonds in a group to create the look of larger stones. Retail prices range from about $100 to $2,000 for these products.

Costume Jewelry

Costume jewelry is mass produced to fill the fashion demand of customers who seek relatively inexpensive jewelry to complete the fashion look of their outfits. The materials used may be plastic, wood, brass, tin, glass, lucite, or any other substance that can be manipulated to achieve the desired effect. Retail prices range widely, from items sold in variety stores to those bearing the names of such companies as Kenneth J. Lane and Miriam Haskell.

The costume jewelry trade has deep roots in Rhode Island. It dates back to colonial silversmiths, who hammered out teaspoons and thimbles and who developed a method in the early 1800s for reducing the cost of jewelry by rolling a thin sheet of gold over a cheaper base. Today this is done by **electroplating,** the process for coating materials with a thin layer of gold or silver.

Economic Importance

Retail sales for women's costume and bridge jewelry in 1994 were more than $4.5 billion. The previous year, domestic producers shipped an estimated $1.5 billion in products at factory value. Jewelry is another segment of the industry in which imports take an increasing share of the market. Products valued at $558 million entered the U.S. market in 1994. Both imports and exports have increased in recent years (*Accessories Market Guide,* 1994, 1995).

Fashion and sport watches, generally considered to be those retailing under $75, have been a growth area. These have accounted for an additional $2.6 billion in retail sales (*Accessories Market Guide,* 1995).

Figures on men's jewelry sales include cufflinks, stud sets, and miscellaneous items (key rings, money clips, tie bars, pens, earrings, and pendants). Retail sales of these products were $50 million in 1994. Cufflink sales vary greatly with trends in how men dress. Younger professionals are reported to consider French-cuff shirts as "dated, tight, and impractical"—the opposite of trends toward more relaxed dress ("Accessories Report," 1995, p. 100).

Some jewelry items, including gold neck chains, earrings, and even fashion/ sport watches, may be sold in unisex retail sources. When this occurs, sales of many of these products are difficult to differentiate by gender.

Other Accessories

Other accessories include glasses, sunglasses, scarfs, belts, handkerchiefs, umbrellas, and wigs. Eye glasses have become very fashionable, sometimes worn by individuals with no vision problems. Optical departments now boast lines by many prominent designers. Sunglasses came into fashion prominence in the 1960s, when then First Lady Jackie Kennedy wore "shades" constantly. They have remained important in fashion, not only for daytime, functional outdoor wear, but also sometimes as accessories for evening. Wigs, falls, and hairpieces, too, have been important accessories at various times, and to some extent their burgeoning popularity coincided with the decline of millinery. Hair ornaments have been an addition to the well-dressed look. Nowadays some women have an entire wardrobe of watches to wear for different occasions.

Belts gain prominence when waistlines are in fashion. Scarfs and stoles fill in low necklines, provide a bit of warmth, add a touch of color, or can be worn to accent broad-shouldered or slender looks, according to how they are draped and according to current fashion requirements. Handkerchiefs, whose utilitarian functions have been taken over by tissues, pass in and out of the fashion picture, tucked into

Table 7–3	Retail Sales of Other Accessories

Accessory Category	Retail Sales in Millions of Dollars
Men's and women's combined[a]	
Sunglasses	$2,226
Women's[a]	
Belts	$678
Hair accessories	320
Scarfs	385
Umbrellas/rainwear	340
Men's[b]	
Ties/neckwear	$1,050
Belts	400
Braces	25
Scarfs	20
Umbrellas	265

Sources: [a]*Accessories market guide.* (1995, December). Norwalk, CT: Business Journals Inc., p. 18.
[b]"Accessories Report" (1995, August). *MR,* pp. 71–119.

breast pockets or sleeves if and when they enhance whatever the "in" look may be. Umbrellas, too, have their fashion ins and outs, sometimes carried with a swagger like a walking stick, sometimes brightly colored to liven up drab days and drab rainwear. Utility sells many umbrellas; fashion, when it touches this field, sells more.

Retail sales figures for some of these other categories of accessories are shown in Table 7–3. Even for items that may seem quite small, total U.S. sales are substantial.

Accessories Designers

"Name" designers in the accessories field are almost exclusively those who have made their mark in the apparel field and who license their names to manufacturers of accessories. The designs themselves may or may not originate with the famous individual whose name is attached to them; they may have come from a design studio run by that luminary, or they may have been created by anonymous employees of the producer and then approved by the licensor.

Very few designers become famous through their work in accessories alone. For the most part, manufacturers have design staffs or use free-lancers; in neither case do they feature the names of these designers. Among the distinguished exceptions are Vera, who began many years ago in scarfs; Elsa Peretti, the house designer of jewelry for Tiffany's; Judith Leiber, a handbag designer; and Paloma Picasso and Kenneth Jay Lane, also in the jewelry field. Robert Lee Morris is an important new accessory designer.

Apparel designers moved strongly into licensed accessories in the 1970s, when the total "look" became important in fashion and consumers began putting together outfits in which the accessories were quite as essential as the apparel if one was to achieve the desired casual or elegant smartness. This trend has brought almost every famous American and European apparel design name into the accessories area. It has brought glamour and useful promotional tools to the field.

It is interesting to note that Liz Claiborne, Inc., whose name had been licensed to Kayser-Roth for a line of accessories in 1986, discontinued this arrangement and opened a new division, Liz Claiborne Accessories. The decision to do this was explained by Jerome Chazen, chairman of Liz Claiborne, Inc., as follows: "Since there has always been a synergistic relationship between apparel and accessories, we have decided to make that relationship closer" ("Claiborne Buys," 1985). Other designers' companies have followed their lead. Many companies also found that marketing their lines themselves was far more profitable than simply licensing their names to other companies.

Intimate Apparel/Undergarments

The segment of the fashion industry that produces loungewear, nightwear, women's and children's undergarments, and body shapers for women is known as the **intimate apparel industry.** This segment of the industry—by this name—applies for women's garments only. For similar products for men, these are simply **undergarments.** The history of women's products is also a history of society's changing perceptions of modesty and feminine beauty. In the nineteenth century and into the early decades of the twentieth, manufacturers in the United States produced, and women wore, an astonishing variety of devices to shape, distort, and even deform the figure to achieve what was considered fashionable for women. It is a matter of amazement that women of the generations that first fought for suffrage and first entered the business world conducted their activities in garments so constricting that people in the trade referred to them in later years as "iron maidens."

Since undergarments in general come into close contact with the body, they have always had sexual connotations. Even though their appearance to the outside observer is secondary, these garments, other than the actual corsets, have generally been characterized by soft fabrics, a great deal of detailing, and many trimmings (Figure 7–7). The Gibson Girl might have worn a corset of tough fabric reinforced with whalebone, but she wore a dainty camisole and lacy petticoats with it.

Recent years have seen renewed consumer interest in intimate apparel. The industry had hit a low point in the 1960s when young women burned their bras as a form of protest and declaration of freedom. This was also the era of tight jeans, worn with minimal or no undergarments.

Nowadays, the intimate apparel industry is thriving. Women have learned they can be both independent and feminine. Many women enjoy the luxurious array of styles and colors provided by the industry today and consider intimate apparel as an equally important part of their wardrobes. Lines of practical, special purpose garments have increased, too. For example, today's concern for fitness has created a need for jogging bras among women who exercise strenuously. Similarly, many types of girdles and other body shaper garments are available for those who want to look more trim and fit than they may actually be.

Although men's undergarments lag far behind women's intimate apparel in terms of design interest and types of products, this segment of the industry has changed, too. The days are gone when men were offered a choice of plain white knit briefs or plain white boxer shorts. Now, men's undergarments come in many colors, fabrics, and patterns. The lower European cut in knit briefs is commonly available. We have seen one notable example of men's undergarments becoming a fashion item that went far beyond the original utilitarian use—namely the popularity of patterned boxer shorts worn by young people in creative layering with the boxer shorts visible.

Figure 7–7

Figure 7–7

The intimate apparel business has become an important segment of the industry. This is good news for the textile firms that supply the fabrics for this segment of the industry.

Source: Reprinted courtesy of Guilford Mills, Inc.

Industry Segments

The industry's products fall into three major categories:

1. **foundations,** which include girdles, brassieres, garter belts, and the shapewear that nowadays replaces corsets;
2. **lingerie,** which includes petticoats, slips, panties, camisoles, and sleepwear such as nightgowns and pajamas;
3. **loungewear,** which consists of robes, negligees, bed jackets, and housecoats. The lines between lingerie and loungewear are not always clear-cut, however, and some in the industry categorize their products as daywear (lingerie and housecoats) and nightwear (sleepwear and negligees, etc.).

Table 7–4	Annual Production in Select Lines of Intimate Apparel and Undergarments (Wholesale Prices)

Garment Line	Production in Millions of Dollars, 1994
Men's and Boys'	
Nightwear and robes*	$ 262
Undershirts*	468
Undershorts and briefs*	503
Thermal underwear*	197
Woven boxer shorts*	220
Women's and Girls'	
Bras	1,409
Foundation garments	390
Nightgowns	728
Panties	853
Slips and other underwear**	293
Infants	
Underwear	55
Nightwear	202

*Data do not include little boys' garments.
**Data do not include little girls' garments.
Source: From *Focus: An economic profile of the apparel industry* (pp. 23–24) by American Apparel Manufacturers Association, 1995, Arlington, VA: Author. Reprinted courtesy of AAMA.

Economic Importance

The intimate apparel/undergarment industry is big business in the United States, with a total output of approximately $6.5 billion, at wholesale. The value of production by some of the categories is shown in Table 7–4. Values given in the table do not add to the total given above because breakouts are not available for all garment lines. The largest portion of this total is produced by the women's and children's undergarment segments of the industry, which employs nearly 52,000 employees and encompasses 475 **establishments.** References to establishments or **plants** include the manufacturing facilities only, and each location is counted separately.[3] The men's underwear and nightwear segment employs approximately 17,500 in 99 plants. Another 6,700 workers in 67 plants produce robes and dressing gowns. Those figures are for plants classified by the SIC system as being in the *apparel* industry—SIC group 23 (AAMA, 1995; U.S. Department of Commerce, 1994).

Additionally, a significant amount of knit underwear (men's, women's, and children's) is made in plants categorized until 1993 under *textile* production, SIC group 22. Now, these are in SIC 23 with other apparel. When knit apparel was categorized in this manner, it meant the garments were made in vertical textile firms. In these

---

[3]Plants or establishments are part of a **firm.** A firm may have many establishments (plants) or could have only one. Today, in many parts of the apparel industry, firms may have *no* sewing facilities but simply contract to have all the manufacturing done by others.

firms, products continue to be made from start to finish within a single company, all the way from knitting fabrics to producing finished garments. However, they are now considered with apparel rather than textiles. Approximately 18,000 employees in nearly 70 plants make knit underwear (AAMA, 1995; U.S. Department of Commerce, 1994).

Marketing

New York City is the major market center for all segments of the intimate apparel industry, and the showings are timed to mesh with those of ready-to-wear. The buyer of intimate apparel is usually a specialist, not involved with the merchandising of outerwear. Nevertheless, the close relationships between undergarments and outwear fashions, and between outerwear fashions and the various categories of at-home wear, make it essential for the intimate apparel buyer to be guided by what the other segments of the fashion industry are presenting.

The intimate apparel industry, which functioned on two markets a year in the days when its major concern was corsetry, now has five seasonal showings: Early Spring in August, Spring in November, Summer in January, Early Fall in March, and Fall and Holiday in May. Market weeks are also held in important regional centers: the Dallas Mart, the Atlanta Mart, the Chicago Apparel Center, and the CaliforniaMart in Los Angeles.

Impact of Fashion

Even in this industry's purely functional garments, the impact of fashion is felt. For example, the length and fullness of outerwear skirts necessarily determines the length and shape of the slips to be worn under them; figure-revealing silhouettes enhance the demand for body-shaping undergarments, whereas relaxed lines diminish their importance; emphasis on the waistline brings waist-cinchers back into production, generally briefly. In recent years, less structured undergarments with fewer seams have been popular with many women. For example, the FormFit Intimates panty, which provides excellent fit without sideseams, is even patented (Figure 7–8). Changes in women's life styles and interests, too, affect the industry's output. A notable example, already cited, is the development of special bras for aerobic dancing, in response to the interest in fitness. In loungewear and nightwear, in which looks are more important than function, the relation to fashion is clear indeed. The customer, consciously or otherwise, tends to seek out the same general effects, the same overall looks, that she has been seeing in apparel displays and on smartly dressed individuals in their areas.

Sometimes ordinary garments can take on a fashion dimension. Earlier, we mentioned men's boxer shorts as an example. Similarly, waffle-knit thermal underwear shirts became a popular casualwear item in the mid-1990s. Thermal underwear knit fabrics were used in other types of shirts, or the fabrics were printed to give a unique look. Popular trends such as these two can have a significant impact on a segment of industry that supplies the products. For example, men's thermal underwear sales increased by about 30 percent in 1994 over 1993—far too much to be explained by a growth in population or colder temperatures.

Importance of Brand and Designer Names

The brand names of producers in this industry have traditionally been so important that store buyers tend to budget their purchases by resource or vendor rather than by merchandise category. This practice goes back to the days when foundation garments

Figure 7–8

The FormFit Intimates seamless panty is made by a patented manufacturing process that produces a smooth, comfortable fit. This FormFit Intimates product is among the few garments under patent protection.

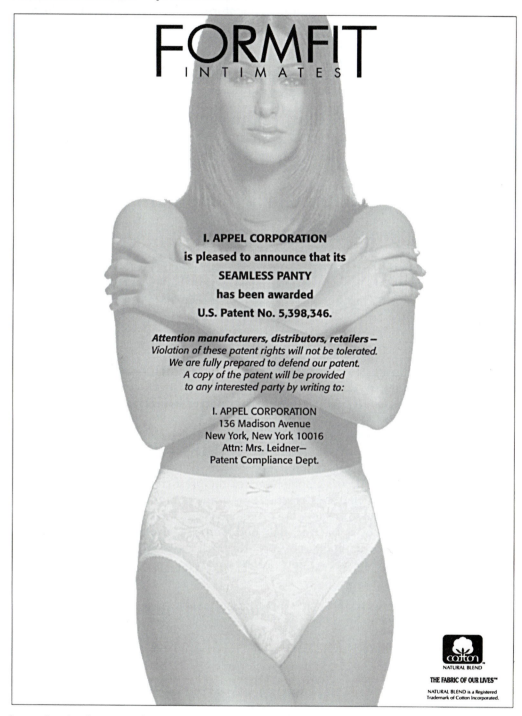

Source: Reprinted courtesy of FormFit Intimates.

had to be carefully fitted to individual customers. Leading manufacturers, in those days, took a major share of responsibility for planning retail stocks and training salespeople in stores that carried their lines.

Among the best-known names in foundations are Warner (the oldest in the field), FormFit-Rogers, Lily of France, Maidenform, Bali, and Playtex. In the lingerie area, well-known brands include Vanity Fair, Barbizon, Vassarette, Natori, Eileen West for Queen Anne's Lace, and Eve Stillman.

As would be expected in a field where brand names are important, producers advertise widely along three fronts: directly to the consumer in print and television, through cooperative advertising with retail stores, and to retail stores through trade publications. Some companies also provide stores with display fixtures, on which their brand names appear, for use in featuring the particular brand in windows and store interiors.

The importance of designer names in marketing fashion merchandise is mirrored in the many licensing arrangements that exist between intimate apparel producers and leading designers of outerwear. Bill Blass, for example, designs robes and loungewear for Evelyn Pearson Company; Christian Dior is licensed to Carol Hochman Designs; and Warnaco licenses Olga, Valentino Intimo, and Ungaro. Previously, Calvin Klein licensed his name in underwear and sleepwear but now Calvin Klein underwear is part of Warnaco.

According to the designers themselves, their objective is to apply to their intimate apparel collections the interpretation of fashion that they present in their ready-to-wear collections. Thus, the seasons' changes in silhouette and fabrication, as they see them, are reflected in intimate apparel as well as in streetwear.

Global Activities

Globalization has affected the intimate apparel industry as it has every other segment of the fashion industry. Imports generally play their greatest role where production is labor intensive, as in intricately sewn and embroidered loungewear and sleepwear, because of the quality of handwork and the advantageous pricing. Bras, for example, have extensive and intricate sewing. Many U.S. apparel manufacturers have their own lines of intimate apparel produced in lower-wage countries, and retailers have goods produced overseas for presentation under their private labels. Direct import of European-brand bras occurs among some of the prestigious fashion stores such as Saks Fifth Avenue, which features French bras from Prima and LeJaby, and Italian bras from LaPerla. The major offshore bra production center, however, is the Philippines, where such companies as Lovable, Bali, and Warner's have their lines produced. In second place after the Philippines is Costa Rica. For robes and dressing gowns, Hong Kong and China are the major import sources.

Readings

The accessories industries and the intimate apparel/undergarment industries have experienced many of the same competitive pressures affecting other segments of the fashion industry. These articles feature successful companies and industry strategies used to be competitive.

Judith Leiber: 30 Years Just the Start

by Amanda Meadus

She may be in the midst of celebrating her 30th year in business, but Judith Leiber, 73, is busy looking to the future.

For the woman considered by many to be the grande dame of handbags, her fourth decade could be her most ground-breaking to date, with the ultimate goal, she said, being "to really develop my name right up in the ranks with Chanel, Hermès and other luxury goods companies."

With backing from her parent company, Time Products PLC, a London-based company, Leiber said she is gearing up to roll out a wide range of luxury goods.

"Within the next 10 years, we'll be doing a full and total line of accessories—scarves, fashion jewelry, eyewear, everything," she said. "There may be luggage, and also maybe shoes, and when the name has become very strong all over the world, a fragrance will be the last step."

And, in the meantime, she's about to be honored for all that she's done up to this point. An upcoming retrospective at the Fashion Institute of Technology will feature her entire body of work, with nearly 400 handbags on display. The show will open with a party on Nov. 14, and the exhibit will be on view through Feb. 4.

In addition, a full-color book about Leiber's work, published by Abrams, is due out next March, and preview softcover versions will be available at the FIT event.

"Judith Leiber has been one of the leaders in bringing a fashion perspective into the handbag business," said Ellen Goldstein, director and chairwoman of FIT's accessories design department. "She also led the way for handbag designers to do the same."

Leiber's influential designs, as well as her versatility, have not been lost on the retailers who have established strong businesses in her goods.

"Her work represents the pinnacle of well-designed and finely crafted handbags," said Dawn Mello, president of Bergdorf Goodman.

"Our business, once focused on the minaudieres and exotic skin cocktail bags, has increased significantly in the evening bags she makes out of fabrics such as antique quilts, Japanese obis, exquisite laces and embroideries," Mello added.

"Her breadth of assortment offers something very important to our customers—options," said Gail Pisano, senior vice president and general merchandise manager of accessories for Saks Fifth Avenue. "She offers whimsy and she also stays more sensitive to price than some people realize. Her customer base is really not so narrow, because she includes smaller items that everyone can afford."

Most importantly, Pisano pointed out, "Her willingness to explore new arenas sets an industry standard, and she doesn't ever rest on her past successes."

The process of expansion has already gotten under way with the development of her day bag business, which, according to her key retail accounts, is already on a growth track. Though she's been producing this line along with her evening pieces ever since she started, it's just now coming into its own, she noted.

"Over the years, I have experimented with everything from cashmere to fish skin, and every time a new material comes along, I have to try it," she pointed out. "People have always linked me with my crystal minaudieres and haven't paid as much attention to my other bags. That's always hurt my feelings a little."

Since Time Products purchased Leiber's firm in March 1993 for $18 million, it has been behind her all the way, she noted. A conglomerate with a strong orientation toward prestige brands, Time Products also handles a full stable of prestige watch brands, including Audemars Piguet, Blancpain, Breguet and Piaget in the U.K.

Time Products posted sales in the year ended Jan. 31, 1994, of $106.8 million (67.1 million pounds) at current exchange, up 13 percent from the year before, and before-tax profits of $18.1 million (11.4 million pounds), up 15 percent.

Though not broken out in Time Product's financial data, annual volume generated by Leiber's business is about $20 million, according to industry sources.

At the time of the purchase, Marcus Margulies, chairman of Time Products, noted, "There is nothing we can do to improve the Judith Leiber business. It's extremely well run. We will simply enhance the brand name and grow the business slowly with a great deal of care."

The relationship has since been developing nicely, Leiber said. "The people at Time Products are very forward-looking and business-minded," she noted.

In addition to expansion of the Leiber brand, cultivation of a retail business is also in the plans and has actually already gotten under way. Two freestanding boutiques were opened in Bangkok last year, and Leiber said more units are scheduled for the Far East and Europe. A store should also be opening in the U.S. in the "not-so-distant future."

In the meantime, Leiber said she is "thrilled" to see the return of femininity to the fashion scene.

"I was never a great friend of the grungy look, though that look didn't really hurt my business, since my customers keep buying regardless of what the trends are," she said. "Grunge just isn't my style; I think glamour is wonderful."

Leiber is also intensely interested in continuing the tradition of craftsmanship that has been such a vital aspect of her career. She herself learned her trade in her homeland of Hungary, and her plan is to develop a workshop-type atmosphere in her own facilities, a place where new generations can practice and perfect their own skills.

"I'd like to eventually set up a whole crew of young designers," she said. "Right now, we're beginning to build up a staff, and we have a designer, a sketcher and three apprentices."

Her peers feel she's already contributed much to the industry.

"Her life and her business are totally inspiring to anyone who's ever had wild ideas about evening bags or any other accessories," said handbag designer Carey Adina. "I remember seeing her when she won the CFDA Lifetime Achievement Award, and she was wearing one of her bags around her neck, like a pendant. It occurred to me that she carries her bags very close to her heart."

Source: From Women's Wear Daily, *October 10, 1994, p. 6. Reprinted by permission.*

Branded Jewelry Sharpens Its Focus

by Amanda Meadus

The branded jewelry business is due for a big turnaround, and targeted merchandise appears to be the way to achieve it.

Now that the worst of the financial woes and other problems that have dogged the big names in branded fashion jewelry business appears to be over, the companies and the retailers who sell their products feel business will recover fully in the next 18 to 24 months—perhaps even sooner—provided they steer their products toward specific consumer demands.

In addition, vendors are turning to such strategies as:

- Cutting back on price promotions, which many feel undermined the business.
- Launching brand extensions.
- Exploring new channels of distribution apart from the traditional reliance on department stores.

Like the rest of the fashion jewelry industry, this segment—which includes The Monet Group, Victoria Creations, Napier and Liz Claiborne—was hit hard over the last two years by a variety of factors, including the minimalist trend and the recession.

But some of these firms were also plagued by financial burdens that made the state of the branded jewelry industry as a whole appear even more dire.

Several firms went through stretches in the red, but perhaps the biggest blow came when The Monet Group was pulled down into Chapter 11, along with the rest of its former parent company, Crystal Brands Inc. The Monet Group, which produces the Monet, Trifari and Marvella brands, is probably the biggest brand name fashion jewelry firm in the country, with an annual wholesale volume of $180 million, according to industry estimates.

Now, however, financial health is returning in most cases, and spirits are lifting along with them. As reported, The Monet Group was lifted from its bankrupt state when Chemical Bank and two private investors purchased it last November for $77.7 million. Others have also begun getting back into the black.

"Brands are still the backbone of the fashion jewelry business for us, and we're positioning them for growth," said Kim White, merchandise manager for jewelry and watches at Federated Merchandising, the merchandising arm of Federated Department Stores.

Although White noted that some of the heavy hitters in the branded category have had their ups and downs, she added that "every one of them is moving in the right direction now. These companies have learned a lot, and they don't operate the same way they did 10 years ago. They have become much more flexible and responsive than they used to be."

At this point, White said, "we're seeing a resurgence in demand for pieces that look like fine jewelry, which is something the brand companies do extremely well." She added that branded designer lines, including Anne Klein II by Swank and Liz Claiborne, have also been hot of late.

Clint Scofield, fashion jewelry buyer for J.C. Penney, said he sees a place for branded lines in the future, although he added that the nature of the business needs to change in order to thrive. Among the major brands Penney's carries are Trifari, Napier, Richelieu and 1928.

"In the Eighties, when the branded lines were so big, there was a real herd mentality in which people wanted the same things everyone else had," Scofield said. "Now, there's a more individualistic approach, in which people are wearing jewelry as a form of self-expression, and targeting these needs is something that can be accomplished very well with private label jewelry.

"If the branded companies work to develop their own niches, there will be a place for them," he added. "Overall, fashion jewelry business has been tough lately, not just because of the minimalism trend, but also because there hasn't been any strong direction."

For their part, the branded firms have been spending the last year or so studying their positions and adjusting them to fit with the times.

"We've been aggressive in modifying and sculpting each of our brands," said Patricia Stensrud, president and chief executive officer of Victoria Creations, which produces the licensed Karl Lagerfeld and Bijoux Givenchy lines as well as Richelieu, its own pearl jewelry brand, and Worthington, J.C. Penney's private label line.

Though it went through an unprofitable period that stretched into several years, the company has been posting financial improvements in its last several quarters. In the fiscal year ended June 30, 1994, the firm posted an operating profit of $183,000 against an operating loss of $981,000 a year earlier. The net loss was cut in half to $2.1 million from $4.2 million. In the most recently reported quarter ended Sept. 30, the firm's sales grew 32.7 percent to $14.7 million, while net profit jumped to $1 million from $165,000.

"The jewelry business has been difficult, because fashion in a much broader sense has been difficult," Stensrud pointed out. "Therefore, fashion products, including jewelry, need to be clearly focused on a specific target customer or end use to have relevance."

Judy Harrison, president and ceo of The Monet Group, said her company spent the first six months of last year making major adjustments to its lines.

"We asked ourselves, 'Why would a consumer want to buy a specific brand of jewelry when everything looks the same?' and then went from there," Harrison said. "Our Monet and Trifari businesses, for instance, are really geared to two very different types of consumers, and once we made that distinction in the lines themselves, we started to see positive results in."

Graham Brewster, executive vice president of sales, marketing and product development for Napier, said his firm has been able to weather the tough times by staying focused on its product.

"And one of the main reasons we've been able to do this is because we haven't had the distractions of being a public company," he noted. "We know right now, for instance, that our target consumer wants merchandise that looks like real jewelry—fairly tailored gold and pearl pieces—and that's one of the things we're known for. We know what we can do well, and don't try to jump too far out of the mold."

The firm, which is based in Meriden, Conn., does an annual wholesale volume of $50 million, according to industry estimates.

"We're very targeted, and we always have been," said Tom Keller, president of Swarovski Jewelry U.S., which makes the Swarovski Jewelers Collection and Savvy brands. "We make crystal jewelry, albeit in two very different lines, and it's what we're known for."

Keller, who said the second half of last year was "extremely strong" for his company, noted that the trends toward glamour and femininity that have recently come onto the fashion scene have only spurred more business.

However, at last month's accessories market, Swarovski did launch an extension of its Savvy line, called Conversations by Savvy, which features novelty pins and necklaces.

"This is an area we can fall back on," he said. "If the glamour trend, for instance, goes away for a long time, we have this product to help supplement."

Though there was moderate growth last year for Liz Claiborne Jewelry, the firm's plan is to keep building up business by courting the same consumers who buy Liz Claiborne apparel, according to Neil Katz, president of Liz Claiborne's jewelry, watch and fragrance divisions. According to Claiborne's most recent annual report, jewelry racked up sales of $25 million in 1993.

"We're going to be broadening our assortment of basic, classic merchandise and fitting it to the demands of the various regional markets, the way we do with our apparel," Katz said, adding that the company hopes to accomplish this by fall.

With fashion's return to the tailored look, he noted, this move to emphasize classics and downplay trend jewelry makes the most sense, Katz said.

"But we're not going to stop there," he added. "The main thing we want to do is meet every jewelry need the Liz Claiborne customer has, so we'll also be looking at how to produce jewelry that goes with her casual, weekend apparel."

Retail consolidation and markdowns are yet other issues that brand jewelry makers acknowledge they will have to deal with on their road to recovery.

"In fact, the consolidation situation can present a lot of opportunities, and it's great when you're in with all the big guys," said Swarovski's Keller. "On the other hand, it's also tremendously painful when you lose even one of them."

Some are also looking to develop new distribution channels as a safeguard measure. The Monet Group, for one, just created a new post, executive vice president of business development, and brought in Russ Giattino, formerly executive vice president of jewelry manufacturer Weingeroff Enterprises, to fill it.

"From our viewpoint, there are so many untapped opportunities out there, and this is our first step toward getting to them," said Harrison.

The markdown and promotion-pricing issue, which has been plaguing fashion jewelry as well as many other segments of the fashion business, is one both merchants and manufacturers are starting to tackle.

"We want to create an environment that's conducive to people buying regular-priced merchandise," said Federated's White. "One of the main ways we plan to do it is by cutting back on promotionally priced merchandise, the $9.99 necklaces and so on, and replace it with goods that have a lot of intrinsic value, such as a pin that retails full-price for $20, but looks as though it costs twice as much."

"Promotion is a fact of life, but it's got to be kept in the right balance and cannot be used as the main reason for selling, particularly in the fashion business," said The Money Group's Harrison.

"Of course, we will all need to keep doing some promotion programs until things improve even more, but they are going to be done with some style and excitement," she added. "The industry just cannot afford to bear any more 'two for $20' deals. There has been too much of it already and it obviously didn't work too well."

Source: From Women's Wear Daily, *February 6, 1995, p. 6. Reprinted by permission.*

Underwear's Power Pair

by Karyn Monget

Two powerhouses of the apparel industry—Calvin Klein and Linda J. Wachner—share a passion for underwear.

Now, nearly a year after The Warnaco Group—Wachner's company—closed the deal to acquire the Calvin Klein underwear businesses for men and women, the duo is poised to make underwear bearing the Calvin Klein name a product as recognizable in the international marketplace as Coca-Cola.

Last week, in a joint interview at the designer's offices, Klein and Wachner were brimming with confidence as they outlined some of the ways they plan to girdle the globe with Klein underwear.

"This is a win-win situation," said Klein. "In this world, fit is so important, and you have to have the resources to produce and distribute the underwear. Linda has that."

"We're the happy couple," said Wachner.

Here are some of the things they have in mind:

- Spending $10 million this year on national print and TV advertising, three times as much as last year's budget.
- Distributing Klein's men's underwear to Japan and Southeast Asia for the first time.
- Expanding his women's underwear to Europe, Japan and Southeast Asia.
- Doubling the number of U.S. department store doors to 1,000.

Warnaco acquired Klein's men's underwear business as well as the trademarks for men's accessories worldwide from the designer's company last March in a deal worth $62.5 million ($38.5 million in cash and $24 million in Warnaco common stock) plus ongoing fees.

As part of the deal, Warnaco took over the women's underwear business at the beginning of this year, after a licensing pact for that category with Heckler Manufacturing & Investment Group expired.

In expanding U.S. department store distribution this year in both the men's and women's underwear businesses, the number of doors will double to 1,000 outlets by August, according to Warnaco executives. The men's and women's underwear will be showcased in separate in-store Calvin Klein boutiques with new white formica fixturing and white packaging.

As part of the strategy to build the Calvin Klein women's underwear business—an area that has been underdeveloped—Klein's concept of items that address lifestyle needs has been expanded for spring to include textured sleepwear and at-homewear items of cotton knit. Shipments for the spring line started in early January.

"We will be spending like crazy to make this a big success," said Wachner, Warnaco's chairman, president and chief executive officer. "We will spend $10 million in 1995 on national print and TV advertising [men's and women's combined]—three times as much as in 1994."

She further noted that this will be the first time Warnaco will do a national TV ad campaign. The commercials, breaking this week, feature Christy Turlington, who, as reported, also appears in the print ads for the underwear.

The image he wants to convey for the women's underwear, Klein said, is "modern and sexy—and with an attitude." He described Turlington as "the woman of right now—not terribly skinny, very approachable, very womanly."

He also said the association with Wachner will be a culmination of a longtime dream of making the Calvin Klein underwear business for women as prominent as the men's underwear business.

"This is very exciting," Klein said, "because I'm at the stage of beginning to realize that something I've wanted to do for a long time is really happening.

"The men's business has really been important," said Klein, who introduced that line of underwear in 1984, "but my frustration has been that I'm known as primarily as a women's wear designer, and we had such an underdeveloped women's underwear business."

The underwear deal was one of three big licensing deals Klein completed last year. His CK Calvin Klein jeanswear business was licensed to a joint venture of Rio Sportswear and Charterhouse Group International, and he entered the home goods arena in a licensing deal with Home Innovations. They will add new dimensions to the continuing bonanza the designer has seen with his licensed fragrance business, Calvin Klein Cosmetics, a unit of Unilever.

For her part, Wachner, who has gleaned a reputation as a hard-as-nails businesswoman, said, "This is really exciting for me, too. The presence of the Calvin Klein underwear business at stores is very important, but the presence of Calvin himself is extremely important—it's bigger, stronger, more recognizable than ever before.

"We think the Calvin Klein fragrance business and underwear business will be very much alike, just sensational," continued Wachner. "We'll be bigger than ever in Europe, Southeast Asia, and we plan to enter Latin America and Mexico for the first time."

Distribution of Calvin Klein men's underwear will be expanded to Japan and Southeast Asia for the first time early this year; deliveries of Klein's women's underwear will be expanded to Europe in May, as well as to Japan and the Southeast Asia. Shipping dates have not yet been decided upon for Latin America and Mexico.

Wachner said she feels so bullish about building the Calvin Klein underwear business for men, she expects to reach the initial sales projection two years from now—not five, as originally planned.

Sales of the men's line are projected to reach more than $100 million this year, doubling sales in 1994, she said.

"We think the men's business can generate annual sales in excess of $300 million by 1997," Wachner added.

She said the women's business "could be bigger at some point in time," but would not be specific. Industry estimates were forecasting a volume of only $16 million for the women's underwear at the start of 1994, when it was still being done by Heckler.

Regarding the acceptance of the Calvin Klein name abroad, Klein said, "It's a good time. Right now people want items that are American. It's cool, hip, and we've had no problems penetrating the European market.

"People are waiting for us to make Calvin Klein underwear available to them," he continued. "As I travel, more people ask me about my underwear, and it has more of an international franchise than my jeans or fragrance. College kids think it's the cool thing to wear. . . ."

Looking at the department store business in the U.S., John Kourakos, president of the Calvin Klein Underwear and Accessories subsidiary of Warnaco, said, "We added 25 employees to the company to act as a support staff to the stores. They make sure the products are merchandised properly, and they also give seminars.

"Our retail philosophy was that the men's and women's underwear be housed in a total Calvin Klein environment, and we've made a significant dollar commitment to stores with the fixturing. In return, we wanted the commitment from the stores that it always be housed as an entire collection."

Source: From Women's Wear Daily, February 6, 1995, p. 3. Reprinted by permission.

Consumer Infidelity

by Robin Lewis

Women are fickle, if not downright promiscuous, when it comes to where they buy their intimate apparel and hosiery. She'll buy a bra in Wal-Mart, Penney's, Nordstrom, or Victoria's Secret, according to whatever tickles her fancy at the moment. She'll buy sleepwear in Saks, panties in Kmart and hosiery at Ann Taylor, depending on the mood that moves her.

Cross-shopping, or the purchase of different apparel items in different stores or retail channels, is here. Store loyalty for the lifetime apparel needs of any one consumer appears to be a thing of the past.

While department stores once had the lion's share of intimate apparel, their position has been under constant fire, mainly by the discounters and specialty stores, which have been steadily taking chunks of their business.

Discounters, in fact, now control the largest share of the intimate apparel category. In hosiery, the discounters and food/drug outlets dominate and, along with direct mailers, continue to capture more share. Department store share continues to slip.

These shifts are clearly consumer-driven, as consumers exploit virtually unlimited shopping options.

If it's a rush to save time, a consumer might seek the convenience of a specialty store nearby. If the goal is spending less, she might pursue discount store options. Or, if her value requirement is for a more fashion-forward item, the consumer may shop across several department and specialty stores.

This is a consumer who is loyal to no one, who has different value needs at different times and is clearly taking advantage of an overabundance of choice.

However, while the consumer may appear to be promiscuous about where she shops, she's actually more discerning than ever. They buy for very specific reasons. They're also smarter and have a clear idea of what an item is worth. Finally, they know precisely where they can get the best value for the least amount of time and effort.

None of this has to do with having a favorite store, although a shopper may have six favorite stores across all distribution channels. In fact, what some see as promiscuity is really polygamy: the new consumer is discriminately married to many different stores for many different occasions and needs.

The same polygamy exists when choosing between the national brands and private label (which includes store brands). Indeed, in every category except bras, private label is growing in market share while the brands are losing. This indicates both a discerning and more intelligent consumer; she makes a purchase decision based on her own specific value equation, as opposed to being lured simply by the lowest price or the more ephemeral promises of a brand's advertising.

The apparent loyalty to the national brands in the bra category, in addition to the fact that women are willing to pay regular price, merely reinforces the concept of the discriminating consumer. Part of this loyalty obviously stems from the consumers' requirements for fit, function and comfort. However, it also points to the fact that the branded suppliers long ago focused on learning what their consumer wanted in a bra and then painstakingly designed, merchandised and marketed their product. Apparently, they are still doing so today. The bra experience provides a clear example of successful strategies that might well be employed by the suppliers and retailers in the other product categories, in order to court the cross-shopper.

As with bras, hosiery brands apparently provide added value over private label. Although the consumer's product requirements are somewhat different than for bras, if she can find those values more conveniently, and at prices she perceives as fair, the type of store she buys from is not a major concern.

This is clearly a product category in which the knowledgeable and discerning consumer has a specific set of value requirements and knows the retail outlets that can deliver them.

In many cases, the stores she chooses are brand names themselves, such as Victoria's Secret, which, from the consumers' perspective, provide value equal to the "national brands." Therefore, this form of private labeling will continue to grow. It provides the consumer with branded value and provides the retailer with greater pricing and margin flexibility.

So, as they improve their sourcing skills, retailers will increasingly compete with the national brands. In effect, they will be marketing their stores as brands. And for those that have outlets nationwide, their sheer physical presence is equivalent to a powerful advertising campaign.

Another indication of a more knowledgeable and discerning consumer is the fact that she is increasingly willing to pay regular price in retail channels that are generally recognized for their lower prices. This describes a consumer who has a clear idea of what something is worth, relative to where she's buying it. It also describes a store that understands this consumer's value equation and knows how to deliver it. Therefore, the consumer will seek the product in that store and happily pay what's asked. These discerning shoppers are also increasing their purchases in these stores at the expense of other retailers who have not responded to the value demands of the consumer.

While the largest share of shoppers across all channels spans the 30-to-64-year-old age group, the 30-to-40 segment is growing at a faster clip. There are also higher incomes across almost all channels, which again signals a heightened selectivity, regardless of traditional perceptions of what a store may have represented in the past. In fact, in the discount tier, consumers with incomes over $60,000 comprise the fastest-growing share. This dramatically illustrates that cross-shopping for different values, across all store types, will be with us well into the next century.

Source: From Women's Wear Daily, *March 13, 1995, p. 2. Reprinted by permission.*

Chapter Review

Key Words and Concepts

Define, identify, or briefly explain the following:

Accessories	Intimate apparel industry	Precious stones
Bridge jewelry	Karats	Private label
Costume jewelry	Last	Small leather goods
Electroplating	Lingerie	Sterling silver
Establishments	Loungewear	24K
Fine jewelry	9802 transactions	Undergarments
Firms	Nonrubber footwear	Uppers
Foundations	Plants	Vamp

Review Questions on Chapter Highlights

1. How do fashions in accessories relate to apparel fashions? Give examples.

2. How would you compare the women's and men's accessories markets?

3. What are four ways accessories firms have attempted to attract customers?

4. What four factors do all of the accessory industries have in common?

5. What is the difference between rubber and non-rubber athletic footwear? Why is this distinction made?

6. Why do you think imports account for such a large portion of the U.S. shoe market?

7. Why are imports less "threatening" to the hosiery industry than they are to other segments of accessories?

8. Why are more vinyl and fabric handbags sold than leather ones?

9. What types of products are included in the term *small leather goods?*

10. What are your thoughts on the future of the millinery/hat industry?

11. Give the three major categories of jewelry and explain the differences among them.

12. Gives examples of designer licensing in each product area of the accessories industry.

13. Name the three major divisions of the intimate apparel industry and give one well-known brand name in each.

14. What is the difference between a plant or establishment and a firm?

References

Accessories market guide '95. (1994, December). Norwalk, CT: Business Journals Inc.

Accessories market guide. (1995). Norwalk, CT: Business Journals, Inc.

Accessories report. (1995, August). *MR,* pp. 71–119.

American Apparel Manufacturers Association (AAMA). (1995). *Focus: An economic profile of the apparel industry.* Arlington, VA: Author.

Claiborne buys its accessories line. (1985, December 23). *Women's Wear Daily.*

The Fairchild 50. (1993, October). *Women's Wear Daily,* Special Report, pp. 1–41.

Footwear: Concept stores. (1988, August). *Stores.*

Footwear Industries of America. (1995, April). *Current highlights of the nonrubber footwear industry.* Washington, DC: Author.

Footwear Industries of America (1996). *Current highlights of the nonrubber footwear industry.* Washington, DC: Author.

McGuire, P. (date unknown). Comments from McGuire, Director, Nike Retail Division.

Millinery Information Bureau. (1995). Author's telephone call with executive director.

Millinery Institute of America. June 24, 1989. Conversations with publicity directors.

National Association of Hosiery Manufacturers (NAHM). (1988). *1987 hosiery statistics and profile.* Charlotte, NC: Author.

National Association of Hosiery Manufacturers (NAHM). (1995). *1994 hosiery statistics and profile.* Charlotte, NC: Author.

1995 national consumer accessories survey. (1995, July). *Accessories,* pp. 36–42.

Pelz, L. R. (1980). *Fashion accessories* (2nd ed.). Indianapolis: Bobbs-Merrill Educational Publishing.

Quimby, H. (1936, December 30). The story of footwear. *Shoe and Leather Reporter, 216*(13).

Treber, J. (1990). Conversation between Treber (chief statistician of Footwear Industries of America) and author.

United States Department of Commerce. (1994). *U.S. industrial outlook 1994.* Washington, DC: U.S. Government Printing Office.

Selected Bibliography

Ball, J., & Torem, D. (1993). *The art of fashion accessories.* Atglen, PA: Schiffer.

Becker, V. (1995). *Art Nouveau Jewelry.* New York: E. P. Dutton.

Boehn, M. von. (1929). *Ornaments: Lace, Fans, Gloves, Walking Sticks, Parasols, Jewelry and Trinkets,* reprint of the 1929 edition. New York: Ayer.

Clark, F. (1982). *Hats.* London: B. T. Batesford.

Cumming, V. (1982). *Gloves.* London: B. T. Batesford.

Gray, M. (1982). *The Lingerie Book.* New York: St. Martin's Press.

Johnson, E. (1980). *Fashion Accessories.* Aylesbuey, Bucks, England: Shire.

Kedley, L., & Schiffer, N. (1987). *Costume Jewelry, The Great Pretenders.* Westchester, PA: Schiffer.

Leather Industries of America, Inc. (annual). *U.S. leather industry statistics.* Washington, DC: Author.

Northampton English Museum. (1975). *A History of Shoe Fashions.* Northampton, England: Museum Pub.

Peltz, L. R. (1986). *Fashion Accessories* (3rd ed.). Encino, CA: Elencoe.

Probert, C. (1981). *Shoes in Vogue since 1910.* New York: Abbeville Press.

Rossi, W. (1988). *Profitable footwear retailing.* New York: Fairchild Books and Visuals.

Schiffer, N. (1987). *The Power of Jewelry.* Westchester, PA: Schiffer.

Swann, J. (1982). *Shoes.* New York: Drama Book.

Tice, B. (1985). *Enticements: How to Look Fabulous in Lingerie.* New York: Macmillan.

U.S. leather industry statistics. (annual). Washington, DC: United States Department of Commerce, Bureau of Census, Industry Division (quarterly). Washington, DC: Author.

The Undercover Story. (1982). New York: Fashion Institute of Technology.

Untracht, O. (1982). *Jewelry Concepts and Technology.* Garden City, NY: Doubleday.

WWD buyer's guide: Women's apparel and accessories manufacturers, 1995. (1995). New York: Fairchild Books and Visuals.

WWD supplier's guide: Women's apparel and accessories manufacturers, 1995. (1995). New York: Fairchild Books and Visuals.

Zucker, B. (1984). *Gems and Jewels: A Connoisseur's Guide.* New York: Thames and Hudson.

Trade Associations

Accessories Council, 522 North St., Greenwich, CT 06830.

American Apparel Manufacturers Association, 2500 Wilson Blvd., Suite 301, Arlington, VA 22201.

American Leather Accessory Designers, Kleinberg Sherrill, 392 Fifth Ave., New York, NY 10018.

Association of Umbrella Manufacturers and Suppliers, 11 W. 32 St., New York, NY 10001.

Belt Association, 330 W. 58 St., #413, New York, NY 10019.

Fashion Accessories Association (Scarf Association), c/o Sharretts, Paley, Carter & Blauvelt, 67 Broad St., New York, NY 10004.

Fashion Accessories Shippers Association, 330 Fifth Ave., New York, NY 10001.

Fashion Footwear Association of New York, 768 Fifth Ave., 17th Floor, New York, NY 10019.

Footwear Industries of America, 1420 K St., NW, #600, Washington, DC 20005.

Handbag Supply Salesmen's Association, 176 Madison Ave., 3rd Floor, Washington, DC 20006.

Intimate Apparel Council, 150 Fifth Ave., Suite 510, New York, NY 10011.

Leather Industries of America, Inc., 1000 Thomas Jefferson St., NW, Suite 515, Washington, DC 20007.

Lingerie and Loungewear Association, 555 Chabanel St. W., #801, Montreal, Quebec H2N 2H8, Canada.

Luggage and Leather Goods Manufacturers of America, Inc., 350 Fifth Ave., New York, NY 10118.

Manufacturing Jewelers & Silversmiths of America, Inc., 100 India St., Providence, RI 02903.

Millinery Information Bureau, 302 W. 12 St., New York, NY 10014.

National Association of Hosiery Manufacturers, 200 N. Sharon Amity Rd., Charlotte, NC 28211.

National Fashion Accessories Association, 330 Fifth Ave., New York, NY 10001.

National Shoe Retailers Association, 9861 Broken Land Parkway, Suite 255, Columbia, MD 21046-1151.

Neckwear Association of America, Inc., 151 Lexington Ave., 2nd Floor, New York, NY 10016.

Shoe Manufacturer's Association of Canada, 4101 Sherbrooke St. W., Montreal, Quebec H3Z 1A8, Canada.

Sunglass Association, 71 East Ave., #5, Norwalk, CT 06851.

Western Shoe Associates, 1040 East Wardlow Rd., Long Beach, CA 90807.

Trade Publications

Accessories Collection, 912 Cheung Sha Wan Road, Kowloon, Hong Kong.

Accessories Magazine, P.O. Box 5550, Norwalk, CT 06856.

American Shoemaking, Shoe Trades Publishing Co., Inc., 61 Massachusetts Ave., Arlington, MA 02174.

BFIA (Body Fashions/Intimate Apparel), 270 Madison Ave., New York, NY 10016.

DNR, 7 W. 34 St., New York, NY 10001-8191.

Fashion Accessories, Trade Media Ltd., GPO Box 11411, Hong Kong.

Fashion Forecast International, 23 Bloomsbury Sq., London WC1A 2PJ, U.K.

Footwear, 7 W. 34 St., New York, NY 10001-8191.

Footwear Forum, Mackirk Publications, 1448 Lawrence Ave., E., Toronto, Ontario M4A 2V6, Canada.

Intimate Fashion News, 307 Fifth Ave., New York, NY 10016.

Jewelers Circular—Keystone, 825 Seventh Ave., New York, NY 10019.

Leather and Footwear in Asia, Benn Electronics Publishing Ltd., Sovereign Way Tonbridge, Kent TN9 1RW, U.K.

National Jeweler, 1515 Broadway, New York, NY 10036.

Shoe Retailing Today, c/o National Shoe Retailers Association, 9861 Broken Land Parkway, Suite 255, Columbia, MD 21046-1151.

Showcase, Luggage and Leather Goods Manufacturers of America, Inc., 350 Fifth Ave., New York, NY 10118.

Travelware, Business Journals, Inc., 50 Day St., Norwalk, CT 06854.

Women's Wear Daily, 7 W. 34 St., New York, NY 10001-8191

World Footwear, Shoe Trades Publishing Co., Inc., 61 Massachusetts Ave., Arlington, MA 02174.

Globalization of the Fashion Industry

*T*oday's fashion industry is being reshaped by **globalization.** Globalization has changed where fashion goods are made, where they are sold, and how each company fits into a network that includes both competitors and partners beyond U.S. borders. Most firms in the fashion industry have found it necessary to restructure their organizations and their operations—either to be *a part* of global activities—or to adjust *because of the effects* of globalization. Although trade among nations has been a fact of life for centuries, today's globalization of business occurs with speed and intensity that transforms the industry in ways never seen before.

Imports and **exports** have long been a major consideration of nations. Each country tries to sustain and expand its economy by exporting products it has in abundance or can produce efficiently and importing those it needs or cannot produce efficiently. As far as fashion merchandise is concerned, international trade in the United States dates back to the country's beginnings. As far back as the eighteenth century, the inventories of our sailing ships listed silks from China, woolens and calicos from England, damasks and velvets from Italy, and embroideries and fine laces and fabrics from Paris. In the nineteenth century, dolls dressed in the latest French fashions were imported by American dressmakers to be used as models of the garments they would create for their wealthy clientele. When advanced printing techniques made possible illustrated magazines, dressmakers turned to such early European magazines as *Peterson's* and *Mrs. Demarest* to see what was being worn in London and Paris—and copied what they saw. Early American fashion retailers, such as Lord & Taylor of New York and Marshall Field of Chicago, bought the models of leading Paris designers, such as Worth and Doucet, as well as European fabrics and trimmings, to copy couture styles in their workrooms.

This chapter provides an overview of how globalization affects the U.S. fashion industry, why this has occurred, some of the issues involved, and the importance of being prepared to function in a global economy. The readings focus on topics related to globalization of the fashion industry. The chapter that follows deals with producers in other countries and regions that are important partners and competitors in the industry.

Overview of Globalization

Although **trade** among nations occurred for centuries, it was a slow and often dangerous matter, particularly in early times. In the earliest days, there were no ways to communicate with people in distant countries. Adventuresome merchants simply took their wares to other countries, or went to buy, embarking on long and dangerous trips by sea. Even after the development of postal services and telephones, communicating with individuals in other countries was slow by mail or costly by telephone. Although airplanes were developed in the early 1900s, early use was limited in areas of trade.

In contrast, advances in modern communications have exploded in the last decade. Computers and fax machines facilitate instant and inexpensive communication among buyers and sellers on different continents. Jets that travel 500 to 700 miles per hour have made it easy, in most cases, to travel to far corners of the globe to conduct business. Other developments have contributed to a global economy. International banks can transfer currency electronically and exchange one country's currency for another with ease. Additionally, international trade bodies develop and oversee rules to guide trade among nations.

All of these advances have led to an **interconnected global economy.** Today, many U.S. fashion firms—both manufacturers and retailers—communicate daily with their partners in Europe or Asia. For apparel manufacturers, product lines may be developed in the firm's U.S. headquarters. Sketches and markers may be transferred electronically to facilities where garments are cut and sewn to meet the manufacturer's specifications (Figure 8–1). If a problem occurs as the product is being made, this is handled through calls, faxes, and electronic mail. For example, if the manufacturer in Thailand believes the neckline is too low, sketches can be faxed back and forth until the issue is resolved.

Retailers have been actively participating in the global economy for many years as they traveled to other countries to buy product lines for their stores. More recently, however, retailers have begun to function much like apparel manufacturing firms. Many major retail firms now have product development staffs who produce their own lines under the store's **private label.** Then, the retailer contracts the production

Figure 8–1

Asian apparel producers communicate regularly with their business partners in other countries through various types of communication technologies.

Source: Kitty G. Dickerson.

with manufacturers. Some private label merchandise is produced domestically. Increasingly, however, retailers contract with manufacturers in other countries. Using contractors elsewhere generally occurs because of lower labor costs in **less developed countries.**

Fashion merchandise can be **global products** in a more complicated sense. A garment may be made of Taiwanese fiber woven into fabric in China and then shipped to the United States. A U.S. firm may cut the garments and send them to the Dominican Republic for sewing operations. After garments are finished, they are re-exported back to the U.S. market for sale. These interlinked stages of production result in products whose origins are hard to identify. These global products result from manufacturing operations in several countries, as shown in Figure 8–2.

Brief Background of Globalization of the Fashion Industry

Although trade in textiles has occurred for centuries, the most dramatic changes have occurred in the second half of the twentieth century. The controversial aspects of this trade began in the 1930s when Japan started selling significant amounts of its textile and apparel products in the European and U.S. markets. At the time, Japan was a low-wage **developing country** that began its economic development by emphasizing textile and apparel production. The trouble began when the nation wanted to earn **foreign exchange** by selling those products outside its own market. Japan began to

Figure 8–2

Global products result from manufacturing operations in a number of different countries.

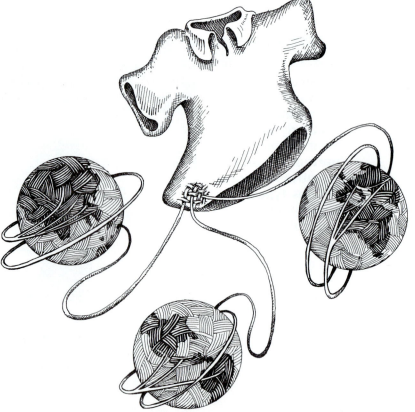

Source: Illustration by Dennis Murphy. Reprinted courtesy of Prentice Hall.

export a substantial amount of textile goods. Although much of Japan's industry was destroyed later in World War II, the country soon rebuilt the industry and began exporting again. By the 1950s, textile producers in the United States and Western Europe worried that Japanese producers were a threat to their businesses. A significant point was that, at that time, Japan had low wages. This meant Japanese products could be sold for less than those made in the U.S. and Europe. Beginning at that time, a series of trade policies was developed to attempt to "protect" the U.S., Canadian, and European manufacturers from competition from imports made in countries with low wages (Dickerson, 1991, 1995).

Other **less developed** nations saw Japan's success in building an economy with the textile/apparel industry, particularly to export the products to **more developed** countries. The less developed countries had little capital or technology to start other industries and had large populations desperately in need of jobs. Many other Asian countries followed Japan's pattern. The newcomers—such as Taiwan, South Korea, Hong Kong, India, and Pakistan—also wanted to export their products to the United States and Europe. These two markets were attractive because of the large number of consumers with enough disposable income to have fairly extensive wardrobes (at least, compared to the rest of the world). Canada and Australia were the other two attractive markets.

As this pattern continued, almost every country in the world developed at least a simple textile and apparel industry. Many nations and individuals built their dreams for a better life around the prospects of making and selling textile/apparel products in the wealthier nations. Textile and apparel firms in the more developed countries feared, however, that imports would drive them out of business. As a result, textile/apparel trade became very hostile. Complex trade policies were initiated to "manage" this sticky area of trade. Exporting and importing nations had diametrically opposing positions. The less developed countries wanted to *ship their products to* the more developed nations. Textile/apparel producers in the more developed countries wanted to do whatever they could to *keep out* the imports they saw as damaging their industry.

As other countries set their sights on the U.S. market, domestic manufacturers began more and more to feel the impact of this competition. Until the 1970s, U.S. manufacturers had a fairly large, captive market to themselves. Consumers bought what U.S. manufacturers produced. As imports made inroads into the market, they were no longer just a *threat*. Imports had become serious competition, taking an increasing share of the U.S. market. Firms found it hard to compete with products made in countries where wages were a fraction of U.S. wages. Many companies went out of business when they were unable to respond to the competition. Many other firms restructured to become more efficient and better positioned to compete (Dickerson, 1991, 1995).

Imports Versus Domestic Production

Although competition from imports is a problem shared by all consumer-oriented domestic manufacturing industries, the fashion industry has been among those most affected by imports. Since 1970, imports have increased faster than domestic output, which means imports account for an increasing share of fashion goods bought by U.S. consumers.

According to the American Apparel Manufacturers Association (1996), U.S. consumers spent about $174 billion on apparel in 1995. Of total purchases, about

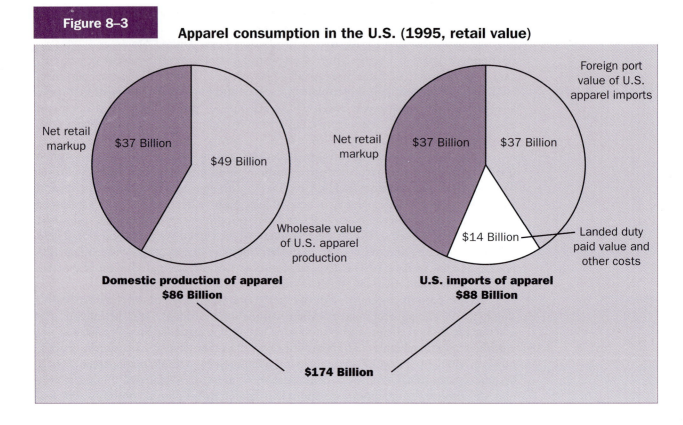

Figure 8–3

Apparel consumption in the U.S. (1995, retail value)

Domestic production of apparel
$86 Billion

Net retail markup — $37 Billion
$49 Billion — Wholesale value of U.S. apparel production

U.S. imports of apparel
$88 Billion

Net retail markup — $37 Billion
$37 Billion — Foreign port value of U.S. apparel imports
$14 Billion — Landed duty paid value and other costs

$174 Billion

Source: From *Focus: An Economic Profile of the Apparel Industry* (p. 4) by American Apparel Manufacturers Association, 1996, Arlington, VA: Author. Reprinted courtesy of AAMA

half were made in other countries. Figure 8–3 shows components that constitute the value at retail for both imported and domestic apparel. It is important to note that although imports cost less initially, duties and other charges are added to those costs.

The level of **import penetration** varies a great deal from one product to another. Because wages are a major factor in determining where garments are made, items requiring more labor input (meaning they are **labor-intensive** products) are more likely to be produced in less developed countries. Items that can be produced on automated equipment that reduces labor input are more likely to be produced domestically. For example, hosiery production is highly automated, with imports accounting for only 7 percent of the U.S. market (National Association of Hosiery Manufacturers, 1995). In contrast, because bras require a great deal of intricate sewing (i.e., are *labor-intensive*), this garment category has a high import penetration level.

Textile and Apparel Trade Deficit

A **trade deficit** is the amount by which the value of imports exceeds exports. In 1995, the United States imported $36.8 billion of apparel and $10.5 billion of textiles, a combined total of $47.3 billion. Although U.S. firms are making greater effort to export now than in the past, the total value of exports is still relatively small compared to imports. Exports were $6.2 billion for apparel and $6.9 billion for textiles. The trade deficit for textiles and apparel combined was $34.2 billion, the highest in history (U.S. Department of Commerce, 1996). The growth of the textile and apparel trade deficit is illustrated in Figure 4–10 on p. 132.

For many years, U.S. fashion producers were in the enviable position of having a large market of consumers who bought their products. Under these desirable conditions, most companies gave little or no thought to trying to sell their products in other countries. In recent years, however, many companies have awakened to the possibilities of selling their products in other parts of the world. Many U.S. fashion products, particularly those with recognizable designer or brand names, appeal to consumers in other countries. The "American look" of jeans, t-shirts, and other casual wear can be observed on every continent. High profile fashion goods names such as DKNY, Ralph Lauren, and Calvin Klein are bought by upscale customers in many countries from Europe to Asia. Consequently, many U.S. firms have started to become more global by selling their products beyond U.S. borders. Exporting textile and apparel products helps offset the high trade deficit in these merchandise areas. However, exporting is a fairly new activity for most U.S. firms in the industry. Therefore, these efforts must grow a great deal from the present level to have significant impact in offsetting the very large trade deficit.

Regulation of Imports

The penetration of imports into the U.S. fashion business has given rise to a highly vocal battle between advocates of protectionism and proponents of free trade. **Protectionism** means the reduction, limitation, or exclusion of merchandise from other countries. **Free trade** means avoiding protectionist measures and letting goods flow freely among countries.

On the protectionist side are many U.S. producers of apparel, accessories, and textiles; the major industry union (UNITE); and most of the manufacturing industry's trade associations. All have a record of continuously lobbying in Washington for more protection from imports. On the other side are the retailers and importers, their trade associations, apparel firms with production in other countries, and some consumer groups.

Officially, at least, the United States supports a free trade position, which means that restrictions on imports are kept to a minimum. This "official" position suggests that excessive restrictions on foreign goods will lower our standard of living (and, as noted in some of these points, affect our relationships with other countries) for the following reasons:

- Trade barriers mean high prices for consumers. Consumers do not get the benefit of competition among countries that leads to the best values in what they buy. Decreased competition may allow domestic firms to charge higher prices.
- Domestic producers that cannot successfully compete in the world market are not entitled to special protection from imports by the government.
- Nations affected by restrictive import measures taken by this country may retaliate against what they consider to be American protectionism and thus damage the export prospects of other U.S. companies. Jobs may be saved in one industry only to be lost in another when foreign countries retaliate by buying less from the United States.
- U.S. firms that rely on imports would be less able to compete and would lose business.
- Erecting barriers to restrict the products of other countries creates political ill will with countries with whom we may need to work on other matters. For example, if

the U.S. wants to maintain a military base in a country, the local government is likely to be less cooperative if their products are restricted from U.S. markets.

The World Trade Organization (WTO)

In 1947, the United States and other major trading nations entered into a new agreement *to reduce trade barriers* that countries were erecting against products from other nations. This trade pact, the General Agreement on Tariffs and Trade, was known as **GATT** and administered by the GATT Secretariat in Geneva, Switzerland. By its active participation in GATT, the United States publicly supported a free trade philosophy of not placing restrictions on trade (Dickerson, 1995). In reality, however, a free trade position for textile and apparel trade did not result, as we shall consider in a section that follows.

In 1995, the members of GATT made significant changes in its agreement that oversees world trade. The GATT was replaced by the **World Trade Organization (WTO)**; the headquarters of the WTO remain in Geneva. Under GATT and now the WTO, a number of basic rules for international trade exist. However, a special and unique agreement has existed for the textile and clothing trade. As part of the 1995 changes for GATT/WTO, this agreement for textiles and apparel is changing, too.

The Multifiber Arrangement (MFA)

A few countries, particularly Japan, became proficient cotton product exporters in the 1950s and 1960s. Japanese cotton goods became a concern for a number of U.S. and West European industry leaders who feared the Japanese shipments would take away sales in U.S. and European markets. U.S. and European textile and apparel leaders applied political pressure and were successful in getting a variety of trade agreements approved by GATT that limited Japanese *cotton* imports.

Until the 1970s, however, the dollar volume of textile and apparel imports coming into the U.S. market was relatively insignificant and therefore created little or no real disruption of domestic textile and apparel industries. As imports began to swell, U.S. industry leaders (and their counterparts in Western Europe) became alarmed, believing the domestic industry could not survive if imports continued at that pace. Consequently, domestic industry leaders were able to persuade policy makers to secure trade agreements that would protect them from imports from low-wage countries. European and U.S. leaders pressed for, and obtained, a new policy under GATT designed to control the flow of textile and apparel imports.

By the early 1970s, *manufactured fibers* had been developed, and limiting only cotton imports was no longer enough. Producers in other countries had cleverly avoided the restrictions on their cotton exports by switching to those made of manufactured fibers. Thus, in 1974, the **Multifiber Arrangement** (*multi*-fiber, to go beyond just cotton products), commonly known as the MFA, was implemented under the auspices of GATT.

The MFA established general rules for the kinds of actions countries might take to protect their industries from disruption by rising imports. Under its provisions, the United States (or other importing nation) might control "disruptive" imports by entering into **bilateral** (two-country) **agreements** that established import **quotas** for that country. For example, the United States could negotiate an agreement that set a limit (quota) on the textile and apparel products from India, another agreement with Hong Kong, another with South Korea, and so on. Quotas established under those bilateral agreements governed the volume of products each country could ship to the U.S. market. In Western Europe and Canada, the other major markets for products from low-wage countries, the systems worked very much the same (Dickerson, 1991, 1995).

Restrictions were applied almost entirely to the products from less developed countries because of the dramatic differences in wages. That is, U.S. manufacturers who paid their workers the minimum U.S. wage felt their products could not compete fairly with those made by workers in less developed countries who earned, in many cases, only a few cents per hour (Figure 8–4). Examples of those wage differences are given in Table 8–1.

As a growing number of less developed countries around the world began producing more and more textile and apparel products, shipments into the United States, Europe, and Canada mushroomed. Each time the MFA was renewed, the restrictions on imports from low-wage countries became tighter and tighter. A trade tug of war resulted. Basically, the less developed countries wanted to send increasing volumes of products to the more developed countries. These exporting countries were most interested in shipping to the *same* countries where textile leaders tried hardest to restrain those imported products from coming in.

In short, almost no countries liked the MFA. The less developed countries felt their exports met with too many harsh barriers under the MFA quota system. These countries became very impatient. After all, the MFA existed under the sponsorship of the GATT— an international body formed *to eliminate* trade restrictions. These exporting nations believed their products were being unfairly "choked off" by the quota system.

At the same time, industry leaders in the wealthier importing countries thought the agreement had not done an adequate job of keeping imports out of their markets. Imports grew phenomenally under the MFA quota system, at a faster rate than the growth of the domestic industry, thus taking a disproportionate share of the market.

Figure 8–4

Garment workers in many less developed countries work for very low wages.

Source: Courtesy of United Nations.

| Table 8–1 | Textile* Labor Cost** Comparisons Among Select Countries |

(Textile industry wages, 1994, in U.S. dollars)	
Japan	$25.62
Switzerland	25.46
Italy	15.65
Canada	13.60
United States	11.89
United Kingdom	10.74
Taiwan	5.98
Hong Kong	4.40
South Korea	4.00
Mexico	3.22
Turkey	2.31
Colombia	1.88
Philippines	0.95
Egypt	0.64
India	0.58
People's Republic of China	0.48
Pakistan	0.45
Sri Lanka	0.42
Vietnam	0.39
Bangladesh	0.26

* Comparable data are not available for the apparel industry; however, apparel wages are generally somewhat lower than those of textiles.
** Includes wages and other costs (e.g., benefits) paid by the employer (that is, this is more in most cases than the wages paid directly to the worker).
Source: Data from "How They Compare," November 1995, *Textile Asia,* pp. 88–89. Based on data from *Spinning and Weaving Labor Cost Comparisons,* by Werner International, 1995, New York: Author.

Additionally, the quota system sets limits on the *quantity* of imports brought into the United States rather than the value (cost) of the merchandise. This meant producers in other countries shifted to higher priced items (known as **upgrading**) to maximize the value of what is shipped under the quota limits. Imports had once been limited to lower priced product lines; however, upgrading meant imports became a threat at upper price points, too (Dickerson, 1991, 1995).

The MFA has been a highly controversial trade agreement. Although it was sponsored by the GATT, it contradicted many of the basic free trade goals of GATT. The less developed exporting countries fought hard to have this peculiar trade policy phased out. After all, no other industry had this kind of special protection provided by GATT.

Eventually, MFA opponents prevailed. In 1995, when GATT officially became the WTO, the clock started ticking toward an eventual phase-out of the MFA and the quota system. Over a 10-year period, quotas on textile and apparel products will be phased out in three stages. By 2005, all products are expected to be traded freely, with no remains of the quota system in place.

Quotas and Bilateral Trade Agreements

The United States has negotiated separate bilateral agreements with each of the textile/apparel exporting nations whose products have been regarded as a threat. These bilateral pacts establish country-by-country quotas, or annual maximums, on hundreds of categories in cotton, wool, and manufactured fiber textiles, and apparel. Each bilateral agreement establishes the quota level on a category-by-category basis, specifies the amount the category can grow in the year, and provides for establishing new quotas in cases that the bilateral agreement does not cover. The chief U.S. textile negotiator, in the Office of the U.S. Trade Representative, negotiates the bilateral agreements on behalf of the United States. The U.S. Customs Service is responsible for keeping track of import levels and quota levels. When more goods are presented for entry into the United States than the quota level allows, that merchandise is denied entry and is warehoused at the port of entry, at the expense of the importer.

Quotas, which vary for different merchandise categories and for different countries, are specified in **square meter equivalents (SMEs),** and all apparel items can be translated into SMEs. For example, customs authorities can convert every dress, shirt, or pair of slacks into square meter equivalents to monitor shipments to be sure the exporting country does not exceed its quota limits.

Under the bilateral agreements, the U.S. government grants each trading partner designated quota levels. Then, each exporting country administers its own quota and makes allocations to individual producers based generally on their past export performance. Allocations can be lost if they are not used within the designated quota year. Manufacturers, however, can and do sell unused quotas to other companies and thus maintain their export rights for subsequent years. Each exporting country has its own system for distributing quota among its manufacturers. In some cases, a board of government and/or industry representatives makes the decisions. In Hong Kong, quota may be bought and sold from one company to another. In some years, when quota was in high demand in Hong Kong, a manufacturer who had large quota allotments might have made as much from selling part or all of its quota as from actually producing apparel.

A manufacturer in another country who plans to export products having quota limits must have *available quota* to be able to ship products into the U.S. market. For example, the Fabulous Frocks company in Indonesia *must hold adequate U.S. quota for those product categories* the company plans to produce and ship to the U.S. market. If Fabulous Frocks wants to ship to a West European country, the company must hold adequate European quota[1] to cover the shipment. Documentation to prove this "ownership" of quota must accompany shipments or they will be stopped in the port of entry by customs authorities.

U.S. fashion firms, whether manufacturers or retailers, having products made in another country must be certain they are working with companies holding adequate quota to cover the products being made for the U.S. firm. Without the quota, the merchandise cannot be delivered to the U.S. company ordering it. This applies, of course, only to those countries and products with quota limits.

Several areas in the world, however, have had no quota restrictions at all for entering the U.S. market—for example, the **European Union.** Exemptions are based on the assumption that (1) these are high-wage industrialized countries whose products are not price-competitive with domestic goods, (2) our exports to these countries balance our imports from them, and (3) their import penetration is not large enough to cause domestic market disruption.

---

[1]This major group of West European countries is now called the *European Union (EU)* and consists of 15 countries that operate as one unit in trade with the rest of the world. Quotas, for example, are designated by the European Union rather than by each specific country (much as the United States government would do for all 50 states). Earlier, this West European group (when it consisted of fewer countries) was known as the European Economic Community (the EEC) and later the European Community (EC).

Mexico and Canada are exempt from the quota limits as a result of the **North American Free Trade Agreement (NAFTA),** which permits free trade among the three countries in North America. As a result of this agreement, Mexico has become a growing source of apparel imports in the U.S. market. This group of countries exempt from quotas is likely to increase as the United States enters into additional free trade agreements in the Americas.

Also exempt from U.S. quotas are other countries in the Caribbean Basin and in Central America (for most product categories) under the Caribbean Basin Initiative, which is discussed in a following section. These countries have been given special treatment in the past because the United States has felt a responsibility to aid many of these very poor countries in their economic development. Additionally, many U.S. government leaders have considered it important to assist with economic opportunity to avoid *political uprising* in nearby countries. Many countries in Africa that are not yet industrialized or even on the road to development are exempt as well. All of these exempt areas are in marked contrast to the quota restrictions placed on more than 90 percent of the textile and apparel products imported from Taiwan, Hong Kong, South Korea, and China. This group, known as the "Big Four," has been the biggest source of supply to U.S. markets over the past two decades.

The 10-year phase-out of the MFA means that quotas are expected to become a thing of the past by 2005. Figure 8–5 shows the progressive removal of quotas during the 10-year phaseout. However, until that time, a significant amount of world trade in textiles and apparel will be governed by the quota system. Therefore, it is important for those working in the fashion field to understand the quota system and its impact on nearly all segments of the industry, from manufacturing to retailing.

Getting Around the Quotas

As might be expected, many producers in other countries have devised ways to "get around" the quota limits imposed by the United States. When an exporting country has used all its quota but is determined to continue shipping products to the U.S. market, foreign producers have been very enterprising.

Often production has been transferred to countries with unused or excess quotas, or to countries without quotas (those that are underdeveloped or that may have a preferential arrangement with no quota). An example of *moving production* has been when some of the Big Four Asian countries have set up garment production in Caribbean or African countries that are free from U.S. quota limits. They produce and ship fashion goods to the U.S. market without the quota restrictions placed on them in their homelands. As one example, 23 South Korean firms have production in Honduras alone ("NAFTA Parity," 1995). Some have even moved operations to a location *within* the United States to avoid quotas. For instance, Hong Kong–based Odyssey International Pte. Ltd. acquired Cal Sport in Yuma, Arizona, a firm producing skiwear, sportswear, and camping equipment. This launched Odyssey's strategy to build or buy a total of 10 to 12 manufacturing facilities in the United States ("Odyssey Begins," 1991).

In addition, **transshipment** has been a common strategy. In this illegal practice, countries with used-up quotas transship products through a third country with quota availability. The countries with available quota are sometimes called "quota havens." For example, China has the ability to produce a volume of garments far in excess of what the country is *permitted* to ship under the U.S. quota limits. To get around this problem, Chinese manufacturers have frequently shipped their merchandise to other places, such as Macau, that have plenty of available quota. The garments bear "made in Macau" labels, and when they arrive in U.S. ports, they appear to have been made

Figure 8–5

MFA quota phaseout schedule

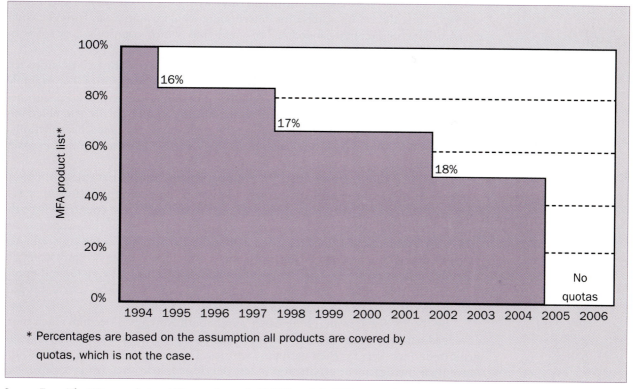

* Percentages are based on the assumption all products are covered by
quotas, which is not the case.

Source: From *The U.S. manufactured fiber market under NAFTA and the WTO* (p. 10) by P. O'Day, September 1994. Presented to the 33rd International Man-Made Fibres Congress. Dornbirn, Austria. Reprinted by permission of Paul O'Day and the American Fiber Manufacturers Association, Inc.

in the third country. The U.S. government has cracked down on these illegal practices and on occasion has penalized China by reducing quota in certain product categories as a result.

In a sense, quotas have created opportunities of export growth for many of the low-wage countries around the world. As demand for inexpensive imports grows, manufacturers and retailers from many countries have of necessity sought sources beyond the quota-limited facilities of the Big Four Asian countries. Many of the most underdeveloped countries would not have the equipment, the know-how, and the market contacts to start up garment production on their own. Start-ups in these poorest countries have required the investment and assistance of industry representatives from more developed countries who are looking for low wages and quota-free production sites. In many cases, as the newest countries become proficient at making garments, quotas are then imposed. Then, manufacturers and retailers sometimes move on to yet another developing country without quotas.

As long as the quota system lasts, it is likely that some producers in exporting countries will try to find illegal means of shipping beyond their legal limits to the more prosperous market countries like the United States. By the same token, as long as the quota system exists, industry representatives working with producers in countries covered by quota will find it critically important to be sure their international partner has *legal access* to quota before signing business contracts.

Country-of-Origin Rules

To curtail quota evasion by transshipment through second countries on categories covered by quotas, new **country-of-origin rules** were established by the United States in 1985. The rules set up criteria for determining which country was truly the country of origin for incoming merchandise—and thus which country's quota was involved.

Traditionally, it had been accepted as legitimate practice for two or more foreign countries to contribute to the making of some apparel categories. For example, in the case of a knitted sweater, yarn could be spun in one country, dyed in another, knit into panels for back, front, and sleeves in a third, and then finally assembled into a garment, labeled, and exported in a fourth. Hong Kong, for instance, has functioned as the assembler and shipper for much of its knitwear, using panels knitted in mainland China.

The 1985 rules required that the country where "substantial transformation" occurred determined the garment's origin.[2] This was, generally, the first manufacturing stages. In the case of garments that were cut from fabrics, the country where the cutting occurred determined the country of origin. In the case of the sweaters cited above, the sweaters came to be regarded, under the 1985 ruling, as having originated in China and would be counted against China's quota, even though Hong Kong did the finishing and shipping. The complication was that China had very limited quota. But, after all, that was the reason U.S. manufacturers had been able to secure this protection—to stop shipments that were mostly made in China.

By the 1990s, Taiwan, Hong Kong[3], and South Korea had become much more advanced nations. Wages in their countries had risen, and it became increasingly difficult to find workers for their garment factories. These countries began to invest and move their own garment production to less developed, low-wage Asian nations such as Indonesia, China, Malaysia, Thailand, Bangladesh, and Vietnam. Operating under the 1985 rules of origin, if Hong Kong manufacturers cut garments in their Hong Kong factories, it could be sewed in mainland China where wages were much lower. Then, when garments were brought back to Hong Kong, they were shipped under Hong Kong quota. This strategy of sending out the cut parts to low-wage areas for the sewing operation is called **outward processing trade (OPT)**. (Many U.S. manufacturers use a similar strategy, which will be discussed in a later section.)

Soon, however, U.S. manufacturers who opposed imports began to realize that OPT was another way of interpreting the rules to export more products to U.S. markets. The biggest concern was that the United States had very restrictive quotas on products from mainland China. However, under the OPT arrangements, a great many products were *actually being made* in China for shipment to the United States, but the products were legitimately labeled as made in Hong Kong.

By 1996, U.S. country-of-origin rules were changed again to limit the OPT arrangements taking place in Asia, particularly in China. Under the new rules, the country of origin is the country in which the garment *assembly* occurs.

Changes in regulations such as the country-of-origin rules make a dramatic difference in how U.S. fashion firms participate in international aspects of business. A partnership with a company in another country can be working smoothly one day and changed totally by the next day. A retail buyer may suddenly discover it is impossible

---

[2]This is a very simplified description of a complex set of rules, which often required a U.S. Customs ruling to settle each case in question.
[3]Technically not a nation, the previously British territory of Hong Kong is part of China as of June 1997.

to do business with an established partner in China or elsewhere because the trade policies have changed. For the fashion goods industries, the trade rules affect where production occurs, what can be produced, and to whom it may be shipped. Therefore, it is critical that professionals in the field learn about and try to have an understanding of these rules and the changes in rules as they occur.

Taxes on Imports: Tariffs/Duties

In addition to the restraints imposed by import quotas, most fashion goods are subject to an import tax. This tax on imports, known as a **tariff** or **duty,** is established and regulated by the U.S. government, paid by the importer, and collected by the U.S. Customs Service. The amount varies for different categories of merchandise, but it is generally *ad valorem,* or a percentage of the **first cost** (invoice cost). Its primary purpose, of course, is to increase the eventual selling price of imported goods and thus protect domestic industries. For many fashion products from the low-wage countries, however, even with the addition of tariffs and shipping costs, the final **landed cost** in the United States is often considerably less than for domestically produced apparel of equal quality.

As part of the 1995 WTO agreement on textiles and apparel, tariffs on imports coming into the U.S. market will decline over the 10-year phase-out period for quotas. However, by 2005, when quotas are to be fully removed, tariffs on textile and apparel goods will remain. In the GATT/WTO negotiations, the U.S. government retained higher tariff levels for textiles and apparel than is generally true for other industries. Similarly, the U.S. textile and apparel industries have more tariff protection from imports than their counterparts in the European Union.

Although many countries that have exported their textile and apparel products to the United States have complained about the quota restraints on their products, many of those countries make it very difficult for outsiders to sell in *their* markets. Because many less developed countries rely so heavily on their textile and apparel industries to support their economies, they do not want products from elsewhere to compete in their markets. Some have very high tariffs; some have other trade barriers; and a few will permit only products that do not compete with their own. This has been a sensitive matter for U.S. and EU manufacturers who would like to sell in those countries. In recent years, many of these less developed countries have started to permit products from elsewhere in their markets. For instance, India had a closed economy until the early 1990s but has since opened the country's market to products from other countries. As a result, fashion manufacturers elsewhere began to consider India as a potential market for their products, particularly to appeal to India's growing upper income groups who would have the means of buying imports.

Preferential Programs: Exemptions from Tariffs or Quotas

The U.S. government also has a number of programs that exempt products from other countries from tariffs or quotas, or in some cases both. Some of these programs are designed to stimulate the economy and encourage trade for less developed countries around the world.

- *The Multifiber Arrangement (MFA)*   As noted earlier, other more developed countries including those in the European Union are exempt from quota restrictions.

This exemption is primarily because the EU is at a similar stage of economic development and wages are comparable to those in the United States. Many of the less developed countries, whose products have been subject to tight restraints, have resented the preferential treatment that the EU and the United States provide one another. Tariffs are, however, levied on textile and apparel products traded between the two.

- *The North American Free Trade Agreement (NAFTA).* Under NAFTA, the United States, Canada, and Mexico moved toward open trade with one another, trade that is free of quotas, tariffs, and most other trade barriers.

  Free trade among the countries in the Americas will continue to expand. In late 1994, President Bill Clinton led an effort in which 33 countries signed an agreement called "Free Trade of the Americas," to be completed by 2005. Even today, many nations in Central and South America have free trade among themselves.

- *The Generalized System of Preferences (GSP).* In 1974, Congress passed the Trade Act, which among other things authorized the Generalized System of Preferences (GSP). The 1984 Trade Act extended the GSP. The purpose of this segment of the act was to give special trade privileges to more than 130 developing countries in Central America, Africa, Asia, the Caribbean Basin, and the Far East. Some 4,000 products made in these designated countries are permitted to enter the United States duty-free. Not surprisingly, most exceptions are in the textile/apparel sector. This has mattered little, however, because even with tariffs added, textile/apparel products made in low-wage, less developed countries are still less costly than those made domestically. The exclusion of textile and apparel products from the GSP illustrates the special protection given the U.S. textile/apparel sector.

- *Special Tariff Provisions: 807/9802 Production.* Under the former U.S. tariff schedule, a special provision permitted U.S. apparel firms to have their garments assembled in other countries, much like the outward processing trade (OPT) described earlier. Under this earlier tariff provision, Item 807.00, apparel firms were permitted to send U.S.-cut garments to low-wage countries for the sewing to be done and then brought back into the United States. Tariffs were charged only on the value added in the production process. Under this provision, garments were still subject to quota limits. Fabrics used in garments could be from any source; only *cutting* in the United States was required (Dickerson, 1991, 1995).

  In 1989, a new Harmonized System of tariff schedules was implemented to give all participating countries the same tariff system. At that time, Item 807 officially became Item 9802. However, in the industry, this strategy for having garments assembled elsewhere is still commonly called 807 production (Figure 8–6).

- *The Caribbean Basin Initiative (CBI).* The CBI is a preferential program developed by the U.S. government to promote economic development in 27 countries in the Caribbean Basin region. Although the CBI provided duty-free access to most products made in those countries, *tariffs remained on textile/apparel products* as a measure to protect the U.S. industry. Basically, the CBI *per se* had no effect on textiles and apparel, except to illustrate again that the industry had special protection.

- *The Caribbean Basin Textile Access Program* (known as **807A production** or "Super 807"). Under this 1986 agreement, Caribbean apparel products are given a more liberal quota system for access to the U.S. market *if fabrics are both made and cut in the United States* (see Figure 8–6). This provision increased U.S. *quota* allotments—known as **guaranteed access levels** or **GALS**—to CBI countries. In short, if garments met the requirements noted above, adequate quota for shipping to the U.S. market was virtually assured. As might be expected, this agreement was

Figure 8–6

How the 807 (9802) and 807A in the CBI Countries works

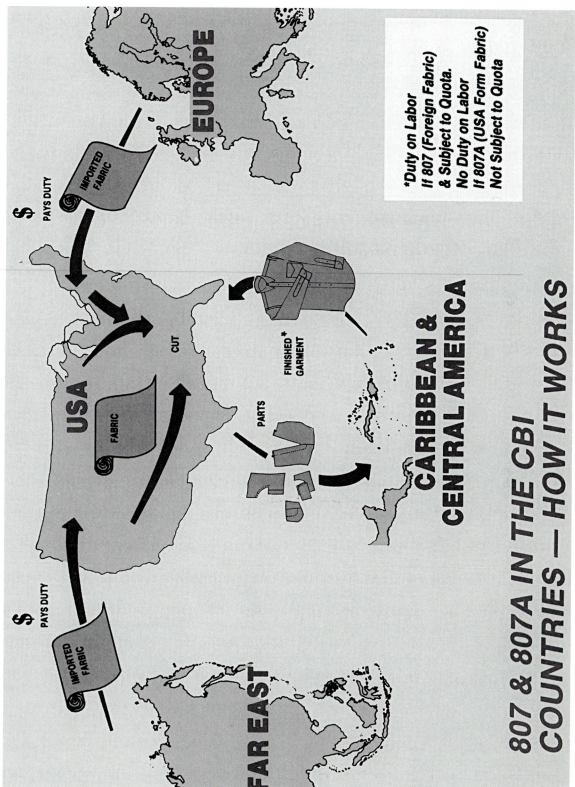

**807 & 807A IN THE CBI
COUNTRIES — HOW IT WORKS**

EUROPE

FAR EAST

USA

CARIBBEAN &
CENTRAL AMERICA

PAYS DUTY

$

IMPORTED FABRIC

PAYS DUTY

$

IMPORTED FARBIC

FABRIC

CUT

PARTS

FINISHED *
GARMENT

*Duty on Labor
If 807 (Foreign Fabric)
& Subject to Quota.
No Duty on Labor
If 807A (USA Form Fabric)
Not Subject to Quota

Source: From *Bobbin* (p. 81), November 1989. Reprinted by permission of *Bobbin.* Copyright © Bobbin Blenheim Media. All rights reserved.

more popular with U.S. *textile* makers because it required the use of U.S. fabrics. The Caribbean Basin Textile Access Program was the provision that led to the greatest growth of apparel production (i.e., assembly) in the region.

- *Caribbean Parity.*   Following the passage of NAFTA, U.S. apparel firms with production in the Caribbean were at a disadvantage compared to those with production in Mexico. Like the Caribbean, Mexico had low wages but also duty-free access to the U.S. market. U.S. firms with production in the Caribbean have fought for parity (equality). They want *duty-free* trade access similar to that provided Mexico under NAFTA.

The Politics of Textile and Apparel Trade

Most of the trade agreements that govern textile and apparel trade have developed for political reasons rather than economic reasons. A major reason for this has been that the textile and apparel industries are so vitally important to nearly every nation's economy. Production has increased in a majority of less developed countries. At the same time, the industry remains a major manufacturing sector in the more developed countries to which the less developed countries wish to export. In both the United States and the European Union, the combined textile-apparel-fiber sectors represent the *largest manufacturing employers* in each. This means that the countries that have been recipients of most of the world's imports have many jobs at stake. In the United States, the combined industry employs nearly 2 million workers; in the EU, more than 2 million. Thus, *jobs* become the main point of argument in trade debates (Dickerson, 1991, 1995).

In the United States, the textile sector is relatively concentrated in the Southeast. Apparel manufacturing occurs in every state. Because of the large number of workers and the geographic spread, the combined industry has a great deal of power in Washington. Virtually no member of the U.S. Congress is without production in his/her district. Consequently, a large number of U.S. political leaders, from presidents to legislators, have found it necessary to take note of the trade problems affecting the industry. In the last four decades, industry leaders[4] have lobbied for protection from imports. These leaders have been very successful in parlaying their clout into special trade agreements to limit imports.

As an example of the strength of the textile/apparel lobby, the industry nearly succeeded in having acts of Congress passed to protect the domestic industry. On three different occasions, when the textile/apparel **lobby** felt U.S. trade policies provided too little protection, members of Congress from the major textile/apparel-producing states introduced bills that would have provided special import protection specifically for these sectors. On three occasions,[5] textile/apparel trade bills failed to pass Congress by only a few votes. This near-success reflected the power of the textile lobby (Dickerson, 1991, 1995).

---

[4]Previously, the textile and apparel industries had a very strong anti-import coalition that worked together to secure protection for the industry. The coalition included a large number of industry associations, unions, and cotton producers.
[5]These "textile bills" were introduced in Congress in 1985, 1987, and 1990.

At the same time that some manufacturers lobbied *to keep imports out*, retailers and importers began to lobby to *eliminate barriers* to imports. Both retailers and importers have grown increasingly dependent on imports for their lines. Therefore, as some manufacturers tried increasingly to limit imports through political avenues, retailers and importers also became politically active to protect their own interests. Each side exerted pressure to protect the interests of its members.

In addition to their lobbying efforts, both sides exhort the general public to add its voice. Statements have been made in newspapers and on TV, petitions are circulated, demonstrations are held, and consumer surveys are made. Both sides have employed consultants and professional lobbyists. Collectively, a great deal of funding and energy has been spent on the political fray.

In recent years, as a growing number of U.S. apparel firms have moved their production outside the country, the apparel industry has been less vocal in fighting imports. This has weakened the previously tight-knit coalition of textile and apparel producers that secured so much protection in the past.

Additionally, as U.S. manufacturers face the reality of having import quotas end, many have changed their strategy. A growing number have begun to think more globally and to look to the markets in other countries as places *to sell their products.*

The politics of textile and apparel trade have changed; however, this sector will probably never be totally free of politics. The reason: too many people have too much at stake. The dilemma over textile and apparel trade will continue and will require many compromises to satisfy retailers, importers, domestic textile/apparel/accessory producers, workers, labor unions, the governments and producers in other nations, global trade officials, U.S. legislators—and the consumer.[6]

Who Imports and Why

There are two major categories of fashion merchandise that the United States imports. One is ready-to-wear fashion merchandise that is totally designed and produced by foreign manufacturers and for the most part is purchased by retail buyers for resale to their customers. The second type is the merchandise that is contracted out to overseas factories for all or part of the production process and is then returned to the United States.

Whenever the domestic market is unable to meet a fashion need, whether it be lower prices, innovation, production capabilities, or whatever, imports have become a means of supplying the need. Each source of supply in another country contributes to the import stream according to its specialized capabilities and its particular area of expertise.

The reasons for the penetration of imports are many and varied. Among them are:

- *Lower prices:* On the price front, the domestic industry has a twofold disadvantage. U.S. labor costs are much higher than in the low-wage countries around the world, and the domestic producer does not enjoy the tax exemptions, rebates, preferential financing schemes, and other profit cushions that many foreign governments provide their exporting entrepreneurs.

---

[6]For further consideration of the positions of each of these groups, see *Textiles and apparel in the global economy* (1995) by K. Dickerson.

- *Availability of hand labor:* Many countries have hand-production capabilities and expertise that the United States may not possess. For example, many foreign countries have generations of skills behind them in such hand operations as laces, embroideries, beading, hand-finished buttonholes, hand-loomed fabrics, and hand-knitted sweaters, to name but a few. They also have a large pool of handicraft workers.

  Hand labor is very expensive in more developed countries. Therefore, low-wage, less developed countries can produce products that involve hand labor, whereas countries like the United States are unable to produce affordable garments with this detailing.

- *Product voids in the United States:* In the category of merchandise that American producers either cannot produce at all or cannot do as well are the cashmeres of Scotland and China, the soft-as-butter leathers of Spain, the linens of Belgium, and the silks of Italy and China. Another example of a product void is the absence of domestically produced fully fashioned sweaters, which is such a labor-intensive process that the American knitwear industry cannot produce them at a salable price.

- *Producers in other countries are more adaptable or cooperative:* Many users of imports feel that foreign producers are more cooperative and responsive to their needs than domestic suppliers. For example the president of Jones New York explained that the firm makes 35 different styles of blouses, which it is able to do overseas without the snafus that would be encountered in the United States. "Here" he said, "they want to mass-produce one style of blouses and factories tell us what their needs are and what we should be doing instead of letting us design and telling them what we want. In the Orient, they are more flexible and less insistent upon large mass cuttings" ("Asia's Lure," 1988).

  And as Art Ortenberg, the former co-chairman of Liz Claiborne, explained it, "When we show a new design to a Japanese sweater knitter, he says, 'Oh, how simple' but the American knitter says 'Oh, how complicated'" ("Asia's Lure," 1988). Many designers also verbalize that it's much easier to work, buy fabrics, and get things done in Europe and the Orient. According to Isaac Mizrahi, Europe has a more nurturing approach toward its talent, and Marc Jacobs says, "It's much easier to work in Tokyo where everyone wants to work with you. Here you go into a fabric company and they give you minimums. How can a young designer be creative here with that kind of attitude? A lot of times I see great fabric but I can't have it because the minimums are so high" ("Asia's Lure," 1988).

- *Exclusive rights:* Foreign purchases also give U.S. companies an opportunity to avoid sameness—assortments that are too much like those of their competitors. Retailers are always in search of new and different merchandise to which they can get exclusive rights, particularly if they can secure these rights without making the massive purchases often required by large, volume-minded U.S. apparel producers. The exclusive items, not available in competing stores, permit the retailer to generate storewide excitement because the merchandise is free from competition. Similarly, it has been almost impossible for apparel producers to obtain exclusivity of fabrics from U.S. textile producers without committing themselves to the purchase of huge runs far in advance of their selling season. Non-U.S. producers of apparel or textiles, which generally are not as large as U.S. manufacturers, do not need or demand big commitments.

- *Fashion cachet of Europe:* Not to be underestimated as a reason for importing fashion goods is the glamour associated with European fashions and labels. From its inception, the U.S. fashion business has been influenced by European fashions and has found inspiration across the Atlantic. It is true that today a circle of American designers get adoring treatment from U.S. retailers and their customers, yet what comes from the European fashion centers will probably always have a special cachet just because of its origin.

Imports by Retailers

A retail firm's success ultimately rests on the strength, balance, and competitiveness of its merchandise assortment. A major responsibility of retail buyers and merchandise managers is, therefore, to seek ideal assortments wherever they can find them. In many situations, imports are an essential ingredient of the retail product mix because they can provide distinctive, competitive, and profitable merchandise.

Although exact figures are not available, published estimates indicate that one-third of foreign-made goods are imported directly by U.S. retailers, one-third by import jobbers, and the remaining third is being produced offshore for domestic apparel producers (AAMA, 1988).

Import Buying Methods

Not all foreign purchases by retailers are made in a single pattern. Procedures vary and may involve anything from sending representatives abroad to placing an order with a foreign source at a showroom in the United States. Among the most common means are the following:

- *Foreign trade shows in the United States.* Many producers from other countries exhibit their collections in the United States. Such showings may be at international trade shows staged in this country or in single-nation shows sponsored by a particular country to court foreign buyers. Buyers who are unable or unwilling to make trips overseas do their buying at such shows. For example, as Turkish apparel producers have attempted to increase their sales in the U.S. market, they have used this strategy.
- *Foreign producers' showrooms in the United States.* Many large overseas producers maintain individual sales forces in showrooms in New York City, as well as in major regional apparel marts, for the convenience of retailers.
- *Store-owned merchandising/buying offices.* Many large retailers maintain offices, independently or in conjunction with their buying offices in the United States, in major cities of Europe and Asia, such as Florence, Paris, London, Hong Kong, Singapore, and Tokyo. These offices keep their principals updated on new producers, important new products, and fashion developments. In addition, they place orders as requested and handle the forms and other procedures that are involved, such as **letters of credit,** quality control checks, and follow-through on shipping arrangements and delivery dates. Retailers that maintain such offices include, for example, Sears, J.C. Penney, Wal-Mart, Kmart, May Company, and Saks Fifth Avenue. Also maintaining foreign offices for the benefit of the retailers they serve are such merchandising/buying offices as Frederick Atkins and the Associated Merchandising Corporation.

    Today, both the store-owned and independent offices located in other countries to serve retailers have evolved from being just buying offices to now assuming more merchandising and product development activities. Frequently the representatives in those offices are closely involved in the manufacturing process for the retailer's lines. This will be discussed further in the following section on securing products for private label lines and in Chapter 11.

Figure 8–7

Ad by foreign commissionaire

> Hong Kong Buying Office
>
> Our overseas buying office has been repre-senting manufacturers of women's leisurewear and sportswear in Hong Kong, Singapore, and Korea for 20 years. We are expanding and looking for additional clients. For information, contact:
>
> More Fashions Far East Ltd.
> 11111 900th St., New York 17777
> 212-111-0000

- *Foreign commissionaires and agents.* Retailers, particularly those of smaller size that are not represented by their own foreign offices in a particular country, use **commissionaires** and agents. These functionaries assist store buyers when they make direct visits to the countries concerned. In return for a fee (i.e., a commission), they direct visiting buyers to suitable producers, handle the necessary export forms, and follow through on delivery and shipping arrangements (Figure 8–7).
- *Foreign trade showings.* Practically every European country and several Asian fashion centers hold seasonal group showings. These shows are attended by thousands of visiting buyers from all over the world who come to buy or observe new developments in foreign fashions and products, or both. Purchases are followed up by either commissionaires or the foreign buying office serving the store concerned. These shows, which are both national and international in nature, are discussed in the following chapter.

Securing Products for Private Label Lines

The move toward import buying by retailers has been accelerated by the renewed retail trend toward featuring **private label** merchandise. Merchants have become disenchanted with designer-name products and national brands because these widely distributed products have lost much of their exclusivity. Designer names and national brands turn up in off-price discount stores that have multiplied like fried chicken and hamburger outlets.

Such store-name or private-brand goods, more often than not, are made overseas by producers that offer favorable comparative values in terms of styling or price, or sometimes both. Nearly all private label merchandise is made to the specifications of the importing retailer (or retail buying group). In **specification buying,** the buyer plans the styles and designs to be produced (Figure 8–8). This is done sometimes by describing the garment, and sometimes by supplying an actual sample for copying or adaptation. The merchant may even supply the fabric, not necessarily from the country in which the garment is to be made. Also specified by the purchaser are the garment's measurements, its trimmings, the quantity, and the negotiated wholesale price. In effect, the retailer fulfills the function of an apparel jobber, and the foreign producer the function of a contractor. Today, many large retail firms have extensive product development staffs who develop lines in much the same way the merchandising staffs in apparel firms do. Moreover, the retailers' representatives are actively involved in the manufacturing process. In this way, U.S. retailers can enjoy both exclusive styles and the favorable prices that are possible when merchandise is made to

Figure 8–8

Specification buying from India

YOUR
Designs
or
Ours...

BOOTHS 2058/2060

A variety of individual and collective PRIVATE LABEL FASHION PROGRAMS for small, medium & large buyers.

Junior, missy, petite & large size sportswear, dresses, lounge wear, scarves and handmade sweaters... Also, men's shirts and sportswear in cottons, rayons, silks, linen and rami-cotton blends.

INDIA IMPORTS
OF CALIFORNIA
P.O. Box 1026, Providence, CA 92901-1026
(999) 272-8600, Telex: 211071INDIARI

NEW YORK SHOWROOM
1400 BROADWAY, SUITE 473, (212) 555-4942

specifications by lower-cost producers in Asia and elsewhere. Private label lines will be considered further in Chapter 10.

Imports by Manufacturers

Even if all retailers were to purchase exclusively from domestic sources, imports would still be a major factor in their merchandise assortments, because U.S. manufacturers also import. The retailer that purchases these imports does so not necessarily because they are imports, but because they satisfy a need in the merchandise assortment and can be sold profitably at a price point attractive to the store's customers.

Direct Imports by Manufacturers

Manufacturers do direct importing of textiles and apparel for the same reasons that apply to retailers—price advantage, exclusivity of product, foreign expertise, and any other fashion or quality factors that may be absent from domestic markets. Fabric mills import yarns not readily available in this country. Fabric jobbers and apparel manufacturers import silks and certain luxurious fabrics that are not produced here. Many sportswear apparel companies import sweaters or leather items to coordinate with their domestically produced skirts, slacks, and other separates. There also are some U.S.-based companies that specialize in importing finished products, such as dresses and skirts, and market them domestically under their own labels (Figure 8–9).

| **Figure 8–9** | **Imports from India and South America** |

> **Pisces Fashions Ltd.**
> **India**
> Looking for importers/wholesalers for woven sleep and loungewear production. We have 10 years experience with top corporations in U.S. market.
> NY contact: 999-555-1234. Overseas: 25 W Gandhi Arena, Delhi, India. 555-5454 TELEX: 22-7114.

> **TEE SHIRTS IN SOUTH AMERICA**
> Large tee shirt manufacturer, high-volume production, offers high-quality services in manufacturing or silk-screening tee shirts on any textiles. Contact Tee-Shirts, 8454 Elk St. Broadhead, NY 00068

Offshore Production

Despite their continuing outcry over the amount of direct importing done by retail buyers, American producers have been steadily increasing their own import practices by having their merchandise produced abroad. For example, all of Liz Claiborne's merchandise is produced by contractors, mostly Asian manufacturers.

To manufacture overseas, domestic producers send electronically the designs, markers, and production specifications that must be exact and clear. Of course, today's communications advances permit easier and faster information exchanges than in the past. The three basic methods used when producing overseas are as follows:

1. **Production package:** In this method, everything but the design is supplied by the contractor, including the fabrics, all of the production processes, finishing, labeling, packaging, and shipping.
2. **Cut, make, and trim (CMT):** In this method, the domestic producer that supplies the designs buys the fabric from one country and then has it shipped to a contractor in another country to be cut and sewn according to specifications.
3. **Offshore assembly:** In this method, fabric is made and cut[7] in the United States and then sent elsewhere for sewing as specified. It is then sent back to the originating company for possibly some finishing and for shipping.

Promotion of Domestic Products

In an effort to offset the deluge of imports coming into the U.S. market, domestic textile and apparel manufacturers developed a campaign to draw attention to domestic products. Financing from textile and apparel firms permitted the industry to form the Crafted with Pride in U.S.A. Council. The Council launched a labeling and promotion

---

[7]As noted earlier, under 807A, manufacturers do not have to face quota limits on products if garments are made of U.S.-made and U.S.-cut fabrics. Consequently, this form of offshore assembly has been more popular in recent years than the original 807/9802 production.

Figure 8–10

The certification mark used by U.S. manufacturers in a voluntary labeling campaign to call attention to U.S.-made products.

Source: Reprinted courtesy of Crafted with Pride in U.S.A. Council, Inc.

campaign to heighten consumer awareness of the advantages of U.S.-made apparel. An easily recognized certification mark identified domestically made garments on labels and hang tags (Figure 8–10). A multimedia campaign featured famous personalities who encouraged viewers to buy U.S.-made garments.

Council members also tried to educate retailers on the bottom-line advantages of domestically produced goods. These advantages include timeliness (i.e., Quick Response), reduced shipping costs, geographic proximity, flexibility in reordering, and having investment tied up in shipments for much shorter time periods.

Later stages of the multimedia campaign emphasized job losses resulting from imports. TV commercials featured families who had to move because the breadwinners lost their jobs as a result of imported merchandise. Others featured unemployed workers, such as those represented in Figure 8–11.

U.S. Penetration of Markets in Other Countries

U.S. textile and apparel producers have been unable to match their exports to the rising tide of imports. Many factors account for this. An important reason discussed earlier is the difference in production costs, resulting largely from different labor costs. Another reason for the trade deficit is that many of the countries that have exported extensively to the United States have been unwilling to accept U.S. products into their markets. Although this has begun to improve in many of these countries in recent years, much room for improvement still exists.

An important factor in limiting U.S. textile and apparel shipments to other countries is that many domestic firms simply have not *thought* about it or *tried* it until the mid-1990s. Although a number of companies have sold their products in other countries for years, many others had been content to sell only in the U.S. market. Many spent more time complaining about imports than thinking about how to

Figure 8–11

This photo from the Crafted with Pride in U.S.A. Council, Inc. portrays textile and apparel job losses resulting from imports.

Source: Reprinted courtesy of Crafted with Pride in U.S.A. Council, Inc.

export. Companies simply have not had an export mentality. Few have had staffs with the multilingual and multicultural skills necessary to work in other countries. These comments could apply to most U.S. industries, however, and were not unique to the textile and apparel sector.

A number of U.S. textile and apparel producers have penetrated the markets in other countries in a variety of ways described briefly in the following sections. Some large companies (e.g., Levi Strauss & Co. and Sara Lee) have used various strategies from one country or region to another (Figure 8–12). Through various strategies, Sara Lee, for example, has become a leader in intimate apparel and hosiery in Europe, Asia, and Mexico. Similarly, Nike has used a variety of strategies to gain significant market share on six continents. Nike's shoes are manufactured and sold in more than 90 countries (Nike, Inc., 1994).

Licensing Agreements

Licensing is a relatively uncomplicated way for a domestic manufacturer to cultivate foreign markets, and it is the least costly. Entering into a legal arrangement, the U.S. company gives the right to use its brand name (trademark) or manufacturing process, or both, to a foreign producer. In return, it receives a fee or royalty percentage on sales.

The foreign producer gains production expertise and the use of a well-known name, or both. The licensing U.S. firm gains entry into a foreign market with little risk or financial investment. In some countries that will not accept imports of U.S. products, this may be the only way to penetrate the market. Often, the foreign producer simply wants to be able to produce and sell a well-known brand. For example, Jockey International was one of the early leaders among U.S. firms in having its products sold in more than 100 countries. In many cases, this occurred through licensing agreements. Producers in other countries were able to make and sell this respected brand. Jockey was able to establish its name in many foreign markets where it would have been unable to sell otherwise.

Pierre Cardin is another widely licensed name. In fact, the name has been licensed for so many products that it has lost some of its cachet. Many U.S. cartoon characters have been licensed around the world. When one of the authors visited the Singapore zoo, more than half the children were wearing clothing with U.S. cartoon characters. In short, enormous amounts of clothing and accessories are produced and sold in other countries that bear well-known American or European designer or brand names. Much of this has occurred under licensing agreements—or, in some cases, companies in those nations have illegally used labels or brand names.

Direct Exporting

When a company is involved in direct exporting, this means it is selling products in other markets directly from the home base. In other words, the company does not have a production base in the region where it is selling. This strategy is one of the most common, and it is less complicated to implement than some others. Direct exporting may be limited, however, by the fairly high cost of U.S. products and the trade barriers in other countries. For example, if a country imposes a tariff as high as 60 or 70 percent on a U.S. product, the increase makes the merchandise very costly to consumers in that market. Nevertheless, many consumers in other countries are attracted to products that are uniquely American and covet the "Made in USA" label. For example, when Levi first began to open stores in India, the company reported running out of merchandise.

Direct exporting may require modifying products for another consumer market. For example, U.S. apparel firms may have difficulty selling garments sized for U.S. consumers in Asian markets where people are smaller, with a slight body build. Sensitivity to cultural differences is important, both in the products sold and how they may be marketed. For example, suggestive Calvin Klein advertisements would be poorly received in conservative Muslim countries.

Although U.S. textile and apparel exports have increased in recent years, these are still very small compared to the volume of imports. To attempt to improve the balance of trade (imports versus exports), the U.S. Department of Commerce has a program to assist U.S. firms in exporting. Staff in the Textile and Apparel Export Expansion Program[8] assist U.S. manufacturers to increase the amount of direct exporting for the sector. Staff coordinate the showing of U.S. merchandise at major trade fairs around the world. For example, merchandise from a number of U.S. apparel firms may be shipped to a trade fair in Europe. The U.S. booth or pavilion at the trade fair features the U.S. garments for viewing by retail buyers from several European countries (Figure 8–13). This provides exposure for the U.S. companies' lines and leads to ongoing business for the companies that exhibited.

Some of the major U.S. textile and apparel manufacturers associations sponsor efforts to assist domestic manufacturers in their export efforts. For example, the American Textile Manufacturers Institute has organized Texport, an export-promotion initiative to help U.S. textile producers export.

Success in exporting may vary greatly depending on **currency exchange rates.** When the dollar is weak relative to other currencies, it is easier to sell U.S. products than when the dollar is strong. When the dollar is weak, this means foreign currencies

---

[8]This program is part of the Office of Textiles and Apparel (referred to as OTEXA) in the U.S. Department of Commerce.

| Figure 8–12 | **Levi Strauss & Co. advertisement for the Dockers family of casual wear which ran in Japan's *Nikkei* newspaper (October 30, 1995, p. 20).** |

Source: Reprinted courtesy of Levi Strauss & Co.

are strong against the dollar and U.S. merchandise is a better value to foreign retailers and consumers.

Joint Ventures

International **joint ventures** are partnerships between a domestic company and a company in another country. Joint ventures are yet another way of entering an overseas market. In many countries, joint ventures are a way of penetrating import barriers. A few countries still limit the percentage of ownership a foreign manufacturer may own in that country. For example, until 1994, Indonesia did not permit an outside firm to own more than 49 percent of a firm located there.

Joint venture partnerships may take various forms. The outside investor firm often provides the technology, expertise, and much-needed capital. The host-country firm provides the local knowledge and marketing skills. For an apparel firm, for instance, the investor firm may provide the capital, the production equipment, the expertise to produce the products, and the brand name. The local firm may provide the workforce, at least some of the management, the knowledge of the country's market, and expertise to sell in that market.

A notable example is the U.S.-based firm of Esprit, which has established Esprit Far East in Asia with a partner in Hong Kong. The Asian partner owns half the com-

Figure 8–12

Continued

Figure 8–13

The Market Expansion Division of the Office of Textiles and Apparel (OTEXA) in the U.S. Department of Commerce coordinates exhibits for U.S. manufacturers who wish to participate in trade fairs in other countries. Exhibiting in a trade fair gives the company an opportunity to show its lines to potential buyers in other countries with hopes of developing long term relationships.

Source: Courtesy of Market Expansion Division of OTEXA. Reprinted courtesy of U.S. Department of Commerce.

pany and serves as its managing director. Esprit Far East is a major exporter of women's and children's casual apparel. Ninety-five percent of its merchandise is produced in Asia. Some of the merchandise is produced in Hong Kong, with the remainder contracted out to factories in other parts of Asia where wages are lower. The U.S. company, however, is involved in every operational step, from design to patterns, to fabric, to quota, to shipping arrangements. Most of the elements that constitute the garments are purchased in Asia—even zippers, labels, and buttons. Esprit Far East also operates its own shops in the region.

Sara Lee's hosiery business in the Asia-Pacific region was boosted by a 1994 joint venture with Shanghai Vocal, which markets sheer hosiery, opaque stockings, and socks under the Vocal brand in China (Sara Lee Corporation, 1995). This is a way for Sara Lee to penetrate the very large Chinese market, which accepts few U.S. apparel imports.

Direct Ownership

Another way to penetrate a foreign market is by a 100 percent investment in a foreign-based operation. This may be just an assembly or production facility, or it may be the ownership of a company complete with production and marketing. Some foreign countries, for economic reasons, offer investment incentives to U.S. companies to establish wholly owned subsidiaries within their borders. As in the case of most joint ventures, the foreign-owned facility provides employment to the host country's labor and often uses at least some local materials.

For example, DuPont Fibers owns more than 20 production facilities in other countries (DuPont, 1995). Plants are located in various regions to make DuPont's fibers available to textile customers there—the weavers, knitters, and carpet producers who make fabrics, carpeting, and other products to sell in local markets. DuPont's plants are located in these areas to serve regional markets and to avoid trade restraints and other costs associated with exporting. Many U.S. apparel firms are now establishing their own plants in Mexico to take advantage of NAFTA. In another case, Sara Lee Corporation has an extensive strategy to penetrate other markets. By buying firms in other countries, the company not only gets to sell the products of the firms purchased but also has almost instant access for its familiar U.S. brands to be sold through channels of distribution used by the acquired firm. For example, owning the European company that produces *Dim* products also gives Sara Lee access to distribution for Playtex, Bali, Hanes, and other company products in those markets.

The Importance of Preparing for Globalization

Globalization is a reality today. Companies and individuals can no longer think in terms of only a domestic market. Those who do will be left behind. Like it or not, technological advances have propelled us into an era in which globalization is a part of everyday business. Today, our business partners may be in another state or, just as readily, in another country. We can communicate with our overseas partners more quickly and more cheaply than we could have exchanges across state lines only 10 years ago. Forward-thinking companies are combining a global vision and new tech-

Source: Reprinted courtesy of QST Industries, Inc.

nology to position themselves to serve a world market, such as the company featured in Figure 8–14.

Individuals who plan to enter any segment of the fashion industry must prepare for this globalized era. This includes having an open mind toward our neighbors in other countries and keeping in mind that the "American way" is not the only acceptable way of doing things. It means respecting the different cultural backgrounds of our global neighbors. U.S. residents must improve on geography skills that have been sorely lacking. Staying abreast of news events, including *global* news events, is critical to being the kind of informed citizen needed to function in a global arena. And, finally, having foreign language skills is more valuable than ever before.

Readings

Globalization is a fact of life for today's fashion industry. Regardless of the segment of the industry in which one is involved, it is important to follow major trends related to trade and trade policies. The following articles highlight examples of important changes a person in the industry needs to follow in trade publications.

As 9802/807 production continues to account for a growing share of imports into the U.S. market, Miami has become the shipping hub. Increasingly, however, this form of contracting has consolidated around fewer and larger firms. This article features two of those large contracting firms.

A change in the country of origin rule now requires that garments be labeled according to the country where the items are assembled rather than where they are cut. This rule, which was designed to keep major Asian producers from sending production to low-wage neighboring countries (to later send the finished products to the United States), created uncertainty for many in the industry.

As companies participate increasingly in global activities, they must be aware of the homework and commitment required. The writer of this article gives tips to companies on how to improve chances of success.

807: Game for Big Players

by Georgia Lee

Despite the large volume of merchandise coming out of 807 programs, the business of 807 contracting has been consolidating around a handful of major players, echoing what has happened in much of the fashion industry.

Apparel exports and imports out of Miami amounted to $4.5 billion in 1994, with 90 percent coming from CBI countries, according to the Beacon Council, a Dade County economic development organization.

Back in the Eighties, as many as 100 small companies here jumped on the 807 bandwagon. While smaller firms still dot the landscape, the business is increasingly being dominated by 12 contractors with the capability to produce more than 5,000 dozen units per week, according to a spokesman for the council.

These companies have built businesses based on the ability to meet the increasing demands of major manufacturers and retailers. Quicker turn-around, varied goods, investment in automation and a knowledge of business in CBI countries are keys to successful partnerships in the Nineties.

Here, WWD profiles two of the survivors—companies that are not just getting by, but growing by adapting to a changing industry.

Bend 'n Stretch

With recent offshore acquisitions, heavy investment in automation and a new in-house customs brokerage department, contractor Bend 'N Stretch is broadening its capabilities for clients looking for a wide variety of services.

In the last six months, Bend 'N Stretch purchased Empire Atlantic, a woven bottoms factory in the Dominican Republic, as well as Carson Manufacturing, a woven shirt factory also in the Dominican Republic.

The acquisitions enable the company, which had produced only knit goods, to assemble each week 100,000 units of woven bottoms, primarily denim, and 48,000 units of woven tops a week.

In addition, Bend 'N Stretch produces 10,000 dozen units of knit goods per week.

"Our customers had been asking for woven goods," said Mano Howard, president. "We did this to better compete with Mexico and also in anticipation of CBI parity."

Bend 'N Stretch can now "make anything except underwear and suits," said Howard. The new production capabilities should bring the company to $38 million in annual sales for 1995, with growth of 25 percent projected for each of the next three years.

Such growth is also a result of the company's commitment to automation—a $1 million investment in each of the next three years.

By October, the company will have four Gerber cutters in its Miami facility, at a cost of about $250,000 per machine. Bend 'N Stretch will also upgrade its 14 Dominican Republic sewing plants with such equipment as electronic sewing machines within 18 months, a project few Miami companies have taken on.

"A lot of people here say they are fully automated but few really are, especially in offshore plants," said Howard. "Handcutting is less expensive short term, but the only way to eliminate the possibility of error is through automation—not just with the goal of flash and dash but with the idea of making the repetitive process work."

Bend 'N Stretch's clients include brand-name vendors and retailers. Private label programs for retailers make up 15 percent of business.

Although retailers are increasingly looking to produce private label goods through Miami-based 807 programs, Howard said these partnerships are the most challenging.

"Some retailers don't understand problems with mills and factories," he said.

Services offered by Bend 'N Stretch range from cutting to full packages that include everything from buying fabric and trim to cutting, sewing, washing, ticketing and delivery.

In the last year, the company has developed an in-house customs brokerage department. Using computers can shorten the customs clearance process—which can take as long as 10 days—to 24 hours.

Howard is a big proponent of CBI parity, describing it not only as a benefit for Miami but as a way to position North America as a worldwide competitor.

Argus International

When Roberto Bequillard founded Argus International Inc. four years ago, he brought with him the know-how that comes from 15 years experience as an industry consultant and an insider's knowledge of manufacturing in Central America.

Bequillard and partner Alfonzo Hernandez, both native Nicaraguans, saw the growth of 807 manufacturing during the Eighties, working in operations and strategy for Kurt Salmon Associates. To take advantage of the opportunity, they founded Argus International, which offers contract cutting services in Miami and a trio of sewing plants throughout Central America for 807 production. Bequillard is president, and Hernandez, chief executive officer.

"The game has changed tremendously over the past 10 years," said Bequillard. "You can't run two-table operations and expect to be successful. It takes the right level of investment, technology, information systems and professional management."

Since 1991, business has doubled each year to a projected $16 million for 1995. The 30,000-square-foot Miami cutting room, which will expand by 50 percent by the end of the year, processes 70,000 dozen panties, 75,000 dozen woven pants and 4,000 dozen shirts a week.

Its three factories are in El Salvador, Nicaragua and Jamaica. The El Salvador plant specializes in pantyhose, assembling 20,000 dozen a week.

"With so much consolidation in the industry, it's become a game of giants," said Bequillard. "Our strategy is to pursue them."

He added that the key to developing strategic partnerships lies in flexible manufacturing.

"Manufacturers are looking for shorter runs, and basic product is feeling the pinch of price competition," he said. "Big stores want to reduce order size and inventory. We have to be able to adapt quickly."

To date, 807 production has been restricted primarily to basic goods. Bequillard noted that "807 programs started out as a low-cost alternative for pioneers such as Levi, Arrow and Van Heusen."

"And, although companies' needs are changing, basics still dominate. The proximity of the Caribbean would make it attractive to do Quick Response fashion items with short seasons, but what is needed is more flexible sewing plants, more sophisticated management and equipment. It's been hard to find both high quality and high flexibility."

However, Bequillard sees a slow but definite evolution toward more fashion-forward merchandise, as fashion companies rely more heavily on 807 manufacturing. With plans to open six more sewing factories over the next five years, Argus will convert its older plants to flexible and modular systems capable of producing more fashion-forward garments, such as skirts and vests, in fabrics such as rayon.

Coming from a family of Nicaraguan manufacturers, Bequillard had an inside track on the workings of factories there. Argus also hires Kurt Salmon to help with plant startups, providing management tools and techniques.

"We are human resource-driven," he said. "We train our managers in eight-week sessions, and retain operators by being concerned with the social aspects of their needs."

Although he feels that his business is well established, Bequillard, like most manufacturers here, feels that passage of CBI parity can only unite the Northern hemisphere in global trade.

"The Americas need to be trading with each other," he said. "Importing from CBI countries offers five months from conception to delivery, as opposed to 10 months from the Orient. It makes sense to me as a U.S. businessman and as a Latin American doing business in the U.S."

Source: From Women's Wear Daily, June 27, 1995, p. 12. Reprinted by permission.

New Origin Rule Spells Confusion for Importers

by Carol Emert

New rules of origin for textile goods published in Tuesday's Federal Register have thrown importers into confusion, and could mean higher prices for some foreign-made apparel, according to importers interviewed.

Starting July 1, 1996, the origin of apparel and other textile goods will be conferred by the country where the products are assembled, rather than where they are cut. The biggest impact is expected to be felt in China, which assembles large quantities of apparel that is cut in nearby Hong Kong, Singapore and Taiwan.

That means that China, which has strict limits on its quota growth, will need more quota and cutting countries will have quota that they can't use. Most of China's quota categories already fill up quickly, leaving many importers wondering how they will fill all their orders.

An example of the quota discrepancy is in men's and women's cotton trousers. China is allowed to export two million dozen pairs to the U.S. each year, while Hong Kong has a quota of million dozen pairs, noted Jim Kilgore, customs and trade director for Levi Strauss Co., San Francisco.

"The major problem [with the new rule] is it creates a lot of uncertainty, which is not good for business," Kilgore said.

One option is to move assembly operations to cutting countries such as Hong Kong, but that would drive up retail prices because labor in Hong Kong and similar nations is much more expensive than in China, said Frank Kelly, vice-president of international trade and customs for Liz Claiborne Inc., Bergen, N.J.

Importers that assemble goods in more than one country were uncertain Tuesday what adjustments they would need to make in their manufacturing operations because Customs did not define which assembly practices it considers "important" or "most important," and which therefore designate origin.

In many cases, fabric may be formed, [garments] cut and partially assembled in China, with final assembly taking place in a second country. The Customs rule did not clarify which assembly processes would be considered "most important," and therefore whether the first or second country would be the country of origin. Such decisions must be made "on a case-by-case basis," the Federal Register notice said.

"Customs recognizes that this may appear to leave importers with a degree of uncertainty," the notice said. "However, Customs believes that a large proportion of multicountry processing is unnecessary from a manufacturing standpoint and thus is done more for quota-engineering purposes, that is, for the primary purpose of avoiding quantitative restraints imposed by international agreements."

Customs suggested that importers request case-by-case "binding rulings" from the agency on specific operations. However, requests for rulings cannot be submitted until October 5 and replies can take 120 days or longer.

"That means it could easily be five months from now" before businesses know whether they need to move their manufacturing operations, said Brenda Jacobs, a trade attorney with Powell, Goldstein, Frazer & Murphy in Washington.

Source: From DNR, *September 6, 1995, p. 3. Reprinted by permission.*

Going Global? Do Homework!

Going global—the new buzz word of the '90s. Expanding your customer base outside of the over-stored, product-saturated U.S. market is tempting, but is it for you?

There is no great mystery in selling overseas customers. All it takes is a little common sense, the right product and lots of patience. The same basic rule applies to selling overseas as selling domestically—customers look at price (value), product differentiation, delivery, etc.

The most common mistake that companies make in approaching export markets is that they don't take the time to understand who will be purchasing their products and why. Answering a few basic questions can save a tremendous amount of time and money.

Is your product (regardless of what it is) able to be identified as "American?" Does it matter to the consumer that the product is made in the United States or can it be sourced anywhere?

In apparel, themes that are associated with America include Western wear, surfwear, military, hunting and fishing, major league and college sports, motorcycle-related apparel, work clothing and outdoor (camping) products. Needless to say, basic jeans and T-shirts also are popular.

American products usually are perceived as being casual, fun and rugged, though not necessarily sophisticated. Leather products, outerwear and accessories are highly sought also.

If your product isn't "American," does it have enough price or product differentiation to stand out in the market (especially after adding duty and freight)?

Are your competitors exporting their products? The easiest way to identify a market is to see what similar lines are being successfully promoted overseas. If the answer is no, then you have to decide whether or not it pays to be the pioneer in your segment of the industry. If the answer is yes, take the time to examine your competitor's success:

- What type of distribution does your competitor have?
- How long has he been selling in the market?

- What segment of his line is popular? Does he make special items for overseas markets?
- How does he market his products overseas? What shows does he attend? Does he have a salesperson selling for him? Does he have an exclusive distributor? Does he advertise overseas? Is he included in fashion editorials in foreign publications?

Have you sold to foreign countries through "domestic" distributors? Another way of discovering whether or not a market is viable is to examine your own successes, regardless of how small, to determine if you can expand these sales through efforts of your own. Many companies fail to examine their sales to see where their products ultimately are sold.

Where to Start

Once you have answered these questions, how do you begin? The same way you would in the United States—you "see the people." Target and then visit the countries you want to sell. Shop the types of stores you sell in the United States, but make sure you look for specialty operations (stores and catalogs) that carry "related" American merchandise. Visit foreign trade shows, before you exhibit, and talk to the U.S. exhibitors about how they distribute their products. Check out competing foreign lines, particularly those who imitate "American" products, to help determine how you want to position yourself in the market.

If you've decided to export, be prepared to make a long-term commitment to the market. Ultimately, relationships will build your business overseas, as they do in the states. Communication, developing trust and following through are the keys to success in going global.

Michael Spiewak is president and chief executive officer of I. Spiewak & Sons Inc., New York, an outerwear manufacturer that exports 30% of its domestic production.

Source: From Apparel Industry Magazine, *July 1993, p. 74. Reprinted by permission.*

Chapter Review

Key Words and Concepts

Define, identify, or briefly explain the following:

Ad valorem tariffs
Bilateral agreements
Caribbean Basin Initiative (CBI)
Caribbean Basin Textile Access Program
Caribbean Parity
Commissionaires
Country-of-origin rules
Currency exchange rates
Cut, make, and trim (CMT)
Developing country
Duty
807/9802 production
807A production
European Union
Exports
Foreign exchange
First cost
Free trade
GATT
Global products
Globalization
Guaranteed access levels
Import penetration
Imports
Interconnected global economy

Joint ventures
Labor-intensive
Landed cost
Less developed countries
Letters of credit
Licensing
Lobby
More developed countries
Multifiber Arrangement (MFA)
North American Free Trade Agreement (NAFTA)
Offshore assembly
Outward processing trade (OPT)
Private label
Production package
Protectionism
Quota
Specification buying
Square meter equivalent (SME)
Tariff
Trade
Trade deficit
Transshipment
Upgrading
World Trade Organization (WTO)

Review Questions on Chapter Highlights

1. Why must we now think more about globalization than in the past?
2. Why has the traditional international trading policy of the United States been based on the principle that excessive import restrictions will lower our standard of living?
3. How has the United States departed from that principle for textile and apparel trade? What led to that departure?

4. Why have the less developed countries become major textile and apparel exporters?
5. What are the regulations that pertain to imports? Explain each one.
6. Do you feel it is appropriate to have quotas on products from some countries and not on others? Explain your answer.
7. Why do you think it is said that textile and apparel trade policies have developed more be-

cause of political reasons than economic reasons?

8. What types of domestic companies import and why?

9. Describe the various methods used by retailers to buy foreign merchandise.

10. What is private label production? How is it done, who does it, and why?

11. Name several major U.S. apparel firms who produce "offshore" and explain why they have their garments made in other countries rather than in the United States.

12. How have U.S. textile and apparel producers tried to draw attention to their domestically made products?

13. Are you a "protectionist" or a "free trader"? What are your reasons for your position?

14. In view of the production capacity and the creative talent in the U.S. fashion industry, why is our textile and apparel trade deficit so large?

15. Some of our textile and apparel producers have found ways to penetrate foreign markets. List those ways, explain each one, and give an example of a company using that strategy.

16. How do you think your future career will be affected by globalization? What are you doing to become prepared to function in a global fashion industry?

References

American Apparel Manufacturers Association. (1988). *Report of the Technical Advisory Committee.* Arlington, VA: Author.

American Apparel Manufacturers Association. (1996). *Focus: An economic profile of the apparel industry.* Arlington, VA: Author.

Asia's lure continues. (1988, February 24). *Women's Wear Daily.*

Dickerson, K. (1991). *Textiles and apparel in the international economy.* Upper Saddle River, NJ: Merrill/Prentice Hall.

Dickerson, K. (1995). *Textiles and apparel in the global economy* (2nd ed.). Upper Saddle River, NJ: Merrill/Prentice Hall.

DuPont. (1995). *Data bank.* Wilmington, DE: Author.

How they compare. (1995, November). *Textile Asia,* pp. 88–89.

Nike, Inc. (1994). *Annual report.* Beaverton, OR: Author.

O'Day, P. (1994, September). *The U.S. manufactured fiber market under NAFTA and the WTO.* Paper presented at the 33rd International Man-Made Fibres Congress, Dornbirn, Austria.

Odyssey begins major U.S. expansion plan. (1991, January). *Apparel Industry Magazine,* p. 10.

Sara Lee Corporation. (1995). *Annual Report.* Chicago: Author.

U.S. Department of Commerce, Office of Textiles and Apparel (OTEXA), online (http://www.ita.doc.gov/industry/textiles/oteka/html).

Suggested Bibliography

Balkwell, C., & Dickerson, K. (1994). Apparel production in the Caribbean: A classic case of the new international division of labor. *Clothing and Textiles Research Journal, 12*(3), 6–15.

Bonacich, E., Chang, L., Chinchilla, N., Hamilton, N., & Ong, P. (Eds.). (1994). *Global production: The apparel industry in the Pacific Rim.* Philadelphia: Temple University Press.

Caribbean/Latin American Action. (annual). *Caribbean Basin databook.* Washington, DC: Author.

Cline, W. (1990). *The future of world trade in textiles and apparel.* Washington, DC: Institute for International Economics.

Dickerson, K. (1991). *Textiles and apparel in the international economy.* Upper Saddle River, NJ: Merrill/Prentice Hall.

Dickerson, K. (1995). *Textiles and apparel in the global economy.* Upper Saddle River, NJ: Merrill/Prentice Hall.

Fairchild Publications. (1995, May 4). Made on the planet earth: The facts, the issues, the future of globalization (special "Infotracs" supplement in both *Women's Wear Daily* and *DNR*). New York: Author.

The GATT agreement. (1994, February). *Textile Horizons,* pp. 16–23.

GATT/WTO. (annual). *International trade.* Geneva, Switzerland: Author.

Grunwald, J., & Flamm, K. (1985). *The global factory.* Washington, DC: The Brookings Institution.

Hamilton, C. (Ed.) (1990). *Textile trade and the developing countries: Eliminating the Multifiber Arrangement in the 1990s.* Washington, DC: World Bank.

Khanna, S. (1991). *International trade in textiles.* New Delhi, India: SAGE.

Naisbitt, J. (1994). *Global paradox.* New York: Avon.

Naisbitt, J. (1996). *Eight Asian megatrends that are shaping our world.* Old Tappan, NJ: Simon & Schuster.

Ohmae, K. (1990). *The borderless world.* New York: Harper Business.

Onkvisit, S., & Shaw, J. (1993). *International marketing* (2nd ed.). Upper Saddle River, NJ: Merrill/Prentice Hall.

Porter, M. (1990). *Competitive advantage of nations.* New York: Free Press.

Textile Institute. (1991). *The globalization of textiles.* Manchester, UK: Author.

Textile Institute. (1994). *Globalization: Technological, economic, and environmental imperatives.* Manchester, UK: Author.

Toyne, B., Arpan, J., Barnett, A., Ricks, D., & Shimp, T. (1984). *The global textile industry.* London: George Allen & Unwin.

United States International Trade Commission. (annual). *U.S. imports of textiles and apparel under the Multifiber Arrangement.* Washington, DC: Author.

Trade Associations

American Apparel Manufacturers Association, 2500 Wilson Blvd., Suite 301, Arlington, VA 22201.

American Textile Manufacturers Institute, 1801 K St., N.W., Washington, DC 20006.

Camara Nacional de la Industria del Vestido (National Chamber of the Apparel Industry), Tolsa No. 54, 06040 Mexico, D.F.

Camara Nacional de la Industria Textil (National Chamber of the Textile Industry), Plinio No. 220, Col Polanco, 11510 Mexico, D.F.

Canadian Apparel Federation, 130 Slater St., Suite 605, Ottawa, Ontario K1P 6E2, Canada.

Canadian Textile Institute, 280 Albert St., Suite 502, Ottawa, Ontario K1P 5G8, Canada.

Caribbean/Latin American Action, 1211 Connecticut Ave., N.W., Suite 510, Washington, DC 20036.

The Textile Institute, 10 Blackfriars St., Manchester M3 5DR, U.K.

Trade Publications

Apparel International, The White House, 60 High St., Potters Bar, Herts EN6 5AB, U.K.

Canadian Apparel Manufacturer, 1 Pacifique, Saint Anne de Bellevue, Quebec H9X 1C5, Canada.

DNR, 7 W. 34 St., New York, NY 10001-8191.

International Business, 500 Mamaroneck Ave., Suite 314, Harrison, NY 10528.

International Textiles, 23 Bloomsbury Square, London, WCIA 2PJ, U.K.

Textile Asia, P.O. Box 185, California Tower, 11th Floor, 30-32 D'Aguilar St., Hong Kong.

Textile HiLights, American Textile Manufacturers Institute, 1801 K St., NW, Suite 900, Washington, DC 20006.

Textile Horizons, 23 Bloomsbury Square, London WCIA 2PJ, U.K.

The Wall Street Journal, 200 Liberty St., New York, NY 10281.

Women's Wear Daily, 7 W. 34 St., New York, NY 10001-8191.

World Clothing Manufacturer, 23 Bloomsbury Square, London WCIA 2PJ, U.K.

World Trade, 500 Newport Center Dr., 4th Floor, Newport Beach, CA 92660.

*F*ashion Producers in Other Countries

*P*roducers of fashion merchandise have proliferated in almost every country of the world and are competing for an ever-increasing share of U.S. consumer dollars. The race is not limited to countries with creative design talent and high-quality products; those with only sewing skills to offer have acquired the know-how to become important players in the world fashion market. In this, most have had the encouragement and support of their respective governments. Eager to promote their foreign trade, their governments have developed export incentive programs as well as help in staging international trade shows to attract buyers from around the world.

This chapter deals with the nature, locations, and fashion operations of the fashion producers in other countries that supply the United States with goods. The readings that follow the text focus on the operations of leading foreign exporting countries and companies.

Different Types of Producers in Other Countries

Fashion producers in other countries fall into three basic categories, each of which is discussed in greater detail further in this chapter.

- *Haute couture houses.* As used in the fashion business, an **haute couture** house refers to a firm whose designer (in French, **couturier** for male or **couturière** for female) semiannually creates and presents for sale a collection of original designs that are then duplicated for individual customers on a made-to-order basis. The important couture houses are located in Paris and Italy. Although men are important leaders in this part of the industry, the business focuses primarily on women's apparel.
- *Ready-to-wear fashion centers in other countries.* Whereas some ready-to- wear was being produced abroad before World War II, it was not until after the war that major ready-to-wear design and manufacturing centers in foreign countries developed and expanded. They did not achieve their present level of design creativity, importance, prestige, and fashion leadership until the 1970s. Paris is still considered a major fashion center in the world; however, there are now other countries whose manufacturers and products have gained recognition as fashion creators and influentials. Italy, England, Germany, and Japan are prominent among them. U.S. designers have risen in importance, relative to many of these, as one of our readings notes.
- *Contractors in other countries—offshore production.* The system of using independently owned outside production facilities—the **contracting system**—plays a major role in the production of ready-made clothing. Since contractors can be located

anywhere in the world where labor is abundant, wages are reasonable, and facilities, machinery, and transportation are available, today there are countless numbers of factories located in low-wage areas such as China, Indonesia, India, Sri Lanka, Vietnam, Mexico, and the Caribbean. They are used by both U.S. and foreign manufacturers and retailers to produce goods from the designs and specifications of those that hire them.

Paris Haute Couture

The fashion leadership of Europe, notably that of Paris, originally derived from a small group of fashion producers known as the haute couture. The founder of the haute couture is generally acknowledged to be Charles Frederick Worth, a brilliant young English designer with a flair for business who was appointed dressmaker to the Empress Eugenie. He established his house (and the Paris couture) in 1858, at about the same time that Elias Howe, in the United States, was busy perfecting his sewing machine.

European haute couture garments are completely different from those of the American firms that produce the high-priced ready-to-wear that is often incorrectly called "couture ready-to- wear." That description is, of course, a contradiction in terms, since *couture* implies clothes made to measure for individual customers, and *ready-to-wear* means garments produced in standard sizes without regard to the individual measurements of the persons who will eventually purchase them. Haute couture garments, moreover, are made of the finest and most luxurious fabrics, use superb needlework and a great deal of handwork, and command astronomical prices. Nothing produced in the United States bears the slightest resemblance to European couture.

Chambre Syndicale de la Couture Parisienne

Shortly after Worth opened his business, a trade association was formed to determine qualifications for a couture house and to deal with their common problems and interests. This was the **Chambre Syndicale de la Couture Parisienne**, founded in 1868. Membership was, and still is, limited to couturiers who met specified qualifications and agreed to abide by a set of rules governing dates of showings, copying, shipping dates, and so on. Membership is reviewed by a commission under the French Ministry of Industry (Fédération Francaise, 1995).

To qualify as an haute couture house today,[1] an establishment must do the following:

- Submit a formal written request for membership in the Chambre Syndicale;
- Employ at least 20 people for production in their own studios;
- Present a collection each year for Spring/Summer (in January) and Fall/Winter (in July) to the media;
- Create a collection of 50 ensembles, consisting of both day and evening designs (previously this was 75 ensembles);
- Present the collection to the clientele of the couture house in places that are arranged for that purpose (Fédération Française, 1995).

For the *newly created houses,* during a transitory period of two years, they must:

---

[1]Criteria were revised in 1992 to foster the development of young designers for a two-year period.

- Employ at least 10 production people instead of 20;
- Present a collection of 25 ensembles instead of 50 (Fédération Francaise, 1995).

The revised number of ensembles required of established houses and the less rigorous requirements for newly created houses reflect the increased financial burden of developing and presenting extensive collections.

Currently the official Haute Couture is composed of 18 houses. In the mid-1990s, the Haute Couture consisted of the houses shown in Table 9–1.

French origin is not a qualification for membership. For example, couturière Hanae Mori is Japanese by birth. Other famous Paris couture designers of the past were not French by birth. For example, Balenciaga was a Spaniard, Dessè was a Greek; Mainboucher was born in Chicago, and Molyneux was an Englishman, as was the founder of the French couture, Charles Frederick Worth.

Chambre Syndicale du Prêt-à-Porter

Originally the Chambre Syndicale limited its membership strictly to haute couture houses. As ready-to-wear operations by couture houses burgeoned in France, the Chambre Syndicale expanded its membership to include some designer-named ready-to-wear (**prêt-à-porter**) companies. Today, there is a subgroup called the *Chambre Syndicale du Prêt-à-Porter des Couturiers et des Créateurs de Mode.* These are described as "having a brand name image which is in a league with the couturiers" (Fédération Francaise, 1995, p. 3). Among these fashion designers who have been designated as *créateurs* are Chloé, Jean-Paul Gaultier, Karl Lagerfeld, Claude Montana, Dorothée Bis, Jacques Esterel, Thierry Mugler, Sonia Rykiel, Balenciaga, Kenzo, and Hermes. Also "held in equal esteem" are Valentino, Romeo Gigli, and Issey Miyake (Fédération Francaise, 1995).

In recent prêt-à-porter showings, foreign designers have been present in unprecedented numbers (more than 30 in 1995). U.S. retailers who shop the French showings have noted the French fashion industry is no longer really French. One store president remarked, "Paris is more important to me as an international city than as the home of French fashion" (Middleton, 1995, p. 18). A store owner noted the new internationalism has many advantages. "Having so many designers represented in Paris is not only more interesting, it's more convenient. . . . If all those people weren't in one place, we'd be running all over the world" (Middleton, 1995, p. 18). Although numerous sources believe France's fashion leadership has diminished, a faithful following still consider it the fashion mecca of the world, as noted by one U.S. store president: "Paris is the place where people go to seek and discover. It's where I go to find the concepts, the spirit, and the mood of the season. I don't go to Paris to decide if green is the color of the month. I go to soak up a gestalt. . . . Milan is more commercial, London is more of a party, but Paris is central to my creative process" (Middleton, 1995, p. 18). The mission of Donald Potard, president of Chambre Syndicale, is to "keep Paris king" (Weisman, 1995b, p. 26).

Activities of the Chambre Syndicale

The Chambre Syndicale provides many services for both ready-to-wear and couture members. It represents its members in their relations with the French government, arbitrates disputes, regulates uniform wage arrangements and working hours, coordinates the opening dates and times of the collections, issues admission cards for the openings to the press, and registers and copyrights the new designs of its members. Unlike the United States, France considers the copying of a registered design punishable by law.

| Table 9–1 | **Paris Haute Couture Directory (Chambre Syndicale de la Couture Parisienne)** |

PIERRE BALMAIN
    Chantal Dannaud-Vizioz*
    44,rue François-Ier
    75008 Paris
    Tel. 47-20-35-34

PIERRE CARDIN
    Monique Raimond*
    82, fg St-Honoré
    75008 Paris
    Tel. 42-66-92-25

CARVEN
    Sophie Favre*
    6, rond-point des Champs-Elysées
    75008 Paris
    Tel. 42-25-66-52

CHANEL
    Véronique Pérez*
    31, rue Cambon
    75001 Paris
    Tel. 42-86-28-00

CHRISTIAN DIOR
    Bernard Danillon and
    Véronique Bénard*
    30, avenue Montaigne
    75008 Paris
    Tel. 40-73-54-44

CHRISTIAN LACROIX
    Laure du Pavillon*
    73, fg St-Honoré
    75008 Paris
    Tel. 42-68-79-00

EMANUEL UNGARO
    Patricia Rivière and Pier
    Filippo Pieri*
    2, avenue Montaigne
    75008 Paris
    Tel. 42-23-61-94

NINA RICCI
    Vanessa Pringle and Sybille
    de Laforcade*
    39, avenue Montaigne
    75008 Paris
    Tel. 49-52-56-00

PACO RABANNE
    Alexandre Boulais*
    6, bd du Parc
    92523 Neuilly
    Tel. 40-88-45-45

TED LAPIDUS
    Elisabeth Caron-Gendry
    and Paule Ouahnoun*
    35,rue François Ier
    75008 Paris
    Tel. 44-43-49-50

GIVENCHY
    Sibylle de Saint Phalle and
    Véronique de Moussac*
    3, avenue George V
    75008 Paris
    Tel. 44-31-50-00

GUY LAROCHE
    Catherine Klein, Eric
    Fournier, and Jean-Paul
    Caboche*
    29, avenue Montaigne
    75008 Paris
    Tel. 40-69-68-00

HANAE MORI
    Max Michel Grand and
    Véronique Dupard*
    17/19, avenue Montaigne
    75008 Paris
    Tel. 47-23-52-03

JEAN-LOUIS SCHERRER
    Alexandra Campocasso
    and Valérie Lebérichel*
    51, avenue Montaigne
    75008 Paris
    Tel. 42-99-05-79

LACOANET HEMANT
    Kuki de Salvertes*
    24, rue Vieille du Temple
    75004 Paris
    Tel. 43-57-63-63

LOUIS FÉRAUD
    Guy Rambaldi, Ghislaine
    Brégé, and Astrid Girod*
    88, fg St-Honoré
    75008 Paris
    Tel. 47-42-18-12

TORRENTE
    Béatrice Manson*
    1, rond-point des
    Champs-Elysées
    75008 Paris
    Tel. 42-56-14-14

YVES SAINT LAURENT
    Gabrielle Buchaert*
    5, avenue Marceau
    75116 Paris
    Tel. 44-31-64-17

*attaché de presse
Source: From Chambre Syndicale de la Couture Parisienne. 1996 update provided through the kind assistance of Pascal Morand, Director General, Institut Français de la Mode in Paris.

Designer-Name Couture Houses

The operations of typical couture firms are fairly uniform. Each establishment is known as a *house,* because it operates in a residential building rather than in a commercial neighborhood. The head of the house is generally the chief designer (the **couturier** or **couturière**), who more often than not is the owner or co-owner. The house usually carries the name of its designer, and its reputation is essentially a one-man or one-woman affair. Occasionally, however, as in the case of Chanel and Dior, the well-known name is retained after the death of the founder, but a new hired designer takes

Figure 9–1

Famous haute couture designers

Cristobal Balenciaga de Eisequirre

Captain Edward Henry Molyneux

Gabrielle Chanel

Paul Poiret

Christian Dior

Mme Vionnet

Elsa Schiaparelli

over. For example, Gianco Ferre designs for the house of Dior and Karl Lagerfeld for Chanel.

There are usually fewer than 25 dressmaking establishments at any given time that are designated as haute couture, and of these, not all achieve worldwide fashion reputations. Among famous couturiers of the past are Paul Poiret, Vionnet, Schiaparelli, Balenciaga, Dior, Chanel, Molyneux, and, of course, Worth (Figure 9–1). Of those who show collections currently, the best known of all is probably Yves

St. Laurent. Among the Paris couturiers, many have made fashion history, each for some innovative contribution.

Semiannual Collections and Showings

Twice a year, the couturiers prepare major collections of sample garments. They work with the most luxurious and expensive materials, some of which cost more than $200 a yard, and trimmings of equivalent quality. Each sample is made to the exact measurements of the model who will show it. In addition, accessories are created for each garment shown—shoes, hats, gloves, perhaps a fur, and generous amounts of jewelry. The cost of preparing such a collection is extreme, as high as $4 million.

The heavy costs of preparing the collections plus the rise in the costs of labor and materials have skyrocketed the prices of the custom-made couture garments. They range from $2,000 to $3,000 for a blouse, $9,000 to $20,000 for a suit, and up to $100,000 for an embroidered evening gown ("Couture's Constant," 1990).

Until 1980 different types of customers, who came from all over the world to attend the openings, included the following:

- Wealthy private customers, to choose styles to be made to their order for their own wardrobes.
- Trade or commercial buyers (i.e., textile producers, designers, apparel manufacturers, retailers), to buy one or several models for the express purpose of having them copied exactly or adapted into ready-to-wear styles to be produced in their respective countries, or both.
- Pattern companies, to buy models or paper patterns to copy as commercial patterns for home sewers.
- Representatives of the press, to whom couture openings were and still are a source of fashion news.

Private customers and the press were admitted without charge, but most houses charged trade buyers a **caution fee** (French for deposit or surety). This right-to-see fee ranged in amount from as low as $500 in some houses to as high as $3,000. In others, the caution took the form of a minimum required purchase, generally one or two models. The caution was then deducted from the amount of whatever purchases were made; if no purchase was made or if purchases did not equal the caution figure, there was no refund.

Trade buyers were traditionally charged more for a garment than a private customer would be asked to pay. The explanation for the higher price was that retailers and producers were actually buying copying rights as well as the garment, whereas the private customer was simply buying for her own use.

Economics of Couture Today: Other Sources of Income

Today, the astronomical prices of couture garments have become prohibitive to all but a relatively few private clients. Trade buyers no longer attend the openings or buy couture clothing for copying. Even the private clientele—extremely wealthy women from all over the world, whose purchases accounted for a sizable majority of couture clothes at its peak—has eroded from 15,000 in the 1950s to about 2,000 (Fédération Francaise, 1995). Of these customers, about 20 percent are American and 40 percent are from Asia (Agins, 1995). Annual couture sales reach $50 million, but this is still a losing proposition for even the most successful houses. This amount involves only the sales of the custom-made apparel produced by the members of the Chambre.

Although the semiannual openings of haute couture houses continue to make world-wide fashion news, the sales of couture garments alone have always cost rather than made money for the houses. To survive, therefore, couture houses have expanded into other, more lucrative ventures, making capital of their names to give luster to more profitable activities, including the following:

- *House boutiques.* Most couture houses have established boutiques in or adjacent to their haute couture premises. These boutiques feature very high priced, high quality accessories such as handbags, lingerie, jewelry, and scarfs, all manufactured exclusively for the house by outside producers. Often the accessories thus offered are identical with those worn or carried by the models when the haute couture collections are shown. The merchandise that is carried in the boutiques is designed by the couturier or a member of his staff and bears the designer's prestigious label.

- *Prêt-à-porter.* Beginning in the 1960s, the decline in couture sales, combined with growing competition from an increasing number of talented ready-to-wear designers, both French and other Europeans, led haute couture houses strongly into the prêt-à-porter field. Although the ready-to-wear lines of the couture houses are designed by the couturiers, production arrangements vary greatly among the different houses, as do the locations of the manufacturing plants. For example, Ungaro's ready-to-wear is manufactured by an independently owned Italian company that also makes Valentino's ready-to-wear. Givenchy's ready-to-wear is produced under licensing agreements by ready-to-wear manufacturing companies in France. The house of Yves Saint Laurent has a separate ready-to-wear division, St. Laurent Rive Gauche, whose merchandise is produced in France by a manufacturing company in which it has a financial interest. In all cases, however, the sales volume of their prêt-à-porter lines is far greater than their couture sales and yields a far greater profit.

- *Franchised boutiques.* Retail boutiques bearing the name of a couturier and featuring his ready-to-wear merchandise made their appearance in the late 1960s and spread worldwide, opening a far-flung consumer market for couturier-designed ready-made clothing. Some of these "name" boutiques are owned and operated by the couture house itself; others are run by independently owned retail stores under a **franchising arrangement.** Under such an agreement, an independent retail distributor—that is, a franchisee—is given permission by a franchising parent company to sell the producer's product in a store that bears the name of the parent company. Especially noteworthy today are the franchising operations of Yves Saint Laurent. He launched his first Rive Gauche ready-to-wear boutique in Paris in 1966, and it met with such enormous success that he now has a worldwide chain of franchised Rive Gauche boutiques that carry only Saint Laurent's ready-to-wear. Some of these boutiques are free-standing stores; others are specialized shops within large stores that carry other merchandise as well. Among the couture designers who followed his lead into franchised boutiques are Dior, Valentino, and Givenchy, with his Nouvelle Boutiques.

- *Worldwide licensing agreements.* In addition to their ready-to-wear operations, major couture houses also license the use of their names on an enormous variety of products—lingerie, shoes, perfumes, stockings, bed linens, luggage, children's clothing, lower-priced women's and men's ready-to-wear, and anything else that is fair game for a well-known designer's name. As in all such **licensing agreements,** the designer sells different manufacturing companies the right to produce and market specific products bearing his or her name. Although the licensed products are supposedly designed, screened, or edited by the couturier whose name appears on them, it does not always work out that way. However, what does work in all cases is the lucrative royalty percentage of wholesale sales that the licensed manufacturer pays to the designer.

Despite frequent predictions of its imminent demise, Paris haute couture seems destined to remain active in the foreseeable future. Although Yves Saint Laurent, for example, claims that his couture garments, each of which sells for many thousands of dollars, are a "gift" to his clients, his business managers do not view his haute couture operation *per se* as a philanthropic venture. As Jean Szware, general director of Yves Saint Laurent, explained it: "As long as the losses align reasonably with the value gained in publicity and image, the couture is worth maintaining. But it is possible, in view of rising costs and declining sales, that a moment could arrive when this is no longer the case" ("Designer's Grumble", 1976). Since Yves Saint Laurent is still continuing haute couture clothing, it seems evident that "the moment" has not yet arrived.

At the very least, however, it seems apparent that haute couture garments have a new business function: to publicize the name of the house in order to provide a well-known, prestigious label for use in the house's other, more lucrative business activities. As Pierre Berge, president of Yves Saint Laurent, said, "No, we don't make a profit on the couture, but it's not a problem. It's our advertising budget" ("Voice of," 1984).

Italian Couture

Although other European countries such as Spain and England have at one time had haute couture houses, the only important couture outside Paris is that of Italy. The Italian couture was organized after World War II along lines similar to those of the Paris couture, but on a much smaller scale. Unlike the French, however, the Italian houses are not headquartered in a single city, but are located in three: Rome, Florence, and Milan. The Italian counterpart of the Chambre Syndicale de la Couture Parisienne is the *Camera Nazionale dell' Alta Moda Italiana*. Its membership of some 13 haute couture houses includes such famous designers as Valentino, Audre Lang, Mila Schon, Galitzine, and Gianco Ferre. Like the Paris couture, the Italian houses present two collections semiannually—in January for Spring/Summer and in July for Fall/Winter, one week prior to the Paris showings.

The experience of the Italian couture parallels that of the Paris houses: couture prices too high for all but a dwindling clientele of the ultrarich; no more trade buyers; and a largely unprofitable couture operation that is subsidized by income from ready-to-wear divisions, franchised boutiques, and licensing fees from perfumes, accessories, and other goods to which a designer's name adds prestige. However, industry experts see the Italians as much more proficient in marketing and knowing the customer than the French.

Ready-to-Wear Fashion Centers

Today, there is hardly a country in the world that does not produce some type of ready-to-wear fashion merchandise that is of interest to foreign buyers. Even though creative talent and productive capacity abound in this country, hundreds of U.S. textile producers, apparel firms, retailers, and fashion reporters travel regularly to Paris, Milan, London, Munich, Düsseldorf, and other, less important **fashion centers** in order to observe new trends or buy merchandise for copying or resale. European designers and their designs continue to hold a special cachet for fashion-forward consumers in the United States and in other countries where the elite can afford them. Table 9–2 illustrates a typical European show schedule for this segment of the industry.

French Ready-to-Wear Industry

The production of ready-to-wear has blossomed into a large, full-fledged industry in France. Contributing to its development were such designer-named producing firms as Sonya Rykiel, Daniel Hechter, Dorothée Bis, Cacherel, and Emanuelle Khanh, many of whom had their beginnings as owner-operated retail boutiques. Such designers began to attract the attention of foreign buyers and the press by developing styles and looks of their own, which were quite different and lower in price than the couture garments.

Many other designer-named ready-to-wear firms have since joined their ranks. Among them are Claude Montana, Angelo Tarlazzi, Thierry Mugler, Jean-Paul Gaultier, Rochas, and Azzadine Alaia. As was mentioned earlier, many of these ready-to-wear designers have been designated as *créateurs* by the Chambre Syndicale and have been admitted as members.

Size of the Industry

The ready-to-wear operations of the Paris couture houses and of the designer-named firms that are members of the Chambre represent only a small part of the industry, in both number of firms and value of output. The **Fédération Française du Prêt à Porter Féminin,** the trade association that represents ready-to-wear producers other than those who belong to the Chambre Syndicale, reports a membership of some 1,200 companies.

Like the industry in most of the more developed countries, the French ready-to-wear industry has a large portion of its garments produced outside the country where labor is less costly. An estimated 50 percent of French garments are produced outside the country in low-wage countries of North Africa, Asia, and, increasingly, in the former communist countries in Central and Eastern Europe. Nevertheless, French designers have provided the creative input for the lines produced in these other areas.

Innovative fashions and mass production have combined to build a ready-to-wear industry that is a very important resource to the American fashion business. Although our dollar purchases of French ready-to-wear amount to only a small percentage of our total imports, our adaptations and copies of their styles and ideas have enormous impact.

Semiannual Collections and Trade Showings

Unlike the American industry, French ready-to-wear producers prepare and present only two seasonal collections a year, as do all foreign-fashion manufacturers. Fall/Winter collections are shown in March, and Spring/Summer collections are presented in October. In its efforts to court foreign buyers, the French ready-to-wear industry stages week-long semiannual **trade shows** in Paris, which are attended by thousands of fashion professionals ("lookers," buyers, and fashion reporters) from all over the world.

Semiannual prêt-à-porter shows, sponsored and coordinated by the Chambre Syndicale, present the ready-to-wear collections of the couturiers and créateurs. These are held in a central Paris area known as Les Halles—which has developed as a cultural center. A 1995 U.S. film, *Prêt-à-porter*, depicted the colorful activities associated with one of these shows.

Table 9–2	This schedule illustrates typical European ready-to-wear show venues for a season.

EUROPE READY-TO-WEAR SHOW SCHEDULES LISTED

MILAN—The schedules for the European designer fall ready-to-wear collections to be shown next month in Milan, London and Paris are as follows.

MILAN
Saturday, March 3
9:30 a.m.	Andrea Sargeant
10:30 a.m.	x Dieci by Luca Coelli
11:30 a.m.	Paola Marzotto
12:30 p.m.	Marina Spadafora
2 p.m.	Harriet Selling
3 p.m.	Massimo Monteforte
4 p.m.	Maurizio Galante
5 p.m.	Emilio Cavallini
6 p.m.	Alma
7 p.m.	Enrica Massei
9 p.m.	Mariella Burani

Sunday, March 4
9 a.m.	Sanlorenzo
10 a.m.	Emporio Armani
11 a.m.	Complice
noon	Chiara Boni
2 p.m.	Max Mara
3 p.m.	Rocco Barocco
4 p.m.	Mario Valentino
5:15 p.m.	Laura Biagiotti
7 p.m.	Gianni Versace

Monday, March 5
9:30 a.m.	Krizia
11 a.m.	Mila Schon
noon	Missoni
1 p.m.	Gianmarco Venturi
2:30 p.m.	Byblos
3:30 p.m.	Salvatore Ferragamo
4:30 p.m.	Erreuno
5:30 p.m.	Blumarine

Tuesday, March 6
9:30 a.m.	Callaghan
10:30 a.m.	Genny
11:30 a.m.	Gianna Cassoli
12:30 p.m.	Basile
2 p.m.	Gherardini
3 p.m.	Sportmax
4 p.m.	Alberta Ferretti
5:30 p.m.	Gianfranco Ferre
7:30 p.m.	Fendi
9:00 p.m.	Filippo Alpi

Wednesday, March 7
9:30 a.m.	Verri
10:30 a.m.	Luciano Soprani
11:30 a.m.	Trussardi
12:30 p.m.	Moschino
2 p.m.	Bill Kaiserman
3 p.m.	Tivioli
4 p.m.	Maurizio Baldassari
5 p.m.	Giorgio Armani
6 p.m.	Giorgio Correggiari

LONDON
Friday, March 9
3:30 p.m.	Caroline Charles
4:45 p.m.	Edina Ronay
6:15 p.m.	Murray Arbeid
7 p.m.	Bodymap

Saturday, March 10
10 a.m.	Red or Dead
Noon	Betty Jackson
12:45 p.m.	Zandra Rhodes
3 p.m.	Workers for Freedom
5 p.m.	Joe Casely-Hayford
6:30 p.m.	Nick Coleman

Sunday, March 11
10 a.m.	Paul Costelloe
Noon	Jean Muir
1:30 p.m.	Bruce Oldfield
3 p.m.	Arabella Pollen
4 p.m.	Ghost

Monday, March 12
10:15 a.m.	Tomasz Starzewski/ Shirin Cashmere
11:30 a.m.	Pam Hogg
5 p.m.	Michiko Koshino
6:30 p.m.	Vivienne Westwood

PARIS
Tuesday, March 13
9:30 a.m.	Claude Barthelemy
11 a.m.	Hiroko Koshino
Noon	Krystyna Bukowska
1 p.m.	Yuki Torii
1:30 p.m.	Corinne Cobson
2:30 p.m.	Kimijima
3:30 p.m.	Emmanuelle Khanh
5 p.m.	Paco Rabanne
6:30 p.m.	Etienne Brunel
7:30 p.m.	Olivier Guillemin

Wednesday, March 14
9:30 a.m.	Barbara Bui
10:30 a.m.	Doby Broda
11:30 a.m.	Elisabeth De Senneville
12:30 p.m.	John Galliano
2:30 p.m.	Junko Shimada
3:30 p.m.	Lolita Lempicka
5 p.m.	Olivier Lapidus
6:30 p.m.	Chantal Thomass

Thursday, March 15
9:30 a.m.	Daniel Hechter
10:30 a.m.	Comme Des Garcons
11:30 a.m.	Angelo Tarlazzi
1 p.m.	Helmut Lang
2:30 p.m.	Yohji Yamamoto
3:30 p.m.	Cerruti
5 p.m.	Jean-Charles de Castelbajac
6:30 p.m.	Thierry Mugler

Friday, March 16
9 a.m.	Givenchy
10 a.m.	Bernard Perris
11:15 a.m.	Karl Lagerfeld

Table 9–2	*(continued)*

12:30 p.m.	Popy Moreni	7 p.m.	Lanvin
2 p.m.	Zucca	8 p.m.	Claude Petin
3 p.m.	Chloe	**Tuesday, March 20**	
4 p.m.	Anne-Marie Beretta	9:30 a.m.	Torrente
5 p.m.	Jean-Paul Gaultier	10:30 a.m.	Guy Laroche
Saturday, March 17		11:30 a.m.	Emanuel Ungaro
9:30 a.m.	Guy Paulin for Tiktiner	2 p.m.	Frederic Castet
10:30 a.m.	Odile Lancon	3:30 p.m.	Hermes
2 p.m.	Gres	4:30 p.m.	Lecoanet Hemant
3:30 p.m.	Balenciaga	5:30 p.m.	Jacqueline De Ribes
5 p.m.	Issey Miyake	7 p.m.	Junko Koshino
6:30 p.m.	Dorothée Bis	9 p.m.	Marithe and Francois Girbaud
8:30 p.m.	Romeo Gigli	**Wednesday, March 21**	
Sunday, March 18		11 a.m.	Yves Saint Laurent
10 a.m.	Matsuda	1 p.m.	Michel Klein
11 a.m.	Enrico Coveri	**By Invitation**	
12:30 p.m.	Martine Sitbon	Christian Lacroix	
2 p.m.	Agnes B	Claude Montana	
3:30 p.m.	I.W.S. Woolmark	Kenzo	
4:30 p.m.	Kansai Yamamoto	**By Appointment**	
6 p.m.	Sonia Rykiel	Pierre Balmain	
8 p.m.	Katherine Hamnett	Carven	
Monday, March 19		Jacques Esterel	
9:30 a.m.	Jean-Louis Scherrer	Louis Feraud	
10:30 a.m.	Chanel	Nina Ricci	
Noon	Hanae Mori	Pierre Cardin	
2:30 p.m.	Christian Dior	Ted Lapidus	
4 p.m.	Jin Abe	Daniel Olivier Favre	
5:30 p.m.	Valentino		

The mass-producing ready-to-wear companies stage their own semiannual shows—the Salon International du Prêt-à-Porter Féminin in the Porte de Versailles, an exhibition building larger than the New York Javits Center. Some 1,300 apparel firms, most but not all French, exhibit their seasonal lines there. In 1989, the Fédération Française du Prêt-à-Porter Féminin introduced a secondary and smaller seasonal show called the Collection Privées.

The French menswear industry also stages its own semiannual seasonal trade shows in the Porte de Versailles. Held in February and September, these are run in conjunction with producers of knitwear and children's clothes.

The Fédération Française du Prêt-à-Porter also organizes French participation in international trade shows held in New York, Düsseldorf, Milan, Tokyo, Munich, and Stockholm. It also maintains a permanent office in New York City. This is the French Fashion and Textile Center, whose major purpose is to promote French ready-to-wear in the United States. It represents all branches of the industry except couture and couture ready-to-wear. Additionally, many of the leading couture houses and larger designer-name ready-to-wear companies have established their own offices in New York, along with sales representation at regional apparel marts.

Summing up, it is obvious that the French are not waiting for fashion buyers to come knocking at their doors. They participate in international trade shows, they franchise designer-name ready-to-wear boutiques worldwide, they have global licensing arrangements, and they maintain individual and group sales offices in the United States.

Italy

Today, the most serious challenger to the fashion leadership of Paris is Italy, which has been attracting foreign fashion buyers since the 1960s. Italy's strengths and competitive advantages derive from the superior quality and design of its fabrics, its workmanship, and the innovative, sophisticated styling of its knitwear, sportswear, and accessories—notably leather shoes and handbags. It has also developed a reputation for its interesting and *avant garde* styling of men's apparel and accessories.

The Italian ready-to-wear industry developed simultaneously with its couture industry and did not depend on Italian couturiers for fashion leadership and design talent. As a result, it started exporting earlier. Today the well-being of the industry relies heavily on its foreign sales efforts, in which it receives encouragement and support from the Italian government.

Semiannual Collections and Trade Shows

When Italy first emerged as a major fashion center, foreign trade buyers went to Florence, where the semiannual collections and showings of ready-to-wear were presented in the luxurious and elegant setting of the Pitti Palace. In the mid-1970s, however, ready-to-wear firms in the north of Italy decided to present their own showings in Milan. The initial handful of firms, among them Basile, Callaghan, Missoni, and Caumont, has grown into an avalanche, and today, Milan has become the major staging ground for Italian ready-to-wear presentations. In fact, many of the Florence ready-to-wear firms have defected to the north and show in both Milan and Florence. Their semiannual showings take place prior to the prêt-à-porter openings in Paris, in early March for Fall/Winter and early October for Spring/Summer. The week-long Milan shows include not only those staged by the country's top ready-to-wear designers, but also Modit, an exhibition at which other countries' apparel manufacturers are invited to show.

Also, like their French counterparts, the Italian industry participates in trade shows in many other countries—among them the New York Pret showings held in early fall and spring. There are many other trade presentations such as Uomo Modo, the semiannual show of menswear manufacturers; an Italian shoe fair staged annually in March in Bologna; the famous textile show, Ideacomo, held in May at Lake Como; and the Mipel accessories show, held in Milan, each January and June. These are but a few of the many trade exhibits staged in Italy.

Leading Designers

Along with those mentioned above, some of the best-known ready-to-wear designer companies in Italy are Krizia, Gianni Versace, Soprani, Complice, Jenny, Biagotti, and Giorgio Armani. All of these have achieved worldwide reputations for their trendsetting fashions. Consider also the names of Gucci and Ferragamo, internationally known for leather products; and Fendi, renowned for innovative fur fashions. Add these names to those mentioned previously in this section and it becomes clear that the fashion story, Italian style, represents serious competition to Paris as the prime source of fashion leadership.

Italy's Fashion Industry

After tourism, the fashion industry is Italy's largest national industry. There are more than twice as many apparel and accessory firms in Italy as there are in France. A significant portion of their annual output is exported, with their largest customers being high income countries of Europe, Asia, and North America. Italian firms, like those in other high-wage countries, are sending many of their garments elsewhere for production. However, Italian producers have been somewhat less inclined to do this than their European counterparts.

It is interesting to note that, because Italian workmanship and fabrics are, on the whole, better and cheaper than they are in France, many French designers are steady customers of Italy. Besides the silks from Como and woolens from Biella, large numbers of sweaters, leather garments, and accessories that come from Italy are sold under French labels.

Like their French counterparts, many Italian companies have established retail boutiques around the world that feature their ready-to-wear. Some of these "name" boutiques are owned and operated by the company itself. Others are owned and operated by franchised retailers. Particularly notable is the worldwide chain of the franchised stores of Benetton. And also like their French counterparts, many of the Italian companies are involved in worldwide licensing agreements. A case in point is the very large Gruppo GFT Italian clothing manufacturer that has put Armani, Valentino, Ungaro, Dior, and other licensed designer labels into closets from Melbourne to Manhattan.

London

The British have long been famous for their tweeds and their men's custom tailoring, but it was not until after World War II that reverberations from their ready-to-wear industry were heard around the fashion world. Their couture effort, which was keyed to the conservative tastes of royalty and the peerage, did not succeed and is nonexistent today.

Fashion Leadership in the 1960s

The British ready-to-wear industry, unlike their couture, did flourish and made a major impact on both men's and women's fashions in the 1960s. The name *Carnaby Street* became synonymous with colorful, uninhibited, *avant garde* clothes for both sexes. The London streets in that area were filled with boutiques carrying unconventional, trendy fashions by new young designers. Their miniskirted dresses, reflecting the free, young spirit of the decade, sent feminine hemlines soaring to incredible highs all over the world. Especially notable was the work of Mary Quant, a young English designer who understood what many other designers around the world were quite late in recognizing: that the young were setting fashions on their own, and that, instead of the young following their elders, the mature folk were following the young.

Classics in the 1970s

In the 1970s, the mood of the "swinging sixties" changed, as did the ready-to-wear offerings of that period. English fashion houses focused on their traditional and classic high-quality woolen fabrics in men's tailored clothing, the excellent workmanship of their rainwear (notably Aquascutum and Burberry), and the fine cotton products of Liberty of London and Laura Ashley.

Revitalization in the 1980s

Led by Jean Muir, Zandra Rhodes, and Ossie Clark, the British fashion industry was revitalized in the 1980s. All kinds of young, highly individualized, and even outrageous fashion statements began coming out of England. Today, the new and exciting exists side by side with the traditional, conservative, and classic clothing for which England has always been known. There could not be anything more radically different from the romantic cotton prints of Laura Ashley than the industrial cottons and futuristic silks of Katherine Hamnett, the bold prints of Betty Jackson, or the unconventional, inventive styles of such other trendsetting firms as Wendy Dagworthy, Rifat Ozbek, Body Map, Jasper Conran, and Vivienne Westwood, for example. These and other new designer talents are leading the British fashion parade today (Figure 9–2).

Even the retail boutiques in London are as inventive as the designers and the styles seen on the streets. For example, there is a shop called the Warehouse, where one can buy white clothes and dye them on the spot, with the dye and washing machines provided for the customer on the premises. In a shop called Spring, clothes are sold Chinese-take-out style.

Size of the Industry

The British fashions have captured the hearts of both the young and the rebellious and their fashion-conscious elders. What is equally important is that they have also captured the dollars (or other currency) of buyers from outside the country. Representatives of many countries attend the semiannual trade showings in March and October.

According to the British Apparel and Textile Confederation (1995), industry output continues at a modest, but respectable, rate of growth. Overall wholesale figures for apparel in 1994 was $4.9 billion and $5.2 billion for textiles. Approximately 400,000 individuals are employed in the industry. In recent years, exports have grown and imports have slowed down. In 1993, textile and apparel imports were valued at $5.9 billion and exports at $3.4 billion, leaving a negative trade deficit of $2.5 billion.

Although British textile and apparel exports to other European Union countries are three times the level of those to non-EU markets, the latter are growing at a very healthy rate (11 to 16 percent annual growth in recent years). Healthy growth of exports to other markets may be attributed to efforts to promote the industry and its products outside the country and to recent favorable currency exchange rates that made British goods even more attractive.

International Shows in West Germany

Germany's apparel industry has long been known for its superior knitting technology and its well-made, moderately priced "middle of the road" clothing. It is only in recent years that a few German companies have begun to make their names and design ideas increasingly felt in the U.S. market. Two companies, Escada and Mondi, are leading their emerging fashion parade, and a number of other companies have begun to follow their lead. Among them is Hugo Boss, who produces a line of fashion-forward clothing for younger men. It is interesting to note that most of these have set up their own retail boutiques in the United States and in Europe.

The country's impact on the fashion world, however, arises from a different source. Germany is famous for the international textile and apparel fashion fairs that are staged there and are probably the most impressive events of their kind in the world. For example, in Frankfurt there is a huge textile trade show, **Interstoff,** sponsored by Messe Frankfurt, at which thousands of fabric producers from many different countries exhibit

Figure 9–2

**London Fashion
Week**

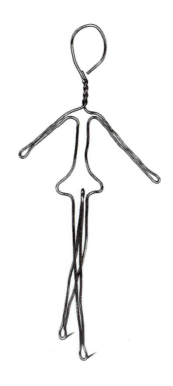

LONDON FASHION WEEK

11-14 March 1995. The London Designers Exhibition and

the catwalk shows for Autumn/Winter '95 will be held at

The Natural History Museum, Cromwell Road, London SW7.

For further information please contact: British Fashion Council 5 Portland Place
London W1N 3AA Tel: (+44) 171 636 7788. Fax: (+44) 171 636 7515.

SPONSORED BY

Source: British Fashion Council. Reprinted courtesy of British Fashion Council.

their wares. Apparel producers from every part of the world attend this show, which now occurs as three specialized shows per season (Weisman, 1995a).

In **Düsseldorf** each spring and fall, there is an international women's show, **IGEDO**, reported to draw some 3,000 producers from 41 countries to exhibit merchandise to a worldwide audience of more than 50,000 potential buyers (Figure 9–3).

Each February and August, Cologne offers a week-long International Men's Fashion Week that attracts some 30,000 buyers to see the lines of an estimated 1,000 exhibitors from 27 countries.

In addition to these, there is an annual International Footwear Fair held in Düsseldorf every March; a semiannual international children's fair in Cologne; and semiannual swimwear and underwear shows in Düsseldorf, which are the only trade fairs of their type in the world. And there are still others. Among them is the Overseas Export Fair, held in Berlin every September.

Figure 9–3
Publicity on the IGEDO show held in Düsseldorf, Germany.

Germany's apparel industry may not be fashion leaders as yet, but its international trade fairs are a major source for new fabric and fashion ideas.

Like other advanced industrialized countries in Europe, the German industry has a large portion of its garments made in lower-wage countries. Turkey has been a popular site for German firms.

Japan

In the not-too-distant past, a label reading "Made in Japan" was usually associated with cheap and poorly made products that were carried in low-priced stores in the United States. Today, however, the Japanese fashion industry has been transformed. This is partly the result of the postwar aid of the United States and partly the fruit of the Japanese determination to become a major industrial democracy. In the process, that country has become an important fashion center for medium and high priced goods, thanks to the presence of many bright, talented designers and to the quality of Japanese products.

In the 1960s and 1970s, Japan began to be recognized as a significant player in the world of high fashion when designers such as Hanae Mori, Kenzo Takada, Kansai Yamamoto, and Issey Miyake first showed their lines at the Paris prêt-à-porter showings. They became a design sensation overnight, and Tokyo was hailed by buyers and the press as the "worldwide fashion capitol" in coming decades. Although Japan continues to play an important role in the global fashion industry, the country's emphasis on other high technology industries may have dimmed the prospects for the fashion industry to be the premier global fashion center once predicted.

High wages in Japan have also affected the fashion industry profoundly. In recent surveys of textile industry wages, Japan has had the highest in the world (Werner International, 1995). Because of these high wages, a very large portion of Japan's garment production occurs in other Asian countries with lower wages. First, Japanese companies transferred production to countries such as South Korea and Taiwan. Now, however, as the wages in those countries have risen, Japan's apparel production has shifted to other locations where wages remain low. These include China, Indonesia, Vietnam, and other less developed Asian countries.

As in the European and North American industries, the creative and marketing aspects of the fashion industry still occur in the home country of the manufacturing firms, i.e., in Japan. Although garment production may occur in neighboring countries, the Japanese quality standards are still evident in products. Because Japan's consumers are very demanding in terms of product quality, this results in products attractive to consumers elsewhere. In his *Competitive Advantage of Nations,* Porter (1990) found that having demanding buyers in an industry's home market forces local firms to meet high standards of product quality, creating a competitive advantage for a country's industry.

Canada

In recent decades, a number of Canadian apparel manufacturers have developed high quality, high fashion lines that have been quite successful in the U.S. market. The sophisticated European styling and quality of Canadian apparel has created a special niche for Canadian producers, whose customers look for distinctive merchandise other than the sameness that characterizes mass-market production. Canadian apparel firms have become experts at producing small runs, making them ideal producers of "limited edition" apparel. Because Canada's population is one-tenth that of the United States and many apparel firms are small, the Canadian Apparel Federation (1995) notes that Canadian firms are well-suited to produce for this smaller, high fashion niche.

Although the United States and Canada have long been important trade partners, two free trade agreements encouraged this commerce even more. First, a Canada-U.S. agreement led to a 10-year phase-out of tariffs on products traded between the two countries. The United States and Canada never had quotas on each other's products because the two countries are at similar stages of development. Second, the North American Free Trade Agreement (NAFTA) fostered trade even more and brought Mexico into the partnership.

The United States is the major destination of Canada's textile and apparel exports. Both countries have increased trade with each other in these sectors since the signing of the trade agreements. Between 1990 and 1994, Canadian apparel exports to the United States nearly quadrupled, increasing from $275.6 million to $944.5 million (Canadian Apparel Federation, 1995).

The **Canadian Apparel Federation (CAF)** is the national association for apparel manufacturers, contractors, and designers. It represents the industry in consultations with the federal government on trade, legislative, and regulatory matters. The CAF provides a variety of assistance to Canadian manufacturers, including marketing and trade expertise, a number of information services, and other support as needed. The Federation can assist in matching the interests of Canadian and U.S. firms (Figure 9–4). The Canadian Textile Institute (CTI) plays a similar role in working with the textile industry.

The Canadian apparel industry requires distinctive fabrics for the types of high fashion apparel being produced by many of its firms. However, like some apparel firms in the United States, Canadian apparel producers feel the domestic textile industry is often unwilling to make the small production runs necessary for more exclusive garments. Yet, when Canadian apparel firms import fabrics from elsewhere, they must pay tariffs on those fabrics. Tariffs raise apparel firms' costs of doing business and make their products less competitive in the marketplace, especially the U.S. market. Because U.S. apparel wages are less than those in Canada, Canadian firms already are operating at a competitive disadvantage. The tariffs, which apparel firms believe are charged to protect the Canadian textile industry from imports, create further disadvantages.

The apparel industry is one of few Canadian manufacturing sectors that can claim it has companies in every province and territory in Canada. However, more than half the total Canadian apparel industry is located in Quebec. Thus, Quebec's continued interest in being a separate country, an effort that barely failed in 1995, has potentially serious implications for the Canadian apparel industry. Separatists vowed to continue their efforts. Considering the close 1995 vote, it is feasible that at some point there will be four countries, rather than three, in North America.

Fashion Producers in Lower-Wage Countries

As was explained in Chapter 5, many ready-to-wear apparel firms do not handle the entire garment production process in company-owned factories. Instead, they contract out some or all of their production to independently owned outside facilities that produce according to given specifications. Many of these contracting

Figure 9–4

The Canadian Apparel Federation provides many services to manufacturers and potential buyers.

Source: Canadian Apparel Federation. Reprinted courtesy of Canadian Apparel Federation.

Figure 9–5

May Department Stores offices in Asia.

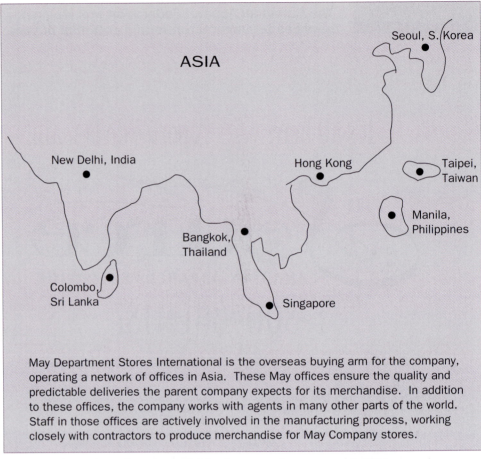

ASIA

Seoul, S. Korea

New Delhi, India

Hong Kong

Taipei, Taiwan

Manila, Philippines

Bangkok, Thailand

Colombo, Sri Lanka

Singapore

May Department Stores International is the overseas buying arm for the company, operating a network of offices in Asia. These May offices ensure the quality and predictable deliveries the parent company expects for its merchandise. In addition to these offices, the company works with agents in many other parts of the world. Staff in those offices are actively involved in the manufacturing process, working closely with contractors to produce merchandise for May Company stores.

Source: Based on author's discussions with May Department Stores personnel, 1995.

operations occur in other countries. In a less common scenario, apparel firms may *own* factories in other countries where wages are lower.

Beginning in the 1970s, apparel firms in the more developed countries of North America and Europe discovered a strategy for competing with low-cost imports coming into their markets. They began to move their own production to countries where wages were lower than in their home countries. Apparel firms soon developed working relationships with factories in Asia, where ready-to-wear could be produced at a fraction of domestic prices. Today, merchandise produced by **overseas contractors** in low-wage countries around the world constitutes the largest percentage of U.S. imports. The product development and marketing activities have remained in the firm's home country.

Both apparel firms and retailers use overseas contractors in low-wage countries. Many retailers are using this strategy to contract directly with firms in other countries to produce their private label lines, *bypassing* domestic apparel manufacturing firms. When retailers use this approach, it means they are becoming somewhat like apparel manufacturers themselves, rather than buying from established apparel firms. In Figure 9–5, for example, we see that the May Department Stores operates offices throughout Asia. Both apparel firms and retailers use overseas contractors for the same reason: to reduce the price of garments.

| Table 9–3 | **Trends in U.S. Apparel Imports by Major Source (Millions of square meters)** |

Country Source	1984		1995		Change In	
					Meters	Percent
Big Four						
People's Republic of China	421		862		441	105%
Hong Kong	848		821		−27	−3%
Taiwan	808		598		−210	−26%
S. Korea	635		343		−292	−46%
Total	2,712	63%	2,624	28%	−88	−3%
ASEAN						
Philippines	197		465		268	136%
Indonesia	108		310		202	187%
Thailand	89		244		155	174%
Singapore	107		84		−23	−21%
Malaysia	54		152		98	181%
Total	555	13%	1,255	14%	700	126%
Other Far East						
Bangladesh	20		519		499	2,495%
India	112		258		146	130%
Sri Lanka	91		281		190	209%
Pakistan	53		154		101	191%
Turkey	13		178		165	1,269%
Total	289	7%	1,390	15%	929	381%
CBI						
Dominican Republic	79		632		553	700%
Costa Rica	28		297		269	961%
Jamaica	8		225		217	2,713%
Guatemala	2		185		183	9,150%
Honduras	9		329		320	3,556%
El Salvador	2		239		237	11,850%
Other CBI	80		71		−9	−11%
Total	208	5%	1,978	21%	1,770	851%
Mexico	72	2%	774	8%	702	975%
All other countries	456	10%	1,234	13%	778	171%
TOTAL APPAREL	4,292	100%	9,255	100%	4,963	116%

Source: From *FOCUS: Economic Profile of the Apparel Industry* (p. 5) by American Apparel Manufacturers Association, 1996, Arlington, VA: Author. Reprinted by permission.

As we can see in Table 9–3, many less developed countries are important sources of U.S. imports. Although European countries provide fashion influence, the bulk of U.S. apparel imports come from elsewhere.

Lower Labor Costs

Apparel production is still one of the most labor-intensive and least automated industries. Producing three-dimensional garments from two-dimensional limp fabrics requires a great deal of hand manipulation. Thus, labor costs are an important element in the manufacture of clothing. In the previous chapter, Table 8–1 provided a comparison of the hourly wages in a number of countries. Many apparel firms in high-wage countries simply could not compete against those odds. Therefore, for the management of many companies, the only means of surviving appeared to be shifting the garment production activities offshore. Although this strategy eliminated many domestic apparel manufacturing jobs, many company executives believe they survived only because they shifted production elsewhere. Those firms were able to maintain in their home countries the management, merchandising, marketing, and other functions that require greater technical expertise and investment.

An additional factor is that in many other countries, the government offers incentives to producers of textiles and apparel for exports. Some provide **subsidies** of various kinds, despite the fact that these are considered illegal because they create unfair competition. In China, for example, the government provides support for the industry because textile and apparel exports are the top priority for helping the country establish itself as a world economic power. Firms in countries not providing this extra assistance cannot compete against products from other countries where manufacturers have received special support. Even when those products have shipping costs and tariffs added, the **landed cost** of the goods is less than production costs in domestic factories. If a U.S. apparel firm is trying to *compete* in the domestic market with garments made by a Chinese firm that sells to a U.S. retailer, the subsidy is a disadvantage to a U.S. apparel firm. On the other hand, if a U.S. firm contracts with a Chinese producer to make its garments, the U.S. company is also likely *benefiting* from that subsidy.

In many of the low-wage countries, governments also have **free trade zones (FTZs)**, where many incentives are given to attract firms there. The FTZs are special enclaves (usually fenced or otherwise enclosed) where goods can be produced under very attractive financial conditions. Business taxes might be eliminated or reduced, and fabrics or other components brought in are often exempt from tariffs. For example, if Indonesia wishes to attract production to the country, especially to provide jobs, the government might establish an FTZ. Many costs of doing business are reduced in the FTZ to lure firms to the country. Firms from anywhere might locate there, and those from countries with higher

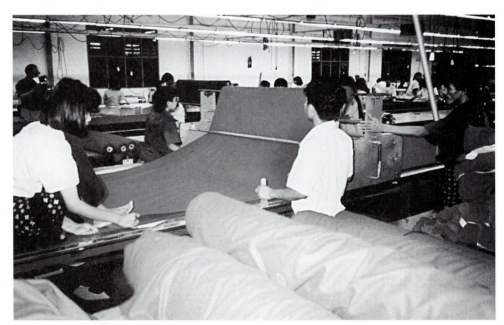

Figure 9–6

Spreading fabrics to cut garments for production in a free trade zone in Indonesia. The plant is a joint venture between a South Korean firm and an Indonesian company.

Source: Photo by Kitty Dickerson.

wages and/or labor shortages are likely to be attracted. For example, it is common to see South Korean apparel firms located in the FTZs in Indonesia (Figure 9–6).

Major Countries of Asia

The Newly Industrialized Countries (NICs)

At one time, apparel made in Asian countries was of such poor quality that it was relegated to the lowest price points of the fashion market. This situation no longer holds true. The **newly industrialized countries (NICs)** of Asia[2], generally considered to include Taiwan, South Korea, Hong Kong, and Singapore[3], have evolved far from where they were in the 1960s and 1970s. In those days, European, U.S., and Canadian apparel firms had garments produced in these countries to take advantage of low wages.

Today, the Asian NICs have become economic powerhouses, resembling in many ways the countries generally considered to be "more developed." The NICs have advanced to a level that makes them far more interested in being involved in high technology, **capital-intensive** economic activities than producing garments for other countries. This is not to say the apparel industry has disappeared in the NICs, but the types of activities have changed markedly. Wages have risen dramatically in these countries, and it has become difficult to find sewing operators for the garment industry. The work is hard and wages in other industries are likely to be higher. Consequently, apparel manufacturers in the NICs have experienced many of the same competitiveness problems as those in Western Europe, the United States, and Canada (Dickerson, 1995).

Although Asia is still a source of lower priced merchandise, much of it is produced in the NICs' neighboring countries. Major cities in the NICs have become *investment and marketing hubs* for the industry in the region. Apparel firms in the NICs are likely *themselves* to be using overseas contractors in low-wage countries.

Beginning in the 1980s, East Asia has led the world economy in terms of average annual growth rates. This economic growth has resulted in a fast rise in incomes and a rapid increase in demand in consumer markets. *Business Week* authors Engardio, Barnathan, and Glasgall (1993) noted that "East Asia is generating its own wealth on a speed and scale that probably is without historical precedent" (p. 100). Growing affluence, plus high population growth, is making East Asian countries major markets themselves rather than the source of low-wage apparel products for firms from other nations.

Hong Kong. For decades, Hong Kong has been producing apparel to order—to the order of the garment trade throughout the world. The apparel and textiles industries are Hong Kong's largest manufacturing sectors, accounting for nearly 40 percent of this city-state's exports (Hong Kong Government Industry Department, 1992). Hong Kong is one of the world's largest apparel exporters; however, this does not mean all the merchandise is produced there. Many of Hong Kong's apparel exports are made through outward processing arrangements (OPT), especially in Shenzhen, an economic zone in southern China just outside Hong Kong. As noted earlier, Hong Kong and the other Asian NICs have become major marketing hubs for the industry. Business deals are signed and production may be coordinated from these centers—but a large portion of the garment production occurs elsewhere.

---

[2]This group is frequently called the "Asian Tigers."
[3]Hong Kong and Singapore are technically city-states, with Hong Kong becoming part of the People's Republic of China in 1997.

Mass producing firms such as Esprit and Liz Claiborne have offices in Hong Kong but contract out virtually all their production. In addition, almost every important retail store in the United States that offers private label fashion goods has offices in Hong Kong to coordinate the manufacturing to its specifications. Traffic between Shenzhen and Hong Kong has increased dramatically. Buses now run daily from Hong Kong to take company representatives to check on production in Shenzhen's factories. Trucks line the highways, transporting components into China and finished merchandise back to Hong Kong.

Quota restraints have encouraged Hong Kong to **upgrade** the products shipped to the United States, Europe, and Canada. Quota limits on the physical quantity of exports, but not the value, encouraged Hong Kong to produce garments of higher quality—and higher price. The Hong Kong industry today is noted for its ability to accommodate style changes and for superior workmanship, for which sources generally pay premium prices. Long runs of low priced staple products are no longer Hong Kong's forte. The Hong Kong industry competes more on the basis of service, quality, and flexibility than on low cost. Leading designers from around the world use Hong Kong for production of high quality goods.

The **Hong Kong Trade Development Council (HKTDC)** has promoted Hong Kong as a major player on the world fashion stage. This includes presenting Hong Kong designers in U.S. and European trade shows, including those in Düsseldorf and Paris. The HKTDC sponsors an annual fashion week, which is billed as "Asia's Largest Fashion Event." Both exhibitors and buyers come from countries on several continents.

Hong Kong's future is somewhat in question. Some business experts are uncertain about Hong Kong's future under communist rule after the return to China in 1997.

Taiwan and South Korea. Taiwan, for many years a major low-wage contracting center for apparel, was an agricultural area called Formosa until Chiang Kai-shek escaped from China, declared Taiwan to be Nationalist China, became its first president in 1949, and remained its ruler virtually until his death. Within a decade, he had transformed Taiwan into an industrial nation.

Taiwan's textile and apparel industry, which the United States and Japan helped to develop, was the major industry on which the country's economy expanded. During the 1970s and 1980s, Taiwan was among the top three apparel producers in the world. Today, however, Taiwan's emphasis is on high technology, capital-intensive industries. Many of the early textile and apparel firms have evolved into large commercial conglomerates with other businesses that include real estate, retailing, and chemical complexes. Among Taiwan's wealthiest elite, a majority began in textiles and apparel. Today, those firms still in this industry are more likely to be producing high technology textile products, including chemical fibers, than assembling garments. All of this reflects the rapid economic and technical advancements in Taiwan.

Although a substantial apparel industry remains in Taiwan, less and less of the production occurs within this island country. Apparel firms' headquarters remain in Taiwan, but much of the labor-intensive garment production is sent to China, Indonesia, or other lower wage countries.

Taiwan's textile and apparel industry receives support and technical assistance in both its production and marketing activities. The government/industry-supported **Taiwan Textile Federation (TTF)** is an umbrella organization for industry groups representing all segments of the business. The TTF provides marketing and export promotion assistance to companies and sponsors exhibits at trade fairs around the world. A design center keeps apparel and fabric makers informed about the latest fashion trends. The talents of young designers are nurtured. Seminars provide business and trade information. In addition to the TTF, the China Textile Institute (also in Taipei) is a center for technical production assistance to the industry.

South Korea has developed much like Taiwan. The garment industry provided the economic foundation for the country's successful industrialization. Today, South Korea is a bustling, advanced nation whose textile and apparel industries are considered less important than in the past. The electronics industry has become important here, as in Taiwan. Still, textiles and apparel represent 20 percent of South Korea's exports (General Agreement on Tariffs and Trade, 1994). South Korea has moved toward the high-tech segments of the textile sector in preference to garment production. Increased wages plus labor shortages and worker discontent add up to mean that garment producers find it increasingly difficult to be competitive in South Korea. Thus, many Korean apparel firms have taken their production to lower wage neighboring countries such as Indonesia and other Southeast Asian locations. A number have built factories in the Caribbean nations to be closer to the U.S. market and to avoid the quota limits they face in their home country if they plan to ship to the United States.

Singapore. The description of the industry in the other Asian Tigers also applies to Singapore, except that Singapore has moved out of garment production more rapidly than the others. Like Hong Kong, limited physical space has permitted minimal development of a textile industry *per se.* Singapore has become an important financial and marketing center for Southeast Asia. This is the main role it plays now for the fashion-related industries. Apparel firms are likely to have offices in Singapore to coordinate the production of garment lines in Indonesia, Malaysia, and other countries in Southeast Asia. Similarly, major retailers have offices in Singapore to coordinate the contract work in that region for private label lines.

Like Hong Kong, Singapore is a major port city and will continue to play a major role in the region's apparel-related industries. Some businesses are eyeing Singapore as an alternative to Hong Kong if conditions become difficult in the latter under Chinese communist rule after 1997. Singapore is positioning itself to be a major trade center in the industry, having opened TradeMart Singapore in 1994. This modern trade mart performs the functions normally associated with regional U.S. marts. Additionally, TradeMart Singapore is prepared to assist manufacturers and retailers from other parts of the world in finding Asian contractors to produce merchandise.

The People's Republic of China

Not long ago, the People's Republic of China (ROC), also known as Mainland China or sometimes Communist China, was isolated from the rest of the world. Once a mighty world power, China entered several decades of isolation following its famous Cultural Revolution. Only since the early 1970s has China engaged once again in foreign relations and trade with the rest of the world.

Today, China is a burgeoning economic powerhouse, whose potential far exceeds what this vast country has demonstrated to the world to date. With 1.3 billion inhabitants, or about *one-fourth the total world population,* China is a rapidly growing giant in the global textile and apparel industry. China is clearly the major producer of apparel exports to U.S. markets, even with a very restrictive quota system that limits China's shipments.

The Chinese government has identified the textile and apparel industries as the top priority sector on which the Chinese economy will be advanced. Textile and apparel exports provide the means for securing badly needed hard currency. Because of the government's priority, the growth of all segments of the textile and apparel industry has been phenomenal. China's enormous population, in need of employment, is willing to work for very modest wages—48 cents per hour in 1994 (Werner International, 1995). These low wages have been a magnet for apparel and retail firms from Western Europe, the United States, Canada, Japan, and other Asian countries seeking low-cost production of garments.

China's manufacturing industries have been aided by investments and technological know-how from Hong Kong in particular. Joint ventures with Hong Kong companies are encouraged by the government in which China supplies the land, facilities, and labor. The Hong Kong partner supplies the machinery, expertise, market access for the products, and often ongoing supervision of production and financial management. Companies from many other countries have similar joint venture or other investment arrangements in China.

China's overwhelming potential has only begun to be tapped. Textile and apparel companies around the world fear the competition that will be unleashed in China when the Multifiber Arrangement's quota system is eliminated. On the other hand, those apparel firms and retailers seeking low-cost production there will be unfettered in their quest for merchandise produced at a bargain.

One thing is certain: textile and apparel industries in every country around the world will be affected by future developments in China's production and trade. With the strong entrepreneurial spirit of the Chinese, China is still a sleeping giant with the potential to flood apparel markets in every part of the world.

Other Low-Wage Production Centers in Asia

As Japan and the Asian NICs became less competitive (and quota restraints tightened), particularly in the production of low-priced apparel, many other Asian countries began to fill the void. The more developed Asian countries have also sought production in neighboring countries where there were fewer quota restraints. Most of the desperately poor nations (often referred to as the **Third World nations**) in Asia welcomed the investments and jobs provided when their more developed neighbors began to move apparel production to their countries. This shift occurred as the more advanced nations could no longer produce competitively in their home countries. Firms from European and North American countries also sought less costly places, other than the NICs, for their contract production. The scenario is nearly always the same as that described earlier: The more advanced nations provide the investment, equipment, technical know-how, and access to markets; the less advanced nations provide the labor, land, and local contacts. Figure 9–7 shows an example of this production.

A number of other very important countries have made their presence known in global textile and apparel markets. Certain members of the Association of Southeast Asian Nations (ASEAN)[4], which includes Thailand, Malaysia, Indonesia, and the Philippines, emerged as major contributors to the global supply of fashion products. Other countries that export a great deal include India, Pakistan, Bangladesh, and Sri Lanka. Newcomers continue to emerge, including Vietnam, Cambodia, and Nepal.

Central and Eastern Europe

In Central and Eastern Europe, a number of countries are placing increasing emphasis on their textile and apparel industries as important cogs in each respective nation's economic development. These countries have a vital interest in the markets of Western Europe and the United States and are making rapid strides in producing for those markets. We shall consider briefly Turkey and the former Soviet bloc countries, reviewing the latter as a group.

---

[4]The ASEAN group includes Thailand, Malaysia, Indonesia, the Philippines, Singapore, and Brunei. The first four are important textile and apparel producers. Brunei has little production because of its wealth from oil, and Singapore is an advanced NIC.

Figure 9–7

Managers in a U.S. apparel firm's sourcing office in Singapore consider specifications for garments to be produced in Malaysia.

Source: Photo by Kitty Dickerson.

Turkey is positioned uniquely between Europe and Asia, with a Middle Eastern heritage similar to its Mediterranean neighbors. The textile and apparel industries have been important to the Turkish economy for decades and have made great strides in exporting in recent years. For many years, the Turkish garment industry has produced for certain West European markets, particularly Germany. More recently, however, a supportive government and strong industry leadership are positioning Turkey's textile and apparel industry to become an increasingly important player on the world stage. The textile-apparel complex is undergoing world-class modernization, making it even more competitive on a global basis. In 1994, textiles accounted for 12.1 percent of Turkey's merchandise exports; apparel, 25.3 percent—*together more than 37 percent of Turkey's total merchandise exports* (World Trade Organization, 1995).

Although most of Turkey's apparel shipments have been directed to the European Union in the past (Figure 9–8), this country has taken steps to increase its shipments to the United States. In the mid-1990s, Turkey's products accounted for less than 1 percent of the U.S. apparel market, but Turkish industry leaders have taken steps to assure their country's significant future growth in the United States.

Many countries of the former Soviet bloc had large textile and apparel industries under the former communist system. However, centrally controlled economies and isolation from the world market resulted in industries out of touch with the rest of the world. The concept of fashion was foreign to garment producers in the region. Factories produced what they were told regardless of what consumers might have wanted. Because no profit incentive existed, industries were inefficient.

Although the people in the former Soviet bloc countries celebrated the fall of the Berlin wall and an end to communism and isolation, painful transition years followed. Unemployment and declining incomes led to difficult conditions for many. As government-controlled factories were **privitized,** the most basic business skills for competing in a global economy had to be developed. Concepts of quality and fashion had to be learned by workers who had been accustomed to producing merchandise that was not competitive in world markets.

Figure 9–8

Turkey is a major apparel supplier to the European Union and will continue to become even more important as a result of favorable new trade agreements with the EU. At the same time, Turkish clothing manufacturers hope to increase exports to the U.S. market.

İMF'96-II
5th İSTANBUL INTERNATIONAL FASHION FAIR
22-25 August 1996
Visiting hours 11:00-20:00
World Trade Center - İstanbul

İstanbul, the buyers' guide to success

A global exporter of ready-wear now on the verge of an even greater breakthrough with her integration in the Customs Union, Turkey is a must on the agenda of every big scale buyer of fashion. And the one name you need to know in Turkey for the hits of the next season is İMF'96-II.

From August 22 to 25, İMF'96-II, the 5th İstanbul International Fashion Fair, will be bringing together the best Turkey has to offer as one of the coming stars of the fashion world. Men's, women's or children's apparels, fancy outfits or down-to-earth, sturdy causal-wear will all be there for you to choose from.

Call your travel agent right away for a ticket to İstanbul, and meet us at the World Trade Center - İstanbul for some glamorous deals!

CNR International Fair Organizations, Inc.
World Trade Center, Atatürk Havalimanı Karşısı, 34830 Yeşilköy -İstanbul / TURKEY
Phone: (+90-0212) 663 08 81 (100 Lines) Fax: (+90-0212) 663 09 75-73
Free bus service, departing every hour on the hour from Atatürk Kültür Merkezi (Culture Center), Taksim.

Source: Reprinted permission of Turkish Clothing Manufacturers Association.

Several of these former communist countries are emerging from the difficult transition years and are becoming important apparel production sites. The apparel industry is playing the same role it has in less developed countries around the world—it is often the first major industry on which the nations' economies are being built. Moreover, wages are low and many workers need jobs.

Central and Eastern Europe are now important production sites for apparel firms in the more developed countries of Western Europe. That is, they are becoming Western Europe's "sewing rooms" through outward processing arrangements similar to U.S. 9802/807 operations in the Caribbean. A number of U.S. apparel firms and retailers have contracted production in this part of Europe also. This region is expected to become increasingly important as a site where firms from countries with high wages and labor shortages will seek production of their apparel lines (Dickerson, 1995).

Latin America and the Caribbean

In addition to Asia, many low-wage production facilities have developed in the Western Hemisphere, where labor is abundant and wages are as low or lower than in some Asian countries. Today, the garment industry is a major sector in the economies of the Dominican Republic, Mexico, Costa Rica, Honduras, El Salvador, Jamaica, Guatemala, Colombia, and others.

The Latin American and Caribbean[5] countries have become increasingly important producers for the U.S. garment industry. As retailers have expected faster and faster responses to their orders, many U.S. apparel firms have turned to *neighboring* low-wage countries to produce apparel. Garments can be made and shipped from this region in a matter of days, whereas shipments from Asia by boat can take a very long time. Merchandise from Asia has often taken six to nine months from the time it is ordered until it is delivered. This time lag in getting products from Asia (unless they are sent by costly air freight) ties up the apparel firm's capital for much longer periods of time and does not permit serving retail customers promptly. Consequently, U.S. sourcing in the Americas is growing more rapidly than in Asia.

In addition, a number of Asian apparel firms have plants in Central America and the Caribbean. Asian manufacturers, plagued by quota restrictions, rising labor costs, and a shortage of labor, have shifted some of their production to the region in order to gain easier entry into the U.S. markets. These Asian producers have also sensed that many U.S. firms prefer the Western Hemisphere over Asia as a place to source.

For all these reasons, apparel from the Western Hemisphere accounts for a growing percentage of U.S. imports, as shown in Figure 9–9. Since the enactment of NAFTA, this trend has accelerated and is expected to continue.

As we noted in Chapter 8, a number of preferential trade policies have favored garment production in the region, particularly in Mexico and the Caribbean countries. These included (1) NAFTA, (2) the 9802/807 provision of the tariff laws, (3) the Caribbean Basin Textile Access Program (807A or "Super 807" with its virtually unlimited quotas if fabrics are U.S.-made and cut), and (4) Caribbean parity continues to be debated in Congress as this book goes to press.

---

[5]For our discussion, this includes Mexico, the Caribbean, Central America, and some South American countries.

| Figure 9–9 | In recent years, apparel produced under 807 and 807A arrangements account for a growing share of U.S. apparel imports. |

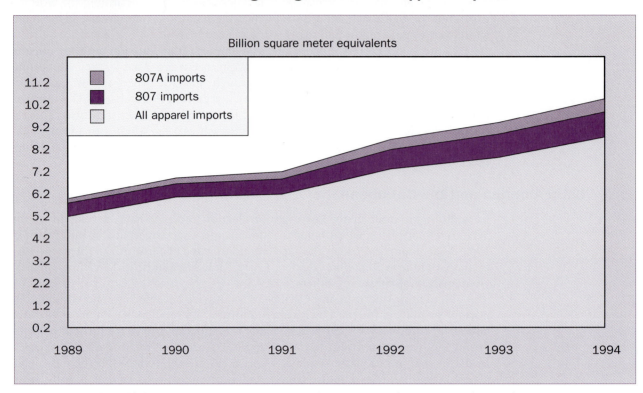

Source: From *Textile Highlights* (p. 28), September 1995. Reprinted by permission of American Textile Manufacturers Institute.

Shift of Foreign-Owned Factories to the United States

The drop in the dollar over the past few years together with rising costs of foreign labor and tight U.S. quota restrictions has made direct investment in the United States increasingly attractive to foreign companies. Some foreign producers are establishing a foothold in the U.S. industry and have shifted some of their production facilities to this country. This strategy puts the producers directly in a major market in which they wish to sell and eliminates costly shipping that would be involved when sending goods from great distances.

Examples include Hong Kong's Odyssey International's expansion in the United States, which was mentioned in the previous chapter. Tai Apparel Ltd., another Hong Kong apparel producer, bought a 900-employee plant in North Carolina from Burlington Industries. The Kienja Industrial Co. of South Korea opened a sweater factory in South Carolina. A number of Asian textile firms have either bought or built production facilities in the southeast United States. Other Asian companies have established operations in New York's Chinatown district and in Los Angeles.

In most cases, the branch factories in the United States are controlled by headquarters in the home country. In some of these cases, designs, fabrics, and other components may be supplied by the home country rather than by segments of the U.S. industry.

Sweatshops: The "Third World" in the United States

The intensely competitive conditions of the apparel sector have led to a shameful dimension of the garment industry. As firms have felt the pressure from low-cost imports, plus the need to respond quickly to market demands, illegal **sweatshops** have sprung up to fill these needs. Found mostly in New York and Los Angeles, these sweatshops frequently prey on new immigrants to provide the workforce. These new immigrants, most often of Asian or Hispanic origin, often lack language or other job skills for other employment choices. They desperately need work to support themselves and their families. Moreover, many immigrants have gained entrance to the United States illegally, which makes them further vulnerable.

Dishonorable entrepreneurs, often of the same ethnic groups they exploit, have taken advantage of this situation by starting sweatshops that provide cheap production for both apparel firms and retailers looking for inexpensive garment contracting. These contractors fill the same role that we have discussed for domestic and overseas contractors. They produce garments on a contractual basis and return finished merchandise to the apparel firm or retailer that contracted with them.

The big difference, however, is that sweatshops operate illegally in a number of ways. Workers are not paid U.S. minimum wages—hence, the attraction to these disreputable firms. Working conditions normally covered by government regulations and benefits expected in the United States today are flagrantly absent. Because workers have few other job options, they are unlikely to report the conditions for fear of losing their only source of income. Many newcomers simply may not know that they should be treated differently; the conditions they suffer in the U.S. sweatshops may be far better than those in the country they left. Illegal immigrants have no option to complain. If they do, they will be deported.

The U.S. public became aware of the sweatshop system in the mid-1990s when authorities discovered a factory in Los Angeles where illegal immigrants from Thailand were being forced to work under slave-like conditions. Tied to an illegal Bangkok operation that promised opportunities to workers to go to the United States, this sweatshop ring isolated immigrants upon their arrival and did not permit them to go outside the factory walls. Workers were exploited by receiving wages as low as those in Third World countries. Most of the workers' meager wages were taken to reimburse Thai ring leaders for the costs of transporting them to the United States. Following the disclosure of this operation, U.S. labor and immigration authorities initiated a crackdown on sweatshop operations. Authorities discovered that sweatshops were not unusual in New York and particularly in southern California.

The sweatshop system, closely resembling that in existence in the late 1800s and early 1900s, can be very complex. The contractor for whom the retailer or apparel firm is working may further **subcontract** the work for actual production. That is, the contractor may or may not actually produce the garments. Some contractors in these schemes are simply "middlemen" (or women) who farm out the work to subcontractors.

Figure 9–10

Members of the Union of Needletrades, Industrial and Textile Employees (UNITE!) stage demonstrations to protest sweatshops in the United States.

Source: Photo by Cara Metz, courtesy of UNITE!

The subcontractors are small sweatshops or even families who produce the garments in their homes. In these arrangements, the individuals who actually do the work are paid woefully low wages to permit those at each stage between the worker and the original owner of the goods to reap profit from the sewing operators' labor.

The contracting system also provides an unfortunate escape route for unscrupulous operators. If the illegal activities are discovered by authorities, each participant claims not to have known about the sweatshop conditions. That is, the manufacturer or retailer claims ignorance of the contractor's illegal activities, and the contractor claims not to know about the subcontractor's illegal operations. In some cases, astute firms truly had not been aware of what happened once they contracted the work, and unfortunately had not inspected production sites.

Following the disclosure of the Thai sweatshop-slavery operation and subsequent sweatshop investigations, a number of major U.S. apparel firms and retailers were identified as having contracted to have garments made in those shops. Many respected firms had their images tarnished by participating in these schemes, sometimes unknowingly. In a few cases, businesses were picketed by individuals who called attention to the company's use of sweatshops; pickets encouraged consumers to boycott merchandise from those companies.

As a result of the negative sweatshop publicity, many apparel firms and retailers developed company policies requiring close monitoring of production conditions. Both the U.S. Department of Labor and the U.S. Immigration and Naturalization Service began more active surveillance of the industry. UNITE, the major industry union, became involved, denouncing these conditions, as shown in Figure 9–10.

In today's globally competitive apparel industry, it is likely there will always be disreputable entrepreneurs who attempt to profit from the unfortunate conditions of vulnerable workers. Professionals in the industry must be on guard to avoid being part of these schemes, no matter how financially attractive they may seem in an industry characterized by cut-throat competition.

Fashion: A Global Business Today

Today, in addition to shopping European countries for new and incoming fashion ideas and for high quality products, knowledgeable manufacturers and retailers travel throughout the world seeking low-wage production partners for apparel and accessories. Representatives of these apparel and retailing firms travel from Shenzhen to San José, from Cairo to Calcutta, from Bogota to Bucharest, and from Kuala Lumpur to Kathmandu, with stops in between. Because apparel and accessory production can occur almost anywhere in the world, the world is a stage upon which contract or other business arrangements occur. Partners in other countries must be able to provide quality, timely deliveries, and appropriate service for these arrangements to be satisfactory. In other words, contracting production halfway around the world cannot be based solely on low labor costs.

The fashion business has indeed become global in all its aspects—design, production, and distribution. In the process, it has made the whole world into a collection of garment centers. Boundaries, borders, hemispheres—these represent no obstacle if there is an idea or facility the fashion world can use.

Readings

Fashion producers from those in the Haute Couture to Third World sweatshops are adapting to a rapidly evolving global market. Producers on each end of this production continuum play an important role in providing fashion products for consumers.

Not So Haute: French Fashion Loses Its Primacy as Women Leave Couture Behind

by Teri Agins

It was a classic Paris "fashion moment." After Christian Lacroix's *haute couture* show of ornate suits and gowns last month, an exhausted but exhilarated Mr. Lacroix took his runway bow, as ladies leapt from their gilt chairs and tossed carnations at him.

But this effusive response obscured the stark truth: Although Paris has been synonymous with high fashion since the late 1800s, when the first French couture houses began charming European royalty with elegant wardrobes, France's fashion supremacy is now largely mystique.

The couture houses, which turned Pierre Cardin, Yves Saint Laurent, Givenchy and Lanvin into household names during the designer licensing boom that began in the 1970s, have lost their leadership position in a fast-moving global market where savvy fashion houses in Italy, the U.S. and Germany have gained international prestige.

And France's new generation of designers, such as Mr. Lacroix, Jean-Paul Gaultier, Claude Montana and Thierry Mugler, have failed so far to turn their avant-garde styles into commercial hits.

Passages

Retail-industry economist Carl Steidtmann calls the waning French influence a "reflection of what happens in the life cycle of all businesses," akin to International Business Machines Corp.'s troubles when computer upstarts came out with innovative products.

"When you look back to the 1950s and 1960s, the Paris designers had an ability to create a fashion look that everyone wanted to have," says Mr. Steidtmann, of the Management Horizons division of Price Waterhouse. "The French felt they didn't need

to market to consumers because their brands were very strong. But the focus has shifted away from designing, and if you have enough money and are good at marketing, you can create a strong brand."

Giorgio Armani, Jil Sander, Prada and Donna Karan are among the non-French labels that have redefined modern fashion by steering clear of the rigid couture tradition of sharply tailored suits and gowns, painstakingly sewn for elite patrons largely by hand. The new designers appeal to professional, globe-trotting women, both affluent and middle class, who demand comfortable, understated wardrobes such as the softly tailored jackets and pants by Armani or the simple black nylon dresses from Italy's Prada.

Socialites and countesses interested in carrying the torch for couture are in short supply—and are no longer the fashion role models for most women. Last month, in the ballroom of the Grand Hotel where the final couture show of retiring designer Hubert de Givenchy was held, the famous clients who attended were American women, a lineup that recalled the society columns of the 1980s, including Mercedes Bass, Susan Gutfreund and Lynn Wyatt.

Still Chic

"France is still the capital for servicing fashion—the best place for holding fashion shows," observes Ralph Toledano, a Paris-based marketing consultant who formerly ran the fashion business of Karl Lagerfeld and now is helping Seventh Avenue's Donna Karan expand in Europe. "But the volume of manufacturing of French goods is down, and it is true that French designers are no longer on top."

But the French fashion establishment still considers itself the pre-eminent player. "Before, France was alone in the world, so it had a privileged position," says Jacques Mouclier, president of the Chambre Syndicale, France's main fashion-industry trade group. "It's not so much that France loses its prestige, but we are finding a market that is more competitive than ever."

Haute couture dates back to pioneering Paris designer Charles Worth—an Englishman—who introduced the bustle dress in the 1860s that liberated women from hoop skirts of the era. Paris later spawned legendary designers such as Coco Chanel, Balenciaga and Christian Dior, whose creations caused a ripple effect around the world. In 1947, Dior's radical New Look of sweeping, ankle-grazing hemlines suddenly rendered every woman's wardrobe of short, straight skirts obsolete.

License in Licensing

But the French never developed a strong apparel manufacturing industry. Even during the designer boom years when their labels reached the mass market, the couture houses didn't make the goods. They licensed their names to the hilt and raked in millions in royalties with a flood of "designer" merchandise, including polyester ties and scarves, vinyl luggage, even Yves Saint Laurent cigarettes.

In 1988, Pierre Cardin had 840 licensees, including bidets and frying pans. Christian Dior had 300 and Yves Saint Laurent had 200. "The French houses overlicensed their names and hurt the image," says Richard Simonin, managing director of Givenchy.

While he is confident about Givenchy's prospects, Mr. Simonin believes many of France's 18 remaining couture houses won't survive in the face of growing international competition. Declining to name names, he predicts: "Half of them will close down over the next few years."

Pierre Berge, the managing director of Yves Saint Laurent, vows that the moment Mr. Saint Laurent, 58 years old, retires, the couture part of his operation will close. "Who cares? Nobody cares," Mr. Berge barks. "The money will be better spent to advertise ready-to-wear [collections] and the perfume."

French perfumes have also lost their sizzle. Fashion houses have traditionally depended on high-profit perfume classics like Nina Ricci's L'Air du Temps, which derived their success from the heavily publicized couture shows. But by the early 1980s,

American perfumers like Estee Lauder, Giorgio of Beverly Hills and Calvin Klein had begun to upstage the French with their heavily advertised fragrances.

"Fifteen or 20 years ago, half to two-thirds of the top 20 fragrances in the U.S. were French," says John Ledes, editor of Cosmetic World, an industry newsletter. Sales of once-popular scents from couture houses such as Rochas, Nina Ricci and Paco Rabanne "have gone down dramatically," Mr. Ledes says.

The stellar exception is the 83-year-old house of Chanel, which was revived by the German-born Mr. Lagerfeld, a plucky marketer who jazzed up Chanel's tweed suits and accessories and made them appealing to well-to-do women under 30. Buoyed by its enduring Chanel No. 5 perfume, the company is estimated to generate retail sales of nearly $1 billion.

But Mr. Lagerfeld agrees that consumers around the world "are no longer impressed with the prestige of Paris. The Italians are very clever marketers," he says, "and the Americans are making modern and interesting clothes, capturing the right mood of today."

Moi and My Calvins

Indeed, American designers are planning aggressive expansion throughout Europe, particularly in France. Calvin Klein Inc. snared Gabriella Forte, a longtime Armani executive with strong ties in Europe, to serve as president, and will introduce Calvin Klein underwear in Galeries Lafayette department store in Paris next month.

A telling sign of the times: On his first day of office in May, French President Jacques Chirac appeared on the cover of Paris Match magazine sporting an Ivy League look: an oxford dress shirt with a Polo/Ralph Lauren logo.

French investors in fashion businesses are even coming to America to underwrite promising fashion talent. In 1990, Chanel bought a controlling interest in the New York fashion house of Isaac Mizrahi, the charismatic, 33-year-old designer now featured in the documentary "Unzipped."

"The French companies think the American designers are bringing ice to the Eskimos, but what they don't realize is that French consumers are thirsty for something new," says Susan Rice, a marketing consultant based in Paris.

And French women are being swayed. "French design is outdated," declares Francoise Aron, president of Paris-based El Dorado advertising agency, whose clients include Hermes, the French purveyor of leather and silk goods, and the Clarins cosmetic company. Ms. Aron says she likes the "simplicity" of designers like Armani, Prada and Donna Karan. As for Mr. Saint Laurent, she concludes: "He reigned all these years, but I find he's less modern, his style is less new, a little old-fashioned."

Better in Italy

The Italian fashion industry poses the most formidable challenge to the French. Italy not only boasts some of the world's finest fabric houses but also a number of top apparel manufacturers such as Gruppo GFT, which makes apparel for, among others, Giorgio Armani and Calvin Klein. It took Gruppo GFT to sell French fashion to Americans: It designs and manufactures Emanuel, one of the few strong French ready-to-wear labels in America, for *couturier* Emanuel Ungaro, under a licensing pact.

"As far as salability, the Italians know how to do it better than the French," says Joan Weinstein, owner of Ultimo, a boutique on Chicago's swank Oak Street. Ms. Weinstein dropped a number of French lines because they were too formal-looking and lacked the variety many women want. "When you are looking for a well-thought-out collection," she says, "there aren't too many of them coming from France."

The French couturiers also took a hard knock when Escada, a 20-year-old German fashion house, beat them at their own game by selling quality French-inspired styles at prices that were still high—$3,000 for an outfit—but lower than the $15,000 made-to-order couture versions.

Escada now operates its fragrance and accessories divisions right in Paris and expects its sales in France to hit $56 million this year, double 1990's.

The French fashion establishment has been slow to change partly because it got a reprieve in new markets in Asia, selling to newly affluent consumers. French fashion companies generate about 40% of their revenue from Asia, up from 25% a decade ago; 20% now comes from the U.S., down from 30%, according to Mr. Mouclier of the French trade group.

This month, French fashion shows in Hong Kong were an "indisputable success," drawing lots of publicity and "all of high society," Mr. Mouclier boasts. The group will put on more fashion shows

next year in other new markets like Beijing, Shanghai, Budapest and Belarus.

But most industry experts agree that the French won't dominate such markets for long. "With Japanese consumers traveling abroad and CNN reaching everyone, women around the world are now exposed to the same trends at the same time," says G. Chrysler Fisher, who formerly ran the U.S. division of Hermes. "Strong brands like Armani and Calvin Klein are getting far more attention than Givenchy. Consumers in emerging markets will look to them for leadership."

Vicky Ross, New York liaison for the Hong Kong-based Joyce chain of 49 Asian boutiques, is unimpressed with what she sees in the French showrooms: "It's the same 10 old men doing a boring rehash of what they've already done, like the hobble skirts that are too tight and are too expensive."

So for France's fashion houses, the name of the game is playing catch-up. Last month, Givenchy hired a spirited young designer, British-born John Galliano, 34, to replace 68-year-old Hubert de Givenchy, who is retiring. And both Givenchy and Christian Dior are pulling back licenses in an effort to restore their exclusive images. Dior's U.S. sales have shrunk to about half of the $1 billion level of the late 1980s.

French fans of couture are putting their faith in Mr. Lacroix, the 44-year-old courtier, who is striving to get his business into the black. Nine years ago, he made his couture debut with the pouf-skirted dress—a look that became *the* party dress of the late 1980s. But the house of Lacroix failed to turn its early fame into fortune, racking up more than $40 million in losses. It stumbled badly in 1991 when its C'est la Vie! perfume flopped.

Lacroix—which, like Givenchy, is owned by LVMH Moet Hennessy Louis Vuitton—is expected to break even in 1996, according to Robert Bensoussan-Torres, the house's managing director. Last year, Lacroix's new Bazar collection of colorful gypsy skirts, vests and sportswear racked up a respectable $20 million in sales. Next up: Lacroix's first designer jeans. Says Mr. Bensoussan-Torres: "Before we launch another perfume, we have to get women into our clothes."

Soon after Mr. Lacroix's fashion show last month, the house received some 30 orders from women for couture ensembles. Lacroix's Mr. Bensoussan-Torres points to these as evidence that couture—while it loses money—is still a valid enterprise. "Haute couture is the pure exercise of design. It is the best, it is untouchable," he declares. "It makes women dream."

But critics say the real dreamers are the French fashion houses. "We are selling products that nobody really needs," says Chanel's Mr. Lagerfeld. The industry must move on "to advertise, to do better marketing. There has to be a next step, and that is the question mark for the future of French fashion."

Source: From The Wall Street Journal, *August 29, 1995, p. 1, A8. Reprinted by permission.*

The Barons of Far East Fashion

by Josephine Bow

The figures are staggering and the stakes equally high. According to GATT statistics, global two-way trade in textiles and garments in 1990 accounted for US$224 billion or a cool 6.5 per cent of the world's total US$3.5 trillion in overall commodities trade.

And Asia accounts for as much as 40 per cent of that amount.

In this arena of profit, Asia's new fashion barons pack a formidable punch. While the region may still lag behind in original fashion design, top-notch manufacturers surge ahead on the retail front—and they sport not only comprehensive technical and production smarts, but important marketing lessons culled from overseas buyers.

The retailing transformation now sweeping Asia leaves no country untouched. Cash-rich Hong Kong, Taiwan and Singapore are studded with modern department stores and exclusive upmarket boutiques, bulging with high-quality Asian-made or -distributed goods.

Developing countries such as Thailand, Indonesia, Malaysia and China are seeing their investment coffers filled. And Asian entrepreneurs, with their particular brand of versatility, creativity and the ability to take calculated risks, are piling up impressive results.

A quick trip around the garment and textile factories of Asia today shows just how rapid the voyage to economic maturity has been. From still-lowly Pakistan to mighty Japan, each country in Asia has climbed the development ladder astride the textile industry.

From nations like struggling Bangladesh, where annual per capita income barely tops US$200, the garment industry has been a lifeline to developing-nation status. In the past 10 years, some 1,600 factories have appeared, and the country hums to the drone of sewing machines.

Countries like Sri Lanka, Nepal and Vietnam tell similar tales. Take the fashionable, impeccably made padded jackets destined for Europe's top shops that are now being churned out, and compare these to the drab Soviet monstrosities Vietnamese factories put together only a few seasons ago, and you understand Asia's astounding growth, both in symbolic and concrete terms.

As a garment-processing country moves up the industry chain, it begins to harness newly developing managerial and financial resources. Local content increases, profits from exports soar, the currency strengthens and then—seemingly overnight—the inevitable occurs: economic factors shift and the country stops being an interesting manufacturing site.

South Korea is one country currently at this crossroads. Garment manufacturers, squeezed by skyrocketing costs and shrinking labor forces, are under pressure from government to move into higher technology sectors. Still they are putting up a good fight to stick with textiles.

Large South Korean companies have gone into lower-cost offshore production, setting up operations in Central America, Indonesia, Vietnam, China and even North Korea. To survive at home, some upmarket South Korean manufacturers have scaled down and done the unthinkable—reduced minimum orders. Production is booked year round, and with consistent quality standards and timely deliveries, buyers aren't complaining over stiff prices.

Taiwan's efforts to save its garment industry haven't seemed nearly as cohesive. So far major companies have set up a hodge podge of overseas operations and seem content to rely on the country's considerable strength in capital and in synthetic textile production.

Still, Taiwanese investment clout is leaving its mark in joint venture textile industry operations all over the region, and the island nation is exhibiting remarkable retailing ingenuity in China.

Meanwhile, the Philippines, Thailand and Malaysia appear to be floundering. While garments and textiles continue to be substantial revenue earners and provide much needed employment, labour costs are rising, capital backing is lacking and long-term commitment is scarce.

The decade's biggest story of the garment business is China, simultaneously possessing the world's largest manufacturing base and its greatest untapped market. The country's new capitalists are eager to duplicate the successes of their overseas cousins, both in manufacturing and retailing. To this end, massive efforts are underway to modernise the nation's lumbering textile plants.

Another growing force in Asia's garment industry is Indonesia, which has enjoyed the advantage of beginning with a clean slate. Flush with revenue from oil earnings in the 1970s, forward thinkers opted from the start for the latest in technology and management. Today, many of the country's garment factories and textile plants are industry models, attracting a host of eager, well-trained Asian expatriate upper level staff.

In the wings stand two other potential contenders, Pakistan and India. Raw cotton exports already represent 60 per cent of Pakistan's economy, although it is still too early to assess efforts to move down the processing chain.

India's industry is similarly cotton dependent and recent dynamic policies aimed at liberalising foreign investment are expected to give the sector a much needed boost.

But Hong Kong is without question the vibrant, pulsating nerve centre of Asia's (and arguably, the world's) garment and textile industry. Second only to Italy for clothing exports, Hong Kong factories employ some 2.5 million workers in southern China alone.

"From Hong Kong you can order garments made anywhere in the world," says David Birnbaum, author of the recently published *Importing Garments from Hong Kong.*

"Hong Kong offers an unequalled level of professionalism, providing access to the world's fabrics, production bases, reliable agents, and the best in modern telecommunications, financial and shipping services, all in one convenient location."

Retailers echo that comment.

"Eventually the Far East will be like a single country," says Jeffrey Fan, chief executive officer of Toppy Ltd. "Regional retail chains will stretch across Asia, with Hong Kong as the trendsetter. Because of greater competition and exposure to the rest of the world, Hong Kong shops will always be the most sophisticated in merchandise, design, and management.

"Even after 1997, China will be proud to let Hong Kong uphold its position as fashion leader."

Source: From Asia Magazine, *33 (K–5), December 2–4, 1994, pp. 9–12.*

Tianjin Factory Life Slowly Changing to Meet the '90s

by Josephine Bow

While U.S. Fortune 500 multinationals such as Motorola and Coca-Cola are happily setting up shop in Tianjin, China's third-largest city located 70 miles east of Beijing, overseas buyers expecting the same entrepreneurial spirit in the garment industry may be in for a disappointment.

First of all, buyers rarely deal directly with factories, but must still go through state-owned import and export trading companies—a phenomenon that is losing ground in the garment hubs around Shanghai and Shenzhen. Tianjin Garments Import & Export Corp., hidden away in an unmarked residential complex, is one of the largest, claiming some $200 million worth of exports in 1994, up 20 percent from 1993.

But a first-time buyer would be hard pressed to believe the company deals in garments. The firm claims to work with over 100 factories, yet there is nary a sample in sight, much less a showroom displaying a selection of wares.

Zhang Gui Chang, North American manager, says that the U.S. usually accounts for about 50 percent of total export market share and that he works mostly through Hong Kong middlemen or direct with U.S. importers, who are, in turn, ordering for a wide variety of often no-name labels.

"We still suffer limited quota to the U.S.," he said. "We never take an order if we don't have the quota, and sometimes I have to turn away buyers." Zhang adds he is losing his low market segment to cheaper factories in countries like Bangladesh and Vietnam. "So we are trying to move into higher, value-added items."

Zhang says new buyers are picked up at the biannual Canton Trade Fair. In recent years he has also tried to pick up contacts at MAGIC, though his group doesn't exhibit.

A buyer who wants to see what factories are capable of will be taken to visit some star factories. Dong-Ta, which specializes in outerwear, is located a solid two-and-a-half-hour drive north in a lightly populated rural country. The factory is indeed impressive, consisting of three well-kept buildings employing over 1,000 workers who last year produced some 1.5 million units, 80 percent destined for export. But on the day of the visit, half the factory was closed because expected raw materials hadn't been delivered on time.

The logistical problems of working with remote factories are daunting. Not only does every garment component, whether sourced locally or from abroad, have to be trucked in on a timely basis, but production surveillance is inevitably spotty.

The best things the factory has going for it are workmanship and price.

Overall communications are more promising at downtown Yu Hua Garments, which employs over 4,000 workers and is one of the few Tianjin companies with direct import/export privileges. Over 50 percent of Yu Hua's annual 3.6-million-unit output is men's shirts, of which 90 percent are destined for longtime U.S. customer Van Heusen. The company says Van Heusen alone accounts for over two-thirds of the I/E Corp.'s precious 20,000 dozen shirt quota—an indication of just how tough it would be for a new customer to break in.

Export manager Chang Chu Liang feels there is more potential in their women's garments. The factory showroom boasts a wide array of well-stitched, mostly synthetic fashion blouses, dresses and jackets, all in imported fabrics, many for customers in the U.S. and Canada, such as Chaus. Making charges vary from $2 to $3 per piece. Although old customers would still have to go through the I/E Corp., new ones could deal directly. Quota for synthetic fabrics is non-critical.

Traditionally representing only 3 percent of China's total garment production, it's hard to say whether garment exports from Tianjin might yet pick up. But with increasing numbers of Korean companies setting up offshore production sites in Northern China and regular shipping runs from Tianjin via Pusan to the U.S., at least shipping services would present no problems.

_____

Source: From DNR, *May 25, 1995, p. 3. Reprinted by permission.*

Chapter Review

Key Words and Concepts

Define, identify, or briefly explain the following:

Canadian Apparel Federation (CAF)
Capital intensive
Caution fee
Chambre Syndicale de la Couture Parisienne
Contracting system
Couturier and couturière
Düsseldorf
Fashion center
Fédération Française du Prêt à Porter Féminin
Franchised boutiques
Franchising arrangement
Free trade zone (FTZ)
Haute couture
Hong Kong Trade Development Council (HKTDC)
IGEDO

Interstoff
Landed cost
Licensing agreement
Newly industrialized country (NIC)
Overseas contractors
Prêt-à-porter
Privitized
Subcontract
Subsidies
Sweatshops
Taiwan Textile Federation (TTF)
Third World nations
Trade show
Upgrading

Review Questions on Chapter Highlights

1. Name the three categories of foreign fashion producers and explain how they differ.
2. What is a haute couture house, and how do its operations differ from those of a U.S. apparel company? Are there haute couture houses in the United States? Explain your answer.
3. What is the prêt-à-porter division of the Chambre Syndicale de la Couture Parisienne, and why did it come into existence?
4. What are the major sources of income for haute couture houses?
5. What are some other centers of high fashion in the world today?
6. What role do the Canadian and U.S. apparel industries play in each other's home market? How has this changed in recent years?
7. Who does overseas contracting and why?
8. Identify the NICs. Describe how the apparel industry has changed in the NICs and why.
9. What single country has the potential to have a great impact on virtually every apparel market

in the world? Why is this country called a "sleeping giant"?

10. Pick one of the other countries discussed in the chapter as an important source for contract production. Locate it on a world map. Go to a library or on-line reference and learn about the country's economic and political situation. How is the economic situation related to the fact that the country does contract production of apparel?

11. Why are the governments in many other countries so eager to develop the apparel industry in their respective countries?

12. What changes have taken place in Central and Eastern Europe in the last decade? What have these changes meant to the apparel industry there?

13. Why have the Latin American and Caribbean countries become important apparel production sites?

14. Describe how you might envision a sweatshop. Why have these developed in the United States? How can sweatshops be eliminated?

15. Why should the person entering the fashion business today have a good knowledge of geography?

16. Why are "boundaries, borders, and hemispheres" no longer obstacles for today's global fashion industry?

17. What is one specific step *you* plan to take to be prepared to participate in today's global economy?

References

Agins, T. (1995, August 29). Not so haute: French fashion loses its primacy as women leave couture behind. *The Wall Street Journal,* pp. A1, A8.

American Apparel Manufacturers Association. (1996). *Focus: Economic profile of the apparel industry.* Arlington, VA: Author.

British Apparel and Textile Confederation. (1995). *TRENDATA: Key statistics of the UK apparel and textile industry, executive summary.* Unpublished report.

Canadian Apparel Federation. (1995). *Canadian Apparel Federation* (information packet). Ottawa: Author.

Couture's constant red ink. (1990, January 18). *Women's Wear Daily.*

Designers grumble but fashion goes on. (1976, July 26). *Women's Wear Daily.*

Dickerson, K. (1995). *Textiles and apparel in the global economy.* Upper Saddle River, NJ: Merrill/Prentice Hall.

Engardio, P., Barnathan, J., & Glasgall, W. (1993, November 29). Asia's wealth. *Business Week,* pp. 100–108.

Fédération Française de la Couture de Pret a Porter des Couturiers et des Creatéurs de Mode. (1995). *La haute couture et le pret-a-porter des couturiers et des createurs de mode.* (Unpublished informational piece, translated by L. Divita).

General Agreement on Tariffs and Trade. (1994). Personal communication with GATT economist.

Hong Kong Government Industry Department. (1992). *Techno-economic and market research study of Hong Kong's textiles and clothing industries 1991–1992.* Hong Kong: Author.

Middleton, W. (1995, August 21). French fashion now (special feature section on Chambre Syndicale). *Women's Wear Daily,* pp. 18–19.

Porter, M. (1990). *Competitive advantage of nations.* New York: Free Press.

Voice of the couture. (1984, December). *Vanity Fair.*

Weisman, K. (1995a, September 12). Interstoff to split shows. *Women's Wear Daily,* p. 21.

Weisman, K. (1995b, October 10). Keeping Paris king. *Women's Wear Daily,* p. 26.

Werner International. (1995). *Spinning and weaving labour cost comparisons.* New York: Author.

World Trade Organization. (1995). *International trade: 1995 trends and statistics.* Geneva, Switzerland: Author.

Suggested Bibliography

American Chamber of Commerce, Hong Kong. (1991). *Doing business in today's Hong Kong.* Hong Kong: Author.

Balkwell, C., & Dickerson, K. (1994). Apparel production in the Caribbean: A classic case of the new international division of labor. *Clothing and Textiles Research Journal, 12* (3), 6–15.

Balmain, P. (1985). *40 Années de Creation.* Paris: Musée de la Mode et du Costume.

Bonacich, E., Cheng, L., Chinchilla, N., Hamilton, N., & Ong, P. (Eds.). (1994). *Global production: The apparel industry in the Pacific Rim.* Philadelphia: Temple University Press.

Calliaway, N. (1988). *Issey Miyake.* New York: New York Graphic Society.

Charles-Roux, E. (1975). *Chanel.* New York: Alfred A. Knopf.

De Graw, I. G.(1975). *25 Years/25 Couturiers.* Denver: Art Publication.

Dickerson, K. (1991). *Textiles and apparel in the international economy.* Upper Saddle River, NJ: Merrill/Prentice Hall.

Dickerson, K. (1995). *Textiles and apparel in the global economy.* Upper Saddle River, NJ: Merrill/Prentice Hall.

Dior, C. (1957). *Christian Dior and I.* New York: E. P. Dutton.

ECHO. (1991). *Textiles and clothing in Eastern Europe.* London: The Economist Intelligence Unit.

Finnerty, A. (1991). *Textiles and clothing in Southeast Asia.* London: The Economist Intelligence Unit.

Giroud, F. (1987). *Dior.* New York: Rizzoli International.

Grunwald, J., & Flamm, K. (1985). *The global factory.* Washington, DC: The Brookings Institution.

Leymarie, J. (1987). *Chanel.* New York: Rizzoli International.

Lyman, R. (Ed). (1972). *Couture.* Garden City, NY: Doubleday.

Milbank, C. R. (1985). *Couture: The Great Designers.* New York: Steward, Tabori and Chang.

Poiret, P. (1931). *Kings of Fashion.* Philadelphia: J. B. Lippincott.

Porter, M. (1990). *Competitive advantage of nations.* New York: Free Press.

Quant, M. (1966). *Quant by Quant.* New York: Putnam.

Rhodes, Z., & Knight, A. (1985). *The Art of Zandra Rhodes.* Boston: Houghton Mifflin.

Rykiel, S. (1985). *Rykiel.* Paris: Herscher.

Saint Laurent, Yves. (1983). *Yves St. Laurent.* New York: Metropolitan Museum of Art.

Saunders, E. (1955). *The Age of Worth.* Bloomington, IN: University Press.

Schaparelli, E. (1954). *Shocking Life.* New York: E. P. Dutton.

Skrebneski, V. (1994). *The art of Haute Couture.* New York: Abbeville Press.

Steele, P. (1990). *Hong Kong clothing: Waiting for China.* London: The Economist Intelligence Unit.

Steele, P. (1988). *The Caribbean clothing industry: The U.S. and Far East connections.* London: The Economist Intelligence Unit.

Steele, V. (1988). *Paris Fashion. A Cultural History.* New York: Oxford University Press.

Toyne, B., Arpan, J., Barnett, A., Ricks, D., & Shimp, T. (1984). *The global textile industry.* London: George Allen & Unwin.

Walker, A. (1995). *West European textiles to 2000: Markets and trends.* London: Financial Times.

Werbeloff, A. (1987). *Textiles in Africa: A trade and investment guide.* London: Alain Charles Publishing Ltd.

Trade Associations

British Clothing Industry Association, 5 Portland Place, London W1N 3AA, U.K.

British Fashion Council, 5 Portland Place, London W1N 3AA, U.K.

Camara Nacional de la Industria del Vestido (National Chamber of the Apparel Industry), Tolsa No. 54, 06040 Mexico, D.F.

Camara Nacional de la Industria Textil (National Chamber of the Textile Industry), Plinio No. 220, Col Polanco, 11510 Mexico, D.F.

Canadian Apparel Federation, 130 Slater St., Suite 605, Ottawa, Ontario, K1P 6E2, Canada.

Canadian Apparel Federation/Design Link, 372 Richmond St. W., Suite 112, Toronto, Ontario M5V 1X6, Canada.

Fédération Française de la Couture, 100–102, Faubourg Saint-Honoré, 75008 Paris, France.

FENECON, P.O. Box 69265, 1060 CH Amsterdam, Netherlands.

Hong Kong Trade Development Council, 38th Floor, Office Tower, Convention Plaza, 1 Harbour Rd., Wanchai, Hong Kong.

Institut Francais de la Mode, 33 rue Jean Goujon, 75008 Paris, France.

Israel Export Institute (Fashion Division), 350 Fifth Ave., New York, NY 10118.

Japan Apparel Industry Council, Room 301 Aoyama Nozue Building, 2-11-10, Kita-Aoyama, Minato-Ku, Tokyo, Japan.

Taiwan Textile Federation, TTF Building, No. 22, Ai Kuo East Rd., Taipei, Taiwan, Republic of China.

Turkish Clothing Manufacturers Association, Yildizposta Caddesi 48/18, Gayrettepe-Istanbul, Turkey.

Trade Publications

Apparel International, The White House, 60 High St., Potters Bar, Herts, EN6 5AB, U.K.

A.T.A. Journal (Asian textiles and apparel), 14/F, Devon House, Taikoo Place, 979 King's Rd., Quarry Bay, Hong Kong.

Canadian Apparel Manufacturer, 1 Pacifique, Saint Anne de Bellevue, Quebec H9X 1C5, Canada.

CAMA (Children's Apparel Manufacturers Association) Parade, 8270 Mountain Sights #101, Montreal, Quebec H4P 2B7, Canada.

DNR, 7 W. 34 St., New York, NY 10001-8191.

Fashion Femme, 1 Pacifique, Saint Anne de Bellevue, Quebec H9X 1C5, Canada.

Fashion Industry News, 250A Eglinton Ave. E., Toronto, Ontario M4P 1K0, Canada.

International Textiles, 23 Bloomsbury Square, London WCIA 2PJ, U.K.

Style Magazine, Suite 301-785 Plymouth, Montreal, Quebec H4P 1B3, Canada.

Textile Asia, P.O. Box 185, California Tower, 11th Floor, 30–32, D'Aguilar Street, Hong Kong.

Women's Wear Daily, 7 W. 34 St., New York, NY 10001-8191.

World Clothing Manufacturer, 23 Bloomsbury Square, London WCIA 2PJ, U.K.

*T*he Retailers of Fashion

*E*ventually all merchandise that is designed and produced must reach the ultimate consumers, and that is the role and responsibility of **retailers.** In the course of buying and selling goods that are acceptable to their customers, retailers also serve the industry as a series of listening posts on the consumer front. At the same time they act as a medium for disseminating information and stimulating demand for fashion products.

Retailers of fashion outnumber fashion producers by more than seven to one and are the largest source of fashion industry jobs. It is estimated that there are approximately 122,000 retailers that specialize in fashion apparel and accessories, and another 38,000 that include some apparel and accessories in their merchandise assortment (National Retail Institute, 1995). Some retailers are giant companies as, for example, Sears and Wal-mart, which are among the world's largest businesses. At the other extreme are small **"mom-and-pop" stores** run by an owner with few or no assistants. Many new **retail formats** are becoming increasingly important.

The first part of this chapter discusses the differing kinds of retail operations and the period and environmental circumstances of their origin. The second part discusses the many changes that have occurred in the retailing of fashion today. The readings that follow the text illustrate some of the new trends and challenges having an impact on retailing today.

Fashion Retailing in the Past

In the early 1800s, there were only about 10 million people in the United States, and most were farmers or pioneers moving westward with the frontier. Except for the few cities established along the Atlantic coast, the country was rural. Transportation was by foot, on horseback, or by horse and wagon. Roads, such as they were, were little more than Indian trails through the wilderness. Retailers that functioned in this environment were small country stores and trading posts, or itinerant peddlers. The last-named group traveled from farm to farm, offering for sale such small conveniences as cutlery, tools, buttons, combs, hand mirrors, needles, and thread. They were welcome visitors to frontier people, because they brought with them bits of news and a touch of civilization. The retailing of ready-to-wear was still in the future, awaiting the development of factory-produced textiles and apparel.

It was not until late in the nineteenth century that significant amounts of ready-made clothing became available for sale in stores. Before that, the fashion operations of stores in the growing cities consisted only of selling fabrics, trimmings, and made-to-order clothing. Although custom-made clothing remained important into the 1920s, it was steadily giving way before the growing and constantly improving ready-to-wear manufacturing industry. At the same time, retailers were learning to deal in ready-to-wear. By the 1920s men's, women's, and children's apparel departments were firmly established in all big-city department and specialty stores, and ready-to-wear was also available through mail-order catalogs to customers in outlying areas.

In the early days of ready-to-wear retailing, owners of the great fashion stores worked creatively with manufacturers to produce ready-to-wear designs that would meet the fashion needs of their customers. Many retailers helped manufacturers get started by bringing them Paris models to copy and providing them with substantial orders. The retailer at that time was the main source of fashion information for consumers as well as manufacturers. There were few movies, few telephones, no television, and only a few publications to keep people up to date on what should be produced or worn. Long before the fashion show, the bridal counselor, and the college shop were commonplace, several prominent stores were publishing fashion brochures that they mailed to their customers. Lord & Taylor began such a publication in 1881, John Wanamaker in 1909, and Marshall Field and Company in 1914. As fashion traveled its long, slow route from Paris to Podunk, customers looked to their oracles, their favorite stores, for advice on what to wear.

Different Kinds of Retail Operations

In the retailing of fashion, as in fashion itself, customers call the tune. Just as fashion keeps changing to reflect changes in consumer wants and needs, so does its retailing continue to change. Historically, new and different forms of retailing have come into being in response to changes in social and economic conditions, and each has initiated certain operational methods that distinguish it from previously existing types. Today, although many once widely disparate kinds of retailing now overlap, many of their distinctive operational characteristics still exist. This is also a time when retailing is being dramatically transformed. Brutal forces are driving out the slow and inefficient. New retail formats are developing. In essence, many retailers are "reinventing" the store (Kurtz, Bongiorno, Naughton, DeGeorge, & Forest, 1995).

SIC Codes for Retailing

In previous chapters, we considered the U.S. government's Standard Industrial Classification (SIC) codes for the manufacturing segment of the fashion industry. Similarly, SIC codes denote specific segments of the retailing industry. Those significant to the fashion industry are given in Table 10–1. As for manufacturing, all government data on the industry (sales, employees, and so on) are grouped according to these categories.

Retail experts at Kurt Salmon Associates (1995) project that the retailing industry as we know it today will change dramatically in the next millennium. Our definitions of different types of retail formats are likely to be modified greatly. In the future, we may think of retailing in basically two formats: **In-store retailing** and **nonstore retailing.** KSA offers these definitions: in-store as "sales made in person through traditional channels; nonstore represents all other forms of retailing where the merchandise is delivered to the customer" (p. 8).

Figure 10–1 shows where U.S. consumers buy their apparel today. In the first part of this chapter we shall consider various types of in-store retailing. This will be followed by a section on nonstore retailing and its growing importance.

Table 10–1	Select Branches of Fashion Goods Retailing by Standard Industrial Classification Code Number

SIC Code	Branch of Industry
53	General merchandise stores
531	Department stores
533	Variety stores
56	Apparel and accessory stores
561	Men's and boys' clothing stores
562	Women's clothing stores
563	Women's accessory and specialty stores, furriers and fur shops
564	Children's, infants' wear stores
565	Family clothing stores
566	Shoe stores
569	Miscellaneous apparel and accessory stores
59	Miscellaneous retail establishments
594	Miscellaneous shopping goods stores
5941	Sporting goods (and bicycle) shops
5944	Jewelry stores
596	Nonstore retailers
5961	Catalog and mail-order houses
5963	Direct selling establishments

Source: From *Standard Industrial Classification Manual* by United States Executive Office of the President, Office and Management and Budget, 1987, Washington, DC: Author.

Figure 10–1

Where U.S. consumers shop for clothes (Market share of apparel sales, 1995).

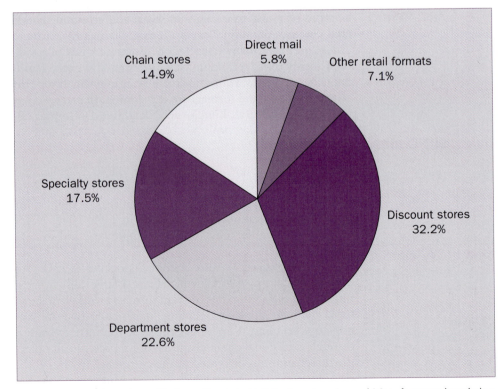

Source: Compiled from *Apparel Industry Trends* (p. 7–8) by American Apparel Manufacturers Association, May, 1996, Arlington, VA: Author.

Department Stores

A **department store** is defined by the Bureau of Census as a retail establishment that employs 50 people or more and that carries a wide variety of merchandise lines, including (1) men's, women's, and children's apparel; (2) furniture, home furnishings, and appliances[1]; and (3) household linens and fabrics. In the trade, however, several other criteria are applied: related categories of merchandise are offered for sale in separate departments; each department is managed as a separate profit center; responsibilities for stocking the department are delegated to a buyer; customers are offered many services, such as credit, return privileges, deliveries, and telephone and mail order. There are usually also such specialized services as restaurants, beauty salons, and jewelry repair, among others. In an earlier era, department stores were one-stop shopping sites for apparel and home furnishings. John Wanamaker in Philadelphia even sold airplanes at one point.

The typical department store chooses as its target group of customers people of middle to upper-middle socioeconomic status, with fairly large discretionary incomes. The fashion appeal of such a store stems from the breadth of assortment it offers in middle to upper-middle prices and in **national brand** and designer names, often augmented by its own brand name. Browsing among its broad stocks and guided by its advertising and displays, the customer can develop his or her own ideas of what to buy. When the choice has been made, the purchase can be consummated with confidence because of the store's refund policies. The offer of money back if the merchandise fails to please has been a cornerstone of department store policy for more than a century.

Department stores provide the "theater" of retailing. Their advertising and displays bring customer traffic and, since these stores cover so many categories of merchandise, they can generate more traffic than a specialized clothing store. The combination of customer traffic and appealing displays often prompts, say, a woman who has come seeking a lamp for her living room to purchase fashion items for herself, even though these were not on her shopping list. Department stores typically do more than half of their total volume in apparel and accessories for women, men, and children. In the fashion business, the department store not only represents an impressive volume of sales, but also is a medium for exposing merchandise to the customer, often with considerable drama.

Figure 10–2 shows a relatively traditional organizational structure for large department stores. Table 10–2 shows the top department and specialty department stores.

Origin of Department Stores

Most of our large, best-known department stores were founded in the middle and late nineteenth century, when mass production was developing and cities were growing. Some of their founders began as peddlers before they opened a store. Some examples

---

[1]A number of large department stores (as they are defined by industry financial analysts) now have little or no furniture. Most do not sell large appliances, such as refrigerators or other "white goods," as they once did. Department stores have dropped a number of product areas they once carried because those departments were not profitable, required large amounts of floor space, or were not consistent with the store's image.

Figure 10–2   **Organization chart of a typical large department store**

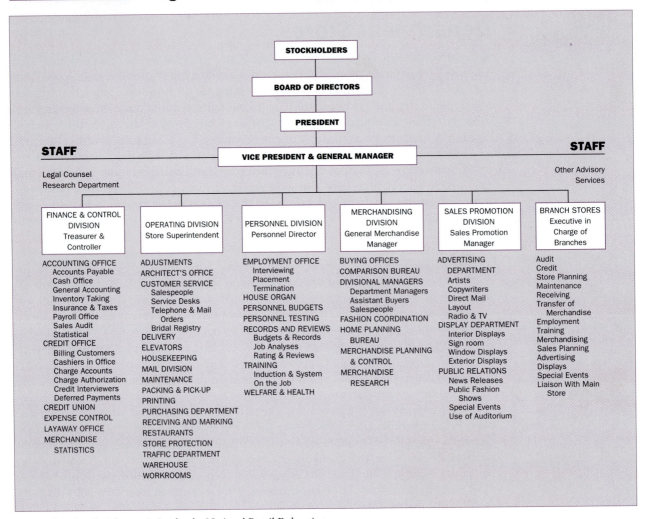

Source: Reprinted with permission by the National Retail Federation.

are Aaron Meier, whose small general store in Portland, Oregon, opened in 1857 and later developed into Meier & Frank; Morris Rich, who peddled notions in Ohio and then moved on to Georgia to open Rich's of Atlanta in 1867; Adam Gimbel, whose descendants built the Gimbel organization on the foundation of the store he opened in Vincennes, Indiana, in 1842. Others had their beginnings as small dry goods stores such as Macy's, New York, which opened in 1858 for the sale of feathers, hosiery, and gloves and added new lines as increasing mass production made them possible (Harris, 1979).

Branches: From Suburban to National

In retailing, when a store well established in one location opens an additional facility in another but operates it from the original parent or flagship store, the new addition is called a **branch store.** Just as the branches of a tree depend on the trunk for nour-

Table 10–2	The Top Department and Specialty Department Stores

Rank	Company	1995 $ Sales (in millions)
1	Sears, Roebuck and Co.[a]	20,133.0
2	Federated Department Stores, Inc.[b,c]	15,048.5
3	J.C. Penney Company, Inc.	14,973.0
4	May Department Stores Company	10,506.9
5	Dayton Hudson Corporation[d]	7,709.0
6	Montgomery Ward	6,573.0
7	Dillard Department Stores, Inc.	5,840.7
8	Nordstrom, Inc.[b]	4,113.5
9	Mercantile Stores Company, Inc.	2,892.1
10	Kohl's Corporation	1,554.1
11	Saks Holding, Inc. (Saks Fifth Avenue)	1,486.0
12	Neiman Marcus Stores[e]	1,398.8
13	Carson Pirie & Scott Co.	1,083.8

[a]Includes sales from outlet store operations.
[b]Includes sales from specialty and outlet store operations.
[c]Includes sales of Broadway Stores, Inc. since the company was acquired on July 29, 1995.
[d]Includes Mervyn's and Marshall Field. Sales figure includes $4,516 from Mervyn's and $3,193 from the Department Stores Division.
[e]Fiscal year ended July 29, 1995.
Note: Sales are for U.S. department store operations.
Source: Company annual reports and Management Horizons.

ishment and growth, so do branch stores depend on the buyers, promotion executives, and other members of the parent store's management team for merchandise and direction.

Where customers go, stores go. When young city families moved out to new suburbs in vast numbers in the 1950s, retailers in the central cities moved out to serve them in branches—free standing at first, but later in the shopping centers that soon developed. By the early 1970s, branches had proliferated to the point that collectively they began contributing more than half the parent firm's total value. By the late 1970s, suitable suburban areas had been exploited to the full by some stores, and these began to expand around the country, into other metropolitan areas. Thus, we find New York's Lord & Taylor with branches in Connecticut, New Jersey, Pennsylvania, Virginia, Texas, and Maryland. Dillard's of Little Rock, Arkansas, has branches in Texas, Missouri, New Mexico, Oklahoma, Florida, Kansas, and Ohio. Bloomingdale's of New York has branches in Massachusetts, New Jersey, Pennsylvania, Texas, Florida, and the Washington, D.C. area.

Competitive Changes by Department Stores

As Figure 10–3 shows, department stores lost market share in the early 1990s while discount merchandisers gained. Department stores have taken bold steps to recapture lost market share, copying many of the strategies used by the discounters. Major cost-cutting efforts have resulted in leaner, more efficient organizations. Many have consolidated divisions, streamlined buying and merchandising operations, and

Figure 10–3

Winners and losers among apparel retailers: Apparel market share trends 1989 vs. 1994

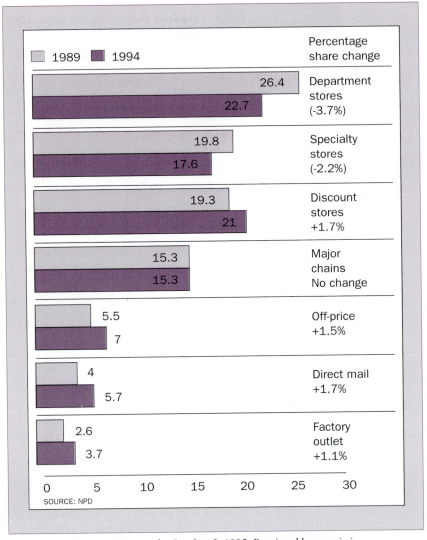

	1989	1994	Percentage share change
Department stores (-3.7%)	26.4	22.7	
Specialty stores (-2.2%)	19.8	17.6	
Discount stores +1.7%	19.3	21	
Major chains No change	15.3	15.3	
Off-price +1.5%	5.5	7	
Direct mail +1.7%	4	5.7	
Factory outlet +1.1%	2.6	3.7	

SOURCE: NPD

Source: From *Women's Wear Daily*, October 5, 1995. Reprinted by permission.

refined tracking and distribution systems, resulting in significant decreases in operating expenses.

Many department store groups have initiated ambitious **private label** programs. Private label merchandise, as used in the fashion industry, refers to goods produced exclusively for one retailer, and it carries only the name of the retailer or one of several brand names owned by the retailer. Private label programs will be discussed later in this chapter. Although department stores will continue to carry well-known national brands, many have found advantages from well-executed private label programs. Retailers have better profit return on private label goods than on national brands. Department stores have more control over their own brands, permitting them to respond more quickly to changing fashion trends, to present exclusive merchandise, and to tailor their lines more precisely for their target markets. Private label merchandise accounts for about 11 percent of department stores' apparel sales, but this percentage is growing (Management Horizons, 1994b).

Table 10–3	May Department Stores: A Store Ownership Group		
Company	**Headquarters**	**Number of Stores**	**1994 Sales**
Lord & Taylor	New York	54	$1.45 billion
Foley's	Houston	49	1.63 billion
Robinsons-May	Los Angeles	52	1.49 billion
Hecht's	Washington, DC	45	1.42 billion
Kaufmann's	Pittsburgh	40	1.30 billion
Filene's	Boston	36	1.16 billion
Famous-Barr	St. Louis	30	947 million
Meier & Frank	Portland, Oregon	8	347 million
Total department stores		314	$9.76 billion
Payless ShoeSource	Topeka, KS	4,435	2.12 billion
Payless Kids stores		635	
Total retail sales			$11,877 billion

Source: Based on information in *May Department Stores Annual Report 1994* (p. 1), 1995, St. Louis: Author.

Like their discounter cousins, some major department stores have made bold growth moves. Unlike the discounters, however, large department stores have been more inclined to buy existing store groups rather than building new ones. These mergers and acquisitions have resulted in powerful store ownership groups, better able to compete against the mammoth discounters and general merchandise chains.

Store Ownership Groups

The founding fathers to today's great department stores operated family-owned and family-run single-unit stores. Today, by means of mergers and acquisitions, nearly every such store is part of a **store ownership group,** which is a corporation that owns a number of autonomously operated retail organizations. Each store division retains its local identity and independence, has its own branches, has its own buyers and merchandise mix, operates under its own name, and presents itself to customers much as if it were still an independently owned institution.

The first and oldest of such groups was the Federated Department Stores, Inc., incorporated in 1929 by a merger of Filene's in Boston, Lazarus in Columbus, and Abraham & Straus in Brooklyn, soon joined by Bloomingdale's in New York. During the decade that followed, other corporate ownership groups were formed such as the R. H. Macy group, Allied Stores, and Associated Dry Goods. The trend continued, giving birth to such other groups as Dayton-Hudson and May Department Stores (Table 10–3).

In recent years, several of these groups were acquired by other groups or merged together, creating giant conglomerates in the department store industry. For example, Associated Dry Goods was acquired by the May Department Stores group. Federated Department Stores and Allied Stores were merged when they were acquired by Campeau Corporation. Following the eventual departure of Mr. Campeau, Federated emerged as a major department store group.

The large Federated Department Stores, Inc. absorbed Macy's in 1994, creating a retail empire with 341 stores. In 1995, Federated added the ailing 82-unit California-based Broadway Stores (formerly known as Carter Hawley Hale Stores) to its empire, and in doing so strengthened Federated's West Coast presence. Analysts expect Federated's annual sales to be nearly $20 billion by 1998 ("Combined Federated," 1994; Moin, 1994, 1995).

The consolidation of the industry through mergers and acquisitions has transformed the department store segment of retailing from what it was 20 years ago. The industry is now so concentrated that *77 percent* of all sales of the top 10 department stores are generated by just *four* companies: Federated Department Stores, Inc., May Department Stores, J.C. Penney, and Sears Roebuck & Co.[2] Because department stores have higher costs of doing business (because of the store environment and services) than specialty stores, one way to reduce those costs has been through the **economies of scale** that result from consolidations. These economies of scale permit department stores to be competitive on prices (Sack, 1995).

As May Department Stores, Inc. and Federated Department Stores, Inc. have acquired additional stores, they have also consolidated divisions and centralized operations to take advantage of their economies of scale. In 1986, May operated 19 department store divisions but by 1994 had streamlined these to eight large regional department store companies (divisions). This consolidation within May saved about $125 million, mostly through job cuts (May Department Stores, 1995; Sack, 1995). For example, a buyer in one of May's new consolidated companies became the buyer for all the stores in what had been two or three companies previously. Instead of buying for 10 stores, the buyer might be buying for 30 stores. Federated Department Stores participated in similar consolidations and also centralized credit operations, data processing, and accounts payable.

Few consumers realize that, for example, Lord & Taylor of New York, Foley's of Houston, and Kaufmann's of Pittsburgh are among the stores owned by the May Department Stores. Similarly, among Federated Department Stores are Bloomingdale's of New York, Burdine's of Florida, Rich's of Atlanta, and others. Indeed, few of this country's largest department stores are now independently owned. Independent and smaller department store groups have an increasingly difficult time competing against the giants; therefore, it is likely the consolidation will continue.

The consolidation of retail power has important implications for the entire fashion industry. These will be discussed further later in this chapter.

Apparel Specialty Stores: Large and Small

In contrast to the department store's wide variety of general merchandise, a **specialty store** is a retail establishment that either deals in a single category of merchandise (such as jewelry, shoes, books, furniture, apparel) or specializes in related categories of merchandise—for example, clothing and accessories for men, women, and children, or sporting equipment and active sports apparel, or television, radios, and VCRs. Compared to the broad appeal of department stores, specialty retailers cater to a particular type of customer and carry narrow lines of merchandise, with a large assortment within each line that is specifically geared for a well-defined targeted customer.

---

[2]Previously J.C. Penney and Sears Roebuck & Co. were not considered department stores. However, as both have repositioned themselves, they are now frequently considered department stores.

Specialty retailers vary widely in size. Some are single-unit "mom-and-pop" stores, some are units of chains, and some are large departmentalized stores with branches. Among consumers, the larger versions are often mislabeled department stores, because they carry wide assortments in the merchandise categories in which they specialize, offer extensive customer services, and are also organized by departments.

Large and small, the specialty shops play an important role in the retailing of fashion today. The fashion impact of giants such as Saks Fifth Avenue and Neiman Marcus makes a great contribution, but so also does the small, independently owned shop that offers convenience, friendliness, and an assortment carefully tuned to the wants of its clientele.

Large Departmentalized Specialty Stores

Like the department stores, many of today's large and prestigious specialty shops began in the second half of the 1800s as small, independently owned enterprises, in small towns or in the then-developing cities. Some expanded into department stores; others simply broadened their assortments in specialized merchandise categories. Filene's of Boston, for example, was founded in 1873 in Lynn, Massachusetts, by William Filene, who later bought a men's store in that city, a dry goods store in Bath, Maine, and two stores in Boston—one specializing in gloves, and the other in laces. Similarly, I. Magnin of San Francisco had its beginnings in 1880, in the modest home of Isaac and Mary Ann Magnin, where wealthy San Francisco ladies came for Mrs. Magnin's exquisite, hand-made, embroidered, and lace-trimmed lingerie, christening dresses, and spectacular made-to-order bridal gowns (Harris, 1979).

Like the department stores, almost every one of these great specialty stores is now part of a store ownership group. To cite but a few examples, Bullock's and I. Magnin are owned by the Federated group and Filene's by the May Company group. And also like department stores, they operate branch stores, either in local suburbs or nationally, or both.

Unlike department stores, however, they are completely dedicated to fashions in the rise and peak stages, and their assortments are both broad and deep in the upper-middle to highest price ranges. Therein lies their competitive strength. They can more easily define their targeted customers; they develop salespeople who are fashion knowledgeable and helpful; and they provide personalized services.

Small Apparel Specialty Shops

It would be hard to find a town so small, or a city so big, that it is without independently owned, small mom-and-pop apparel or accessories shops. These are the stores owned and managed by one or two people and employing fewer than three salespeople. Each of the stores so defined generally has annual sales volume of half a million dollars or less; they neither have branch stores nor are part of a chain. The attrition rate among them is high, but so also is the rate of replacement by new entrepreneurs. Their collective impact in the fashion business, however, is important. Bureau of the Census figures continue to show that a substantial part of fashion retailing is done in just such outlets.

From the consumers' point of view, small fashion retailers offer convenience of location and intimate knowledge of their customers' needs and tastes. Their owners know the way of dressing in the communities they serve, and more often than not, they will buy with individual customers in mind.

From the producer's point of view, according to manufacturers interviewed by the authors, the importance of these stores goes far beyond the amount of business they place. For one thing, they are loyal to the firms from which they buy. In the larger stores, the buyers may not be the same from one year to the next, and they do not have that same loyalty.

With some manufacturing firms, small specialty shops may account for a major portion of their business. With others, such as Liz Claiborne or Esprit, the minimum quantities demanded on an order will rule out the small retailer entirely. Levi Strauss & Co. created quite a stir among small retail firms when the company established a policy of selling only to companies that purchased at least $10,000 in Levi merchandise. For the industry as a whole, which is a stronghold of small manufacturing firms, the collective buying power of the small, specialized apparel retailers is very significant.

Boutiques

The term **boutique** is French for *little shop,* and for many years it referred only to those intimate shops within Paris couture houses where the customer could buy perfumes and accessories carrying the house label. In the United States the term *boutique* designates a small shop that carries highly individualized and specialized merchandise intended for a narrow, well-defined customer segment.

The proliferation of boutiques in the United States (and in London, where the trend began) was an outgrowth of the anti-establishment "do your own thing" attitudes of the 1960s. Some of today's boutiques, like their 1960s forerunners, cater to the *avant garde* young, others to more mature customers. Many feature merchandise at astronomical prices; others sell at more moderate levels. Some deal only in designer clothes; others deal in hand-crafted fashions; some deal in trendy accessories; and still others deal in antique clothing.

The early independently owned boutiques of the 1960s were often established by creative fashion enthusiasts to sell merchandise that expressed their individual point of view—even if they had to design or possibly produce the merchandise themselves. Generally the merchandise was too advanced, too limited in appeal, for large stores to handle; only boutiques could do the job.

Independently owned boutiques made such an important place for themselves in the mid-1960s that large stores sought ways to appeal to boutique customers. Many stores established and still maintain groups of small, highly specialized shops on their floors in which they feature merchandise assortments keyed to a particular "total look" in apparel and accessories.

The boutique approach gained further impetus as European couture designers ventured into ready-to-wear and established their own boutiques, either free standing or within stores selected for the franchise, or both. Among the luminaries whose ready-to-wear is offered in boutiques in free-standing stores or within larger stores are Cardin, Givenchy, Valentino, Yves Saint Laurent for his Rive Gauche collections, and such Americans as Calvin Klein, Ralph Lauren, Anne Klein, and Donna Karan. In addition, many ready-to-wear designers from other countries have entered the U.S. market by way of their own boutiques in fashionable areas—for example, the Soprani boutique on Rodeo Drive in Los Angeles and the Giorgio Armani on New York's Madison Avenue.

Today, the boutique concept is widely accepted and used by most large department and specialty stores, not only for current fashions, but also for bath accessories, gourmet food and cookwear, and whatever else captures customer interest.

Chain Store Retailing

A chain is understood to be a retail organization that owns and operates a string of similar stores, all merchandised and controlled from a central headquarters office. Multi-unit chains developed during the late 1800s, as transportation and communication improved. Among the early chains were the A & P (Great Atlantic & Pacific Tea Company), Woolworth's, and J.C. Penney. Each started with a single store, gradually added others, and demonstrated the feasibility of the multistore concept and the economies of centralized buying.

Chains that sell apparel are either (1) general merchandise retailers, such as Sears and Montgomery Ward, whose product categories are similar to those of department stores, or (2) specialized apparel or accessory chains that focus on one or more related categories of apparel. Chains may be national, regional, or local in location. Their highly centralized, uniform store operation is quite different from what prevails among departmentalized stores that have branches or are autonomously operated retail stores that are part of the store ownership groups discussed earlier.

In the trade, the characteristics that distinguish **chain store** operations from those of typical department stores are as follows:

- There is no one big city flagship or main parent store, as in the case of a multi-unit department store with branches.
- The store units are standardized and uniform in physical appearance and in the merchandise they carry.
- The buying is done by buyers in the chain's central office, i.e., they have **centralized buying,** and each buyer is responsible for a specific category of merchandise—as contrasted with buying for an entire department.
- Merchandise is usually distributed to the units of a chain from its central or regional warehouses.
- The buying function is separate from the selling function.
- Selling is the responsibility of centralized sales managers and the managers of the individual store units.

However, as the number of branches operated by a departmentalized store increases, the parent store usually adapts several of a chain's operations, notably the separation of the selling function from the buying function. Selling becomes the responsibility of centralized store managers.

As an indication of the important role that chains play in the business of fashion, consider the following facts.

- Wal-Mart, Kmart, Sears, and J.C. Penney—the four largest general merchandise chains—are considered to be the "Big Four" of retailing (Table 10–4). Their combined 1994 annual sales of $166 billion had grown by 65 percent over what this group's sales were only five years earlier. Wal-Mart clearly leads the pack, having more than tripled its annual sales volume in five years. Wal-Mart is the largest retailer in the world.

Table 10–4	The "Big Four" General Merchandise Chains	
Company	**1994 Sales**	**Number of Stores**
Wal-Mart	$82,494,000,000*	2,684
Kmart	$34,025,000,000	3,834
Sears	$29,451,000,000	1,817
J.C. Penney	$20,380,000,000	960

*Includes supercenters and Sam's Clubs
Source: Sales figures are from "Analysis of Retail Performances for Fiscal 1994," August 1995, *Women's Wear Daily,* p. 6. Number of stores from "State of the Industry" by Management Horizons, August 1995, *Chain Store Age,* p. 3A.

Table 10–5	Select Specialized Apparel Chains	
Company	**1994 Sales**	**Number of Stores**
Melville*	$11,285,561,000	7,378
The Limited**	$ 7,320,492,000	4,867
The Gap	$ 3,722,940,000	1,508
Edison Brothers***	$ 1,476,400,000	2,761
U.S. Shoe****	$ 2,598,308,000	2,349
Charming Shoppes	$ 1,272,693,000	n.a.
Talbots	$ 879,585,000	n.a.
Merry-Go-Round	$ 782,816,000	n.a.

n.a. = Not available
* Includes Marshall's, which is now owned by TJX.
** Before dividing into two companies.
*** Before selling off stores as a result of Chapter 11 action.
**** The women's specialty store group was sold to La Leonardo Finanziaria in 1995.
Source: Sales figures are from "Analysis of Retail Performances for Fiscal 1994," August 1995, *Women's Wear Daily,* p. 6. Number of stores from "State of the Industry" by Management Horizons, August 1995, *Chain Store Age,* pp. 3A–7A.

- The combined sales of the eight top specialized apparel chains shown in Table 10–5 were more than $29 billion in 1994. The Limited alone had sales of more than $7.3 billion in 1994 before splitting into two entities: one from its core women's apparel group and the other from its lingerie and personal care businesses.

Specialized Apparel Chains

In terms of the fashion business, the decade of the 1920s was the beginning of apparel retailing by chain stores. Before then, there were a few retail chains of "waist stores," as blouse shops were then called. Their targeted market was low-income customers seeking prices below those offered in department and specialty stores. In about 1919, as blouses went out of fashion, producers of waists began to make low-priced dresses that the waist chains added to their assortments. With department and specialty stores catering to middle- and upper-middle-income families, there was little competition for chains featuring low-priced apparel. This period saw the start of many low-priced apparel chains that catered to the new class of "working women" who had entered the workforce during the manpower shortage of World War I.

Figure 10–4

Composite organization chart of an apparel chain

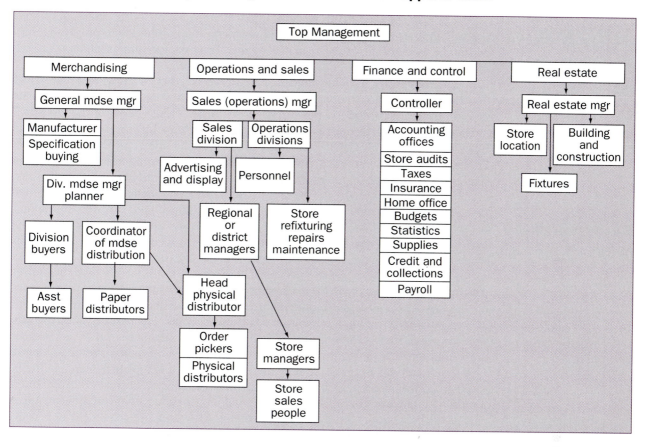

A notable example of an early waist chain is the Lerner Shops, which got its start in those years and by 1984 had 800 stores, with sales of $700 million primarily in low-priced fashions ("The Super," 1986). In 1985 this chain was acquired by The Limited stores. Other types of chains that sprang up and developed in the 1920s included millinery chains, men's hat chains, and family clothing stores. Fashion leadership was not their forte.

Chains took a different direction in the 1970s. There are now new **apparel specialty chains,** quite different from any of their predecessors. Regional or national in scope, they operate stores of relatively small individual size, and feature highly selective lines of contemporary and often trendy fashions in middle price ranges. Their aim is toward mainstream American juniors, misses, and young men's sportswear customers.

Today's apparel chains derive their strength from their ability to focus on a particular segment of the consumer market and the fashion interests of that market. Unlike department stores, they are not burdened by the need to serve a broad section of the public; they concentrate strictly on the target market they have identified for themselves. As in all chain retailing, their operations are highly centralized; their store units are generally uniform in design and merchandise presentation; and they usually operate under the same name in all locations (Figure 10–4). Many have a **store ambiance** designed to appeal to the customer the store wants to attract. Typical are The Gap, The Limited, Talbots, Eddie Bauer, and Casual Corner.

Such chains feature mainly their own private brands. Additionally, their buying power is so large that they can specify color, patterns, styles, fabrics, designs, and whatever else they consider important.

These specialized chains became, and still are, a major source of competition to department stores since their merchandise categories and moderate price ranges are within the scope of this older form of retailing. Their competition is felt most directly in casual sportswear for juniors, misses, and young men.

Specialty stores have lost market share in recent years, as shown in Figure 10–3. Too many have been competing for the same customers in their teens through early thirties and have not changed as this consumer matured. This segment of the industry is crowded, with a high degree of overlap among stores competing for the same shoppers. Even stores under the same ownership compete for the same customer. The Limited Stores, Express, and Lerner, all owned by The Limited corporation, have competed in the same markets, and frequently in the same malls. Many of the apparel specialty stores established their early successes around having a few "hot" items that attracted young customers. Now that consumers are becoming more individualistic, fewer are responding to these items. Specialty retailers are finding it harder and harder to find these big fashion hits. As the stores try to avoid big mistakes in identifying these "hot" items, many resort to filling their stores with "safe" choices like denim and khaki. This has led to the "sameness" in specialty stores that have caused consumers to ask themselves, "Wasn't I just in this store?" (Management Horizons, 1994a).

Specialty retailers are finding it harder to continue to compete by using another strategy that gave them an edge over department stores. For two decades, specialty retailers made their success by being faster and more nimble than their department store colleagues. Specialty retailers were able to zero in on their customers, identify new trends, and by using the latest technology produce and replenish merchandise far more quickly than could their large, slower-moving department store cousins. For example, The Limited could identify trends and have products delivered in fast cycles that department stores could not begin to match. However, as department stores have developed partnerships with suppliers and become more proficient in producing their own private label assortments, specialty stores no longer have this advantage (Management Horizons, 1994a).

The weak retailing climate of the early 1990s has caused several retail reorganizations. A number of major specialty apparel chains have filed petitions under **Chapter 11** of the U.S. Bankruptcy Code. Chapter 11 is the legal process that provides an opportunity for companies burdened by excessive debt to continue operations while plans are made to restructure the company and reschedule debt payments. This often involves selling off some divisions. All such decisions are made in negotiations with creditor and stockholder committees and are subject to approval and supervision of a federal bankruptcy judge who oversees the situation.

Among specialty store groups that have filed for Chapter 11 are Edison Brothers Stores Inc., which had 2,700 units. (Store units are often referred to as **"doors"** in the industry.) In the restructuring, about 500 unprofitable doors were closed down (Wilner, 1995). The company's Oaktree division was merged into its Jeans West Division. Other Edison Brothers Stores include: 5-7-9 Shops, J.Riggins, JW/Jeans West, Zeidler & Zeidler/Webster, Coda, Repp Big & Tall, Bakers/Leeds, The Wild Pairs, and Precis.

One-time top performer, Merry-Go-Round stores, is another specialty store chain that operated for a time under Chapter 11. Other specialty chains that ran store-closing sales during out-of-court restructuring included Charming Shoppes and Gateway Apparel. All of these once-thriving specialty chains suffered from the sluggish retail climate and the crushing competition of the 1990s.

Apparel Retailing by General Merchandise Chains

The mass general merchandising chains have also become a factor in fashion distribution. The Penney chain had apparel and accessories from the start, but Montgomery Ward and Sears had functioned primarily as catalog houses until the 1920s. With transportation improving and the rural customer no longer completely dependent on the mail, they moved into store operations. Sears began in 1925, with a single store located in its Chicago mail-order facility. Ward's soon followed. Both companies started with stores that featured equipment and supplies primarily of interest to men. Only gradually did their stores move into apparel, and then it was for their typical customer, of modest means and modest clothing budget.

It was not until the 1960s that the big **general merchandising chains** came of age as major factors in the fashion business. In response to the increased affluence and greater fashion awareness of their targeted customers, they broadened their assortments and extended their price ranges upward. They also gave prime main floor locations to apparel and accessories.

Both J.C. Penney and Sears Roebuck have emphasized apparel more in recent years than was true in their earlier company histories. In the 1980s, J.C. Penney shifted to apparel for a greater portion of its store merchandise assortment, dropping some of its hard lines such as furniture and large appliances. In the 1990s, Sears ended years of floundering to redefine itself, settling on apparel as its primary focus. In this transformation, Sears adopted an award-winning "Softer Side of Sears" apparel campaign, which became so successful for its women's clothing that it was extended to men's and children's clothing. The retailer expanded its assortment of national and private brands, offering customers trendier and more updated merchandise. The new emphasis on apparel proved to be a winning strategy for Sears in its 800 stores throughout the country (Palmieri & Kaplan, 1995).

With their enormous buying power, these great chains can have merchandise produced to their specifications and styled exclusively for them. They may not have, or even attempt to have, the fashion authority and leadership shown by department and specialty stores and by the new breed of specialized apparel chains. But what they can do, and do very well, is move a great deal of merchandise and control a substantial percentage of the fashion market. It is generally estimated in the trade that apparel and accessories represent at least 30 percent of these chains' total volume. On that basis, the combined fashion goods business of the big chains amounts to many billions of dollars, a decidedly important share of the fashion market.

Discount Retailing: Underselling Operations

Shortly after World War II, discounters added a new dimension to the world of retailing by adopting the operational techniques originated by food **supermarkets** in the 1930s. These techniques entailed offering lower food prices to depression-weary customers by using self-selection selling, low-rent locations, inexpensive decor, and cash-and-carry terms.

As generally understood in the trade, the term **discounter** applies to a retail establishment that *regularly* sells its merchandise at less than conventional prices, concentrating mainly on national brands. By operating with self-service and other expense-saving techniques such as no mail or telephone orders, no free deliveries, low-rent locations, and limited return privileges (in some cases), they can operate profitably on markups lower than those that prevail among other types of retailers.

The success of discounters in the 1950s stemmed from their selling of nationally advertised branded appliances at prices below the manufacturers' suggested retail prices. This was in the period just after World War II, when men returning from military service spearheaded a boom in family formation, suburban living—and babies. The two-earner household in that period was relatively rare, and incomes had to be stretched to accommodate the pent-up demand for everything young families needed, from refrigerators to ready-to-wear. As the suburban communities burgeoned, so did the discounters. They opened stores in both cities and suburbs, and broadened their merchandise assortments to include low-priced, unbranded apparel.

As these households and their children prospered, many of them retained their active interest in buying at favorable prices. They were in a position to enjoy the good life—but they enjoyed it more at a bargain. This was in marked contrast with the attitude of earlier generations, among whom comfortable incomes were equated with freedom from price consciousness. Underselling retailing in various forms became more and more firmly entrenched in the 1960s, 1970s, and 1980s, without regard to business cycles, employment statistics, or consumer income figures. Value-conscious consumers of the 1990s emphasized this trend even more than had been true earlier.

Full-Line Discount Stores

Full-line discount stores, called *discounters,* have had a powerful impact on the retail industry in recent years. These stores generally sell name brand merchandise, as well as their own store brands, at prices lower than those of the traditionally priced department or specialty stores. The major discounters are Wal-Mart, Kmart, Target (part of Dayton-Hudson), Ames, Bradlees, Caldor[3], and Venture Stores (formerly part of May Company). These stores are economy versions of the old fashioned store where customers could fulfill a large portion of their shopping needs in one place. Today's discounters often have more merchandise than the traditional department stores.

Although the discounters are not the fashion leaders, they are the most powerful presence in the industry today. As consumers have become more value-conscious **cross-shoppers,** who may shop at department stores for some items and at less expensive stores for others, discounters have been the winners. Most notably, Wal-Mart has roared onto the scene, going from a small midwestern discount chain to the world's largest retailer. Today, Wal-Mart is also the largest apparel and accessories retailer in the world, with more than 2,600 stores, and it is adding about 100 stores per year.

Discount chains, like other mass merchandisers, have massive buying power that wields a great deal of influence in the industry. Because they buy huge quantities, they can negotiate competitive prices with suppliers that permit the discounters to pass savings along to the consumer. The appetites of major discounters such as Wal-Mart are so great that some manufacturers may produce all their merchandise for only one giant chain (a strategy with many risks if that single retail customer decides to change suppliers). In fact, some of these chains are so large that few manufacturers have the production capacity to fill a major discounter's needs, even for a single product line. Consider, for example, that over 2,600 dresses are required to have only

[3]Both Bradlees and Caldor filed for Chapter 11 status.

one of a single type in each Wal-Mart store. To offer a range of sizes and styles in a line quickly adds up to hundreds of thousands of items required by just this one retailer. Buyers for the discounters work in narrowly specialized apparel categories and are responsible for millions of dollars in sales annually.

Discount chains continue to take market share from other retailers—at least a percentage or more of the market each year. The growth of discounters compared to department stores and specialty stores is shown in Figure 10–3. Although a percentage or two of the market may seem slight, it is significant when one percent represents more than $1 billion. Discounters, particularly Wal-Mart, have been criticized for hurting small businesses in communities where stores are opened. As Wal-Mart opens **supercenters** with 175,000 or more square feet of space, these have been estimated to equal the sales volume of 100 typical small businesses (Barrett, 1994).

Discounters continue to seek well-known branded apparel to enhance sales and store image. Selling brands such as Gitano, Catalina, White Stag, Faded Glory, and Hanes continues to make discounters a growing force in apparel retailing. Wal-Mart's introduction of the Kathie Lee Collection, using Kathie Lee Gifford as the spokesperson, was a monumental success for the Arkansas-based discounter.

Wal-Mart may have started as a small-town operation, but the company is now legendary for many of its efficient and state-of-the-art operations that keep costs to a minimum. These efficiencies, which are translated into attractive prices for consumers, include use of technology and logistics to provide efficient warehousing, transportation, and delivery systems.

Hypermarkets and Supercenters

Adopting a retailing format popular in Europe, several **hypermarkets** were opened in the United States. These hypermarkets are gigantic full-line discount stores and supermarkets combined, with 200,000 to 300,000 square feet of selling space and selling as many as 100,000 items. Stores sell everything including clothing, home furnishings, tires, appliances, gardening supplies, and food and offer services such as haircuts, restaurants, banking, and free supervised play areas for children. Employees often move about these megastores on skates.

These sprawling hypermarkets began to appear in France in the 1960s and subsequently spread to a number of other European countries. Once touted as the next big boom in U.S. retailing, hypermarkets did not meet retailers' expectations in this country. U.S. consumers appeared to be overwhelmed by the size of hypermarkets. Bigger did not appear to be better in this case. This retail format has succeeded in Europe, particularly in France, apparently because other mass retailers do not compete as vigorously as in the United States. Two French retailers, Carrefour and Leedmark, opened hypermarkets in the United States but closed them. Kmart's partnership with Bruno's supermarket to form hypermarkets in the South was not successful. To date, Wal-Mart remains the only major retailer operating hypermarkets, four of them, in the United States (D'Innocenzio, 1992).

The supercenter concept has been much more successful than hypermarkets. Both Wal-Mart and Kmart have been successful with this format, combining a very large, full-line general merchandise discount store with a supermarket. Supercenters, carrying thousands of **SKUs,** are more streamlined and user-friendly than the hypermarkets. Wal-Mart appears to be placing major growth emphasis on the supercenter concept, building those rather than smaller stores in areas where population demographics show these can be successful.

Warehouse Clubs

The **warehouse clubs,** also called membership warehouses or price clubs, originated in Europe as cash-and-carry wholesalers for small businesses. In the United States, these clubs serve small businesses but also have expanded their clientele to include customers who pay a small membership fee to join. The major warehouse club groups are Sam's Club (owned by Wal-Mart Stores Inc.) and Price Club/Costco. The former Pace Membership Warehouse, owned by Kmart, was purchased by Sam's Club. Little or no advertising, stark industrial decor, low-rent locations, cash-and-carry transactions, and very fast inventory turns keep their expenses very low. The warehouse atmosphere of these clubs and their low pricing policies attract the value-conscious customer—a category that includes almost everyone who shops for commodities.

Although the warehouse clubs specialize in selling branded commodity goods in bulk, they also sell basic apparel, footwear, and home textiles. Casual wear, sportswear, and undergarments are the most frequently found apparel items, with an occasional find in designer lines. Dressing rooms are generally unavailable.

Most of the time upscale brand merchandise appears in these stores under legitimate conditions, but sometimes it gets there through **diverters.** Because many manufacturers of prestige goods do not want their status labels weakened by being sold in cut-rate stores, they refuse to sell to these retailers. However, enterprising individuals too often find ways of bending the rules, and diverters sometimes play that role in this case. In this scheme, other stores will intentionally overbuy these prestige items, with the intent of selling the merchandise to warehouse clubs or other low-cost retailers. The merchandise is "diverted" to a retailer other than the one to whom the manufacturer sold it.

Despite their popularity, warehouse clubs have not been as profitable as expected. The future of this retail format is still uncertain.

Category Killers

The retail landscape has been changed dramatically in the past decade by the "**category killers**"—retailers that specialize in tremendous assortments of a single kind of merchandise. They get their name from destroying competitors who sell the same merchandise. Like discounters, these stores offer substantial savings because of high volume and low margins. Traditionally these stores have been huge, stand-alone stores. These cavernous stores are also sometimes called **superstores** or "big box" retailers. Sometimes when Wal-Mart is included in a group with these stores, these are called the *power retailers*.

Some of the major names among the category killers are Home Depot, Toys 'R' Us, Barnes & Noble, The Sports Authority, Circuit City, Office Depot, and Bed Bath & Beyond. Although this is an exceedingly important group of retailers, industry experts generally do not identify fashion retailers in this category.

A new retail phenomenon began to occur in the mid-1990s, which some described as "demalling" or "the invasion of the category killers" (Edelson, 1995b, p. 8). As hundreds of small specialty stores close annually[4], malls are filling their spaces with the big box stores. This move is a historical change in the classic mall concept with a few **anchor stores** surrounded by specialty stores. Traditional de-

---

[4]Edelson (1995b) notes that apparel retailers alone lost an estimated one million square feet of mall space in 1994.

partment store anchors then will be forced to compete against the category killers inside their own malls. This means the department stores must rethink their merchandising and consider eliminating categories the big box retailers sell. Edelson (1995b) noted that "what appears to be threatening department stores may end up benefiting them in the long run. Observers see the big box invasion as creating a hybrid retail environment that could reverse negative traffic patterns at malls across the country" (p. 8).

Off-Price Apparel Chains

Underselling stores that offer quality and fashion apparel have been on the scene for many years, but only recently have they blossomed into a major force in retailing. One of the earliest among them, Loehman's, was founded in Brooklyn in 1920 and is now a national chain of 77 stores. Others that came into the field later followed the same course, starting as individual stores and developing into national chains.

Known in the trade today as **off-price retailers,** the fashion apparel discounters came into their own in the late 1970s, growing at a much faster rate than more conventional retailers (Table 10–6). What distinguished these new fashion discounters from their predecessors was that they specialized in high-quality brand- and designer-name clothing, at deeply discounted prices—and they still do.

The target customers of these operations are the price-conscious middle class. Among them are also consumers who formerly bought top-quality merchandise without really questioning price. When apparel prices skyrocketed, some of these consumers sought the discounters—not for cheaper grades of merchandise, but for the familiar "names" and qualities at lower prices. For example, they are willing to spend $100 on a dress, sweater, or handbag, but they want one that normally sells for $150 to $200 in department and specialty stores. In these stores, the selection is limited, and returning merchandise is often more difficult than at other stores.

Restructuring is occurring in this segment of the industry also. For many years, Marshalls was the largest apparel discounter, with 495 stores and sales of $2.8 billion in 1994. However, TJX bought the Marshalls division from Melville in 1995 ("TJX Buys," 1995).

The impact of underselling apparel retailing on conventional retailers has been more than just competition. Today one can walk into well-known department and specialty stores at the height of the selling season and find numerous off-price sales

Table 10–6	Off-Price Apparel Chains: Big Names in Bargain Clothes	
Company	**1994 Sales**	**Number of Stores**
TJX Companies, Inc.	$3,842,818,000	1,098
Burlington Coat Factory	1,468,440,000	195
Ross Stores	1,262,544,000	n.a.
Filene's Basement	608,303,000	n.a.
Dress Barn	457,324,000	n.a.

n.a. = Not available
Source: Sales figures are from "Analysis of Retail Performances for Fiscal 1994," August 1995, *Women's Wear Daily,* p. 7. Number of stores from "State of the Industry," by Management Horizons, August 1995, *Chain Store Age,* pp. 6A–7A.

Figure 10–5

Examples of deep discounts on name brand merchandise at offprice apparel stores.

being featured. The distinction between conventional and discount retailers has become blurred, and it has become increasingly harder to determine where conventional retailing ends and off-price operations begin.

Factory Outlets

Another important form of off-price apparel retailing has become an important force across the country—**factory outlets** owned and operated by manufacturers of top brand and designer-name clothing. These outlets originally served as a dumping ground for out-of-season merchandise and odds and ends of factory stock, but have evolved far from that.

Today, there are nearly 12,000 outlet stores in all parts of the United States, compared to 3,682 in 1988. More than 500 manufacturers operate outlet stores, many with a "chain" of outlet stores. Most of these are clustered in fast-growing **outlet centers,** or outlet malls. Outlet store decor, services, merchandise assortments, and locations have been upgraded, becoming good-looking, professionally run retail stores with total sales in 1994 of $11.4 billion (Figure 10–6). Growing faster than many of their retail competitors, sales growth in outlet centers increased 15 percent in 1994 compared to a 5 percent growth for department stores (Edelson, 1995c; "Outlet Industry," 1995).

Initially located on the factory grounds, these outlets began to cluster in outlet centers, which were located in outlying areas not in conflict with the shopping areas of their major retail accounts. If a major department store buys from a manufacturer, the retailer resents having the supplier establish its own store nearby and undersell

Figure 10–6

A factory outlet center

Source: Photo by Anthony Magnacca/Merrill/Prentice Hall

the department store on the same merchandise. Outlet centers are now trying to build a more consistent base of repeat customers, and to do so, they are locating closer to traditional malls. Whereas outlet centers were 45 miles from traditional malls in 1990, they now average 28 miles. Outlet center shoppers were found to spend twice the amount of time at outlet centers as in a traditional mall. When they invest the time to get there, it is a planned event (Edelson, 1995).

Factory outlets generally do very little advertising, thus avoiding conflict with their retail accounts, but they do leave labels in the garments. In the past, outlet stores typically received manufacturers' new lines after they had been shipped to other retail customers a month or so earlier. Increasingly, however, outlet stores are featuring in-season merchandise, treating outlet centers as another distribution channel, not a place to get rid of excess inventory or seconds. In some cases, manufacturers produce merchandise specifically for their outlet stores. With the popularity of outlet stores, discounts have dwindled from more than 70 percent below the normal retail price to sometimes as as low as 10 to 15 percent below. The norm now appears to be 20 to 25 percent below retail (Edelson, 1995c).

During the early years of outlet centers (the 1980s), merchandise tended to be from middle-of-the road manufacturers that appealed to the mass market. Today, outlet developers are courting a more affluent clientele. Outlet centers have attracted fashion-forward designers including Ralph Lauren, Donna Karan, Calvin Klein, Henry Grethel, Harvé Benard, and Kenar. One center has a European store featuring merchandise from Armani and Emanuel. With the upscale orientation, the shopping environments and amenities have improved, more closely resembling traditional malls.

Retailers are even trying to get in on the successful outlet mall trend, opening outlet stores near their flagship stores. For example, Saks Fifth Avenue's clearinghouse outlet, Off-5th—Saks Fifth Avenue Outlet, opened near its Manhattan store.

Some retail experts question whether outlet centers can continue their fast-paced expansion. One writer noted, "the outlet mall boom is sowing the seeds of its own decline" (Rudnitsky, 1994, p. 46). Because of the growth of these malls, this segment of the industry, like several others, is becoming rapidly **overstored**. Total consumer spending has not increased enough to keep pace with the growing number of stores. Outlet malls are succeeding by taking market share from other retailers, but consumers may eventually lose some of their zest for outlet stores.

Franchised Retailing

Franchised operations are familiar to the public through such organizations as fast-food outlets like McDonald's and KFC, through automobile dealerships, restaurants such as Howard Johnson's, and national networks of real estate offices like Century 21.

In a **franchise** arrangement, the **franchisor** (a parent company) provides a **franchisee** (owner-operator of a retail unit) with exclusive use of an established name in a specific trading area, plus assistance in organizing, training, merchandising, and management, in return for a stipulated consideration. The nature of the agreement varies widely from company to company. For example, the franchising company may provide an operating program complete in every detail, or the agreement may simply specify that the franchisor will provide merchandise for the franchisee. The uniform appearance of many franchised retail outlets often gives the impression to the public that they constitute a chain, but in actuality, each store is run by an individual entrepreneur who owns the business, meets his or her obligation to the franchisor, and retains the remaining profits.

Designer-Name Franchised Boutiques

As described in the previous chapter, European ready-to-wear designers have been operating their own franchised name boutiques for the last two decades, among them the Rive Gauche franchised boutiques of Yves Saint Laurent and the Nouvelle Boutiques of Givenchy. Beginning in the 1970s, franchising arrangements began to be visible in the domestic apparel retailing field. Among the earliest and most successful were the maternity shop franchises such as Lady Madonna and Maternally Yours. Other examples are the Tennis Lady shops and the hundreds of Athlete's Foot franchised outlets.

In the 1980s, American name designers began to follow the lead of European designers, and today American designer-franchised boutiques have burgeoned in major cities throughout the United States. An outstanding example is Ralph Lauren, who has pioneered a multimillion-dollar retail business with worldwide franchises in the United States and throughout affluent areas in Europe and Asia. The growth and future role of retail stores controlled by their designer franchisors is one that bears watching.

Shopping Centers and Malls

A major retail phenomenon growing out of the migration to suburbia that followed World War II was the development and proliferation of shopping centers. A **shopping center** is a preplanned, architecturally coordinated grouping of retail stores, plus a parking area that is generally larger than the area occupied by the stores themselves. Medical facilities, banks, restaurants, and sometimes theaters and skating rinks may be part of the mix offered the shopper. These centers are usually developed by real estate interests and occasionally by the real estate divisions of very large retailers. The centers have their own managements, promotional activities, and merchants' associations to weld their stores into a cohesive group.

Since the 1960s, when shopping centers emerged as major retail sites, they have provided a prime area of expansion for department stores, chain stores, large and small specialty stores, and sometimes off-price retailers. More recently, even the category killers are locating in malls. By 1995, there were 40,368 shopping centers in the United States. California has the largest number, with 5,350, followed by Florida with 3,086 and Texas with 2,824 (International Council of Shopping Centers, 1995).

The retail climate of the 1990s has had an impact on the development of shopping malls. A slow-growing economy and reluctant consumer spending have resulted in a slowdown of new mall construction. An excessive amount of retail capacity (space available)—known as overstoring—exists in the United States. Some 18 square feet of retail space exists for every man, woman, and child in the country, more than enough to accommodate reasonable population growth in the future (Sack, 1995). Figure 10–7 shows the extent to which shopping center growth rates have out-paced population increases, leading to market saturation.

Figure 10–7

Shopping center growth outstrips population rise. (Index, 1964-100)

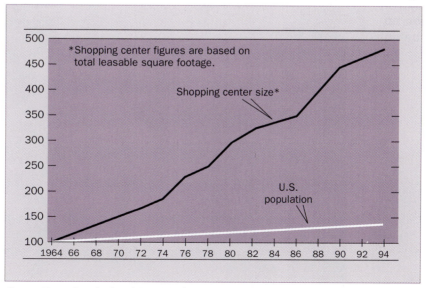

Source: From *Standard and Poor's Industry Surveys: Retailing* (p. R63) by K. Sack, 1996, New York: Standard & Poor's. Reprinted by permission.

Because of the glut in retail space, new shopping center construction has slowed. During the 1970s, about 25 new regional shopping centers opened in a typical year. That pace slowed to five malls in 1993 and four in 1994 (Sack, 1995).

Numbers alone do not tell the whole story of shopping centers, however. Over the years, they have changed from open-air centers, laid out horizontally with on-site parking, into multilevel, enclosed, and climate-controlled **malls,** where shoppers can spend an entire day shopping, resting, eating, even skating or seeing motion pictures. And they are no longer purely suburban phenomena; they are now in center city areas—often those associated with urban renewal enterprises. An outstanding example of an urban enterprise is Trump Tower, located on Fifth Avenue in New York. This is a 68-story building consisting of 49 floors of apartments, 13 floors of office space, and a 6-floor atrium around which are some of the most prestigious fashion stores in the world. Another example is the Water Tower in Chicago.

Another large type of shopping center has emerged on the scene in recent years. Sometimes called a **megamall,** the largest of these in the United States is the Mall of

Figure 10–8

Camp Snoopy provides various forms of entertainment to Mall of America shoppers. The Snoopy Bounce is 38 feet tall and 28 feet in diameter. Inside the giant inflated beagle, children can frolic on an air-filled cushion.

Source: Courtesy of Knott's Camp Snoopy.

America, located in Bloomington, Minnesota, near Minneapolis/St. Paul. With 4.2 million square feet, 10 times the size of an average regional mall, the Mall of America is large enough to hold seven Yankee Stadiums. Total store front footage of 4.3 miles, distributed among more than 400 stores on several levels, makes this a shoppers' paradise. Referring to itself as "the world's premier retail and entertainment center," the mall attracted an estimated 700,000 tourists from other countries in its first year. The area near the mall is designed to accommodate visitors who come for more than a brief shopping trip; 6,500 hotel rooms are nearby. Tour groups often identify the Mall of America as their destination; over 12,000 organized tour groups and 400 Japanese groups visited in the mall's first year (Mall of America, 1994).

The Mall of America is the leading example of another retail phenomenon—*combining shopping with entertainment.* Complete with Knott's Camp Snoopy, which features seven acres of year-round theme park entertainment, the Mall of America sets the trend in creating large-scale entertainment-oriented shopping centers (Figure 10–8). As consumers have shied away from shopping and spend less and less time at malls, shopping center developers have added entertainment components to create more of a "destination." The goal is to entice the consumer to spend more time in the mall. With 45 restaurants, 9 nightclubs, 14 theater screens, and even a wedding chapel (with full wedding planning services), visitors have plenty of ways to be entertained at the Mall of America. The strategy appears to be working for at least some stores in the megamall. For example, the Nordstrom store there has surpassed all the company's other stores in the country in sales and profits ("At Retail," 1995).

Nonstore Retailing

As consumers continue to be pressed for time, many are expected to be increasingly attracted to the convenience of various types of nonstore retailing. Consumer research also indicates that this time-pressured consumer is frustrated with shopping in malls (Sack, 1995). Options that permit shopping in the convenience of one's home are becoming increasingly appealing to weary consumers. Retail consultants Kurt Salmon Associates (1995) predict that over the next 10 to 15 years, there will be a massive shift to nonstore retailing of all types. Figure 10–9 illustrates the shift KSA predicts from in-store retailing to nonstore retailing.

Although changes in consumers' attitudes toward shopping are critical to these predicted shifts, technology advances have created nonstore shopping options undreamed of a decade ago. Interactive technology provides access to vast amounts of information and choices, and this will increase exponentially in coming years. Consumers' televisions and computers now offer vast potential as places to shop as manufacturers and retailers discover ways to sell effectively through these media. The new wave of electronic retailers has just begun.

Mail-Order Houses

By census definition and trade usage today, a **mail-order house** is a retail establishment that does the bulk of its selling to the consumer primarily through the medium of a catalog as a result of orders placed mainly by mail or phone. The concept of selling through a catalog rather than over the counter of a store was pioneered by Aaron Montgomery Ward in 1872, to be followed by Richard Sears, who issued the first

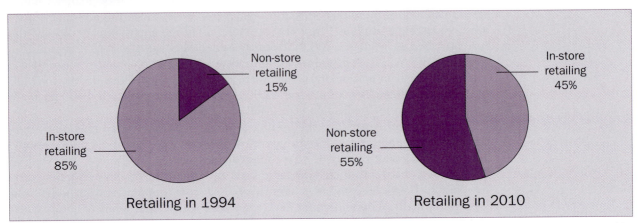

Figure 10–9

In-store vs. non-store retailing

Source: Based on information in *Vision for the New Millennium. . . Evolving to Consumer Response* (p. 8) by Kurt Salmon Associates, 1995, Atlanta, GA: Author. Adapted by permission of Kurt Salmon Associates.

Sears Roebuck & Company catalog in 1893, although he had been in business before that time.

Among the conditions that paved the way for this nineteenth-century innovation in retailing was the then-predominantly rural nature of the country. Stocks of country stores were limited, and transportation to the developing fashionable city stores was difficult. More to the point, rural free delivery had just been introduced by the post office.

These early catalogs were the standbys of rural customers for generations. Although the fashions offered were not exciting, the prices and assortments surpassed those in rural stores, and they were a delight to the country clientele they were intended to serve (Figure 10–10). In the eyes of these customers, the catalogs indeed earned the name that came to be applied to them: "the wish book." So well, indeed, did the mail-order houses meet the needs and broadening interests of rural customers that by 1895 the Sears catalog consisted of 507 pages, and the company's annual sales exceeded $750,000 ("Merchant to," no date).

As one early mail-order company, Jones Post & Co., told its customers: "Your home, or ranch, or farm, is never so far distant that you are shut out from the great throbbing world with its mammoth commercial establishments. No longer are you forced to be satisfied with the small stock and slim assortment (of country stores) from which to make your selection at exorbitant prices" (Kidwell & Christman, 1974, p. 162).

Growth of Mail-Order Retailing

Beginning in the 1970s, catalog sales have been increasing rapidly and show every sign of continuing to do so. Catalog sales to consumers have climbed by 5.5 percent per year between 1990 and 1995 to $38.6 billion. Department stores and other general retailers account for only 2.4 percent of the consumer catalog direct order sales; however, this is the fastest growing catalog industry segment (Direct Marketing Association, 1995). In 1994, some 13 billion catalogs were mailed; this was 51 for every man, woman, and child in the United States (Sack, 1995). More than half

Figure 10–10   **1897 Sears Roebuck & Company catalog page**

Source: Courtesy of Sears Roebuck & Co.

the adult population made at least one purchase by telephone or mail ("Mail-Order,"1994).

This "buying from catalog" phenomenon results from several factors: the rise of two-earner families, in which neither spouse has much time for shopping in stores; affluent singles, whose active working and social lives leave little room for shopping; the time crunch for working mothers; crowded stores and their often inexperienced and hard-to-find salespeople; and the advent of toll-free 800 telephone numbers. The result has been an explosion not only in the number of catalog companies, but also in the variety of goods that can be bought from catalogs. Today mail-order houses range from large, well-known retailers such as Spiegel, which sells designer-name fashions, to small specialty operations such as the Collins Street Bakery in Texas, which sells fruitcake. In fact, mail-order sellers of both apparel and other consumer products have multiplied to such a degree that there is even a publication called *Shop-at-Home-Directory* for consumers who want information about the various mail-order houses and the merchandise that each features.

The largest in terms of dollar sales are the general merchandise catalogs of J.C. Penney and Spiegel. Targeted at mainstream America, they sell everything to furnish a home, clothe a family, and equip every type of activity. For a century, Sears Roebuck & Company published its beloved "wish book." However, the company dropped the catalog in 1993 as part of a major restructuring. Following the end of Sears' "big book," many other catalog firms scrambled to secure pieces of that mail-order business. Sears has since returned to the mail-order business with specialty catalogs.

Mail-Order Apparel Specialists

Although apparel has been featured in mail-order catalogs since their inception, it is only in recent years that there has been a great emphasis on upscale fashions. Many highly specialized apparel mail-order houses have proliferated, each of which focuses its effort on a clearly defined targeted group of consumers. Some, such as the Horchow Collection, concentrate on high-priced, sophisticated luxury items of wearing apparel and accessories. Other similar operations of this type are Trifles, J.A. Bank Clothiers, and the specialized fashion-forward books of Spiegel. Hartmarx's Barrie Pace catalog is directed to professional women. Another group of catalog fashion retailers specialize in classic and casual wear for men and women. Perhaps among the best known of this type is Lands' End which mails millions of catalogs annually and whose sales are reported as $992 million ("Analysis of," 1995). Examples of others in this category include Johnny Appleseed, Eddie Bauer (owned by Spiegel), L.L. Bean, and Talbots (Figure 10–11). There are also catalogs devoted to off-size apparel, such as King Size for men and Brylane for large-size women's apparel. Spiegel's E style is a catalog for African-American women (Chandler, 1994). A number of mail-order shoe firms specialize in hard-to-find sizes.

The operations involved in the buying and selling of fashion goods by mail are quite different from those of stores. The preparation of a catalog is a lengthy process, and merchandise must be bought close to a year in advance of a selling season. Since apparel producers do not have their seasonal lines ready that far in advance, mail-order houses must work with fabric suppliers and apparel manufacturers to develop the kinds of merchandise they want for their targeted customers. However, because most catalog retailers print and distribute millions of catalogs, their tremendous purchasing power enables them to have merchandise made expressly for them.

Figure 10–11

The appeal of shopping by catalog

Source: Courtesy of L.L. Bean

Catalog Operations by Department and Specialty Stores

At this point, it may be well to reread the definition of a mail-order house. Some catalog retailers may have one or more retail stores. Talbots, for example, operates over 400 stores and plans to double that number by the year 2000. However, if the bulk of a retailer's business is done through catalog sales, it is considered a mail-order house.

Originally, the primary purpose of the catalogs of conventional department and large specialty stores was to attract customers into the store. Nowadays, the same elements that led to the growth of mail-order retailing have encouraged such retail stores to increase the frequency and distribution of their catalogs and improve the efficiency with which they handle mail and telephone responses. These days, although not to be classified as mail-order houses, mail and telephone business accounts for a more and more substantial portion of the conventional stores' business. Precise figures are not readily available, but these may illustrate the point: Bloomingdale's-by-Mail is now referred to as the "second largest store" in their multi-unit operation.

Catalog Showroom Retailing

A **catalog showroom retailer** is an underselling company that sells from a catalog and also maintains a showroom where samples of the merchandise can be seen and ordered. There are no deliveries, but usually the purchases can be picked up immediately at the showroom or from an adjoining warehouse. Very large, prepackaged stocks of the catalog items are on hand.

The mainstay of the merchandise assortment is usually branded housewares, appliances, TVs, stereo equipment, electronics, toys, and sporting goods at prices well below those prevailing in conventional stores. Items of apparel, cosmetics, children's sleepers, men's underwear, and jewelry are also carried, but often are not featured or listed in the catalogs. Prices reflect the low operating costs. In addition to their bare-bones operation, catalog showrooms are usually in low-rent areas. Few salespeople are needed, because customers select their items from samples and catalogs, then make out purchase slips and pick up their packages from the warehouse.

Retail operations of this type began in the late 1960s and achieved a growth in sales ranging from 30 to 40 percent during the 1970s. The largest of these is Best Products, with sales over $1.5 billion.

The impact of such stores on the fashion business has been negligible thus far; but so was the impact of other forms of underselling stores at first. Whether or not these minimum-service retailers will make a place for themselves in fashion still remains to be seen.

Electronic Retailing

Although most goods are still being sold through stores and mail-order catalogs, various forms of electronic shopping are expected to become increasingly important. No one can really predict the future of these forms of retailing, but nearly all industry experts agree that more and more consumers will participate in electronic shopping, viewing merchandise on either television screens or on a personal computer. In short, home shopping is going high tech ("Electronic Shopping," 1994).

The electronic retailing trend reflects the same social factors that explain the growth of mail-order sales—the number of working women and individuals' interest in spending spare time in more relaxed ways than shopping. The use of credit cards—i.e., the "plasticizing" of the purchase process—has facilitated easy purchases from almost anywhere. Added to this, the advent of 800 numbers, WATS lines, fax machines, computers, United Parcel Service, and Federal Express, shopping and shipping occur with the ease of a call or a few strokes on a keypad. Moreover, these systems have almost eliminated geographical shopping boundaries (Bartlett & Peterson, 1992).

Electronic retailing occurs in basically three formats: (1) **home television shopping,** (2) **on-line computer services,** and (3) **CD-ROM shopping** with a compact disk run on a CD-ROM drive to show catalog collections. Each of these is discussed below.

Home Television Shopping

TV shopping shows have been around since the late 1970s, but most authorities date the real emergence and increasing importance of home shopping channels to the mid-1980s.[5] Home shopping channels are cable or satellite TV channels entirely devoted

---

[5]Home Shopping Network was founded in the late 1970s and QVC in 1986.

to selling goods and services. Most TV shopping works like mail order; the consumer calls an 800 number after viewing the product. As cable and satellite companies upgrade to offer hundreds of channels and become interactive, home shopping has the potential of tapping into a "video mall"—offering consumers a chance to browse through channels, ask for information, order, and pay without ever leaving home.

Until the early 1990s, television shopping had featured moderate-priced merchandise directed to the masses. Major retailers had shown little interest because this medium was not being directed toward the more urban and suburban upscale customer many merchants wanted to attract. However, a major change occurred in the TV home shopping industry when Barry Diller, who had started Fox Broadcasting Co. and made it a powerful fourth network, took the helm at QVC, the second-largest home shopping channel at the time. Diller rapidly transformed QVC into a high-profile medium attracting both manufacturers and retailers catering to a range of customers.

Under Diller's leadership, QVC became a more fashion-oriented shopping channel. Fashionable Saks Fifth Avenue made astonishing sales, confirming that upscale shoppers were attracted to this form of retailing. Other upscale stores including Bloomingdale's, Nordstrom, and Williams-Sonoma explored TV home shopping. Numerous designers have sold merchandise on QVC, including Arnold Scaasi, Donna Karan, Calvin Klein, and Diane von Furstenberg. Diller created a second channel, Q2, aimed at sophisticated professionals. For many manufacturers and retailers, the sales volume per hour was phenomenal—far beyond what could have been anticipated based on previous TV shopping history. One survey found that home shoppers were younger, more educated, and more style-conscious than believed earlier; nearly half were men (Zinn, DeGeorge, Shoretz, Yang, & Forest, 1993). MTV's home shopping venture, "The Goods," featured designers such as Isaac Mizrahi, Todd Oldham, and Marc Jacobs.

Instead of thinking of TV home shopping as a competitor, for a time some retailers saw this medium as having potential to help reduce the costs associated with store retailing—namely, rent, sales help, and advertising. Even J.C. Penney, whose earlier home shopping network failed, remained open to the future of this retailing option. A number of retailers explored having their own shopping channels but most eventually backed off.

During Diller's two-year stay at QVC, TV home shopping was heralded as the most important shopping format of the future. Sales were astonishing. After the initial hype, however, enthusiasm waned. Although Home Shopping Network and QVC each have annual sales of well over $1 billion, fewer high-profile designers and retailers appear to be attracted to this medium. TV home shopping has two constraints that reduce its appeal: (1) The customer must adapt to the TV schedule, watching lengthy programs to see only a few items displayed—hardly the time-saving feature today's time-starved consumers want, and (2) TV home shopping does not permit fashion products to be presented with enough clarity and detail to make satisfactory purchase decisions (Edelson, 1995a).

Shortcomings may be reduced if TV home shopping takes on more interactive features, turning the experience into an active rather than passive one. Interactive features might let the viewer point and click on products of specific interest—e.g., shoes, jewelry, or undergarments—rather than having to watch what the network chooses to show. Interactive features could permit the shopper to zoom in on the product. Both TV home shopping and on-line computer shopping have the potential to offer these interactive features; time will tell which becomes the medium of choice.

On-Line Computer Services

Computer technologies permit consumers to use the Internet and on-line services like Prodigy, CompuServe, and America Online to shop in cyberspace. As growing numbers of consumers have home computers, this will be a growing medium for the fashion industry. Limitations are that graphics are less clear than photographs, and the consumer can be in only one "store" at a time, making comparison shopping difficult. Advantages include immediate update of products, and many companies provide a chance to order directly via the computer.

Examples of consumer shopping venues include: Internet Mall, Shopping 2000, MCI Marketplace, Shopping In, and a growing number of options offered by individual companies (Figure 10–12). Sara Lee has "One Hanes Place." Mail-order firms Lands' End and L.L. Bean have electronic catalogs; these join J.C. Penney, Burlington Coat Factory, and a growing number of firms with World Wide Web home pages (DeWitt, 1995).

Although on-line shopping is still in its infancy, many believe this will be an important new frontier of retailing. Although companies do not necessarily believe this form of shopping will replace catalogs, it may permit them to reach potential customers who use computers but do not read catalogs.

CD-ROM Computer Shopping

This retail format involves use of a CD-ROM disk holding offerings from 25 to 45 companies. Several companies specialize in developing these disks, which are purchased by consumers. The consumer may click on icons and word commands to browse through the catalog "pages" on the screen. Shoppers may type in the names of specific items and retrieve selections from various catalogs on the disk. This format is more limited than on-line services because new product offerings occur only when the consumer obtains a new disk. On the horizon is the new digital versatile

Figure 10–12

Shopping by computer

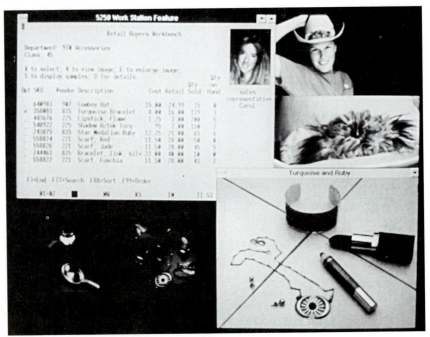

Source: Courtesy of International Business Machines Corporation

disk (DVD), which will be used in computers known as DVD-ROMs. Although the disk looks like a CD, it holds many more times the information a CD holds.

Flea Market Retailers

A **flea market** is a location, either indoors or out, in which a wide variety of independent sellers rent space on a temporary basis. Flea markets are growing all over the country, both in number and in size. Some are open every day, others only on the weekend. Any vendor may sell at these markets. All that is needed is merchandise and the money to rent a booth or table.

The merchandise offered for sale may be new or old, antiques and near-antiques, clothing, accessories, furniture, kitchen utensils, hand-crafted and ready-made products, high-priced and penny-priced merchandise. Some flea market sellers even specialize. One may sell only used jeans, another may sell only jewelry, and so on. The variety is infinite—and this is part of the attraction for shoppers hunting for possible treasures, bargains, or unique items.

Direct Selling: Door-to-Door and Party Plans

Modern versions of the early peddlers are the **direct-selling retailers** who operate without stores. A *direct-selling* establishment is one that sells merchandise by contacting customers through either *door-to-door* approaches or some form of *in-home party plan.* Direct selling is not new in the fashion field; in the period before World War II, silk hosiery and custom-made foundation garments were successfully sold this way.

Door-to-door retailing encompasses many different types of products. Working on commission, a salesperson calls on a customer at home and attempts to make the sale. In the household goods field, such names as Electrolux and Fuller Brush are familiar; they use this method exclusively. In fashion-related fields, Avon is perhaps the best-known operation of this kind. Starting with door-to-door selling of cosmetics, it now includes jewelry as well as apparel and accessories in its merchandise mix.

The **party plan** of selling depends on the company's representative getting a local woman to organize a party of her friends and neighbors, at which the salesperson presents the company's merchandise. The hostess receives a gift, usually provided by the salesperson. This method of selling in the home is most closely associated with Tupperware, but it has also been used effectively in the fashion field by a firm such as Sarah Coventry for jewelry. Doncaster is an example of fashion apparel sold by this means.

In most instances, salespeople who represent direct-selling firms use a company-produced catalog to supplement the relatively limited assortment of samples from which they sell.

The Changing Dimensions of Fashion Retailing

Very few periods in history have seen as many changes in the world of retailing as the decades of the 1980s and 1990s. Although the fundamental role played by retailers in the business of fashion has not changed—the buying and selling of fashion products to the ultimate consumer—almost everything else about them has.

Until 1980, major retailers of fashion could still be easily classified as department stores, specialty stores, chains, mail-order houses, discount houses, and the like, according to their distinctive operational characteristics. Since the 1980s, however, retailers moved in so many different directions that they can no longer be so neatly defined. *Acquisitions, verticalization, globalization, partnerships, buyouts, private labels, on-line retailing, restructuring, consolidation,* and *superstores* have become retailing buzzwords. Today, the retail marketers of fashionable merchandise come in an almost infinite variety of shapes, sizes, corporate ownership, pricing strategies, and merchandise assortments.

The section that follows covers major changes that are revolutionizing soft goods retailing.

Growth of Private Labels: Retailers into Manufacturing

In the late 1970s, as designer and manufacturers' national brand names proliferated, it seemed as if every type of retailer was featuring the same nationally advertised names—department and specialty stores, mail-order houses, chain store retailers, and hordes of off-price apparel specialists that were underselling these well-known names. In order to have merchandise that was unique to their stores and to regain their freedom from price competition, many large department and specialty stores increasingly developed and promoted their own private-label fashion products in men's, women's, and children's apparel and accessories. *Private label* merchandise, as used in the fashion industry, refers to goods that are produced exclusively for one retailer, and it carries only the name of the retailer or one of several brand names that are owned by the retailer. Recent years have witnessed a steady expansion of private label operations, and today the fashion business is inundated with so many different names and labels that it is hard to know whether a specific name is that of a manufacturer's national brand, a designer's name, or a retailer's private label.

In a special "Infotracs" supplement on brands in *Women's Wear Daily* and *DNR,* these industry distinctions were given:

- *National/designer brand.* A label that is distributed nationally to which consumers attach a specific meaning. Typically a national brand represents a certain image, quality level, and price-point range to consumers. Examples are Lee, Ralph Lauren, Hanes, and Fruit of the Loom.
- *Private label brand.* A label that is owned and marketed by a specific retailer for use in their stores. Examples are Stafford, Arizona, Jaclyn Smith, and Kathie Lee Gifford.
- *Retail store brand.* A name of a retail chain that is, in most cases, used as the exclusive label on the items in the store. Examples are The Gap, L.L. Bean, and Victoria's Secret.
- *All other brands.* Miscellaneous labels that are not included in the categories above; these included licensed brands. Examples include Mickey & Co., Looney Tunes, August Silk, and Wilson.
- *Nonbrands.* A label to which consumers attach no significant identity, awareness, or meaning (Lewis, 1995, p. 3).

A survey for the "Infotracs" feature found that consumers do not make distinctions among what the industry views as different types of brands. Rather, consumers think in terms of *brands* (which include all the first four above) and *nonbrands.* Nearly three-fourths of the female respondents defined certain store labels as "brands," and two-thirds identified certain private labels as "brands."

In the same "Infotracs" feature, a survey of retailers revealed that *financial reasons* (increasing revenues and margins and reducing costs) and *differentiation* were the major reasons merchants had developed private label programs. Fulfilling a consumer need or niche was rated lower in importance (Lewis, 1995).

Today, as a result of expanding private label operations, large retailers are deeply involved in the production process and have assumed roles that traditionally belong to manufacturers—the purchase of fabrics and the styling and production of merchandise. Most have established special **product development** departments that create their own lines of merchandise and work with manufacturers or contractors in this country and abroad to produce their private brand merchandise according to their specifications.

The May Department Stores, for example, has a staff of nearly 100 people who perform product development functions, just as a product development staff at an apparel manufacturing firm would do. They develop private label lines like the Valerie Stephens line and contract production both domestically and overseas. Many other large retail firms, including J.C. Penney, have staffs who are doing the same. Today on the classified pages of industry publications, retailers' help-wanted ads for product developers compete with those of manufacturers for the same designers and production coordinators. A large retail store product development department uses all the new computer technology for design, marker making, and so on that a modern apparel firm will have. Other stores work with producers that specialize in creating and producing private label programs. Moreover, a Private Label Expo provides an opportunity to find firms willing to produce for these programs (Figure 10–13)

Although it is generally estimated that about 70 percent of private label merchandise is produced offshore by contractors in low-wage countries, many major domestic manufacturers with strong national brands of their own are now also producing private label merchandise. Rather than lose business to foreign sources of supply, they are supplying retailers with exclusive merchandise to be sold under the store's own labels. While continuing to produce their own nationally branded products, they are developing private label divisions within their own companies. More often than not, the merchandise is manufactured in the same factories by the same workers who make their national brands and is sold side by side in the same stores. Examples include the Vanity Fair division of VF Corporation (producers of its own Vanity Fair and Vassarette lines plus at times private label merchandise for Victoria's Secret) and the Mansco division of Manhattan Industries. Even a high priced fashion producer such as Tahari has entered the field and produces for the Privé-Collection label of Saks Fifth Avenue.

Another development is the licensing and use of a designer or other well-known name as one of a store's private labels. For example, The Limited has a licensing agreement for the Moods by Krizia line. Other examples are the agreement between Kathie Lee Gifford and Wal-Mart (Figure 10–14) and between Jaclyn Smith and Kmart.

Although retailers build their own brands for greater profit, more distinctive assortments, and greater control over their merchandise, most merchants continue to sell name brands alongside their private label brands. Sometimes retailers have to be concerned that their private label products do not destroy the market for name brands they have carried successfully, damaging the long-term relationships they have built with name-brand manufacturers over time. J.C. Penney's Arizona jeans is a good example of a private label line that is compatible alongside the strong Levi brand. The Arizona label sells more than $500 million annually; however, Levi sales in Penney stores continue to grow at a healthy pace.

Figure 10–13

The private label expo trade show provides an opportunity for companies to develop private label business relationships.

Source: Reprinted courtesy of The Schimel Company.

The proportion of private label goods to other labels varies from store to store, but for many, the range is 10 to 20 percent of all apparel (Lewis, 1995). Figure 10–15 on p. 430 shows the percentage by major apparel categories and how private label merchandise accounts for an increasing share of all apparel sold. Among chains whose store names are the same as the apparel brand, well over half the total stock, or in some cases all, may be privately branded merchandise.

In the early days of private label merchandise, only a few specialty and discount chains used this strategy in securing merchandise assortments. Today, however, private label development has proliferated into a high-volume, high-profile enterprise at major retail firms everywhere. Private label programs have become more comprehensive, covering more categories and SKUs. The explosion of private label programs has occurred at a time when the U.S. apparel market is already over-saturated. Growing imports have added to this excess of products in the market. The oversupply of apparel has occurred as consumers have slowed in their clothing expenditures. As these trends converge, the result is an apparel market glut in which markdowns

Figure 10–14

The Kathie Lee Collection was developed exclusively for Wal-Mart.

Source: Photo by Anthony Magnacca/Merrill/Prentice Hall

are required just to sell the merchandise, and both manufacturers' and retailers' profits suffer.

Concentration of Retail Power

As we have discussed in earlier sections of the chapter, consolidations through buyouts and mergers have resulted in larger and more powerful retail firms. This concentration of power and clout has many advantages as retailers respond to a bruising economic environment. Large merchants can consolidate functions such as buying, product development, and logistics to reduce costs and improve efficiency. The massive buying power of the retail giants permits them to demand very competitive prices on merchandise. These competitive prices permit the megamerchants to offer merchandise to their customers at attractive prices and to improve their own profit margins. For some retailers, even major ones, this consolidation has rescued firms that were gradually sinking into bankruptcy. Industry experts predict that the retail consolidations will continue, and by 2000 half of today's retailers will disappear (Ostroff & Emert, 1995).

Although retail consolidations have many advantages for the industry, these changes may have limitations, also. For example, as consumers complain of too much "sameness" in stores, consolidation of buying may add to that. For example, if Federated's buyers are now making all the buying decisions for stores that were once made by Macy's buyers, this reduces prospects for variety in merchandise in the Federated/Macy's stores.

Figure 10–15   **Dollar share of private label merchandise by category**

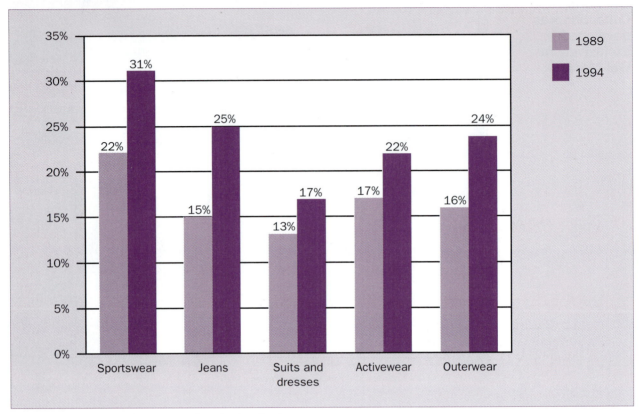

Source: *Women's Wear Daily* (1995, April 26) Section II. p.8.

Retail consolidations may also create challenges for manufacturers who sell to the new breed of giant merchants. As retailers get larger, they are positioned to make increasing demands on their suppliers. As retailers have experienced profit difficulties, they tend to squeeze suppliers. The consolidation means that the suppliers now have fewer potential retail customers. The remaining retailers buy very large quantities of merchandise; therefore, manufacturers generally want part of that business. Of course, powerful retailers know this. Consequently, large, powerful retailers continue to press suppliers to give better and better prices and to provide more and more services to the retailer. For example, stores now expect manufacturers to **preticket** merchandise, to ship it floor-ready, and to hold the extra inventory. Retailers continue to demand more **chargebacks,** financial penalties imposed for transgressions ranging from errors in purchase orders to failure to deliver merchandise floor-ready ("Manufacturers Howl," 1995). All of these demands add cost to the manufacturer to the advantage of the retailer.

A number of retail giants have added another difficult dimension for manufacturers. Several retailers have concentrated their purchasing to a limited group of vendors, in a strategy called **matrix buying.** This preferred vendor list, called *the matrix,* consists of suppliers who can provide the products, service, and pricing that retailers need to execute their particular strategies. For large powerful retailers, this is likely to consist of manufacturers who give attractive prices on merchandise that fits into the store's merchandising plan and provide the services the retailer demands.

Increasingly, it is the largest apparel manufacturers who can meet the demands of the giant retailers. For example, if retailers want the supplier to hold the bulk of the inventory and send replenishment items as needed, this **Quick Response** strategy may not be possible for small suppliers. Quick Response requires sophisticated electronic data interchange (EDI) technology that small apparel firms are not likely to have. Considering the consolidations in both the retailing sector and the manufacturing sector and the proficiencies each requires of the other, it is possible there will be a time when "the elephants dance only with the elephants."

Partnerships in the Softgoods Industry

As competition and a sluggish economy have created challenging business conditions for both retailers and manufacturers, both have learned there are advantages to developing closer working relationships with each other. Both are serving the same end-use consumer. Moving away from a feeling of animosity toward one of cooperation has led to a more integrated softgoods industry, at least for companies that choose to develop these partnerships.

As a means of serving customers more effectively and in reducing costs, retailers and manufacturers work together through Quick Response programs. The aim of QR programs is the quick replenishment of fast-selling items and to have merchandise in stock when consumers want it. The electronic linkages between suppliers and retailers rely on shared data. When the retailer sells an item, the only way the supplier knows to replenish that item is by having access to the retailer's sales data. In other partnerships, the retailer tracks sales by style, size, and color and transmits that information to the manufacturer. The apparel firm uses the information to tailor its production to match retail sales so they can replenish stock quickly and spot trends fast. Linkages are also set up between apparel companies and textile companies so they also can tune into retail sales. The linkages are also important in retailers' development of private label lines, as shown in Figure 10–16.

Globalization of Retailing

Retailers have traditionally attached great significance to "thinking locally"—that is, developing relationships between merchants and consumers and tailoring merchandise assortments to each local clientele. Although retailers must continue to address the needs of local markets, many large retail firms are now thinking in much broader terms. A number of major retailers are developing *global* strategies.

Globalization of retailing is occurring for a number of reasons. First, many borders and barriers have vanished. The NAFTA pact has encouraged firms in North America to think increasingly in terms of one market rather than three. Increased integration of the European Union means there are fewer borders to penetrate to sell in Europe. The fall of the Berlin Wall has opened vast markets in Central and Eastern Europe.

Second, advances in communication technology and transportation make it much easier to do business in other parts of the world. Fax machines and electronic mail permit low-cost communication with business partners worldwide. Satellite television, movies, and travel have resulted in a degree of converging tastes among consumers on all continents. Consumers almost everywhere recognize McDonald's, Mickey Mouse, Coca-Cola, Levis, and Pizza Hut. Although cultural differences continue to exist among the peoples of the world, an amazing number of consumers everywhere want U.S. jeans and sneakers.

Figure 10–16

J.C. Penney uses electronics to develop private label lines.

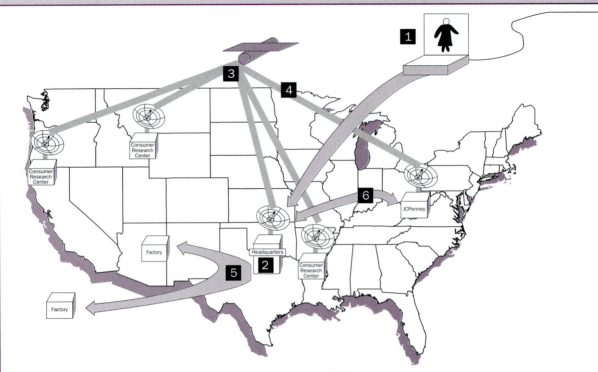

1 J.C. Penney fashion scout in Europe sees a new design, transmits a color photo via telephone lines to headquarters in Dallas.

2 At headquarters, a J.C. Penney version of the product is designed on a computer-aided design system.

3 Using satellite links, designs are shown to consumers at J.C. Penney testing centers around the U.S. The consumers "vote" on the products on personal computers. The results are tabulated at headquarters within 24 hours to help decide if the company should sell the product.

4 Using the company's direct broadcast system, merchandise is shown to buyers at 700 J.C. Penney stores nationwide. They can provide instant feedback.

5 Design and production information about the garment is transmitted electronically to factories in the U.S. and Asia. Photographs of samples may be transmitted back to headquarters for quality-control checks.

6 Sales results are tabulated daily at J.C. Penney stores and are transmitted to headquarters over phone lines. When sales of a product reach a certain level, a computer in the store may automatically reorder it. In some cases, these reorders are transmitted directly from the store to the manufacturer.

Third, changes in the economies in various regions of the world have resulted in a difference in spending potential or spending willingness. In the 1980s a number of European retailers opened stores in the United States to sell in what much of the world sees as a large, affluent market. These included Benetton, Laura Ashley, and Body Shop International Plc. However, as we have discussed previously, the U.S. fashion market changed in the 1990s. Consumers slowed their spending on apparel and other products as a result of demographic changes and shifting priorities. Therefore, the U.S. market, like that in most of the other more developed countries, has offered very little growth potential for ambitious retail chains looking for opportunities to expand. As U.S. domestic growth leveled off, a number of other regions of the world experienced high rates of both economic and population growth, particularly in Asia and some parts of Latin America. In the past, as retailers in the more developed countries wanted to expand their international markets, they added stores in *other* more developed countries. That is no longer the case. The rapidly expanding economies of countries once considered less developed are the new targets for retail expansion.

Many familiar U.S. retailers are rapidly expanding in other countries; these include Talbots, J.C. Penney, Foot Locker, Wal-Mart, Kmart, and others. L.L. Bean now issues its catalogs in more than 145 countries. Compared to European and Asian retailers, retailers in the Americas have been slow to globalize; however, many are actively pursuing expansion strategies today. Management Horizons (1994c), a retail consulting firm, predicts that by the year 2000, 90 percent of the 100 largest retailers of the world will be operating as global retailers.

Although this worldwide retail expansion is expected to continue, individuals involved will find it necessary to recognize and respect the cultural differences in other countries. Although a "westernization" of life styles is occurring, marketers must realize that many tastes and preferences will differ. Just as Coca-Cola offers flavor variations in other countries and McDonald's burgers are made from a different mixture of ingredients in other nations, apparel preferences will vary also. Consumers have different views on what constitutes attractive colors and styles. Fit preferences are different; some residents in other countries may view U.S. clothing as sloppy and vulgar. Acceptable exposure of the body varies greatly among the peoples of the world. Sizes must accommodate different stature. For example, U.S. size ranges are not suitable for Asian markets where individuals have a smaller build.

Global retailing offers many potential opportunities for those firms willing to take risks, study their markets carefully, work closely with local representatives who know the market, and remain committed for the long term. Global retailing will not be easy, but it may very well distinguish the winners from the losers among retailers in the decades to come.

Relationship Marketing

At the same time that retailers are expanding globally, many retailers are also striving for **relationship marketing**, that is, building a closer relationship with the domestic customer. Retailers realize that to prosper, they must strive to meet the needs of an increasingly demanding consumer. As consumers are less and less inclined to think of shopping as an enjoyable social activity, they increasingly focus on a specific destination for what they need. As consumers tire of the "sameness" in retailing, this will require a move away from *mass* merchandising.

As retailers attempt to meet these new demands, they must attempt to know and understand their target market. Using computers, retailers can build databases on customers to an extent unheard of until recent years, permitting **database marketing.**

These computer files can amass a great deal of information on a consumer's demographic and psychological characteristics and life style; these files may be developed by the retail firm or purchased elsewhere. This specific information allows the retailer to develop offerings of special interest to specific customers and to build a relationship with those consumers.

New technology allows retailers to increasingly **customize** their merchandise offerings and service to more narrow niches of the domestic market. Providing products specific to consumers' needs will use **micromarketing** techniques. This requires differentiating stores, merchandise within those stores, and thinking at the lowest level of aggregation. Retailers who manage this in the domestic market may be better prepared to function successfully in global markets.

Specialty mail-order firms have used these database marketing techniques for years to reach specialized niches. Women who wear large-size apparel may find that they are deluged by catalogs from retailers specializing in large sizes, or the individual with hard-to-find shoe sizes may suddenly receive dozens of catalogs. When these strategies lead to ongoing relationships between the consumer and the retailer, the resulting information is useful to manufacturers also. That is, the whole softgoods chain is better able to serve specialized markets through various micromarketing techniques.

Readings

Retailers face many challenges today. Some of these matters require introspection to change the way a type of retail format or company does business. Other challenges are related to the way in which vendors and retailers work together. The following articles focus on a variety of these issues.

Stanley Marcus at 90: The Great Gadfly

by Holly Haber

Home shopping TV shows? Only a cut above snake-oil peddlers. Department stores? In desperate need of an overhaul. The state of fashion? Ugly.

When retail guru Stanley Marcus holds forth, he doesn't mince words. And why should he? The man has been a power in the retail industry for almost 70 years.

Marcus, who celebrates his 90th birthday April 20, was to the store born. His father, Herbert Marcus, and aunt and uncle, Carrie Marcus Neiman and Al Neiman, founded Neiman Marcus in 1907. Little Stanley grew up amidst display cases and clothing, playing on the floor of the store. His official tenure began in 1926, when he quit Harvard Business School to become secretary, treasurer and director in the family business.

"In retrospect, I think I lived in the golden age of retailing—by pure luck, not through anything I did—when retailing was a personalized business and even in large operations, managers were owners," reflected Marcus.

"There were great names to emulate, like Marshall Field and John Wanamaker. It was a period when merchants were trying to make their mark and build their communities. It also was much easier to develop merchandise that fitted your concept and personality. You didn't have established lines that were cut in concrete. Today, buyers are buying what satisfies the manufacturer, and that makes it much more difficult to have unique product. I don't think they even strive for uniqueness anymore."

But Marcus isn't sitting around pining for the good old days. Ensconced in his office overlooking the jagged Dallas skyline, he demonstrates the fast pace of his schedule by holding up a calendar that's packed with appointments through May.

Marcus is a retail consultant, publisher of miniature books, and public speaker. And he has co-founded a new business: Narrowcasting, a targeted marketing service that's stockpiling data on the shopping habits of wealthy Americans. The enterprise has amassed lots of data on Dallas's rich; now it's working on the rest of the country.

Marcus speaks slowly, walks with a cane, but his vision of the retail business is analytical, futurist.

Department stores, he reasoned, are floundering because they exact the same markup as specialty stores but don't offer as much service and ambience. They are isolated between discounters and specialty stores, satisfying few and losing customers to both.

"In the 21st century, I think the department store will have to be redefined and reinvented," Marcus predicted. "It serves a very important place in the American distribution economy, but it's out of date. Across the country, with few exceptions like Macy's and Bloomingdale's, department stores are dismal places to be in. They're overcrowded with fixtures and merchandise, offer no service to speak of, no ambience or anything exciting. They don't even have the charm of a warehouse."

His remedy?

"The department store needs to be reborn with a fresh, contemporary design that will enable them to sell goods at about 28 percent markup," he asserted. "That will still put them ahead of discounters, but I think there are people who will be willing to pay more than discounters who aren't willing to buy all the services that go with the specialty stores.

"The department stores would stock the same type of merchandise as now, but in order to get a drop in the cost of operations, they would have to reduce selling costs. And that comes down to the development of friendly vending machines. There are a lot of products that could be sold through vending machines, such as hosiery, certain cosmetics, men's underwear and shirts."

Such machines would have to have a Disney-esque sense of humor or entertainment so they'd be fun to use, he pointed out.

"I also think the whole selling function is so badly conceived and supervised, which is management's fault, not the staff," Marcus said.

"They are terrifically inefficient. My guess is that no department store gets more than 25 percent of a customer's spending ability, because they have ignored that selling is an important skill that has to be honed. There is no cream that you can rub on the hand that makes a person give good service. It's something that has to be constantly taught and constantly supervised."

When it comes to home shopping, Marcus sees potential, but he's disgusted by current TV merchandising programs.

"Home shopping is just a step above the old snake-oil business where they promised the moon," he asserted. "It's scandalous they've been able to get away with what they've done."

Marcus predicted home shopping via computers or video could grasp as much as 10 to 15 percent of the retail market in the next century—not enough to seriously threaten stores.

"Home shopping will eventually be a greatly refined system where the TV will bring you into the store to buy things," he said. Marcus cited a system developed by Oracle Corp. that enables a viewer to peruse merchandise on TV by store and category, and order goods for delivery. It's being tested in Fairfax County, Va., and London.

"It's a very realistic scenario and could be tremendously useful for sending gifts, but not for buying fashion, which requires trying it on," Marcus observed.

Existing home shopping shows, like mass merchandisers, offer watered-down styles with the widest possible appeal, he pointed out.

"Fashion is a commodity, and when you're making for a mass market, you are making something that has a broad common denominator. The mass market is expanding greatly; the high-quality market is fairly static, although there is more wealth in the country.

"These mass-produced lines have democratized clothes just as rayon democratized fashion and liberated it from the confines of cotton, wool or silk and brought prices way down. And it made it more possible for people to wear clothes that satisfied them at prices they can afford."

Does that mean quality is less important?

"A big portion of the market has never had experience with the things that make for good quality because they were brought up on popular-brand merchandise that's produced for the income level that they can afford," Marcus reasoned. "I have great respect for whoever makes a garment that everybody can wear. But to say this is a fine-quality garment is relative. It may be fine quality next to something made in Yugoslavia, but it's not fine quality compared with something that was made by hand."

A longtime champion of elegance, Marcus had virtually no kind words about today's fashions—even at the designer level. Some of the blame he dished to the media.

"Fashion is ugly," Marcus declared. "Designers are all mixed up and suddenly conceive of themselves as great artists and they're making an ego statement. They're hoping to write a book or sign a movie contract, and they've lost a sense of purpose of making clothes that are attractive. They're so eager to get their name in the paper and in Vogue that they make extreme things, many of which never get into production, but get into photographs.

"The media is a willing participant in the charade. I remember years ago when I was in business, Vogue always had the skill of picking things that were never produced. It made a good picture, but it never got worn. And this is an even further extreme. I know lots of women who are probably spending one-tenth of what they would spend if they could find clothes that they liked."

The diffusion of styles and lack of trends in the fall collections will make it even harder for retailers to push fashion, Marcus said.

"I think it's always harder to sell clothes when you can't grab onto a trend," he pointed out. "I think women are confused. What is probably happening is that so many women of affluence find it difficult to find clothing they like that they're not buying clothing and are finding other places to spend their money and get greater satisfaction.

"And as they begin to find they can get greater satisfaction by spending money on travel, or gardening or collecting, suddenly clothes begin to have less importance. This drop in the apparel business may be a confirmation that this is already occurring."

As for the former family business, the chairman emeritus demurred. He retired from Neiman's in 1976, and isn't closely involved anymore. He did say he sometimes shops incognito at Neiman's in other cities and has found they maintain one of the best standards of service in the U.S.

Marcus takes pride in the legacy he left: elevating the local Dallas store to the status of an internationally respected retailer. He was the first fashion retailer outside New York to place ads in national magazines, such as *Vogue*—in 1932. "The fact that we dared to advertise in a national magazine made news itself, and as a result *Time* and *Life* magazine came to see me to find out what kind of store it was," he recalled.

The rationale for nationally publicizing a lone Dallas specialty store was two-fold. Marcus realized his oil-rich customers travelled frequently, so his competition included top stores in New York. More subtly, he figured that Dallasites visiting big cities would be plagued with provincial insecurity, and would feel more accepted if their local shopping spot were recognized as a fine retailer.

Folk and fine art from around the world dot his office, and Marcus said if he could imagine himself in any other career, it would be as an art dealer or architect.

Retire? Never. "My mother lived to be 97, and I asked her how she maintained good health," Marcus recalled. "She said, 'I try to learn something new every day and keep my mind occupied.' I decided life was too exciting. I've had fun, and I'm still having fun."

Source: From Women's Wear Daily, *April 12, 1995, pp. 8–9. Reprinted by permission.*

Talbots Thrives with Innovative Synergies, Consumer Research

by Susan Reda

When executives at Talbots decide where to open a new store, as they plan to do scores of times this year, they use a road map that sometimes leads them to locations that other techniques of market analysis would have overlooked.

Talbots' method, which has worked with almost complete success in recent years, calls for placing stores in clusters of ZIP codes where the company's catalog customers have already spent $150,000 on classic women's and children's apparel.

That store-location strategy is a good example of the Hingham, Mass.-based company's innovative efforts to take advantage of synergies between its retail and catalog businesses.

Such policies, along with a commitment to intensive consumer research and a clearly articulated stylistic vision, have enabled Talbots to thrive and expand in the face of the ongoing slump in the women's apparel business.

Last year, while other women's apparel chains selling flimsy floral dresses, sheer blouses and other trendy items eked out comparable-store sales increases of just 1 percent to 2 percent, Talbots' classic blue blazers, white cardigans and khaki slacks yielded store-for-store sales gains of 9.5 percent, a 19 percent hike in net sales to $879.6 million and a 30 percent increase in net income.

Even as many of their competitors are pulling the reins in on store expansion and merchandising experimentation, Talbots plans to open 65 new stores this year, debut five shoe and accessory stores, introduce infant and toddler sizes at the burgeoning Talbots Kids units and increase the company's presence internationally.

"We're a very focused company. We are classic women's clothing," says president and chief executive officer Arnold Zetcher. "That's what we've been and that's what we're going to be in the future."

"Women have reached a point in their lives where they don't want to light a match to their closet every other season," he explains. "They have a different set of priorities than they had five or six years ago. Today it's exceptional quality at reasonable prices, a comfortable shopping experience and knowledgeable service that they value."

Zetcher, who took the helm in 1988, just as Jusco, a Japanese retail conglomerate, bought the chain from General Mills, makes clear that the company's success did not happen overnight. A brief foray into fast-changing fashion in 1990 caused operating profits to slump by 40 percent and led to a $7 million loss.

The company quickly shifted gears and regained its footing, though, and the slip-up taught Zetcher a valuable lesson.

Ever since, building and maintaining close relationships with shoppers has been the watchword at Talbots, whose founding credo—"Do what's right for the customer"—originated in 1947. Consumer focus groups held throughout the year are attended by the whole senior management team, and an annual benchmark survey in which customers voice their likes and dislikes is required reading.

"We've constantly got our ear to the ground to find out what our shoppers want. They've been very loyal to us and we're willing to do whatever we can to keep it that way," says Zetcher, whose company was ranked first among specialty store retailers in a 1994 survey by Consumer Reports.

Continually probing shoppers' needs and wants has led to many changes and new avenues of growth for the company. A decision to increase the proportion of private label to 95 percent and a commitment to making the stores more comfortable with amenities such as spacious fitting rooms both were fueled by customer dialog.

In addition, the recently launched Talbots Babies collection was conceived during a focus group. Next month a 700- to 800-sq.-ft. area within four to five Talbots Kids stores will be assigned to the new baby merchandise.

Talbots' trump card is the opportunity created by the combination of catalog and store operations, which are run as an integrated business. Utilizing the customer information and demographic data gathered from the catalog database, executives have managed to substantially increase the efficiency of the total business. They have also been able to reduce out-of-stock positions and lessen the risk associated with brand extensions and new store locations.

"By using our catalog database to determine where to open new stores, we have taken virtually all of the risk out of store site selection. We know exactly where our customers are," explains Zetcher, who reports that the company has opened several highly profitable stores in markets that might otherwise have been ignored.

Generally, once catalog sales in an area exceed $150,000, it can support a store. Over the past four years, 95 percent of Talbots' new stores have become profitable in their first year of operation.

Exploiting this synergy between catalog and store-based retailing has also served the company in the development of new business lines. The expansion of petites and the introduction of Talbots Kids and Talbots Intimates stores were all based on the strong acceptance those merchandise categories first received in the catalog.

The latest catalog spinoff, Talbots Shoes and Accessories, will debut this fall. Plans call for four to five stores to open adjacent to Talbots' misses units.

Although retail analysts aren't sure whether Talbots' expansion into new fields will be successful, they do seem convinced it will continue to defy the slump in women's apparel. Harry Ikenson, senior director of New York-based Rodman & Renshaw, estimates total sales growth of 12 percent in 1995, to $990.9 million, and a 5.5 percent increase in comp-store sales.

"There are a number of facets to Talbots' business that point to continued growth," explains Ikenson. "They have a fair pricing policy, which reinforces their credibility with shoppers. They have superior customer service that is professional and knowledgeable without being pushy. And they've figured out how to update their classics with enough fashion to keep it interesting but not so much that it alienates today's somewhat less fashion-forward shopper."

In the first quarter of this year, Talbots once again posted industry leading figures. The company tallied $230.6 million in sales—a 13 percent increase compared with the first quarter of the previous year, and store-for-store sales in units open for at least a year were up 3.7 percent.

Talbots is also planning to continue expanding internationally. It opened a store in Britain last September, and plans to open two more stores this fall. In Canada, where the first Talbots store debuted in 1991, four new stores are planned, bringing the total there to 16.

In addition, there are 12 Talbots stores in Japan. These units are operated by Jusco, which retains a 63 percent stake in the publicly traded company.

Source: From Stores, *July 1995, pp. 34–35. Reprinted from Stores Magazine, NRF Enterprises, Inc., 1995.*

Outlet Malls Look to Lure More Male Shoppers

by Eileen Courter

Outlet developers are taking Phillips-Van Heusen Corp.'s mass closing of 200 stores (DNR, Sept 14, Page 1) as a wakeup call that it's time to do more to attract men to their off-price centers.

And they're doing something about making them more user-friendly for men.

Outlet operators are already fine-tuning their mix of tenants to sign on more high-visibility sportswear designer names and brands. And the developers are adding special perks to lure men into existing and new outlet malls—sporting goods stores, electronics, putting greens, and more.

Their reason for arranging their building blocks this way is pure and simple: Men's wear is among the top performers in outlet centers nationally. They want to keep it that way.

As for the P-VH situation, the giant dress shirt and sportswear manufacturer/retailer, which currently has close to 1,000 outlet units, will reportedly balance the store closings with new openings in the same period. What's more, the shuttering of the 200 stores will take time.

P-VH's impending move could actually turn out to be a wash, according to outlet developers. They have been told by P-VH executives that the outlets to be closed within the next few years will be replaced by new units with possibly new names and merchandise.

But the closings aren't being taken lightly and developers admit they signal the fact that outlet centers certainly aren't immune from the lumps that other retail formats are taking.

Discussing P-VH's plans to close stores, William Carpenter Jr., president and chief operating officer, Prime Retail, the Baltimore-based outlet developer, says he is "keeping the move in perspective."

"Look, the entire picture of men's wear outlet retailing must be tucked into proper context." As for the P-VH closings, Carpenter stresses that, over the years, P-VH has closed 40 to 50 stores a year, "but continues to do an enormous amount of business.

"I met with Walter Rossi [chairman, P-VH retail group] the day the closings were announced. From what he indicated to me, it has little or no effect on our portfolio. They have nearly 1,000 stores. When they finish this, and you add on the new stores opening with us, I venture to say it will probably be a wash.

"I think what they're doing is cleaning up their portfolio. But nobody really knows because they have not pinpointed that yet."

J. Dixon Fleming Jr., board chairman of Factory Stores of America, which merged last summer with Charter Oak Group Ltd., a subsidiary of Rothschild Realty, reports P-VH has been Factory Stores' single-biggest men's wear tenant.

The newly combined operation is the largest factory-outlet real estate investment trust in the U.S. and Ralph Lauren is one of the hot names added to the Factory Stores tenant roster with the merger.

As for the P-VH cutbacks, Fleming states, "My guess is some of that is a result of the move toward casualwear. And the company's primary focus, of course, has been men's dress shirts. Those guys who have been in the casual business, as some of our tenants are, have done fairly well."

The executive indicates that even before the cutbacks, P-VH had discussed with his company plans to convert some outlets to the Izod and Gant units, brands P-VH recently acquired from Crystal Brands. Those conversions were discussed some six months ago during lease negotiations.

Factory Stores agreed to allow P-VH to close eight stores, notes Fleming. Five have already been replaced. And this could be an indication of what the future will bring.

One developer who refuses to mention P-VH by name is Gary Geisler, vice-president, chief operating officer, HGI Realty Inc., Muskegon, Mich., which was formed this year when Horizon Outlet Centers Inc. merged with McArthur/Glen Realty Corp., McLean, Va.

Like Carpenter, Geisler states he wants to put men's wear sales in perspective.

"We haven't analyzed all our numbers, but the first quarter was quite strong for the 'Tommy Hilfigers' who have gotten into the outlet business recently. Without a certain tenant [Geisler shies away from identifying the tenant but doesn't deny the tenant's initials are P-VH] that has been having troubles

across the board—and if we pull those numbers out—the first quarter was up about 12 percent against last year."

Geisler suggests that the tenant he doesn't want to name could dramatically improve its sales by changing how it's presenting its product lines. He understands the closings will actually take place over three years, with no closings in HGI malls for at least two years.

Turning to men's business at HGI centers, he states, "I don't have the analysis of the second quarter yet. But it's my perception, from what I've seen from the stores doing well, men are looking for newness and more fashion. They're tired of the same polo-shirt look. They're looking for fresh colors and styling."

Geisler states that homewear has been the top performer, "thanks to the cocooning influence. Women's wear continues to be the weakest category, although manufacturers tell me they're looking for a strong fall season."

Commenting on the state of men's wear outlets at the Prime centers, Carpenter asserts, "Even in a traditional retail setting, the pure men's wear category is relatively small in the overall mix." But he points out that this slice of Prime's portfolio has been performing fairly well.

"Through July, which was one of our bigger months, we were running about 7.6 percent ahead in the men's wear category over the same period and same store a year ago. However, from January through July, the stores were running about 2 percent below last year." Most retailers do the major portion of their business in the second half.

Carpenter is confident that with the kinds of sales trends happening and the amount of traffic shopping at Prime's centers, business may be solidly in the black by the end of the year.

He adds, "That would be better than the women's popular-to-high-priced business throughout the country, not only in regular-priced stores, but also in the outlet side of the retail business."

Why will men's wear beat the overall sales trend line? Carpenter credits the shift to corporate casual for boosting men's wear sales at outlet centers. He considers these stores the perfect environment for men to piece together new workday wardrobes. Prime Retail itself offers employees casual Fridays.

"I know when I'm out buying I'll think about our casual dress Fridays. The garment I'm looking for may not be a polo shirt, but it might be a casual/dress type of shirt. I'm looking at different things than I did a few years ago. And so are our employees," Carpenter explains.

He adds that his own search for more relaxed apparel that still fits into an office setting extends to shoes and accessories. "I'm looking for something between Dockers and Allen Edmonds."

Men's wear retailers and manufacturers operating outlet stores—including Brooks Brothers, Polo/Ralph Lauren, J. Crew and Liz Claiborne with its Claiborne for Men—refused to comment on trends in their outlet operations. But it's clear from current successes at outlet centers that Tommy Hilfiger or Bugle Boy labels will ride the dress-down trend more readily than a store showing suits.

Fleming at Factory contends he's "cautiously optimistic" approaching the holiday season. He suggests consumer optimism has already boosted big-ticket sales such as cars and houses. "Electronic sales have also been robust. Those categories may have lured dollars away from men's wear. But if consumer optimism remains strong, some money will likely shift back into soft goods as the Christmas season approaches.

"The summer itself was pretty good. We saw sales up 4 to 5 percent. Back-to-school, as best as I can tell, was a little disappointing. Sales were pretty flat. As for expectations for the fall, most folks think they can perhaps make up what they missed during the back-to-school season.

"We are fortunate in our portfolio in that for the most part we have anchored projects. We have some larger stores that have continued to do well, and they pulled along some of the other guys."

Addressing one of the core problems facing all developers, Carpenter at Prime Retail mentions the problem of bringing men into outlet malls, especially those who avoid shopping whenever they can. Prime just opened the Arizona Factory Shops in New River, Ariz., its 16th venture, and the focus was to create attractions for men.

"Outlet shopping is a family affair," Carpenter indicates. "We are looking for things men like to do. As a company we're putting in Black & Decker, Sony, Bose—some of the hard goods names men would be attracted to in addition to the men's wear shopping they may do.

"We're installing putting greens. In San Marcos, Texas, we're adding a sports court where you can buy golf clubs, then go out and drive balls to try the clubs. We're exploring that as a venue to enhance the shopping trip.

"In our sports courts we're looking at building almost clubhouse-type places where men can sit down and watch sports on television. We're the only outlet mall developer who builds large food courts with 500 to 600 seats.

"You don't necessarily want to put television sets in there because you need to turn tables over. But we're almost creating rest stops for the male consumer so he's not bored."

Especially those with an appetite for new sportswear.

Source: From DNR, *October 6, 1995, pp. 1, 5. Reprinted by permission.*

Wal-Mart: To Sell or Not To Sell?

Moderate apparel manufacturers could soon be faced with a king-size dilemma: whether or not to sell Wal-Mart.

If they do, they get a colossus of a client: one with a solid credit rating, giant volume and huge consumer traffic. But they also risk their business with other retailers, including not inconsequential chains like J.C. Penney and Sears, Roebuck, in addition to department stores.

Doing business with Wal-Mart, said one apparel executive, could be "the kiss of death" as far as his other customers are concerned because "nobody wants to compete with Wal-Mart."

The news that Wal-Mart is looking for more brands for its apparel departments, as reported here Thursday, is likely to produce new strategies for the manufacturing and retail communities.

"Wal-Mart is sending out a message to brand-name manufacturers that it's interested in selling more brands," said Robert Adler, president of Kellwood Co.'s Halmode division, which does about $75 million with mass retailers. "The problem is, if you have a branded department store business, you have a big decision to make, because once you sell to Wal-Mart, you can kiss your department store business goodby."

It was Donald Soderquist, vice chairman and chief operating officer to the Bentonville, Ark.-based Wal-Mart, who on Wednesday told a group of advertising executives that the company was actively seeking to increase the amount of national apparel brands it carries.

"Wal-Mart is going after everybody" within the discounter price limits, said one competitor. "They would like to have every brand name in the store at any cost. They're more competitive than most retailers. But they really haven't done it yet. In sportswear, it's really just Gitano and Bonjour, and in lingerie, Hanes Her Way."

Kmart is also after more brands.

"It's something we are always pursuing," said Jerry Steinberg, Kmart's divisional merchandise manager of women's apparel. "There are people we have approached that did not want to sell us. They wanted to keep brand names in department stores, and when we approached them, they said they would like to sell to us but perhaps use another name."

Kmart's branded business has been growing mainly by expanding from jeans, innerwear and hosiery, areas where brands are most important at Kmart, into other categories.

Chic, Sasson and Bonjour, major jeans labels for many years at Kmart, have become major sportswear resources at the chain in the last two years, Steinberg said. Chic, Sasson and Brittania are the three top jeans brands at Kmart, followed by Bonjour and Gitano.

Hanes Her Way and Mickey Unlimited are two brands that have branched into sportswear, and have been successful at Kmart. This fall, Kmart has been testing Fruit of the Loom sportswear, hoping to capitalize on its success with FTL lingerie.

"Where we have success in brands is where we're giving more real estate," Steinberg said. "But at the same time, private label is also very important. We must offer customers a choice of both."

Reportedly, Wal-Mart's apparel sales rose 29 percent in the first half of this year—several points higher than its overall sales gain of about 25 percent. Hard goods are still Wal-Mart's strength, and many analysts said the rise in apparel was fueled by women's foundations.

Nevertheless, Marie Beninati, director of retail market strategy for Kurt Salmon Associates, a research firm, said the improved apparel results show that Wal-Mart is already reevaluating its approach to clothes and is implementing tactics to build that business.

"Wal-Mart's agreement with Dillard's is another indication that Wal-Mart is making a move to more moderate-priced apparel," she said.

Three weeks ago, Wal-Mart and its Arkansas neighbor, Dillard Department Stores, announced a joint venture to open Dillard's units in Mexico.

Wal-Mart is already a partner with Mexico's largest retailer, Cifra, in 47 discount stores, supercenters and warehouse clubs south of the border.

"This has to cause other retailers to reassess their own apparel strategies and to find ways for customers to differentiate between them and Wal-Mart," Beninati added. "And the other retailers will certainly consider dropping their more marginal vendors that sell to Wal-Mart."

She noted that Wal-Mart should not have a problem attracting national brands because of the volume it commands. Wal-Mart will push for and most likely get better prices because of that volume.

"Some major manufacturers might be able to develop brands specifically for Wal-Mart," she speculated.

Other observers said a more likely scenario would be that Wal-Mart would be able to get brands that have been lackluster performers in department stores, but still have retained their cachet.

Wal-Mart is the world's largest retailer, with 1993 sales of $67.3 billion and projections of $83 billion this year. The company operates more than 2,500 stores and is expanding, with the addition of 100 discount stores and 100 supercenters—units that combine general merchandise and groceries—domestically next year. Besides its Mexican and Canadian operations, it is opening new international markets, including South America, Hong Kong and China.

It is not unprecedented for department stores to drop a brand that suddenly appears in a mass chain. R.H. Macy & Co. stopped buying Levi Strauss products when the sportswear and jeans maker began supplying Penney's and Sears. Levi's apparently left too big a hole in Macy's assortments, however, and the chain brought the brand back last year, after an 11-year absence.

Dillard's buyers reportedly have orders not to shop vendors that sell to Penney's. There was speculation that when Leslie Fay began selling its signature label to Penney's this year, Dillard's would drop the brand. That, however, has not happened.

Retail consultant Kurt Barnard said he's been expecting this move by Wal-Mart for some time.

"Wal-Mart has been eyeing Target's success in apparel and it wants to capture market share wherever it can," he said. "Wal-Mart also realizes that many Americans want good value in a pleasant environment, and they don't mind going to stores like Wal-Mart for apparel."

Barnard added that this move will give Wal-Mart one more dimension of strength and will allow the retailer to gain significant market share.

"A lot of people have been bringing more and more of their dollars to stores like Wal-Mart, so we mustn't prejudge what they'd be willing to spend on apparel there," he continued.

Kurt Salmon's Beninati said there is a limit to how much the Wal-Mart customer will pay for clothes, but said the limit is only a function of where Wal-Mart wants to focus.

"Who's to say Wal-Mart won't reinvent itself in a few years, and spin off a new format?" she asked. "They certainly have the capital to do so."

"If Wal-Mart says they are going to do it, they'll do it," said Steve Louis, partner in Andersen Consulting. "They're too smart. They don't do things on a whim. The bigger issue is what manufacturers are going to do. They'll have to figure out how to maintain market share in department stores, but how can anyone turn down a $70 billion outlet?"

He said manufacturers could end up making "subtle product changes" to sportswear lines to differentiate what they sell to department stores and discounters, as they currently do in hard goods.

Wal-Mart and other discounters sell plenty of brands, particularly in denim, innerwear, and activewear, but he noted there are opportunities in more casualwear brands.

Some apparel executives said Wal-Mart is not easy to do business with because of the many strict requirements the firm places on vendors and its hard-bargaining tactics.

"Wal-Mart didn't used to be so demanding, but they are becoming tougher in terms of deliveries and service," said one denim supplier. "If you give them something for $10 one season, they want it for $9.50 the next."

Those difficulties are discounted by Linda J. Wachner, president, chief executive officer and chairman of The Warnaco Group and president of Authentic Fitness Corp., whose White Stag sportswear and Catalina swimwear brands are on Wal-Mart's shelves.

"It is a pleasure doing business with them," Wachner said, declining to elaborate.

Many manufacturers concurred that Wal-Mart is making the right move to add more brands.

Halmode's Adler said his firm has been making Bobbie Brooks sportswear and dresses for Wal-Mart for several seasons. Bobbie Brooks, once a huge independent brand, is owned by Wal-Mart and distributed only in its stores.

Adler, whose company does about half of its $150 million in volume with mass chains like Sears and Kmart, said he sees Wal-Mart's strategy as reviving existing brands, as it has with White Stag, as well as developing and creating more store brands, such as Bobbie Brooks.

"They don't want to start selling brands that are already widely distributed at Kmart or Target," Adler said. Robert Luehrs, president of Chic jeans, which does not sell to Wal-Mart, said he thinks the store is on the right track to emphasize branded apparel, which he feels is as much of a draw for customers as price.

"Every Sunday, in every paper in this country, there's a circular," he said. "They all look the same, whether it's Venture, Kmart or Caldor. All they emphasize is price, price, price. I feel the discounter does not do a good job selling brands. There's no display, no effective signage.

"We don't sell Wal-Mart because we believe, rightly or wrongly, that our accounts buy more from us because we don't sell Wal-Mart," Luehrs said.

Tropic-Tex International, a misses' and junior resource, sells to Wal-Mart under private label. Its own brands are Croquet Club and Airplane.

"Wal-Mart has been very successful in creating its own brands or building labels like Gitano and White Stag," said Jennifer Mead, vice president of sales and marketing. "It has tremendous internal brand development already, so I don't think it will affect us."

She added that Wal-Mart's quest for brands should not affect the junior market that much.

"The junior customer is not so brand-driven. She wants the latest look and the best price," Mead said. "It may have more impact on other markets, like misses', where the customer is more brand-conscious."

Because of the sensitive nature of dealing with Wal-Mart, several prominent manufacturers declined to speak for attribution.

"There's a reason Leslie Fay went into J.C. Penney and risked its business with Dillard's—1,100 stores versus 200 stores," said one moderate-price vendor. "I have department store accounts that are angry because I sell to Sears. And Sears asks me outright if I sell to Wal-Mart, and that if I do, they won't do business with me. But the bottom line is, if you're hot, everyone wants you."

The source said he wants to increase the amount of business he does with stores like Wal-Mart because "they are very creditworthy, in a market that is seeing fewer retailers with good credit."

"Would I give them my brand, or go under a different label?" he asked. "It would all depend on the kind of volume we would do."

Not all manufacturers are enamored of the idea of selling to Wal-Mart.

"We have absolutely no plan to increase our distribution by going into the mass chains with any of our brands," said Gary Wolkowitz, president of Hot Sox Inc., which manufactures its own brand of socks and tights, as well as its licensed Ralph Lauren Hosiery and Ralph by Ralph Lauren hosiery.

"If my competitors choose to, that would only strengthen my position in department stores," Wolkowitz added. "As more brands jump over the line into mass distribution, the more we have to gain."

Source: From Women's Wear Daily, *November 4, 1994, p. 12. Reprinted by permission.*

A 12-Step Program to Revive Fashion

Complaints come easily about the sorry state of the apparel business.

Solutions, however, are elusive.

Each season there's a new scapegoat: bad economy, hesitant consumers, lack of newness, off-the-wall fashions, no direction, poor timing—and, of course, the weather.

Scapegoats aside, what can be done to breathe life back into stores and into clothes, and start cash registers ringing again?

WWD polled dozens of executives from retailing, manufacturing and financial circles and asked them to suggest solutions for the major problems facing the fashion industry. Their responses lead to a 12-step recovery program that covers everything from creativity to customer service.

The challenges are formidable. Observes say the industry still needs to confront and overcome fundamental cultural changes.

Among them:

- The priorities of baby boomers have shifted: They are more interested in spending disposable income on home and family and less on wardrobes.
- The 21st century will bring less disposable income to households in the U.S., according to Kurt Salmon Associates. Rising health care costs, higher taxes and other cost-of-living hikes will continue to outpace income growth, and the likely victim will be consumption of things like apparel.
- Consumers are spending less time in the stores; in fact, they spent two-thirds less time in malls in 1994 than they did in 1980.
- According to an Arthur Andersen study, 64 percent of women surveyed consider shopping "a drudgery," while only 6 percent said it was a "favorite pastime."

Here, culled from dozens of interviews, a revival plan.

1   Take the Lead

Fashion needs to lead, not follow.

Years ago, when Yves Saint Laurent said "short," women wore short. When Giorgio Armani introduced soft tailoring, it revolutionized the look of women in the workplace. And in the mid-Eighties, when Donna Karan said "body dressing," women followed her edict in droves.

No longer. Yes, companies like Prada can show skinny belts and before you know it, they're on everyone else's runway. But somewhere along the way the consumer lost confidence in fashion and the occasional runway trend hasn't really convinced her to buy. Instead, self-reliance, practicality and value have won out.

The result of retailers playing to an insecure fashion consumer has been a lack of sustained and coherent direction, observers say.

While no one has much hope for the return of seasonal obsolescence—when women regularly bought clothes to avoid looking like yesterday's latex—a little industry backbone might give a consumer the confidence to try something new.

Some feel it's good that women have plenty of options and can put their own look together. But in what started as a good-faith response to a consumer-driven economy, the industry unwittingly created a problem by trying to respond to what women "really wanted." The problem? Women didn't know what they wanted, and the result has been a change in buying behavior.

They buy more like men. With no true direction, they often look for safer, investment clothes, the "classics" that won't go out of style next season.

Some observers feel the need to reestablish command—if not exactly a dictatorship, at least a more authoritative image. The industry prospered when it told people, with authority *and* credibility, what to wear.

They say the only way to revive consumerism, ironically, is to re-create the idea of pressure: Make people feel they must have a certain thing to look good or fit in.

2   Get a Grip on Casual

Face it: Women aren't going to wear ripped denim shorts to the office.

The "dressing down of America," most dramatically expressed in casual attire for the workplace, has been a boom for the men's wear business but a flop for women, mainly because women's manufacturers don't understand it and retailers don't know how to merchandise it.

With 75 percent of American women working outside the home, women's career apparel is a $10 billion a year business. There is a major opportunity in casual attire—but the industry has to define it. By telling the consumer what to wear to the office on "dress-down Friday," makers and stores will capitalize on one of the biggest lifestyle changes to come along in years.

Stores overdosed on casual this spring because they bought the wrong stuff—weekend wear, as opposed to casual workwear, which is in high demand. Consequently, piles of shorts and T-shirts are crowding selling floors across the country. Some executives even say the too-casual revolution is killing fashion.

3   Exploit Global Opportunities

Levi's has become such a worldwide brand that it is used as currency in some places. The jeans giant has been way ahead of the game in global marketing and sourcing. Last year, its international volume was $2.3 billion out of the company total of $6 billion.

There's lots of room for other players, from jeans makers, like VF Corp. and Guess, to designer collections.

The Gap has opened in France and has plans for Italy and Germany. Other prominent names on the American fashion scene, like Calvin Klein and Tommy Hilfiger, have launched licensing programs to spread their names around the world. Polo/Ralph Lauren's worldwide business generates more than $1.5 billion a year.

The world has a growing appetite for the hot names in American and European fashion, and it's a good thing, because the U.S. market is becoming over-saturated with stores and labels. Today, according to Tactical Retail Solutions, there are nearly 20 square feet of retail space per capita in the U.S., compared with 12.3 in 1985—and people are shopping less.

The market can only support so much business, particularly at the high end.

Companies throughout apparel and retailing are seeking opportunities around the world, particularly in China, with its billion-plus population, where the economy is expected to grow 10 percent a year through the end of the decade. Included on lists of prospective markets are the Far East, Latin America and India. These are areas with vast populations, some concentrations of wealth, small middle classes and enormous lower classes, whose personal income is gradually rising.

In Brazil, for example, the gross national product grew 4.9 percent in 1994 over 1993, and per capital GNP grew 8.6 percent, according to DRI/McGraw Hill.

More evidence of growth in emerging markets: According to the World Bank's 1994 World Development Report, the average growth in per capita GNP has been 3.1 percent for India and 7.6 percent for China from 1980 through 1992 (the latest year for which figures are available).

You might get bruised at first. For example, China is just beginning to learn about capitalism and requires foreigners to take on a Chinese business partner. There are also disputes about intellectual property rights. The black market is rampant throughout Russia, and it's difficult or impossible to take money out of those countries. But getting involved in emerging growth markets can be the ticket to big sales and future profits.

An example is Mexico. The NAFTA-inspired rush to get into that market created a lot of interest in Mexican retailing and sourcing. Apparel and textile imports from Mexico soared 72 percent in March, propelling that nation into the third spot among the top suppliers of these goods to the U.S.

When the peso took a hit this year, sending the economy into a tailspin, some businesses decided to approach their expansions there more cautiously. But executives maintain that it is still a viable country in which to do business, and say the experience gained there is useful in developing businesses in other nations. Mexico, particularly, is cited as the gateway to Central and South America, and trade agreements with Brazil and Chile are not so far in the future.

4   Offer Newness

"Homogenized" is good in milk but it's deadly on the retail sales floor.

The very thing that should invigorate sales—creativity—is often the first to go as big-store bottom line pressures heighten. Whether it's a merchandising concept, like Ralph Lauren's Polo Sport, or an innovative new product, like CK One, creativity is still the fastest way to seduce a shopper.

Saturation of major brands and lookalike private brands leads to stale floors and every department store looking the same. And as the big companies get bigger, the small get smaller or disappear, leading to further saturation by the commodity crowd.

But creativity doesn't have to be a third sleeve on a jacket or some other radical silhouette. It can be as easy as adding color.

It sounds simple, but walking into a sea of neutral shades or black in a department store can be a big yawn. New Yorkers' obsession with black, for example, makes many things look the same. Designers would do well to remember that New York is not America. Apparel makers should take chances with some color, combinations of colors, prints—anything to make the stores more lively and visually interesting.

There is money out there, but the lack of newness in women's apparel has inhibited spending.

Retreating to the safe haven of such basics as Gap jeans and plain white shirts was fashion's answer to the cocooning/nesting phenomenon of the early Nineties, when many people needed a breather from the glitz and hustle of the Eighties.

Now it's time to wake up the customer.

5   Revamp the Timing of Deliveries

Designers have been wailing about it for years. The entire coat industry has been battling it forever. It's an evergreen gripe: The timing of the industry is out of whack with real-life needs of the consumer.

Donna Karan, at a recent trunk show at Bergdorf Goodman, asked a group of her best customers: "When do you want to buy your fall clothes? Do you want to buy a tweed suit in July?" The unanimous—and highly vocal—response was that consumers don't want to look at fall styles until September.

The timing of deliveries perpetuates price slashing, and consumers know it. A woman can see a wool coat in a department store on a sweltering August afternoon, and know that, chances are, the same coat will be hanging when she returns in October, when the weather has just started to cool down—only this time, big red signs top the racks, offering discounts of 20 or 30 percent.

Executives from all areas of apparel have been singing the same tune.

People don't buy their wardrobes months in advance anymore, and merchandise should be delivered when the customer needs it.

"Right now we deliver summer when there's snow on the ground and fall when it's 90 degrees and humid," said Ken Zimmerman, chief executive officer of Kenar Enterprises. "This schedule automatically throws everything into a markdown mode."

When women shopped more for pleasure, manufacturers could get an early read on merchandise, and that's why they wanted to be the first in the stores.

"Now, with lead times so much longer due to worldwide sourcing and production, early reads aren't as relevant anymore," he said. "Today's customer isn't coming into the stores to give you an early indication. Right now, we are adhering to what the stores want, but it's like putting ice cream out in the sun. It's going to melt."

He added: "Summer should go on sale in July and August and fall should hit the stores around Sept. 15. Then discounters will get the merchandise at the right time and truly be discounters."

Linda J. Wachner, president, chairman and chief executive officer of the Warnaco Group, offered: "More compact lines should be shipped more frequently to retailers.

"For example, instead of five lines a year, a manufacturer should ship seven lines a year—or more—so merchandise constantly looks fresh at stores."

6   Manage the Matrix Better

It's no secret that manufacturers love matrix buying when they're on the system, loathe it when they're excluded, and fear it almost all the time.

That dreaded matrix—a list of vendors that department store companies pick from and stick to almost religiously, with little or no room for variation—can lead to lack of creativity, overbuying and too much promotion.

On the positive side, the matrix evolved as a tool for better inventory management, more efficient business practices, and fast replenishment of commodity items.

But if retailers get too dependent on the matrix for programmed buying decisions, a sameness infects the stores that leads to stale-looking floors and merchandise that sits until it's marked down to a no-profit price.

Federated Department Stores, a pioneer of matrix-style buying, is making a major effort to avoid a homogeneous look by hosting vendor fairs and setting aside time each month to see new resources.

"While we have an approval process, I would not confuse it with what has been called a matrix by other companies," Terry Lundgren, chairman and ceo of Federated Merchandising, said. "It has mostly to do with flexibility and open-mindedness. In fact, our strongly stated objective is to add new resources."

7   Give the Little Guy a Chance

In many cases, smaller is better.

Smaller stores, with their mom-and-pop merchandising, are unique entities. They offer the consumer an alternative to cookie-cutter assortments often found in the big department stores, and win the rewards for attentive service and uncommon apparel choices.

The specialty store thrives on distinctive mixes, but this is not solely the domain of the tiny operation. Large retailers—Nordstrom, for example—have been successful partly because of their regional buying policies. A Nordstrom on the East Coast is merchandised differently from one in the Midwest or in the Pacific Northwest. Local merchandising takes into account the needs and preferences of local people.

Specialty stores, in fact, were able to maintain a stable percentage of frequent shoppers from 1990 to 1994, while in the same period the number of consumers who shop often—once a month or more—at department stores fell to 19 percent from 33 percent, according to a study by Management Horizons.

8   Define Your Niche

So you're a supercenter, and you're everything to everyone and retailing's future. Congratulations.

But for the rest of you, take note: It's important to define your niche and why you are in business. You have to stand for something.

Narrowing the focus of business has been a mantra in corporate America for a few years. It's part of knowing who your customer is, and serving her properly.

Some retailers have grasped the knack of niche marketing. Victoria's Secret, Bath & Body Works, Authentic Fitness Speedo Shops, Warner Bros. Studio Stores, The Body Shop, the Gap and Banana Republic are prime examples of firms that have managed solid growth and overall profitability in tough times by staying focused on their *raison d'etre.*

However, being focused doesn't necessarily mean being a small specialty store. Such category killers as Home Depot, Toys "R" Us and Bed Bath & Beyond prove that bigger can be better—as long as it's focused. Even mega-retailer Wal-Mart, which is on top of the supercenter trend and the world's largest retailer, doesn't lose sight of its mission and the customer it serves.

One obvious illustration of the opposite is Kmart Corp., which engaged in a strategy that drove down both profits and stock price, and cost its chief executive his job. Kmart virtually ignored its core discount stores in favor of its glamorous specialty superstore concepts—Sports Authority, Office Max, Borders/Waldenbooks, Builders Square. Kmart sold stakes in Sports Authority and Office Max, and a public offering is planned for Borders as well. These concepts prospered at the expense of the Kmart discount stores, and now the company is committed to rebuilding that business.

Retail consolidations have been rampant, and many observers agree the process is not over. While the instinctive reaction to consolidation is "fewer accounts to sell means less business," a little Darwinism makes the entire industry stronger and healthier.

"We have yet to recognize as an industry that things have permanently changed," said Robert Buchanan, analyst for NatWest Securities. "There are certain retail executives who still think it is the Eighties and are still talking to shareholders and associates about unrealistic goals like 20 percent top-line growth.

"May Department Stores has had the proper focus for the last several years. It's been closing marginal stores and boosting return on invested capital, while relegating top-line growth to a backseat role.

Now they're at the point where they have their core assets remaining and can try to grow off that smaller base. This paring down process is one that the industry continues to put off.

"One way or another, capacity is going to be reduced. It will either be the result of rational strategies or the result of carnage in the form of Chapter 11s."

Manufacturers, too, must develop a strong identity, project that vision consistently and stay on top of what their customers want. Like retailers, when makers are obsessed with rapid growth, they lose the focus on the customer and product. The result? Mediocrity.

9 Improve In-Store Service and Visual Display

You might have most ingredients for success: a good location, well-made merchandise—abundant and in-season—that's priced to move and an attractive store environment. But the salesperson is either rude, doesn't know about the product, or is nonexistent, and you've lost the sale—maybe even the customer.

In-store service and presentation are paramount to closing the sale. They are what gets that message to the consumer and are the subtle cues that encourage her to pull out her wallet.

Not every store can, or should, go the extreme of a Warner Bros. Studio Store or Nike Town. But these are huge examples of retailers that make it fun to come in and shop. These stores attract consumers because they have lively, well planned, exciting environments.

Sales associates—the ambassadors of the store—must follow through by being thoroughly familiar with the product and showing the customer how to work with new looks. The right presentation and a friendly, accessible sales staff can defuse the price issue. Consumers are sometimes willing to pay a little more for a delightful shopping experience.

Department stores that have become too focused on the bottom line have cut badly needed staff, reduced training and sacrificed expenditures on visual presentation. This can cost sales, but more important, thwarts efforts to build a loyal customer base.

10 Stop the [Markdown] Madness

Markdowns are the bane of manufacturers' existence and after a disappointing Christmas and a dis-

mal spring, the pressure from stores has intensified across all vendor segments.

"The stores make an error in buying and we have to give them money for it," noted one manufacturer. "But there's no such thing as 'markup money' when something sells really well."

Markdowns are a self-perpetuating problem, leading to unrealistic pricing and poor inventory management. A manufacturer, knowing he has to build markdown into his wholesale price, adds several percentage points to his cost. His price is doubled at the retail level, and ends up being marked down to a sale price, which is what the garment should have been tagged in the first place.

11 Offer Realistic Pricing and Value

There's a reason the Kathie Lee collection is blowing out at Wal-Mart, with annual volume projected to cruise past $250 million: value for the price.

It's another solution that sounds obvious, but, as Pierre Bergé, president of Yves Saint Laurent, declared, "[Clothes] must be very well made; they must be priced reasonably, and they must be wearable. If we can manage to create fashion in this manner, then we'll get out of the fashion depression."

One of the biggest problems in fashion retailing has been the lack of intrinsic value in merchandise—and it has been a problem for several years. It has fueled the volcanic growth of the mass merchants, by driving the department store customer to the giant discounters, because she's shopping for price.

Many consumers equate value with price. If further proof is needed, look at the erosion in consumer prices in women's apparel: In May, they dropped a seasonally adjusted 0.5 percent against April, and were off 4.4 percent against May 1994.

But it's not only about price. Perceived value is also important, and that comes in the forms of brand name, presentation and convenience as well.

"We've created an illusion about price," said Richard Elias, president of Renlyn Suits.

"The customer is tired of being ripped off. She wants to buy at the real value of the garment, and she knows if she waits long enough, it will be marked down."

12 Communicate

"Partnering" and "interfacing" are among the buzzwords of the Nineties, and many executives feel improving communication between vendor, store and consumer is the way to avoid mistakes, enhance design, track sales, manage merchandise distribution, monitor stock levels and keep assortments current.

Advances in technology—particularly electronic data interchange, allowing vendors and merchants to manage and replenish inventory more efficiently—play a key role in improving communication.

For example, Massimo Ferretti, chairman of AEFFE SpA, said his firm provides a 24-hour on-line service to its buyers with real-time information about what items are available and ready for shipping from their warehouse.

Interactive video communications is another method by which retailers can simultaneously communicate with their own divisions and store groups.

Focus Networks, for example, has developed a format where retailers can share management as well as vendor messages with branches on everything from sales training and line introductions to point-of-purchase ideas, via satellite, according to Dan Owen, chairman.

And Paul Kaess, president of Certified Fashion Guild, said the firm's Rag-Net satellite data interchange and marketing system allows it to link its member retailers and a network of manufacturers and transmit text and high-resolution pictures within four seconds.

Source: From Women's Wear Daily, *July 21, 1995, pp. 1, 6–9. Reprinted by permission.*

Chapter Review

Key Words and Concepts

Define, identify, or briefly explain the following:

Anchor stores	Factory outlet	Outlet center
Apparel specialty chain	Flea market	Overstored
Boutique	Franchise	Party plan
Branch store	Franchisee	Preticketing
Catalog showroom retailer	Franchisor	Private label
"Category killers"	General merchandising chain	Product development
CD-ROM shopping	Global retailing	Quick Response
Centralized buying	Home television shopping	Relationship marketing
Chain store	Hypermarket	Retail format
Chapter 11	In-store retailing	Retailer
Chargebacks	Mail-order house	Shopping center
Cross-shoppers	Mall	SKUs
Customization	Matrix buying	Specialty store
Database marketing	Megamall	Store ambience
Department store	Micromarketing	Store ownership group
Direct-selling retailer	Mom-and-pop store	Supercenter
Discounter	National brand	Supermarket
Diverters	Nonstore retailing	Superstore
"Doors"	Off-price retailer	Warehouse club
Economies of scale	On-line computer shopping	

Review Questions on Chapter Highlights

1. In what types of retail establishment do you prefer to shop and why? What types do you avoid and why?
2. Why is the SIC category system important when studying retailing?
3. Describe the targeted customer of the typical department store.
4. What is a store ownership group? How does it differ from chain operations?
5. What are the competitive advantages of apparel specialty stores compared with department stores?
6. Compare the operations of a department store and its branches with chain store operations. How are they similar and how do they differ?
7. How can off-price retailers such as Marshall's undersell conventionally priced retailers? What are their sources of supply?
8. How are large department and specialty stores meeting the competition of the underselling retailers?
9. Why do you think full-line discount stores are taking apparel market share from other retailers?
10. What is the difference between a hypermarket and a supercenter?

11. What do you think accounts for the success of the "category killers"? How are they a threat to conventional retailers?
12. Describe the evolution of outlet centers. What is your prediction for their future success?
13. List several kinds of nonstore retailing. Which do you believe holds the most success for the future and why?
14. Why is mail-order retailing so important today? Name different types of retailers that are in the mail-order business.
15. What are your predictions regarding the type of electronic retailing that will grow most? Why?
16. What is the difference between private label and national brands? How do consumers compare the two?
17. What does it mean to say "the elephants will dance only with the elephants"? In the context in which this is used, what are the problems associated with this trend?
18. Why are industry partnerships important to retailers?
19. Why is global retailing likely to increase in the future?
20. How can retailers balance the two ideas that seem very different: globalization and customization?

References

American Apparel Manufacturers Association. (1996, May). *Apparel Industry Trends.* Arlington, VA: Author, pp.7–8.

Analysis of retail performances for fiscal 1994. (1995, August 31). *Women's Wear Daily,* pp. 6–7.

At retail, it's a Barnum & Bailey world. (1995, May 3). *Women's Wear Daily,* pp. 1, 8, 9.

Barrett, J. (1994, August 11). Capitol Hill turns up the heat on discount retailers. *DNR,* p. 10.

Bartlett, R., & Peterson, P. (1992). A retailing agenda for the year 2000. In Peterson, R. (Ed.). *The future of U.S. retailing: An agenda for the 21st century.* New York: Quorum Books.

Chandler, S. (1994, September 12). Spiegel's book is a real page-turner. *Business Week,* pp. 74, 76.

Combined Federated/Macy's will hit sales of $17.5B by '98. (1994, September 1). *DNR,* pp. 2, 9.

DeWitt, J. (1995, September). Sourcing the cyber way. *Apparel Industry Magazine,* pp. 56–62.

D'Innocenzio, A. (1992, November 24). Hypermarkets: A very big idea that never grew. *Women's Wear Daily,* pp. 1, 9.

Direct Marketing Association. (1995). *Economic impact: U.S. direct marketing today* (unpublished fact sheet).

Edelson, S. (1995a, November 8). Fashion reevaluates flickering fortunes of TV home shopping. *Women's Wear Daily,* pp. 1, 8, 9.

Edelson, S. (1995b, August 9). The great mall makeover. *Women's Wear Daily,* pp. 8–9.

Edelson, S. (1995c, April 4). Once a poor relation, outlets go legit—and trouble looms. *Women's Wear Daily,* pp. 1, 8, 9.

Electronic shopping. (1994, October). *Consumer Reports,* p. 623.

Harris, L. (1979). *The merchant princes.* New York: Harper & Row.

International Council of Shopping Centers. (1995, November 14). Author's telephone conversation with Council staff member.

Kidwell, C., & Christman, M. (1974). *Suiting everyone: The democratization of clothing in America.* Washington, DC: Smithsonian Institution Press.

Kurt Salmon Associates. (1995). *Vision for the new millennium . . . evolving to consumer response.* Atlanta, GA: Author.

Kurtz, M., Bongiorno, L., Naughton, K., DeGeorge, G., & Forest, S. (1995, November 27). Reinventing the store. *Business Week,* pp. 84–96.

Lewis, R. (Ed.). (1995, November). What's in a name? Is it a brand, a private label, or a store? "Infotracs" special supplement to *Women's Wear Daily,* pp. 1–35.

Mail-order shopping. (1994, October). *Consumer Reports,* pp. 621–627.

Mall of America. (1994). *Press kit.* Bloomington, MN: Author.

Management Horizons. (1994a, August). *Retail review: Softgoods, 11,* pp. 4–5.

Management Horizons. (1994b, December). *Retail review: Softgoods,* pp. 12–13.

Management Horizons. (1994c). *Retail world: Window of opportunity.* Columbus, OH: Author.

Management Horizons. (1995, August). State of the Industry. *Chain Store Age,* pp. 3A–7A.

Manufacturers howl as retailers pile on more chargebacks. (1995, July 25). *Women's Wear Daily,* pp. 1, 6, 7, 31.

May Department Stores. (1995). *May Department Stores annual report 1994.* St. Louis: Author.

Merchant to the millions. (no date). Chicago: Sears Roebuck and Co.

Moin, D. (1994, July 15). Macy's/Federated: It's a deal. *Women's Wear Daily,* pp. 1, 10, 11.

Moin, D. (1995, August 15). Federated shocker: Makes deal to buy all Broadway Stores. *Women's Wear Daily,* pp. 1, 31.

National Retail Federation. (1996, April 25). Faxed communications to author.

National Retail Institute. (1995). *Retail industry indicators.* Washington, DC: Author.

Ostroff, J., & Emert, C. (1995, June 15). More consolidation around the corner, IAF parley is warned. *Women's Wear Daily,* pp. 1, 8.

Outlet industry data. (1995, Spring). *Value retail news convention newsletter.*

Palmieri, J., & Kaplan, D. (1995, May). Retail scorecard. Special supplement to *Women's Wear Daily,* pp. 1–14.

Rudnitsky, H. (1994, August 15). Too much of a good thing. *Forbes,* pp. 46–47.

Sack, K. (1996). *Standard & Poor's industry surveys: Retailing.* New York: Standard & Poor's.

The super specialists. (1986, August). *Stores Magazine.*

TJX buys Marshalls. (1995, November). *Stores,* p. 9.

Wilner, R. (1995, November 6). Edison Bros. Stores files Chapter 11, will close 500 units in next 3 months. *DNR,* pp. 2, 15.

Zinn, L., DeGeorge, G., Shoretz, R., Yang, D., & Forest, S. (1993, July 26). Retailing will never be the same. *Business Week,* pp. 54–60.

Suggested Bibliography

Barry, M., Warfield, C., Cavender, D., & Henton, J. (1993, March). Apparel retailing in the USA. *Textile Outlook International,* pp. 9–41.

Berman, B., & Evans, J. (1995). *Retail management: A strategic approach* (6th ed.). Upper Saddle River, NJ: Prentice Hall.

Brough, J. (1982). *The Woolworths.* New York: McGraw-Hill.

Burnstiner, I. (1994). *How to start and run your own retail business.* New York: Carol.

Donnellan, J. (1995). *Merchandise buying and management.* New York: Fairchild.

Fairchild Publications. (1990). *A statistical analysis of retailing.* New York: Author.

Falk, E. (1994). *1,001 ideas to create retail excitement.* Upper Saddle River, NJ: Prentice Hall.

Fetterman, R., & Byrne, H. (1995). *Interactive selling in the '90s: Applying information, technology, multimedia, and electronications to the sales process.* San Diego, CA: Ellipsys International.

Friedman, H. (1992). *No thanks, I'm just looking: Professional retail sales techniques for turning shoppers into buyers.* Dubuque, IA: Kendall/Hunt.

Gold, A. (1978). *How to sell fashion* (2nd ed.). New York: Fairchild.

Harris, L. (1979). *Merchant princes.* New York: Harper & Row.

Hoge, C. (1988). *The first 100 years are the toughest: What we can learn from the century of competition between Sears and Wards.* Berkeley, CA: Ten Speed Press.

International Council of Shopping Centers. (1988). *Increasing retailer productivity.* New York: Author.

International Council of Shopping Centers. (annual). *The scope of the shopping industry in the United States.* New York: Author.

Israel, L. (1994). *Store planning/design: History, theory, process.* New York: Wiley.

Kirkpatrick, G. (1994). *Shops and boutiques.* New York: Rizzoli International.

Kunz, M., Bongiorno, L., Naughton, K., DeGeorge, G., & Anderson, F. (1995, November 27). Reinventing the store. *Business Week,* pp. 84–96.

Lewison, D. (1994). *Retailing* (5th ed.). Upper Saddle River, NJ: Prentice Hall.

Mahoney, T., & Sloane, L. (1974). *The great merchants* (2nd ed.). New York: Harper & Row.

Mallory, C. (1991). *Direct mail magic.* Menlo Park, CA: Crisp Publications.

Management Horizons. (1990). *Retailing 2000.* Columbus, OH: Author.

Marcus, S. (1974). *Minding the store.* Boston: Little, Brown.

Marcus, S. (1979). *Quest for the best.* New York: Viking Press.

National Retail Institute. (annual). *Retail industry indicators.* Washington, DC: Author.

Ostrow, R., & Smith, S. (1984). *The dictionary of retailing.* New York: Fairchild.

Pegler, M. (1991). *Visual merchandising and display* (2nd ed.) New York: Fairchild.

Peter, G. (1992). *It's not my department!* New York: Berkeley.

Peterson, R. (Ed.). (1992). *The future of U.S. retailing: An agenda for the 21st century.* New York: Quorum Books.

Rating the stores. (1994, November). *Consumer Reports,* pp. 712–721.

Reid, T. (1991). *What Mother never told ya about retail: A small store survival guide* (2nd ed.). Amite, LA: Retail Resources.

Rossi, W. (1988). *Profitable footwear retailing.* New York: Fairchild.

Seelye, R., & Moody, O. (1993). *The selling starts when the customer says no: The 12 toughest sells—and how to overcome them.* Chicago: Probus.

Spector, R., & McCarthy, P. (1995). *Customer service the Nordstrom way.* New York: John Wiley & Sons.

Sroge, M. (1995). *101 tips for more profitable catalogs.* Lincolnwood, IL: NTC Publishing Group.

Sroge, M. (1985). *How to create successful catalogs.* Lincolnwood, IL: NTC Publishing Group.

Standard & Poor's. (annual). *Industry surveys: Retailing.* New York: Author.

Stevens, M. (1979). *Like no other store in the world: The inside story of Bloomingdale's.* New York: Thomas Y. Crowell.

Stone, K. (1995). *Competing with the retail giants.* New York: John Wiley & Sons.

Traub, M. (1993). *The Bloomingdale's legend and the revolution of American marketing.* New York: Random House.

Vance, S., & Scott, R. (1994). *Wal-Mart.* Old Tappan, NJ: Macmillan.

Wardell, P. (1993). *Successful retailing: Your step-by-step guide to avoiding pitfalls and finding profit as an independent retailer* (2nd ed.). Dover, NH: Upstart Publishing.

Weil, G. (1977). *Sears, Roebuck, U.S.A.* New York: Stein & Day.

Trade Associations

Apparel Retailers of America, 2011 Eye St. NW, Suite 300, Washington, DC 20006.

Association of Retail Marketing Services, 3 Caro Ct., Red Bank, NJ 07701.

Confederation National Dos Directoes Loj, Rua Acre, 83 Andar, Rio de Janiero, RJ 20081, Brazil, S.A.

Direct Marketing Association, 1120 Ave. of the Americas, New York, NY 10036-6700.

Direct Selling Association, 1776 K St., NW, Suite 600, Washington, DC 20006.

FENALCO Presidencia Nacional, Carrera 4a No. 19-85 piso 7o, Bogota, D.E. 440, Colombia, S.A.

Footwear Distributors & Retailers of America, 1319 F St., NW, Suite 700, Washington, DC 20004.

General Merchandise Distributors Council, 1275 Lake Plaza Dr., Colorado Springs, CO 80906.

International Association of Department Stores, 72 Boulevard Haussman, Paris F-750-08, France.

International Council of Shopping Centers, 665 Fifth Ave., New York, NY 10022-5370.

International Franchise Association, 1350 New York Ave., NW, #900, Washington, DC 20005.

International Retail Advertising and Marketing Association, 500 N. Michigan Ave., Suite 600, Chicago, IL 60611.

Japan Retailing Center, Building 1-15-3 Minami Aoyama, Minato-Ku, Tokyo 107, Japan.

Jewelers of America, Inc., 1185 Ave. of the Americas, New York, NY 10036.

Le Consell Quebecois Du Commerce De Detail, 550 Sherbrook St., West, #1000, Montreal PQ H3A 1B9, Canada.

Mail Order Association of America, 1877 Bourne Ct., Wantagh, NY 11793.

Menswear Retailers, 2011 Eye St., NW, Washington, DC 20006.

National Association of Catalog Showroom Merchandisers, P.O. Box 725, Happauge, NY 11788.

National Association of Display, 468 Park Ave. S., Rm. 1707, New York, NY 10016.

National Association of Men's Sportswear Buyers, Inc., 500 Fifth Ave., New York, NY 10110.

National Retail Federation, 325 7th St. NW, Washington, DC 20004.

National Retailers Association of Mexico, Homero No. 109-11 Piso, Mexico City, D.F., 11560.

National Shoe Retailers Association, 9861 Broken Land Pkwy., Suite 255, Columbia, MD 21046.

Private Label Manufacturers Association, 369 Lexington Ave., New York, NY 10017.

Retail Council of Canada, 210 Dundas St. W. #600, Toronto, Ontario M5G 2E8, Canada.

Swedish Retail Federation, Sveriges Kopmannaforbund, S-105-61 Stockholm, Sweden.

Trade Publications

Apparel Merchandising, 425 Park Ave., New York, NY 10022.

Apparel Strategist, The, 101 E. Locust St., Fleetwood, PA 19522.

Catalog Age, 911 Hope St., Bldg. 6, Stamford, CT 06907.

Chain Merchandiser, Rt. 1, Box 95C, Baker City, OR 97814.

Chain Store Age Executive, 425 Park Ave., New York, NY 10022.

Current Business Reports: Annual Retail Trade, U.S. Bureau of Census, Department of Commerce, Washington, DC 20233.

The Discount Merchandiser, 233 Park Ave. S., New York, NY 10003.

Discount Store News, 425 Park Ave., New York, NY 10022.

DNR, 7 W. 34 St., New York, NY 10001-8191

Inside Retailing, 425 Park Ave., New York, NY 10022.

Loeb's Retail Report, P.O. Box 1155, New York, NY 10018.

Private Label Development, 19 W. 21 St., #403, New York, NY 10010.

MMR (Mass Market Retailers), 220 Fifth Ave., New York, NY 10001.

Retail Asia, 60 Martin Rd. #07-33, TradeMart Singapore, Singapore 0923.

Retail Business Review: The Executive, 100 W. 31 St., New York, NY 10001.

Retail Performance Monitor, 195 Smithtown Blvd., Nesconset, NY 11767.

Retail Review: Softgoods, Management Horizons, 41 S. High St., Columbus, OH 43215.

Retailing Today, Box 249, Lafayette, CA 94549.

Shopping Center World, 6151 Powers Ferry Rd. NW, Atlanta, GA 30339.

Shopping Centers Today, 665 Fifth Ave., New York, NY 10022-5370.

Stores, National Retail Federation, Inc., 325 7th St., NW, Washington, DC 20004.

The Retailer and Marketing News, P.O. Box 191105, Dallas, TX 75219.

Value Retail News, 15950 Bay Vista Dr. #250, Clearwater, FL 34620.

Women's Wear Daily, 7 W. 34 St., New York, NY 10001-8191.

*A*uxiliary Fashion Enterprises

*O*f *vital importance in the* fashion industry are the services of a variety of independently operated auxiliary enterprises that act as advisers, sources of information, and propagators of fashion news. Some of these enterprises devote their full energies to observing and analyzing the fashion scene, and assist producers and retailers in clarifying their own thinking about it. Others aid by getting a coherent fashion message to the consuming public, thus giving impetus to trends in the making. Among these fashion business auxiliaries are fashion information and advisory services, the news media, fashion video producers, advertising and publicity specialists, and resident buying offices. Consultants who assist firms in importing and exporting have also become important to the industry.

This chapter discusses such enterprises, how they function, and the part they play in the fashion business. The readings that follow the text are concerned with the activities of companies that operate in this segment of the fashion business.

Fashion Information and Advisory Services

Although all fashion producers and retailers of any size have experts of their own within their firms, many use outside specialized sources of fashion information against which to check their own analyses and conclusions.

Fashion Information Services

Beginning in the late 1960s and growing in importance ever since then, a number of comprehensive **fashion information services** have developed. Their clients are worldwide and include fiber companies; textile producers; producers of men's, women's, and children's wear; retailers; buying offices; and accessories and cosmetics companies. So all-pervading is the influence of fashion, however, that their clients also include some producers of small appliances, cars, home furnishings, and other consumer products.

In a business environment where time and timing are ever more important, these services offer specific, timely, concise, and complete worldwide information, often tailored to each client's specific needs.

The number of firms offering these services is constantly increasing, but the following are among the most important:

- Nigel French, headquartered in London. Their fabric reports cover the major fabric seasons—Spring/Summer and Fall/Winter—including the Interstoff and American fabric showings. They also issue separate color and knitwear brochures, report on New York and European designer collections, and present major season styling issues.

- The Fashion Service, known as TFS, whose reports cover fashion information from all over the world. Information is also available in CD form. Examples of TFS trend information are shown in Figure 11–1.
- The *International Colour Authority* (published in London) and the Color Association of the United States (with headquarters in New York) are important sources of color trend information. These are available for both women's wear and menswear (Figure 11–2).
- Here and There, whose reports cover U.S. ready-to-wear, couture collections, Japanese Prêt collections, Italian and French knitwear shows, fabric fairs (Interstoff, Ideacomo, Premier Vision, Prato), and a special feature that translates high fashion looks for mass markets.
- Promostyl, which began as a children's wear service in 1967. They now have offices or agents in 23 cities worldwide, and publish 31 different handbooks annually.
- Stylists' Information Service (SIS). Their reports include "The Boutique Forecast" (twice a year), "The Children's Forecast" (twice a year), "The Eveningwear Forecast" (once a year), "The Menswear Forecast" (twice a year), "The Lingerie Forecast" (once a year), "The Women's Actualwear Forecast" (twice a year), and "The Trimming and Finishing Book" (once a year).
- Karten for Kids is published eight times a year, and Karten for Little Kids (or infants and toddlers to the age of two) is published twice a year.

Fashion Consultants

A **fashion consultant** is an independent individual or firm hired by fashion producers and retailers to assist them in some phase of their fashion operation. Probably the oldest still in existence is **Tobé Associates,** founded in 1927 by Mrs. Tobé to service

Figure 11–1

Examples of TFS, The Fashion Service, forecasting information. TFS is an international company that specializes in color, trend, and fashion forecasting.

Source: Courtesy of TFS, The Fashion Service.

Figure 11–2   **Examples of trend information provided by the International Colour Authority, a London-based organization.**

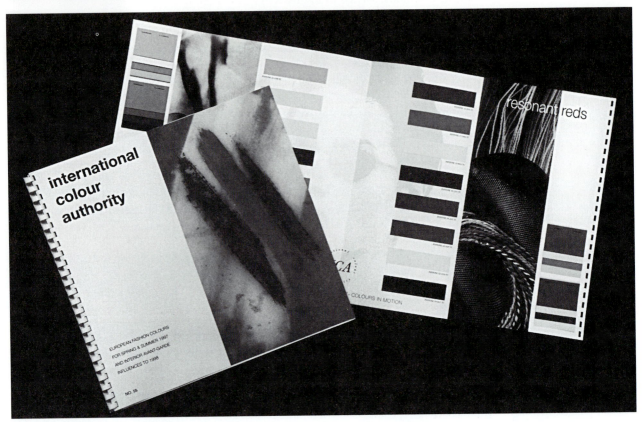

Source: Courtesy of ITBD Publications.

retailers. The firm sends to its paying clients a multipage, illustrated weekly brochure that contains information on current and coming trends, illustrated by specific style numbers with the names of the producers and the wholesale prices. As Tobé herself once described the function of her consulting firm,

> We are the reporters and interpreters of the fashion world speaking to the fashion-makers and the fashion sellers. . . . Our job is to tell the makers what the sellers are doing and vice versa. Most of all, we interpret and evaluate for each what is happening to fashion itself. . . . We make it our business to stay abreast of those economic, social, and art trends which I maintain are the great formative currents of fashion. . . . From all these we try to pick the significant trends that will change our lives, and hence our fashions. . . . We keep an eye on what those in the fashion vanguard are wearing and doing and seeing. This not only means reporting on what smart people wear. . . . It also means keeping abreast of what plays, films, and TV presentations they are seeing, which are successful, where they travel, and what books they read. . . . All of this information flows into our offices, where it is digested, sorted out, evaluated, and then disseminated through a weekly report. . . . Our clients—department stores throughout

America, specialty stores in Europe, a wool manufacturer in Finland, the Export Institute in Israel—they can all shop the Fifth Avenue stores, the Paris showings, the Seventh Avenue showings, without budging from their desks. They can keep track of resort life without going to Monaco or Florida or the Caribbean. They can read about the fads, as well as the foundations of fashion, without spending much time or effort in research.

So it is our business as a whole to interpret the current scene to the makers and sellers of fashion wares (Tobé, 1957).

A reading at the end of this chapter gives specific information about what Tobé Associates does and how it does it.

Another example of a retail consultant is Merchandising Motivation, Inc. (MMI), which is operated on a similar but smaller scale. There are also many other consulting firms, usually headed by former fashion practitioners, whose services are available, for a fee, to retailers or producers, or both. These firms usually deal with specific areas of the fashion industry, such as accessories, fibers, fabrics, children's wear, and menswear.

Merchandising, Buying, and Product Development Organizations

This group of organizations evolved from companies that were once known as **resident buying offices.** These began as a paid service for retailers to help them locate desirable goods in the market. They played an equally important but unpaid service for manufacturers by bringing their merchandise to the attention of retailers when it met their needs and standards.

Originally, almost every large store outside New York City was affiliated with an independent buying office, either serving that store alone or serving many noncompeting retailers. Buying office functions included reporting market information, acting as a representative of its client stores, and performing related services for its retail clients. Today, as they did then, these organizations keep stores informed of fashion, price, and supply developments, and act as eyes and ears for the client stores.

Today, however, the term *resident buying office* is only somewhat applicable to these organizations as they have evolved to meet the needs of a changing retail industry. Rather than being buying offices, these groups have become organizations with other kinds of services to help retail clients. They assist retailers far beyond the buying function, and some no longer function as *buying* offices at all. Among the newest and now one of the most important services rendered by these organizations is **product development,** whereby the design staff of the buying office develops private label merchandise specifically tailored to the needs of their client stores. Some of these organizations have become broad-based business consulting organizations (i.e., **consultants**) to assist retailers with merchandising activities, sourcing, **logistics** related to importing, **management information systems (MIS),** and a range of other areas. Retail giants may have their own internal staffs who perform these roles, but for smaller retailers, these consulting organizations provide the expertise and assistance needed to remain profitable in today's competitive retail environment.

The organizations that provide the merchandising and product development services to retailers (what were formerly just buying offices) i.e., **merchandising, buying, and product development organizations,** fall into two major categories: (1) those that are independently owned enterprises and receive fees from the stores they serve and (2) those that are store owned or corporate owned.

Independently Owned or Fee Organizations

Independently owned organizations, which were known as salaried or **fee offices** when they were buying offices, are run as private enterprises. Member or subscribing stores pay a yearly fee, usually based on a percentage of annual sales volume. Most such offices concentrate on serving specialty stores that carry all or most types of apparel and accessories. Others specialize in such narrow categories as large, petite, or tall sizes; bridal, maternity, or junior wear; off-price apparel; fabrics or accessories; men's and boys' wear; or home furnishings. A few concentrate on filling the needs of small department stores, representing them in all the markets of interest to these clients.

Because buying offices exist to serve the retail community, the mergers and acquisitions that have changed retailers' ownership in recent years have seen an accompanying phenomenon in what were strictly buying offices. Some of the long-standing buying offices have closed, and others have been acquired by large firms. The Doneger Group has emerged as the largest independent apparel buying office in the country (Palmieri, 1994). This group, which now operates 10 specialized divisions, assists client firms with many aspects of business that go beyond the traditional buying function. The term *buying office* is actually too limited. One article in the readings section of the chapter reports on this company's expanded services to retailers. Among the 10 divisions are the Doneger Buying Connection, Doneger Kids, Doneger Menswear, Doneger Tall Buying, and D³Doneger Design Connection. The Doneger Group assists clients in such areas as domestic and international market coverage, product development, trends in color and style changes, direct mail programs, information on sources of store supplies, and many others.

When buying offices were first established in New York, they were vital since they offered store owners (outside the marketplace) access to new and current information, increased purchasing power because of their size, and an opportunity to share or exchange information. Today, as major retailers grow bigger and their buying clout also grows bigger, buying offices must change their service menu. One of their major roles now is to facilitate imports and private label programs. Another major function is to provide personalized services such as executive searching and personal market service with and without the presence of the store owner, and to seek out new and unusual resources to provide smaller stores with unusual merchandise.

Store-Owned Organizations: Cooperative Groups

Unlike the privately owned, profit-oriented fee offices, the organizations that are store owned are controlled and supported by the stores they serve. Their major objectives are to provide market expertise and whatever additional services the supporting stores require to assist them in operating profitably.

A **cooperative merchandising organization** (formerly a **cooperative buying office**) is one owned and maintained by a group of stores that it serves exclusively. This type of office was also known as an *associated office*. Membership in the store group is by invitation only, and all the participants in such groups are major retailers within their respective areas.

One of the major and best known of such offices is the Associated Merchandising Corporation (AMC), founded in 1918 by Filene's of Boston; F. & R. Lazarus of Columbus, Ohio; J. L. Hudson of Detroit; and Rike's of Dayton. Other stores, such as Abraham & Strauss of Brooklyn, Bloomingdale's of New York, Shillito's of Cincinnati, Foley's of Houston, Sanger-Harris of Dallas, and Burdine's of Miami, soon joined. Membership grew, attracting both U.S. stores and some in other countries. Today, AMC is owned mostly by Dayton-Hudson and Federated Department Stores, but it does have several other members (Bertsch, 1995). Others include Avon, Carson Pirie Scott & Co., Marshall's, Parisian, Saks & Company, Strawbridge & Clothier, and Warner Bros. (Associated Merchandising Corporation, 1995).

Today, AMC, whose headquarters are in New York, focuses primarily on sourcing and development of exclusive products for member stores. As the largest and most comprehensive overseas sourcing and product development organization of its kind, AMC has a staff of over 600 professionals with offices in more than 30 locations outside the United States. In these offices in other countries, staff members coordinate the production of merchandise being sourced from that region (Figure 11–3). **Overseas merchandise representatives** make major contributions to product management, in the selection and development of merchandise. The representative's knowledge of local markets is vital, and he or she often works one-on-one with individual store merchants who travel the world in search of unique product assortments and look to AMC's overseas staff for guidance and direction. These representatives have the client's best interests in mind as they monitor production for quality and prompt timing of deliveries (Figure 11–4). Each office is staffed with quality control personnel who test products to see that they meet the retail client's expectations (Associated Merchandising Corporation, 1995). One of the readings at the end of the chapter describes AMC's current activities in more detail.

The other major cooperative organization is Frederick Atkins, Inc., which like the others we described has evolved from being a buying office to an entirely different type of business. The company describes itself as "a store owned merchandising and product development organization. A cooperative with 28 retail corporations located throughout the United States, Mexico, and South America" (Frederick Atkins, 1995, p. 1). This cooperative is an international retail merchandising and marketing organization that provides market direction, exclusive merchandise programs,

Figure 11–3

AMC overseas merchandise representatives coordinate the overseas production of private label apparel for member companies.

Source: Photo by Kitty G. Dickerson.

Figure 11–4

Overseas merchandise representatives follow through on orders after buyers have left the overseas production site.

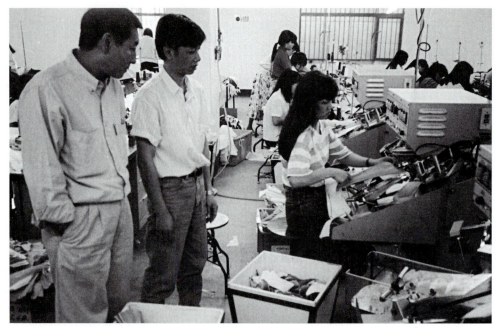

Source: Photo by Kitty G. Dickerson.

management information, and merchandising counseling to a group of independent and general merchandise retailers. The combined total annual sales volume of the member stores in North America in 1993 was over $13 billion. Frederick Atkins, Inc. engages in product development and distribution of exclusive private brand merchandise as well as national brands to the member firms. With a staff of more than 400 associates, Atkins has divisions that parallel those in a department store, indicating they provide assistance on a range of retail activities. The goal is to maximize the market share, productivity, and profitability of its stockholders. Among the members are the Bonton, Dillard's Department Stores, Inc., Emporium, and Jacobsons Stores, Inc. The company's international division has commissionaires in 30 countries. The commissionaires help develop and maintain resource relationships in other countries, assist office and store personnel on overseas trips, set up meetings, and follow through on orders after the buyers have left (Frederick Atkins, 1995).

Corporate Offices

Another very important type of office is the **corporate merchandising/buying office**, which is owned and financed by a store ownership group and services only the stores of that group. Unlike the homogeneous mix of stores served by cooperative offices, some of the store ownership groups consist of both large and small stores. Examples are May Department Stores, Mercantile Stores, T. Eaton, Belk Stores, and Batus Corp. In the case of each of these corporate offices, the combined volume of the stores it serves makes it a very important entity in the marketplace.

The large corporate merchandising/buying offices have evolved into multifaceted units, as we have discussed for the previous groups that began as buying offices. Rather than focusing exclusively on searching the markets for products for the stores in the corporation, these offices have also become heavily involved in designing, product development, and sourcing of private label merchandise. Today's **market representatives** are frequently performing both roles.

Changes in the May Department Stores Company reflect shifts that have occurred for corporate buying offices for store ownership groups. The company's buying office, May Merchandising Company, was previously located in New York. Staff in that office searched the market for all the May companies, working with buyers from various stores in planning and securing merchandise. In the early 1990s, May Merchandising Company was moved to St. Louis to be at the corporate headquarters. May Merchandising Company "identifies emerging fashion developments and merchandise trends for the department store divisions" and "closely collaborates with the operating companies to enhance their merchandising programs" (May Department Stores, 1995, p. 22). The company's central merchants and creative group work with the design and technical center (i.e., the product development group with nearly 100 staff members) and May Department Stores International to develop private label programs. May Department Stores International is the overseas buying arm of May Merchandising. It operates a network of eight offices in Asia and works with agents in numerous other countries. The reader may wish to refer back to Figure 9–5. May is one of only a few domestic department store companies[1] that owns and manages its own overseas operations, a structure which the company feels is vital to the quick response of May's import programs to merchandising trends (May Department Stores, 1995).

Management Consultants

In addition to the organizations we have just discussed, another type of consulting group has become increasingly important to many manufacturers and retailers. Although the groups just discussed have worked primarily with retailers and have specialized more in the past on merchandise-related areas of expertise, some others also provide various types of management and marketing assistance.

Another group consisting of **management consultants** focuses more specifically on management and market research areas, specializing in the softgoods and consumer goods distribution industries. These consulting firms tend to focus more on helping companies with management issues such as broad strategic planning, market strategy analysis and planning, merchandising, and operations strategies, rather than on product trend analysis and selection. Examples of these include:

- *Kurt Salmon Associates, Inc.* (KSA) specializes in working with companies in the softgoods industries. Some of their divisions work more specifically with textile and apparel manufacturers, and others specialize in retailing. KSA has offices in several parts of the United States and in numerous other parts of the world. This consulting firm often conducts in-depth studies of an industry sector in a country but also works with individual firms in analyzing their operations to become more efficient and profitable.

- *Management Horizons* is a division of Price Waterhouse, the well-known accounting firm. Management Horizons is a worldwide management and market research consulting firm specializing in retailing and consumer goods distribution industries. This company does extensive research and reporting on the retail industry in general and works with retail clients on an individual basis to improve

---

[1] May Department Stores is one of the few department stores to do so; however, a number of mass merchandise retailers maintain their own offices.

competitiveness and profitability. Management Horizons has been a leader in conducting studies of global retailing trends.

- *Deloitte & Touche*, another major accounting and consulting firm, has a division, the TRADE/Retail and Distribution Services Group. This group works specifically with the retailers, wholesalers, and apparel and textile companies. In fact, Deloitte & Touche claims to be the largest consulting group to the retail sector (Braun, 1995). More than 400 professionals in North America and over 1,000 worldwide devote their efforts to serving clients large and small, public and private. This group serves many of the largest retailers, including 37 of *Fortune*'s top 50 retailers. The Garr Consulting Group, a division of TRADE, provides engineering assistance related to logistics problems involved in retail and wholesale distribution (Braun, 1995). Additionally, Deloitte & Touche's consulting division works with many major softgoods manufacturers.
- *IBM Corporation* has a Consulting Services and Distribution Industries division devoted to working with the retailing sector. Because of the nature of IBM's product areas, this consulting is obviously related to technology in some way. However, IBM's consultants consider broader areas of management and market analysis, which in many cases has implications for computer technology use.

Consultants in Technical Areas

Consultants who wish to sell their services to textile/apparel manufacturing and retailing firms offer an almost unlimited menu of expertise. Many of the organizations described in previous sections have staff qualified to provide assistance in specialized technical areas. However, some consulting firms offer services *only* in specialized areas such as the following:

- *Information technology.* Consulting firms offer a range of assistance in areas related to information technology, including CAD systems, product data management systems, Quick Response, POS systems, bar coding, production of CD-ROM "catalogs," establishing shopping sites on the Internet, and on and on. Information technology is being applied increasingly throughout the softgoods industry, as shown in Figure 11–5. Because many of the information technology systems are quite technical to put in place and adapt to a company's specific use, consultants can help firms obtain maximum benefit from the investments.
- *Logistics.* Some consulting firms specialize in assisting businesses with the distribution processes involved in getting merchandise moved quickly and efficiently from the manufacturer to the customer. Some of the firms may operate only within the country, while others are involved in logistics related to importing and exporting.

Import and Export Consultants

The globalization of the fashion industry has added new dimensions to the business of producing and selling fashion goods. The complexities of sending merchandise from one country to another require specialists who stay abreast of the trade laws, documentation, and business strategies associated with importing and exporting. Although large firms may have some of these specialists on their staff, even those firms often use the services of trade specialists. Smaller firms will almost surely need to hire experts in these areas to be sure goods are delivered as expected, that trade laws are followed, and that payment occurs as intended. Because of the complexities of

Figure 11-5

Application of information on technology throughout the fashion pipeline.

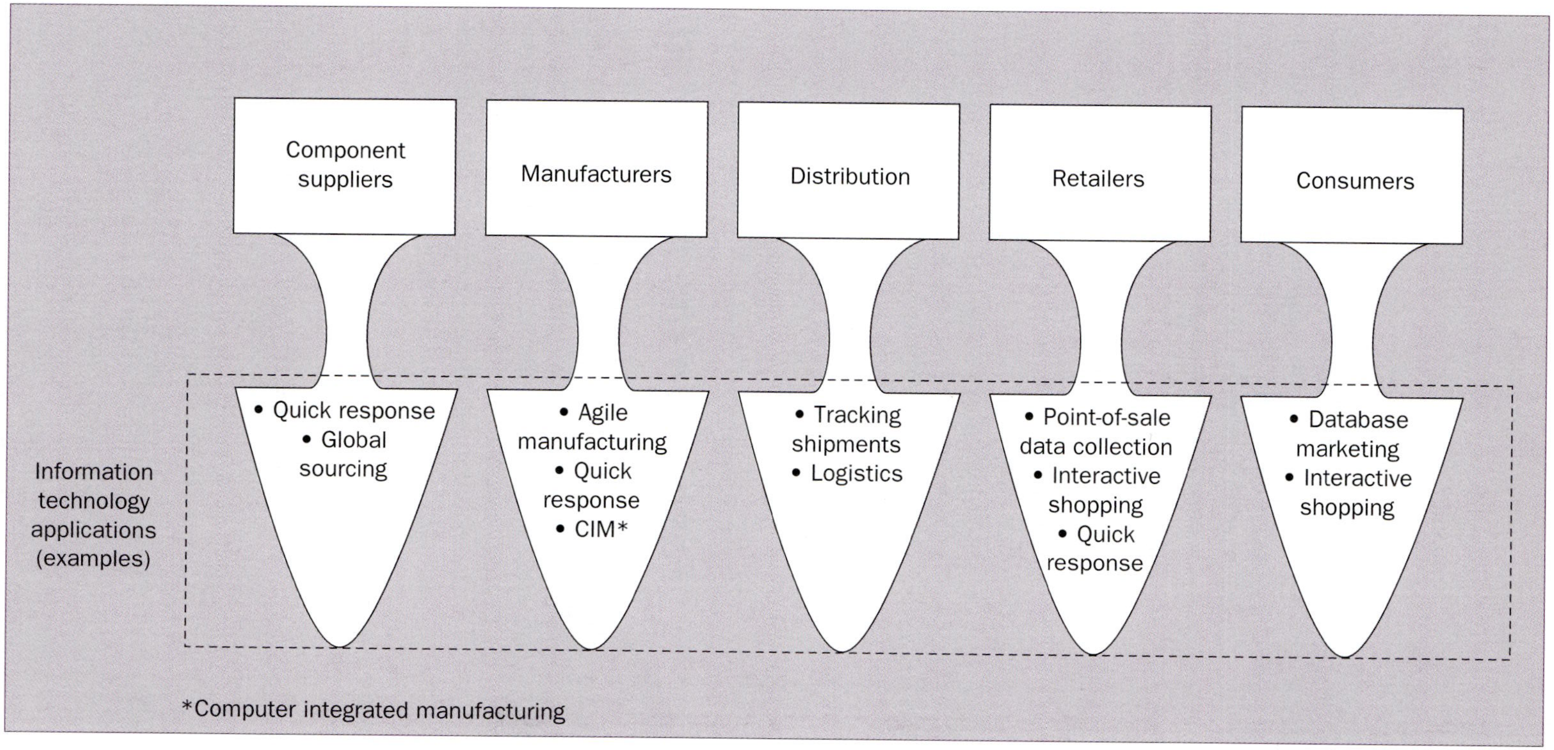

| Component suppliers | Manufacturers | Distribution | Retailers | Consumers |

Information technology applications (examples)

- Quick response
- Global sourcing

- Agile manufacturing
- Quick response
- CIM*

- Tracking shipments
- Logistics

- Point-of-sale data collection
- Interactive shopping
- Quick response

- Database marketing
- Interactive shopping

*Computer integrated manufacturing

importing and exporting, fees paid to these consultants may actually save money and valuable time in the long run. Examples of these consultants include:

- **Import brokers** coordinate the details of importing merchandise made in other countries for buyers in the United States.
- **Trade attorneys** provide legal assistance related to importing and exporting. Trade attorneys can help companies in advance of international business activities to help firms understand the potential risks and costs involved. Some law firms may even specialize in trade laws for specific regions. For example, the Sandler & Travis firm is particularly well known for helping companies with 9802/807 production and other business related to imports from the Caribbean region.
- **Export specialists** can help firms both in marketing to make sales in other countries and then in the technical details related to shipping merchandise once it is sold.
- **Lobbyists** are law firms or consulting firms, generally located in Washington, D.C., that attempt to influence policymakers on trade policies that benefit the companies or groups who are paying them. For example, some textile firms want tough trade policies to limit imports, so lobbyists hired by this group work to try to get policies passed to restrict imports. Other lobbying firms may represent retailers, the governments of other countries that want to ship more merchandise to the United States, or even some large apparel firms that import some or all of their products; these lobbyists try to influence policymakers toward freer trade.

Fashion in the News Media

Fashion is news, and the news media cover it, both in editorial treatments and in paid advertising messages. This statement applies not only to newspapers and magazines but also to broadcast media. Thus, a vital means of communication between the industry and the consumer, and between related parts of the industry, is activated in the daily newspapers, news magazines, women's and men's magazines, specialized fashion publications, those segments of the trade press that affect the fashion business, radio, and television. The impact is enormous.

Fashion Magazines

Fashion magazines, whose major activity is to report and interpret fashion news to the consumer, together with additional features for balanced reading fare, have been functioning in this country for more than a century. *Godey's Lady's Book,* which was started in 1830, carried pictures of the latest fashions, gave advice on fabrics, contained other helpful hints, and, of course, included advertising. Its distinguished editor, Sara Joseph Hale, gave early proof that a woman could have a successful career in the business world even in the days of hoop skirts and cinched waists. Its masculine counterpart, *Burton's Gentlemen's Magazine,* also had an editor whose name acquired luster: Edgar Allan Poe. His editorial career there was brief, however—from 1839 to 1840.

The present-day roster of fashion magazines is in the midst of an explosive change. The old tried and true magazines such as *Harper's Bazaar, Vogue, Glamour, Mademoiselle,* and *Seventeen* have suddenly been subjected to a barrage of competition from new and exciting magazines. The entrance of *Elle* as an important fashion book started an avalanche that now includes *Mirabella* (headed by Grace Mirabella, the long-time editor of *Vogue*), *Vanity Fair, Details, M, Inc., Savvy, Model, Taxi, La Style, In Fashion,* and others (Figure 11–6). How many will stand the test of time is hard to say, but the competition for fashion readership is keen, and the established older books are experimenting with new formats and features to try to keep their circulation and revenue figures up. In menswear, *GQ* (*Gentlemen's Quarterly*) and *Esquire* remain the major purveyors of fashion news.

Role of Fashion Magazines

The role of fashion magazines is a many-sided one. As fashion reporters, their editors shop the wholesale markets both here and abroad, to select and feature styles they consider newsworthy for their individual audiences. As fashion influentials, these editors sometimes take an active part in the production of merchandise by working closely with manufacturers to create merchandise that they consider acceptable to their readers. They participate in distribution by contacting retailers and urging them to carry and promote the designs they feature and to emphasize the trends endorsed editorially. Finally, they provide their readers with information not only about the styles they recommend, but also about who produces them and who sells them at retail.

Figure 11–6

Selected examples of fashion magazines.

An important tool of their activities, and of other consumer magazines that cover fashions to a lesser extent, is the **editorial credit.** This is how it operates: The editors select garments and accessories that, to their minds, exemplify fashion news. They photograph and show these styles in their pages, identifying the makers and naming one or more retail stores in which the consumer can buy them, and usually citing the approximate price. The magazine's sponsorship and the editorial mention encourage the makers to produce the garments in good supply, the retailers to stock them, and the customer to buy. Even in stores that do not have editorial credits for it, a fashion item featured in a strong magazine may be given special attention. If the magazine concerned has a good following among the store's customers, the editorial sponsorship becomes a selling point of the garment not only to consumers but also to the merchant. The style is then stocked, advertised, and displayed, and the magazine's name is usually featured in ads and displays. Hangtags on the garment and magazine blow-ups in the displays remind the customer that this is the style he or she saw in the publication. The magazine, of course, provides the tags and the blow-ups.

Dependence on Advertising Revenue

Like most publications, fashion magazines derive their principal revenue from the sale of advertising space. In 1996, a single black-and-white page in *Vogue, Mademoiselle,* or *Glamour* ranged in price from $37,180 to $58,320, and a four-color page began at $54,020 and went up to $82,190. In general magazines such as *Reader's Digest,* the rates were about $156,000 a page in black and white, and $182,000 for a four-color ad. *McCall's* was $87,560 for a black and white page and $103,305 for color (Standard Rate and Data Service, 1996). Naturally, a high ratio of advertising to editorial pages means a prosperous magazine. Although conditions vary from issue to issue and from year to year, advertising generally accounts for nearly half the total number of pages in a consumer fashion magazine.

Dependency on dollars from advertisers instead of dollars from subscribers is not always conducive to unbiased fashion reporting; it can result in a conflict between editorial comment and advertising interests. Editorial mentions of merchandise bring to producers highly desirable publicity and prestige, since the editorial pages tend to have more authority in the reader's eyes than do pages devoted to paid advertising. Thus, firms that buy space in a magazine and contribute toward keeping it profitable are likely to protest if they are not given adequate editorial attention. Such a clash of interests often makes objective fashion reporting difficult, if not impossible.

The money the advertiser spends for a page is, in simplest terms, spent to influence customers to buy its product. If a publication can show tangible evidence that it can move merchandise into the retail store and then out into the consumer's hands, its chances of selling advertising space improve.

Magazines confirm that to attract advertisers, nothing is more important to fashion magazines than their relation to stores. This fact accounts for the increasingly large staffs of departments almost unknown to their readers—promotion and merchandising. The merchandising editors act as the liaison between the fashion editors, the advertising staff, and the retail stores. Their job is to ensure that editorialized and advertised merchandise will be placed in retail stores where readers can buy it. They do this by telling the retailers what the magazine is featuring and why—and where to purchase it. Then they list for their readers' information the names of stores where the merchandise can be found. This service to the reader also helps impress the advertisers with the magazine's selling power among retailers.

Services to the Industry

The closer their relationship with both the producers and retailers, the easier it is for magazines to attract advertising. To cement these relationships, many free services are offered by fashion publications. Their staff members keep fabric and apparel producers informed on new trends and advise them on ways and means of selling merchandise. The fashion editors encourage them to manufacture items for which they anticipate a demand and, secure in the knowledge that the items will be featured by the editors, the producers will plunge ahead. The merchandising and promotion departments provide advertisers with "as advertised" blow-ups to distribute to their retail accounts. In addition, most magazines that are active in fashion prepare, well in advance of each season, fashion forecasts of their color predictions for the guidance of manufacturers and retailers alike. These forecasts show the colors, specific styles, and resources that will be featured in the magazine.

In developing a close relationship with retail stores, the fashion magazines make themselves a source of information for them. To make their editorialized and advertised merchandise desirable to retailers and, ultimately, to their customers, the merchandising departments prepare elaborate retail store kits that, along with the list of sources for featured garments, contain suggestions for advertising, fashion shows, and display. The kits also include selling aids such as hangtags, signs, and other promotional materials. If an important retailer requests the service, the magazine will send a representative to commentate a fashion show. Members of the magazine staff are also available in their offices at almost any time to show samples of merchandise to retailers who call, and thus encourage buyers to visit the producers of the featured apparel and accessories.

Most of the consumer magazines, including those primarily concerned with fashion, also maintain research departments. A function of these departments is to survey the readers of the magazine and compile information about their buying power, living patterns, and merchandise preferences. *Glamour,* for example, surveys young career women and college students periodically and compiles reports for retailers and manufacturers about what these women buy, how much they spend, and similar information. The fashion magazines, then, not only interpret the fashion for their readers but also interpret their readers for their industry. In the process, they serve as a clearinghouse for information in the fashion field.

Compared with consumer magazines of general interest, such as *Reader's Digest,* with a circulation of more than 16 million in 1995, or women's magazines such as *McCall's,* with a circulation of about 4.6 million, the fashion magazines have smaller circulations. *Glamour,* the largest, has a U.S. circulation of 2,081,212, another 206,618 in Italy, and 108,244 in France. *Seventeen* has 1,850,000, followed by *Vogue* with a readership of 1,219,958 in the United States and another 76,420 in Australia, and *Mademoiselle* has 1,219,159. *Esquire* has a U.S. circulation of 702,611 and another 90,514 in Great Britain. *GQ (Gentleman's Quarterly)* has a circulation of 711,476 (*Standard Periodical Directory,* 1995; *Ulrich's International Periodical Directory,* 1995).

The fashion magazines' influence in the fashion business, individually and collectively, is great and far out of proportion to their actual circulation. Fashion editors ignore styles and designers in whom they have little faith but give a great amount of free publicity to those they favor. Ordinarily, however, what they do is try to pick the most dramatic, the most exciting fashions—not always the most wearable, but the ones that will attract attention.

Newspapers and General Magazines

As mentioned earlier, almost all newspapers devote space to fashion. Coverage varies, of course, in both amount and depth. A paper with the resources of the *The New York*

Times may have its experts report on the Paris openings and express opinions that are read by consumers and trade professionals alike. A small-town paper, on the other hand, may assign its society editor to fill out the fashion pages with items about fashion, clipped from what the wire services send, what comes in by way of press releases, or what the local retailers supply. Each paper's policy and the interests of its readers determine how much space the publication devotes to fashion news.

Among magazines not in the fashion-magazine category there is also coverage of fashion, and it varies with the nature of the publication. Fashion editors of such media, looking at the fashion scene through the eyes of their average reader, will select for illustration and comment only the items of interest to the young mother, the working woman, the ageless city sophisticate, the sportsman, the young male executive, or whoever the particular audience may be.

Some of the general magazines show merchandise and give editorial credit; others, like the *New Yorker,* show no merchandise but sometimes discuss what the shops are showing. The activities of their fashion editors, as in the case of newspapers, vary according to the importance that each publication and its readers attach to fashion information.

Trade Publications

There is a special field of journalism known as business or **trade publishing.** Some business newspapers and magazines in the fashion field concern themselves with a particular classification of merchandise, from raw material to the sale of the finished product. These publications are not addressed to the ultimate consumer but to the fashion professionals concerned with the manufacturing and distribution of that merchandise. Typical examples are *Textile World,* and *Bobbin* magazine. Other business publications devote themselves to only one aspect of production or retailing and have a horizontal readership. Examples of these publications are *Stores* magazine, which goes to store management, and *Chain Store Age,* for chain store management. Fairchild's **Women's Wear Daily,** which is published five times a week, covers the fashion waterfront in the women's fashion business—raw materials, manufacturing, retailing, and how the trend setters among the consuming public dress. Founded in 1890 by E. W. Fairchild, it has headquarters in New York City and maintains offices in cities throughout the United States, Europe, and Asia. *Women's Wear Daily* reports collections, trade conventions, fashion events, new technical developments at all stages of production, personnel changes at the executive level, the formation of new fashion businesses—and the wardrobes and activities of prominent individuals. It is often called the industry's "bible" and no women's fashion enterprise is without its copy of *Women's Wear Daily.* The Fairchild counterpart for the textile and men's wear industry is the *Daily News Record,* now referred to as *DNR.*

Trade publications are not aimed at the general public and are inclined to discourage subscriptions from people not active in the fields they serve. They seldom appear on newsstands, except for the Fairchild dailies in the garment district. Their circulations are quite small compared with those of consumer magazines, and their advertising rates are correspondingly small, approximately $10,640 a page. *Women's Wear Daily,* with a circulation of 56,249 in 1995, is a giant in the field. *DNR* has a circulation of 23,000, with a black-and-white rate of $10,080 a page (Standard Rate and Data Service, 1995).

The capacity of trade papers for disseminating fashion information is out of all proportion to their size. Their readership, it should be kept in mind, is concentrated among people dealing in the merchandise they cover. They talk shop to such people. And, in terms of the amount of merchandise involved, when a manufacturer or merchant responds to information on fashion, that response moves a great deal of merchandise.

Trade paper editors are usually in their markets every day of the business year, and they cover every nook and cranny of their fields. They analyze fashion trends for their readers and show sketches or photos of actual merchandise, identified as to source and style number, to assist buyers and store owners in keeping abreast of the flow of new products. In addition, trade publications discuss business conditions and contain articles on how to manufacture, promote, or sell the industry's products. They analyze and report on the markets in other countries, cover conventions and other meetings of interest to the trade, report on legislative developments of interest, and write up merchandising and promotion operations of retail stores.

Market research is also part of a trade publication's work. These magazines and papers make estimates of the size of their markets, survey subscribers on buying responsibilities and attitudes toward current problems, publish directories of manufacturers, help retailers and manufacturers find sources of supply, and report on seminars and conventions appropriate to their fields.

It is important to keep in mind that trade publications are available in many other countries. Some have an international perspective, such as those published in London by ITDB Publishers (Figure 11–7).

Within their particular fields, trade paper editors and reporters are extremely well informed. Reading their articles is like listening to a group of experts indulging in shop talk.

Electronic Media

The impact of electronic media is tremendous, and the potential for new types and new uses in the fashion industry are almost without limits. Several forms are already familiar, and many others are in their infancy. All of these require a cadre of professionals who prepare and present merchandise through these media.

Television advertising is a powerful medium but expensive to use. Until recent years, one saw and heard little more of fashion advertising on the home screen than the institutional messages of fiber companies or the local promotions of retailers. In the late 1970s, a few retailers such as J. C. Penney began to use network TV advertising to tell their fashion stories. Today, however, both retailers and manufacturers are harnessing the power of network TV. New brands of jeans, notably Jordache and Calvin Klein, became familiar names through saturated use of this medium. Mass merchandisers including Wal-Mart, Kmart, and J. C. Penney use television advertising extensively. Sears' TV campaign to promote the "Softer Side of Sears" assisted in this major retailer's dramatic turnaround from rapid decline to success. Many producers use TV advertising; among them are Hanes, Fruit of the Loom, Russell, Levi, and Lee. Cotton Incorporated has advertised extensively to extoll cotton's comfort and utility.

Since MTV and its superstars such as Madonna and Michael Jackson have demonstrated how quickly they can create demand for new fashions, fashion firms are aware of the impact the home screen can have on their customers. Particularly for young audiences, shows with models going down the runway are now old hat compared with the new fashion presentations, in which entertainment is the key word and the emphasis is on imagination and excitement, not merely the particular outfits.

As noted in the previous chapter, home television shopping gained a great deal of attention in the 1990s. A number of well-known designers and retailers have at least tried selling on the leading shopping channels, Home Shopping Network and QVC. An entirely new cadre of fashion professionals has emerged as a result of the

| Figure 11–7 | Trade publications with an international perspective, some multilingual, published by ITBD Publications in London. |

Source: Reprinted courtesy of ITBD Publications.

growing popularity of home television shopping. These include not only the television personalities who present the merchandise on the air, but also many representatives of firms whose products are being shown in a TV segment. Those individuals play important coordinating roles in having the appropriate merchandise on hand and in perfect condition to present on the air. This requires close communication with the manufacturers or retailers whose products are being presented. If a firm's products are shown regularly, a full-time representative of that firm may work at the net-

Figure 11–8

Industry professionals fill numerous roles at home shopping television networks and within the companies whose products are shown on the programming segments.

Source: Courtesy of QVC.

work's facilities (Figure 11–8). Numerous other specialists are required to handle the technical details of producing the program segments and assuring that home viewers can see closeup details of garments, jewelry, or other merchandise.

Fashion videos have been useful in a number of ways. Designers, among them Donna Karan, Ralph Lauren, Ann Klein, and Nicole Miller, have used videotape to capture the excitement and sales appeal of their fashion shows for their retail customers, who present the videos on their selling floors with the actual merchandise. Videotapes are used to support sales in larger stores as salespeople and consumers see the collection from the designer's point of view.

Videos have been used for in-store merchandising in another way by companies such as J. C. Penney. Videotapes were sent from company headquarters to individual stores where local department managers made merchandise selections for their stores. A shortcoming of this system, however, was that store personnel found it necessary to view a total videotape, even if they needed to order only select items. CD-ROM technology has replaced videotapes for this purpose, because the local department manager can view only those product lines for which there is a need in the local store.

Electronic **kiosks** have been used in a variety of ways in retail stores. Some of these simply run videotapes so the customer may view new products or to learn how to use certain items, such as creative ways to use scarfs. Other kiosks are interactive so customers can learn about merchandise or order specific sizes and styles. Lee Company has used interactive kiosks to help customers learn how to determine proper size and fit for jeans purchases. Some major bra manufacturers have also used this means to assist customers. Like other forms of electronic media, specialized professionals develop these units and adapt the technology to specific fashion products.

Many new auxiliary fashion enterprises will continue to develop around the burgeoning computer technologies of the 1990s. These include forms discussed in the previous chapters: on-line computer shopping, CD-ROM[2] catalogs, and so on. These are being applied at various stages in the softgoods pipeline: manufacturers are showing fashion lines to retailers through these formats, and, similarly, retailers are showing lines to consumers.

Video conferencing is being used more and more in the industry. Saving the time and costs associated with travel, buyers now have the option to watch new lines presented at the CaliforniaMart without having to go there. Through video conferencing, executives at Levi Strauss & Co.'s San Francisco headquarters can visit with plant managers at Levi plants across the country, or Levi executives at remote locations may be interactive participants in key company meetings held at the headquarters.

Even the fax machine is used as a selling or solicitation device. Attendees who go to major trade shows[3] may receive faxes from U.S. firms or those in a host of other countries who are seeking business partners. Sometimes headhunter firms seek candidates for executive positions through fax solicitations.

Electronic media of various forms will play an increasingly important role in the fashion industry in the next millennium. These developments will not only change the way we do business but will also offer many new employment options for individuals seeking careers in the industry.

Advertising and Publicity Agencies

There are two ways in which producers and retailers use space in print media or time in broadcast media to get their message across to the trade or to the public. One way is paid **advertising**. The other is **publicity**—time or space given without charge by the medium because it considers the message newsworthy.

Advertising Agencies

An **advertising agency** is a service agency whose original function was simply to prepare and place ads in magazines or newspapers for its clients. Today its job encompasses much more: research of the client's consumer markets, advice on promotional needs, planning of promotional campaigns, preparation of print and broadcast advertising, preparation of selling manuals, and creation of selling aids, labels, signs, and packaging—anything that helps increase the sale of the client's product and makes the advertising itself more effective.

An advertising agency may consist of one talented, hard-working executive with a few small clients, or it may be an organization with a staff of hundreds and clients with hundreds of millions of dollars to spend each year. Approximately 65 percent of agencies' revenue is derived primarily from commissions. These are paid, not by the client, but by the media from which the agencies purchase advertising space or time. Custom has fixed the rate at 15 percent. The balance of their income is received directly from clients, generally in the form of fees for special services such as market research, and as part of the cost for producing a product for the client—for example, photography, typography, art, and layout.

When an advertising agency bids for a client's account, it studies the firm's operation thoughtfully and draws up a presentation that outlines the campaign the agency sug-

---

[2] The CD-ROM catalogs may be replaced by the newer DVD (digital versatile disk) catalogs, used on DVD-ROM computers.
[3] Companies may buy a registration list or secure individuals' names as attendees register with exhibitors.

gests and the varied services that the agency performs. When awarded the account, the agency may delve into package design, market research, and creation of selling aids and sales training material—plus its original function of preparing and placing advertising in publications, in broadcast media, and, in some cases, in transit and outdoor media.

In the fashion industries, it is usually only the largest producers of nationally or internationally distributed merchandise that make use of advertising agencies. These include some makers of finished apparel, accessories, and fragrances, plus the giant fiber and fabric sources. In recent years, however, fashion companies have made bolder use of ads on billboards and buses, as well as other media. Retailers whose audience is local or regional usually maintain their own complete advertising departments that handle their day-to-day newspaper advertisements.

Fashion Expertise

Some agencies, often among the smallest in the field, specialize in fashion accounts. In such agencies, and in those of the larger ones that serve fashion accounts, it is important to have personnel who are expert in the language and background of the fashion business: account executives who work with clients and coordinate what is done, art directors who visualize the fashion advertising, copywriters who are familiar with fashion appeals, and stylists or fashion coordinators who are responsible for the fashion slant of the ads.

The work of the fashion expert in an agency is not necessarily limited to fashion accounts. If a man's or woman's figure appears in an ad for automobiles, cigarettes, or soap, it is most likely that a fashion adviser has checked the model's outfit to make sure it is in tune with the current fashion picture as well as with the occasion and level of society being represented. Agency people also realize that fashion is a quick way to identify with whatever group of customers the advertiser seeks to reach: young, dashing, mature, conservative, or whatever. This is especially noticeable in television advertising, where the advertiser has only a few seconds in which to establish rapport with the particular viewers it wishes to influence. Compare the clothing of the characters in an investment firm's commercials, for example, with those of the characters in commercials for soft drinks. The one seeks to project a conservative image; the other a carefree, young, with-it attitude.

Thus, the advertising agency, whether or not it has a fashion account on its roster of clients, becomes involved, directly or indirectly, in the business of fashion.

Publicity and Public Relations Firms

Publicity, unlike advertising, cannot be controlled in relation to where, when, and how a particular message will appear—if, indeed, it appears at all. The publicity practitioner's control over the fate of the story he or she wishes to place with a medium rests primarily in the ability to convince the particular editor that the material is truly news of interest to that medium's audience.

Publicity's purpose, like that of advertising, is to enhance the client's sales appeal to potential customers. The space or time supplied by the media, in this case, is free, but the public relations firm's services are not. Working on a fee basis, with provision for expenses, the publicity agency develops news stories around the client's product or activities and makes these stories available to editors and broadcasters.

The key word in effective publicity is *news*. The publicity expert's first job is to find or "create" news value in a product, activity, or personality to be publicized. Next, he or she considers the media that might conceivably find this news of interest to their readers and writes the story (called a press release) in a form appropriate to the media that constitute the target. If they are likely to use illustrations, a suitable photograph may be included.

Typically, publicity activities include getting editorial mentions in consumer and trade publications, "plugs" on television and radio, school and college tie-ins, running fashion shows or other events (often with admission charges that go to a charity organization), feature articles in newspapers and magazines, and anything else that makes the products or the client's name better known and more readily accepted by the consumer—or by an industry, if that industry is the client's customer.

The publicity firm does more than merely use its contacts to place material for its client. It also prepares press releases, distributes photographs, writes radio and TV scripts, sometimes works out an elaborate fashion show, and hires and coaches professional actors to sing, dance, and model for the audience. If a medium, whether print or broadcast, is working on a special feature touching the client's field, the public relations people swing into action to provide the writer of the feature with facts, photos, and other help. Many fashion editors in smaller towns depend on press releases and photographs for the content of their fashion pages.

A broader term than publicity is **public relations.** A public relations firm does not limit its efforts to getting the client or the product mentioned in the media through press releases and similar efforts. It may supply expert advice on how to improve the client's public image and may develop some potent but less obvious ways of getting publicity for the client: suggesting him or her as a speaker at conventions of appropriate groups, or having the client give scholarships and establish awards and foundations, for instance.

There are many independent publicists and public relations agencies that specialize in fashion publicity. As in the case of advertising agencies, their clients are generally fiber, fabric, or apparel producers instead of retailers, since retailers usually maintain their own internal publicity staffs. Insofar as the fashion business is concerned, the public relations and publicity fraternity performs the very useful function of feeding information about the industry to the news media and thus stimulates business by keeping fashion in the limelight.

Mall/Property Management Specialists

Behind the scenes of large shopping malls and other properties where fashions are sold are teams of individuals who manage and promote a group (or groups) of stores. These **mall/property management specialists** are responsible for the operation of the mall or other property, assuring that facilities are clean, attractive, and safe for shoppers. Most property management groups have a marketing staff responsible for efforts to attract shoppers to a mall or other facility. The marketing staff plays an important role in creating a lively atmosphere, filled with activities that encourage shoppers to think of that mall as a destination for a pleasant shopping experience. A staff, headed by a director of marketing, is responsible for staging special events to draw customers and doing whatever it takes to create a positive image in the community for that mall. These may range from sponsoring a visit from Santa Claus or the Easter bunny, to organizing a teen board, to coordinating theme weeks for the mall or fashion shows, to hot air balloon liftoffs to promote a special sale. The mall staff also has a vital role in helping property tenants feel a part of the "mall family" through newsletters and various events. The mall marketing staff often develops advertisements to represent the mall as a total entity; these ads may be for the print media, television, or radio (Figure 11–9).

Property management offices play a critical role in having attractive sites for the retailing of fashion goods. Individuals in these offices keep the mall industry functioning effectively, which makes them important players in the fashion industry. In an era when consumers are less likely to think of shopping as a pleasant experience, mall

Source: Courtesy of St. Louis Galleria.

staffs have a particularly challenging role. Moreover, property management represents yet another group of career options. Numerous management positions are involved. Among them, marketing departments in these offices may offer potential for individuals who are creative, versatile, and resourceful and have a high energy level.

Trade Show Enterprises

A number of businesses exist for the purpose of organizing trade shows for various segments of the industry. Some of these are companies that exist solely for this purpose. Others, such as Bobbin-Blenheim, sponsor trade shows such as the annual Bobbin Show for the apparel industry and also have other business activities, including publishing *Bobbin* magazine. Some trade shows are organized for the fashion segments of the industry, which retail buyers attend to secure lines for their stores (Figure 11–10). Others may be textile shows. Some are for retailers for purposes other than buying fashion merchandise (e.g., exhibitors may show computer systems, security systems, and other products or services related to store operations), textile manufacturing equipment, trims, and so on. Large trade shows require masterful coordination and need the competencies of individuals who specialize in this type of work. The activities of these trade show enterprises are important in providing a venue where different segments of the industry come together to transact business important to keeping the industry functioning.

Trade Associations

Trade associations also play important roles in the fashion industry. Each trade association represents businesses and business executives with interests in common. These associations are composed of members who pay dues to support the operation of the group and to carry out the common goals of the members. Each organization is set up

A number of trade show enterprises exist to organize trade shows for all segments of the industry. These may range from shows that feature apparel lines, such as the one in this figure, to those that are for textile machinery exhibitors.

Source: Courtesy of The Larkin Group.

as a medium for such purposes as disseminating trade and technical information, doing research into markets or methods of operation, analyzing relevant legislation, doing public relations work for the industry or trade, and lobbying on legislation or other political matters. Some of the largest trade associations associated with the fashion industry are the National Retail Federation (NRF), the American Apparel Manufacturers Association (AAMA), and the American Textile Manufacturers Institute (ATMI). As many as 200 U.S. trade associations are related to the fashion industry. Some are large with fairly heterogeneous memberships such as the three large ones named. However, some are quite small or may represent narrowly specialized groups such as hosiery manufacturers, yarnspinners, importers and/or exporters, intimate apparel producers, the leather industries, millinery firms, sportswear, children's wear producers, uniform manufacturers and distributors, or cotton growers. There are also associations for advertising and publicity specialists, fashion writers, individuals in shopping center management, and fashion designers, among many others.

The Fashion Group International

The Fashion Group International is a professional association of women who represent every phase of fashion manufacturing, retailing, merchandising, advertising, publishing, and education. Organized in 1931, its purpose was, and is, to serve as a national and international clearinghouse for the exchange of information about what is going on in the business of fashion.

Headquartered in New York, it has 34 regional chapters in major cities throughout the United States and in other countries. Its membership exceeds 6,000. The Fashion Group International describes itself as a "global non-profit organization" whose mission is:

- To advance professionalism in fashion and its related life-style industries, with a particular emphasis on the role and development of women;
- To provide a public forum for examination of important contemporary issues in fashion and the business of fashion;
- To present timely information regarding national and global trends that have an effect on the fashion industries;
- To attain greater recognition of women's achievements in business;
- To encourage women to seek career opportunities in fashion and related industries; and
- To provide activities and programs that enhance networking skills and encourage interpersonal contacts so as to further the professional, social and personal development of members (Fashion Group International, 1995).

Although many may question the female-only membership, perhaps the intent of this stipulation has been to provide networking opportunities that have long been available to men through many other organizations.

Other Fashion Enterprises

There are enterprises of many other types that play important behind-the-scenes roles in the business of fashion. Their activities, however, are too varied and too highly specialized to be described in detail. For example, display consultants design and construct fashion display materials for manufacturers, retailers, and fashion magazines. Consultants in the fields of sales promotion and marketing are also retained on a fee basis by manufacturers and retailers. Market research agencies do consumer surveys for retail stores, publications, and manufacturers, or retail surveys for producers. Among the research agencies that do work for the fashion field are Audits and Surveys, which has made some interesting studies of the buying patterns of retail store customers, and Yankelovich, Skelly and White, which is noted for its demographic and psychographic research.

In short, there is a whole arsenal of auxiliary services that contributes to making the fashion business what it is today and that will undoubtedly contribute to its growth in the future.

Readings

Because the auxiliary fashion enterprises exist to serve the industry, it means that as the manufacturing and retailing industries have restructured, this segment of the industry has changed also. These readings give an inside view of some of these businesses that work behind the scenes to serve the fashion industry.

Doneger: Tailored to Fit the Times

by Susan Reda

By now the tale is familiar. Dogged by anemic sales, continued consolidation, Chapter 11 filings and obstinate consumer malaise, apparel retailers are searching for solutions and pursuing every opportunity for growth.

Not so familiar, however, is the role that some buying offices are performing as they attempt to help mitigate retail acts that in the past were fresher in terms of bottom-line results. Much like accounting firms, which no longer simply keep the books and have in fact become broad-based business consultancies, buying offices are attempting to play bigger parts in their customers' businesses.

"The term 'buying office' is limited in scope," stresses Abbey Doneger, president of The Doneger Group, a New York-based resident buying group. "Our services extend far beyond what a buying office traditionally provides. We delve into all areas of merchandising and marketing. Our objective is to help retailers generate increased sales and profits, gain market share and realize their full potential."

With an extensive client list that runs the gamut from high-end department and specialty stores to middle-market mass merchants and one-price budget formats, The Doneger Group operates from a unique perspective. Management is able to assess opportunities and obstacles from both a broad industry-wide outlook and a narrow vertical view.

"We use them [The Doneger Group] in certain areas a lot. Before we go out into the market, we go to Doneger first for trend information and vendor direction," says Mark Minsky, senior vp. gmm [general merchandise manager], Caldor.

"When we started a dress business a few years back, we were able to soak up a lot of information from them. For this fall, they helped us by recommending resources and honing in on key items from ladies' leather outerwear, a new category for us," Minsky adds.

With pricing more important than ever in today's market, it is not surprising that Price Point Buying, Doneger's off-price service, has taken on a more critical role at the company.

This division, formed in 1988 and now headed by merchandise manager Marvin Goldstein, specializes in opportunistic buying of overruns and merchandise made available because of canceled orders.

The scope of Price Point Buying has been amplified recently as mass merchants test new programs, plug up holes in their assortments and work to keep the selling floor stocked, despite the squeeze of skittish factors that have become somewhat overprotective of their accounts receivable.

"Large-scale retailers typically do not have the flexibility to react to the opportunities of off-price purchasing because the size of their businesses dictate that product development and orders be set well in advance," explains Thomas Burns, senior executive vp and gmm of The Doneger Group.

"The current retail environment has, however, opened some new doors for us. With retailers planning inventory much closer to the vest than in previous seasons, they sometimes find themselves on the short end of supply," says Burns. "We have the capacity to go into the market, find what they're looking for at the price they want to pay and deliver it to them in an efficient time frame."

Among the items Goldstein and his staff of eight have been chasing for fall are denim jumpers and vests. Typically, Goldstein relies on both his buyers and those in the women's sportswear area of Doneger to piece together a working list of vendors who have product available at the right price.

"For retailers, the name of the game is right product, right price and right time. They have to have something when it's hot—particularly since key items have been few and far between," says Goldstein. "For us, it's a question of synergy—of working with the other divisions under the Doneger umbrella of services to respond to a retailer's needs."

In the wake of several Chapter 11 filings at a number of retail chains across the country, Doneger's Price Point Buying team has been called upon to help fill in some gaps on the selling floor. According to Burns, once a factor puts up a red light, merchants have to seek out new resources that are willing to be supportive. Merchants, overwhelmed by the task of finding manufacturers that meet their quality, value and price parameters, rely on Doneger's expertise. Rose's, which successfully emerged from bankruptcy protection in May, was one of the companies that utilized Doneger's sourcing skills when it needed help stocking its shelves.

Selling is of course a two-way street. A red light at one chain translates into manufacturers being left with fast-depreciating inventories. Vendors call on the Price Point Buying division to rid themselves of the merchandise quickly and cut their losses.

"Price Point Buying is essentially a push and pull business," says Burns. "The push comes from the market side as manufacturers look to sell off in-season product, which tends to lose value every day. The pull comes from retailers who have specific needs and are looking to secure product."

When recent changes in quotas and issues surrounding labor resulted in the canceled parts of retailers' product development programs, merchants looking for immediate sourcing—Montgomery Ward and Pamida, for instance—tapped Doneger's services.

Price Point Buying is also used by retailers attempting to better serve particular demographic and/or ethnic customer bases via micromarketing. According to Burns, the company has worked with a number of regional discounters who believe this is a critical component of differentiation.

"Different items surface in different parts of the country, and it's very difficult for a buyer who is making broad purchasing decisions for 200 or more stores to hone in on small pockets of opportunity. Still they [retailers] recognize the importance of developing these unique portions of their businesses," says Burns, who expects retailers to pursue micromarketing more aggressively as time goes on. "We can call upon the network of resources and information we have here to help them succeed."

According to Goldstein, the fuel that drives the engine when it comes to Price Point Buying and other services provided by The Doneger Group is communication.

"The more buyers share with us about what they're trying to accomplish, who their customers are and what their specific business objectives are, the more we can focus our expertise on helping them to attain their goals."

In one form or another, that tenet has run throughout The Doneger Group since the company was founded in 1946 by Abbey's father, Henry. Today, the company consists of 10 specialized divisions serving 850 retail clients.

On a simplified level, the diversity of Doneger services includes three tiers: long-term fashion direction and product development, seasonal market analysis and presentations and the chance to fill-in via incentive buying in-season.

To actualize these objectives, the company's services include the Doneger Information Network, which provides newsletters, merchandising concepts, market overviews and new resource information to clients. Retailers working with The Doneger Group can also tap into the buying group's direct mail prowess and into the worldwide sourcing opportunities and administrative support provided by HDA International, the company's import/export division, which serves both domestic and international retailers.

Doneger is especially proud of the D3 Doneger Design Direction division, which specializes in color trend forecasting. Like every service at Doneger, D3 is used by clients dealing at all price point levels.

"D3 is the fashion service for realists who regard fashion as a business instead of an art form," says Doneger. "Our merchandising experts travel the globe gathering information and soaking up emerging trends. Then they package their findings in the 'D3 Box.' Complete with color charts, yarn and fabric swatches, and fashion sketches, the D3 Box becomes their tool caddie."

While much of what The Doneger Group does revolves around assessing trends and recommending and buying product, retailers sometimes look to the company for advice or to act as a sounding board, according to Doneger.

Recently, Doneger executives spent time with discount stores such as Hills and ShopKo to give them some direction on how to develop a career business.

"These retailers are casual-driven, but they're beginning to realize that they have an opportunity in unconstructed careerwear because of the sheer volume of women shopping in their stores and the fact that 75 percent of them are in the work force," says Burns.

With one discounter, Burns recommended that the long skirts and knit tops, which the retailer already had on the selling floor, be pulled together to create "outfit dressing" in a cohesive setting.

"Discounters are starting to realize that they don't have to relinquish the career business to other retailers. By having a few key items on hand that shoppers can buy for work, retailers will reduce the amount of cross-shopping and keep shoppers in the store for a longer period of time," explains Burns.

Perhaps one reason why The Doneger Group understands its retail clients so well is that it shares some formidable challenges. The first is dealing with a shrinking marketplace. The second is adapting to the changes that have become so much a part of daily retailing.

"We're constantly adapting to this changing marketplace and to new ways of doing business," says Doneger. "Since 1946, we've been reinventing our services to be more in sync with the needs of our retail clients, and we continue to do that today."

Looking ahead, Doneger feels that technology, with its ability to gather information with speed and accuracy, will play an increasing role in the buying group's services. The bottom line is that Abbey Doneger, an aggressive, energetic executive, and his team want to stay on the cutting edge.

Source: From Apparel Merchandising, *October 16, 1995, pp. A12, A14. Reprinted by permission.*

All About AMC

by AMC (Associated Merchandising Corporation) Staff

AMC is a not-for-profit corporation, owned by its shareholders, who are leading department stores and specialty operations around the globe. These shareholders are also AMC's principal clients. In addition, AMC's client roster includes major mass merchandisers, promotional department stores and manufacturers.

With the world at our fingertips, we provide our clients with the most comprehensive global market coverage available with a worldwide network of quality control. Our focus is on the future, as we seek to predict what's ahead in merchandise trends and fashion direction, in our development of exclusive products, in merchandising and marketing concepts, or in new and emerging markets.

The following briefly describes various aspects of the AMC, reflecting many years of worldwide leadership in merchandising and retail marketing.

Global Sourcing and Production
Sourcing

If the international aspect of AMC is its strength, then merchandise is its lifeblood. A global philosophy embodies our commitment to check the pulse of the world's markets constantly. Sourcing, investigating, evaluating and reporting our findings to our clients provides them with a competitive edge in their merchandise selection. This work is coordinated worldwide by a team of product specialists who implement:

- Advance Product Research—Ongoing research is done on all aspects of product: from testing new materials to assessing the capability of individual factories.
- Global Product Evaluation—Due to a strong network of worldwide offices, AMC is able to utilize

a global approach to product evaluation. This enables AMC to place each item in the country and factory best suited to its manufacture.

- Remote/Supplemental Market Purchasing—In cases where traditional key markets become overutilized, AMC works in remote and/or supplemental locations. AMC coordinates the transfer of piecegoods and trim as well as all aspects of production and quality control.

Production

With regard to production, AMC is constantly looking for ways to improve our quality control [QC] by:

- Taking the position that we will only place orders in countries where we have QC coverage.
- Adding Production Engineers who check and ensure that top quality is being built into our products at the factory level.
- Hiring Fabric Technologists to coordinate all aspects of fabric quality, pricing, research, and development.
- Approaching product development with a corporate focus on quality at all stages.
- Integrating state of the art Production Tracking Systems, which follow each item from preproduction to final inspection.

From the communication of a fashion concept through the design, manufacture and delivery of top quality products, the Sourcing and Production staff works to keep our clients at the forefront of the retail industry.

The Bureau of Standards/ Quality Assurance

The Bureau of Standards (BOS) plays a pivotal role in AMC's commitment to uncompromising quality and performance for all merchandise, wherever it is produced. With headquarters in New York and major regional offices in Italy, Hong Kong, Singapore, Korea, and Taiwan, the BOS maintains an international staff of technical experts, in both hard and softlines, whose functions range from textile analysis to the development of size specifications. Further, its laboratory and unique testing procedures set the pace for the retail industry in the area of quality control. The BOS Department at AMC New York has implemented Lectra Systems computer-aided design for patternmaking and grading.

Quality assurance is the paramount objective of the Bureau of Standards. Beyond testing, staff members provide technical training for all offices, supporting a cadre of local AMC inspectors who conduct on-site factory inspections overseas.

The staff is also involved in virtually every stage of the product development process. Their practiced eye assures that special sizes are accurately scaled, and that a style or look can be translated overseas or in the United States to meet specifications of size, fabric, workmanship, and, where applicable, safety. Theirs is the final word that ensures compliance with government regulations and safety requirements (flammability, care labeling, food and drug regulations, etc.) for all merchandise, including AMC stores' own direct imports.

Product Development

AMC's Product Development Organization is structured to provide balanced, cost-efficient, focused, client-driven service to shareholder stores. Our objective is to develop superior quality/value merchandise in response to shareholder needs and merchandising strategies. In achieving this objective, we are dedicated to:

- Focusing on product classifications in which private label fills assortment voids identified in shareholders' merchandising strategies.
- Partnering with shareholders in concept development and product execution across division lines to help ensure competitive differentiation as well as consistency of shareholders' private label style, quality and value message.
- Understanding client objectives through regular store visits.
- Balancing clients' needs for purchasing efficiency against the widespread desire for more individualized service.
- Providing the vital trend and color research necessary for the effective evolution of shareholders' private label assortments.
- Utilizing technology, wherever possible, to achieve maximum time and cost efficiency.

There are numerous specialists within the arena of Product Development. All work together to create the desired end product.

Product Managers (PMs) develop merchandise for group programs tailored to the needs of AMC clients and their customers. Focusing their energies on overseas markets, PMs work with their colleagues in the AMC stores to plan objectives for seasonal import programs. They travel to appropriate overseas markets, assessing and selecting vendors who manufacture quality merchandise. The PMs know the technical aspects of their commodities and they are highly skilled at negotiating the best prices for the stores they represent.

Account Executives (AEs) function in the same manner as Product Managers, except they develop merchandise for a specific store(s).

Overseas Merchandising Services

The Overseas Merchandising Services (OMS) division is the newest of the AMC merchandising areas, formed in 1983 to handle the unique foreign market needs of mass merchandisers, promotional department stores and specialty operations.

Because the AMC is committed to protecting the confidentiality of both our department store and OMS shareholders, a separate OMS staff is maintained. By understanding this need and observing discretion in all client matters, AMC has won the respect and confidence of its members.

The OMS Product Managers (PMs) develop product for the OMS stores. They serve as the liaison between AMC's worldwide offices and the individual OMS store. They also spend a substantial percentage of their time in the stores analyzing assortments, price line emphasis and stock balance, and offering merchandise and strategy recommendations to their retail counterparts. Because of the volume requirements of our OMS clients, the OMS Product Managers work with each store on an individualized basis, rather than as a total group.

Creative Services

The *Creative Services* of AMC work in conjunction with the merchandising areas to forecast emerging fashion and color trends, to develop exclusive product (from concept through final samples), and to create exclusive prints and patterns, as well as private label packaging and hangtags.

The Fashion Office provides color and trend direction for all apparel-related areas. In-house design staff creates exclusive product, print or patterns based on current or future fashion and color trends.

The *Computer Aided Design (CAD)* department creates original prints and patterns and recolors existing prints. Prints and patterns can be applied to silhouettes to assist the focus group in determining colorways, color rolls, pricing and deliveries.

The Home Furnishings Design Studio provides emerging fashion and color direction for the Home Furnishings merchants. An in-house design staff creates original artwork that will be applied to a wide array of products, from Tabletop/Housewares to seasonal opportunities, such as Christmas Trim.

Graphic Services sets the standards for all printed materials throughout AMC worldwide and works in conjunction with the merchants to develop point-of-sale materials, such as hangtags, private label packaging and marketing ideas, when appropriate.

International Operations

As the largest and most comprehensive overseas sourcing and product development organization of its kind, AMC's International Operations boasts a staff of over 600 professionals. Known throughout the world for its integrity and high standards, it ranks #1 in the marketplace. The staff's experience and reputation represent an invaluable "plus" to shareholder stores. As part of the AMC, they receive priority consideration in the mills and factories of the world.

There are other advantages as well. Because AMC owns its overseas operation, it is able to control costs carefully and still maintain a high level of professionalism. AMC is unique in its position as a global sourcing company; it is the only organization which maintains its own offices throughout the world.

Overseas Services

Altogether, AMC is represented in over 30 locations outside the United States, with well-established retail merchandising offices in most of these markets. Overseas offices may be headed by a Regional Division Vice President or a Managing Director, with a core of seasoned merchants to provide the most comprehensive market coverage possible.

In addition, each office is supported by experienced Quality Control personnel (more than 200 throughout the world) and an administrative team that is responsible for all aspects of overseas business, including transportation, customs, freight, and consolidation. Our international communication network utilizes advanced technology to speed information and merchandise from individual regions to the stores.

Overseas Merchandise Representatives (OMRs) in local overseas offices make major contributions to product management, in the selection and development of merchandise. Their great strength comes from their market knowledge, their understanding of the competition and their ability to detect new emerging markets.

Frequently, OMRs work one-on-one with individual store merchants who travel the world markets in search of unique product assortments and look to AMC's overseas staff for guidance and direction.

North and South American Operations/U.S. Office

The North and South American Operations/U.S. Office handles the merchandising, order placement and delivery/quality control for orders placed through either Landed Duty Paid (LDP) or Domestic Product Development (DPD) programs by the Shareholder Stores. Also, all export orders placed by our Overseas Shareholder Stores are handled through this office.

Merchandise Representatives (MRs) shop the U.S. and Canadian markets for the Overseas Shareholder Store Buyers, reporting on trends and resources specifically geared for exporting to Europe, South America, Australia and Asia. The MR works directly with the Store Buyers and Merchandise Managers, accompanying them to market appointments, facilitating order placement and confirming the details of the purchase order with local manufacturers.

A production team, made up of a manager and production coordinators, is responsible for production tracking and follow-up of all orders placed for AMC private label programs and for export to the Overseas Shareholder Stores. It also serves as liaison between the New York staff and AMC's South American commissionaires.

A Production Engineer supplies technical guidance to the New York office, coordinates all domestic inspections and regularly audits shipments arriving from overseas to assure that quality standards have been met.

Washington, D.C. Trade Office

The AMC Trade Office provides major support of overseas activities, by disseminating critical information on all facets of international trade that may affect AMC's import programs. The AMC trade rep-

resentative is actively involved in educating government officials and legislators about sourcing needs and in providing background for trade negotiations, often serving in an advisory capacity.

AMC Washington also supplies all offices with regular reports on apparel quota, including details of quota negotiations, changes in visa or tariff requirements, yearly quota levels, warnings or countervailing duties. By acting as an early warning system and by providing an ongoing education program for AMC and its member stores on matters affecting imports and overseas markets, the Washington office constitutes a vital link in the AMC network.

Merchandise Support Operations

Management Information Systems (MIS)

Capitalizing on new technology, MIS reflects AMC's effort to facilitate the swift flow of information between stores and the AMC worldwide. As a global effort, it includes the automation of Order-Status Reports from all foreign offices, and the development of a production tracking system that will permit stores to follow orders throughout the manufacturing and delivery process.

The automation of order placement speeds the information process. Currently, most data exchange between AMC stores and staff is handled on an electronic basis.

Import Transportation Services

This division has the overall responsibility for developing and maintaining the most economical and efficient methods of transporting store imports. It plays a key role in international operations by determining principal freight forwarders and transportation routes. This includes consolidating shipments to save on transportation costs and brokerage fees, expediting shipments through U.S. Customs, auditing all import billing, and handling store claims against foreign vendors and carriers.

In addition, Import Transportation administers a Guaranteed Landed Cost (GLC) program from all areas of the world, which allows shareholders to know the landed cost of merchandise purchased at the time they place their orders. This, together with an enhanced EDI capability, provides member stores with worldwide UPC bar-coded, retail priced preticketing, thereby speeding the flow of merchandise to the selling floor.

AMC maintains a number of U.S.-based stock programs. These warehouse programs have been particularly valuable for products which vendors will ship in full container load quantities only. Through AMC's maintenance of these inventories, stores have reduced their carrying costs for large inventories, have accessed "quick response" order processing, and have reduced their out-of-stock position.

As with our overseas purchasing, AMC's volume and size are a distinct advantage in securing the best possible transportation terms. Our position in the industry translates into significant savings for our clients.

Financial Services

With headquarters in New York and major financial centers in Hong Kong and Florence, the financial group is concerned with accounting and financial reporting, financial analysis, expense payment, budget administration, expense control, and merchandise payments worldwide. This latter function requires a vast knowledge of international monetary matters, involving the management of Letters of Credit and the transfer of funds between AMC member stores, AMC New York and vendors worldwide.

Since AMC does not operate for profit, through the efficiencies of our financial services and conservative budget planning, many millions of dollars have been returned to AMC shareholder stores over the years.

Human Resources

Like every division of the AMC, Human Resources seeks to support the business by helping managers address and resolve significant business issues.

Toward this end, it contributes a wide range of personnel activities including recruiting, employment, performance management, career development, training, and benefits administration, for both the United States and the overseas offices.

Human Resources assists managers and employees with performance issues, career counseling, benefits and policy and procedure questions. Additionally, it provides a wide range of technical training, with a special focus on systems technology such as the Merchandise Processing System, Production Tracking, Inquiry Reports, and E-Mail. The importance of all Human Resources efforts is reinforced by senior management, which encourages the use of new knowledge and skills on the job.

Source: From All About AMC *(pp. 1–15) by Associated Merchandising Corporation, 1995, New York: Author. Reprinted by permission.*

Stepping Out

by Rosemary Feitelberg

Apparel, fragrance and cosmetic companies are storming the streets with ads on buses, billboards and telephone kiosks.

"Fashion as a category has never been more bold. The format is, 'Hey guys, here it is—look at this,'" said Chris Carr, vice president of the Gannett

Outdoor Group. "How else can companies make a seasonal statement overnight and get the message out to everybody?"

For 1995, Gannett expects outdoor advertising sales for fashion, fragrance and cosmetic companies to grow 20 percent over last year, according to Carr.

At TDI, meanwhile, second-half bookings for outdoor advertising for fashion are running 10 percent ahead of last year's $14 million business. And additional growth is expected, according to Jodi Yegelwel, senior vice president of TDI, the largest diversified out-of-home media company in the U.S.

"There was a time when out-of-home advertising was made for tobacco and liquor companies," she said. "Now the fashion industry is putting excellent, creative magazine-type advertising on the streets. The perception of the medium is turning around."

Men's and women's products each account for 30 percent of the category, and generic campaigns such as those for CK One, Banana Republic and Champion comprise the remaining 40 percent, she said.

Yegelwel pointed to Calvin Klein's underwear ads featuring Christy Turlington, DKNY's Hollywood campaign and Banana Republic's skin care shot as lasting images in advertising.

The Gap, Barneys and Daffy's have also waged eye-catching campaigns, she said.

Gannett's Carr cited ads for Nike, Levi's for Women and CK One as some of the most effective campaigns on the street.

With Nike, Reebok and Gilda Marx already in the outdoor advertising game, the category should be the most competitive in the months ahead, he said. The interest in activewear has triggered some

beverage makers such as Evian to advertise outdoors, Carr noted. The market for watchmakers is also opening up, he said.

According to Yegelwel, in recent years retailers have entered the outdoor market somewhat cautiously. While Barneys, Banana Republic, Brooks Bros., Coach, Daffy's and The Gap are now squaring off in the streets, the category should become more important in the years ahead, she said, adding that cosmetic makers should also tap into the outdoor market.

Fragrance ads, which accounted for about $1.5 million of TDI's overall volume, have become a hot category, Yegelwel noted. In the last year, Tommy Hilfiger, Calvin Klein and Ralph Lauren have introduced ads for their scents.

"First they put all their efforts behind the core of their business. Now they're having so much success with their apparel that they're looking to invest in their fragrances," she said. "If you really like a restaurant for dinner, you might give it a shot for lunch."

The focus of outdoor advertising has shifted from billboards to buses because they penetrate urban centers from shopping districts to upscale residential areas, Yegelwel noted.

"With buses, advertisers are able to reach people who are too busy to read a magazine," she explained. "Buses are a quick read and they should be visually pleasing. They're very different from a magazine ad that allows you to hold the impression eight inches away from your face to really examine it."

Source: From Women's Wear Daily, *June 1995, p. 4. Reprinted by permission.*

Chapter Review

Key Words and Concepts

Define, identify, or briefly explain the following:

Advertising
Advertising agency
Consultant
Cooperative merchandising organization (formerly cooperative buying office)
Corporate merchandising/buying office
DNR
Editorial credit
Export specialists
Fashion consultant
The Fashion Group International
Fashion information service
Fashion magazine
Import brokers
Kiosks
Lobbyists
Logistics

Mall/property management specialists
Management consultants
Management information systems (MIS)
Market representative
Merchandising, buying, and product development organizations
Overseas merchandise representative
Product development
Public relations
Publicity
Resident buying office
Tobé Associates
Trade association
Trade attorneys
Trade publication
Women's Wear Daily

Review Questions on Chapter Highlights

1. List the different types of information provided by fashion information services. What types of firms subscribe to them? Why and how are they used?
2. Why would a Japanese company and a U.S. company subscribe to and use the *same* fashion information service?
3. Describe the transformation that has occurred in what were once called buying offices. What are some of the newer forms of assistance being provided by these organizations? What is the reason for this change?
4. Who might use the services of the Doneger Group? Who uses the services of AMC?
5. What role do AMC and Frederick Atkins play in today's global economy?
6. How do the activities of May Merchandising Company differ from those of AMC or Frederick Atkins?

7. How do management consultants differ from fashion consultants if they are working for a fashion firm?
8. Why might a retail firm use the services of consultants in the areas of information technology or logistics?
9. Describe the roles of import and export consultants. Who uses these services?
10. Explain the relationship and services of a fashion magazine to each of the following: (a) apparel producers, (b) retailers, (c) consumers.
11. What types of information are found in trade publications such as *Women's Wear Daily* and *DNR*? How does a trade publication differ from a fashion magazine?
12. Why and how are fashion firms using electronic media?

13. Why are mall/property management specialists important to the fashion industry?
14. What is a trade association? Give the names of trade associations that have been mentioned in previous chapters of the book and describe their activities.

References

Associated Merchandising Corporation. (1995). *All about AMC.* New York: Author.

Bertsch, D. (1995, November). Telephone conversation with author.

Braun, H. (1995, June 14). *Speaking globally: Information systems on a worldwide scale.* Unpublished paper presented to the International Apparel Federation, Washington, DC.

The Fashion Group International. (1995). Unpublished Fashion Group International press release.

Frederick Atkins, Inc. (1995). *The organization of Frederick Atkins, Inc.* New York: Author.

May Department Stores Company. (1995). *May fact book 1995.* St. Louis: Author.

Palmieri, J. (1994, October 10). Retail pool keeps shrinking, but Doneger Group keeps growing. *DNR,* p. 8, 12.

Standard Periodical Directory (V. 18). (1995). New York: Oxbridge Publications.

Standard Rate and Data Service. (1995, November). *Business publication advertising source, Part 1,* 77(11) 348, 353, 354. Wilmette, IL: Author.

Standard Rate and Data Service. (1996, May). *Consumer magazine advertising source.* Wilmette, IL: Author.

Tobé. (1957, April 25). Address before Harvard Graduate School of Business Administration, Cambridge, MA. Reprinted with permission of the late Tobe Coller Davis in the 1965 edition of this book.

Ulrich's International Periodical Directory (33rd ed.). (1994–1995). New Providence, NJ: R. R. Bowker.

Suggested Bibliography

Beaton, C. (1968). *The best of Boston.* New York: Macmillan.

Dolber, R. (1993). *Opportunities in fashion careers.* Lincolnwood, IL: NTC Publishing Group.

Edelman, A. (1990). *Fashion resource directory.* New York: Fairchild.

Everett, J., & Swanson, K. (1995). *Guide to producing a fashion show.* New York: Fairchild.

Falk, E. (1994). *1,001 ideas to create retail excitement.* Upper Saddle River, NJ: Prentice Hall.

Kelly, K. (1972). *The wonderful world of* Women's Wear Daily. New York: Saturday Review Press.

Pegler, M. (1995). *Visual merchandising and display* (3rd ed.). New York: Fairchild.

Perna, R. (1987). *Fashion forecasting.* New York: Fairchild.

Russell, J. (Ed.) (annual). *National trade and professional associations of the United States.* Washington, DC: Columbia Books.

Snow, C. (1962). *The world of Carmel Snow.* New York: McGraw-Hill.

Visual Merchandising and Store Design (Eds.). (1994). *Great store design.* Rockport, MA: Rockport Publishers.

Visual Merchandising and Store Design (Eds.). (1995). *Great retail displays.* Rockport, MA: Rockport Publishers.

Winters, A., & Goodman, S. (1984). Fashion advertising and promotion. New York: Fairchild.

Winters, A., & Milton, S. (1982). *The creative connection: Advertising copywriting and idea visualization.* New York: Fairchild.

Trade Associations

American Advertising Federation, 1225 Connecticut Ave., NW, Washington, DC 20036.

American Association of Advertising Agencies, 666 Third Ave., New York, NY 10017.

Color Association of the United States, 409 W. 44 St., New York, NY 10036.

The Fashion Group International, 597 Fifth Ave., New York, NY 10017.

International Council of Shopping Centers, 665 Fifth Ave., New York, NY 10022.

Magazine Publishers of America, 575 Lexington Ave., New York, NY 10022.

Public Relations Institute, 350 W. 57 St., New York, NY 10019.

Public Relations Society of America, 33 Irving Place, 3rd Floor, New York, NY 10003.

Trade Publications

Advertising Age, 740 North Rush St., Chicago, IL 60611.

Fashion Calendar, 185 E. 85th St., New York, NY 10028.

Fashion Forecast International, 23 Bloomsbury Square, London WC1A 2PJ, England.

International Colour Authority, 23 Bloomsbury Square, London WC1A 2PJ, England.

Public Relations Journal, 845 Third Ave., New York, NY 10022.

Standard Rate and Data Service, Inc., 5201 Old Orchard Rd., Skokie, IL 60076.

Visual Merchandising, 407 Gilbert Ave., Cincinnati, OH 45202.

*F*ashion Business Glossary

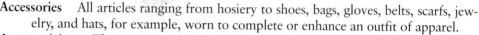

Accessories   All articles ranging from hosiery to shoes, bags, gloves, belts, scarfs, jewelry, and hats, for example, worn to complete or enhance an outfit of apparel.

Accessorizing   The process of adding accessory items to apparel for display, for models in fashion shows, or for customers' clothes on request.

Accounts Payable   The financial obligations owed *by* a company to its suppliers.

Accounts Receivable   The financial obligations owed *to* a company by its customers.

Acquisition   A company purchased (acquired) by another firm.

Ad Valorem **Tariff**   An import tax as a percentage of the price of the product.

Adaptation   A design that reflects the outstanding features of another design but is not an exact copy.

Advertising   A nonpersonal method of influencing sales through a paid message by an identified sponsor. Advertising appears in media such as newspapers, magazines, television, and radio.

Advertising Credit   The mention of a store name (one or several) in a producer's advertisement, as a retail source for the advertised merchandise.

Agile Manufacturing   Quick Response with a higher order of flexibility, or QR made-to-order (Clune, 1993).

Anchor Stores   The department store (or other similar major stores) in a shopping mall.

Apparel   An all-embracing term that applies to men's, women's, and children's clothing.

Apparel Jobber   A firm that generally handles all the processes but the sewing, and sometimes the cutting, and that contracts out these production processes to independently owned contractors.

Apparel Manufacturer   According to the Bureau of Census, a firm that buys fabrics and does the designing, patternmaking, grading, cutting, sewing, and assembling of garments in factories that it owns. Today industry use of the term has a much broader interpretation to include any firm that develops garments, controls production, sells to retailers (or directly to end-use customers), and ships and bills for merchandise. Firms may or may not buy the fabrics to be used. Today, mostly only small apparel companies conform to the census definition for apparel manufacturers.

Apparel Mart   A building that houses the regional showrooms of apparel companies.

Avant Garde   In any art, the most daring of the experimentalists; innovation of original and unconventional designs, ideas, or techniques during a particular period.

Bar Code   A series of vertical bars that identify a merchandise category, the manufacturer, and the individual item.

Bilateral Agreements   Trade agreements between two countries.

Bilateral Treaty   A treaty between two countries.

Boarding (Hosiery)   Heat-setting process used to give hosiery a permanent shape.

Body Scanning   A futuristic concept to scan an individual's body electronically to make a custom-made pattern.

Boutique   From the French word meaning "little shop." A free-standing shop or an area within a retail store, devoted to specialized merchandise for special-interest customers.

Branch   In retailing, an extension of a parent or flagship store, operated under the same name and ownership.

Brand   A trade name or symbol that distinguishes a product as that of a particular manufacturer or distributor.

Bridge Jewelry   Jewelry that in price and materials is between costume and fine jewelry.

Buyer   An executive (retail) who is responsible for the selection and purchase of merchandise and for the financial performance of that person's assigned merchandise area.

Canton Trade Fair   A textile trade show held in Canton (now generally known as Guangzhou), China.

Caribbean Basin Initiative (CBI)   A U.S. trade policy that gives special privileges to countries in the Caribbean Basin.

Caribbean Basin Textile Access Program   Provides virtually unlimited quotas for Caribbean-made garments made of U.S. fabrics and cut in the United States.

Caribbean Parity   Having apparel trade privileges for the Caribbean countries equal to those for Mexico.

Catalog   A promotional book or booklet in which merchandise is offered for sale.

Catalog Showroom Retailer   An underselling establishment that prints and distributes a catalog and maintains a showroom where samples of the merchandise can be seen and ordered.

"Category killers"   Retailers that specialize in extensive assortments of a single kind of merchandise at prices below those of conventional retailers.

Caution   French term for admission or entrance fee charged to trade customers by haute couture houses.

CD-ROM Shopping   Viewing products compiled from catalogs or other sources on a compact disk.

Centralized Buying   When all buying is done by merchandise staff from corporate headquarters.

Chain Stores   A retail organization that owns and operates a string of similar stores that are merchandised and controlled from a central headquarters office.

Chambre Syndicale de la Couture Parisienne   The French trade association that represents the haute couture houses of Paris.

Channel of Distribution   A network of organizations (and/or individuals) that performs a variety of interrelated functions in moving products from origination to consumption/use destinations.

Chapter 11   The legal process that provides an opportunity for companies burdened by excessive debt to continue operations while plans are made to restructure the company and reschedule debt payments.

Chargebacks   Financial penalties retailers demand of vendors for various reasons.

Chief Executive Officer (CEO)   The individual in a firm who has the final decision making power for the company.

Chief Operating Officer (COO)   The individual in a firm who is head of all day-to-day operations for the company; this individual reports to the CEO.

Classic   A particular style that continues as an accepted fashion over an extended period of time.

Closeout   An offering of selected discontinued goods by a vendor to a retailer at reduced prices.

Collection   A manufacturer's or designer's group of styles or design creations for a specific season. The season's total number of styles of designs, accumulated for presentation to buyers, constitutes a collection.

Commissionaire   An independent retailer's service organization that is based in another country (or countries) and is used to represent importers abroad.

Competition   In its marketing context, it is a form of business activity in which two or more parties are engaged in a rivalry for consumer acceptance.

Computer Aided Design (CAD)   Employs software to assist in product development by saving time required to create a prototype garment. When CAD systems are linked to automatic marker making and cutting, a sample can be produced in a matter of hours.

Computer Integrated Manufacturing (CIM)   Links together via computers many aspects of a company's activities associated with developing and producing a line.

Concentration (or Industry Concentration)   The amount of an industry's business handled by a small number of the largest firms.

Confined   A line or label that is sold to one retailer in a trading area on an exclusive basis.

Conglomerate   A company consisting of a number of subsidiary divisions in a variety of unrelated industries.

Consumer   The ultimate user of goods or services.

Consumer Obsolescence   The rejection of something that retains utility value in favor of something new.

Consumer Orientation   A business gives primary attention to serving and pleasing the consumer.

Consumer-Ready   Customized products are sent directly from the manufacturer to the consumer.

Contract Tanners   Business firms that contract hides and skins to the specification of leather converters.

Contractor (Apparel)   A garment production operation that does the sewing and often the cutting for other apparel producers or retailers (so called because this work is done under a contractual arrangement). The contractor may, in some cases, be responsible for securing the fabrics.

Converter (Leathers)   A company that buys hides and skins, farms them out for processing to contract tanneries, and sells the finished product.

Converter (Textile)   A firm that buys or handles the greige goods (i.e., unfinished fabrics) from mills and contracts them out to finishing plants to have them finished (i.e., dyed, printed, etc.).

Cooperative Advertising   Advertising, the cost of which is shared by a firm and its customer for the benefit of both.

Cooperative Merchandising Organization (formerly a Cooperative Buying Office)   A service operation owned by a group of store to assist those stores in developing (i.e., product development) and securing merchandise for their stores; other services may also be available.

Corporate Merchandise/Buying Office   A modern version of what was once the corporate buying office only; now assists stores in a store ownership group with a broader range of merchandising services (often including product development) as well as buying.

Corporation   An artificial legal entity.

Cost Price   The price at which goods are billed to a store, exclusive of any cash discounts that may apply to the purchase.

Costume Jewelry   Jewelry made of nonprecious materials.

Country-of-Origin Rules   The laws that determine the official country of origin for purposes of quota use.

Couturier   French word for (male) designer, usually one who has his own couture house. Couturiere (female).

Craze   A fad or fashion characterized by much crowd excitement or emotion.

Cross-Shoppers   Consumers who may shop across all retail channels; they may, for example, buy outerwear at department stores and undergarments at discount stores.

Currency Exchange Rates   The number of units (i.e., the "price") of one currency in relation to another. For example, one British pound (£) may be worth $1.50 at a certain time, depending on fluctuating currency exchange rates.

Custom Made   Apparel made to the order of individual customers; cut and fitted to individual measurements as opposed to apparel that is mass produced in standardized sizes.

Customization   Tailoring products and services around the needs of individual customers.

Customized Products   Those produced for a consumer's specific needs.

Cut, Make, Trim (CMT)   Contracting to have garments cut, sewn, and trimmed as a "package" agreement.

Cutting-Up Trades   The segment of the fashion industries that produces apparel (i.e., apparel producers).

Data Base   An information system, generally computerized, in which a variety of factual data are organized and stored

Database Marketing   Using computer files containing a great deal of information on consumers' demographic and psychological characteristics and life style to target market efforts to a narrow group of consumers.

Demographics   The study of vital and social statistics of a population.

Department Store   According to the Bureau of Census, a retail establishment that employs at least 50 people and that carries a wide variety of merchandise lines, including home furnishings, apparel for the family, and household linens and dry goods. Today, however, few department stores carry home furnishings or major appliances.

Design   An arrangement of parts, form, color, and line, for example, to create a version of a style.

Designers   Individuals responsible for the creative aspect of product development.

Developing Country   A poor country in early stages of economic development.

Direct Marketing   A term that embraces direct mail, mail order, and direct response.

Direct Seller   A retailer that sells merchandise by contacting customers either through door-to-door approaches or through some form of in-home party plan.

Discounter (Off-Price)   An "underselling" retail establishment that utilizes self-service combined with many other expense-saving techniques. This term is commonly used to refer to the mass merchandising discount chains.

Display   A visual presentation of merchandise or ideas.

Diverters   Questionable businesses that "divert" merchandise to a retailer other than the one to whom the manufacturer sold it. This strategy puts luxury or name brand goods in off-price retail stores to whom the manufacturer will not sell.

Domestic Market   When referring to origin of goods, *domestic* means manufactured in one's own country as opposed to foreign-made.

Domestics   Merchandise essentially for the home including sheets, pillows, towels, blankets, table linens, and other textile products.

"Doors"   An industry term for the number of stores. A chain might have 200 "doors," or a vendor might be selling to 100 "doors."

Duty   (also known as a tariff) A tax on imports.

Economies of Scale   The savings associated with manufacturing or selling on a large sale.

EDI   Electronic data interchange: the exchange of business data between two parties electronically.

EDI Mailbox   Where data are stored on a third party's computer, when a receiving computer is incompatible with a sending computer.

EDI Third Party   A company that provides EDI mailboxes.

EDI Trading Partner   A company with which one exchanges data electronically.

Editorial Credit   The mention, in a magazine or newspaper, of a store name as a retail source for merchandise that is being editorially featured by the publication.

807/9802 Production   A provision in the U.S. tariff rules that permits garments to be cut in this country and sewn elsewhere. When garments are returned to the United States, tariffs are paid on only the value added during the assembly process. Technically, this rule is now 9802, but much of the industry still refers to this as "807 production."

807A Production   Using U.S.-made fabrics that are cut into garments in the United States, assembled in the Caribbean, and returned virtually quota-free to the U.S. market.

Electronic Retailing   Selling by means of an electronic device such as television or interactive computers.

Entrepreneur   A person who organizes, launches, and directs a business undertaking and assumes the financial risks and uncertainties of the undertaking.

Establishment   Generally synonymous with *plant*, which refers to a single production facility. If the business is large, many establishments may be part of a *firm*.

European Union (EU)   These are the major countries of Western Europe, which have formed an integrated area with common trade policies, common agricultural practices, and free movement of labor and capital among members.

Exclusivity   Allowing a company sole use within a given trading area of a product.

Export orientation   An attitude and business orientation that emphasizes the importance of exporting for a firm or country.

Exports   Products or services that one country sells and ships to another.

Factor   Financial institution that buys accounts receivable from sellers, assumes the risks and responsibilities of collection, and charges a fee for this service.

Factory   A manufacturing plant.

Factory Outlet   A manufacturer-owned retail outlet. In earlier decades the major purpose was to dispose of the manufacturer's excess inventory. Now, many manufacturers see this as another place to sell their merchandise.

Fad   A minor or short-lived fashion.

Fashion (or Fashions)   (1) The prevailing style(s) at any particular time. When a style is followed or accepted by many people, it is a fashion. (2) A continuing process of change in the styles of dress that is accepted and followed by a large segment of the public at any particular time.

Fashion Bulletin   Written report on significant fashions prepared by fashion specialists.

Fashion Clinic   Meeting of a group of persons interested in fashion (under the direction of a fashion specialist) for the purpose of presenting or discussing significant fashion trends. Clinics are usually held at the beginning of new fashion seasons.

Fashion Consultant   A person who gives professional fashion advice or services.

Fashion Coordinator (or Director)   A person charged with the responsibility for keeping abreast of fashion trends and developments, and acting as a source of fashion information to others in his or her organization. Other responsibilities vary from place to place, as do job titles.

Fashion Forecast   A prediction as to which fashions or styles will be popular during a future period.

(The) Fashion Group   A national association of women engaged in the fashion business.

Fashion Image   The impression the consumer has of a retailer's (or manufacturer's) position on fashion leadership, quality, selection, and prices.

(The) Fashion Press   Reporters of fashion news for magazines, newspapers, broadcast media, and so on.

Fashion Retailing   The business of buying fashion-oriented merchandise from a variety of resources and assembling it in convenient locations for resale to ultimate consumers.

Fashion Show or Showing   Formal presentation of a group of styles, often in connection with showing the season's new merchandise.

Fashion Trend   The direction in which fashion is moving.

Firm   The overall business, or company. A firm may have many establishments (plants) or could have only one. Today, a number of apparel firms have no production facilities but are simply marketing companies that contract to have manufacturing done by others.

First Cost   The price a retailer pays to the producer in another country for merchandise.

Flea Market   A location in which a wide variety of independent sellers periodically rent space.

Floor-Ready   Manufacturers send merchandise to retailers with packaging and ticketing that permits moving goods directly on to the selling floor.

Focus Groups   Small consumer groups brought together to discuss their views and preferences regarding certain products or services.

Foreign Exchange   The currency one country uses to buy from another.

Franchise   A contractual agreement between a wholesaler, manufacturer, or service organization (the franchisor) and an independent retailer that buys the right to use the franchisor's product name or service for a stipulated fee. In return, the parent company provides assistance, guidelines, and established business patterns.

Franchisee   The owner-operator of a retail unit for which there is a franchise arrangement with a franchisor, the parent company.

Franchisor   The parent company which provides the franchisee with exclusive use of an established name in a specific trading area, plus assistance in organizing, training, merchandising, and management in return for a stipulated consideration.

Free Trade   Trade without barriers.

Free Trade Zone (FTZ)   An area within a country where goods may be imported and garments produced without being subject to taxes and customs duties.

Garment Center (SA)   The area to the East and West of Seventh Avenue in New York City, in which many of the women's ready-to-wear industry showrooms are located.

GATT   General Agreement on Tariffs and Trade. This has now been replaced by the World Trade Organization (WTO) which is located in Geneva, Switzerland.

Gemstones   A mineral found in nature that is used in jewelry because of its beauty, clarity, rarity, and other attributes.

General Merchandise Stores   Retail stores that carry a wide range of merchandise lines including apparel, hardware, furniture, home furnishings, and many other products.

Global Marketing   Operations through which produced goods are exported and marketed in foreign countries.

Global Products   Those with components or production from multiple countries.

Global Retailing   The expansion of retailing operations on a global scale.

Global Sourcing   Utilization of worldwide production.

Globalization   A shift from a time when countries did business within their own borders to one in which almost all countries' economies are connected by various production and marketing networks.

Grainline   The direction of the warp and weft yarns in a fabric.

Greige Goods   Unfinished fabrics.

Haute Couture (literal French translation: "The finest dressmaking")   As used in the fashion business, this refers to a firm whose designer creates a collection of original designs that are then duplicated for individual customers on a made-to-order basis.

Hides   Animal skins that weigh more than 25 pounds when shipped to a tannery.

High Fashion   A fashion that is in the stage of limited acceptance.

Home Television Shopping   Selling goods and services via television, primarily on cable or satellite home shopping channels.

Hypermarket   A superlarge retailing establishment that brings food and general merchandise together in an immense area.

ILGWU   International Ladies' Garment Workers' Union, which became part of UNITE.

Import   Merchandise brought in from another country for resale or other purposes.

Import Broker   An agent middleman who brings buyers and sellers together to facilitate the buying and selling of goods from other countries in a domestic market.

Import Penetration   The portion of a domestic market taken by imports.

Income   The returns that come in periodically from business, property, labor, or other sources (i.e., revenue).

Industrialization   The social and economic changes associated with having products made by machinery rather than by hand.

Initial Markup (Mark On)   The difference between the cost price of merchandise and its original retail price.

Initial Public Offering (IPO)   The shares of stock offered by a company on the stock market when the company first becomes a publicly held firm.

Intercolor Association of representatives of the worldwide fashion industry who meet in Paris twice annually to analyze color cycles and project color palettes for seasons two years in advance.

Interconnected Global Economy The close linking of the economies of many countries.

International Colour Authority A color trend service published by ITBD Publishers in London. This service is based on the predictions of color experts, and forecasts are available for fiber, yarn, fabric, and apparel producers. Color trend information is published separately for womenswear, menswear, and building interiors.

International Marketing See Global Marketing.

Interstoff An important textile trade fair held in Frankfurt, Germany.

Jewelry Articles of personal adornment made of either precious or nonprecious materials.

Job Lot A broken, unbalanced assortment of discontinued merchandise reduced in price for quick sale. Also called odd lot.

Jobber See Apparel Jobber.

Kips Animal skins weighing from 15 to 25 pounds when shipped to a tannery.

Knock-Off The copying of another manufacturer's fashion design.

Labor-Intensive A product that involves a great deal of labor to produce.

Landed Cost The cost of an imported product, which includes the cost of the merchandise, transportation, and duty.

Last A form in the shape of a boot over which shoes are built.

Lead Time Time necessary to produce merchandise from receipt of order to delivery time.

Less Developed Countries Another term for developing countries; this term incorporates countries that have advanced beyond the poorest levels.

Letters of Credit Typical form of payment for merchandise produced in other countries.

Leveraged Buyout (LBO) The purchase of a public company's stock made by a group of investors who borrow money from an investment firm using the company's assets as collateral.

Licensee The person or organization to whom a license is granted.

Licensing An arrangement whereby firms are given permission to produce and market merchandise that bears the name of a licensor, who receives a percentage of wholesale sales (i.e., a royalty) in return for the use of his or her name.

Licensor The person or organization who grants a license.

Line A collection of styles and designs shown by a producer in a given season.

Line-for-Line Copy Exact copy of a style first developed by an original designer.

Lobby A group that works together to put political pressure on policymakers to attempt to have the group's wishes carried out.

Logistics The process of moving merchandise from manufacturers to retailers to consumers in the most efficient way possible, with concerns also for prompt delivery.

Mail Order A firm that does the bulk of its sales through a catalog.

Mail-Order House A retailing organization that generates the bulk of its business through merchandise catalogs.

Mall See Shopping Centers.

Management Consultants Business specialists (and companies) that assist client firms on broad strategic planning, market strategy analysis and planning, merchandising and operations strategies (in contrast to fashion consultants, who assist with trend analysis and merchandise selection).

Management Information Systems (MIS)   A computerized system for managing data and putting it in meaningful form so that it is useful to management in making good decisions.

Manufactured Fibers   Known previously as "man-made" fibers, they are produced from chemical substances in contrast to fibers produced in nature (natural fibers).

Markdown   Reduction from an original retail price.

Market   (1) A group of potential customers. (2) The place or area in which buyers and sellers congregate.

Market Representative   (1) A market specialist in a corporate merchandising/buying office who covers a segment of the wholesale market and makes information about it available to client stores. (2) Similarly, a market specialist for a store ownership group or corporation who seeks merchandise lines for that company's stores.

Market Segmentation   The subdivision of a population (frequently ultimate consumers) whose members share similar identifiable characteristics (e.g., age, wealth, education level, marital status, life style).

Market Weeks   Scheduled periods during which producers introduce their new lines for an upcoming season.

Marketing   The total business interaction that involves the planning, pricing, promotion, and distribution of consumer-wanted goods and services for profit. A marketing orientation means that a company builds this around the consumer's needs.

Marketing Concept   Recognizing the importance of the ultimate consumer in the buying and selling process.

Marketing Environment   All the factors that affect how a company is able to meet its goals in developing and maintaining successful business relationships with its target customers.

Marketing Mix   The combination of factors related to product, price, place, and promotion that a company puts together to serve its target market.

Marketing Strategy   The approach a company uses to identify its customers' needs and the company's ability to satisfy those needs.

Markup   The difference between the cost price of merchandise and its retail price. Usually expressed as a percentage of the retail price.

Mart   A building or building complex housing both permanent and transient showrooms of producers.

Mass Merchandising   The retailing of goods on a very large scale.

Mass Production   Production of goods in quantity—many at a time rather than one at a time.

Matrix Buying   A strategy used by retailers in which they develop a list of preferred vendors who can supply the products, service, and pricing that retailers need to execute their respective strategies.

Megamalls   Jumbo malls several times larger than the typical regional mall.

Merchandisers   (1) In large firms, these individuals are responsible for developing new lines. Merchandisers plan the overall fashion direction for the coming season and give directions to the design staff about seasonal themes, types of items to be designed, and colors. (2) In recent years, this title is also being used for individuals who represent a manufacturer and work with retailers to assure that the apparel firm's line is being displayed and otherwise represented effectively within the store setting.

Merchandising   The activities involved in planning and development (or buying) of a merchandise line for targeted customers, providing them with what they want, when they want it, at prices they can afford and are willing to pay.

Merchandising, Buying, and Product Development Organizations   The operations that have evolved from the "buying office" concept. Because most of these enterprises are involved in product development, sourcing, and activities that go far beyond buying, the old buying office term is too limited for most of these today.

Merger   A joint agreement of two or more companies to merge their business into one.

Microfibers (Microdenier Fibers)   Fibers of less than one denier per filament; this fineness gives yarns and fabrics greater softness and more silk-like characteristics than traditional fiber filaments provided.

Micromarketing   Using a data base to break the consumer market into smaller and smaller segments to provide increasingly specialized products and services for those small consumer groups.

Mode   Synonym for a fashion.

Modular Production Systems   One way in which garments may be produced in a factory. In this arrangement, a small empowered team (module) produces garments from start to finish, setting its own goals and often its own work rules to get the job done.

Mom-and-Pop Store   A small store generally operated by husband and wife with limited capital and few or no hired assistants.

More Developed Countries   Those with relatively high incomes and standard of living.

Multifiber Arrangement (MFA)   A trade policy responsible for the textile/apparel quota system.

Multinational Company   A firm that conducts a portion of its business in two or more countries.

National Brand   Brand owned by a manufacturer, which is a trade name or symbol, that is nationally advertised.

National Retail Federation (NRF)   A trade association of the leading department, specialty, and chain stores in the United States.

Needle Trades   Synonym for apparel industry.

Newly Industrialized Country (NIC)   Countries that not long ago were developing countries but now have significant industrialization and fast-growing economies.

Nonrubber Footwear   All footwear that contains less than 50% rubber in the upper part of the shoe.

North American Free Trade Agreement (NAFTA)   A free trade policy between the United States, Canada, and Mexico.

Off-Price Retailing   The selling of brand and designer-named merchandise at lower than normal retail prices.

Offshore Assembly   Having cut garments assembled in another country.

Offshore Production   Production of goods by a domestic manufacturer (including retailers) in another country.

On Line Computer Shopping   When consumers use on-line computer services to view and order merchandise.

Openings   Fashion showings of new collections by apparel producers at the beginnings of a season.

Open-to-Buy   The amount of money that a buyer may spend on merchandise to be delivered in a given period.

Outside Shop   See Contractor.

Outward Processing Trade (OPT)   Sending garments to another country for some or all of the assembly.

Overseas Merchandise Representatives   Individuals in other countries who assist their retail clients in the selection, development, and delivery of merchandise (i.e., sourcing) produced in that overseas region.

Overstoring   The excess retail space available, relative to the population, in the United States.

Pelt   Skin of fur-bearing animal.

Plants   The same as *establishments;* that is, a single production facility that may or may not be part of a larger firm.

Policy   A clearly defined course of action or method of doing business deemed necessary, expedient, or advantageous.

POS   Point-of-sale. In retailing, that area of the store or department where the customer pays for the merchandise and the sale is recorded. This information is processed by computers and provides the basis for Quick Response systems.

Preproduction Operations   Those between the time a style is accepted for the line and when a style is ready for the sewing floor. Glock, R., & Kunz, G. (1995). *Apparel manufacturing: Sewn product analysis* (2nd ed.). Englewood Cliffs, NJ: Prentice Hall.

Press Kit   A collection of facts, figures, photographs, and other promotional materials assembled into a compact package and distributed to the press.

Press Release   A written statement of news that has occurred or is about to occur, specifying the source of the information and the date after which its use is permissible.

Prêt-à-Porter (French term meaning, literally, "ready-to-carry")   French ready-to-wear apparel, as distinguished from couture clothes, which are custom made.

Preticketing   The vendor puts the price on merchandise before shipping it to the retailer. Many retailers are now requiring vendors to do this.

Primary Market   Producers of fibers, textiles, leather, and furs.

Private Label   Merchandise that is produced exclusively for one retail firm and identified by one or more "names" or brands that are owned by the retailer.

Privately Held Companies   Those owned privately by individuals or groups rather than shareholders.

Privatized Industries   Those previously operated by the government but now have been transferred to private ownership such as those in the former Soviet Union.

Product Developer   A person employed by a manufacturer to develop product lines or a retailer to create private label merchandise for their exclusive use.

Product Development   The part of apparel manufacturing (also used increasingly by retailers) that develops the line and monitors its production to assure that garments meet expectations

Product Manager   An executive who functions as the head of the product development team responsible for the planning and development of a particular product, product line, or brand.

Production Orientation   A company's focus on producing what the company wants to produce or can produce, in contrast to a marketing orientation, which focuses on customers' needs and wants.

Production Package   Contracting out the complete production of garments from cutting to finishing.

Productivity   The amount of factory output per employee. This is a measure of efficiency of a manufacturing company.

Profit   Total revenue and sales less all costs and expenses.

Progressive Bundle System   The traditional way of producing garments in assembly-line fashion; workers perform specialized tasks and then pass the garment on to the next operators.

Protectionism   Strategies to restrain imports from one's market.

Psychographics   The study of people's attitudes and values.

Public Corporation   A business that sells shares of its stock on the stock market to the public.

Publicity   A nonpaid message—verbal or written—in a public-information medium about a company's merchandise, activities, or services.

Publicly Owned   A corporation whose shares are available for sale to any person who chooses to purchase these shares; this means the shareholders (stockholders) collectively own the company.

Pull System   Determining the consumer's needs and wants and basing production on that information.

Push System   Force feeding a product line through the manufacturing and marketing process in hopes the consumer will like it.

QR (Quick Response)   A computerized partnership between different segments of the industry. Its purpose is to supply customers with products or services in the precise quantities required at exactly the right time. Computer technologies are important in quick response systems.

Quota   Quantitative restrictions placed on exporting countries on the number of units of specific product categories that may be shipped to a particular importing country over a specified period of time.

Rapid Replenishment   A Quick Response system that permits quick replacement of items sold by the retailer. When an item is sold, the manufacturer has a replacement item in the retailer's stock in a matter of days.

Ready-to-Wear   Apparel that is mass produced in standardized sizes as opposed to apparel made to a customer's special order (custom made).

Real Time Merchandising   The continuous analysis of fashion direction, consumer style testing results, and current retail sales that permits manufacturers and retailers to operate in "real time" (much closer to the selling season) rather than having merchandise tied up in the pipeline for months.

Relationship Marketing   Identifying the needs of a specific group of customers, customizing merchandise assortments around those customers' needs, and maintaining an ongoing relationship with those consumers.

Reorder Number   A style number that continues to be ordered by buyers.

Resident Buying Office   Formerly, a service organization located in a major market center that reports market information, acts as market representative, and renders other related services to a group of stores who have their own buyers. Today, these organizations provide other kinds of services (e.g., product development, merchandising, and sourcing) and may do no *buying* at all.

Resource   A vendor or source of supply.

Restructuring   The changes a sector or company goes through in its efforts to remain competitive in response to changing market conditions.

Retailing   The business of buying goods from a variety of resources for resale to ultimate consumers.

Royalty   A compensation paid to the owner of a right (name, brand, etc.) for the use of that right.

Sales Operations   Carry out the firm's marketing and merchandising plans by physically selling the line to retail customers.

Sales Promotion   Any activity that is used to influence the sale of merchandise, services, or ideas.

Sample   The model or trial garment (may be original in design, a copy, or an adaptation) to be shown to the trade or perhaps made to check the design effectiveness and fit of the garment.

Season   In retailing, a selling period.

Secondary Fashion Centers   Regional market centers outside New York City; examples include Los Angeles, Dallas, and Chicago.

Secondary Market   Producers of finished consumer fashion products (dresses, coats, suits, accessories, and the like).

Sell Through   A measurement of the amount of merchandise sold of a particular merchandise category or style.

Seventh Avenue   An expression used as a synonym for New York City's women's apparel industry (actually, a street on which the showrooms of many garment manufacturers are located).

Shareholders (also referred to as *Stockholders)*   The individuals who own a publicly held company because they own stock in the firm.

Shopping Centers   A group of retail stores and related facilities planned, developed, and managed as a unit.

Showing   See Fashion Show or Showing.

Silhouette   The overall outline or contour of a costume. Also frequently referred to as *shape* or *form.*

SKU   Stock-keeping unit.

Smart   Having a fashionable appearance.

Socioeconomics   Pertaining to a combination or interaction of social and economic factors.

Sourcing   For retailers as well as manufacturers, the process of determining how and where merchandise (or components) will be obtained. In apparel manufacturing and retailing this term is often used to refer to where garments will be manufactured (assembled).

Specialty Store   A retail establishment that deals either in one category of merchandise or in related categories of merchandise.

Specification Buying   Occurs when a retailer contracts the production of private label merchandise, providing precise specifications for the end product. In recent years, as retailers have essentially become manufacturers themselves (developing product lines and monitoring closely the production), this term understates the responsibilities now assumed by many retailers in the manufacturing process.

Square Meter Equivalent (SME)   A measure for tracking textile and apparel imports to restrict shipments according to quota levels.

Standard Industrial Classification (SIC)   A U.S. system established by the U.S. Office of Management and Budget to classify establishments into industry groupings on the basis of their primary economic activity.

Store Ambience   The look and feeling of the retail store that a consumer experiences upon entering and shopping there.

Store Ownership Group   A retailing organization consisting of a group of stores that are centrally owned and controlled in terms of broad policy making but are operated autonomously.

Style (noun)   A type of product with specific characteristics that distinguish it from another type of the same product.

Style (verb)   To give fashion features to an article or group of articles (as to style a line of coats and suits, for example).

Style Number   An identification number given to an individual design by a manufacturer. The retailer uses the number when ordering the item and for stock identification.

Style Piracy   The use of a design without the consent of the originator.

Style Testing   A strategy to determine consumer interest in new apparel or other products by introducing a few items and carefully watching the extent to which consumers buy them.

Stylist   One who advises concerning styles in clothes, furnishings, and the like.

Subcontracting   When contractors distribute the garment production even further; subcontracting often occurs in very small shops or in homes.

Subsidies   A form of government payment or support to exporters so they may compete more effectively in world markets.

Supercenters   A combination of discount store and supermarket with a total of 175,000 or more square feet of selling space.

Superstores   The "big box" stores that carry extensive product lines and undercut other retailers in price. These include the "category killers" or "power retailers."

Sweatshops   Illegal garment production facilities that do not meet U.S. government standards for wages, benefits, and healthy working conditions.

Target Market   A particular segment of a total potential market selected by a company as the object of its marketing efforts.

Tariff   A tax leveled against imported products,, also known as *duty*.

Telemarketing   Sales of products and services via an interactive system or two-way television or via telephone.

Texitalia   An important textile trade show held in Milan, Italy.

Textile Mill Products   That segment of the industry that converts fibers into finished fabrics; this includes spinning and texturing yarns; knitting, weaving, and tufting; and dyeing, printing, and other finishing.

Third World   The poorer countries of the world. These are also sometimes known as the less developed countries (LDCs) or the developing countries.

Trade   The sale of goods or services from one country to another.

Trade Association   A nonprofit voluntary association of businesses having common interests.

Trade Attorneys   Specialists in trade law who assist their clients in importing and exporting activities.

Trade Balance   The difference between a country's imports on one hand and exports on the other. A negative balance (deficit) means the country receives more imports than it exports; a positive balance (surplus) means the country exports more than it imports.

Trade Deficit   A condition in international trade in which the value of a country's imports is in excess of the value of its imports.

Trade Publications   Newspapers or magazines published specifically for professionals in a special field.

Trade Show   Periodic merchandise exhibits staged in various trading areas by groups of producers.

Transshipment   When a country that has used all its quota sends products to another with available quota so the shipment appears to come from the second country.

Triangle Shirtwaist Fire   A fire that occurred in the Triangle Shirtwaist factory in 1911 and took 146 lives. The tragedy was the turning point in the "sweatshop" era because it awoke the public conscience to the labor conditions in the garment industry.

Trunk Show   A producer's or designer's complete collection of samples brought into the store for a limited time to take orders from customers.

UNITE   The Union of Needletrades, Industrial & Textile Employees. In 1995, the International Ladies Garment Workers Union (ILGWU) and the Amalgamated Clothing and Textile Workers Union (ACTWU) merged to form UNITE.

UPC   Universal product code. A special bar-code symbol that has been adopted as a standard for the retail industry. The code consists of a one-digit merchandise category code, a five-digit UPC vendor number, a five-digit item number, and a one-digit check digit.

Upgrading   When countries "trade up" to ship higher priced products so they maximize what they can send under quote restrictions.

Vendeuse   French term meaning saleswoman.

Vendor   One who sells; resource from which a retailer buys goods.

Volume   Amount of dollar sales done in a given period by a retail store or other mercantile establishment.

Warehouse Club   A retail establishment that specializes in bulk sales of nationally branded merchandise at discount prices.

Women's Wear Daily   Trade publication of the women's fashion industries. (The textile and menswear counterpart is *DNR*, previously known as *Daily News Record*.)

World Trade Organization (WTO)   The international body that promotes free trade among nations and spells out reciprocal rights and obligations for member countries.

The Influential Designers

These are the people who have had the greatest design impact on the fashion industry during this century. Some of them are superb craftsmen and women whose knowledge of fabric, cut, and production have enabled millions to be clothed with taste and style. Others have raised fashion design to the level of art. In all cases, they have either created lasting trends, established standards of excellence, or been a major influence on future generations. (*Authors' Note:* The name of Geoffry Beene, considered by many to be one of America's most creative designers, was inadvertently omitted from this article. Known for his innovative combination of textures, fabrics and unusual designs. Among other influential designers who have emerged are Christian Lacroix, Todd Oldham, Joseph Abboud, Nicole Miller, Isaac Mizrahi, Patrick Kelly, Romeo Gigli, Matsuda, and Byblos.)

Adolfo Began as milliner, added separates, custom blouses, long skirts in late '60s . . . devoted following of status dressers.

Gilbert Adrian MGM's top designer, 1923–1939, for stars such as Crawford, Hepburn, Garbo . . . wide shoulders, tailored suits.

Azzedine Alaia Sexy clothes that cling to every curve from this contemporary Paris ready-to-wear designer.

Walter Albini Early Italian rtw designer.

Hardy Amies British couturier for men and women, noted for his tailored suits, coats, cocktail and evening dresses.

Giorgio Armani Major Italian rtw force for men and women . . . beautifully tailored clothes . . . now at peak of his powers.

Laura Ashley Romantic Victorian looks in fabrics and fashion . . . built a London-based empire in clothes and home furnishings.

Cristobal Balenciaga One of century's greatest . . . innovations include semifit jacket, cocoon coat, balloon skirt, bathrobe coat, pillbox hat . . . desciples include Givenchy, Courreges, Ungaro.

Pierre Balmain Opened own Paris house in 1945 . . . classic daytime looks, extravagant evening gowns.

Patrick De Barentzen "Daring" member of Italian couture in the '60s . . . whimsical . . . enormous Infanta skirts.

Jean Barthet Influential milliner of the '50s and '60s . . . customers ranged from Princess Grace to Sophia Loren.

Bill Blass Mr. Fashion Right . . . taste, durability and a consistent high level of talent since the late '50s.

Marc Bohan Joined House of Dior in the early '60s and was there until 1989. Replaced by Gianfranco Ferre (couturier for Dior).

Source: Adapted from *WWD: 75 Years in Fashion 1910–1985*. Reprint permission granted.

Donald Brooke   Most successful period was the '60s . . . also did much work for Broadway stage.

Stephen Burrows   Body-conscious clothes in vibrant colors . . . noted for his draped matte jerseys.

Roberto Capucci   Started in Rome at age 21 . . . very hot in the '50s . . . known for drapery, imaginative cutting.

Pierre Cardin   King of the licensing game . . . top innovator of the '50s and '60s, became first Paris couturier to sell his own rtw . . . now involved in everything from rock to restaurants.

Hattie Carnegie   Influential in the '30s and '40s . . . began as milliner, then designed custom and rtw . . . influenced Norell, Trigere, McCardell.

Bonnie Cashin   An American sportswear original—casual country and travel clothes in wool jersey, knits, tweeds, canvas, leather.

Antonio Del Castillo   The Infanta silhouette . . . designed for Lanvin from 1950 to 1963, then opened his own house in Paris.

John Cavanaugh   One of Britain's best in the '50s . . . headed Curzon St. . . . known for nipped-waist, full-skirt New Look.

Coco Chanel   Chanel No. 5 . . . the house on the rue Cambon . . . the Chanel suit: braid-trim, collarless jacket, patch pockets . . . feminism before it was fashionable . . . the one and only.

Aldo Cipullo   Jeweler for Cartier's in the '70s . . . elegance, but with a light approach.

Liz Claiborne   Contemporary sportswear . . . executive dressing . . . great commercial success.

Ossie Clark   Enfant terrible of British fashion in the '60s . . . HotPants, maxi coats . . . started '40s revival in 1968.

Sybil Connolly   Ireland's most prestigious designer.

Andres Courreges   The Basque tailor . . . hot in the '60s, with suits and roomy coats . . . Tough Chic . . . the great white way.

Angela Cummings   Designed jewelry for Tiffany's, now on her own . . . inventive and tasteful.

Lilly Dache   From the '30s to '50s, U.S.'s top milliner . . . draped turbans, brimmed hats, snoods . . . fantasies for films.

David Dart   Contemporary California designer of the '90s . . . winner of many design awards for his chic contemporary designs.

Donald Davies   English shirtmaker who is based in Dublin and went to shirtdresses in the '60s . . . he used featherweight Irish tweed in a variety of colors.

Christian Dior   Launched the New Look in 1947, becoming fashion's most famous name until his death 10 years later.

Jean Dresses   Designed from 1925–1965 . . . his Jean Dresses Diffusion, a lower-price line for America, the start of mass production by a French couturier.

Perry Ellis   Appeared in the '70s as one of the avant-garde young sportswear designers . . . gave classics a high-fashion twist.

Alberto Fabiani   One of Italy's top couturiers of the '50s . . . "surgeon of coats and suits" . . . conservative tailoring . . . wed Simonetta Visconti.

Jacques Fath   Enfant terrible, showman, ran own Paris house from 1937–1954 . . . sexy clothes, hourglass shapes, plunging necklines.

Salvatore Ferragamo   Italian shoemaker who became international success . . . pioneer of wedge heel, platform sole, Lucite acrylics heel.

Gianfranco Ferre   Architectural approach has turned him into one of Italy's leading rtw designers.

Anne Fogarty   Spearheaded the revolution in junior sizes in the early '50s.

Fontana Sisters   One of Italy's leading couture houses in the '50s, started by mother, Amabile, in 1907, continued by daughters Zoe, Micol and Giovanna.

Federico Forquet   Big in the '60s in Rome, noted for coats and suits in blocks of bold color . . . went into interior design in 1972.

Mariano Fortuny   Mushroom-pleated silk tea gowns . . . his clothes now are collectors' items.

James Galanos   Born in Philadelphia, studied in New York, worked in Paris, opened own business in Los Angeles . . . one of America's most elegant fashion creators.

Irene Galitzine   Palazzo pajamas of the '60s an important concept . . . now in cosmetics, furs, linens.

Jean-Paul Gaultier   One of Paris's trendiest and more controversial rtw designers for men and women.

Rudi Gernreich   Avant-garde sportswear . . . maillots . . . topless swimsuit, 1964 . . . see-through blouses . . . the No-Bra.

Hubert de Givenchy   A major couturier since he opened own House in Paris in '52 . . . influenced by Balenciaga . . . most famous client: Audrey Hepburn.

Alix Gres Originally a sculptress . . . couturiere since 1934 . . . known for statuesque and molded gowns "sculpted" on live model.

Aldo Gucci Head of Florence-based family business . . . manufacturer and retailer of leathers, luggage and apparel . . . GG.

Halston Began as milliner at Bergdorf's, did Jacqueline Kennedy's pillbox hat, 1961 . . . opened couture business in '68, rtw in '72 . . . simple classics . . . name licensed by J.C. Penney.

Norman Hartnell London's biggest couture house in the '30s . . . coronation gowns for Queen Elizabeth.

Edith Head Probably Hollywood's best-known designer.

Jacques Heim Successful Paris couturier from 1923 until the early '60s . . . designer of Atome, the first bikini.

Stan Herman Designer and owner of Mr. Mort during the '60s and '70s . . . popularized "fashion at a price" . . . revived chenille as a fashion fabric in the '80s and '90s . . . leading uniform designer of the world . . . three-time Coty Award winner . . . President of the Council of Fashion Designers of America.

Barbara Hulanicki Mod look, the early '60s . . . a founder of Biba . . . the Total Look: coordinated color in clothes, cosmetics, hose.

Irene Top designer for movie starts for many decades, also had own rtw business in the '60s.

Charles James The Eccentric One . . . ran own custom business in the '40s and '50s . . . innovative shapes . . . the Dali of design.

Mr. John One of America's best-known milliners, especially in the '40s and '50s—the heyday of hats.

Betsey Johnson Big in the '60s . . . low prices, offbeat fashions . . . designed for Paraphernalia, co-founded Betsey Bunky, Nini.

Stephen Jones London's extraordinary milliner who designs hats for such notables as Lady Di.

Norma Kamali Her contemporary sweatshirt clothes made high fashion affordable by a young audience.

Jacques Kaplan Headed Georges Kaplan, New York furrier . . . innovator and promoter . . . a pioneer of "fun" furs.

Donna Karan Anne Klein's assistant, then her successor . . . now on her own . . . high-fashion, elegant sportswear.

Rei Kawakubo Comme des Garcons . . . one of the first of the New Wave from Japan in the '80s.

Kenzo Left Japan for Paris in 1965 . . . light, whimsical rtw.

Emmanuelle Khanh One of the first major rtw designers in Paris in the '60s . . . kicky, young clothes.

Charles Kleibacker Journalism, show business, then fashion . . . opened own business in New York in 1960 . . . known for bias cuts . . . later fashion educator.

Anne Klein A major American sportswear designer . . . associated with Junior Sophisticates, 1951–1964 . . . classic sportswear.

Calvin Klein Pure American looks in sportswear and rtw . . . clean lines, sophistication and a wide range of prices.

Karl Lagerfeld Outspoken, controversial, avant-garde . . . designed for Chloe, now for Fendi and Chanel.

Jeanne Lanvin One of earliest Paris couturiers . . . peak years between two World Wars . . . her perfumes: My Sin and Arpege.

Ralph Lauren Noted for his Americana-influenced designs . . . the western look for men and women.

Lucien Lelong Great name in Paris couture from the '20s to '40s . . . didn't design himself, but inspired workers such as Dior, Balmain, Givenchy and Schlumberger.

Jean Louis Not only a successful Hollywood designer, but also headed his own couture firm.

Claire McCardell Perhaps the most profound influence on American sportswear design . . . hot in the '40s and '50s.

Mary McFadden Socialite who first started designing exotic jewelry . . . her pleated evening dresses became the rage in the late '70s.

Mainbocher One of America's first custom designers in Paris . . . dressed Duchess of Windsor . . . specialized in quiet quality.

Germana Marucelli Avant-garde Milanese couturiere of the '50s and '60s.

Vera Maxwell Pioneer of American sportswear.

Missoni One of the early Italian rtw families . . . known for knits in original colors and designs.

Issey Miyake Avant-garde Japanese designer, predated Japan's New Wave.

Anna Molinari Italian designer whose fashion is a mix of sensation and cultural influences, revisiting the past while divining the future for the romantic and glamorous woman. Lines include her name line, Blumarine, Blugirl, and Blumarine Vomo (the last for men).

Capt. Edward Molyneux   From the '20s to '40s, his purity of line drew the rich and famous to his Paris salon. Brief revival in the '60s.

Claude Montana   Contemporary French rtw . . . big shoulders . . . leathers . . . architectural shapes.

Hanae Mori   Comes from Japan, shows in France . . . tasteful clothes in beautiful colors . . . innovative beading.

Digby Morton   Early British couturier . . . opened house in 1933 . . . specialized in tailored suits, cableknit sweaters, Donegal tweeds.

Thierry Mugler   Tongue-in-chic fashion from one of Paris's New Wave designers.

Jean Muir   Started in the '60s in London . . . elegant, intricately detailed young clothes.

Norman Norell   Brought American fashion to the level of Paris couture.

Frank Olive   Sophisticated and slick hats have been his forté since the '60s.

Andre Oliver   Associated with Pierre Cardin since 1955 . . . created clothes for men and women.

Paquin   One of the first Paris couturiers . . . house opened in 1891 and lasted until 1956.

Mollie Parnis   One of the most successful women designers and manufacturers on SA.

Jean Patou   A businessman and showman as well as a designer of elegant, ladylike couture clothes in the '20s and '30s.

Mme. Paulette   Leading American milliner in the '50s and '60s . . . associated with Saks Fifth Avenue.

Sylvia Pedlar   Put high fashion into loungewear . . . founded Irish Lingerie and designed there 40 years.

Elsa Peretti   Revolutionary jewelry designer . . . diamonds by the yard . . . made small diamonds fashionable . . . innovator in silver.

Robert Piquet   Ran his Paris couture house from 1933 to 1951 . . . influenced Givenchy and Dior, both of whom were employed by him.

Paul Poiret   One of first French couturiers to free women from constraints of underpinnings . . . leader of early 20th century.

Thea Porter   Anti-establishment London designer of the '60s and '70s . . . fantasy long clothes . . . Orientalia.

Anna Potok   A key influence in fur design . . . founder of Maximilian.

Emilio Pucci   His prints on thin silk jerseys revolutionized Italian fashion in the '50s and '60s.

Lilly Pulitzer   Her printed-cotton shift, the "Lilly," swept the nation in the '60s and '70s . . . floral prints . . . Palm Beach.

Mary Quant   A miniskirt pioneer synonymous with the "swinging London" look of the '60s . . . Carnaby St.

Madeleine de Rauche   Renowned sportswoman who created sports clothes for herself and friends . . . made functional clothes in the '30s.

Oscar de la Renta   Came to U.S. to work for Elizabeth Arden in the early '60s . . . one of SA's "luxury" designers.

Zandra Rhodes   A London original . . . outrageous evening looks . . . fantasy colorings for hair and makeup.

Jacqueline de Ribes   A socialite-turned-designer . . . her love of couture quality is reflected in her rtw.

Nina Ricci   Opened her house in Paris in 1932 . . . dressed mature, elegant women . . . pioneered showing lower-priced clothes in a boutique . . . her fragrance: L'Air du Temps.

John Rocha   One of Britain's most successful designer exports of the '90s, going to Paris, but returning to London . . . known for innovative, experimental use of fabric and color, layering of textures, and simplicity of silhouette . . . designs sometimes viewed as "nonfashion" fashions.

Marcel Rochas   Elegant French Couture of the '30s and '40s . . . packaged a perfume called Femme in black lace.

Sonia Rykiel   The genius of sweater dressing.

Yves Saint Laurent   One of the century's greatest influences on fashion and taste.

Count Fernando Sarmi   Beautiful evening clothes . . . chief designer at Elizabeth Arden, 1951–1959, then head of his own business.

Jean-Louis Scherrer   His soft, refined dresses popular in the '60s . . . opened own Paris house in 1962.

Elsa Schiaparelli   The Great Schiap . . . one of the true avant-garde designers in Paris from the '30s to '50s.

Jean Schlumberger   Legendary jeweler whose exuberant fantasies have pleased women such as

Bunny Mellon and Babe Paley since the late '40s.

Mila Schoen   Important Italian designer of the '60s and '70s.

Ken Scott   Expatriate from Indiana who settled in Milan . . . fabric and dress designer since 1956 . . . Art Nouveau influenced.

Simonetta   One of the first of the Italian couture designers . . . married Albert Fabiani.

Adele Simpson   One of SA's durables . . . in her own business since 1949 . . . known for conservative good taste.

Stephen Sprouse   Contemporary, controversial designs, strongly influenced by the '60s.

Gustave Tassell   Started own business in Los Angeles, 1959 . . . refined, no-nonsense clothes.

Pauline Trigère   A pioneer American designer . . . started own business in 1942, still going strong.

Emanuel Ungaro   Once known as "the young terrorist" of fashion, now does some of the most seductive clothes in Paris.

Valentina   Russian-born, opened own couture business in America in 1928 . . . dramatic clothes . . . dressed Garbo, whom she resembled.

Valentino   The Chic . . . one of the most important European couturiers since the mid-'60s . . . taste, elegance, timelessness.

Philippe Venet   Givenchy's master tailor, 1953–1962, then opened own business . . . noted for lean suits, rounder shoulders.

Gianni Versace   Italian rtw . . . an innovator for men and women in leathers and other fabrics.

Sally Victor   From mid-'30s to mid-'60s, one of America's most prominent milliners.

Madeleine Vionnet   The inventor of the bias cut and a major influence on fashion since early in the century.

David Webb   Known for his enamel-and-jeweled bracelets in the '60s.

John Weitz   Women's sportswear with menswear look . . . big in the '50s and '60s . . . now only in men's wear . . . once "designed" a cigar.

Vivienne Westwood   Contemporary, controversial English designer . . . runs World's End, off-beat London boutique.

Charles Frederick Worth   Dressmaker for Empress Eugenie and "founder" of French couture when he opened his own house.

B. H. Wragge   Owner-designer of Sydney Wragge, pioneered concept of sportswear separates . . . important in the '40s and '50s.

Yohji Yamamoto   Oversize, dramatic Japanese clothes.

Ben Zuckerman   The master tailor . . . major influence on American coats and suits.

*S*ources of Current Statistical Information

From the U.S. Government

- *Statistical Abstracts of the United States.* Annual. Provides historical as well as fairly current data on a wide variety of subjects. Uses both government and private sources. From the U.S. Department of Commerce, Washington, DC 20233. In most libraries.
- *Survey of Current Business.* Monthly. Provides little historical data but much fairly current data from a variety of sources. U.S. Department of Commerce.
- *U.S. Industrial Outlook.* Annual up through 1994. Provided figures and interpretive comment on many industries, but did not cover every industry each year. U.S. Department of Commerce.
- *Population Profile.* Annual. Summarizes data on population by age, sex, area, income level, and so on. U.S. Department of Commerce.
- *Monthly Labor Review.* Contains data on the workforce, consumer price index, wholesale prices, and so on. U.S. Department of Labor, Washington, DC 20212.
- *County Business Patterns.* Contains pertinent industry data on various sectors. Data are available for national, state, and county levels. U.S. Department of Commerce.
- *Retail Census.* Every five years, the U.S. Department of Commerce publishes a *Census of Retail Trade: Establishments and Firm Size.*

The listed publications are a good starting point for research. For greater detail about specific subject areas, consult the following sources:

- *Industry production:* Write the Bureau of the Census, U.S. Department of Commerce, Washington, DC 20233, for whatever is currently available on the particular product or industry operation with which you are concerned.
- *Retailing:* Write the Bureau of Census (same address as above) for current information on the retailing industry.
- *The consumer:* Contact the Bureau of the Census for its most recent population reports on whatever phase interests you most (income, education, ethnic origin, metropolitan area versus nonmetropolitan, etc.). For information on how much the public spends on various categories of goods and services, ask the Office of Business Economics, U.S. Department of Commerce, for its latest annual report on personal consumption expenditures. Also check the Bureau of Labor Statistics, U.S. Department of Labor, Washington, DC 20212, for possible studies of urban family budgets and expenditures.
- *Foreign trade:* Monthly reports, with annual figures in the December issue each year, from the Department of Commerce, Bureau of the Census. FT110 on imports and FT410 on exports are good starting points.

On-Line Sources of Government Information

Increasingly, up-to-date government data are becoming available through the Internet and World Wide Web. These have many advantages over publications in that they can be updated constantly. One example providing a tremendous amount of data is the National Trade Data Bank, through which extensive information on countries and trade may be found. When using the World Wide Web, the following are examples of keywords that generate extensive listings of information sources:

- Apparel industry
- Textile industry
- Retail industry
- Fashion industry
- Textile trade
- Apparel trade

Private Research Organizations

Supported by their subscribers, private research organizations often develop useful research publications, some of which may be compendiums of statistics gathered from many sources.

- *Dun & Bradstreet Companies, Inc., 299 Park Ave., New York, NY 10171.* This is a credit reporting agency, primarily concerned with business enterprises.
- *The Conference Board, 845 Third Ave., New York, NY 10022.* Funded by business firms, makes studies of economic conditions, consumer attitudes, and so on. Presents statistics from government sources in graphic form.
- *Standard & Poor's, 25 Broadway, New York, NY 10004.* A service subscribed to by financial and investment concerns to provide information on individual companies whose stocks are listed on the various exchanges. Has detailed information on producers and retailers; makes annual surveys of textile and apparel industries, "Textiles, Apparel and Home Furnishings." Another Standard & Poor's survey, "Retailing," covers all retailing including supermarkets, drugstores, hard lines, and so on.

  Standard & Poor's also publishes *Stock Reports,* which provides periodic reports on the performance of publicly held companies' stock. Reports on a company also provide assessments of the financial outlook for that company and indicate whether the company is a good prospect for investment. This reference is available in most university and college libraries as well as many public libraries.
- *Value Line, 220 E. 42 St., New York, NY 10017-5891,* is another source for following a publicly held company's performance and gives important

data on the company's financial status. *Value Line* also charts the company's stock performance, generally over a longer period of time than Standard & Poor's similar review. This source is also found at most libraries.

Each chapter of this book includes a list of trade-related associations functioning in the sector of the industry being covered. For additional organizations, check with your library for its latest available directory of trade associations.

Indexing Services

The following sources have indexed a wide range of publications related to the fashion industry. Each provides the necessary citation information to find full articles or other sources of information.

- *Clothing & Textiles Arts Index,* HuTech, P.O. Box 1300, Monument CO 80132 USA. This is an extensive source of citations related to fashion, ranging from industry information to theoretical pieces. Citations from 2,500 English periodicals, serials, and monographs from around the world, in addition to journals regularly reviewed. Available on CD-ROM.
- *Textile Technology Digest,* The Institute of Textile Technology, 2551 Ivy Rd., Charlottesville, VA 22903-4614, provides an updated monthly index with abstracts from current periodicals, books, journals, and pamphlets in textile technology and textile business. Available in printed form, on CD-ROM, and on-line. Over 250,000 abstracts on a variety of textile subjects are stored on a single CD; 9,600 abstracts are added each year.

Periodicals

Publications that sell advertising usually have research departments, which are sources of information on the publication's readers and on the market it serves. Each chapter of this book includes an appropriate list. For additional sources, check with your library for its latest directory, such as *Ulrich's International Periodicals Directory, Standard Rate and Data Service,* or *IMS/Ayer Directory of Publications.*

Career Opportunities in Fashion

Fashion is everywhere, and so are career opportunities for those who combine a knowledge of the fashion business with their own talent, ambition, and ability. Consider that a fashion career may open up anywhere along the road from raw materials to the final consumer purchase; stores, mail-order houses, other forms of retailing, manufacturing companies, advertising agencies, newspapers, magazines, commercial photography studios, and public relations firms are among the student's targets in the quest for a foothold in fashion.

Personal attributes suggest the direction a beginner should take. An outgoing personality helps in sales work at all levels, in showroom work, in public relations, and especially in jobs such as that of fashion coordinator, in which one often needs persuasive skills to sell one's ideas to other executives in the organization. The gift of a great figure (or physique, for men) or a photogenic face can make modeling a possibility and, through that work, a chance to learn from inside many other phases of the fashion business. Visually creative people do well in design, display, advertising, photography, and sketching for designers and fashion information services. Analytical minds adapt well to the multiple problems of managing retail fashion assortments or planning factory production, and thrive on market research.

The rewards of fashion careers are as varied as the jobs themselves. Some pay fabulously; others provide only a modest living. Some positions demand worldwide travel, to buy or observe, or to do both. Virtually all positions in the industry require an understanding of textiles and apparel in the global economy, even if one does not actually travel.

Some jobs permit one to live at home and commute to an office, retail store, or manufacturing establishment. But all of them, and hundreds more, offer the student of fashion a chance to work, learn, and grow in the endlessly exciting, unceasingly stimulating business of fashion.

The following is a guide to entry-level jobs in the fashion industry. It was originally prepared by Phyllis Madan and Marilyn Henrion of the Placement Department of the Fashion Institute of Technology, New York. For this edition of the book, these positions have been updated and modified somewhat.

Entry-Level Jobs for Fashion Design Graduates

- Assistant designer
- Cutting assistant
- Sketching assistant
- Sketcher (assistant to designer)
- Sketcher/stylist
- Junior designer

The personal qualities needed for all of the following jobs in the design room are similar. Applicants must be well-organized, flexible, fast workers, and must have the ability to work under pressure in often cramped working conditions. Fashionable grooming and neat appearance are essential. Most jobs require creativity and a good eye for trends in silhouette, color, and fabric. It is also important to have an understanding of the fashion industry (i.e., the "big picture") and the economic aspects of producing a line—that is, the enterprise must be *profitable* as well as creative to stay in business.

Assistant Designer

An individual in this role is responsible for executing designers' ideas by creating a first pattern from CAD computer files, slopers, or draping. Instructs and supervises the work of samplehands. Often required to keep records, order fabrics and trim, and do follow-up and clerical work. Although job is primarily technical in nature, one may be asked to shop stores for trends, sketch, possibly consult with designer about fabric choices and designs.

Requirements: Fashion Design degree, good knowledge of garment construction (sewing), computer skills, strong technical skills (making first patterns, draping, and sketching). Beginners must have a portfolio.

Cutting Assistant

This may be a beginning assistant position in companies where there are several assistant designers. Cuts samples, alters patterns, generally assists in design room. Once ability is proven, may have opportunity to assist patternmaker or do draping.

Requirements: Fashion Design degree preferred, computer skills, good patternmaking skills, draping skills helpful, knowledge of garment construction.

Sketching Assistant

In this position an individual sketches principally for designers' records—precise technical sketches of constructed garment swatched with fabric and trim. May sketch freehand or by computer. May sketch and prepare artwork for presentations. Writes specification sheets on how garments are constructed. Usually orders fabric, handles a variety of clerical and follow-up duties. May do market research.

Requirements: Fashion Design degree and computer skills necessary. Ability to do precise technical sketches rapidly, either by computer or by hand, sometimes both. Portfolio required.

Sketcher (Assistant to Designer)

This person sketches freehand or computer illustration-quality sketches for designers' ideas, may be asked to contribute own design ideas, may deal with buyers, do promotional work. Hours are often long and irregular. Must be available to run errands and generally assist the designer.

Requirements: Fashion Design degree a must. Ability to do computer or freehand illustration-quality sketches at a fast pace. Outstanding portfolio required.

Sketcher/Stylist

An individual in this position works directly with principals of firm and product development staff. Shops stores for current trends, sketches ideas, works with patternmaker in developing these ideas, may not do technical work of draping and patternmaking. Participates in fabric selection, coordination of the line; may be involved in working with buyers in merchandising the line.

Requirements: Fashion Design degree, excellent portfolio, good eye for trends in silhouette, color, and fabric.

Junior Designer

This person sketches original designs, executes own first pattern, frequently sews sample. Does market research in fabrics and trends. Must be able to provide company with new design ideas and make accurate predictions on what will be salable in coming season. Must be able to design garments within company's price range. Job is fast-paced and a high-risk position since continuation of employment may be based on success of line.

Requirements: Fashion Design degree required. Strong creative ability as well as excellent computer and technical skills (draping, patternmaking, sewing). Good eye for trends (silhouette, color, fabric). Portfolio must show evidence of strong creative ability in designing coordinated line of apparel.

Entry-Level Jobs for Textile/Surface Design Graduates

- Textile/surface designer
- Colorist
- Assistant to stylist
- Lace and embroidery designer
- Screen print artist
- Woven fabric designer
- Painted woven designer
- Knit designer
- Assistant stylist

Jobs for Textile/Surface Design graduates are available in textile converting houses, vertical manufacturing (garment manufacturers that produce their own fabric), textile/surface design studios, department stores (private label), architectural firms (interior fabrics, wall coverings, carpeting), rug manufacturers, contract manufacturers/consultants, paper products manufacturers, china and giftware companies, color forecasting services, and computer graphics design firms.

Requirements: Degree in Textile/Surface Design. Excellent portfolio of designs exhibiting versatile skills and ability to meet professional standards. Must have strong computer skills, as much of this design work is done on computers today. Other requirements include initiative, reliability, following instructions, and meeting deadlines.

Textile/Surface Designer

Does original textile designs; may also do color combinations and repeats.

Colorist

Does various combinations for existing designs or products and may do original designs.

Assistant to Stylist

Not to be confused with assistant stylist, an upper-management position. Sets up appointments for stylist, acts as liaison with mills, works with clients and salespeople in stylist's absence, keeps clerical records.

Lace and Embroidery Designer

This position requires providing detailed technical drawings on graph paper of designs for lace and embroidery. Limited use of color.

Screen Print Artist

A person in this role executes designer's ideas through screen print process. Knowledge of color separations, layouts, repeats, and sample printing is required. An understanding of color and a knowledge of color formation is mandatory. Designers express themselves through the screen print process as a means of executing screened croquis and custom printing (limited or exclusive yardage) for both home furnishings and apparel. Again, much of this work is done on computers today.

Woven Fabric Designer

This individual does original designs and executes designer's ideas on handloom. Acts as an aide to stylist, sends out mill specs, does quality control, research, and resource work.

Painted Woven Designer

This person executes painted woven designs and colorations using ruling pen and airbrush; designs may be developed on computers.

Knit Designer

In this role, an individual executes knit swatches and designs on knit machines for apparel. Knitting skills are required. An understanding of the production process is necessary.

Assistant Stylist

This is a managerial position in a design firm or studio. Works with stylist in compiling lines, preparing storyboards, and forecasting; acts as liaison among stylists, designers, and clients.

Entry-Level Jobs for Advertising Design Graduates

- Paste-up and mechanical artist
- Layout artist
- Assistant art director

Jobs for Advertising Design graduates can be in either advertising or graphic design areas.

Advertising artists may work on trade or consumer accounts in advertising agencies, in-house advertising departments, or printing firms. They may work in print (magazines or newspaper) or television advertising.

Graphic designers develop "collateral material," which may consist of brochures, annual reports, packaging, logos and trademarks, corporate image projects, and so forth. They also may work in publishing, doing editorial layout for books and magazines. Board persons do the finished art to prepare it for the printer. They may work in either advertising or graphic design companies.

Jobs require creativity, computer skills, and other graphic design skills.

Paste-Up and Mechanical Artist

This artist prepares art for printer by pasting together elements of layout (type, illustration, photography), does color separations using T-square and ruling pen. May work for advertising agency, graphic design studio, service studio, printer, publication, or in-house corporate art department.

Requirements: Advertising Design degree or Illustration degree. Must have computer skills. Must have taken course in paste-ups and mechanicals and have portfolio demonstrating precision and accuracy in executing mechanicals and color separations.

Layout Artist

This person designs layout for ads, usually under the supervision of the art director. Specifies typeface, does "comp" rendering to indicate what finished ad will look like when printed. May do own mechanicals.

Requirements: Advertising Design degree, portfolio demonstrating advertising layouts, thorough knowledge of typefaces, computer expertise, skill at "comp" rendering and mechanicals, neat and precise work habits.

Assistant Art Director

The individual in this role works directly with art director. May perform any or all of the following duties depending on the size and structure of the agency or firm: assist in developing concepts for advertising campaigns, rough and finished "comp" renderings, specifying type, mechanicals, paste-ups, layout, and graphic design.

Requirements: Advertising Design degree, strong portfolio indicating thorough development of creative concepts through fast, crisp "comp" rendering; computer skills.

Alternate Entry Jobs for Advertising Design Graduates

Because of the highly competitive nature of most of the jobs just noted, graduates sometimes begin their careers by accepting nonart positions in the field such as Guy or Gal Friday, advertising assistant, or advertising production/traffic assistant. This is an excellent way to gain experience and contacts and get a foot in the door.

Entry-Level Jobs for Fashion Illustration Graduates

- Free-lance illustrator
- Staff illustrator
- Sketcher

Free-Lance Illustrator

Jobs in illustration tend to be free-lance rather than full-time. Free-lance illustrators may do work for advertising agencies, retail stores, manufacturers, textile and fiber houses, pattern companies, display houses, and publications.

Requirements: Illustration degree required. Must have excellent portfolio indicating distinctive illustration style and creativity. Computer skills necessary today. Should be well organized and have ability to run own free-lance business (negotiating contracts, setting rates, billing, keeping own records). Must work successfully from photographic references, as models are not provided in the industry.

Staff Illustrator

Staff illustrators may work for buying offices, retail stores, pattern companies, and some publications. However, most illustration work is done on a free-lance basis. Increasingly, these illustrations require at least some use of computers.

Requirements: Illustration degree required. Must have excellent portfolio. Computer skills increasingly important.

Sketcher

Apparel manufacturers may hire sketchers on a free-lance or full-time basis to sketch garments for their records. These sketches are not used for reproduction and are not considered illustrative. They are tight sketches showing clear details of garment construction. Computer product data management programs fill this role increasingly.

Requirements: Illustration or Fashion Design degree, knowledge of garment construction, ability to do detailed sketches with tight hand, computer skills.

Entry-Level Positions for Fashion Buying and Merchandising (FBM) Graduates

Career possibilities for FBM graduates fall into these general categories:

- 1) Retail stores and 2) merchandising, buying, and product development organizations (formerly resident buying offices)
- Manufacturers

1) Retail Stores and 2) Merchandising, Buying, and Product Development Organizations

Management Trainee

Most department stores and some specialty chains have formal executive training programs. Firms recruit trainees as potential managers and buyers. Each store has a limited number of openings for the training program, and competition is keen. For the majority of training programs, a bachelor's degree is necessary (especially with department stores). Each training program is unique and includes components of on-the-job training and formal instruction. Trainees are given exposure to merchandising as well as management areas.

Requirements: A high grade point average (especially in math) (a minimum grade point is required by some department stores [e.g., 2.8 to 3.0, depending on the company].), analytical ability, computer skills, strong communication skills, leadership ability, initiative, high degree of motivation and energy, maturity, fashionable grooming.

Long-Range Career Goal: Buyer, retail store manager, or other retailing executive positions.

Department Manager

Many stores hire candidates directly for managerial positions. Previous experience in sales and management in the store for which they are hired is desirable. A bachelor's degree may be necessary depending on the prerequisites of the firm. Responsibilities are training and supervising sales associates, handling all department operations such as opening and closing the register(s), scheduling, merchandising and displaying goods, some direct customer contact.

Requirements: Similar to that of management trainee.

Long-Range Career Goal: Retail store manager, buyer, or other management positions.

Assistant Store Manager

These positions are available with specialty chain stores. Duties vary depending on the size and structure of the company and store, but usually involve assisting the manager in all phases of running the store. Positions *do not* usually lead to buying careers.

Requirements: Strong retail sales background. Computer familiarity. Duties are similar to those of department manager. With a small chain store or boutique, the manager must understand the needs of customers and provide buyers with feedback about sales and inventory. After a proven success record of store management with a specialty chain store, career growth into a district or regional manager position is possible. (Ultimately, the responsibility for growth and volume with a designated number of stores rests with the district manager.)

Long-Range Career Goal: Store manager, possibly district manager.

Buyer's Clerical

This is usually an entry-level position more commonly found in some of the few remaining large central buying offices (CBO). The job duties are often consistent with clerical duties of an assistant buyer trainee in a smaller firm and include keeping accurate records, scheduling appointments, follow-up work, possibly answering phones.

Requirements: A high degree of detail orientation is essential as well as strong math aptitude, computer skills, and communication skills.

Long-Range Career Goal: Assistant buyer and beyond.

Assistant Buyer Trainee (or Assistant Market Representative)

Often an entry level position in some of the few remaining CBOs. The trainee works directly with the buyer and performs a variety of duties such as keeping unit control records, accompanying the buyer to the market, scheduling appointments, placing reorders, and following up on shipments. Usually the position is a five-day workweek, although overtime may be required during peak seasons.

Requirements: Necessary qualifications are similar to those of buyer's clerical.

Long-Range Career Goal: Market representatives (or buyers)—make trips to the market and spend a large portion of time researching trends, merchandise, and resources. Qualifications include a high degree of communication skills, solid math aptitude, ability to analyze data and make sound business judgments. A good fashion and color sense is also important.

Distribution Planner

Usually a position found in a large retail firm or CBO. Includes working with computer to determine distribution of merchandise to branches of the retail firm. Additional responsibilities include keeping records of unit-control, communicating with buyers and merchandise coordinators. Computer skills are essential.

Requirements: Strong problem-solving and analytical skills as well as computer skills are essential.

Long-Range Career Goal: Head distribution planner, buyer, or controller.

Product Development Trainee

Jobs in product development combine business, technical, and creative aspects and can be found in large retail organizations, private label apparel manufacturers, or independent consulting firms. Entry-level jobs may include preparing specs, handling paperwork and follow-up, dealing with clients, overseas communications, and fashion research. As training progresses, additional responsibilities will include working with product development manager and buyers in coordinating garment styles or lines that meet buyers' expectations in regard to delivery, quality, and price point. Once orders are placed, duties include completing the necessary paperwork, providing breakdown information (sizes, colors, quantities), and approving samples for fit, color, and quality. Communications with overseas or domestic production facilities, approval of production samples, and development of yarn and fabric blends and resources are also included in product development. The job may eventually involve travel overseas, negotiating with factories on pricing, working out delivery schedules, and investigating new factories for possible future sourcing.

Requirements: Understanding of merchandising and fashion trends, basic knowledge of garment construction, textile science, and apparel manufacturing processes. Computer skills. Ability to do technical sketches, excellent communication and organizational skills, analytical and problem-solving ability, strong business sense, high energy level. Ability to interact effectively with staff in other countries.

Long-Range Career Goal: Head of a retail company's product development division.

Manufacturers

Positions with manufacturers involve work in the following general areas: (1) promoting or selling the product line, (2) merchandising or planning the line, and (3) overseeing the production and operations of manufacturing the line. In smaller companies, career positions may include duties in several of those areas, such as sales plus merchandising. In a larger

firm, positions may fall more neatly into one particular area. Many jobs involve on-the-job training with regular workweeks (occasional overtime during peak seasons).

Entry-Level Positions

- Showroom sales trainee
- Showroom receptionist
- Clerical assistant
- Product development trainee

All of the positions just listed may be very diversified depending on the size and nature of the firm. Responsibilities include any of the following—showing and selling the line to clients, dealing with buyers in person and on the phone, reception, greeting clients, keeping sales records, faxing, follow-up on deliveries, writing up orders, possibly modeling garments, and attending meetings.

Requirements: Necessary qualifications include fashionable appearance, assertive personality, excellent oral and written communication skills, computer skills, and a high level of organization. Past sales experience is often helpful.

Long-Range Career Goals: Showroom sales and showroom manager—responsible for sales with own list of clients. If manager, supervise showroom sales force and staff; coordinate sales meetings. Road salesperson—sales outside of showroom in a particular geographic territory. Usually occurs with a large company after proven showroom sales record.

Retail Sales Coordinator

These positions are unique in that they provide an opportunity to gain exposure to manufacturing as well as retailing. One facet of the job involves duties in the showroom (usually serving as the home base) such as showroom sales, coordinating sales among retail store locations, analyzing inventory reports, and ordering and reordering goods for retail store locations.

A second facet of the position includes promoting the manufacturer in a retail department store setting through customer service, displaying and merchandising the goods, and preparing sales and inventory.

Requirements: Excellent interpersonal and communication skills, high energy level, math aptitude, flexibility, sales ability. Computer skills. Past sales experience can be helpful.

Long-Range Career Goal: Potential growth as merchandiser or in sales.

Merchandising Assistant

Duties include working with the merchandiser in planning upcoming product lines; researching the market for trends and colors; keeping records; dealing with sales force, design staff, and customers.

Requirements: Ability to be highly organized and detailed is essential. Good fashion and color sense, team worker, analytical aptitude, and follow-through ability are important. Computer skills. Sketching skills may be helpful.

Long-Range Career Goal: Merchandiser, with responsibilities for planning the overall line, investigating colors and fabrics, giving direction to the design staff, estimating prices. In a smaller firm the owner or designer usually fulfills the role of merchandiser.

Assistant Piece Goods and Trim Buyer

Duties include assisting with ordering fabrics and trims, keeping track of inventory and records, maintaining swatch file and samples, accompanying buyer on trips to fabric market to learn resources.

Requirements: Interest in textiles, detail oriented, well organized, ability to make good business judgments. Course work in textiles or garment construction may be helpful.

Long-Range Career Goal: Piece goods and trim buyer—to resource piece goods and trim market, price and cost goods, make purchases in conjunction with needs of design staff, possibly give direction to design staff for fabrics and trims.

Production Assistant

Duties involve assisting production manager in keeping records relating to production, sales, shipping, and inventory; keeping track of orders; writing up cutting tickets; costing garments; acting as liaison among factory, sales staff, and customers; heavy phone contact with factory. If production is done overseas, may assist in coordinating imports.

Requirements: Important qualifications include high degree of organization, tolerance for stress, communication skills, planning, follow-up and problem-solving ability, math aptitude, computer skills. Increasingly, second language skills are valuable.

Long-Range Career Goal: Production manager—coordinates and supervises all aspects of producing the line. Usually works out of factory. If overseas manufacturer, makes regular visits to factory to check quality and coordinate production and importing.

Administrative Assistant

This position can be very diversified and usually involves assisting an executive of the firm (vice president, sales manager) in the following capacities: scheduling appointments, keeping records, filing, follow-up work, coordinating information, typing memos. For a college graduate, this is generally a job one takes just to get a foot in the door, with an eye toward moving to a more career-oriented position.

Requirements: The ability to organize efficiently is essential. Detail orientation, strong communication skills, computer skills, and potential for advancement are also important.

Long-Range Career Goal: Upper level management—position in a specialized area (sales manager, operations manager) involved in policy making and overall managing of the firm.

Entry-Level Jobs for Apparel Production (or Manufacturing) Management Graduates

- Production control assistant
- Import coordinator
- Junior industrial engineer
- Costing analyst
- Quality control specialist
- Assistant plant manager

Graduates of an apparel production management program generally work for apparel manufacturing and importing firms. Increasingly, however, product development divisions in large retailing firms also seek graduates with this preparation. The work site may be based in a corporate office or at a manufacturing plant. Jobs in the office may or may not involve some travel to factory sites, domestically or overseas.

Production Control Assistant

Working in the corporate office as assistant to the production manager, this entry-level position may include any combination of the following responsibilities: serving as liaison between marketing and production, expediting orders, preparing cutting tickets, maintaining production records, piecegoods and trim inventory, ordering piecegoods and trim, following up on and coordinating shipments, receiving and allocating goods, dealing with contractors, production scheduling and follow-up, maintaining fax and e-mail communications with overseas resources, preparation of cost sheets, overseeing of sample production, quality control, entering and retrieving computer data.

Requirements: Organizational ability, quantitative aptitude, computer skills, accuracy, thoroughness, assertiveness, high stress tolerance, good communication skills, detail orientation, problem-solving ability.

Import Coordinator

A person in this role coordinates and monitors overseas production and shipments. Constant interface is required with shipping, warehousing, merchandising, and design areas. This individual makes certain production schedules are met, coordinates deliveries with sales orders, and meets completion dates. Other duties include: prepares specifications and documentation, obtains duty rates, adds quotas, figures markups, prepares data for computer entry. Maintains daily electronic communications with overseas resources and contractors. May be involved in matters pertaining to customs regulations, trade policies, and payment methods (e.g., letters of credit).

Requirements: Organizational ability, quantitative aptitude, computer skills, accuracy, thoroughness, assertiveness, high stress tolerance, good communication skills, detail orientation, problem-solving ability, appreciation for cultural differences in other countries, an understanding of textiles and apparel in the global economy. Facility with other languages a valuable asset.

Junior Industrial Engineer

A person in this role works at an apparel manufacturing plant studying operations and practices. Does time and motion studies, methods analyses, rate setting, plant layout, monitors efficiency of plant. Reports findings to management and makes recommendations for improvements.

Requirements: Maturity, organizational skills, strong analytical problem-solving and mathematical ability, computer skills, good at details and followthrough.

Costing Analyst

This position requires breaking down cost of manufacturing garments and taking into account such factors as piece rates, materials costs, import duties, and so forth.

Requirements: Good mathematical skills, analytical ability, computer skills, good at details.

Quality Control Specialist

An individual in this position usually works for an apparel manufacturer or importer, though jobs may also be found in large retail organizations with centralized buying. The person examines garments (may include fiber, textile, color, as well as sewing construction) to see that production specifications are met. The person must check assembly operations, identify problems, and work with production staff and management to correct problems. May develop specifications and inspect merchandise as it comes in from overseas as well as from domestic sources. Job often involves travel to factories.

Requirements: Detail oriented, good at followthrough, ability to work under pressure, high energy level, good communication skills, analytical and problem-solving ability, computer skills. Ability to work effectively with individuals from very different backgrounds from one's own. Second (or more) language skills are an asset.

Assistant Plant Manager

An individual in this job assists in running a factory—oversees work flow, maintains production schedules, distributes and keeps track of work. He or she assists in staffing plant and supervising various plant operations including cutting, sewing, pressing, warehousing, shipping.

Requirements: Must be a self-starter, have strong interpersonal skills, supervisory and organizational ability, high energy level, ability to work well under pressure, problem-solving ability, computer skills.

Entry-Level Jobs for Textile Development Graduates

- Assistant converter
- Assistant stylist (fabric or yarn)
- Product development assistant (textiles)
- Textile technologist
- Sales trainee
- Fabric librarian

Since textiles constitute a key component of the apparel industry, graduates of this major have a broad range of career options related to both business and technology. The entry-level jobs listed here represent some of the more typical ones available, but by no means cover the entire range of possibilities.

Assistant Converter

This individual assists the converter in overseeing and expediting the various processes involved in the transition of greige goods to finished fabric (dyeing, printing, finishing). Serves as liaison among mills, dyeing and finishing plants, knitters, and clients; heavy phone work. Projects greige goods needs, figures yardage and poundage, prepares dye orders, schedules printing, tracks yarn and finished goods. Processes customer orders and follows up on orders to see that deadlines are met. Figures costs, losses; maintains inventory control.

Requirements: Good at details and followthrough, problem solving, gathering and analyzing data, computer skills, oral communications, working with figures, memorizing, confronting, mediating.

Assistant Stylist (Fabric or Yarn)

In this role, a person may work for textile firm or yarn producer. He or she assists in developing seasonal lines and colorations. Duties may include any of the following, alone or in combination: surveys competitors and forecasts, researches market trends. Assists in preparing presentation boards and sales aids. Works with customers on development and refinement of patterns and colors. Places lab dips, follows up on sample yardage. Works with artists to make sure work is done on time. Obtains approval from customers. Maintains fabric library, keeps it current and organized, locates samples and data. Handles administrative and follow-up details related to line development.

Requirements: Excellent color sense, fashion awareness, organizational ability, communication skills, good at details and followthrough.

Product Development Assistant (Textiles)

This position requires one to be involved in knit or woven fabric development. The person helps develop product from technical point of view, prepares specification graph layouts to be executed at mill level and art room level. Translates clients' and salespeople's ideas into what is technically feasible, advises as to machine capabilities. Has samples made up, checks yarns, follows up on production, sees that finished goods are executed properly. May involve some travel to mills.

Utilizes market research findings, maintains records, handles follow-up work, serves as liaison between design room and mill. Maintains phone contact with mills and factories to make certain piece goods shipments are met. Reviews fabric lines brought in by textile salespeople or may go out into market to assist in piece goods selection. May order piece goods, trims, and notions, and may make substitutions when goods are unavailable. Maintains electronic communications with overseas resources.

Requirements: Analytical ability, organizational skills, fashion awareness, color sense, strong communication skills, problem solving related to purchase orders and reorders. Skills in negotiating, confronting, record keeping, handling details and followthrough, gathering and analyzing data, use of computer, problem solving, juggling multiple demands, organizational ability, color sense.

Textile Technologist

In this role a person may work for a testing laboratory, retailer, or manufacturer. Responsibilities may include any of the following duties, depending on the setting: performs various lab tests on fabrics, yarns, fibers, and garments to determine color fastness, washability, shrinkage, and so forth. Textile components may be tested before and/or after being made into garments. Analyzes fabric construction, fiber content, finishing properties; compiles data; prepares reports on findings. Identifies problems, helps maintain standards. Develops and verifies care labeling.

Requirements: Systematic, good at details, well organized, able to follow instructions and work alone. Good communication skills; oral, written, and analytical ability; computer skills.

Sales Trainee

This individual may work for a textile mill, converter, or yarn producer. He or she calls on manufacturers (or textile firms) to sell the line and service accounts. Training may include visit to mill or assisting in showroom. Initially will be given list of accounts to work with; ultimately will be expected to generate new accounts. May deal with designers, merchandisers, piece goods buyers, or production people. May suggest end uses for product, explain properties. Gathers information and provides feedback to management on customer needs in terms of styling, product development. Follows up on orders and shipments, services accounts.

Requirements: Initiative, outgoing personality, excellent communication and interpersonal skills, problem-solving ability, good memory, color sense, high energy level, self-starter, competitive spirit.

Fabric Librarian

In this role, a person may work for a fiber or textile firm, trade association, or pattern company. Responsibilities may include any combination of the following duties: maintains up-to-date fabric library, prepares sample cards and seasonal presentations. Works with color file system, runs groups of colors in response to requests. Researches and compiles fabric resources list, may go out to review fabric lines at various resources and select appropriate fabrics for library. Assists users in locating, identifying, and selecting appropriate fabrics for library. May work in a setting that serves as a resource for internal design staff only, or may deal with clients representing other firms.

Requirements: Knowledge of textiles, excellent color sense, design and fashion awareness, ability to match textile products and potential end uses, organizational ability, systematic, good memory, good communication skills.

Index

Note: **Boldface** page numbers indicate definitions or descriptions of designers and companies.

About the Authors

Jeannette Jarnow is Edwin Goodman Professor and Professor Emeritus, Fashion Institute of Technology in New York. Ms. Jarnow founded the Fashion Buying and Merchandising program under the Edwin Goodman Chair at the Fashion Institute of Technology. Prior to entering academe, Ms. Jarnow had a successful career in fashion retailing; she was merchandise manager and buyer with Abraham and Straus. Additionally, she has served as a consultant to a number of leading companies in the industry. She is a member of the Board of Directors of Shenkar College of Textile Technology and Fashion in Israel. Ms. Jarnow was the lead author in developing the first edition of *Inside the Fashion Business*, launching a book that remains today the most comprehensive text on the fashion industry.

Kitty G. Dickerson is Department Chairman and Professor, Department of Textile and Apparel Management, University of Missouri-Columbia. Dr. Dickerson is a Fellow in the International Textile and Apparel Association and has served as president of that group. She was named to *Textile World's* "Top Ten Leaders" list and has received numerous other academic and industry awards. She serves on the Board of Directors of Kellwood Company, a Fortune-500 apparel firm. With previous experience in retailing, Dr. Dickerson's work focuses on the total soft-goods industry. Also author of *Textiles and Apparel in the Global Economy*, Dr. Dickerson was an early leader in focusing on globalization of the industry. She has published widely in scholarly and trade journals and has been invited to address academic and industry groups in the United States and in other countries.

Cotton Farms
No. in U.S.: 43,000
Acreage: 10,000,000

Cotton Farm
Production: 1.5 bales/acre
Size: 500-1000 acres

Farmer
Avg. No. of Farms: 4
No. of Employees: xx

Cotton Module
Production: 14,000 lbs.
to 16,000 lbs.
Cotton Field No.: xx

Cotton Gins
Operational (U.S.): 1,500

Cotton Gin
Capital Cost: $xx
Production Rate: 30-40 bale/hr.
Annual Production:
  11,000 bales
Baling Charge: $42.50/bale
Capacity: 700-100K/yr

Cotton Bale
Weight: 480 lbs.
Worth: $370

Cotton (Classification) Sample
Bale ID (Gin Ticket): xx
Fiber Length: xx inches
Length Uniformity: High
Trash: xx%

Harvest Cotton

PROCESS TIME 6-8 WEEKS

72¢/lb.

TRANSIT TIME: 1 DAY

Cotton Module

Compress Into Bale

Remove Seed, Trash, and Lint

Cleaned Cotton

Band and Wrap

Transportable Cotton Bale

Cotton Bale

Tag with Gin Ticket

123

INSPECTION

Unique Cotton Bale

Stored Bale

Store in Gin Warehouse

TRANSIT TIME: 2 DAYS

Stored Bale

WAIT TIME 6 MONTHS

Store in Consolidator Warehouse

INSPECTION

Stored Bale

TRANSIT TIME: 1 DAY

Store at Yarn Manufacturer Staging Area

WAIT TIME 21 DAYS

Bale to be Processed

INSPECTION

Carding

Carded Cotton

INSPECTION

Opening and Blending Bale

INSPECTION

Blended Cotton

Ring Spinning

Consolidating Warehouse
Capacity: 225K bales
Cost to Store: $xx
Cost to Handle: $xx

Cotton Merchant
Margin: x%
Market Share: xx%

Finish Garment Includes: Pressing and Ticketing

PROCESS TIME 4-5 DAYS Sew, Finish, Fold and Package

Finished Garment

Package to Ship

PROCESS TIME 1 DAY

Package for Sewing Plant

PROCESS TIME 2 DAYS Spread and Cut

Spread

INSPECTION

Spread Fabric

TRANSIT TIME: 1 DAY

Package Garment

Pallet
No. of Units: 500

TRANSIT TIME: 1 DAY

Pallet

Fold Garment

INSPECTION

Folded Garment

Sewn Garment

INSPECTION

Ga

Unpack

INSPECTION

Floor-Ready Garment

Apparel Packing Center
Location: Anytown
Avg. Throughput: xx Cartons/Yr.

Apparel Finished Product Inventory
Quantity: xx
Carrying Cost: $xx
Replenishment Policy: Production Plan

PROCESS TIME 1-6 DAYS Pick, Label, and Pack

Pick for Retailer Order

Assembled Order

TRANSIT TIME: 1 DAY

Stock on Shelves

Floor-Ready Garment

TRANSIT TIME: 1 DAY

Assembled Order

Label with Retailer Specific Labels

Bulk Retailer Distribution Center
Avg. Throughput: xx units

Recieved Carton
Avg. Weight: 40 lbs.
Quantity: xx units

Carton

Label and Cross Dock